THE CONSTRUCTION LAW LIBRARY FROM WILEY LAW PUBLICATIONS

ALTERNATIVE CLAUSES TO STANDARD CONSTRUCTION CONTRACTS
James E. Stephenson, Editor

ALTERNATIVE DISPUTE RESOLUTION IN THE CONSTRUCTION INDUSTRY
Robert F. Cushman, G. Christian Hedemann, and Avram S. Tucker, Editors

ARBITRATION OF CONSTRUCTION DISPUTES
Michael T. Callahan, Barry B. Bramble, and Paul M. Lurie

ARCHITECT AND ENGINEER LIABILITY: CLAIMS AGAINST DESIGN PROFESSIONALS
Robert F. Cushman and Thomas G. Bottum, Editors

CONDOMINIUM AND HOMEOWNER ASSOCIATION LITIGATION
Wayne S. Hyatt and Philip S. Downer, Editors

CONSTRUCTION ACCIDENT PLEADING AND PRACTICE
Turner W. Branch, Editor

CONSTRUCTION BIDDING LAW
Robert F. Cushman and William J. Doyle, Editors

CONSTRUCTION CLAIMS AND LIABILITY
Michael S. Simon

CONSTRUCTION DEFAULTS: RIGHTS, DUTIES, AND LIABILITIES
Robert F. Cushman and Charles A. Meeker, Editors

CONSTRUCTION DELAY CLAIMS
Barry B. Bramble and Michael T. Callahan

CONSTRUCTION ENGINEERING EVIDENCE
Loren W. Peters

CONSTRUCTION FAILURES
Robert F. Cushman, Irvin E. Richter, and Lester E. Rivelis, Editors

CONSTRUCTION INDUSTRY CONTRACTS: LEGAL CITATOR AND CASE DIGEST
Wiley Law Publications Editorial Staff

CONSTRUCTION INDUSTRY FORMS (TWO VOLUMES)
Robert F. Cushman and George L. Blick, Editors

CONSTRUCTION INDUSTRY INSURANCE HANDBOOK
Deutsch, Kerrigan & Stiles

CONSTRUCTION LITIGATION FORMBOOK
David M. Buoncristiani, John D. Carter, and Robert F. Cushman

CONSTRUCTION LITIGATION: REPRESENTING THE CONTRACTOR
Robert F. Cushman, John D. Carter, and Alan Silverman, Editors

CONSTRUCTION LITIGATION: REPRESENTING THE OWNER (SECOND EDITION)
Robert F. Cushman, Kenneth M. Cushman, and Stephen B. Cook, Editors

CONSTRUCTION LITIGATION: STRATEGIES AND TECHNIQUES
Barry B. Bramble and Albert E. Phillips, Editors

CONSTRUCTION RENOVATION FORMBOOK
Robert F. Cushman and John W. DiNicola, Editors

CONSTRUCTION SCHEDULING: PREPARATION, LIABILITY, AND CLAIMS
Jon M. Wickwire, Thomas J. Driscoll, and Stephen B. Hurlbut

CONSTRUCTION SUBCONTRACTING: A LEGAL GUIDE FOR INDUSTRY PROFESSIONALS
Overton A. Currie, Neal J. Sweeney, and Randall F. Hafer, Editors

DESIGN PROFESSIONAL'S HANDBOOK OF BUSINESS AND LAW
Robert F. Cushman and James C. Dobbs, Editors

DRAFTING CONSTRUCTION CONTRACTS: STRATEGY AND FORMS FOR CONTRACTORS
Samuel F. Schoninger

HANDLING FIDELITY, SURETY, AND FINANCIAL RISK CLAIMS (SECOND EDITION)
Robert F. Cushman, George L. Blick, and Charles A. Meeker, Editors

HAZARDOUS WASTE DISPOSAL AND UNDERGROUND CONSTRUCTION LAW
Robert F. Cushman and Bruce W. Ficken, Editors

1990–1991 DIRECTORY OF CONSTRUCTION INDUSTRY CONSULTANTS
Wiley Law Publications, Editors

1991 WILEY CONSTRUCTION LAW UPDATE
Steven M. Goldblatt, Editor

PROVING AND PRICING CONSTRUCTION CLAIMS
Robert F. Cushman and David A. Carpenter, Editors

SWEET ON CONSTRUCTION INDUSTRY CONTRACTS
Justin Sweet

TROUBLED CONSTRUCTION LOANS: LAW AND PRACTICE
Stanley P. Sklar, Editor

SUBSCRIPTION NOTICE

This Wiley product is updated on a periodic basis with supplements to reflect important changes in the subject matter. If you purchased this product directly from John Wiley & Sons, Inc., we have already recorded your subscription for this update service.

If, however, you purchased this product from a bookstore and wish to receive (1) the current update at no additional charge, and (2) future updates and revised or related volumes billed separately with a 30-day examination review, please send your name, company name (if applicable), address, and the title of the product to:

Supplement Department
John Wiley & Sons, Inc.
One Wiley Drive
Somerset, NJ 08875
1-800-225-5945

DESIGN PROFESSIONAL'S HANDBOOK OF BUSINESS AND LAW

ROBERT F. CUSHMAN, Esquire

JAMES C. DOBBS, Esquire

Editors

Wiley Law Publications

JOHN WILEY & SONS, INC.

New York • Chichester • Brisbane • Toronto • Singapore

This publication is designed to provide accurate and authoritative information in regard to the subject matter covered. It is sold with the understanding that the publisher is not engaged in rendering legal, accounting, or other professional services. If legal advice or other expert assistance is required, the services of a competent professional person should be sought. *From a Declaration of Principles jointly adopted by a Committee of the American Bar Association and a Committee of Publishers.*

Library of Congress Cataloging-in-Publication Data

Design professional's handbook of business and law / Robert F. Cushman, James C. Dobbs, editors.
p. cm. — (Construction law library)
Includes bibliographical references.
ISBN 0-471-52284-8 (cloth)
ISBN 0-471-55232-1 (paper)
1. Architectural contracts—United States. 2. Engineering contracts—United States. 3. Construction industry—Law and legislation—United States. I. Cushman, Robert Fairchild, 1918– II. Dobbs, James C., 1944– . III. Series.
KF902.D45 1991
343.73'07869—dc20
[347.3037869] 91-3267
CIP

Printed in the United States of America

10 9 8 7 6 5 4 3 2 1

PREFACE

Time and time again architects and engineers ask the same business, financial, management, and legal questions of their lawyers and professional advisors. To field these recurring but complex questions is by no means an easy task because few, if any, individuals have the training, background, and knowledge to do justice to problems of so broad a scope, and fewer still the ability to render answers clearly and practically. The design profession is a profession caught up in an era of growth in corporate partnering, commercial, industrial, and power plant upgrading, and mushrooming environmental and infrastructure problems, making accurate answers a necessity.

The design professional desiring to proceed with understanding and confidence has hungered for readily available and readable information and answers to these key questions in a single source. This need could only be met through concerted action, a collaboration of well-qualified specialists.

To accomplish the purpose of this handbook, it first became necessary to compile a list of the problems and questions most frequently asked by the design community. We have tried, we hope successfully, to superimpose upon our personal preferences the knowledge and experience of many prominent professionals associated with the industry to develop those most worthy of inclusion.

The 26 chapters of this guide, each representing a key question, are organized to address issues pertinent to the initial formation of the design entity, as well as accounting, record keeping, and tax concerns. The first section addresses business organization. This is followed by a section that addresses financing and insurance matters. The next section is concerned with the problems and pitfalls pertaining to contract procurement including chapters on current and pertinent federal regulations. This is followed by a section on contract documentation and administration and then a section on contract performance with an emphasis on the rights, remedies, and liabilities of design professionals. The last section of the handbook deals with the special problems architects and engineers face in the 1990s. Although some chapters within a section are interrelated, each chapter can be read and understood on its own.

The accountants, bankers, contractors, engineers, insurance consultants, and lawyers who have been selected to author these chapters were chosen with two criteria in mind: first, they had to be outstanding authorities within their field with proper qualifications and expertise to write their particular chapter and second, they had to be able to write in understandable, nontechnical language.

We believe that we have chosen wisely and well and that through the generous effort and skill of the distinguished contributors, we have, in this handbook, presented those who advise the design and engineering community with a reference work that could never have existed without cooperative effort.

The compiling of this handbook represents the work, advice, and encouragement of many. We are indebted to each of the contributors, whose reward is filling the void.

May 1991

ROBERT F. CUSHMAN
Philadelphia, Pennsylvania

JAMES C. DOBBS
Wakefield, Massachusetts

ABOUT THE EDITORS

Robert F. Cushman is a partner in the international law firm of Pepper, Hamilton & Scheetz in Philadelphia, Pennsylvania, and is a recognized specialist and lecturer on all phases of construction and real estate law. He serves as legal counsel to numerous trade associations and construction, development, and bonding companies. Mr. Cushman is the editor and coauthor of several books about construction, including the following John Wiley publications: *Construction Litigation: Representing the Owner* (2d ed.); *Construction Defaults: Rights, Duties, and Liabilities; Construction Failures; Proving and Pricing Construction Claims;* and *Alternative Dispute Resolution in the Construction Industry.* A member of the Pennsylvania bar, he is admitted to practice before the United States Supreme Court and the Court of Appeals for the Federal Circuit. Mr. Cushman has served as executive vice president and general counsel to the Construction Industry Foundation, as counsel to the American Construction Owners Association, and as regional chairman of the Public Contract Law Section of the American Bar Association. He is permanent chairman of the Andrews Conference Group's Construction Litigation and Hazardous Waste superconferences and is a charter member of the American College of Construction Lawyers.

James C. Dobbs is vice president and general counsel of Metcalf & Eddy, Inc., in Wakefield, Massachusetts. He is responsible for providing legal and regulatory counsel on a variety of environmental services in the water, wastewater, solid waste, industrial, and hazardous waste markets. He has written and lectured extensively on environmental issues for businesses and professional groups and for educational institutions. Mr. Dobbs is a director of the Privatization Council, Inc., chairman of the Committee on Privatization of the ABA's Natural Resources Section, and vice chairman of the Environmental Values Committee of the America Bar Association's Administrative Law Section. He holds a B.A. degree from Georgetown University, a J.D. magna cum laude from New York Law School, and a master of laws degree from New York University Law School.

SUMMARY CONTENTS

DETAILED CONTENTS

SHORT REFERENCE LIST

Short Reference	*Full Reference*
AGC	Associated General Contractors
A/E	architect/engineer
AIA	American Institute of Architects
ARCS	alternative remedial contract strategy
CADD	computer-aided design and drafting
CAS	cost accounting standards
CASB	Cost Accounting Standards Board
CERCLA	Comprehensive Environmental Response Compensation and Liability Act (Superfund)
CGL	comprehensive general liability
EJCDC	Engineers Joint Contract Documents Committee
E&O	errors and omissions
EPA	Environmental Protection Agency
ESOP	employee stock ownership plan
FAR	Federal Acquisition Regulation
GAO	General Accounting Office
GSA	General Services Administration
HVAC	heating, ventilation, and air conditioning
IFB	invitation for bids
IRC	Internal Revenue Code

Short Reference	*Full Reference*
IRS	Internal Revenue Service
NCP	National Contingency Plan
OFPP	Office of Federal Procurement Policy
PCs	professional corporations
P&L	profit and loss
PRPS	potentially responsible parties
RCRA	Resource Conservation and Recovery Act
RFP	request for proposal
RFQ	request for qualifications
RULPA	Revised Uniform Limited Partnership Act
SARA	Superfund Amendments and Reauthorization Act of 1986
SF	standard form
TINA	Truth-in-Negotiations Act
UCC	Uniform Commercial Code
ULPA	Uniform Limited Partnership Act
UPA	Uniform Partnership

PART I

BUSINESS ORGANIZATION

CHAPTER 1

NEW DIRECTIONS FOR DESIGN PROFESSIONALS

James C. Dobbs

James C. Dobbs is vice president and general counsel of Metcalf & Eddy, Inc., in Wakefield, Massachusetts. He is responsible for providing legal and regulatory counsel on a variety of environmental services in the water, wastewater, solid waste, industrial, and hazardous waste markets. He has written and lectured extensively on environmental issues for businesses and professional groups and for educational institutions. Mr. Dobbs is director of the Privatization Council, Inc., chairman of the Committee on Privatization of the ABA's Natural Resources Section, and vice chairman of the Environmental Values Committee of the American Bar Association's Administrative Law Section. He holds a B.A. degree from Georgetown University, a J.D. magna cum laude from New York Law School, and a master of laws degree from New York University Law School.

§ 1.1 Introduction

Design professionals confront enormous challenges in the 1990s, as they move their practices into the twenty-first century. Growing concerns about the environment, a decaying infrastructure, and overall quality of life, combined with the continued rapid development of technology and communications, make it more difficult than ever for the design professional to build and develop a successful business. Because the practices of the past are no longer adequate to meet the professional, financial, and entrepreneurial needs of today, design professions are in flux, searching for the right mixture of technical competence, organization, and incentives to nurture their growth.

Faced with demands from all sides—clients, employees, government regulators, and a public's changing attitude toward professionals in general—the obstacles facing the design professional are formidable. However, as in every time of uncertainty, there are many significant opportunities. This decade will be one of rapid change, with increased requirements for competence and cost-effective products and services. The growth in domestic and international markets and expanding competition from foreign firms will create unique challenges for the design professional. This handbook is intended to help design professionals understand the diverse demands on their profession and harness the human, financial, and organizational resources necessary to meet the challenges ahead.

§ 1.2 The Past

Design professionals have always been an integral part of civilization, taking their scientific knowledge of materials and the forces of nature and using them for the benefit of society.[1] From the designers of the Parthenon and the Roman aqueducts to the builders of the Great Wall of China and the great cathedrals in Europe, structures created by design professionals have represented civilization, reflecting not only the existing society but also its hopes and dreams. Today that is still true.

Some of our earliest American leaders were by training or avocation design professionals. George Washington, a surveyor, and Thomas Jefferson, an architect, practiced well-recognized "learned professions." Only 100 years ago, master builders, architects and engineers, created the Erie Canal, the Brooklyn Bridge, and the transcontinental railroads, projects that moved America westward and bound it together into one nation. Despite the closing of the frontier in the 1890s, the importance of the design

[1] Robinson, *Major Engineering Disciplines,* Consulting Engineering Practice Manual 15 (S. Cohen ed. 1985).

professional continued to grow as the country poured its efforts into developing new territories. There was an insatiable demand for bridges, tunnels, skyscrapers, dams, irrigation systems, and transportation systems for an exploding population.

At the same time, major advances in technology occurred that led to an increase in the size, technical complexity, and aesthetic requirements for these new facilities and structures. This forced major changes in how design professionals practiced their profession and provided services to their clients. Originally, services were provided by individuals or small groups under the strong leadership of one or two professionals. Toward the second third of this century, design practice moved to a partnership form, both large and small. Starting in the 1950s, design professionals began to convert themselves into business corporations.

§ 1.3 The Present

Design professions, like many other institutions in the last half of this century, have been faced with increasingly complex and contradictory requirements, forcing dramatic changes in the way design businesses are organized and operated and professional services are performed. Six important trends have emerged that have had a significant impact on how design professional services are produced and delivered today. They are:

1. The loss of overall project control
2. Increased specialization
3. Separation of the design professional from the construction process
4. The growth of large, interdisciplinary firms
5. The need for business development ability
6. Increasing vulnerability to liability claims.

These trends have created a bewildering number of choices, while following one trend or another has contributed to both successes and failures.

§ 1.4 —Loss of Project Control

The most important trend for design professionals in this century has been the loss of overall project control, resulting in fragmentation of the construction process. As the technical and political complexity of projects has increased, less and less need for a master builder has been perceived. This has led to a dramatic change in the way design professional services are purchased by clients who, for the sake of efficiency, quality control, and competitive pricing, attempt to divide design services into individual packages that can be put together in various combinations.

This fragmentation affects the entire construction process, separating designer and constructor and insisting that each service be performed in discrete phases to enable the client to maintain better control of the final product. Today, a design professional firm must provide a complete menu of services from which its clients can pick and choose, including studies and reports, permitting, designs, both preliminary and final, construction services, construction management, startup and trouble-shooting, and, most recently, program management. Each of these services can be purchased individually or bundled together.

This type of procurement has produced a steady erosion in the long-term professional-client relationship, which had allowed the design professional to focus on understanding the client's needs and insuring they were met. Instead, combined with increasingly lower margins from price competition, the subdivision of the construction process by the owner creates a situation in which no active participant takes control and responsibility for the overall project. This leaves the owner, who is frequently unprepared, to oversee and manage the project from the conceptual phase to the completion of construction. Inevitably, when problems or defective work occurs, each party blames the other parties. The more design professionals and contractors working on a project, the less responsibility each takes and the more difficult it becomes to understand who and what caused a problem. This delays the proper corrective action, dramatically increasing the cost to the owner and the other parties, including design professionals.

In many cases, the division of a project into separate phases is not mandated by technical requirements, but by sociopolitical decisions. For example, in the area of studies and reports, the earlier comprehensive preliminary study is now divided into many separate phases, from planning to feasibility to design studies and special environmental impact statements. Many of these services are driven by the dramatic growth of legislation and regulations during the past 50 years. The Federal National Environmental Policy Act,[2] its state counterparts, and other environmental laws demand an increasing number of reports and studies on the environmental impact of a project, including studies of the project's effect on the wildlife habitat of endangered species, land planning, wetlands depletion, transportation, and even archaeological factors. Because of this regulatory explosion, many projects today live or die on the basis of studies and reports, most unheard of 30 years ago.

The design phase also is frequently broken down into several discrete parts. Enormous effort is expended in the permitting process to complete the various regulatory and other reviews required before a project can be

---

[2] 42 U.S.C. §§ 4321 *et seq.* (1988).

initiated. In the design process itself, changes today are as much the result of regulatory or other political requirements as of technical or aesthetic considerations. Unfortunately, with multiple governmental reviews, it seems many can criticize and modify the design or implementation of a project without anyone taking ultimate responsibility for its success or failure.

§ 1.5 —Increased Specialization

A second major trend is the increased specialization of design professionals resulting from the great explosion of knowledge and information in the twentieth century. Many projects also have created new technical issues, leading to an expansion in the types of scientific and technical services design professionals provide. No more is an individual simply an engineer or architect. Among engineers there are many categories, including mechanical, chemical, civil, industrial, transportation, environmental, structural, and energy. Even within these designations there are further subdivisions. For example, energy engineering includes specializations in generation, distribution, utilization, and electrical engineering. The disadvantage of this specialization is that it fosters a more narrow, myopic view among professionals, making it harder to coordinate information and provide comprehensive project services.

Modern projects also require the expertise of design professionals who did not exist 100 years ago. Unusual geotechnical problems, hazardous waste contamination, urban planning and traffic, biological evaluations, environmental studies, and computer design systems require the expertise of design professionals unheard of a generation ago. In the last few years, the services of new professionals in meteorology, zoology, and archaeology have become necessary if a project is to obtain the required public and regulatory approval.

To counteract the specialization of design professionals, a new generalist, the project manager, has been created. The project manager ideally incorporates all the virtues of a businessperson, technical manager, and client relations specialist capable of guiding a project from start to finish. In today's design professional firm, the project manager has a pivotal role in providing design services effectively and profitably.

§ 1.6 —Separation from the Construction Process

A third trend influencing design professional practice is the separation of the design professional from the construction process. Previously, the architect or engineer not only conceived and designed a project, but also in many cases was the actual builder. In the last 100 years that concept has changed radically, so that now there is a clear distinction between the services provided by the design professional and those furnished by the contractor. The contractor is now in charge of the actual erection of the facility, implementing the design and specifications created by the design professional, who provides only advisory services during the construction phase.[3]

In the past decade, however, the pendulum has begun to swing back toward the earlier concept of master builder, whereby the design professional or another entity plays the leading role in constructing the project. This idea never completely died out, but for many years it was limited to certain mega-projects, such as dams, petrochemical facilities, and nuclear power plants. Today, the weakness of divided responsibility has become apparent to many clients; disagreements among the various design professionals, contractors, equipment suppliers, and subcontractors have created a Tower of Babel in which no one takes responsibility for the work and any resulting mistakes.

Consequently, new organizational forms have been created to centralize the responsibility for managing a project through completion. The most well-known is *construction management.* Although there are many variations and definitions of construction management, the concept basically involves one entity ensuring that the entire building process is properly managed, controlling time, cost, and quality. The construction manager uses modern management techniques to cut across the barriers that have grown up between design professionals and construction contractors,[4] thus performing many of the services that the traditional master builder provided a century ago.

Another variation of this management approach is the *design-build contractor.*[5] Under this concept, the owner directly or through a design professional provides a series of performance specifications for the facility desired. Thereafter, the design-construct entity has the responsibility for developing the total design, constructing a facility that meets the performance specifications within the time and budget constraints set by the owner. A traditional way of providing industrial facilities during the last decade, the design-build concept has expanded widely to commercial buildings and government facilities.

Finally, there is the *program management concept.* Although often confused with construction management, program management is a step up in the threshold of responsibility whereby the program manager, in effect,

---

[3] Kahn, *Introduction: The Changing Role of the Architect,* 23 St. Louis U.L.J. 216 (1979) [hereinafter Kahn].

[4] T. Kavanaugh, F. Muller, & J. O'Brien, Construction Management, A Professional Approach 7 (1979) [hereinafter T. Kavanaugh].

[5] Kahn, 217 n.2.

becomes the alter ego of the owner and is brought into the process early on.[6] The program manager deals with the initial conceptual planning, study phase, predesign, design, construction, and startup, directly providing or closely managing the procurement of all services. The program manager may choose to provide the required studies, design services, equipment, construction, startup, and even operation and maintenance personally or may subcontract some or all of these services. The primary mission of the program manager is to use modern management techniques to help the owner develop a project concept and then to execute the design and construction in a cost-effective manner, thus coming as close as possible today to the master builder concept. Once limited to the mega-project, program management has made great strides in the marketplace. From managing the expansion and renovation of airports in New York to solid waste resource recovery facilities in California, program management has gained increased credibility in the public and private sectors with clients looking for professional management and a single point of responsibility for the creation and completion of a project.

§ 1.7 —Growth of Interdisciplinary Firms

A fourth trend affecting design professional practice is the growth of large interdisciplinary firms furnishing a wide range of design professional services. Since World War II, a number of architectural, engineering, and geotechnical firms have grown rapidly as suppliers of a wide array of design professional services, both nationally and internationally. Today, over 25 firms have design billings alone in excess of $200 million, not including construction management and program management services.[7] These firms are multidisciplined, containing dozens of professional services provided by multiple offices spread across the country and around the world. These large firms grew in response to a demand for specialized services in a multidisciplinary environment to handle technically complex projects.

Despite this trend, the design professional industry remains more fragmented than most major industries in the United States, in part because of its generally low entry costs. The essence of a design professional—offering technical services directly to clients—enables many small entrepreneurial organizations to be created, grow, and flourish. Although these smaller firms do not have all the resources to execute very large projects, there is still an enormous amount of business, both public and private, that does not require the resources of large firms. In many cases, the small firm

---

[6] T. Kavanaugh, 2 n.4.

[7] *The Top 500 Design Firms,* 224 Engineering News-Record 48 (1990).

specializing in a small number of disciplines has a competitive technical and cost advantage over the large multidisciplinary firms.

Small, local firms that are on the scene and accessible also have tremendous psychological and logistical advantages. Because the design professional's practice is a service business, the personal contacts and the ability to react quickly and be at the scene of a project or in a client's office gives a small firm a significant edge.

To bridge the competitive gap between large and small firms, the last two decades have seen an increasing use of joint ventures to win projects. A joint venture, properly structured, provides a "win-win" situation for both parties. See **Chapter 4**. In a joint venture, each party has certain strengths, such as technical expertise, office location, client relations, and computer resources which, bundled together, enable the joint venture to compete against otherwise stronger firms or joint ventures.

In the past, joint ventures were looked upon as anticompetitive, reducing the number of players in the marketplace. Today the joint venture is considered a competition enhancer, enabling more firms to join together and compete against each other in many otherwise inaccessible markets.

§ 1.8 —Need for Business Development Ability

A fifth requirement now imposed on design professionals is business development ability. The one indispensable item for every design professional firm is clients. Determining who they are and how to get and keep them is an art that may be the most important factor in building a successful business.

Until recently, design professionals were chosen solely on the basis of qualifications, reputation, and experience.[8] Marketing was done through well-established professional societies, technical papers, and individual contacts. In the 1990s, a firm's selection is more likely to be based on a competitive price and the ability to get the job done on time and within budget.

§ 1.9 —Vulnerability to Liability Claims

The final and most publicized trend in the last two decades is the increasing vulnerability of design professionals to liability claims from their clients, construction contractors, and unrelated third parties. Driven by articles, seminars, and highly publicized cases in an increasingly litigious society, liability mania is a top concern for many design professional

[8] Crawford, *The Work of the Consulting Engineer,* Consulting Engineering Practice Manual 12 (S. Cohen ed. 1985).

firms. The traditional legal definition of liability revolving around the concept of negligence is rapidly changing to incorporate other legal theories, such as implied warranties and strict liability. Headlines touting million-dollar verdicts and unlimited environmental liability are causing design professionals to deal with problems conservatively and limit innovation and risk taking.

Although it is essential that design professionals spend time on liability issues and exposure, more effort should be applied to risk management and control. For instance, contract documents should be updated to provide a more equitable risk/reward equation with clients. Increased attention also should be placed on project and technical quality control. If the project manager is the crucial organizational unit, who is reviewing that individual's work and competency?

Nevertheless, the traditional underlying principles of a successful professional practice are still the keystone of successful risk management. Careful and accurate performance of a design professional's services must be the top priority, in other words, "doing it right the first time." Now, as in the past and as it will be in the future, there is no substitute for competence.[9]

§ 1.10 The Future

Successful design professionals must be competent businesspersons as well. No matter how large or small the firm, the design professional must be technically qualified, able to maintain high professional standards, and capable of managing a profitable business.[10] Without some foundation in technical, financial, administrative, marketing, human, and other business problems, even the best technical firm may become a total business disaster.

The management of a business is as much a profession as designing the tallest building in the world. Managers of design professional businesses are professional managers: managers of technology, people, finance, liabilities, and the other business realities. The certainty of the past decades is gone, replaced by a strong entrepreneurial drive and confidence that the scientific and technical tools of today and tomorrow will enable design professionals to address people's needs and requirements in the twenty-first century. The purpose of this handbook is to give design professional managers a starting point with which to deal with the problems faced by their firms each day in the 1990s. The ability of the design professional firm to address management issues is crucial for survival and successful growth in the future.

---

[9] Kahn, 218 n.2.

[10] Ratliff, *Preface,* Consulting Engineering Practice Manual ii (S. Cohen ed. 1985).

CHAPTER 2

REGISTERING TO DO BUSINESS

James C. Dobbs

James C. Dobbs is vice president and general counsel of Metcalf & Eddy, Inc., in Wakefield, Massachusetts. He is responsible for providing legal and regulatory counsel on a variety of environmental services in the water, wastewater, solid waste, industrial, and hazardous waste markets. He has written and lectured extensively on environmental issues for businesses and professional groups and for educational institutions. Mr. Dobbs is director of the Privatization Council, Inc., chairman of the Committee on Privatization of the ABA's Natural Resources Section, and vice chairman of the Environmental Values Committee of the American Bar Association's Administrative Law Section. He holds a B.A. degree from Georgetown University, a J.D. magna cum laude from New York Law School, and a master of laws degree from New York University Law School.

§ 2.1 Introduction

Because a design professional's practice is both a business and a profession, the difference between business and professional registration gives rise to much confusion. Many design professionals find that changes in the registration form and requirements from state to state are contrary to their training and inherent nature for orderliness and uniformity.

Professional registration laws themselves do not help much in this regard. In our federal system, the regulation of professions has been left to the states. Despite the rise of many model codes and laws and the best efforts of many professional groups, a standard set of definitions and regulations for licensing the various design professions has eluded us. With more than 55 state and territorial legislatures, an equal number of blue-ribbon committees, advisors, and literally hundreds of draftsmen who believe everything previously written can be improved, today we have a discordant set of rules and regulations, confusing sometimes and conflicting in details from jurisdiction to jurisdiction.

Nevertheless, for the design professional it is imperative that these rules be complied with despite the difficulty, paperwork, and cost. Fortunately, the registration laws applicable to business and professional activities did not evolve in a vacuum. With the help of national organizations such as the National Council of Engineering Examiners and other professional organizations, most laws dealing with professional registration contain many of the same principles, elements, and objectives. The differences occur in their implementation.

This chapter discusses these requirements, emphasizing the basic tenets and structure common to the regulations adopted for the design professional and identifying the nuances and quirks that can assist or cause havoc to a practice.

One distinction must be understood: the difference between the registration necessary to operate a business and the professional registration essential to practice a design profession. A lack of understanding here can have dire consequences, both businesswise and professionally. Every type of business, especially if it is in a corporate form, must be registered to do business. From manufacturing cars to selling shoes to designing wastewater treatment plants, nationwide a business is required by law to be registered, normally with the secretary of state, in each jurisdiction where it does substantial business. There are also totally separate and specific legal requirements for individuals and for the partnerships, corporations, or other entities in which design professionals practice their professions to register with duly constituted boards or organizations designated by a state to regulate a specific design profession. As a result, design professionals and their businesses are faced with two or three distinct registration requirements in every jurisdiction where they conduct business. Failure to understand and comply with these laws can result in civil and criminal penalties plus the loss of the right to practice one's profession.

§ 2.2 Business Registration

"If I am a licensed engineer in Connecticut, and my firm is also registered with the state board, why do I have to register to do business?" This question is asked hundreds of times a year, mostly in response to some tax or client requirement. Yet the rationale for requiring design professional firms to register to do business is easy to understand.

Every design professional corporation and some partnerships and sole proprietorships are registered by law to do business in one jurisdiction automatically, the state in which they are incorporated or otherwise organized. By being created under a particular state law, each firm or sole proprietorship is subject to that state's laws and appoints the secretary of state or some other person designated by the state as the firm's resident agent for service of process in a legal action and for other official notices that may have to be given.

The difficulty occurs when a firm begins to practice in a jurisdiction different from that in which it was created. Each firm or corporation is a creature of the state law in which it was established and has no legal existence in other states, where it is considered to be a foreign corporation or business entity. When a firm solicits and performs work for clients in another state, it must secure that state's consent to operate in its jurisdiction by complying with the laws on business registration. This is generally termed "qualifying to do business."[1] As such, it applies to all businesses irrespective of their product or service.

This emphasis on a business's domicile originated from the separate and independent identities of the states when the United States was organized. Today, after the country has developed into one large marketplace, the rationale for these requirements is twofold: the protection of local citizens and businesses by enabling them to serve legal process on foreign businesses and the collection of substantial revenues from state taxes and franchise fees.

Consistent with certain constitutional limitations, states can impose various registration and reporting obligations on businesses that operate within their boundaries. In practice, most states prescribe similar registration requirements, including an authentication of the firm's original incorporation or organization in its home state, the firm's continued good standing in its

[1] B. Tomson & N. Coplan, Architectural & Engineering Law 43 (2d ed. 1967).

home state, and the designation of a state official or other recognized business entity, such as CT Corporation or Prentice-Hall, upon whom legal process may be served. In addition, some states require the filing of corporate capital structure and financial information and all states require yearly taxes or franchise fees as a levy on this right to do business.[2]

Foreign registration is not required in all business transactions. The performance of incidental work on an occasional basis is generally held not to transgress these state registration laws. Thus, a business that occasionally performs services in or provides work or articles from a home office to another state has little to worry about. If, on the other hand, the amount of work is significant and requires work over an extended time in a state, a business is normally found to be doing business in that state and is subject to its business registration and taxation laws.[3]

The courts have characterized business activity that is substantial and continuous as engaging in business within a jurisdiction. However, over the years these requirements have been watered down to the point where even a single contract or project, especially if sizable and performed over an appreciable period of time, is sufficient contact for a state to impose registration burdens.[4]

Failure to register to do business was once more serious than it is today. Some states held that contracts with unregistered business entities were void or unenforceable. In other cases, a business could be subject to criminal penalties, but today such draconian penalties are mostly gone.[5] Nevertheless, in many states, failure to register to do business when required still invokes a harsh penalty, prohibiting the foreign business from enforcing its legal rights in that state's court. Work can be performed in a foreign state but, unless properly registered, a business is barred from suing for monies owed or from seeking other legal relief.[6] This can be especially disastrous when dealing with local businesses or government entities that cannot be sued in a business's home state.

There is relief in some states that permit a business to register after the transaction is completed, but only after the payment of penalties and substantial embarrassment.

---

[2] CT Corporation System has published an excellent summary of the various states' definitions of "doing business" plus discussion of the effect of such requirements on various businesses. CT Corporation System, What Constitutes Doing Business (1985) [hereinafter CT Corporation].

[3] *See* CT Corporation at 59–67.

[4] B. Tomson & N. Coplan, Architectural & Engineering Law 44 (2d ed. 1967).

[5] *Id.* at 50–51.

[6] CT Corporation at 4–9.

§ 2.3 Individual Professional Registration

For many design professionals, the symbol of their professional practice is their professional registration, won after an arduous process of education, training, and examination. It is worn like a badge of honor, posted prominently on the wall and abbreviated conspicuously after their names. This has led some design professionals to become registered in more than a dozen states.

Professional registrations are more than a ticket necessary to show others one is entitled to practice a profession. The registration process, from granting licenses and renewals to enforcement, goes to the heart of what the design professions are all about: performance of competent services for the public.

In July 1981, a major structural failure occurred at the Hyatt Regency Hotel in Kansas City. Between 1,500 and 2,000 people on two walkways suspended in a large atrium were hurled to the ground floor when the walkways collapsed. With 114 dead and over 180 injured, the National Bureau of Standards called this accident the most devastating structural collapse in United States history.[7]

After an unprecedented investigation, which determined that the cause of the accident was the failure to review shop drawings by the structural engineers, the Missouri Board for Architects, Professional Engineers and Land Surveyors took action to revoke the professional engineering licenses of two engineers and their corporate employer. In looking at the engineers' conduct, the board found their actions constituted gross negligence, incompetence, and misconduct. Even the engineers' attempt to limit their responsibility and liability for shop drawing review was held to be unprofessional conduct violating Missouri's professional engineering registration laws.[8]

In upholding the board's action, the Missouri Court of Appeals held:

> The statutory provisions make clear that Missouri has established a stringent set of requirements for professional engineers in the state. The thrust of those requirements is professional accountability by a specified individual certified engineer. These requirements establish the public policy of the state for the protection of the public. . . . Design of connections is, under

---

[7] Jackson & Kaskell, *The K.C. Hyatt Regency Disaster: What Went Wrong,* 56 Def. Couns. J. 415 (1989).

[8] Duncan v. Missouri Bd. for Architects, Professional Eng'rs & Land Surveyors, 744 S.W.2d 524, 533–37 (Mo. Ct. App. 1988). *See generally* Note, *Defining the Engineers' Scope of Responsibility: The Missouri Architects Commission Hands Down a Decision on the Hyatt Case,* 55 UMKC L. Rev. 108 (1986).

> the statute, a matter for which the engineer is responsible. Custom, practice or "bottom line" necessity cannot alter that responsibility.[9]

State regulation of registration of design professionals has occurred only since the early 1900s. Following the lead of medicine and law, the technical professions waged a long campaign to induce states to adopt registration laws for these learned professions. In 1907, Wyoming adopted the first law regulating the practice of engineering.[10] The objective was to enhance the level of competence of each profession by setting minimum standards for education and on-the-job training culminating in the successful completion of a written examination and the issuance of a formal license to practice a profession.

The rationale for adopting these licensing laws was the valid exercise of police power by the state to safeguard the public's health, safety, and welfare. In Alabama, today's architecture registration statute declares it

> to be a matter of public interest and concern that the architectural profession merit and receive the confidence of the public and that only qualified architects be permitted to practice [and that] to safeguard life, health and property, and to promote the public welfare, no person shall practice architecture in this state or use the title "Architect" . . . unless such person shall comply with the [regulation] provisions of this chapter.[11]

Similar wording is found in almost every design profession registration law.

Those who have felt the lash of rejection or attempted to perform technical services that were thwarted by judicial enforcement of professional registration laws have argued that the real purpose of such laws was anticompetitive, restricting the number of individuals who practice in a particular state. Although that was certainly a consideration of those championing restrictive registration laws, the main goals were those of competence and protection of the public from unethical and incompetent practitioners. The emphasis on personal liability in these statutes reflects the strong impetus to protect the public, the ultimate beneficiary of professional services. Today there is little quarrel that the purpose of these statutes in raising the standards of professional education and conduct has been achieved.

---

[9] Duncan v. Missouri Bd. for Architects, Professional Eng'rs & Land Surveyors, 744 S.W.2d 524, 533–34 & 536 (Mo. Ct. App. 1988).

[10] Stitt, *Corporate Practice of Engineering,* 14 Bus. Law. 969, 972 (1959) [hereinafter Stitt].

[11] Ala. Code § 34-2-31 (1985).

§ 2.4 Different Design Professions

Design professional is a generic term encompassing several recognized professions whose functions deal primarily with the use of science, scientific principles, and mathematics to understand and manipulate the natural environment. The end result of this activity is to create an improvement to the physical surroundings, by which human activities are enhanced. Over the years, each design profession has developed its own concept of what constitutes the practice of that profession. This is reflected in the definitions that have been enacted by state legislatures and interpreted by the courts over the years. Although there are many different variations in legislation adopted by the individual states, these laws contain the same elements and characterization of activities that define a particular profession.

In registration statutes, the initial definition of a profession is then amplified by another term defining the practice of that profession. This turns the concept of a professional into one who provides a group of services and creative work which is that profession's hallmark. No state statute can be called typical, but similar definitional threads on what constitutes a profession and its practice run throughout all these laws. State laws on registration of design professionals are listed in **Table 2–1** in **§ 2.9**.

An example of the definition of architectural services is expressed in this Massachusetts statute:

> [The] performing [of] professional services in connection with the design, construction, enlargement or alteration of a building including consultations, investigations, evaluations, preliminary studies, aesthetic design, the preparation of plans, specifications and contract documents . . . administration of construction contracts and any other similar service or combination of services in connection with the design and construction of buildings.[12]

It is easy to recognize that architecture practice revolves around design services for buildings and structures but does not have this field wholly to itself. Architecture and engineering practice overlap, with a distinction hard at times to ascertain. Thus, many laws contain a proviso that the practice of architecture "shall not include the practice of engineering" as further defined.[13]

A typical definition of professional engineering was adopted by Connecticut:

> [A] person who is qualified by reason of his knowledge of mathematics, the physical sciences and the principles of engineering, acquired by professional

[12] Mass. Gen. L. ch. 112, § 60A (1988).

[13] *Id.*

> education and practical experience, to engage in engineering practice, including the rendering or offering to render to clients any professional services such as consultation, investigation, evaluation, planning, design or responsible supervision of construction, in connection with any public or privately-owned structures, buildings, machines, equipment, works or projects wherein the public welfare or the safeguarding of life, public health or property is concerned or involved.[14]

As all-encompassing as this definition may seem, some states such as California have seen fit to further subdivide engineering into specialties including civil, electrical, and mechanical engineering.[15] As defined in most statutes, engineering encompasses more than the design of structures and equipment. Investigations, reports, planning, and supervision of construction are normally mentioned in the definition of engineering practice.

Another long-standing profession is land surveying, which has had an important part in the settlement and development of this country. In tune with the adoption of new laser technology, the definition of land survey has grown from the determination of land boundaries and rights of way to the broader and more comprehensive characterization adopted by Connecticut:

> [A] person who engages in the practice [of] surveying and measuring the area of any portion of the earth's surface, the lengths and directions of bounding lines and the contour of the surface, for their correct determination and description and for conveyancing or for recording, or for the establishment or reestablishment of land boundaries and the plotting of land and subdivisions thereof.[16]

The geologist has been an important contributor to the exploitation of minerals in the West. Several states recognized the geologist's significance by adopting legislation regulating his practice as a professional. As new emphasis was given in the 1980s to the use and misuse of our natural resources, other states adopted laws regulating geological services. Today, over 18 states have such legislation. In Maine, geology is defined as the science that investigates the composition of the earth and its constituent rocks, minerals, liquids, and gases. The practice of geology becomes "the performance of geological work or service . . . including . . . consultation, investigation, surveys, evaluation, planning, mapping or inspection of geological work [for] the safeguarding of life, health, property and the environment."[17]

---

[14] Conn. Gen. Stat. Ann. § 20-299(1) (West 1989).

[15] Cal. Bus. & Prof. Code §§ 6731, 6702, 6702.1, 6702.2 (West Supp. 1990).

[16] Conn. Gen. Stat. Ann. § 20-299(2) (West 1989).

[17] Me. Rev. Stat. Ann. tit. 32, § 4902 (1988).

The rapid growth of environmental concerns in the last decade has given impetus to development and recognition of a related profession: soil scientist or soil classifier. Dealing with the specialized knowledge of physical, chemical, and biological sciences required for the proper study and evaluation of soil conditions has created a whole new professional classification of geotechnical engineer, reflecting the adaptability and growth of the design professions in response to society's changing needs. In Virginia, practice of soil science consists of "the evaluation of soil by . . . observation, investigation, and consultation on measured, observed and inferred soils and their properties; analysis of the effects of these properties on the use and management of various kinds of soil; and preparation of soil descriptions, maps, reports and interpretive drawings."[18]

Finally, most states have defined landscape architecture as a distinct profession. In California the practice of landscape architecture involves "landscape preservation, development and enhancement [through] consultation, . . . planning, design, preparation of drawings, construction documents and specifications and responsible construction observation."[19] Many statutory definitions of landscape architecture emphasize the aesthetic and functional use of land and its natural features.

Unfortunately, actual practice sometimes creates a situation in which the performance of professional services by one type of licensed professional includes activities of a different profession. This happens primarily in the architect-engineer fields, where overlapping services regularly occur. Many times an engineer designs buildings or structures to accommodate a certain process or equipment he has designed. Similarly, in a building designed by an architect, there are electrical and mechanical systems whose design is technically within the scope of engineering. Most states accommodate this conflict with language that permits engineers and architects to perform the other's professional services only if incidental to their own work.[20] Thus, an engineering firm can design a structure around industrial equipment and architects can lay out the electrical system of a home without fear of violating professional registration laws.

There are situations in which individual design professionals undertake to provide more than incidental services and end up practicing another profession. In those cases, enforcement action is taken by the appropriate state board or agency to enjoin such illegal activity. Recently in Massachusetts, legal proceedings were commenced against the leading industrial designer of electric chairs and other execution devices on the basis that the president of the company was practicing engineering without a professional

---

[18] Va. Code Ann. § 54.1-2200 (1988).

[19] Cal. Bus. & Prof. Code § 5615 (West 1988).

[20] *See* Ala. Code § 34-11-1(4) (1985) (engineering); *id.* § 34-2-32(d) (architecture).

engineering registration. Normally, such proceedings are sufficient to police the occasional transgression.

Courts have sometimes found it hard to referee the squabbling that has occurred between architects and engineers over alleged trespass by one profession practicing in the other's backyard. The decisions have raised more confusion instead of a clean demarcation between the practice of these two disciplines. All have noted the significant overlap in the statutory definition and in actual practice in the real world. In most cases, courts are reluctant to act either by injunction or in a punitive manner except in the most egregious cases.[21]

However, in New Jersey the conflict over cross-practice of professions was raised to full-scale warfare. Architects in New Jersey, through their professional association, filed a series of lawsuits charging various engineers with the unlawful practice of architecture. After several years of combat, including victories by the architects,[22] the state legislature in 1990 passed legislation to resolve the dispute over practice coverage.[23]

The New Jersey legislation recognized that there are areas of concurrent practice between the practice of architecture and the practice of engineering. After first redefining the practice of both professions more specifically than before, the legislature adopted two methods to reduce interprofessional conflict. First, in one portion of the Building Design Services Act, all buildings and structures were placed into certain classifications with an approved matrix designating which profession could provide design services to which classification.[24] Next, the Act went on to create a Joint Committee of Architects and Engineers to mediate disputes referred from the professional architect and engineering societies. After a period of investigation and evaluation of an allegation of unlicensed practice of architecture or engineering, the Joint Committee is obligated to provide a declaratory ruling on the complaint to the appropriate professional state board for disciplinary action.[25] With membership consisting of two architects, two engineers, and one board member appointed by the governor who is not a licensed architect, engineer, or in a closely allied profession, the stage is set for continued conflict, though ideally at a more reduced level.

Although some states have adopted legislation providing for the joint practice of architecture and engineering by one firm, providing it contains principals licensed in both professions, the New Jersey legislation strengthened the wall separating the professions by specifically prohibiting

---

[21] *See* State v. Beck, 156 Me. 403, 407, 165 A.2d 433, 435 (1960).

[22] *See* State Bd. of Architects v. North, 197 N.J. Super. 385, 484 A.2d 1297 (1984).

[23] Building Design Services Act, N.J. Stat. Ann. §§ 45:B-1 *et seq.* (West Supp. 1990).

[24] *Id.* at § 45:4B-7.

[25] *Id.* at § 45:4B-5.

businesses offering services by one profession from practicing the other profession except in very limited and specific situations.[26]

The battle goes on. In Pennsylvania, engineering companies had offered comprehensive engineering and architectural services. The architectural services were beyond those incidental to the practice of engineering. In rejecting the engineers' argument that the distinction between the professions had become increasingly blurred and that clients were demanding "total service" firms, the Pennsylvania Supreme Court decided that the legislature intended architectural services to be practiced only through architectural firms meeting Pennsylvania's restrictive shareholder ownership and control standard. The rationale for such requirements is that projects undertaken by architectural firms must "be closely supervised by licensed architects who occupy eminent positions in their firms." The court said this would ensure that services to the public are offered only through competent firms, furthering the protection of the public's health and safety.[27]

One must wonder whether the Pennsylvania legislature and courts were concerned only about the public's health and safety in architectural services, because similar ownership and control requirements were not imposed on other design professions. New Jersey and Pennsylvania laws reflect the wide division between professions on the issue of joint practice and the barriers that are being erected under the guise of public health and safety concerns to prevent a worldwide trend toward total service firms from interfering with architectural business.

§ 2.5 Corporate Practice

With the increase in complexity and magnitude of design projects in this century, it became more and more difficult to provide the necessary design professional services in the traditional sole practitioner and partnership organizations. As professional organizations became larger, reflecting a multidisciplinary approach to projects, and as practices spread across the country in various branch offices, the advantages of corporate organizational form became apparent.[28] Nevertheless, the issue of practicing professional design services through a corporate form has been very contentious.

---

[26] *Id.* Louisiana has adopted a statute creating an Architecture-Engineering Corporation to practice both professions. The corporation must be licensed by both the state architectural and engineering boards. La. Rev. Stat. Ann. §§ 12:117 *et seq.* (West Supp. 1990).

[27] Consulting Eng'rs Council v. State Architects Licensure Bd., 560 A.2d 1375, 1377–78 (Pa. 1989).

[28] Lunch, *Professional Practice and Organization of Engineering Firms: The Regulatory Framework,* Handbook of Engineering Management 63 (J. Ullman ed. 1986) [hereinafter Lunch]; Stitt at 971.

The opponents of corporate practice by design professionals argued that members of a learned profession required a relationship between the individual professional and the client, whereby the professional was personally responsible for the quality of the work product. Somehow, many believed organizing responsible licensed professionals into a corporate form would subvert or diminish this concept of individual professional responsibility.[29] This argument ignores the provision in all professional registration laws that holds the individually licensed professional personally liable for the work he performs or that is performed under his supervision and direction, no matter through what business organization such services are provided. Moreover, the economic facts of the practice of many professions, including accountancy, medicine, and law, reflect an ever-increasing trend toward group and corporate practice.

Opponents also argued that corporate practice of professional services would have harmful economic effects, making a practice by individuals and small firms difficult. They also claimed that using a corporate organizational form would place the ultimate authority and responsibility for professional decisions in the hands of owners and business managers who may not be licensed professionals.[30]

Today, the advantages of corporate practice by design professionals are well recognized. The corporate form allows larger and more complex arrangements of professionals and nonprofessionals focused on dealing with the large, complex projects today's world demands. There are significant tax and employee benefit plan advantages to corporations, which enable these entities to attract and compensate their staff, thereby keeping competent professionals. The corporation also can develop financial strength and resources by accumulating capital and generating working funds necessary to retain a large staff and to execute large projects. Finally, the corporate form can ensure the continuity of the business by enabling one group of owners and managers to pass control to another without the business and financial disruptions a partnership form may engender.[31]

This battle has continued for a long time. The first laws permitting the corporate practice of engineering were passed in 1921.[32] Today, most jurisdictions permit design professionals to practice in the corporate format. Almost every state permits engineers to engage in corporate practice, and a vast majority apply the same principles to architects. In other design professions such as surveying and soil science, more and more states are adopting legislation recognizing the right to practice as a corporation. State laws on corporate practice are identified in **Table 2–2** in **§ 2.10**.

---

[29] Stitt at 979.

[30] *Id.* at 981; Lunch at 65.

[31] Stitt at 971, 977–78; Lunch at 64–65.

[32] Stitt at 972.

Such state authorization does, however, impose requirements and regulations on those who practice as corporations. The typical state statute requires that the practice of professional services by corporations, and sometimes also by partnerships, be conducted under the direct control, supervision, and direction of an officer or principal who is a duly licensed professional in that state. These principals and officers are specifically designated to be in "responsible charge" of the activities of the firm. Such individual or individuals specifically undertake to be in charge and to direct that company or firm's professional practice.[33]

Responsible charge has been defined to mean a position requiring:

> [I]nitiative, skill and independent judgment, and implies such degree of competence and accountability gained by technical education and experience of a grade and character as is sufficient to qualify an individual to personally and independently engage in and be entrusted with the work involved in the practice of engineering or land surveying.[34]

Most statutes also go on to state that individual licensed professionals are not relieved of their personal responsibility for work they or their firm perform by reason of its organization or structure.[35]

Some states limit the corporate practice of design professional services to specially created "professional corporations" or "professional associations." These entities were created pursuant to state law to enable incorporated professionals to take advantage of favorable federal tax and pension rules, but still restrict participation in the business to the licensed professionals only. Under most professional corporation statutes, all owners or shareholders of a professional corporation must be individually licensed to practice the design profession in that state. In many cases, that requirement applies to all, or at least to a majority, of directors and officers. The laws also restrict the transfer of ownership interest only to licensed professionals eligible to be shareholders under the statute. Each law has a provision stating that the professional corporation does not alter the personal liability of the shareholders, directors, officers, and employees to the public. In many cases, besides reaffirming the individual liability of the management, the corporation is held to be liable for its employees' professional activities up to the full value of its assets.[36]

---

[33] *See* Ala. Code § 34-2-37 (1985); Cal. Bus. & Prof. Code § 6738(3) (West Supp. 1990); Pa. Stat. Ann. tit. 63, § 153 (Purdon Supp. 1990); Tenn. Code Ann. § 62-2-601(a) (1990).

[34] Pa. Stat. Ann. tit. 63, § 149(ii) (Purdon Supp. 1990).

[35] *See* Colo. Rev. Stat. § 12-4-110(b) (Supp. 1990); S.D. Codified Laws Ann. § 36-18-31.1(3) (1986).

[36] *See* Lunch at 66–67; Colo. Rev. Stat. § 12-4-110 (Supp. 1990); D.C. Code Ann. § 29-602 (1988).

Even a few years ago, it could be stated that the issue was not whether corporations should be allowed to practice engineering, but whether engineers properly registered should be permitted to perform such services through the corporate form.[37] Today, however, many states are requiring design professional firms to obtain their own separate registration. In the engineering profession alone, over 20 states now require separate, distinct registrations by a corporation or partnership for the entity and its employees to practice engineering. A lesser number of states have similar requirements for architectural or other design professional firms.[38] A typical statute requires the corporation, either business or professional, to obtain a certificate of authority from the professional regulatory board or commission by submitting an application according to procedures adopted by the board or commission. These applications include basic information about the corporation, its organizations, its officers, and directors, and those officers, directors, and employees who are licensed to practice in that state, with particular emphasis on designating those who are in responsible charge of the professional practice.[39] In a disciplinary action arising from the collapse of the Kansas City Hyatt Hotel (see **§ 2.3**), the Missouri Board for Architects, Professional Engineers and Land Surveyors revoked the corporate license to practice of the structural engineering firm and the individual licenses of its president and the employee responsible for the walkway connection design.

§ 2.6 Practice Variations

Today, design professionals can practice their profession through many different business entities. Whether the form of practice is a sole proprietorship, partnership, professional association, professional corporation, or business corporation, the principles of professional responsibility and personal liability are constants. The same cannot be said for the rules and regulations applicable to design professional practice in this country. Not only do the rules vary from state to state, but also within a state each profession may be treated somewhat differently. Engineers are given the greatest latitude in the method of practice, architects are more restricted, and other professions often are treated as being practiced only by sole practitioners or small partnerships. This creates a mosaic of requirements that must be understood to traverse the regulatory obstacle course to become licensed to practice a profession.

---

[37] Lunch at 64; Stitt at 976.

[38] See **Table 2-2** in **§ 2.10**.

[39] *See* S.D. Codified Laws Ann. § 36-18-31.2 to 31.5 (1986).

Only two jurisdictions prohibit all practice by design professionals through business corporations. The District of Columbia became the battleground over the corporate practice of engineers. The federal court, in *Potomac Engineers, Inc. v. Walser,* decided that only a natural person could meet the definition of professional engineer and comply with the citizenship, education, and examination requirements of the regulation statute: "It may be added that traditionally only natural persons can practice a learned profession, because only natural persons can be charged with the moral responsibility that the practice of a learned profession requires."[40] In practice, the concept of natural persons was expanded to include partnerships made of natural persons, each duly licensed in the District of Columbia. The professional registration law was later modified by the adoption of a Professional Corporation Act, enabling those who practice a profession that can only be rendered lawfully pursuant to an individual license and "could not by law or custom be rendered by a corporation" to form a professional corporation, duly registered with the District.[41] This enabled architects and engineers practicing in the District of Columbia to benefit from the pension, benefits, and tax advantages enjoyed by owners and employees of corporations, while still retaining personal liability to those benefitting from such services.

Puerto Rico follows a similar rule for its design professionals, but without the benefit of a professional corporation statute. Under the Puerto Rico law regulating the practice of engineering, architecture, and surveying, practice is limited to natural persons.[42] Though the word "person" is not defined, in 1962 the Puerto Rico Supreme Court interpreted an earlier version of this statute to refer only to individuals because only they can meet the requirements for academic training and examination required by the law.[43] Therefore, by implication, corporations were not persons for professional registration purposes. Luckily for the existing design professional firms, the court was able to uncover a separate statute that could be interpreted to permit them to form partnerships.[44] Puerto Rico also has adopted one unique requirement: only individuals who are legal residents of the Commonwealth of Puerto Rico may be licensed. Moreover, this remains in effect only while the license holder remains a resident. If he subsequently becomes a nonresident, the license automatically becomes inactive and the individual cannot practice in Puerto Rico until he resumes resident status.

---

[40] 127 F. Supp. 41, 42 (D.D.C. 1954), *aff'd,* 223 F.2d 95 (D.C. Cir. 1955).

[41] D.C. Code Ann. § 29-602(2) (1988).

[42] The previous law was found at P.R. Laws Ann. tit. 20, §§ 681 *et seq.,* originally adopted in 1954. This statute was superseded by Act No. 173 (Aug. 12, 1988) (Escrutinio Legislativo, Inc.—unofficial translation).

[43] Raza Eng'g Corp. v. Daubon, 86 P.R.R. 182 (1962).

[44] *Id.* at 186 n.1.

Some states regulate the corporate practice of design professionals by enacting ownership and management restrictions requiring that design professionals licensed in that state have an equity interest in the corporation and an active role in its management. For example, in Ohio engineers and surveyors can use a business corporation to practice only if at least 50 percent of the directors and 50 percent of the officers are licensed in Ohio.[45] Michigan has adopted similar restrictions but requires that two-thirds of the officers and directors be licensed.[46] The rationale for this provision is that it gives more assurance that properly trained and qualified engineers and surveyors who understand the local conditions, customs, codes, and ethical standards have control over all the business and professional activities of the corporation. It is also thought that the cognizant licensing authorities have more leverage and control through strict monitoring to ensure that statutory professional standards are met.

Architects are faced with these restrictions more often than other design professionals. Pennsylvania requires a business corporation practicing architecture to have one-third of its stockholders be licensed architects and two-thirds of its directors be registered architects, engineers, or landscape architects.[47] No similar obligation is imposed on corporations practicing engineering. Several other states impose similar requirements on architects. Iowa, unique among licensing jurisdictions, requires one-third of directors of architectural corporations to be licensed as architects or engineers in Iowa or another state whose licensing requirements are "equivalent" to Iowa's and increases this requirement to two-thirds if the other state's licensing requirements are only "substantially equivalent" to Iowa's standards.[48]

New York, on the other hand, has adopted a different way to limit the practice of architecture and engineering by business corporations. Only corporations organized before April 15, 1935, and with continuous existence are permitted to practice engineering in New York State.[49] Architects are under similar restrictions.[50] Like restrictions on taxi cab medallions in New York City, also adopted during the Depression, the primary result of such legislation is to increase the value of such corporations, making them salable commodities like rare coins and paintings. Vermont also has adopted similar restrictions requiring any corporation that commenced the practice of engineering after July 1, 1986, to do so as a professional corporation.[51]

[45] Ohio Rev. Code Ann. § 4733, 18(D) (Baldwin Supp. 1990).

[46] Mich. Stat. Ann. tit. 63, § 18.425(2010) (Callaghan 1986).

[47] Pa. Stat. Ann. tit. 63, § 34.13 (Purdon Supp. 1990).

[48] Iowa Code Ann. § 118.21 (West Supp. 1990).

[49] N.Y. Educ. Law § 7209(b) (McKinney Supp. 1990).

[50] *Id.* § 7307(4) (McKinney 1985).

[51] Vt. Stat. Ann. tit. 26, § 1186 (1989).

§ 2.7 Registration Procedures

Each state's registration requirements, although varying in details, generally require that the design professional graduate from a four-year college or university with a degree in his specialty. Next, there is a period of apprenticeship during which the design professional obtains practical experience under the supervision of a licensed professional. Finally, the design professional must pass a written and sometimes an oral examination. In certain disciplines, the written examination is prepared by a national organization such as the National Council of Engineering Examiners. Upon completion of these requirements a license is issued.[52]

For those design professionals who have become registered in one state and wish to practice in another, most states provide for reciprocity or comity. This allows a professional to register in another state without taking a second examination. Normally, to be eligible for reciprocity a person must be licensed under a state's law whose registration requirements are equivalent to the educational, experience, and examination requirements of the admitting state.[53] Some states provide an alternative method for reciprocal licensing based upon many years of experience by permitting design professionals to take a "practical" examination that is shorter and more focused than the national examinations. This latter method is helpful to those individuals whose professional training and licensing took place in a foreign country.[54]

State registration laws contain a variety of exemptions that permit design professionals to practice in specific, restricted areas without the necessity of formal registration. The most widely adopted exemptions are for employees of the federal government, employees or subordinates working under the supervision of a licensed professional, and employees of a corporation or business who perform professional services for that business. Many states also provide exemptions for limited practice by nonresidents and for new residents who have filed a proper application for a license.[55]

Each state creates an independent board, commission, or state authority to administer professional registration laws. Some states have a separate board for each design profession; others regulate one or more professions with a single board. Procedures are established to register, monitor, and punish members of each profession. Members of these boards are appointed in a variety of ways, but they usually include representatives of the licensed profession plus members of the public at large.

---

[52] For example, *see* Ala. Code § 34-2-33 (1985). *See* Waggoner, *Professional Relations,* Consulting Engineering Practice Manual 148–49 (1982); Lunch at 66.

[53] *See* Lunch at 67–68.

[54] Pa. Stat. Ann. tit. 63, § 34.9(b) (Purdon Supp. 1990).

[55] Lunch at 68–69.

§ 2.8 Enforcement

Because competence and the public's health and safety are the stated purpose of registration laws, the process of ensuring compliance with their provisions is a primary activity of the boards and authorities created by these laws. Since the Kansas City Hyatt accident in 1981 (see **§ 2.3**), the professions as a whole have taken the issue of competence more seriously and rejuvenated the enforcement activities of many state registration boards.

In most states, violation of the registration provisions of the statutes is a criminal offense. Individuals who practice a design profession without being registered, use the title of the profession in a business name, falsely claim to be registered, or use an expired or revoked certificate of registration are guilty of a crime, usually a misdemeanor, and are liable for imprisonment up to six months and a fine prescribed by law. These criminal penalties apply equally to individuals, partnerships, corporations, and other business entities.[56]

Criminal convictions are few today. Most professional practice violations result in an injunction action by which the state regulatory board seeks an order from a court to make the violator cease further improper practice of a profession. Violation of an injunction will lead to contempt of court charges that can result in imprisonment and fines.[57]

A more effective deterrence is the rule recognized in all jurisdictions that contracts for professional services performed by individuals who are not registered in a state where the services are rendered are unenforceable in court. Over the years, no matter how unfair the result, court after court has held such contractual obligations invalid and void, enabling the recipient of the services to avoid payment. These decisions are based upon the understanding that professional registration laws were designed to protect the public from the unauthorized practice of the profession by incompetent and unqualified persons. Therefore, any services provided by unregistered individuals are against public policy, and the courts hold any contractual obligations to such persons illegal, preventing recovery of any monies due.[58] In this instance, the power of the purse may be mightier than the sword.

This principle has been applied recently in several cases in which the corporation was not properly licensed in the state where the services were performed, although the plans and specifications were signed and sealed by a properly registered employee.[59] The same result occurred even when the

[56] *See, e.g.,* Ark. Stat. Ann. § 14-40-102 (1987); Cal. Bus. & Prof. Code § 5536 (West 1990).

[57] Lunch at 69–70.

[58] *Id.* at 70.

[59] Dalton, Dalton, Little v. Mirandi, 412 F. Supp. 1001 (D.N.J. 1976).

president and chief engineer were licensed but the corporation was not. In the latter case, the court pointed out that the registration requirements in Missouri for foreign corporations to render architecture, engineering, and land surveying services are different and distinct from the requirement for individuals to be licensed. Each is required to obtain his own certificate before rendering professional services.[60]

To ameliorate the harsh result of this rule, some courts have decided that an unregistered out-of-state firm can recover the fair value of its services on the basis of quantum merui. In Louisiana, a corporation provided architectural services for a school board. The Louisiana Supreme Court held the school board could declare the contract void and unenforceable, but the court volunteered that the corporation may have a claim for unjust enrichment on the basis of quantum merui theory.[61]

Enhancement of professional standards is increasingly being maintained through the rigorous enforcement of disciplinary standards and sanctions contained in professional registration laws. Under these provisions, the licensing authorities are empowered to reprimand, censure, sanction, or, in extreme cases, revoke a design professional's license. In some instances, disciplinary action can be taken to place a licensed professional on probation, reporting regularly to state licensing authorities, limiting his practice to certain designated areas, and undertaking additional professional education.[62]

The most common grounds for disciplinary action are fraud and deceit in obtaining a certificate of registration, conviction of a crime (frequently limited to those involving moral turpitude or affecting the ability to practice the profession), violations of the registration statute, and negligence or incompetence in practicing the profession. An important ground for discipline is signing and sealing any plans, specifications, or drawings not personally prepared by the licensed professional or under his personal supervision.[63] In many large firms, professionals are asked to sign and seal documents because of their position or the unavailability of other registered professionals licensed to practice in a particular state. This is one request to avoid. The personal and professional responsibility undertaken by this action is serious. The personal injuries and property damage that can arise out of professional work are substantial. Not being able to testify that a design professional spent some reasonable amount of time reviewing or supervising the preparation of documents he subsequently signs and seals

---

[60] Haith & Co. v. Ellers, Oakley, Chester & Rike, Inc., 778 S.W.2d 417 (Mo. Ct. App. 1989). *See also* Wheeler v. Bucksteel Co., 73 Or. App. 495, 698 P.2d 995, *review denied,* 704 P.2d 513 (Or. 1985).

[61] West Baton Rouge Parish School Bd. v. T.R. Ray, Inc., 367 So. 2d 332, 335 (La. 1979).

[62] *See* Ind. Code Ann. § 25-31-22.1(e)(5) (Burns Supp. 1990).

[63] *See id.* § 25-31-22.1(b)(7).

leaves the design professional defenseless against certain personal, professional, and possibly criminal liabilities. Such irresponsible action goes to the heart of what these laws are designed to achieve: protection of the public through competent performance of professional services.

In the case dealing with the revocation of the licenses for the engineers and their corporation arising out of the Kansas City Hyatt collapse, the court noted that the Missouri statute placed "a non-delegable duty of responsibility" on the engineer for work on which he affixed his seal. This action imposed responsibility for the whole project. Thus, the president of the structural engineering corporation by "his refusal to accept a responsibility so clearly imposed by statute manifests both the gross negligence and unprofessional conduct found by the Commission."[64]

Grounds for disciplinary action have been expanded to meet the changes occurring in today's society. Additional grounds for action have been adopted for alcohol and drug abuse, failure to keep abreast with current professional theory and practice, lewd and immoral conduct, and failure to report any malpractice claim brought against any individual, partnership, or corporation.[65]

As the public demands more and more of its professionals, the enforcement of registration laws by state regulatory bodies will take on more importance for design professionals. Only effective and public enforcement of such laws will allow design professionals to maintain their place as a group that is valued and respected for the services it provides to the public and the contribution it makes to society's advancement.

§ 2.9 Registration Laws

Table 2–1 is a state-by-state listing of registration laws for design professionals.

Table 2–1

State Design Professional Registration Laws

ALABAMA	
Architects	Ala. Code §§ 34-2-1 *et seq.* (1985)
Engineers and Land Surveyors	Ala. Code §§ 34-11-1 *et seq.* (1985)
Landscape Architects	Ala. Code §§ 34-17-1 *et seq.* (1985)
Soil Classifiers	Ala. Code §§ 34-32-1 *et seq.* (1985)

[64] Duncan v. Missouri Bd. for Architects, Professional Eng'rs & Land Surveyors, 744 S.W.2d 524, 542 (Mo. Ct. App. 1988).

[65] *See* Colo. Rev. Stat. § 12-25-108(i)(j), (k) (1985); Ind. Code Ann. § 25-31-22.1(4), (5) (Burns Supp. 1990).

Table 2–1 *(Continued)*

ALASKA	
Architects, Engineers, and Land Surveyors	Alaska Stat. §§ 08.48.011 *et seq.* (1987)
ARIZONA	
Architects, Assayers, Engineers, Geologists, and Surveyors	Ariz. Rev. Stat. Ann. §§ 32-101 *et seq.* (1986)
ARKANSAS	
Architects	Ark. Stat. Ann. §§ 17-14-101 *et seq.* (1987)
Engineers	Ark. Stat. Ann. §§ 17-27-101 *et seq.* (1987)
Landscape Architects	Ark. Stat. Ann. §§ 17-29-101 *et seq.* (1987)
Soil Classifiers	Ark. Stat. Ann. §§ 17-40-101 *et seq.* (1987)
Surveyors	Ark. Stat. Ann. §§ 17-41-101 *et seq.* (1987)
CALIFORNIA	
Architects	Cal. Bus. & Prof. Code §§ 5500 *et seq.* (West 1990)
Landscape Architects	Cal. Bus. & Prof. Code §§ 5615 *et seq.* (West 1990)
Professional Engineers	Cal. Bus. & Prof. Code §§ 6700 *et seq.* (West 1975)
Soil Engineers	Cal. Bus. & Prof. Code §§ 6736.1 *et seq.* (West Supp. 1990)
Geologists and Geophysicists	Cal. Bus. & Prof. Code §§ 7800 *et seq.* (West 1975)
Land Surveyors	Cal. Bus. & Prof. Code §§ 8700 *et seq.* (West 1975)
COLORADO	
Architects	Colo. Rev. Stat. §§ 12-4-101 *et seq.* (1985)
Engineers	Colo. Rev. Stat. §§ 12-25-110 *et seq.* (1985)
Surveyors	Colo. Rev. Stat. §§ 12-25-201 *et seq.* (1985)
Geologists	Colo. Rev. Stat. §§ 34-1-201 *et seq.* (1985)
CONNECTICUT	
Architects	Conn. Gen. Stat. Ann. §§ 20-288 *et seq.* (West 1989)
Professional Engineers and Land Surveyors	Conn. Gen. Stat. Ann. §§ 20-299 *et seq.* (West 1989)
Landscape Architects	Conn. Gen. Stat. Ann. §§ 20-367 *et seq.* (West 1989)
DELAWARE	
Landscape Architects	Del. Code Ann. tit. 24, §§ 200 *et seq.* (1987)
Architects	Del. Code Ann. tit. 24, §§ 301 *et seq.* (1987)
Professional Land Surveyors	Del. Code Ann. tit. 24, §§ 2701 *et seq.* (1987)
Professional Engineers	Del. Code Ann. tit. 24, §§ 2801 *et seq.* (1987)
Geologists	Del. Code Ann. tit. 24, §§ 3601 *et seq.* (1987)

Table 2–1 *(Continued)*

DISTRICT OF COLUMBIA	
Architects	D.C. Code Ann. §§ 2-201 *et seq.* (1988)
Professional Engineers	D.C. Code Ann. §§ 2-2301 *et seq.* (1988)
FLORIDA	
Engineers	Fla. Stat. Ann. §§ 471.001 *et seq.* (West Supp. 1990)
Land Surveyors	Fla. Stat. Ann. §§ 472.001 *et seq.* (West 1981)
Architects	Fla. Stat. Ann. §§ 481.201 *et seq.* (West Supp. 1990)
Landscape Architects	Fla. Stat. Ann. §§ 481.301 *et seq.* (West Supp. 1990)
Professional Geologists	Fla. Stat. Ann. §§ 492.101 *et seq.* (West Supp. 1990)
GEORGIA	
Architects	Ga. Code Ann. §§ 43-4-1 *et seq.* (1988)
Geologists	Ga. Code Ann. §§ 43-19-1 *et seq.* (1988)
Landscape Architects	Ga. Code Ann. §§ 43-23-1 *et seq.* (West Cum. Supp. 1990)
Professional Engineers and Land Surveyors	Ga. Code Ann. §§ 43-15-1 *et seq.* (1988)
HAWAII	
Professional Engineers, Architects, Surveyors, and Landscape Architects	Haw. Rev. Stat. §§ 464-1 *et seq.* (Supp. 1989)
IDAHO	
Architects	Idaho Code §§ 54-301 *et seq.* (1988)
Engineers and Surveyors	Idaho Code §§ 54-1201 *et seq.* (1988)
Environmental Health Specialists	Idaho Code §§ 54-2401 *et seq.* (1988)
Geologists	Idaho Code §§ 54-2801 *et seq.* (1988)
Landscape Architects	Idaho Code §§ 54-3003 *et seq.* (1988)
ILLINOIS	
Architects	Ill. Ann. Stat. ch. 111, para. 1201 *et seq.* (Smith-Hurd 1978)
Professional Engineers	Ill. Ann. Stat. ch. 111, para. 5201 *et seq.* (Smith-Hurd Supp. 1990)
Structural Engineers	Ill. Ann. Stat. ch. 111, para. 6601 *et seq.* (Smith-Hurd 1978)
Landscape Architects	Ill. Ann. Stat. ch. 111, para. 8101 *et seq.* (Smith-Hurd 1978)

Table 2–1 *(Continued)*

INDIANA	
Architects	Ind. Code Ann. §§ 25-4-1-2 *et seq.* (Burns Supp. 1990)
Landscape Architects	Ind. Code Ann. §§ 25-4-2-1 *et seq.* (Burns Supp. 1990)
Geologists	Ind. Code Ann. §§ 25-17.5-1-1 *et seq.* (Burns 1982)
Professional Engineers and Land Surveyors	Ind. Code Ann. §§ 25-31-1-1 *et seq.* (Burns Supp. 1990)
IOWA	
Professional Engineers and Land Surveyors	Iowa Code Ann. §§ 114.1 *et seq.* (West 1984)
Architects	Iowa Code Ann. §§ 118.1 *et seq.* (West 1984)
Landscape Architects	Iowa Code Ann. §§ 118A.1 *et seq.* (West 1984)
KANSAS	
Architects, Engineers, Land Surveyors, and Landscape Architects	Kan. Stat. Ann. §§ 74-7001 *et seq.* (1985)
KENTUCKY	
Professional Engineers and Land Surveyors	Ky. Rev. Stat. Ann. §§ 322.010 *et seq.* (Michie/Bobbs-Merrill 1990)
Architects	Ky. Rev. Stat. Ann. §§ 323.010 *et seq.* (Michie/Bobbs-Merrill 1990)
Landscape Architects	Ky. Rev. Stat. Ann. §§ 323A.010 *et seq.* (Michie/Bobbs-Merrill 1990)
LOUISIANA	
Architects	La. Rev. Stat. Ann. §§ 37:141 *et seq.* (West 1988)
Civil Engineers and Surveyors	La. Rev. Stat. Ann. §§ 37:681 *et seq.* (West 1988)
MAINE	
Architects and Landscape Architects	Me. Rev. Stat. Ann. tit. 32, §§ 211 *et seq.* (1988)
Engineers	Me. Rev. Stat. Ann. tit. 32, §§ 1252 *et seq.* (1988)
Geologists and Soil Scientists	Me. Rev. Stat. Ann. tit. 32, §§ 4901 *et seq.* (1988)
Professional Land Surveyors	Me. Rev. Stat. Ann. tit. 32, §§ 13901 *et seq.* (Supp. 1990)
MARYLAND	
Architects	Md. Bus. Occ. Code Ann. §§ 3-101 *et seq.* (1989)
Landscape Architects	Md. Bus. Occ. Code Ann. §§ 9-101 *et seq.* (1989)
Professional Engineers	Md. Bus. Occ. Code Ann. §§ 14-101 *et seq.* (1989)

Table 2–1 *(Continued)*

Professional Land Surveyors	Md. Bus. Occ. Code Ann. §§ 15-101 *et seq.*(1989)
MASSACHUSETTS	
Architects	Mass. Gen. L. ch. 112, §§ 60A *et seq.* (1988)
Professional Engineers and Land Surveyors	Mass. Gen. L. ch. 112, §§ 81D *et seq.* (1988)
Landscape Architects	Mass. Gen. L. ch. 112, §§ 98 *et seq.* (1988)
MICHIGAN	
Architects, Land Surveyors, and Professional Engineers	Mich. Stat. Ann. §§ 18.425(2001) *et seq.* (Callaghan 1986)
MINNESOTA	
Architects, Engineers, Surveyors, and Landscape Architects	Minn. Stat. Ann. §§ 326.02 *et seq.* (West 1981)
MISSISSIPPI	
Architects	Miss. Code Ann. §§ 73-1-1 *et seq.* (1989)
Landscape Architects	Miss. Code Ann. §§ 73-2-1 *et seq.* (1989)
Engineers and Land Surveyors	Miss. Code Ann. §§ 73-13-1 *et seq.* (1989)
MISSOURI	
Practice of Geology	Mo. Ann. Stat. §§ 256.501 *et seq.* (Vernon 1990)
Architects, Professional Engineers, and Land Surveyors	Mo. Ann. Stat. §§ 327.011 *et seq.* (Vernon 1990)
Landscape Architects	Mo. Ann. Stat. §§ 327.600 *et seq.* (Vernon Supp. 1990)
MONTANA	
Architects	Mont. Code Ann. §§ 37-65-101 *et seq.* (1989)
Landscape Architects	Mont. Code Ann. §§ 37-66-101 *et seq.* (1989)
Engineers and Land Surveyors	Mont. Code Ann. §§ 37-67-101 *et seq.* (1989)
NEBRASKA	
Professional Engineers and Architects	Neb. Rev. Stat. §§ 81-839 *et seq.* (1987)
Land Surveyors	Neb. Rev. Stat. §§ 81-8,108 *et seq.* (1987)
Landscape Architects	Neb. Rev. Stat. §§ 81-8,184 *et seq.* (1987)
NEVADA	
Architects	Nev. Rev. Stat. Ann. §§ 623.010 *et seq.* (Michie 1986)

Table 2-1 *(Continued)*

Landscape Architects	Nev. Rev. Stat. Ann. §§ 623A.010 *et seq.* (Michie 1986)
Professional Engineers and Surveyors	Nev. Rev. Stat. Ann. §§ 625.010 *et seq.* (Michie Supp. 1990)
NEW HAMPSHIRE	
Engineers, Architects, and Land Surveyors	N.H. Rev. Stat. Ann. §§ 310-A:1 *et seq.* (1984)
NEW JERSEY	
Architects	N.J. Stat. Ann. §§ 45:3-1 *et seq.* (West Supp. 1990)
Engineers and Land Surveyors	N.J. Stat. Ann. §§ 45:8-1 *et seq.* (West Supp. 1990)
Landscape Architects	N.J. Stat. Ann. §§ 45:3A-1 *et seq.* (West Supp. 1990)
Building Design Services	N.J. Stat. Ann. §§ 45:4B-1 *et seq.* (West 1978)
Professional Planners	N.J. Stat. Ann. §§ 45:14A-1 *et seq.* (West 1978)
NEW MEXICO	
Architects	N.M. Stat. Ann. §§ 16-15-1 *et seq.* (1987)
Engineers and Land Surveyors	N.M. Stat. Ann. §§ 61-23-1 *et seq.* (1987)
Landscape Architects	N.M. Stat. Ann. §§ 61-24B-1 *et seq.* (1990)
NEW YORK	
Engineers and Land Surveyors	N.Y. Educ. Law §§ 7200 *et seq.* (McKinney 1985)
Architects	N.Y. Educ. Law §§ 7300 *et seq.* (McKinney 1985)
Landscape Architects	N.Y. Educ. Law §§ 7320 *et seq.* (McKinney 1985)
NORTH CAROLINA	
Architects	N.C. Gen. Stat. §§ 83A-1 *et seq.* (1990)
Landscape Architects	N.C. Gen. Stat. §§ 89A-1 *et seq.* (1990)
Engineers and Land Surveyors	N.C. Gen. Stat. §§ 89C-1 *et seq.* (1990)
NORTH DAKOTA	
Architects	N.D. Cent. Code §§ 43-03-01 *et seq.* (1978)
Professional Engineers and Land Surveyors	N.D. Cent. Code §§ 43-19.1-01 *et seq.* (1978)
Professional Soil Classifiers	N.D. Cent. Code §§ 43-36-01 *et seq.* (1978)
OHIO	
Architects	Ohio Rev. Code Ann. §§ 4703.01 *et seq.* (Baldwin Supp. 1989)
Landscape Architects	Ohio Rev. Code Ann. §§ 4703.30 *et seq.* (Baldwin 1988)

Table 2–1 *(Continued)*

Professional Engineers and Surveyors	Ohio Rev. Code Ann. §§ 4733.01 *et seq.* (Baldwin Supp. 1989)
OKLAHOMA	
Architects and Landscape Architects	Okla. Stat. Ann. tit. 59, §§ 46.1 *et seq.* (West 1989)
Engineers and Land Surveyors	Okla. Stat. Ann. tit. 59, §§ 475.1 *et seq.* (West 1989)
OREGON	
Architects	Or. Rev. Stat. §§ 671.010 *et seq.* (1989)
Landscape Architects	Or. Rev. Stat. §§ 671.310 *et seq.* (1989)
Professional Engineers and Land Surveyors	Or. Rev. Stat. §§ 672.002 *et seq.* (1989)
Geologists	Or. Rev. Stat. §§ 672.505 *et seq.* (1989)
PENNSYLVANIA	
Architects	Pa. Stat. Ann. tit. 63, §§ 34.1 *et seq.* (Purdon Supp. 1990)
Landscape Architects	Pa. Stat. Ann. tit. 63, §§ 901 *et seq.* (Purdon Supp. 1990)
Engineers and Land Surveyors	Pa. Stat. Ann. tit. 63, §§ 131 *et seq.* (Purdon 1968)
PUERTO RICO	
Engineers, Surveyors, and Architects	Act No. 173 (Aug. 12, 1988) (Escrutinio Legislativo—unofficial translation)
RHODE ISLAND	
Architects	R.I. Gen. Laws §§ 5-1-1 *et seq.* (1987)
Engineers	R.I. Gen. Laws §§ 5-8-1 *et seq.* (Supp. 1990)
Land Surveyors	R.I. Gen. Laws §§ 5-8.1-1 *et seq.* (Supp. 1990)
SOUTH CAROLINA	
Architects	S.C. Code Ann. §§ 40-3-10 *et seq.* (Law. Co-op. 1986)
Engineers and Land Surveyors	S.C. Code Ann. §§ 40-21-10 *et seq.* (Law. Co-op. Supp. 1989)
Soil Classifiers	S.C. Code Ann. §§ 40-65-10 *et seq.* (Law. Co-op. 1986)
Geologists	S.C. Code Ann. §§ 40-77-10 *et seq.* (Law. Co-op. Supp. 1989)
SOUTH DAKOTA	
Engineers, Architects, and Land Surveyors	S.D. Codified Laws Ann. §§ 36-18-4.1 *et seq.* (1986)
Landscape Architects	S.D. Codified Laws Ann. §§ 36-18-44 *et seq.* (Supp. 1990)

Table 2–1 *(Continued)*

TENNESSEE	
Architects, Engineers, and Landscape Architects	Tenn. Code Ann. §§ 62-2-101 *et seq.* (1990)
Geologists	Tenn. Code Ann. §§ 62-36-101 *et seq.* (1990)
TEXAS	
Architects	Texas Rev. Civ. Stat. Ann. art. 249a, §§ 1 *et seq.* (Vernon Supp. 1991)
Landscape Architects	Texas Rev. Civ. Stat. Ann. art. 249c, §§ 1 *et seq.* (Vernon Supp. 1991)
Engineers	Texas Rev. Civ. Stat. Ann. art. 3271(a), §§ 1 *et seq.* (Vernon 1973)
Land Surveyors	Texas Rev. Civ. Stat. Ann. art. 5282(c), §§ 1 *et seq.* (Vernon Supp. 1991)
UTAH	
Architects	Utah Code Ann. §§ 58-3-1 *et seq.* (1990)
Professional Engineers and Land Surveyors	Utah Code Ann. §§ 58-22-1 *et seq.* (1990)
VERMONT	
Architects	Vt. Stat. Ann. tit. 26, §§ 121 *et seq.* (1989)
Professional Engineers	Vt. Stat. Ann. tit. 26, §§ 1161 *et seq.* (1989)
VIRGINIA	
Architects, Surveyors, and Landscape Architects	Va. Code Ann. §§ 54.1-400 *et seq.* (1988)
Geologists	Va. Code Ann. §§ 54.1-1400 *et seq.* (1988)
Soil Scientists	Va. Code Ann. §§ 54.1-2200 *et seq.* (1988)
VIRGIN ISLANDS	
Architects, Engineers, and Land Surveyors	V.I. Code Ann. tit. 27, §§ 281 *et seq.* (Supp. 1990)
WASHINGTON	
Architects	Wash. Rev. Code Ann. §§ 18.08.235 *et seq.* (1989)
Landscape Architects	Wash. Rev. Code Ann. §§ 18.96.010 *et seq.* (1989)
Engineers and Land Surveyors	Wash. Rev. Code Ann. §§ 18.43.010 *et seq.* (1989)
WEST VIRGINIA	
Architects	W. Va. Code §§ 30-12-1 *et seq.* (Supp. 1990)
Landscape Architects	W. Va. Code §§ 30-22-1 *et seq.* (1986)
Engineers	W. Va. Code §§ 30-13-1 *et seq.* (1986)
Land Surveyors	W. Va. Code §§ 30-13A-1 *et seq.* (1986)

Table 2–1 *(Continued)*

WISCONSIN	
Architects, Professional Engineers, Designers, and Land Surveyors	Wis. Stat. Ann. §§ 443.01 *et seq.* (West 1988)
WYOMING	
Architects	Wyo. Stat. §§ 33-4-101 *et seq.* (1987)
Surveyors and Engineers	Wyo. Stat. §§ 33-29-114 *et seq.* (1987)

§ 2.10 Corporate Practice Laws

Table 2–2 is a state-by-state listing of corporate practice laws for design professionals.

Table 2–2

State Design Professional Corporate Practice Laws

ALABAMA	
Architects	Ala. Code § 34-2-37 (1985)
Engineers and Land Surveyors	Ala. Code § 34-11-9 (1985)
Landscape Architects	Ala. Code § 34-17-4 (1985)
Soil Classifiers	Ala. Code § 34-32-4 (1985)
ALASKA	
Architects, Engineers, and Land Surveyors	Alaska Stat. § 08.48.241 (1987)
ARIZONA	
Architects, Assayers, Engineers, Geologists, and Surveyors	Ariz. Rev. Stat. Ann. § 32-141A (1986)
ARKANSAS	
Architects	Ark. Stat. Ann. § 17-14-303(a) (1987)
Engineers	Ark. Stat. Ann. § 17-27-301(5) (1987)
Surveyors	Ark. Stat. Ann. § 17-41-201(c) (1987)
CALIFORNIA	
Architects	Cal. Bus. & Prof. Code §§ 5536 & 5610 (West 1990)
Professional Engineers	Cal. Bus. & Prof. Code § 6738 (West Supp. 1990)
Land Surveyors	Cal. Bus. & Prof. Code § 8729 (West Supp. 1990)

Table 2–2 *(Continued)*

COLORADO	
Architects	Colo. Rev. Stat. § 12-4-110 (Supp. 1990)
Engineers	Colo. Rev. Stat. § 12-25-104(a) (1985)
CONNECTICUT	
Architects	Conn. Gen. Stat. Ann. § 20-298(b) (West 1989)
Professional Engineers and Land Surveyors	Conn. Gen. Stat. Ann. § 20-206(a) (West 1989)
Joint Architect-Engineer Corporation	Conn. Gen. Stat. Ann. § 20-206(b) (West 1989)
DELAWARE	
Architects	Del. Code Ann. tit. 24, § 303(b)(4) (1987)
Professional Engineers	Del. Code Ann. tit. 24, § 2821 (1987)
FLORIDA	
Engineers	Fla. Stat. Ann. § 471.023 (West Supp. 1990)
Architects	Fla. Stat. Ann. § 481.219 (West Supp. 1990)
Landscape Architects	Fla. Stat. Ann. § 481.319 (West Supp. 1990)
Professional Geologists	Fla. Stat. Ann. § 492.111 (West Supp. 1990)
GEORGIA	
Architects	Ga. Code Ann. § 43-4-10(c) (1988)
Geologists	Ga. Code Ann. § 43-19-25(a) (1988)
Landscape Architects	Ga. Code Ann. § 43-23-14 (1988)
Professional Engineers and Land Surveyors	Ga. Code Ann. § 43-15-23.1 (Supp. 1990)
HAWAII	
Professional Engineers, Architects, Surveyors, and Landscape Architects	Haw. Rev. Stat. § 464-12 (Supp. 1989)
IDAHO	
Architects	Idaho Code §§ 54-307 & 316 (1988)
Engineers and Surveyors	Idaho Code § 54-1235 (Supp. 1990)
ILLINOIS	
Architects	Ill. Ann. Stat. ch. 111, para. 1206 (Smith-Hurd 1978)
Professional Engineers	Ill. Ann. Stat. ch. 111, para. 5223 (Smith-Hurd Supp. 1990)
Structural Engineers	Ill. Ann. Stat. ch. 111, para. 6619 (Smith-Hurd 1978)
INDIANA	
Architects	Ind. Code Ann. § 25-4-1-27 (Burns Supp. 1990)
Professional Engineers and Land Surveyors	Ind. Code Ann. § 25-3-1-18 (Burns 1982)

Table 2–2 *(Continued)*

IOWA	
Professional Engineers and Land Surveyors	Iowa Code Ann. § 114.26 (West 1984)
Architects	Iowa Code Ann. § 118.21 (West 1984)
KANSAS	
Architects, Engineers, Land Surveyors, and Landscape Architects	Kan. Stat. Ann. § 74-7036 (1985)
KENTUCKY	
Opinion of the Attorney General § 322.060, May 2, 1957 (No company shall be registered; admission to practice shall be determined upon the basis of individual, personal qualifications).	
LOUISIANA	
Civil Engineers and Surveyors	La. Rev. Stat. Ann. § 37:689 (West 1988)
Architect-Engineering Corporation	La. Rev. Stat. Ann. §§ 121:1171 *et seq.* (West Supp. 1990)
MAINE	
Architects and Landscape Architects	Me. Rev. Stat. Ann. tit. 32, § 220 (1988)
Engineers	Me. Rev. Stat. Ann. tit. 32, § 1253 (1988)
Geologists and Soil Scientists	Me. Rev. Stat. Ann. tit. 32, § 4904 (1988)
MARYLAND	
Professional Engineers	Md. Bus. Occ. Code Ann. § 14-302 (1989)
MASSACHUSETTS	
Architects	Mass. Gen. L. ch. 112, § 60L (1988)
Professional Engineers and Land Surveyors	Mass. Gen. L. ch. 112, § 81D (1988)
MICHIGAN	
Architects, Land Surveyors, and Professional Engineers	Mich. Stat. Ann. § 18.425(2010) (Callaghan 1986)
MINNESOTA	
Architects, Engineers, Surveyors, and Landscape Architects	Minn. Stat. Ann. § 326.14 (West 1981)
MISSISSIPPI	
Engineers and Land Surveyors	Miss. Code Ann. § 73-13-43 (1989)

Table 2–2 *(Continued)*

MISSOURI	
Architects, Professional Engineers, and Land Surveyors	Mo. Ann. Stat. § 327.401.2 (Vernon 1990)
MONTANA	
Landscape Architects	Mont. Code Ann. § 37-65-303(1) (1989)
Engineers and Land Surveyors	Mont. Code Ann. § 37-67-320(2) (1989)
NEBRASKA	
Professional Engineers and Architects	Neb. Rev. Stat. § 81-854 (1987)
NEVADA	
Professional Engineers and Surveyors	Nev. Rev. Stat. Ann. § 625.240 (Michie Supp. 1990)
NEW HAMPSHIRE	
Engineers, Architects, and Land Surveyors	N.H. Rev. Stat. Ann. § 310-A:20 (1984)
NEW JERSEY	
Architects	N.J. Stat. Ann. § 45:3-18 (West Supp. 1990)
Engineers and Land Surveyors	N.J. Stat. Ann. § 45:8-27 (West Supp. 1990)
NEW MEXICO	
Engineers and Land Surveyors	N.M. Stat. Ann. § 61-23-21 (1987)
NEW YORK	
Engineers and Land Surveyors	N.Y. Educ. Law § 7209(6) (McKinney Supp. 1990)
Architects	N.Y. Educ. Law § 7307(4) (McKinney 1985)
NORTH CAROLINA	
Architects	N.C. Gen. Stat. § 83A-8 (1990)
Engineers and Land Surveyors	N.C. Gen. Stat. § 89C-24 (1990)
NORTH DAKOTA	
Engineers and Land Surveyors	N.D. Cent. Code § 43-19.1-27(3) (1978)
OHIO	
Architects	Ohio Rev. Code Ann. § 4703.18(E) (Baldwin Supp. 1989)
Professional Engineers and Surveyors	Ohio Rev. Code Ann. § 4733.18(D) (Baldwin Supp. 1989)

Table 2–2 *(Continued)*

OKLAHOMA	
Architects and Landscape Architects	Okla. Stat. Ann. tit. 59, § 46.9 (West 1989)
Engineers and Land Surveyors	Okla. Stat. Ann. tit. 59, § 475.21 (West 1989)
OREGON	
Architects	Or. Rev. Stat. § 671.041 (1989)
Professional Engineers and Land Surveyors	Or. Rev. Stat. § 672.060(a) (1989)
PENNSYLVANIA	
Architects	Pa. Stat. Ann. tit. 63, § 34.13 (Purdon Supp. 1990)
Engineers and Land Surveyors	Pa. Stat. Ann. tit. 63, § 153 (Supp. 1990)
RHODE ISLAND	
Architects	R.I. Gen. Laws §§ 5-1-7 & -8 (1987)
Engineers	R.I. Gen. Laws § 5-8-21(d) (Supp. 1990)
SOUTH CAROLINA	
Architects	S.C. Code Ann. § 40-3-100 (Law. Co-op. 1986)
Engineers and Land Surveyors	S.C. Code Ann. § 40-21-405 (Law. Co-op. Supp. 1989)
SOUTH DAKOTA	
Engineers, Architects, and Land Surveyors	S.D. Codified Laws Ann. § 36-18-31.1 (1986)
TENNESSEE	
Architects, Engineers, and Landscape Architects	Tenn. Code Ann. § 62-2-601 (1990)
Geologists	Tenn. Code Ann. § 62-36-101 (1990)
TEXAS	
Architects	Texas Rev. Civ. Stat. Ann. art. 249a, § 10(i) (Vernon Supp. 1991)
Engineers	Texas Rev. Civ. Stat. Ann. art. 327(a), § 18 (Vernon 1973)
Land Surveyors	Texas Rev. Civ. Stat. Ann. art. 327(a), (Vernon Supp. 1991)
UTAH	
Professional Engineers and Land Surveyors	Utah Code Ann. § 58-22-10(b) (1990)
VERMONT	
Professional Engineers	Vt. Stat. Ann. tit. 26, § 1186 (1990)

Table 2-2 *(Continued)*

VIRGINIA	
Architects, Surveyors, and Landscape Architects	Va. Code Ann. § 54.1-411 (1988)
VIRGIN ISLANDS	
Architects, Engineers, and Land Surveyors	V.I. Code Ann. tit. 27, § 291(4) (Supp. 1990)
WASHINGTON	
Architects	Wash. Rev. Code Ann. § 18.08.420 (1989)
Engineers and Land Surveyors	Wash. Rev. Code Ann. § 18.43.130 (1989)
WEST VIRGINIA	
Architects	W. Va. Code § 30-12-12(e) (Supp. 1990)
Engineers	W. Va. Code § 30-13-9 (1986)
Landscape Architects	W. Va. Code § 30-22-9 (1986)
WISCONSIN	
Architects, Professional Engineers, Designers, and Land Surveyors	Wis. Stat. Ann. § 443.08(2) (West 1988)
WYOMING	
Surveyors and Engineers	Wyo. Stat. § 33-29-134 (1987)

CHAPTER 3

CHOOSING A BUSINESS FORM

Rodger W. Charin

Rodger W. Charin has a private practice in Fairfax, Virginia, specializing in business tax consulting. He formerly was a tax partner in the Washington, D.C. office of the international accounting firm of Ernst & Young, where he was a member of the firm's entrepreneurial services practice and coordinated tax services for the Construction Industry Group. He is a frequent lecturer on tax planning for startup and closely held businesses and has been a national instructor on subchapter S corporations. Mr. Charin is a member of the District of Columbia Institute of Certified Public Accountants, the American Institute of Certified Public Accountants, and the Associated General Contractors of America.

§ 3.1 Introduction

One of the most important decisions confronting design business owners is selecting a business form. Each form, whether it be a sole proprietorship, partnership, or corporation, has its advantages and disadvantages and selection should be based on the objectives and circumstances of a particular business and its owners.

Taxation and liability protection are often key factors in the selection process, but the choice of form affects numerous other business considerations. These include the ability to raise capital, managerial control, the transfer and sharing of ownership, administrative and operating costs, and accounting periods and methods. Additionally, design firms must pay special heed to the rules of state regulatory boards and professional organizations, as well as the statutes that specifically govern professional firms. All these factors should be weighed in choosing a business structure. In certain instances, even a combination of forms may be appropriate. Moreover, the form that is best at start-up may not remain appropriate as the enterprise evolves or the business environment changes. An individual starting a design firm might begin as a sole proprietor, change the form to a partnership to bring in co-owners, and then convert to a corporation to raise capital for expansion. Revisions in tax or other laws also may make it wise to change to a different form.

This chapter looks at three primary business forms: the sole proprietorship, the partnership, and the corporation. The corporate section examines corporations generally, with special attention devoted to the professional corporation. The corporate financing techniques of private placements, public offerings, and employee stock ownership plans (ESOPs) are reviewed. Taxation of all three business forms also is examined, including the taxation of S corporations.[1] The final sections discuss the selection of tax accounting methods and a tax period.

§ 3.2 Sole Proprietorships

Sole proprietorship is the simplest business form for the lone design professional operating a firm. With the sole proprietorship, the business is, in effect, inseparable from the individual owner. A sole proprietorship can

---

[1] This chapter includes federal tax law changes through the Revenue Reconciliation Act, Pub. L. No. 101-508, 104 Stat. 1388 (1990).

have only one owner, but that is the only size restriction. Revenues can grow to any amount and there can be any number of employees.

The owner is in charge; there are no issues of control. Assets are titled in the owner's name and the owner has direct financial liability for the obligations of the business. General contract, tort, property, and agency law and rules apply. Because the business and the owner are inextricably linked, when the owner dies the business ends.

In most states there are few, if any, registration requirements for establishing a sole proprietorship, particularly compared to formation of a corporation. As with any business, however, general requirements such as obtaining local licenses or permits and filing for a federal identification number must be fulfilled. Further, regardless of entity choice, the design professional must meet special state licensing and registration requirements. Virtually every state's statutes require registration of a design business and/or licensure of the individual professional with a state regulatory board.[2]

Because there is a single owner and minimal registration requirements, there is no need to draft and maintain formal organizational documents. This can mean significant cost savings, particularly in the formation of a new business. Operational costs are also generally low. Accounting is normally required only for tax and internal reporting purposes, although more formal reporting will probably be necessary if financial institutions have provided financing.

The business itself does not pay taxes or file a return; the owner does that. The business's income and expenses must be reported separately on a Schedule C on the sole proprietor's tax return. As with any business, the sole proprietorship is subject to the general rules governing tax accounting methods, as discussed in **§ 3.15**. The business's accounting method may differ from the individual's normal method, but design professionals can, and usually do, use cash accounting in both instances.

Whatever accounting methods are used, the business's net income is mixed with the owner's other sources of income and deductible expenses to determine taxable income. There is generally a single level of tax. There is no entity level federal tax and typically no entity level state or local tax. Although some state and local jurisdictions impose an unincorporated business income tax on sole proprietorships,[3] this levy is unlikely to be sufficient to affect the selection of entity.

When the sole proprietorship generates losses from business operations, they can offset the owner's taxable income from other sources. The use of business losses as an income offset is particularly valuable in the start-up phase of an operation when losses are most likely. Further, there are no

---

[2] See **Ch. 2**.

[3] *E.g.*, New York City and the District of Columbia.

adverse tax consequences for withdrawing money from a sole proprietorship, and termination of the business is generally as simple as origination. The sole proprietorship also lends itself to easy conversion to partnership or corporate form.

Until recently, there were a number of tax incentives that made incorporation attractive to an individual business owner. When the Internal Revenue Service (IRS) indicated in 1969 that it would treat corporations organized under state professional association acts as corporations for tax purposes, many one-person businesses chose to incorporate. Subsequent changes in tax law have eliminated many of the beneficial aspects of incorporation.

Sole proprietorships can now establish tax-favored retirement plans comparable to those formerly available only to corporations.[4] These plans permit self-employed individuals to make tax deductible contributions generally equal to those allowed to shareholder-employees of corporations.[5] Contributions remain untaxed until distribution.[6] The top individual tax rate of 31 percent is currently lower than the top corporate rate of 34 percent, and the benefit of graduated corporate rates is not available to corporations defined as personal service corporations for federal tax purposes (the status that will often apply to corporate design firms, as discussed in **§ 3.12**). Additionally, sole proprietors can now deduct 25 percent of qualified medical insurance payments.[7]

In summary, the sole proprietorship may be particularly desirable for the design professional first starting a professional practice. It is simple and inexpensive to form and maintain. There is a single level of tax. It may serve as the best structure throughout a firm's life, but should business needs change, it easily can be converted to a partnership or corporation. However, there are disadvantages as well. The owner is directly responsible for all business liabilities, although insurance can mitigate this risk. Growth may be constrained by the owner's personal financial resources and ability to borrow. Additionally, conversion to another form may be required to accommodate the growth and needs of key employees.

§ 3.3 Partnerships

When two or more design professionals decide to own and conduct a business together, formation of a partnership is the alternative to incorporation.

---

[4] Retirement plan benefits available to sole proprietors, partners, and S corporation shareholders were equalized with those available to regular corporation shareholders by the Tax Equity and Fiscal Responsibility Act, Pub. L. No. 97-248, 96 Stat. 324 (1982).

[5] I.R.C. §§ 401(c), 404(a)(8) (West 1990).

[6] *Id.* §§ 401(a), 501(a).

[7] *Id.* § 162(1).

General partnerships have a long history of use by all types of professionals, including architects and engineers. Limited partnerships are rare in the design industry, but may be useful in special circumstances. **Sections 3.4** through **3.7** primarily address the general partnership and briefly examine limited partnerships and joint ventures.

§ 3.4 —General Partnerships

The law of general partnerships is governed in virtually every state by the Uniform Partnership Act (UPA) or some variation thereof. In general, any business activity carried on for profit by two or more co-owners is considered a general partnership under the UPA.[8] A general partnership may be as simple as two individuals who agree to share equally in all financial and managerial aspects of a business or as complex as hundreds of individuals (or other entity types) with varying managerial and economic rights. Some of the largest professional firms in the world are structured as general partnerships.

Design partnerships generally are subject to state regulation and attendant design professional registration and licensing requirements for the entity and individual partner.[9] However, most states have few other statutory reporting and compliance requirements for the formation and operation of general partnerships. Even a written partnership agreement is not required under the UPA. However, a well thought-out and thorough partnership agreement that sets forth the rights and obligations of the individual partners should be drafted with the assistance of competent counsel. Depending upon its complexity, the cost of drafting a partnership agreement often exceeds that of drafting formal corporate documents.

The partnership form allows substantial organizational flexibility. Managerial control can be crafted in virtually any fashion and almost any economic or managerial arrangement can be embodied in a written partnership agreement. In large partnerships, management is usually vested in one or two individuals or a committee. Smaller partnerships typically seek to assure that control follows ownership interests. Profit and loss sharing can be based on straight ownership percentages or on special allocations tied to performance or other criteria. All partners in design partnerships normally are active participants in the business, and the ability to construct varied organizational structures to meet the needs and desires of the partners is a particularly desirable characteristic. Statutory requirements that generally apply to corporations (see **§ 3.9**) do not exist. The potential benefits are most dramatic when contrasted with the strict organizational

[8] 6 U.L.A. 1 (1969).

[9] See **Ch. 2**.

eligibility requirements that must be met to elect and maintain S corporation status. See § **3.13**.

In many respects, a partnership is merely an aggregation of its separate partners. However, the entity is considered separate and distinct for certain purposes and generally will be perceived as such by outside parties. A partnership technically has a limited life and "dissolution" is automatic under the UPA when a partner dies, retires, is expelled, or otherwise departs the organization.[10] However, the continuity of the partnership as a business can be assured in most circumstances by provisions in a written partnership agreement.

The ability to control the admittance of new partners and the transfer of the interests of withdrawing or deceased partners is important to professional partnerships and should be carefully considered in drafting a design firm's partnership agreement. Professional partnerships normally prohibit the transfer of partnership interests from an existing partner to a new partner. New partners are brought into the organization by the issuance of a partnership interest by the partnership itself. The partnership interest of departing or deceased partners is retired. The unrestricted transferability of interests that can characterize the corporate form is not associated with general partnerships. Because individual partners frequently leave and professional partnerships often break up as individual partners or groups of partners seek other professional opportunities, partnership agreements should set forth the rights and obligations of the partners and the partnership when such events occur.

The most frequently cited disadvantage of the partnership structure is the unlimited personal liability of each partner for the financial and legal obligations of the business. Partners are jointly and severally liable for negligence and other torts committed by partners, employees, or other agents of the business. In most states, joint and several liability extends to all partnership contractual obligations as well. As with the sole proprietorship, insurance can greatly mitigate this risk. Nevertheless, there is always the possibility that personal assets have to be forfeited to satisfy the partnership's obligations. Partnership law binds each partner to the acts of co-owners through the doctrine of mutual agency; therefore, the honesty, competence, and good faith of potential partners should be given major weight in determining whether to enter into a partnership or to admit new partners.

Accounting requirements are usually more extensive for a partnership than a sole proprietorship because the financial obligations and rewards of individual partners must be clearly spelled out. Moreover, the need to account at the owner's level as well as the entity level can make partnership accounting more costly and difficult than corporate accounting. This is true even though, in contrast to corporations, partnerships have few nontax

---

[10] Unif. Partnership Act § 31, 6 U.L.A. 1 (1969).

reporting requirements mandated by statute or regulation. Partnership accounting can be particularly complex when there are special allocations of profits and losses or uneven withdrawals and contributions of capital. Further, a partnership will frequently borrow directly from outside sources and creditors may demand an accountant's report on the partnership's operations. Regardless of specific requirements, it is obviously in the best interests of all partners that good accounting records be maintained.

Capital resources of general partnerships are constrained by the financial means of the individual partners and the borrowing that their business and personal assets will support. Creditors are apt to lend greater amounts to a partnership than a sole proprietorship because there are multiple parties that can be held liable for the debt if the business fails to meet its obligations. For the same reason, partnerships may have greater access to borrowing than many closely held corporations unless individual shareholders are willing to personally guarantee loans. However, there are financing sources that are available to corporations that are not available to partnerships. See § 3.11.

§ 3.5 —Limited Partnerships

Although general partnerships have long-established roots in common law, limited partnerships are statutory creations of state law. Consequently, they are subject to far more procedural and operating requirements than general partnerships. Limited partnerships are governed by either the Uniform Limited Partnership Act (ULPA)[11] or the Revised Uniform Limited Partnership Act (RULPA)[12] in the District of Columbia and every state except Louisiana.

A limited partnership must have two or more partners, at least one of whom is a general partner subject to unlimited liability. Limited partners are limited in two ways: their liability is limited to the amount of their capital contributions, and their management rights are restricted. The same basic tax rules that apply to general partnerships apply to limited partnerships.

Limited partnerships are generally established to attract equity investors who would otherwise not participate in a venture because of exposure to liability. The characteristics of limited liability and favorable partnership tax treatment have made limited partnerships particularly attractive in the real estate and oil and gas industries. Although generally inappropriate for professional organizations, this partnership form can be useful in the design industry when a firm's activities include actual construction. In this case, a limited partnership can be used to raise financing for specific

---

[11] 6 U.L.A. 1 (1969).

[12] 6 U.L.A. (Pocket Part 1969).

projects. The design firm typically participates as the general partner, retaining control and management. Limited partners, both professional and nonprofessional, provide financing in return for potential tax and investment rewards.

§ 3.6 —Joint Ventures

Two or more design firms may join together to provide services on a specific undertaking. An arrangement of this nature is referred to as a *joint venture.* It is usually temporary, and upon project completion the venture is dissolved.

Joint venture arrangements are common in the design industry. They can make sense for a variety of reasons. For example, a project may require financial resources or expertise that the firms lack individually. A firm moving into a new geographical area may find it desirable to engage in a joint venture with a local firm before undertaking projects on its own. Two firms considering a merger might undertake a joint venture to get a better feel for each other's skills and style.

For most nontax and tax purposes, a joint venture is a form of general partnership. As such, it is subject to the same rules and requirements as any general partnership. Care should be taken to clearly define the rights and obligations of the parties, and the tax rules discussed in **§ 3.7** apply.

§ 3.7 —Taxation of Partnerships

The federal taxation of partnerships is governed by the provisions of Subchapter K of the Internal Revenue Code (IRC). Unlike a corporation, which is treated as a separate taxable entity, the partnership is regarded as a pass-through entity. Income and deductions generated by the partnership's operations are taxed at the partner's level only.[13] As with sole proprietorship, this single level of tax gives partnerships a significant advantage over corporations. State and local income taxes on unincorporated businesses apply in some jurisdictions[14] and must be given consideration. They are unlikely, however, to have more than a marginal impact on the choice of business form.

A partnership does have certain characteristics of a taxable entity. It is required to file an annual information return, Form 1065, that accounts for its operations and the allocation of taxable items to individual partners.

[13] I.R.C. § 701 (West 1990).

[14] *E.g.*, New York City and the District of Columbia.

The fundamental tax accounting is performed at the partnership level and most tax elections are made at the partnership level.[15] Because the partnership is a conduit, the individual partners are taxed whether or not distributions are made. Items of income, deduction, and credit must be separately stated by the partnership (that is, ordinary income or loss, investment interest, passive income or loss, charitable contributions) to be treated appropriately at the individual partner's level.[16]

A partnership has a number of other favorable tax characteristics. In contrast to S corporations (see **§ 3.13**), income and loss can be allocated to individual partners in virtually any fashion as long as the allocations have "substantial economic effect."[17] Losses can be passed through to a partner to the extent a partner has basis in the partnership and is considered at risk.[18] A partner's basis continually changes after the initial investment. It is adjusted upward for additional capital contributions and annual taxable income. It is adjusted downward for distributions and tax losses.[19] A partner generally is considered at risk to the extent her basis is positive. A general partner also has basis and is considered at risk for her share of the partnership's recourse liabilities and certain nonrecourse liabilities.[20] Nonrecourse liabilities are included in determining the at-risk amount when the lender's only security is real estate, a situation that can apply to design firms owning their own building(s). The inclusion of the entity's liabilities in determining loss allowances represents an important distinction from the S corporation. Also, partners now enjoy the same access to qualified retirement benefits as corporations.[21]

Consistent with the single level of tax concept, contributions to and withdrawals from a partnership generally do not result in taxable gain or loss. The avoidance of tax applies both at the initial formation of the partnership and when assets are transferred to an existing operation.[22] Even property that has appreciated generally can be transferred to a partnership without yielding an immediate taxable gain. In this instance, however, special accounting may be necessary to assure that the gain, when ultimately recognized, is allocated only to the contributing partner.[23] One exception to the

---

[15] I.R.C. § 703 (West 1990).

[16] *Id.* § 702.

[17] *Id.* § 704(b).

[18] *Id.* §§ 704(d), 465.

[19] *Id.* § 705(a).

[20] *Id.* § 752.

[21] As a result of the Tax Equity and Fiscal Responsibility Act, Pub. L. No. 97-248, 96 Stat. 324 (1982).

[22] I.R.C. § 721 (West 1990).

[23] *Id.* § 704(c).

nonrecognition rule may occur when contributed property is subject to liabilities that exceed the property's tax basis.[24]

Distributions to partners, including liquidating distributions, generally are not taxed unless the partner receives cash that exceeds her partnership basis,[25] which is particularly advantageous when contrasted with the adverse tax consequences that typically occur when distributions are made to C corporation shareholders. Distributions of appreciated property usually can escape tax, an important advantage over both C and S corporations. In addition, there is a beneficial provision in partnership law that permits payments to withdrawing partners upon death or retirement to be treated as paid from pretax dollars.[26] Taxable gain or loss may have to be recognized under partnership rules if a partner receives a distribution of both ordinary income and other assets that differs from her proportionate share of such assets held by the partnership.[27] This exception frequently can apply to professional partnerships because ordinary income assets in the form of accounts receivable normally represent a large portion of the asset base. Gain or loss on the sale or exchange of a partnership interest usually will be recognized as a capital transaction.[28] The gain or loss is measured by the difference between the proceeds received and the partner's basis.

It must be remembered that partnership tax law is extremely complex and there will be circumstances when these general rules do not apply. Competent tax professionals should be consulted, particularly on nonroutine transactions, to avoid undesirable results. In many cases, careful planning will mean the difference between taxable and nontaxable transactions. Tax matters also should be given careful consideration in crafting the partnership agreement.

§ 3.8 Corporations

Sections 3.9 through **3.13** examine the characteristics of corporations generally and professional corporations (PCs) specifically. Some states permit design firms to incorporate only as PCs; a few permit incorporation only as general business corporations. Many jurisdictions now allow design firms to choose between establishing a PC or operating as a general business corporation.

One of the most important advantages of the corporate form to the design industry is access to financing sources unavailable to the other forms.

[24] *Id.* § 752(b).

[25] *Id.* § 731(a).

[26] *Id.* § 736(a).

[27] *Id.* § 751(a).

[28] I.R.C. § 741 (West 1990).

Sources include private placements, public offerings, and ESOPs. General corporate taxation is discussed (see **§ 3.12**), as is the taxation of S corporations (see **§ 3.13**). The emergence of the S corporation as a popular tax vehicle has been an important development for closely held businesses in all industries.

3.9 —General Corporate Characteristics

Corporations are creatures of statute, formed and organized under state law. Unlike the partnership and the sole proprietorship, a corporation is a separate legal entity distinct from its shareholder-owners and it is required to pay taxes separately. It also shields its owners from liability in most cases.

Corporations must be formally organized and adhere to strict statutory requirements governing their formation and operation. To form a corporation, a corporate charter must be drafted and filed with the appropriate state agency. Formation also entails the issuance of stock, the drafting of bylaws, the election of a board of directors, and the appointment of corporate officers. Periodic board of directors meetings are usually required to make key decisions. Minutes, books, and records must be maintained and annual filings with the state normally must be made. Violation of statutory requirements can jeopardize corporate existence. Maintenance of corporate records can be costly and time consuming. These burdens should be considered when deciding to incorporate. Too often, the inconvenience of these rules causes owners of closely held corporations to take unwise risks by ignoring them.

Important characteristics generally shared by all corporations include the following:

1. **Limited liability.** Shareholders normally are not personally liable for corporate obligations except to the extent of their actual investment in the corporation. For most industries, this is the most commonly cited reason for selecting the corporate form. Under common law, however, a professional, including a design professional, generally remains liable for her own wrongful practices when performing services as an employee of a corporate entity. The professional is also liable for wrongful practices of those performing professional services under her supervision and control. The professional's status as an officer, director, or shareholder does not affect this concept. Most states have codified this common law principle in PC statutes[29] and, in some instances, have extended liability to other professional shareholders of

---

[29] *See, e.g.*, N.J. Stat. Ann. § 14A:17-8 (West Pocket Part 1990); N.Y. Bus. Corp. Law § 1504(a) (McKinney 1986).

the corporation, as discussed in § **3.10**. For design firms, therefore, the corporate liability veil may not be as valuable as it is to nonprofessional businesses. In addition, business creditors frequently will seek shareholder guarantees that effectively negate the corporate shield. This is particularly true in the early stages of a closely held business when the risks are greatest. Despite the limitations, the protection that the corporate structure can provide should be weighed in the entity selection process.

2. **Continuity of life.** Corporations, once established, generally have a perpetual existence. Thus, they are unaffected by changes in shareholder-owners. This is often cited as a benefit not shared by sole proprietorships and partnerships. This attribute has limited value when a corporation is owned by a single shareholder or only a few partners. Partnership agreements can be drafted to provide similar continuity and large professional partnerships typically have such provisions.
3. **Transferability of interests.** Corporate ownership is evidenced by corporate stock that is normally freely transferable under state law. Many corporations, particularly smaller ones, will restrict this right to transfer shares (often through the use of buy/sell agreements stipulating to whom shares can be sold, under what circumstances shares can or must be sold, and, generally, the method for determining the sale price). Nevertheless, this attribute is particularly valuable when the ability to raise equity capital is considered. Various equity instruments, such as preferred stock, can be created to facilitate capital requirements. Free transferability greatly enhances the ability to share and transfer ownership. However, specific statutory restrictions often apply to PCs, as discussed in § **3.10**.
4. **Management and control.** Specific rights and responsibilities generally are assigned by law to the board of directors (selected by shareholders) and corporate officers (appointed by the board of directors). The establishment of corporate policy and overall management is the responsibility of the directors. Management of day-to-day operations is the province of the corporate officers. Management responsibilities thus tend to be centralized and more clearly defined than with partnerships, although partnerships often create similar structures. Classes of stock with different voting rights normally can be created if desired to assure that control is retained by specific shareholders.

§ 3.10 —Professional Corporations

Professional corporations (PCs), referred to as professional associations in some states, were created to enable professionals in the "learned professions" to enjoy pension and other benefits formerly available only to corporate employees under federal tax law. Regular corporate status, particularly liability protection, had been viewed as inappropriate to the client/professional relationship. PC statutes have been enacted in every state and the District of Columbia to meld the demand from professionals for tax benefits with the public policy of holding professionals liable for their work.

PC statutes vary from state to state, but some common elements generally apply. PCs are subject to general corporate law as well as PC statutes, with the PC provisions controlling when there is a conflict. Most significantly, PC statutes normally provide that a shareholder or other professional employee remains liable for her own professional acts.[30] Most states specifically provide that a professional employee's liability extends to professional acts performed by those under the professional's supervision and control.[31] A number of jurisdictions, however, do provide that liability for a wrongful professional act does not extend to shareholders who were not associated with the act giving rise to the claim.[32] Other jurisdictions are silent as to whether shareholders not associated with an act are still liable, which indicates that liability does not attach because PC law normally falls back on general corporate law when there is no specific PC provision.[33] Consistent with general corporate concepts, shareholders and other employees generally are not held accountable for liabilities related to nonprofessional matters. Thus, while the corporate veil is not without value, its benefit to PCs is diminished by specific statutory provisions.

Most PC statutes place certain restrictions on the ownership and activities of the corporation: (1) PCs normally can render only one type of professional service (architecture, professional engineering, and, frequently, landscape architecture tend to be considered one type for this purpose, but not in all jurisdictions);[34] (2) Generally, all shareholders must be licensed to practice the profession being rendered, effectively limiting the transferability of interests,[35] although some states permit a minority percentage in the design profession to be nonprofessionals;[36] and (3) Nonprofessional activities are generally restricted to passive investments. The corporation itself

---

[30] *See, e.g.*, N.C. Gen. Stat. § 55B-9 (1990); Tex. Bus. Corp. Act Ann. tit. 18, ch. 32, art. 1528e, § 16 (Vernon Pocket Part 1991).

[31] *See, e.g.*, N.J. Stat. Ann. § 14A:17-8 (West Pocket Part 1990); N.Y. Bus. Corp. Law § 1504(a) (McKinney 1986); Fla. Stat. Ann. § 621.07 (Harrison 1986).

[32] *See, e.g.*, N.J. Rev. Stat. Ann. § 14A:17A (West Pocket Part 1990); Fla. Stat. § 621.07 (Harrison 1986).

[33] *E.g.*, Illinois and New York.

[34] *See, e.g.*, N.Y. Bus. Corp. Law § 1503(a) (McKinney 1986); Va. Code § 13.1-543(B) (Michie 1989).

[35] *See, e.g.*, Fla. Stat. § 621.09 (Harrison 1986); N.Y. Bus. Corp. Law § 1511 (McKinney 1986).

[36] *See, e.g.*, Va. Code § 13.1-543(6) (Michie 1989); La. Rev. Stat. Ann. tit. 12, ch. 16, § 12:1090(B) (West Pocket Part 1990).

and/or its shareholder-employees normally must register with the applicable licensing board.

With the equalization of pension benefits, incorporating solely to qualify for the few tax deductible benefits remaining available to corporate owner-employees (see **§ 3.12**) is rarely worthwhile. Further, in those states where design professionals can choose to incorporate as either a regular corporation or a PC there appears to be little reason to choose restrictive PC status. A firm already organized as a PC should consider switching to regular corporate status if the option is made available by statute. Virtually the only reason to choose PC status over regular corporate status is to ensure that the business retains its focus and does not stray from professional activities. When PC status is the only corporate option available, it may make sense to incorporate for the limited liability protection that does exist if a high value is placed on this attribute.

§ 3.11 —Sources of Corporate Financing

Most design firms operating in corporate form are closely held corporations, that is, the stock is held by relatively few shareholders who are all employee-owners.[37] PCs are generally required by statute to be set up in this fashion. There are definite advantages to operating as a closely held corporation, particularly the ability to maintain management and control. Stock ownership can easily be controlled and restricted and professionals own and operate the business, which is consistent with the general practice of the professions.

There may come a time, however, when a design firm's capital requirements make outside equity or other funding attractive. For example, ambitious expansion plans may require capital resources that exceed those of the owners and the ability of the corporation to borrow. Large regional and national design firms frequently seek outside equity financing to achieve their business goals. Nevertheless, professional organizations tend to seek such outside financing less often than other types of businesses because of the forfeiture of professional control.

Equity funding is usually obtained in one of two ways: through a private placement or by a public offering. The employee stock ownership plan (ESOP), a form of qualified retirement plan, also presents an opportunity to raise significant capital and has recently become a popular financing vehicle. These sources of capital are only available to corporations. Larger design firms may choose corporate status solely to gain access to funds in

---

[37] The term *closely held corporation* is used here in its generic sense and should not be confused with corporations formed under close corporation statutes available in some states such as California and Delaware. These statutes are infrequently used.

one or more of these ways. Use of these financing sources normally will prevent a corporation from qualifying to be a S corporation because of S corporation restrictions on the type and number of shareholders.

Private Placements

A private placement is an offering of securities that is exempt from registration filing requirements with the Securities and Exchange Commission (SEC) because it meets certain prescribed rules as to the number and/or type of investors who can participate.[38] It is normally directed at sophisticated investors, such as venture capitalists having familiarity with specific industries. Private placements are attractive due to the relatively quick access they provide to equity capital. The onerous procedures and ongoing filing requirements associated with a public offering are avoided. The extent of outside ownership can be controlled, which is highly desirable for professional corporations. This benefit may be diminished if sophisticated investors demand oversight rights, such as a board of directors position, and periodic financial data, including audited statements.

The vast majority of private placements are governed by Regulation D of the Securities Act of 1933,[39] which details the dollar value and participation ranges for three different categories of private offerings:

1. Rule 504: Up to $1 million of securities can be issued by nonpublic companies over a 12-month period to an unlimited number of investors.[40]
2. Rule 505: Up to $5 million of securities generally can be issued over a 12-month period to an unlimited number of accredited investors and no more than 35 nonaccredited investors.[41]
3. Rule 506: An unlimited amount of securities can be issued to an unlimited number of accredited investors and no more than 35 nonaccredited but sophisticated investors.[42]

Accredited investors are those that fit into one of eight categories, which include insiders such as directors and executive officers, certain high-net-worth individuals, certain high-income individuals, and institutional investors such as banks, broker dealers, and insurance companies.[43]

[38] Securities Act of 1933, § 4(2), 15 U.S.C.A. § 77(d)(2) 1990.

[39] 17 C.F.R. §§ 230.501–506 (1990).

[40] *Id.* § 230.504.

[41] *Id.* § 230.505.

[42] *Id.* § 230.506.

[43] *Id.* § 230.501.

Nonaccredited but sophisticated investors are those who are financially astute and experienced and are capable of evaluating the merits and the risks of the investment.[44]

In addition to the legal limits, there are practical limits to the funds that can be obtained through private offerings. Private placements generally are perceived as relatively high-risk investments. The universe of investors is restricted and securities are not readily marketable because they cannot be traded on public markets. Nevertheless, private placements have become an increasingly important source of capital in recent years. They are frequently the first vehicle for outside equity financing before a public offering.

A private placement may involve significant expenses, but it is generally far less costly than a public offering. There are also a number of reporting requirements. Such an offering escapes federal registration requirements, but registration may be required by state law. Federal anti-fraud laws apply equally to private placements and public offerings,[45] so it is necessary to provide potential investors with accurate and detailed information about company operations. A limited filing with the SEC, a Form D, is required. In addition, an offering document is often required and a broker's fee may be involved. Competent counsel and accountants should be retained.

Public Offerings

If a private placement seems unlikely to meet corporate needs, a public offering may make sense. A public offering expands the universe of investors and has the potential to bring in considerably more money than a private placement. However, the decision to go public should not be taken lightly. It is a long process and significant expenditures are certain. It is a strategy for a growing and prosperous business, not for one desperate for cash.

In addition to bringing desired equity infusions, a successful public offering can have a number of other favorable results. The company should be able to borrow at better rates. The stock's marketability and readily determined market price can facilitate acquisitions and compensation arrangements such as stock option plans. Existing shareholders should benefit by an increased value in their investment and a market for their shares. It also may help bring in business by boosting a company's prestige and raising its public profile—an attraction to potential customers who will feel more secure dealing with a well-known firm. Once a company has gone public and performed successfully, it should be able to bring in more funds through additional offerings.

---

[44] *Id.* § 230.506.

[45] Securities Act of 1933, §§ 12(2), 17, 15 U.S.C.A. § 77(1) and (q) (1990).

Notwithstanding the benefits, taking a company public can be a mixed blessing. In addition to the cost, it means a significant sacrifice of privacy and control. New disclosure requirements will mean that previously private financial information and other business arrangements must be made public. Outside investors will place new demands on management that may conflict with long-range business plans and objectives.

The process itself is governed by the Securities Act of 1933[46] and administered by the SEC. It begins with the filing of a registration statement that includes all information necessary for an investor to evaluate the company. Regulation S-K governs the nonfinancial statement requirements.[47] The financial disclosure requirements are contained in Regulation S-X.[48] Forms S-1 and S-18 are generally used for initial offerings. S-18, which has less stringent disclosure requirements, is only available for offerings of up to $7.5 million. The registration statement must include such items as a preliminary prospectus, which provides a detailed discussion of the company's operations, management structure, financial status, and potential risks. Audited balance sheets and income statements for prior years are also required. The process requires that an underwriter be chosen, preferably with experience in the industry. Attorneys and accountants also must be engaged. The company's information and planning systems, as well as its management structure, will have to be reviewed and possibly revamped to make sure it can handle the requirements of a public company.

Once the company has gone public, it will have to comply with a number of government reporting requirements. A Form 10-K, an annual statement including audited financial statements and specified nonfinancial disclosures similar to those included in the offering documents, must be filed by all companies in their initial public year. Companies required to register under the Securities and Exchange Act of 1934 because they are listed on a national stock exchange or meet shareholder and asset size thresholds must file a Form 10-K and a quarterly report, Form 10-Q, in all subsequent years as well. Future stock transactions by the corporation and its officers also will be subject to government securities regulations.

Employee Stock Ownership Plans

An ESOP represents an alternative to seeking capital from outside investors. An ESOP is a qualified retirement plan that invests primarily in employer securities.[49] Through the Internal Revenue Code, ESOPs have been granted

---

[46] 15 U.S.C.A. § 77(g) (1990).

[47] 17 C.F.R. § 229 (1990).

[48] *Id.* § 210.

[49] I.R.C. §§ 401(a), 4975(e)(7) (West 1990).

more favorable tax benefits than other qualified plans to encourage corporations to transfer ownership to employees. An ESOP can be leveraged or nonleveraged. It is the leveraged ESOP that presents corporations with a highly favored financing opportunity.

Nonleveraged ESOPs involve the contribution of employer stock or cash to buy employer stock. The employer gets a deduction equal to the fair market value of the stock or the cash contribution. Other than the investment in employer stock, it functions similarly to other qualified retirement plans.

A leveraged ESOP, as the name implies, involves the borrowing of funds from an outside party. In a typical leveraged ESOP, an ESOP trust is established to buy employer securities. A lending institution loans the funds to the trust to make the purchase and loan repayment is guaranteed by the employer. Annual contributions are made by the employer to the ESOP for use in making interest and principal payments. As the payments are made, stock held by the trust is allocated to individual employee accounts.

An ESOP loan is the only type of loan for which a tax deduction is allowed for both principal and interest. A deduction is allowed the employer for principal payments of up to 25 percent of the participant's annual payroll. Interest costs to service the loan are fully deductible.[50]

ESOPs have other favorable characteristics. They typically require less sacrifice of control than equity offerings. Financial institutions lending to ESOPs that hold more than 50 percent ownership of all classes of stock also get a tax break because they can exclude 50 percent of the interest received from their taxable income.[51] The lender generally turns back part of this savings to the employer by charging a lower rate on the ESOP loan. Qualified stockholders making a sale to an ESOP that holds more than 30 percent of all classes of stock can defer tax recognition of their gains by reinvesting in qualified securities.[52]

On the negative side, ESOPs can be expensive to establish and operate. Annual appraisals are required and there are recurring administrative costs as well. A financial institution is likely to consider an ESOP loan only if the corporate guarantor has a proven financial history. The guarantor will have to record the liability on its financial statements, giving the company a less healthy balance sheet than an equity offering would. ESOPs, nonetheless, have become an extremely popular financing tool and are viewed positively by employees. The stock plans also have become popular in financing buyouts.

---

[50] *Id.* § 404(a)(9).

[51] *Id.* § 133.

[52] *Id.* § 1042.

§ 3.12 —Corporate Taxation: C Corporations

Corporations other than S corporations are referred to as *C corporations* and are treated as separate taxable entities. Corporate earnings are taxed once at the corporate level and again when distributed to shareholders in the form of dividends, redemptions, or liquidation proceeds. Although losses experienced by partnerships and sole proprietorships can be used to offset an owner's other income, C corporation losses are only available to offset corporate income.

It is the double tax potential that usually makes the C corporation the least attractive business structure from a tax standpoint. C corporations frequently seek to reduce or eliminate the double tax by providing employee-shareholders with deductible distributions in the form of compensation. This device is limited by the requirement that the compensation be reasonable. This is rarely a problem for firms that earn revenue exclusively from the provision of professional services because these businesses can argue that the earnings directly reflect services rendered by their employees. It is a harder case for larger companies in which there is substantial invested capital, there are other sources of income, and/or compensation follows stock ownership ratios. Even with smaller firms, particularly cash-basis businesses, significant year-end accounting is required to drain the firm of its profits in order to avoid taxation.

C corporations are subject to a top tax rate of 34 percent. Certain C corporations are eligible for graduated rates (15 percent on the first $50,000 of taxable income; 25 percent on the next $25,000). The lower graduated rates are phased out, however, through the use of a 5 percent surtax on income between $100,000 and $335,000.[53] The graduated rates are not available to certain C corporations classified as personal service corporations. For this purpose, personal service corporations are defined in the Internal Revenue Code by the same function and ownership test that permits them to use the cash basis of accounting. See **§ 3.15**. The income of corporations meeting this definition, which often include design firms, is always taxed at a flat 34 percent rate.[54]

Although more complex than with partnerships, formation of a C corporation generally can be accomplished tax free to both the corporation and the shareholders if properly structured.[55] However, as with a partnership, the contribution to a corporation of property subject to liabilities in excess of its basis will incur a tax on the contributor.[56] Unlike partnerships, contributions of appreciated property to an existing corporation are also likely to

---

[53] I.R.C. § 11(b)(1) (West 1990).

[54] *Id.* § 11(b)(2).

[55] *Id.* § 351.

[56] *Id.* § 357(c).

result in a tax for the contributor unless the transferor is the sole corporate shareholder.

Once assets are put in corporate form, it is difficult to get them out without significant tax costs. The distribution of appreciated assets creates corporate taxable income (for both S corporations and C corporations) equal to the difference between the fair market value at the date of distribution and the tax basis.[57] In addition, C corporation shareholders will pay a second tax upon receipt of these assets.

The tax effects of corporate ownership are most harshly felt upon the sale of a business interest. Although the sale of stock will generate only a single level of tax at the owner's level, the result is normally worse than a partner's sale of a partnership interest or the sale of stock by an S corporation shareholder. In all three cases, taxable gain or loss is measured by the difference between the proceeds of the sale and the tax basis of the interest sold. However, the basis of a partner's interest or an S corporation shareholder's stock is adjusted for earnings that were not withdrawn from the business. There is no such adjustment for undistributed C corporation earnings.

Due to the elimination of the so-called "General Utilities doctrine"[58] by the Tax Reform Act of 1986,[59] the corporate tax effect is even more dramatic when a sale of corporate assets is followed by a corporate liquidation. The General Utilities doctrine allowed the avoidance of taxable gain at the corporate level in the case of a complete liquidation even if the liquidation was preceded or followed by a sale of assets.

Under current law, a gain at liquidation is recognized at the corporate level unless the shareholder is a controlling corporation.[60] In the case of a sale of assets, the gain is determined by the difference between the sale proceeds and the assets' tax basis. If there is no sale, the gain is equal to the difference between the fair market value of the distributed assets and their tax basis.[61] A second gain (or loss) is incurred at the shareholder level on the difference between the fair market value of the asset and/or the cash received and the basis of the shareholders' stock.[62] By contrast, there is only a single level of tax—at the individual level—upon liquidation of an S corporation or a partnership. The same is true of a sole proprietor, which can only sell assets.

There are some other disadvantages associated with C corporations. Two "penalty" taxes can apply: the accumulated earnings tax and the personal

---

[57] *Id.* § 311(b).

[58] General Utils. & Operating Co. v. Helvering, 296 U.S. 200 (1935).

[59] Pub. L. No. 99-514, 100 Stat. 2085 (1986).

[60] I.R.C. § 336(a), (d)(3) (West 1990).

[61] *Id.* § 336(a).

[62] *Id.* § 331.

holding company tax. The *accumulated earnings tax* is applied to large amounts of undistributed earnings that are held with no business purpose.[63] This tax was enacted to prevent the intentional avoidance of the double tax. The *personal holding company tax* is a tax on certain closely held corporations that earn 60 percent or more of their income from so-called passive sources such as interest, dividends, and rents.[64] Also included among these is income from *personal service contracts.* This is income derived from services performed by a shareholder who owns 25 percent or more of the corporation and is specified by contract as the only individual who can render the services.[65] Passive income of this type may frequently be received by a closely held design firm.

As with all taxable entities, C corporations are subject to the alternative minimum tax,[66] a separate, parallel system to the regular tax system. The computation of alternative minimum taxable income starts with regular taxable income. Specified adjustment and preference items, such as generally shorter depreciation lives, are then added or subtracted.[67] The alternative tax rate, currently 20 percent for C corporations[68] and 24 percent for other taxpayers,[69] is applied to the total. The higher of the alternative minimum tax or the regular tax applies.[70] However, certain preferences and adjustments apply only to C corporations. Most important among these is the adjusted current earnings (ACE) adjustment.[71] The ACE adjustment entails substantial calculations, particularly with respect to recomputing depreciation.

C corporations do offer some tax advantages. Deductions for certain employee benefits are available only to C corporation owner-employees. These benefits include (1) group-term life insurance up to $50,000;[72] (2) up to $5,000 in death benefits paid directly by the employer;[73] (3) health and accident plan expenses,[74] and (4) cafeteria plan benefits.[75] The availability of a 25 percent deduction of health and accident insurance costs for partners,

---

[63] *Id.* §§ 531–537.

[64] *Id.* §§ 541–547.

[65] *Id.* § 543(a)(7).

[66] I.R.C. § 55 (West 1990).

[67] *Id.* §§ 56, 57.

[68] *Id.* § 55.

[69] Revenue Reconciliation Act, Pub. L. No. 101–508, 104 Stat. 1388 (1990).

[70] I.R.C. § 56(c) (West 1990).

[71] *Id.* § 56(g).

[72] *Id.* § 79.

[73] *Id.* § 101(b).

[74] *Id.* §§ 105, 106.

[75] *Id.* § 125.

S corporation employees, and sole proprietors partially offsets the corporate benefit of a full write-off for health and accident plan expenses.[76]

Special provisions are available to corporations that allow them to effect mergers and other reorganization transactions in a tax-free manner.[77] These provisions, combined with other corporate attributes, make corporations an attractive vehicle for growth through acquisition. Corporate stock is also an effective tool for use in tax-favored stock option plans.

Finally, general corporate tax law permits the filing of a consolidated return by a holding company and any number of subsidiaries if certain ownership requirements are met.[78] Thus, a complex structure of multiple corporations can be set up without concern that the losses of any company will not offset the income of other group members. Large design firms operating as general business C corporations often use a holding company structure and file a consolidated tax return. This may be desirable for various reasons, including shielding members of the group from liabilities incurred by other members. Although individual professionals still will not be shielded from potential liability for professional acts, the assets of group members may be shielded from liabilities, related to professional and other matters, of other group members.

§ 3.13 —S Corporations

Certain corporations can elect to be treated as a pass-through entity, known as an *S corporation,* that generally is not subject to federal income tax at the corporate level.[79] Qualifying firms may find the S corporation an appealing option because it combines the nontax advantages of a C corporation with many of the tax benefits associated with noncorporate entities. For all nontax purposes, an S corporation is legally indistinguishable from a C corporation. Thus, tax benefits are enjoyed without sacrificing desirable nontax corporate attributes such as liability protection.

To qualify for S status, a corporation must be a domestic corporation with 35 or fewer qualifying shareholders. A husband and wife are counted as one shareholder for this test. Although certain trusts and estates can hold shares in S corporations, shareholders generally must be individuals. Individual shareholders must be either United States citizens or residents. Corporations and partnerships cannot be shareholders of an S corporation. An S corporation may not have control of an active subsidiary in which it

---

[76] I.R.C. § 162(1) (West 1990).

[77] *Id.* § 368.

[78] *Id.* § 1501.

[79] I.R.C. § 1363(a) (West 1990).

has ownership interest of 80 percent or more. An S corporation is permitted only one class of stock, but that stock can have differences in voting rights.[80] In all other respects, including dividend rights and liquidation preferences, the economic rights of shareholders must be equal.[81]

S Corporations are taxed much like partnerships. Income, loss, and credit, while determined at the entity level, are reported to individual shareholders and taxed by the federal government and most states only at the shareholder level.[82] At the federal level, an S corporation shareholder is taxed at a top rate of 31 percent, rather than the 34 percent corporate rate. Deductible losses, however, are limited to a shareholder's basis in her stock plus (in contrast to a partnership) loans made to the corporation by the shareholder.[83] Some state and local jurisdictions do not honor S corporation status and treat the S corporation as a regular corporation for income tax purposes.[84] This diminishes the advantages normally associated with S corporation status, but the significant federal tax benefits remain.

As with a partnership, a shareholder's basis changes continually after the initial investment. It is adjusted upward for taxable income and additional capital contributions. Downward adjustments are made for tax losses and distributions.[85] Unlike a partnership, a shareholder does not receive basis for loans by outside parties to the S corporation, even if the shareholder is a guarantor. If borrowing is necessary, it is often wise for the shareholder to create basis by borrowing directly from the lender and, in turn, re-lending or contributing the funds to the corporation.

An S corporation election requires the consent of all shareholders and must be made on or before the fifteenth day of the third month of the taxable year for which the election is to be effective.[86] The election can be made by a newly formed corporation or an existing C corporation. An S election can be revoked prospectively at any time by a majority of the shareholders and automatic termination occurs as soon as a corporation fails to meet any of the eligibility requirements discussed in this section.[87] It is critical to guard against unintended termination. Most importantly, stock transfers should be restricted and dividend distributions should always be pro rata to ownership. Unlike a partnership, special earnings

---

[80] *Id.* § 1361 contains the S corporation eligibility requirements.

[81] Prop. Treas. Reg. § 1.1361-1(1), 55 Fed. Reg. 40872 (1990).

[82] I.R.C. § 1366 (West 1990).

[83] *Id.* § 1366(d).

[84] *See, e.g.,* D.C. Code Ann. §§ 47-1810.1(a)(2), 1801.4(16) (1990) and Tenn. Code Ann. § 67-4-806(a), -805(a)(2) (1989).

[85] I.R.C. § 1367 (West 1990).

[86] *Id.* §§ 1362(a), (b).

[87] *Id.* § 1362(d).

allocations cannot be made.[88] However, reasonable special compensatory allocations may provide a similar result.

An existing corporation making the S election may be subject to several adverse tax provisions. One of these is a tax, at the shareholder level, on distributions that are deemed to come from corporate earnings and profits that existed at the date of conversion.[89] However, distributions are considered to first come from the earnings of the S corporation;[90] thus, they are only taxable to the extent they exceed S corporation earnings.

Most importantly, a special toll charge referred to as the *built-in gains tax* also may apply to converting corporations.[91] The built-in gains tax is designed to prevent corporations from avoiding double tax on appreciated assets existing at the conversion date. C corporations switching to S status are subject to corporate level and individual level tax on any net built-in gains existing at the time of the switch that are recognized as taxable income in the following 10-year period.[92] Net built-in gains equal the difference between the fair market value of assets and their tax basis at the date of conversion.[93]

Many C corporations will have built-in gains from items such as goodwill or real estate, but many will avoid tax on these gains because the assets are not disposed of during the 10-year recognition period. Cash-basis firms—and many design firms are in this category—are not as fortunate. Accounts receivable are considered a built-in gains item to the extent they exceed accounts payable.[94] Generally, they will be recognized in the first S corporation year and taxes will be due. Cash-basis firms considering conversion to S corporation status must determine whether the benefits of such a move outweigh the immediate tax costs.

The primary disadvantage of S corporations is the strict statutory rules that can severely restrict business options. Because an S Corporation can have no more than 35 shareholders, its ability to bring in additional owners is limited. For example, an S Corporation with 20 owners is precluded from a merger that would add more than 15 new owners to its ranks. This limitation is a common reason for professionals to choose a partnership structure rather than organizing as an S corporation.

Nevertheless, the S corporation is often appropriate for qualifying design firms, particularly those that value nontax corporate attributes. The

---

[88] Prop. Treas. Reg. § 1.1361-1(l), 55 Fed. Reg. 40872 (1990).

[89] I.R.C. § 1368(c)(2) (West 1990).

[90] *Id.* § 1368(c)(1).

[91] *Id.* § 1374.

[92] *Id.* § 1374(d)(7).

[93] *Id.* § 1374(d)(1).

[94] H.R. Rep. No. 100-795, 100th Cong., 2d Sess. 63, and Treas. Announcement 86-128, 1986-51 I.R.B. 22.

popularity of S corporations has grown dramatically since the Tax Reform Act of 1986,[95] which provided an annual tax savings for S corporation owners by setting the top individual tax rate lower than the corporate rate. By overturning the General Utilities doctrine,[96] the Act also made S corporations the only corporate form that can avoid a double tax upon liquidation. The sale of S corporation stock has always received better tax treatment than the sale of C corporation stock because its tax basis is adjusted upward for earnings and not withdrawn from the company.

§ 3.14 Tax Accounting

In addition to choosing a business form, every new enterprise must select tax accounting methods and an accounting period. The choice of favorable tax accounting methods can make an important contribution to the financial success of a business. Accounting methods should be chosen with care because they are generally difficult to change at a later date. Any permissible method can be chosen upon the filing of a business's first return. IRS approval must be obtained for any subsequent change in accounting methods, except when changes are required or specifically permitted by tax law.[97] Although the options available can be affected by the business form chosen, usually they are controlled more by the nature of the business itself. Tax accounting methods frequently differ from methods used for financial statement purposes. The tax accounting period can differ from the financial statement period but seldom does.

§ 3.15 —Tax Accounting Methods

Taxable income is normally computed under one of the two fundamental methods of accounting, the *accrual method* or the *cash method.* Firms whose activities extend to the performance of long-term contracts must account for these contracts under special rules. This section first considers the choice between the accrual and the cash method for those firms that do not perform such contracts. It then addresses the special considerations for those firms that do.

The *accrual method* of accounting records revenues at the earliest time the taxpayer has the right to receive payment for goods or services. Likewise, deductions are usually recorded as soon as an obligation to pay for goods or services arises. Revenue recognition thus often precedes the actual

---

[95] Pub. L. No. 99-514, 100 Stat. 2085 (1986).

[96] General Utils. & Operating Co. v. Helvering, 296 U.S. 200 (1935).

[97] I.R.C. § 446(e) (West 1990).

receipt of cash and cash outlays generally come after expense recognition. The accrual method is normally considered the best measure of the economic performance of a business.

By law, the accrual method must be used for tax purposes in businesses in which inventory is an income-producing factor.[98] The decisive factor in this instance is the nature of the business, not the entity form. If a taxpayer is engaged in two separate businesses, one employing inventory and one of a service nature, a hybrid method can be used—accrual for the inventory business and cash for the service business—as long as separate books and records are maintained. When there are two separate trades or businesses, it is often preferable to separate them into separate legal entities to avoid IRS challenge. A design firm with a business that has inventory, such as an interior design firm that sells furniture and other items, may find it advantageous to segregate that business from the provision of its professional services.

Regardless of the nature of the business, certain C corporations are required to use the accrual (or other acceptable noncash) method of accounting.[99] As a general rule, C corporations (or partnerships with C corporation partners) with average annual gross receipts exceeding $5 million in the prior three taxable years may not use cash accounting. Gross receipts are measured by aggregating related taxpayers; thus, the segregation of a business or businesses generally will not defeat the statute. Qualified personal service corporations, however, can use the cash method.[100] This is true regardless of the amount of gross receipts, an exception that will benefit many design firms. To qualify for the exception, both function and ownership tests must be met. The *function test* requires that substantially all (greater than or equal to 95 percent) of the activities of the corporation are in one of eight designated fields, among which are architecture and engineering. The *ownership test* requires that substantially all (greater than or equal to 95 percent) of the corporate stock be held by owner-employees (and certain retired employees and their estates and heirs) engaged in providing qualified services.[101]

Although most firms use the accrual method for financial statements, the *cash method,* when permitted, is almost always preferable for tax purposes. The cash method recognizes income at the time payment is actually received. Expenses are recognized when amounts are actually paid. As a result, firms on the cash basis normally will defer income to later periods than those on the accrual method. Additionally, firms typically will be able to control the recognition of taxable income to some degree by accelerating

---

[98] Treas. Reg. § 1.446-1(c)(2)(i) (as amended in 1987).

[99] I.R.C. § 448 (West 1990).

[100] *Id.* § 448(b)(2).

[101] *Id.* § 448(d)(2); Temp. Treas. Reg. § 1.448-1T (1987).

payments and deferring billings. When a taxpayer maintains financial statements on the accrual basis but reports taxable income on the cash method, reconciling entries should be made in the books or kept in supplemental work papers. Failure to do so could cause forfeiture of the cash method.[102]

Design firms whose activities include entering into contracts for the construction of real property or the manufacture of unique items are likely to be subject to special tax accounting rules for long-term contracts.[103] The phrase *long-term contract* is somewhat misleading because any contract whose performance spans more than one taxable year is considered long term. Thus, a two-day contract that begins on December 31 and ends on January 1 is a long-term contract if performed by a calendar-year taxpayer. As a general rule, long-term contracts must be accounted for on the *percentage of completion method.*[104] This method requires that the expected profit or loss on a contract be recognized as the contract is performed. Recognition is based on actual costs incurred at year-end as a percentage of total projected contract costs. Tax law requires that numerous overhead costs be allocated to contracts for this purpose.[105]

The percentage of completion method is not required for contracts that meet a "small contract" exception. This exception applies if (1) a contract is expected to be completed in less than two years, and (2) the entity performing the contract has had average gross receipts of less than $10 million over the prior three years. Related entities must be aggregated when calculating gross receipts.[106] When this exception applies, the *completed contract method* is allowed, permitting profit deferral until the end of the contract. The completed contract method generally allows significant deferrals, in contrast to the percentage of completion method. This benefit is diminished, however, because alternative minimum tax calculations must use the percentage of completion method.[107]

When an entity performs both contract and noncontract activities, the noncontract activities are governed by general tax accounting rules. A design firm performing long-term contracts and professional services, therefore, can use the cash basis for the service activities as long as it otherwise meets the cash basis requirement. Note, however, that the existence of contract activities is unlikely to permit a C corporation to qualify as a personal service corporation eligible for the cash method.

---

[102] Treas. Reg. § 1.446-(1)(a)(4) (as amended in 1987).

[103] I.R.C. § 460 (West 1990).

[104] *Id.* § 460(b).

[105] *Id.* § 460(c).

[106] *Id.* § 460(e).

[107] *Id.* § 56(a)(3).

Design firms that engage in long-term contract activities almost certainly can be expected to perform the related contract design services. The IRS has recently made clear that in such instances the design services are considered part of the contract. Thus, they are subject to contract accounting rules.[108] Design services of the same taxpayer, not related to the subject matter of any of that taxpayer's long-term contracts, are carved out for treatment under the general rules.

§ 3.16 —Tax Accounting Periods

As a general rule, sole proprietorships, partnerships, and S corporations must use the calendar year as their tax year. C corporations, except certain personal service corporations, can select the tax year of their choice.[109]

A partnership is normally required to adopt the year-end that conforms to the tax year of the partners that own a majority of the capital and profits.[110] When the partners are individuals, a calendar year almost always results. S corporations and personal service corporations also are normally required to have a calendar tax year.[111] The definition of personal service corporation for this purpose is broader than the definition governing the availability of the cash basis of accounting. If the principal activity is personal services that are substantially performed by employee-owners who own more than 10 percent of the corporation's stock, a C corporation is defined as a personal service corporation for tax year purposes. Personal services specifically include architectural and engineering services.[112]

Partnerships, S corporations, and personal service corporations, however, can choose an alternative year that ends no more than three months than the normally required tax year.[113] This generally means they can choose a tax year that ends in September, October, or November. The period between the tax year-end and the calendar year is referred to as the *deferral period.* S corporations and partnerships choosing an alternative year are required to make payments to an "escrow account" held by the federal government.[114] Payments into the account are based on calculations intended to approximate the tax savings resulting from postponing the reporting of income due to the deferral period. A similar result is achieved with personal service corporations by preventing compensation deductions

[108] Gen. Couns. Mem. 39,803 (Nov. 16, 1989).

[109] I.R.C. § 441(b), (c) (West 1990).

[110] *Id.* § 706(b).

[111] *Id.* §§ 1378, 441(i).

[112] *Id.* § 441(i); Temp. Treas. Reg. § 1.441-4T (1987).

[113] I.R.C. § 444 (West 1990).

[114] *Id.* §§ 444(c), 7519.

when insufficient distributions have been made to employee-owners before the end of the deferral period.[115] Significant accounting is required if one of the alternative periods is chosen.

Some S corporations, partnerships, and personal service corporations may have other year-ends, retained under grandfathering rules.[116] A different year-end can be granted by the IRS if a natural business year can be demonstrated based on facts and circumstances or if a mechanical test can be met.[117] A natural business year is almost never granted for a service company on the basis of facts and circumstances. The mechanical test requires four years of history showing that the gross receipts in the last two consecutive months of the requested fiscal year are the most gross receipts received in any two-month period and represent more than 25 percent of that year's total gross receipts.

---

[115] *Id.* §§ 444(c), 280H.

[116] *Id.* § 441(b)(3).

[117] Rev. Proc. 87-32, 1987-2 C.B. 396.

CHAPTER 4

JOINT VENTURES FOR DESIGN PROFESSIONALS

Robert H. Garb

Robert H. Garb is senior counsel—special projects at Bechtel Corporation in San Francisco,where he is involved in project development and international transactions including privatization projects and the negotiation of joint ventures and joint stock companies. He has held several overseas field assignments with Bechtel in Australia and Papua, New Guinea, and recently was head of the legal section in Gaithersburg, Maryland. For several years, Mr. Garb was chairman of his legal department's Committee on Joint Associations. He received his bachelor's and law degrees from the University of Michigan.

§ 4.1 Rationale for Forming Joint Ventures

Joint ventures in the architect/engineering (A/E) industry are primarily used to enhance the participating firms' chances of being awarded a contract. One marketing reason for forming a joint venture among two or more A/E firms is to merge specialists in complementary skills important to the particular project. As an example, Bechtel National, Inc. entered into a joint venture agreement with the Australian A/E firm of WBM-Stalker Pty. Ltd. in 1988 to design a free-piston shock tunnel, which is used for research on very high-speed gas flows. WBM-Stalker is the designer of the world's only free-piston shock tunnels and is a patent holder on portions of the design. Through this arrangement, Bechtel was able to complement its diversified A/E skills on civil works projects and its knowledge of potential United States-based clients for such shock tunnels with WBM-Stalker's unique expertise in designing free-piston shock tunnels.

The Thai landbridge planning study is another example in which a joint venture was established to combine the strengths of companies from three countries. In this case, Bechtel Ltd. entered into a joint venture with Nippon-Koei of Japan and two Thai A/E firms, Asian Engineering Consultants Corp. Ltd. and South East Asia Technical Co. Ltd. Bechtel Ltd. brought the know-how for master planning of mega-projects; Nippon-Koei brought access to Japanese financing sources; and the local Thai firms brought cost-competitive design capability and knowledge of local requirements.

Political reasons are another market-driven motivation for two or more A/E firms to form a joint venture. For example, a small, local, and highly competent A/E firm may be very well known by the client's evaluation team; however, the firm may not have the capacity to do a large design project. The client may, in fact, recommend to the local A/E firm that it team up with X or Y so it can participate in the client's proposed project. When Bechtel Ltd. was considering performing A/E services for the director general of civil defense for Saudi Arabia regarding the upgrading of existing civil defense facilities there, Bechtel became aware that the civil defense agency was familiar with and had a high degree of confidence in the ability of a Saudi A/E group, Al-Zaid Engineering Consultants. Al-Zaid maintained an office in Riyadh, Saudi Arabia, of highly qualified architects and engineers. Although Al-Zaid was too small a firm to have any real chance of being awarded the contract at issue, Bechtel recognized the synergy to be gained by combining resources with this firm. An additional benefit to joint venturing with Al-Zaid was its ability to provide Arabic-speaking technical personnel.

Other motivating factors for forming a joint venture among two or more design professionals are:

1. To extend the market reach of a specialty A/E organization. For example, a foreign firm may be unfamiliar with a potential United States client and thus find it advantageous to combine with a known

United States A/E firm that has an excellent record with prospective clients.

2. To enhance one's position in a narrow field of specialized competitors. For example, as is frequently the case, a limited number of A/E firms may be invited to submit qualifications or a proposal. By two of the bidders' forming a joint venture, the chances of success may be increased. Of course, there are potential antitrust considerations that must be evaluated because forming the joint venture means that the coventurers will not be competing among themselves for the proposed work. See § **4.3**.
3. To present a centrally managed, strongly qualified entity and not merely a multiheaded association of firms to a prospective client.
4. To spread costs and risks. A single A/E firm may not have or may not wish to commit all the financial resources required to undertake a particular design project, or it may not want to undertake all the financial risk associated with a particular opportunity. For example, this reluctance may stem from the costs of obtaining professional liability insurance at the limits required by the client's invitation for bids or the incurrence of excessive liquidated damages associated with late completion.
5. To continue a prior joint venture relationship. For example, in the early 1960s a joint venture was formed by the A/E firms of Parsons Brinckerhoff Quade & Douglas, Inc., Tudor Engineering Co., and Bechtel (the PBTB Joint Venture) to perform design services for the San Francisco Bay Area Rapid Transit District's (district) then-proposed BART system. The job was completed in the early 1970s and the joint venture then terminated. Subsequently, on January 17, 1979, a fire occurred in one of the facilities designed by the PBTB Joint Venture, the Trans-Bay Tube. The district sought an A/E to assess the damage, if any, done to the tube and to suggest any remedial measures. Having initially designed and managed the construction of the Trans-Bay Tube, the three A/E firms felt morally obligated to again reconstitute themselves as a joint venture and bid for this emergency work.

§ 4.2 Hypothetical Scenario: Central Artery Project

The Commonwealth of Massachusetts, acting by and through its Department of Public Works (DPW), and with federal highway fund support, plans to construct an extension of the Massachusetts Turnpike (Interstate 90) from its present terminus at the Central Artery, across Boston Harbor, to a new terminus at Logan International Airport. The project consists of a Seaport Access Roadway through South Boston connecting to a Third Harbor Tunnel running from South Bay to Logan at Bird Island Flats and Route 1A in East Boston (Central Artery Project). The management consultant, the Bechtel/Parsons Brinckerhoff Joint Venture, has divided the work into section designs. One of the sections is the Third Harbor Tunnel, which will carry four vehicular lanes and will be 4,200 feet long. This highway tunnel would be three to four times wider than the typical subway tunnel structure. The DPW's preference is for immersed tube construction, consisting of 12-shell binocular tube tunnel sections with a 26-foot wide, 2-lane roadway in each barrel. The DPW is soliciting qualifications from interested A/E firms to be the section designer of the immersed tube. The DPW is using as its design consultant contract a form that reflects compensation on a cost-reimbursable basis with a total estimated cost ceiling. The estimated construction cost is expected to be approximately $300 million. The design period is estimated to be 12 months.

Potential Bidders

Design Management Associates (DMA), a large A/E firm based in New York City, has highly skilled technical and managerial personnel, who have a nationally known reputation for controlling costs and meeting schedules. Although DMA has had extensive experience in subway tunnel design for the New York City Transit Authority and the Washington Metropolitan Area Transit Authority, DMA has never undertaken the design of a highway immersed-tube project to date. DMA is very interested in broadening its expertise into this line of activity because of the extensive highway immersed-tube work envisioned for several major cities in the near future. DMA has never done an assignment with the DPW.

To determine if DMA is interested in bidding, DMA has obtained the invitation-to-bid package for the design of the Third Harbor Tunnel. One of the requirements of the package is for the bidder to carry a $10 million professional liability insurance policy covering claims that may arise out of acts, errors, or omissions in the performance of the design services. DMA has a master professional liability insurance policy of this magnitude, so they believe that they satisfy this tender requirement.

Assume that four other Boston-based design firms have specific expertise in the design of immersed-tube tunnels, and DMA believes they could reasonably be expected to be serious contenders for the Third Harbor Tunnel design work. The only one of these four firms with which DMA is familiar is TJA Associates. A minority-owned firm, TJA has an outstanding local reputation as an A/E firm. Most of these firms, including TJA, recently have had, or now are engaged in, highway tunnel immersed-tube design work for the DPW.

Assessing Whether to Form Joint Venture

DMA's management considers the following issues:

Despite DMA's lack of highway immersed-tube design experience, should it submit qualifications to go it alone?

Could DMA strengthen its position by:

Seeking out TJA and/or perhaps other Boston-based design firms to form a joint venture to undertake the immersed-tube design work?

Seeking out TJA to serve as the prospective prime section design consultant with DMA serving as a subconsultant?

Seeking out TJA to serve as a prospective design subconsultant to DMA?

Because only four Boston-based firms have expertise in highway immersed-tube design, and DMA is contemplating taking TJA out of the market by having it team up with them, are there any antitrust implications in adopting this approach?

If DMA chooses to form a joint venture agreement with TJA, what should be DMA's proposed working arrangements with TJA regarding management, responsibilities of the parties, budgeting procedures, bank accounts, insurance matters like the required $10 million professional liability policy, termination, and the resolution of claims and disputes? What contractual arrangements are necessary to address these concerns?

Should DMA do nothing and forget the job?

DMA concludes that the DPW is looking for one entity with the capability of being totally responsible for the job. DMA likes this scenario because DMA generally has performed most of its work alone. DMA has a general aversion to working in joint venture arrangements because of the loss of control, joint liability, and increased management time and effort required in administering such arrangements. However, in this particular situation, without having had any experience in immersed-tube tunneling design, DMA would not likely obtain the job if it bid for this job alone or was the prime consultant, even with one or more of the Boston-based firms serving as DMA's subconsultants. Furthermore, in the political climate in which large design projects are awarded by the DPW, it appears that an out-of-state firm unknown to the DPW's evaluation team would not have a good chance of being the prime consultant.

However, working as a subconsultant to TJA does not appeal to DMA because of the following factors:

One of the main contributions that DMA can bring to the arrangement is its management skill in completing projects on time and within budget, so DMA's skills in this regard should be exercised as a prime consultant rather than as a subconsultant.

DMA wants to gain credibility in the performance of design of immersed-tube tunneling design projects; thus, DMA would better further this goal by being a prime consultant.

DMA concludes that a joint venture with TJA would be the ideal approach to bid for the Third Harbor Tunnel design because of the following:

DMA's strong managerial and cost-control skills will match well with TJA's strengths in the design of immersed-tube tunnels.

TJA has the resources to quickly mobilize the necessary committed staff.

Coventuring with TJA, a disadvantaged business enterprise, should give DMA a competitive edge in the DPW's selection process.

DMA can present a centrally managed, strongly qualified single entity as the contracting party.

Based on its previous few joint ventures, DMA recognizes that the most important single consideration in forming a joint venture is choosing the right coventurer. DMA has enough experience to know that problems with potential coventurers cannot necessarily be resolved by contractual language incorporated into a joint venture agreement or by the way the joint venture is to be structured. Accordingly, DMA must take the necessary time to make an evaluation of TJA's financial condition, reputation in the Boston A/E community, and its technical strengths in immersed-tube design work.

§ 4.3 Antitrust Considerations

Because the formation of the DMA/TJA joint venture means that these coventurers will not compete among themselves in seeking the Third Harbor Tunnel design work, DMA must address antitrust concerns in assessing the feasibility of forming the proposed joint venture with TJA.

A fundamental premise on which the antitrust laws are based is that competitors should compete, as opposed to cooperate, with each other in those activities that are, in essence, a corporation's reason for being. The basic rationale underlying this premise is that, through vigorous competition based upon price, quality, and services, optimal levels of efficiency will be attained and the best products and services will be made available to the consumers at the lowest price possible.[1]

[1] T.K. Vakerics, Antitrust Basics, Release 6, at 10-1 (1990) [hereinafter Vakerics].

Most joint ventures among design professionals typically will be evaluated under § 1 of the Sherman Act[2] or under § 7 of the Clayton Act.[3] Section 1 of the Sherman Act prohibits contracts, combinations, and conspiracies that unreasonably restrain trade. It is important to note that the joint venture agreement itself may constitute a contract or combination, as that term is defined under the Sherman Act, so that the establishment of a joint venture automatically may meet one element required for a Sherman Act violation. The only remaining question regarding compliance with the Sherman Act would be whether the venture unreasonably restrains trade.[4] If the proposed venture results in the elimination of existing or potential competition between the venturers and is not justified by a need to join forces to provide services that the venturers were not providing on their own, the venture faces a possible per se violation of § 1 of the Sherman Act.[5]

Section 7 of the Clayton Act prohibits entities from mergers and acquisitions that would be likely to cause a substantial reduction in competition or that tend to create a monopoly. If it is determined that the joint venture has eliminated a significant, potential entrant into the market, a key element of a Clayton Act violation will have been met.[6]

If the formation of the DMA/TJA joint venture is in violation of United States antitrust law, the United States Department of Justice may seek an injunction requiring the dissolution of the joint venture. More importantly, competitors of the venture can recover three times their damages plus reasonable attorneys' fees in a civil suit if the formation of the venture can be proven to have violated the antitrust laws. Under some circumstances, criminal penalties may be imposed on the venturers and their officers.

The leading judicial authority on the evaluation of loss of competition due to joint venture formation is the United States Supreme Court decision in *United States v. Penn-Olin Chemical Co.*[7] In that decision, the Supreme Court noted that a joint venture is similar to a merger in that, in both instances, two or more previously independent entities are pooling all or a portion of their individual talent and resources to create a separate entity. The Court ruled that joint ventures should therefore be evaluated under § 7 of the Clayton Act, as a corporate merger.

The *Penn-Olin* litigation commenced because Pennsalt Chemicals Corporation and Olin Mathieson Chemical Corporation formed a joint venture to produce and sell sodium chlorate in the southeastern United States.

---

[2] 15 U.S.C. § 1 (1988).

[3] 38 Stat. 731 (1988).

[4] Vakerics at 10-4.

[5] Antitrust Adviser 205 (C.A. Hills 3d ed. 1985).

[6] *See* Vakerics at 10-12, 10-13.

[7] 378 U.S. 158 (1964).

Before the creation of the joint venture, neither coventurer had produced or sold sodium chlorate in the southeastern United States. The government sought an injunction to dissolve the joint venture because it allegedly violated both § 7 of the Clayton Act and § 1 of the Sherman Act. The trial court found no violation of § 1 of the Sherman Act because there was no division of the market among the venturers. The Supreme Court upheld the trial court's ruling that there had been no violation of § 1 of the Sherman Act, as there was no proof of specific intent to use Penn-Olin as a vehicle to eliminate competition.[8]

With respect to the Clayton Act issues, the Supreme Court agreed with the trial court that there was not a reasonable probability that both Pennsalt and Olin would have built a plant to produce sodium chlorate in the relevant market area. However, the Supreme Court noted that it is not necessary that *both* joint venturers might have independently entered the market and competed against each other in order to find a violation pursuant to § 7 of the Clayton Act. The Supreme Court ruled that the trial court should have considered the possibility that either venturer would have entered the market in the absence of the venture, while the other "remained at the edge of the market, continually threatening to enter."[9] This analysis became loosely known as the *potential competition* doctrine. On subsequent retrial to consider the potential competition issues, the trial court addressed (1) whether either venturer would have entered the southeastern market for sodium chlorate alone, and if so, (2) whether the other would have retained such an interest in the market as to be a significant potential competitor. The trial court found insufficient proof that either venturer would have entered such market alone and the Supreme Court, in reviewing the trial court findings, upheld the legality of the joint venture.[10]

Using the tests provided by *Penn-Olin,* DMA's management analyzes its proposed joint venture with TJA to determine whether there is or is not a reasonable probability that DMA and TJA would have bid for the Third Harbor Tunnel design work independently (Clayton Act issue) and whether there was a justifiable need to join forces to provide services that the coventurers were not providing on their own (Sherman Act issue). As part of making such analysis, it is noted that although TJA had previously engaged in highway tunnel immersed-tube design work in the Boston area, it never had engaged in one of the magnitude of the Third Harbor Tunnel design. TJA did not have the wherewithal to assume the risks associated with this project, including satisfying the requirement for a $10 million professional liability insurance policy, nor did they have strong managerial and cost-control skills to independently undertake a project of this magnitude.

---

[8] *Id.* at 788 (1964).

[9] *Id.* at 787 (1964).

[10] United States v. Penn-Olin Chem. Co., 389 U.S. 308 (1967).

Because DMA had never undertaken the design of a highway immersed-tube project and did not have any political clout in Boston, it was not conceivable that it would seek such initial work outside of its home base, New York City, on a project of the magnitude of the Third Harbor Tunnel design. DMA's management review concludes that neither DMA nor TJA acting alone represented a potential effective competitor for the Third Harbor Tunnel design work, and hence there appeared no anticompetitive purpose in joint venturing that would be in violation of the Clayton Act. By joint venturing, the parties were accomplishing a bona fide integration of skills, in effect promoting competition by introducing into the market a new entity that combined the individual unique resources of each party. Accordingly, the parties were not combining in restraint of trade in violation of the Sherman Act.

§ 4.4 Terms of Joint Venture Arrangement

Having concluded there are positive business reasons for settling on the joint venture approach and having evaluated TJA's financial capability and its particular strengths for undertaking the Third Harbor Tunnel design work, DMA selects TJA as its proposed joint venture partner. DMA's president then contacts the president of TJA, Daren Reed, regarding his interest in such a joint venture. Mr. Reed appears enthusiastic because he, too, believes that the combined strengths of DMA's organization, when matched with TJA's, result in a bidder with unique credentials for success in obtaining the Third Harbor Tunnel design work. In addition, Mr. Reed has evaluated DMA's financial condition and technical strengths and was pleased with the results.

Allocation of Work

Now, the parties discuss the overall terms of their working relationship. First is the allocation of the work. The intent is that the parties will *not* work as an integrated team, but each will perform its respective scope of work at its individual offices with a goal of achieving an approximate equal split of the job. The decision as to whether DMA's proposed joint venture is to be an integrated or nonintegrated joint venture is an important one in terms of shaping the structure of the joint venture agreement. For example, one would treat differently liability to the client and to subcontractors for design deficiencies and damages and to third parties for personal injuries and property damages depending upon whether it is an integrated or a nonintegrated arrangement. In a *nonintegrated joint venture,* each party will generally be responsible for its respective portion of the Third Harbor Tunnel work, although some sharing of certain costs, such as common business development costs expended in securing the work, may be necessary. With respect to a nonintegrated joint venture, it may be possible to have the client pay each of the coventurers directly for its specific portion of the work. However, the more frequent arrangement is to have each coventurer send its invoices to the leader or sponsor of the joint venture, who will in turn forward them to the client for payment.

The even split in interests between DMA and TJA could result in some hard negotiations as to which party will, in fact, be the leader or sponsor of the joint venture and have the right to appoint the project manager, who will have the responsibility for the day-to-day management of the work. If this becomes a real sticking point in the negotiations, one means of possibly solving the problem in a nonintegrated joint venture is to have a separate project manager chosen by DMA and TJA for their respective scopes of work. Each of the selected project managers will be the spokesperson for the DMA/TJA joint venture in meeting with the DPW when the scope of work of his employer is being addressed.

Finalizing Arrangement

Depending upon the complexities of the proposed joint venture agreement and the time remaining to bid submission, DMA's president will be advised by its legal advisors/contracts group to confirm its arrangements with TJA either on a two-step basis, that is, a memorandum of understanding to cover the period up to award of the design professional's agreement followed by a formal joint venture agreement after award, or on a one-step basis, that is, immediately entering into the formal joint venture agreement. If TJA is already teamed up with Firm X, one of DMA's competitors, on a nonexclusive basis for the particular job, DMA will be forced to follow the two-step process. TJA would not want to firm up a joint venture agreement with DMA until it knows whether its bid with Firm X or with DMA is the one that was awarded the project. Whether DMA goes the two-step or one-step approach, it is important that DMA's initial agreement address all major issues to avoid disputes that may arise after award, and that both firms execute the document before the bid is submitted.

Integrated and Nonintegrated Arrangements

It was noted earlier that in DMA's negotiations with TJA, it was decided that DMA would not work with TJA as an integrated team. The nonintegrated arrangement is typically used when the design professionals teaming together have specialized areas of expertise or assigned work responsibilities, such as when an A/E firm that specializes in designing science museums teams up with a design professional that specializes in designing large aquariums. The counterpart to this is the *integrated arrangement,* wherein the design professionals essentially agree to perform their work as if they were a single corporation with several shareholders. In this case, all monies received from the client would go into a joint venture bank account. The joint venture would share profits and losses in accordance with a previously agreed ratio. Both parties' personnel would work together under the supervision of one or more of the joint venturers in accomplishing the A/E services.

In an integrated arrangement, DMA should allocate liability to each coventurer in accordance with its proportionate interest in the joint venture, even though one of the joint venturers was negligent and the other was not. The concept here is that with an integrated team it will be difficult to pinpoint liability to a particular joint venturer. Furthermore, an integrated arrangement is not conducive to finger pointing, unless one of the parties has been grossly negligent. In the case of the nonintegrated relationship, it should be quite easy to identify which joint venturer caused the injury and to have that party bear the full responsibility for the design deficiency, property damage, or personal injury.

§ 4.5 —Agreement Forms

As a base format for the agreement with TJA, DMA's legal/contracts group selects the American Institute of Architects (AIA) Document C801, Joint Venture Agreement for Professional Services. This form provides for the following two methods of compensation:

> **Division of compensation.** This method assumes that the services provided by the a/e firms and the compensation received will be divided between the parties as agreed at the outset. The profit for each party is therefore dependent on individual performance. This method is based on the parties' working on the project on a nonintegrated basis.
>
> **Division of profit/loss.** This method is based on each party's performing work and billing the joint venture on the basis of cost-plus overhead. The ultimate profit or loss of the joint venture is divided between the parties at the completion of the project. This method is premised on the parties' working on the particular project as an integrated team.[11]

Apart from the compensation terms, following are several of the key issues addressed in the part of the AIA Document C801 that uses the division of compensation method:

1. **Preliminary expenses.** All preliminary expenses incurred by any party before the date of the joint venture agreement are to be borne by the party who incurred such expenses.

---

[11] *Documents Synopses,* 3 The Architect's Handbook of Professional Practice 7 (1987).

2. **Exclusivity.** Neither party will enter into any separate agreement with the owner to perform professional services in connection with the project without the approval of the other party.
3. **Description of the services to be provided by each party.** This section also defines where the work is to be performed.
4. **Interest of the parties.** A statement is included as to each of the parties' respective percentage interests in the compensation and liabilities under the prime contract with the client. All working capital required for the performance of the prime contract should be contributed by the joint venturers in accordance with their respective interests.
5. **Resolution of disputes.** All disputes between the parties arising out of or relating to the joint venture agreement are to be decided in accordance with the Construction Industry Arbitration Rules of the American Arbitration Association, unless the parties otherwise mutually agree.[12]

As noted, in formulating the joint venture agreement, AIA Document C801 may be helpful to serve as DMA's base format. However, DMA should supplement the form by including a number of other provisions tailored to its particular project. For example, the prime contract with the DPW most likely will require that each of the joint venturers assume joint and several liability for their work. Because DMA is entering into a nonintegrated arrangement with TJA, such prime contract liability should be indicated in the joint venture agreement with TJA by including a cross-indemnity clause requiring that each party indemnify and hold harmless the other party from and against claims from the client or third parties caused by the indemnitor's acts or omissions. Such a clause is needed because in an increasing number of jurisdictions architect/engineers can be liable to a variety of third parties despite the lack of any privity of contract. For example, in *M. Miller Co. v. Dames & Moore,*[13] a contractor was allowed to sue a soils engineer with whom he had no contractual relationship for negligence because the soils report failed to reveal unstable material beneath the construction site. The report had been made available to the contractor bidding on the project, and the contractor relied on the report in submitting a bid that was substantially lower than his actual costs. Of course, the value of a cross-indemnity clause depends upon the respective parties' financial strength.

---

[12] *AIA Document C801—Joint Venture Agreement,* 4 The Architect's Handbook of Professional Practice, C-Series Documents 1-13 (1987).

[13] 198 Cal. App. 2d 305, 18 Cal. Rptr. 13 (1961).

If a joint venturer fails or is unable to provide its proportionate share of the funds required by the joint venture, its interests in the profits of the joint venture should be decreased to the proportion that its actual contribution bears to the total amount of the funds provided by all joint venturers. However, its share of any losses in the joint venture should remain intact.

Each joint venturer also should assign sufficient competent professional and administrative personnel to the services allocated to each of them. It would be prudent for the joint venture's policy board to review the candidates slated for key joint venture management positions.

When a joint venturer invoices the joint venture for the compensation to which it is entitled, the invoice should be supported by the documentation required by the prime contract and by the joint venture's policy board. Unless there is a statutory requirement that the prime contractor must pay its subcontractors within a reasonable time, the joint venture should not be obligated to pay any joint venturer until it has received the corresponding payment from the client.

A joint venture bank account should be established in a bank agreed upon by the joint venturers. The books of the joint venture should be held by a mutually agreeable sponsor member of the joint venture. The books should be maintained in accordance with generally accepted accounting practices and be open to examination by the respective representatives of the coventurers at any reasonable time. It would be prudent to maintain the books on an accrual basis of accounting for management purposes and on a cash basis for tax purposes. A statement of the financial condition of the joint venture should be issued to the joint venturers on a regular basis, such as monthly.

There should be prior agreement on the types and amounts of insurance coverage to be carried by the joint venture. In general, insurance should cover the responsibility of the joint venture as a legal entity, either by endorsement of the insurance of each of the joint venturers or by a separate policy covering the joint venture.

At the outset, it may be desirable to commit each joint venturer to secrecy with respect to the know-how transmitted, especially if the coventurer is a potential competitor. Each joint venturer should be committed not to use the other joint venturer's know-how at any time without the prior approval of the joint venturer who owns such know-how. It should be stipulated that such secrecy provisions should survive the termination of the joint venture agreement.

One should never enter into a joint venture relationship without developing an exit strategy. When the project is completed as determined by the joint venture's contract with the client, the joint venture should terminate. It should be settled in the joint venture agreement how the joint venture's property will be disposed of at the conclusion of the relationship. There also should be provisions that would allow for a joint venturer to be terminated for default. This exit strategy should go beyond removing the other coventurer only if it goes into bankruptcy or liquidation or commits a criminal or other act materially affecting the operations of the joint venture. It also should encompass a mechanism for forcing out the other coventurer, if a material breach of any key obligation is committed or if a deadlock of irreconcilable differences occurs between the coventurers.

A joint venturer whose participation is terminated for default should remain liable for any losses incurred by the joint venture. Furthermore, the surviving joint venturer should be solely entitled to all compensation arising from work done after the date of such default by the defaulting venturer. The defaulting joint venturer should be obligated to turn over to the surviving joint venturer all technical and other documents relating to the project, which are in its possession or control.

§ 4.6 —Budgeting Procedures

Because the compensation for the proposed DMA/TJA joint venture work will be on a cost-reimbursable basis, subject to a price ceiling, the joint venture will need to seek in its proposed agreement with the DPW provisions that allow for adjustments to the ceiling for changes, force majeure events, and other conditions beyond the joint venture's control. To effectively operate within the price ceiling, DMA and TJA need to mutually agree on a budget covering the respective costs and fees that they each expect to expend in performing their portions of the Third Harbor Tunnel design work. It is recognized that this budget will be subject to revision during the course of the design work to reflect changes in the scope of the project and for schedule extensions. As part of this budget allocation, there should be agreement on the direct costs and overhead rates to be charged by each firm.

If the contemplated joint venture is an integrated arrangement, consideration should be given to the possibility of having the joint venture itself be a payroll entity, because this may allow for lower overhead rates and the development of a more competitive price to the client. One could envision, for example, the majority of the joint venture personnel being comprised of design engineers hired specifically for the new work and who would be terminated when the work was completed. In this scenario, such design engineers, while employed on the joint venture's payroll, would not have to be afforded the full range of fringe benefits that each of the coventurers ordinarily would have to provide to their own employees. In this way, a more competitive overhead rate could be developed. Because DMA and TJA are contemplating a nonintegrated joint venture, this proposed structuring probably would not have particular appeal to them.

As noted earlier, the proposed joint venture between DMA and TJA contemplates that each party will perform its portion of the Third Harbor

Tunnel design work at its respective offices. In this regard, the joint venture agreement should reflect a requirement for DMA and TJA to report each month to the joint venture's project manager the engineering and other labor hours and funds budgeted to date and actually expended to date by their respective organizations for the work. Such project progress reports also should reflect monthly the percentage of the work scheduled to be completed and what was actually completed to such date by each firm. The report should make reference to the total budget and the current estimate of such budget at completion. There should be a procedure in the joint venture agreement for DMA and TJA to consult and adopt mutually agreed-upon corrective measures when the monthly status reports indicate that the current estimate at completion figures will exceed the total budget by a particular percentage.

§ 4.7 —Management of Joint Venture

The management issue is another key consideration of the coventurers' working relationship. AIA Document C801 envisions that each party is to designate a primary representative to serve on a policy board. The policy board should review the technical and financial status of the project on a periodic basis and should make overall decisions regarding project performance, such as approving budgets and schedules, reviewing the selection of key management personnel, and determining the allocation of work to subconsultants. Decisions on all substantive issues regarding the project, such as the acceptance of change orders, the determination of working capital needs, the opening of bank accounts, the approval of key joint venture personnel to be engaged on the project, and the proposed settlement of claims all should be made by unanimous vote of the board's representatives.

The policy board appoints a project manager and, if required, an assistant project manager, who are responsible for the direction and management of the work in accordance with the policies and procedures established by the board. To enable the project manager to assume these responsibilities, he or she must be given commitment and signature authority by the policy board. The project manager's duties should include the administration of the joint venture's contract with the client, the administration of the joint venture agreement, the day-to-day direction of the work, and control of the money flow.

Because this hypothetical situation indicates that TJA is the A/E firm with the specific expertise in highway tunneling design and with an outstanding local reputation as a qualified A/E firm, it appears that TJA has the marketing leverage to insist that it be the leader of this joint venture with the right to appoint the project manager. Accordingly, the issue for DMA to assess is whether by relinquishing such leadership position, it would still have an important say in the joint venture, especially regarding any issues that may have financial or legal implications for DMA or that might affect DMA's reputation.

In this scenario, as well as when DMA has a minority interest in a proposed joint venture arrangement, DMA should as a minimum strive to achieve the following understandings with its coventurer:

There should be unanimous agreement among the joint venturers on the proposal and its qualifications before it is submitted to the client.

Whenever possible and practicable during the proposal phase, both parties should initial all proposed joint venture correspondence to the client.

Both joint venturers should be entitled to participate in any resulting negotiations with the client and/or any third party in connection with the proposal. No joint venturer should be entitled to make any commitment regarding the other joint venturer without first obtaining the other joint venturer's prior written approval.

Each joint venturer should have the right to refuse to lower its prices or to accept terms and conditions other than those contained in its proposal if a joint venturer determines that making such changes exposes it to unacceptable risks and liabilities.

If the proposal is accepted, the resulting contract with the client should be signed by both joint venturers.

The policies of the joint venture should be established by the policy board.

During the joint venture's operational phase, neither joint venturer shall have the power to bind the joint venture except to the extent specifically authorized in writing by the joint venturers.

The joint venture's books and accounts should be subject to inspection at any reasonable time during the term of the joint venture by either joint venturer or its designated representatives, including independent auditors, at any reasonable time.

DMA probably won't be able to achieve all of these wish-list items, but it must achieve most of them if it is to obtain control over the joint venture in essential matters.

§ 4.8 —Professional Liability Insurance Coverage

Another major issue that DMA must address with TJA is the requirement for professional liability insurance in the DPW's invitation for bids. The invitation for bids requires all bidders for the particular package to carry a $10 million professional liability insurance policy covering claims that may arise out of acts, errors, or omissions in the performance of the design services.

Assume that even though DMA initially thought it met this requirement, upon reading the conditions of its errors and omissions policy, DMA noted that it had the typical *joint venture exclusion*. This exclusion applies to "liability of any kind based upon, involving or arising out of the conduct by an individual, corporation, partnership or joint venture of which the Insured is a partner, officer, member or employee which is not designated in the Declarations as a named Insured, unless specifically endorsed hereon."[14] Such exclusion sometimes reads as follows: "professional services performed by 'you' as part of a joint venture or by any other member of such joint venture, unless named in this policy."[15] Simply put, this exclusion precludes coverage to any entity other than those listed in the policy. This exclusion was introduced in the 1960s because of an increasing number of cases in which one or more members of the joint venture had no liability insurance and the insured member or member(s) of the joint venture bore the entire brunt of claims against the joint venture.[16] This historical situation still exists today. The American Consulting Engineers Council's Tenth Annual Professional Liability Survey Results, issued in October, 1988, indicates that 21 percent of all United States engineering firms are operating without professional liability insurance. ACEC Director of Liability Issues Bob Fogle, attributes this phenomenon to "smaller firms . . . being forced to operate at tremendous risk because many can no longer afford professional liability insurance."[17]

The only manner in which DMA could get the benefits of professional liability insurance coverage with respect to its contemplated joint venture with TJA is to advise the insurance carrier who is carrying its basic practice coverage of DMA's joint venture with TJA. DMA should request an endorsement on such policy that would cover the joint venture arrangement with TJA, should the joint venture be favored with an award of the Third Harbor Tunnel work.

However, the issue still is not completely resolved. The joint venture endorsement will not provide coverage for the entire joint venture, but rather will apply only to DMA's participation in it.[18] DMA must make sure that TJA obtains its own professional liability insurance policy endorsement covering its participation in the contemplated joint venture. For a small

---

[14] R. Cushman & T. Bottum, Architect and Engineer Liability: Claims Against Design Professionals 49 (John Wiley & Sons 1987).

[15] Continental National Assurance, Specimen Design Professionals Policy § II.A.3, CNA Form 1-887503-A (Mar. 1988).

[16] *Professional Liability Insurance for Joint Ventures Between Design Professionals,* VI Guidelines for Improving Practice—Architects and Engineers Professional Liability 1 (1976).

[17] American Consulting Engineers Council, *Consulting Engineers Paid Over $250 Million in 1988 for Professional Liability Insurance,* Liability Report (Oct. 1988).

[18] *See* R. Cushman & T. Bottum, Architect and Engineer Liability: Claims Against Design Professionals 42 (John Wiley & Sons 1987).

firm like TJA, this may not be easy, because obtaining a professional liability insurance endorsement at higher limits could become prohibitively expensive. One has to keep in mind that professional liability insurance represents the second largest operating expense to A/E firms, exceeded only by payroll.[19] According to the American Consulting Engineers Council, design professionals' liability insurance costs in 1988 reached an average high of 4.5 percent of gross billings. This data was based on a survey of approximately 1,800 design firms of all disciplines. The coverage for structural engineers only was 8.31 percent of gross billings.[20] However, TJA won't have to obtain the full $10 million endorsement to its basic practice policy, because it will only have to maintain an endorsement covering its percentage participation in the contemplated joint venture billings. As a rough guide, the additional premium for a joint venture endorsement will be approximately 5 percent of the firm's total billings to be derived from the joint venture.[21] It is recommended that the contemplated joint venture coverage be added as soon as possible after the joint venture with TJA is formed, but in any event before the date when any drawings and specifications for the Third Harbor Tunnel Project are ready for release by the joint venture to the DPW. If coverage is not placed in force before such date, it will be too late to provide effective coverage. Also, undue delays in obtaining such coverage may mean that higher rates will be in effect when the endorsement is actually requested.

DMA also should recognize that professional liability policies are issued only on a claims made basis. This means that the carrier will honor only claims made during the policy period. If a claim is made under the policy based on the proposed joint venture's tunneling design, DMA must recognize that it will most likely arise during construction or when the tunnel goes into operation. Accordingly, both DMA and TJA will have to purchase a tail onto their respective professional liability policies to account for claims made long after the joint venture's work has been completed, that is, during the discovery period.

§ 4.9 —Finalizing Key Issues

After several negotiating sessions with TJA representatives, DMA must then go through a mental checklist to see where it stands on several of the

[19] W. McInerney, Jr. & F. Yap, Architect and Engineer Liability: Claims Against Design Professionals 16 (John Wiley & Sons Supp. 1990).

[20] *See Professional Liability Insurance for Joint Ventures Between Design Professionals,* VI Guidelines for Improving Practice—Architects and Engineers Professional Liability 2 (1976).

[21] *See* American Consulting Engineers Council, *Consulting Engineers Paid Over $250 Million in 1988 for Professional Liability Insurance,* Liability Report (Oct. 1988).

key issues it initially addressed. With respect to whether the arrangement with TJA should be on a two-step or one-step basis (see § **4.4**), DMA decides that only a one-step process is necessary. TJA plans to work only with DMA in the submission of a bid for this work and, hence, the firm is prepared to enter into a joint venture agreement with DMA at this time. To firm up this understanding, there should be a broader exclusivity provision set forth in the joint venture agreement than contained in AIA Document C801 (see § **4.5**). Such provision would provide that each party agrees to exclusively work with the other party in the submission of a proposal for the Third Harbor Tunnel work.

As to the management arrangement, DMA and TJA agree to change AIA Document C801 to indicate that the project manager will be nominated by TJA rather than the policy board. They also decide that the scope of the project does not justify having an assistant project manager. In exchange for giving TJA the right to appoint the project manager, TJA agrees to include in the joint venture agreement the following list of key management decisions that would have to be decided by the policy board by unanimous vote:

Approval to enter into the design consultant contract with the DPW and any subcontracts with engineers, consultants, or anyone else concerning the Third Harbor Tunnel work

Assignment of a coventurer's interest to a third party

Any commitment to DPW that could materially affect the joint venture's financial condition, liability exposure, or performance obligations

Assignment or release of any claim of debt owed to the joint venture, except upon payment in full.

As to the insurance issues, TJA and DMA agree that they will obtain endorsements onto their existing professional liability insurance policies to cover their proposed work as a joint venture on the Third Harbor Tunnel design. Considering the long construction period associated with the entire Central Artery Project, the parties agree that these endorsements will include a seven-year tail.

Agreement with TJA is also reached that DMA and TJA will specifically request reimbursement in their bid prices for the premium costs of the professional liability endorsement with a seven-year tail needed specifically for this project. Having addressed all key issues, DMA is now prepared to enter into its joint venture agreement with TJA for the Third Harbor Tunnel work.

PART II

FINANCE AND INSURANCE

CHAPTER 5

FINANCIAL ADMINISTRATION AND CASH MANAGEMENT

Eileen Dinn
John Jackson
Charles Wetherill

Eileen Dinn is the assistant controller of the Consulting Engineering and Design Division of Metcalf & Eddy, an international environmental treatment and services firm in Wakefield, Massachusetts. She graduated from Stonehill College with a degree in accounting and is pursuing an M.B.A. in the executive program at Northeastern University. Ms. Dinn has over 11 years of both domestic and international experience.

John Jackson is the vice president/controller of the Consulting Engineering and Design Division of Metcalf & Eddy in Wakefield, Massachusetts. He graduated from Bentley College with a degree in accounting and has 15 years of systems and accounting experience in the service industry.

Charles Wetherill is the assistant controller of Metcalf & Eddy's Corporate Division in Wakefield, Massachusetts. He graduated from Wagner College with a major in business administration, and he earned an M.B.A. in accounting from Pace University and is a Certified Public Accountant. Mr. Wetherill has over 25 years' experience in this field.

---

§ 5.1 Introduction

The professionals in a design firm who are responsible for financial administration and cash management must be guided by the firm's overall goals and philosophy and its shifting short-term and long-term strategies. It is often helpful if the firm has a *mission statement* outlining its objectives and philosophy. The mission statement should be tailored to the specific firm, but many contain statements such as:

1. The firm's primary role is satisfying the needs of its clients. Customer service is everyone's job.
2. The firm will provide the highest quality service consistent with the needs of the client, competitive pricing, and making a fair profit.
3. The firm will strive to be the number one or two firm in the primary markets in which it competes.
4. The firm will be a responsible contributor to society and will protect the environment.
5. The firm will encourage its staff to take prudent business risks, will match responsibility with authority, and will link compensation to performance.

The firm also should have clear and concise manuals of its policies and procedures, including technical and administrative areas as well as finance functions.

Financial management has the same basic function as all management: planning, organizing, leading, and controlling. Historically, a greater emphasis has been on the controlling function; hence, the head of the finance function carried the title "controller." Today, the broader managerial scope of the finance function is generally recognized and the title *chief financial officer* (CFO) is commonly used.

The financial officer has primary responsibility for safeguarding the assets of the firm and ensuring its fiscal health through sound business practices. Thus, the finance function must be an integral part of the top management team. More businesses fail due to financial issues than for any other reason.

§ 5.2 Typical Financial Activities

All design firms require financial record-keeping activities such as cash receipts and disbursements, payroll, job costing, billing, taxes, and general ledger accounting. Many progressive firms also include budgeting, treasury, financial reporting and analysis, and internal auditing activities. Following is a more detailed description of these functions:

1. **Cash receipts.** This activity records the checks received by the design firm, primarily from its customers, in a cash receipts register,

deposits the receipts into the firm's bank account(s), and records the payments into client account receivable ledgers or other appropriate accounts.

2. **Cash disbursements.** The disbursements function is responsible for preparing checks to pay for the firm's obligations to suppliers and employees. This function prepares cash disbursement register(s) and records the distribution of payments to jobs and accounts. See § **5.18**.
3. **Payroll.** The payment of salaries and wages to the firm's employees is the primary payroll function. Preparation of payroll registers, both for employees and taxing authorities, and recording payroll changes to jobs and accounts is also required. See § **5.17**.
4. **Job costing.** Costs that are directly attributable to client contracts are recorded in job ledgers for each contract. The job cost records should segregate labor and other direct costs in sufficient detail to provide billing details for clients. Job cost records also should contain budget information at a level of detail sufficient to manage the progress of the job.
5. **Billing.** This function produces the invoices and any supporting documents that are sent to the firm's clients. See § **5.20**.
6. **Taxes.** The preparation of the firm's tax returns for all types of taxes, except payroll taxes which are generally a payroll function, falls under the tax function. See § **5.18**.
7. **General ledger accounting.** This function maintains the firm's summary or general ledger(s) that ties together all the accounting transactions recorded in the ledgers of subsidiary functions such as cash receipts, cash disbursements, payroll, and job costs.
8. **Budgeting.** The budgeting function is responsible for the preparation and maintenance of the firm's financial plan. See § **5.12**.
9. **Treasury.** Treasury activities include maintaining banking relationships, such as opening and closing accounts, and monitoring cash flow and investing excess cash or borrowing to cover cash requirements.
10. **Financial reporting and analysis.** This function prepares and analyzes reports for project and administrative management. The reports can be standard or ad hoc, historical or forecasts. See § **5.20**.
11. **Internal auditing.** This activity checks the firm's compliance with its financial and operational policies and procedures to assure that the firm's financial reports are accurate and its assets are safeguarded. See § **5.22**.

Some firms may add procurement, data processing, and office administration activities under the finance function. Publicly traded firms also have external reporting requirements.

Many factors affect the organizational structure of the finance function, such as the size of the firm, availability of staff resources, divergent service offerings and number of locations. However, if the financial structure does not match the objectives, philosophy, and strategies of the firm, there will be serious problems. For example, if the business strategy is to emphasize delivery of the firm's total service offerings on a regional basis and measure performance regionally, financial resources should be organized to support that strategy. If the finance organization is structured to support only each separate service line, there will be considerable inefficiencies and possible reductions in regional accountability.

Among the organizational decisions to be made are which financial activities should be performed internally or purchased externally, centralized or decentralized, and computerized or done manually.

§ 5.3 —Internal versus External

At smaller design firms, the finance function may be the part-time responsibility of the proprietor or one of the principals. A Boston-area consulting firm offers the following guidelines for when to hire in-house financial personnel:

Firm Size	Finance Personnel
5–10	Part-time bookkeeper
20	Full-time bookkeeper
40	Full-time accountant and bookkeeper
60	Controller and accounting staff
125	Vice-president of finance, controller, and staff

Many larger design firms have sizable financial staffs to perform most, if not all, customary financial activities internally. Other firms rely on outside services for certain activities such as payroll or taxes.

A cost/benefit analysis is useful to determine whether it is advantageous to buy services rather than to use internal resources for a particular activity. Among the factors to be considered when purchasing outside services are:

1. The activity should involve specialized capabilities that either are not available in-house, or the in-house personnel will provide a better return in other activities. Examples of specialized capabilities include tax advice covering unusual circumstances or business in other states or countries, auditing services, if required by clients, and overhead rate, procurement, or pricing analyses, if required for governmental agencies.

2. The activity should not be highly integrated into the firm's financial reporting systems. If extensive, externally prepared information has to be re-entered into internal systems, apparent cost savings may soon disappear.
3. The outside services should be less costly in the long term.

§ 5.4 —Centralized versus Decentralized

Many financial activities can be performed outside the accounting department, such as billing, collection, and vendor invoice approvals. As a general rule, decentralized activities tend to be more flexible and responsive to client needs and centralized activities tend to be subject to more control. Each financial activity should be reviewed with respect to the issue of control versus responsiveness. The finance function often has a bias for control but should strive for the proper balance to best meet the firm's objectives.

§ 5.5 —Computerized versus Manual

Today, very few firms can manage without some computerization of their financial records. In fact, lack of computerization may indicate a lack of control. Repole Associates of Boston suggests that small firms of 20 persons or less may be able to employ manual or one-write systems, which use specialized disbursement checks with carbon paper that produces the check register when the check is written. However, larger firms should mechanize their accounting systems. Determining the proper level of sophistication of a firm's computerized financial systems should be, again, a matter of cost/benefit analysis and business objectives.

Automation of financial information systems can provide benefits in two major areas: (1) productivity—doing things better, such as reducing work cycles, and (2) innovation—doing better things, such as providing better management tools and reports.

When evaluating a computerized financial system, the key is defining functional requirements. Prepare a list of what capabilities are required within a computerized system to accomplish what the firm needs. This is often a list of what is currently being done manually. The following criteria should be considered:

1. Functionality. Does it meet defined requirements in all material respects?
2. Ease of use. Does the system work the way the employees currently work? Is training relatively easy? Is error correction simple?
3. Flexibility. Can the system meet a variety of business requirements for the same function, such as multiple billing types? Can it be easily

changed to meet changing internal and external requirements? Can it accommodate the planned growth of the firm?

4. Modular yet integrated. Can different people learn just their piece, but have all pieces fit together so data is entered once and updates all affected modules?
5. Vendor support. Is the vendor stable? Does it have good support services?
6. Cost. Can the total cost, including implementation, training, and ongoing maintenance, be justified?

§ 5.6 Cash versus Accrual Basis Accounting

Many small firms with sole proprietors or few partners use the *cash basis method* of accounting for tax purposes. This method records only cash receipt and disbursement transactions and does not reflect any uncollected billings or unpaid vendor invoices in periodic profit-and-loss statements. The *accrual method,* on the other hand, recognizes revenue in the period when "earned" and expenses when "incurred." All design firms should use the accrual method for internal management reports because it reflects a more accurate picture of what has occurred in the reported period.

§ 5.7 Internal Controls

The accounting profession has a formal definition and explanation of internal controls in its Statement on Auditing Standards No. 1. Essentially, there are three types of internal controls:

1. *Administrative controls* to "promote operational efficiency, and encourage adherence to prescribed managerial policies"
2. *Accounting controls* to "check the accuracy and reliability of . . . accounting data"
3. *Physical controls* "to safeguard assets."[1]

Administrative controls include management policies on such things as authorizations and approvals, segregation of duties, and operational budgets and forecasts. Accounting controls include procedures to ensure that transactions are executed and recorded in accordance with management's policies. Physical controls include restricting access and supervisory checking.

[1] American Institute of Certified Public Accountants, Statement on Auditing Standards No. 1 (1972).

§ 5.8 Budgeting and Planning

A plan is a tool used for setting goals for the future and determining the course of action required to achieve those goals. Plans are generally prepared for the upcoming year; however, longer- or shorter-range plans also may be appropriate. Plans take on a variety of forms and should depend upon each other. **Sections 5.9** through **5.13** contain examples of the types of plans that should be developed to set expectations and then measure performance. **Table 5–1** illustrates a budgeting and planning process flow.

Table 5–1

Budgeting and Planning Process Flow

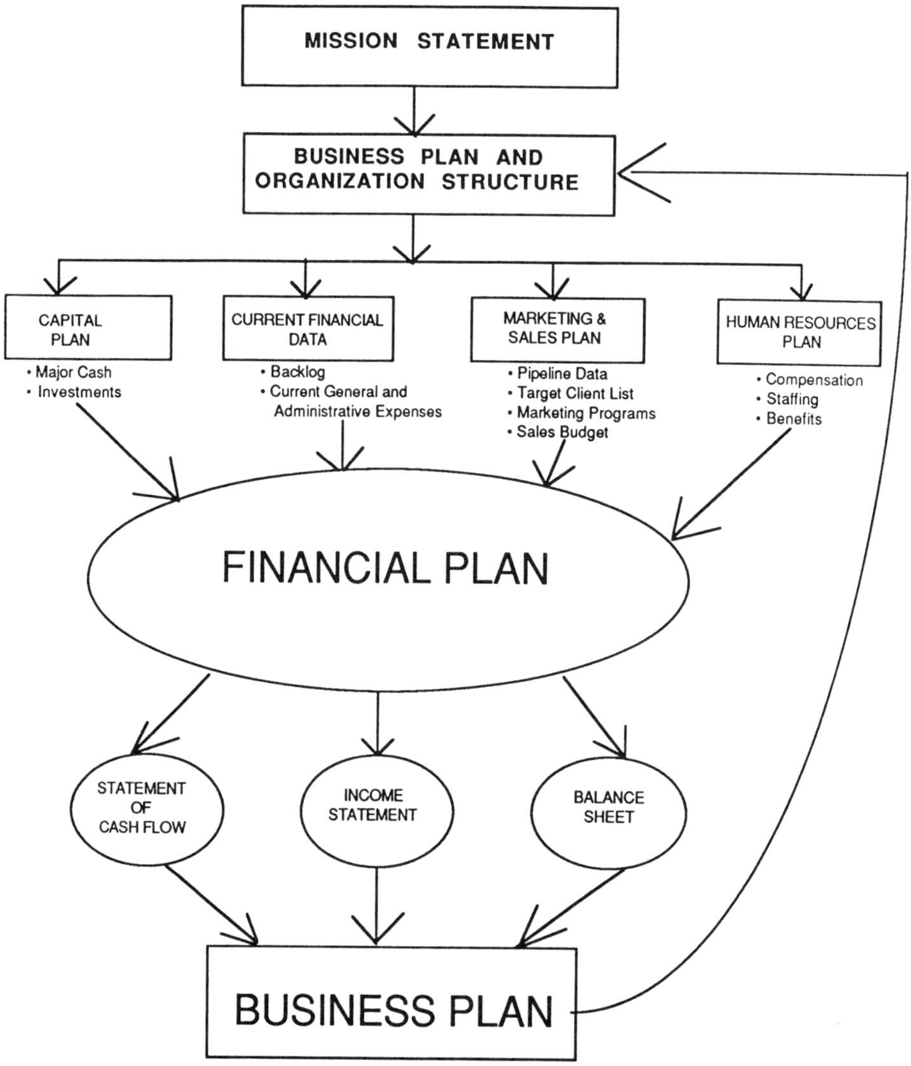

§ 5.9 —Business Plan

A *business plan* defines and sets the overall objectives of the firm and usually incorporates both long- and short-term goals. To prepare a business plan, the design professional must define the mission of the firm and then set goals.

Following is a list of questions to consider when preparing a business plan:

1. What is the trend in the design firm community?
2. What clients have funding?
3. Are the types of services you offer still in demand by your clients?
4. Do you need to redefine your markets or market niches in which you operate?
5. Are you successfully penetrating the market?
6. Should you invest in vertical integration of multiple product lines within the business?
7. Do you need to repackage your product or your image?
8. Is your sales staff effective?
9. Can the current management team lead you into the future?
10. Do you have a qualified work force to provide the service your customers demand?

Sample Business Plan

OBJECTIVE

To grow after-tax profits of 25 percent annually

BUSINESS STRATEGY

Increase share in key market niches (list niches)
Achieve new market penetration (list markets)
Add research and development and introduce proprietary technology
Achieve higher profit margins through improved contract performance
Reduce general and administrative costs by improved productivity and better controls
Manage sales force efforts and assign sales targets
Provide training to key technical staff.

A dollar value should be identified with each business objective.

§ 5.10 —Marketing Plan

After determining the firm's business objectives, the next step is to define how to achieve those objectives. The *marketing plan* should define the market or niche to be penetrated, identify the client base, and set a strategy for winning contract awards. The marketing plan should include the following items:

1. Understand and identify the trends in the market(s) both at the national and local level. Is there legislation pending that may impact the business favorably or unfavorably?
2. Target your client base. Identify your sales force and assign responsibility. Will you primarily sell to industrial clients, municipal clients, or the federal government? What size client do you plan on serving: large, national firms or small, local businesses? small towns and communities or large regional/municipal clients? Is your role to be a subcontractor or a prime contractor?
3. Define your product and/or service. Know what your targeted clients' needs or requirements are and be prepared to respond. There may be a need, but is there adequate funding? Can you provide alternative solutions at an affordable price?
4. Develop a detailed list (pipeline) of potential clients and identify potential contracts. Assign the person responsible for marketing to the client.
5. List the marketing and sales programs anticipated to be implemented. Identify major advertising campaigns, direct mailing efforts, brochure productions, conferences, and trade show attendances. Each of these should be listed and assigned a dollar value for inclusion in the financial plan.

Keep in mind that marketing, both selling and proposal preparation, carries a high dollar cost. Be sure to determine that the investment is cost effective.

§ 5.11 —Human Resources Plan

Depending on the size of the firm, there may or may not be a separate human resources department. As a general rule, if there are more than 90 employees, then the firm should employ a human resources professional. For every additional 100 people, an additional human resources professional should be added to the staff.

The human resources function is typically responsible for:

1. Wage and salary administration
2. Maintenance of fringe and benefit programs
3. Recruiting and relocating employees
4. Regulatory agency compliance
5. Employee communications.

The business strategy and projected growth of the firm will set the basis for establishing a *human resources plan.* The human resources plan should be done in conjunction with the financial plan. Input from the human resources department for recommended salary increases, projected benefit costs per person, and an estimate for recruiting and relocating costs will be needed for the financial plan.

§ 5.12 —Financial Plan

Quantifying the business and marketing plans is done through the *financial plan.* A financial plan includes a *profit-and-loss plan* (P&L) and a *balance sheet/cash-flow plan,* both of equal importance. Financial plans are most commonly prepared for a 12-month cycle, with revenues and costs allocated by month. Setting a monthly plan allows management to monitor the business operations in a timely fashion to address areas of concern before they become a crisis.

The financial plan should be prepared with input from various sources and management levels within the firm. Both a *top-down* and *bottom-up* approach should be used in the actual preparation of the financial plan. The top-down approach should be communicated from executive level management. The top-down plan should highlight the key items identified in the business and marketing plans and provide projections on the anticipated growth projections for the firm. The bottom-up approach takes the plan a step further and requires a detailed analysis of the various components of the firm's operations.

In preparing the bottom-up financial plan, five items must be evaluated to accurately determine the projected financial picture of the firm:

1. Business and marketing plans, to accurately determine the costs of implementing these strategies.
2. Current clients and the marketing pipeline, to accurately forecast the revenue stream and associated costs such as direct labor, subcontractors, consultants, and other direct costs (to calculate gross

margin). Analysis of the gross margin should be grouped into six categories:

a. Backlog (balance of work on existing contracts)

b. Add-ons (anticipated change orders or additional work a current client is expected to need without going out for competitive bid)

c. Selections (work for which the firm has been selected but contract has not yet been negotiated)

d. Proposals (work proposed on with a get or win percent of at least 50 percent)

e. Leads (potential work that has been identified but not yet proposed)

f. Unknown (typical value of work received "over the transom").

These categories will help define the risk associated with the plan. Typically, a design firm will generate 60 to 70 percent of its revenues from backlog and add-ons. **Tables 5–2** and **5–3** provide sample worksheets for gross margin analysis.

3. Employee labor hours, to categorize the amount of time each employee will be working on marketing efforts (selling and proposal preparation), administrative functions, training and professional education, and—a key factor—direct contract labor. Identifying the direct contract labor, marketing, and administrative time spent by staff will assist in evaluating the additional resources required to support the growth projections. This process needs to be an iterative one, where the direct labor identified through review of the marketing pipeline and the firm's existing contract backlog (gross margin analysis) must be tied to the direct labor resulting from existing employee evaluations and the new staffing plan. **Table 5–4** provides an example of a schedule for preparing a labor analysis breakdown. After the hours and category are identified, the hourly rates are applied to calculate the dollars. The direct labor dollars calculated total $338,128, which is $78,372 short of the amount ($416,500) required to complete the projects identified in the gross margin analysis (**Table 5–2**). Therefore, less time must be spent on indirect functions or additional staff will be required to meet the projected needs. Consideration must be given to the level and years of experience and the timing of the new hire. In **Table 5–5**, new hires have been added to meet the projected workload.[2]

4. Current selling, general, and administrative items, to assess the baseline requirements for typical overhead costs required to operate a business, such as rent, telephone, supplies, and equipment. A tool

---

[2] R. Stross, Recovering Indirect Costs (1988).

Table 5–2

Gross Margin Analysis Sample Worksheet
Jan. 1, 1991–Dec. 31, 1991

DESCRIPTION	START DATE	END DATE	NEW ORDERS	REVENUES	SUBCONTRACTORS	DIRECT PROJECT EXPENSES	NET REVENUES	DIRECT LABOR	GROSS MARGIN	MULTIPLIER
BACKLOG										
CONTRACT ABC		06/01/91	0	100,000	7,000	5,000	88,000	29,000	59,000	3.03
CONTRACT DEF		12/31/91	0	350,000	15,000	25,000	310,000	105,000	205,000	2.95
CONTRACT 123		05/01/91		100,000	10,000	15,000	75,000	25,000	50,000	3.00
TOTAL BACKLOG			0	550,000	32,000	45,000	473,000	159,000	314,000	2.97
ADD – ONS										
CONTRACT ABC	01/01/91	06/01/91	25,000	25,000	10,000	2,000	13,000	4,500	8,500	2.89
	05/01/91	12/31/91	300,000	300,000	40,000	10,000	250,000	79,000	171,000	3.16
TOTAL ADD–ONS			325,000	325,000	50,000	12,000	263,000	83,500	179,500	2.89
SELECTIONS										
CLIENT GHI	02/01/91	06/01/92	200,000	100,000	10,000	4,000	86,000	28,500	57,500	3.02
CLIENT JKL	04/01/91	08/01/92	550,000	50,000	5,000	2,000	43,000	14,000	29,000	3.07
CLIENT MNO	05/01/91	04/01/93	750,000	75,000	10,000	2,500	62,500	22,000	40,500	2.84
TOTAL SELECTIONS			1,500,000	225,000	25,000	8,500	191,500	64,500	127,000	2.97
PROPOSALS										
CLIENT PQR	02/01/91	08/01/91	125,000	75,000	15,000	2,000	58,000	19,000	39,000	3.05
CLIENT STU	03/01/91	10/01/91	50,000	50,000	10,000	4,000	36,000	12,000	24,000	3.00
TOTAL PROPOSALS			175,000	125,000	25,000	6,000	94,000	31,000	63,000	3.03
LEADS										
CLIENT VWX	06/01/91	03/01/92	125,000	95,000	5,000	2,000	88,000	29,000	59,000	3.03
CLIENT YZZ	08/01/91	02/01/92	100,000	75,000	5,000	5,000	65,000	21,500	43,500	3.02
TOTAL LEADS			225,000	170,000	10,000	7,000	153,000	50,500	102,500	3.03
UNKNOWNS	01/01/91	08/01/91	100,000	100,000	10,000	3,000	87,000	28,000	59,000	3.11
GRAND TOTAL			2,325,000	1,495,000	152,000	81,500	1,261,500	416,500	845,000	3.03

Table 5–3

Gross Margin Worksheet
Direct Labor Requirements

DECRIPTION	JAN	FEB	MAR	APR	MAY	JUN	JUL	AUG	SEPT	OCT	NOV	DEC	TOTAL
CONTRACT ABC	8,000	7,500	6,000	4,500	3,000								29,000
CONTRACT DEF	8,750	8,750	8,750	8,750	8,750	8,750	8,750	8,750	8,750	8,750	8,750	8,750	105,000
CONTRACT 123	10,000	8,000	4,000	3,000									25,000
BACKLOG	26,750	24,250	18,750	16,250	11,750	8,750	8,750	8,750	8,750	8,750	8,750	8,750	159,000
CONTRACT ABC	100	1,800	1,700	700	200								4,500
					7,500	7,500	8,500	10,000	12,000	12,000	15,000	6,500	79,000
ADD-ONS	100	1,800	1,700	700	7,700	7,500	8,500	10,000	12,000	12,000	15,000	6,500	83,500
CLIENT GHI		800	1,200	2,200	4,500	4,500	4,500	4,500	3,300	1,300	1,200	500	28,500
CLIENT JKL				500	800	1,600	1,600	1,900	2,000	1,800	1,800	2,000	14,000
CLIENT MNO					2,750	2,750	2,750	2,750	2,750	2,750	2,750	2,750	22,000
SELECTIONS	0	800	1,200	2,700	8,050	8,850	8,850	9,150	8,050	5,850	5,750	5,250	64,500
CLIENT PQR		1,200	1,200	1,200	1,800	1,800	2,200	2,300	2,500	1,800	1,500	1,500	19,000
CLIENT STU			1,200	1,200	1,200	1,200	1,200	1,200	1,200	1,200	1,200	1,200	12,000
PROPOSALS	0	1,200	2,400	2,400	3,000	3,000	3,400	3,500	3,700	3,000	2,700	2,700	31,000
CLIENT VWX						4,143	4,143	4,143	4,143	4,143	4,143	4,143	29,000
CLIENT YZZ								4,300	4,300	4,300	4,300	4,300	21,500
LEADS	0	0	0	0	0	4,143	4,143	8,443	8,443	8,443	8,443	8,443	50,500
UNKNOWNS	2,333	2,333	2,333	2,333	2,333	2,333	2,333	2,333	2,333	2,333	2,333	2,333	28,000
TOTAL LABOR	29,183	30,383	26,383	24,383	32,833	34,576	35,976	42,176	43,276	40,376	42,976	33,976	416,500

Direct labor spread based on estimated start/end dates of contracts and assumptions for estimated labor volumes.

often employed is that of *zero-based budgeting,* the concept that all costs are zero until identified and justified. Historical trend analysis is another method commonly used. **Table 5–6** provides a sample worksheet that identifies typical selling, general, and administrative items. Many of the items are generated from other schedules. The indirect labor and compensated benefits are from the labor analysis and the depreciation expense is from the capital worksheet discussed in **§ 5.13**.

5. Current facilities and equipment, to determine if they adequately support both the existing staff and any additional head-count that may be required. Facilities and equipment are significant investments and are fixed costs whether set by lease or through depreciation. Real estate market conditions and growth projections over several years should be considered before sizable investments are made.

§ 5.13 —Capital Expenditures Plan

In the normal course of operating a business, certain capital expenditures are incurred, whether in the form of a direct purchase or a long-term commitment of funds, such as leases. Typically, design firms have not been capital intensive. Their most expensive asset has been their employees. However, in today's computer-literate environment, a heavy investment in computer equipment is necessary. What was once done on the drafting table is now done on the computer-aided design and drafting (CADD) system; what was once done on 13-column accounting paper is now done on sophisticated software programs that require personal computers, minicomputers, or even mainframe systems.

Categories of assets typically found in a design firm include:

1. Leasehold improvements
2. Furniture and fixtures
3. Office equipment, telephone, fax machines, copiers
4. Computer equipment
5. Field equipment
6. Automobiles.

Capital expenditures usually carry a high dollar value and require a substantial cash layout. Policies and procedures should be in place to ensure that management approves all capital expenditures. **Table 5–7** provides an example of a capital expenditure worksheet. Step one is to analyze the current capital (fixed) assets to determine the depreciation expense associated with each item. Detailed records of the date and amount purchased should be kept in the accounting files. Each asset should be listed

Table 5–4

Current Employees Labor Analysis Sample Worksheet
Breakdown by Hours

					****** HOURS		******					* BREAKDOWN OF INDIRECT		HOURS *	
		ANNUAL	HOURLY	TOTAL	EST	EST	EST	VAILABL	EST	DIRECT	INDIRECT	GENERAL			TOTAL
NAME	TITLE	SALARY	RATE	RS YEA	SICK	HOLIDAY	ACATIO	HOURS	DIRECT %	LABOR HRS	HOURS	ADMIN	ROPOSAL	SELLING	INDIRECT
	PRESIDENT	135,000	64.90	2,080	16	80	120	1,864	55.0%	1,025	839	239	150	450	839
	VICE PRESIDENT	100,000	48.08	2,080	16	80	120	1,864	70.0%	1,305	559	129	151	280	559
	SR PROJECT MGR.	85,000	40.87	2,080	40	80	120	1,840	75.0%	1,380	460	100	262	98	460
	PROJECT MGR.	65,000	31.25	2,080	40	80	120	1,840	75.0%	1,380	460	100	262	98	460
	ENGINEER	48,000	23.08	2,080	40	80	120	1,840	80.0%	1,472	368	80	288	0	368
	ENGINEER	45,000	21.63	2,080	80	80	80	1,840	80.0%	1,472	368	80	288	0	368
	JR ENGINEER	38,000	18.27	2,080	80	80	80	1,840	90.0%	1,656	184	20	164	0	184
	SECRETARY	30,000	14.42	2,080	80	80	80	1,840	50.0%	920	920	520	400	0	920
	TOTAL	546,000	13.13	16,640	392	640	840	14,768	71.8%	10,610	4,158	1,268	1,965	926	4,158

Breakdown by Dollars

NAME	TITLE	ANNUAL SALARY	HOURLY RATE	TOTAL RS YEA	······DOLLARS* EST SICK	EST HOLIDAY	EST ACATIO	*······ VAILABL DOLLARS	EST DIRECT %	DIRECT LABOR $'S	INDIRECT DOLLARS	* BREAKDOWN OF INDIRECT DOLLARS GENERAL ADMIN	ROPOSAL	SELLING	TOTAL INDIRECT
	PRESIDENT	135,000	64.90	2,080	1,038	5,192	7,788	120,961	55.00%	66,539	54,441	15,499	9,736	29,207	54,441
	VICE PRESIDENT	100,000	48.08	2,080	769	3,846	5,769	89,615	70.00%	62,731	26,885	6,183	7,259	13,442	26,885
	SR PROJECT MGR.	85,000	40.87	2,080	1,635	3,269	4,904	75,192	75.00%	56,394	18,798	4,087	10,707	4,005	18,798
	SR PROJECT MGR.	65,000	31.25	2,080	1,250	2,500	3,750	57,500	75.00%	43,125	14,375	3,125	8,188	3,063	14,375
	ENGINEER	48,000	23.08	2,080	923	1,846	2,769	42,462	80.00%	33,969	8,492	1,846	6,646	0	8,492
	ENGINEER	45,000	21.63	2,080	1,731	1,731	1,731	39,808	80.00%	31,846	7,962	1,731	6,231	0	7,962
	JR ENGINEER	38,000	18.27	2,080	1,462	1,462	1,462	33,615	90.00%	30,254	3,362	365	2,996	0	3,362
	SECRETARY	30,000	14.42	2,080	1,154	1,154	1,154	26,538	50.00%	13,269	13,269	7,500	5,769	0	13,269
	TOTAL	546,000	13.13	16,640	9,962	21,000	29,327	485,712	69.61%	338,128	147,584	40,336	57,531	49,716	147,584

DIRECT LABOR REQUIRED FROM GROSS MARGIN WORKSHEET 416,500

SHORTFALL (78,372)

Table 5–5

New Hire Labor Analysis Sample Worksheet
Breakdown by Hours

					••••••	HOURS	••••••					• BREAKDOWN OF INDIRECT	HOURS •		
DATE OF HIRE	TITLE	ANNUAL SALARY	HOURLY RATE	TOTAL RS YEA	EST SICK	EST HOLIDAY	EST ACATIO	VAILABL HOURS	EST DIRECT %	DIRECT LABOR HRS	INDIRECT HOURS	GENERAL ADMIN	ROPOSAL	SELLING	TOTAL INDIRECT
2/91	PROJECT MGR.	60,000	28.85	1,907	40	72	80	1,715	75.00%	1,286	429	150	199	80	429
5/91	ENGINEER	45,000	21.63	1,387	24	64	40	1,259	82.00%	1,032	227	60	167	0	227
7/91	ENGINEER	45,000	21.63	1,040	16	48	20	956	85.00%	813	143	40	103	0	143
2/91	P/TIME BOOKKEEPER	15,000	14.42	953	40	72	40	801	11.82%	95	707	706	0	0	706
	TOTAL	165,000	86.54	5,287	120	256	180	4,731		3,225	1,505	956	469	80	1,505

Current Employees Labor Analysis Sample Worksheet
Breakdown by Dollars

					****** DOLLARS *			******				* BREAKDOWN OF INDIRECT DOLLARS			
NAME	TITLE	ANNUAL SALARY	HOURLY RATE	TOTAL RS YEA	EST SICK	EST HOLIDAY	EST ACATIO	VAILABL DOLLARS	EST DIRECT %	DIRECT LABOR $'S	INDIRECT DOLLARS	GENERAL ADMIN	ROPOSAL	SELLING	TOTAL INDIRECT
2/91	PROJECT MGR.	60,000	28.85	1,907	1,154	2,077	2,308	49,462	75.00%	37,096	12,365	4,317	5,740	2,308	12,365
5/91	ENGINEER	45,000	21.63	1,387	519	1,385	865	27,231	82.00%	22,329	4,902	1,297	3,605	0	4,902
7/91	ENGINEER	45,000	21.63	1,040	346	1,038	433	20,683	85.00%	17,580	3,102	865	2,236	0	3,102
2/91	P/TIME BOOKKEEPER	15,000	14.42	953	577	1,038	577	11,558	11.82%	1,366	10,192	10,192	0	0	10,192
	TOTAL	165,000		5,287	2,596	5,538	4,183	108,933	71.95%	78,372	30,561	16,671	11,582	2,308	30,561
ADD: Bal from current employees		546,000		16,640	9,962	21,000	29,327	485,712	69.61%	338,128	147,584	40,336	57,531	49,716	147,584
GRAND TOTAL		711,000		21,927	12,558	26,538	33,510	594,644	70.04%	416,500	178,145	57,007	69,113	52,024	178,145

Table 5–6

Selling, General, and Administrative Analysis
Sample Worksheet

Category	Plan
Indirect Labor	
Admin Labor	57,007
Bus. Dev. Labor	69,113
Down Time	52,025
Total Indirect Labor	178,145
Compensated Absences	
Vacation	33,510
Holiday	26,538
Sick	12,558
Tot Comp Absences	72,606
Employee Benefits	
FICA	30,000
FUTA	3,000
SUTA	5,500
Health Insurance	20,000
Profit Sharing	10,000
Bonus	50,000
Tot Employee Benefits	118,500
Travel & Entertainment	
Travel	18,000
Meals	3,000
Meetings	2,500
Entertainment	5,000
Tot T & E	28,500

Table 5–7

Capital Expenditures Analysis Sample Worksheet

	CURRENT CAPITAL ITEMS			ADDITIONS TO CAPITAL ITEMS					GRAND TOTAL FY 91	
	CAPITAL AMOUNT	ESTIMATED USEFUL LIFE	DEPRECIATION EXPENSE		DATE OF PURCHASE	CAPITAL AMOUNT	ESTIMATED USEFUL LIFE	DEPRECIATION EXPENSE	CAPITAL AMOUNT	DEPRECIATION EXPENSE
LEASEHOLD IMPROVEMENTS										
INCURRED 1/89	200,000	20	10,000	NONE		0	0	0	200,000	10000
FURNITURE & FIXTURES										
PURCHASED 1/89	10,000	8	1,250	FOR NEW HIRES	2/91	4,000	8	500	14,000	1750
PURCHASED 1/90	7,000	8	875		5/91	2,000	8	250	9,000	1125
					7/91	2,000	8	250	2,000	250
FIELD EQUIPMENT				OVA EQUIPMENT	2/91	3,000	5	600	3,000	600
PURCHASES 4/90	4,300	5	860						4,300	860
COMPUTER EQUIPMENT				PC FOR BOOKKEEPER	2/91	5,000	5	1,000	5,000	1000
PURCHASES 5/89	6,800	5	1,360	CADD SYSTEM	3/91	45,000	5	9,000	51,800	10360
AUTOMOBILES				NONE		0	3	0	0	0
PURCHASED 1/89	34,965	3	11,655						34,965	11,655
OFFICE EQUIPMENT				FAX MACHINE	2/91	1000	5	200	1,000	200
PURCHASED 1/89	45,000	5	9,000						45,000	9,000
GRAND TOTAL	308,065		35,000	GRAND TOTAL		62,000		11,800	370,065	46,800

with the appropriate useful life assigned. For purposes of illustration, typical lives have been identified and the straight-line method for depreciation has been chosen. Depreciation expense represents a full year in the year of purchase, regardless of the date of purchase. These assumptions are used for financial reporting purposes only. There are specific IRS tax regulations regarding depreciation. These issues should be discussed with an accountant. Step two is to list all new items anticipated to be purchased in the upcoming year and to calculate the associated depreciation expense. Adding together the depreciation from the prior year's assets and the projected purchases will provide the basis for the depreciation expense on the profit-and-loss (P&L) plan as well as the additions to capital assets on the balance sheet.

The *capital expenditures plan* must be prepared in conjunction with the financial plan because each depends upon the other. Capital expenditures impact both the P&L and the balance sheet. Additional depreciation expenses must be reflected in the P&L, and the recognition of the capital asset must be reflected on the balance sheet.

With the accumulation of the data from the previous worksheets, the P&L plan can be completed. **Table 5–8** provides an example of a typical P&L for a design firm. **Table 5–8** reflects a full-year plan. However, in most instances it is advisable to break down the plan into smaller time frames, such as monthly or quarterly.

Once the P&L plan has been completed, the balance sheet and cash-flow plans can be prepared. The *balance sheet* is the measure of the financial condition of the firm at a given point in time. A *cash-flow statement* takes the accrual-based statements and reports the increase or decrease in the cash position of the firm. It identifies the sources from which the cash was received and the uses for which it was spent.

Although the P&L statement is typically considered the most important financial statement for a business, the balance sheet offers management a tool for assessing the composition of its assets, liabilities, and net worth. The objectives of the firm must be evaluated again when preparing a *balance sheet plan.* If growth will require additional capital, then sources must be considered. Should the capital come from internal resources through aggressive asset management (that is, faster billing and shorter collection time), or should it come from external sources, such as a public offering or a loan or credit linc from a bank? The balance sheet plan is generated from the current year ending balance sheet and adding in the impact of the other plans. **Table 5–9** identifies a typical balance sheet for the design professional.

Cash is important to all businesses. Preparing a cash budget is necessary to determine the resources available to meet the current obligations of the firm. On an ongoing basis, firms typically prepare some form of a cash budget, usually monthly and often weekly. During the planning process, it is important to review the cash budget to determine the requirement for additional financing. The cash budget is commonly referred to as the *statement*

Table 5–8

Design Firm Sample Profit-and-Loss Statement

Actual FY 90	Category	Plan FY 91
200,000	New Orders	2,325,000
550,000	Backlog	1,380,000
800,000	Revenues	1,495,000
90,000	Subcontractor Costs	152,000
40,000	Direct Project Expenses	81,500
10,000	Contract Reserves	0
660,000	Net Revenues	1,261,500
215,000	Direct Labor	416,500
445,000	Gross Margin	845,000
	S,G & A Expenses:	
90,000	Indirect Labor	178,145
40,000	Compensated Absences	72,606
60,000	Employee Benefits	118,500
15,000	Travel & Entertainment	27,500
13,000	Supplies & Postage	21,000
8,000	Telephone Expenses	13,500
5,000	Recruitment & Relocation	15,000
5,000	Publ, Memb, & Training	9,000
10,000	Promotional	35,000
8,000	Outside Consultants	16,000
6,000	Bad Debt Expense	0
15,000	Computer Expenses	19,000
10,000	Equipment Rental & Maint	13,000
25,000	Insurance Expense	47,000
30,000	Building Rent, Util & Maint	35,000
35,000	Depreciation	46,800
4,000	Other	7,000
379,000	Total S, G & A	674,051
(12,000)	Interest Income/(Expense)	(15,000)
8,000	Other Income	2,000
6,000	Other Expense	7,000
56,000	Income Before Taxes	150,949
2,800	State Taxes	7,547
18,620	Federal Taxes	50,191
34,580	Net Income	93,211
	Ratios	
3.07	Multiplier	3.03
70.5%	Utilization	70.0%
176.3%	Indirect Cost Rate	161.8%
4.3%	Return On Sales	6.2%

Table 5–9

Design Firm Balance Sheet Worksheet
December 31, 19XX

ASSETS

Current Assets	
Cash	72,749
Accounts Receivable	295,000
Unbilled Sales	200,000
Prepaid Expenses	10,251
Total Current Assets	578,000
Property, Plant and Equipment	370,065
Less: Accumulated Depreciation	(115,065)
Net Property, Plant & Equipment	255,000
Total Assets	833,000

LIABILITIES AND OWNERS EQUITY

Current Liabilities	
Accounts Payable	50,000
Wages Payable	0
Fees Billed Not Earned	100,000
Short term portion of long term Loan	50,000
Interest Payable	40,000
Total Current Liabilities	240,000
Loans Payable	375,000
Total liabilities	615,000
Owners Equity	218,000
Total Liabilities and Equity	833,000

of cash flow. In November of 1987, the Financial Accounting Standards Board (FASB) issued FASB No. 95, addressing the required format for producing a statement of cash flow. The FASB allows for two methods of presentation, the indirect and direct method, but recommends the direct method. **Table 5–10** is an illustration of the direct method.

Review and analysis of the data are critical. The planning process provides management a tool not only for assigning a dollar value to future earnings, but also for establishing the required contract pricing guidelines. The financial plan sets the basis for calculating the company's overhead rate(s) and also serves as an opportunity for tax planning. In most cases, a plan is a requirement when seeking financial assistance from outside resources.

Table 5–10

Sample Worksheet
Statement of Cash Flow
(000's)

Cash flow from Operating Activities	
Beginning Cash Balance	50,000
Add:	
Collections from customers (Est)	1,000,000
Other Income	2,000
Net cash available	1,050,000
Less Cash Disbursements	
Subcontractors	125,000
Direct Project Expenses	75,000
Direct Labor	416,500
Total S,G&A (less non-cash items)	627,251
Other Expenses	7,000
Interest Expense	15,000
State Tax	3,500
Federal Tax	21,000
Total Disbursements	1,290,251
Total Cash available from Operating Activities	(240,251)
Cash Flow from Investing Activities	
(Purchase)/Sale of Investments	0
(Purchase)/Sale of Capital Assets	(62,000)
Net Cash used in Investing Activities	(62,000)
Cash Flow from Financing Activities	
Proceeds from issuance of Long-Term Debt	375,000
Payment of Short term note	(100,000)
Net Cash provided from Financing Activities	275,000
Net Increase/(Decrease) in Cash	(27,251)
Cash at Beginning of Year	100,000
Cash at End of Year	72,749

§ 5.14 Ratios

There are several financial ratios that are specific to the design industry. The ratios aid in determining the validity of the planning process and assess the comparative strength of the firm.

A comparative implies that there are standards against which design firms can be measured. Practice Management Associates, Ltd., publishes the *Professional Services Management Journal Financial Statistics Survey.* It is exclusively for design firms and provides results of statistical surveys of the financial conditions of hundreds of design firms. The survey is also organized so that comparisons can be made against firms of a similar size, discipline, and geographic area.

Ratio	Common Definition
Multiplier	The multiplier is the net reserves divided by direct contract labor. It is the effective rate at which the firm's labor dollars are covered with overhead and profit. A design firm with an overhead rate of 150 percent wishing to achieve 10 percent profit on labor and overhead would want to maintain a 2.75 effective multiplier.
Overhead Rate	Also referred to as an indirect cost rate, overhead rate is the firm's total indirect costs divided by direct contract labor. It is the rate at which labor must be increased to break even. A firm with an overhead rate of 150 percent must sell at 250 percent (2.50 multiplier) to break even.
Labor Utilization	Labor utilization is the percent of either total salaries or available salaries that are directly chargeable to a client contract. On an individual employee basis, it is often termed *billability.* Many firms use total salaries as the demoninator. Total salaries include direct contract labor, indirect labor, sick time, and holiday or vacation time. Available labor excludes all time associated with absences from work.
Return on Sales (ROS)	ROS is commony the firm's net income after taxes divided by revenues. It is often calculated using pretax income or net revenues.
Return on Assets (ROA)	ROA is the firm's after-tax income divided by total assets. It is not very common to the design industry, as design firms generally do not use assets to generate revenue. Design firms do, however, generate revenues from their employees, as employees are the real assets of a design firm. Net revenues to

Ratio	Common Definition
	total staff is a more commonly used indicator, replacing ROA.
Net Revenues to Total Staff	Calculated by dividing net revenues by total staff. Variations on this are net revenues to technical staff or project managers.
Direct Labor Per Day	Direct labor per day is calculated by dividing direct contract labor by the number of work days in the period being analyzed. This ratio is helpful in comparing results for differing periods, most often not of the same duration.
Quick Ratio or Current Ratio	This ratio measures the financial strength of a firm over the short term as current assets (those assets that will turn over within a year) divided by current liabilities (obligations due within a year). The results of the calculation provide a quick analysis of the firm's ability to meet short-term obligations or incur losses.
Debt-to-Equity Ratio	Calculated by dividing the firm's debt by its total equity (capital plus retained earnings). Banks will require certain ratios to be maintained when borrowing. Little or no equity implies to the bank that one of two things have occurred: 1. Profits have been channeled away from the firm rather than being made available for reinvestment. 2. The firm is not profitable and will have difficulty meeting its obligations.
Total Collection Time	Total collection time is the time it takes to invoice costs to clients and collect what was invoived. Total collection time is commonly measured by analyzing the last three months' reserves and dividing the analyzed amount by 360 days. The resultant one-day sales are then divided into total unbilled sales plus total accounts receivable.

§ 5.15 Pricing

The standards for pricing in design firms come in various forms and depend upon the market, the client, and type of contract. Pricing policies are commonly determined by management and are variable in nature. Many factors influence contract pricing: market conditions, client restrictions, federal government regulations, and the firm's own requirements for profitability. These profitability requirements were defined during the planning process. Return-on-sales expectations developed in the planning process must be validated against the market's willingness to pay the prices that grant those expectations. If a firm does a significant amount of cost-plus fixed fee work for federal or public clients, profit expectations must be reduced as risk is reduced. Niche players, risk takers, and firms doing fixed-price work are rewarded with greater as-sold profit margins.

The finance organization is responsible for the control, analysis, interpretation, and reporting of costs. The finance organization should have the responsibility for reporting to management key pricing information so management can make an informed decision on price. Typical types of data include:

1. Annual and interim overhead rate calculations (break-even point)
2. Average salaries per discipline or grade
3. Profitability by client type
4. Profitability by market segment.

In design firms, a common basis for costing requires the development of an *overhead rate.* The overhead rate is a percentage calculation based on total overhead costs divided by a most common factor for all contracts: total costs or total direct labor. In design firms, the typical calculation would be total overhead costs divided by total direct labor costs. The overhead rate represents the break-even point for the company, so that for every dollar of direct labor sold, one must charge an additional percentage (the overhead rate) to recover costs.

The overhead rate includes all costs that are not charged directly to contracts and cannot be specifically identified to a direct final cost objective. Some clients will not allow specific components of indirect costs to be included in an indirect cost rate. The federal government, for example, will not allow interest, bad debt, promotional, or entertainment type costs,[3] to name a few. It is important to remember that nonfederal clients may pay for these costs, and if market rates are favorable, all components of the firm's costs should be included in pricing.

In developing a pricing strategy, it is also important to consider the cost of support functions. For example, should the cost of personal computers, reproduction, word processing, or field equipment be charged to the client or be included in overhead and charged as part of the indirect cost rate(s)?

If support costs are to be charged to clients as direct costs, specific accounting treatment must be adopted. *Service centers* is the term used most

---

[3] 48 C.F.R. § 31.2 (1990).

frequently in the industry to describe the various pools of costs associated with each support function.

All costs applicable to a service center must be easily segregated from other costs. A method that most equitably allocates the cost from the service center to a specific client contract must be chosen. Personal computer usage is generally acceptable to clients when charged on a per-hour basis, while copy costs are acceptable on a per-copy basis.

It is important to apply the chosen methods consistently and to all pieces of equipment. It would be incorrect to charge copy costs to one project and not another. It also would be incorrect to charge usage of one copy machine and not the other if the cost of all machines was used as the cost basis for the allocation.

It is important to include only allowable costs in the cost pools. For example, interest costs associated with the purchase of a copy machine on credit is an unallowable cost when doing business with the federal government or when the contract references the Federal Acquisition Regulations (FAR). All allowable costs should be considered for each service center, but practicality and price also should be considered. Costs most often used are depreciation, maintenance, supplies, training, occupation/space costs, and software.

The total annual costs of the service center divided by the total expected annual usage provides the rate to charge the final cost objective (that is, direct client contract or overhead function). These rates should be reviewed annually, at a minimum, for large fluctuations in anticipated costs and/or usage. The variances, frequently referred to as *over* or *under absorptions* created by the allocations methodology, can either be credited or charged back to the final cost objectives or left in the overhead pool where all clients will absorb the benefit or extra charge. Large variances of 25 percent or more should not be left in the overhead pool.

Competitive pricing issues and the clientele with which the firm does business will most likely dictate the use of service centers. Finance should be responsible for ensuring that there are written policies and procedures for pricing contracts and that these policies are updated regularly and enforced.

§ 5.16 Cost Control and Disbursements

Traditionally, the finance function addresses issues of cost control more often than issues of revenue control. The three major components of a design firm's costs are labor, suppliers, including subcontractors and consultants, and taxes. Disbursements for labor costs are normally a payroll function and disbursements for suppliers and taxes are an accounts payable function.

§ 5.17 —Payroll

Payroll often represents the largest cost component. Although it may appear that this is a relatively easy area to control, there are a number of factors that add considerable risks if the payroll function is not properly managed. These factors include compliance with:

1. Local, state, and federal wage laws that determine when, where, and how employees must be paid
2. Internal Revenue Service (IRS) and other taxing authorities' definitions of employees and independent contractors
3. IRS and other taxing authorities' definitions of taxable compensation, including such items as company cars, subsistence, tuition, relocation, and life insurance
4. IRS and other tax filing requirements
5. Workers' compensation insurance classifications
6. Client billing requirements
7. Governmental record-keeping requirements.

Good payroll accounting begins with proper records with earnings and deduction information for each employee. These employee files also should include data for labor classification, pay grade, workers' compensation classification, equal employment opportunity (EEO) status, birth, hire, and review dates, and other personnel requirements, unless separate personnel files are maintained.

Time worked by all employees should be recorded on time sheet forms signed by the employees and their supervisors. Time sheets should be filled out daily, specifying hours worked on each project, both regular time and overtime. For several important reasons, time sheet requirements should be mandatory:

The time sheet is a legal contract between the employee and the firm.

The time sheet is the basis for both determining the employee's pay and charging labor costs to specific projects.

Proper documentation is required for both internal (management) and external (clients, IRS, auditors) review.

Controls for labor costs should include formal policies on compensation and overtime and criteria for merit raises, fringe benefits, and standard labor classifications so that employees can be treated fairly and consistently within the firm and measured against the competitive market. Other controls should be instituted that ensure the confidentiality of payroll information and provide that all statutory record-keeping and retention requirements are met.

§ 5.18 —Accounts Payable

Cash disbursements are the tail end of a process that involves many people in the firm, both inside and outside the finance function. The firm should have written policies and procedures identifying:

1. Which persons/positions have authority to commit company funds and what are their dollar limits
2. Appropriation request forms and procedures for capital expenditures and major expenses, as well as purchase requisition forms and procedures for other procurements
3. Criteria for vendor qualification and selection
4. Purchase order forms and procedures
5. Receiving report forms and procedures
6. Procedures for matching purchase orders, receiving reports, and vendor invoices
7. Payment procedures ensuring that the firm's (not necessarily the vendor's) payment terms are met.

Accounts payable is an area in which the firm has control over the timing of its cash disbursements. For large subcontractors and consultants, contractual agreements should specify that the sub/consultant gets paid for its work only after the firm gets paid by the client for such work, if this is legally valid in the jurisdiction in which the contract is to be enforced. In addition, agreements should specify a retention holdback of 10 percent (or more or less) from each sub/consultant's invoice until the project has been completed and the client has approved all work. Generally, payment terms on other vendors should be extended so that they receive payment just before 60 days from their invoice date. This will keep the firm off the vendor's over-60-day accounts receivable agings, which could be important for good credit references. Therefore, procedures to improve cash management must be balanced with maintaining good vendor relationships.

Control procedures should be instituted to provide proper segregation of duties in cash disbursements. Ideally, separate individuals should perform each of the following duties: approve payments, process payments, maintain unsigned checks, sign checks, and reconcile checks. If limited resources require some combination(s) of functions, firms should, at a minimum, segregate approval/check signing from processing/maintaining checks and from reconciling checks.

Records must be maintained to comply with regulatory requirements, such as reporting to the IRS all payments in excess of $600 per calendar year to nonemployee individuals, and reporting, on some governmental contracts, procurements from minority-owned business enterprises (MBE), women-owned business enterprises (WBE), or small business enterprises (SBE).

§ 5.19 —Tax Disbursements

One of the more exacting financial functions is taxes. In many firms, payroll-related taxes are managed by the payroll function and income-related taxes are managed either separately or by the general accounting function.

At one time, payroll taxes involved applying the proper tax rate tables and paying and filing on time. In theory this is still true, but changes in tax laws have added new complexity to determining taxable compensation and applicable withholding requirements. Disbursement schedules for payroll taxes depend on the size of the firm's payroll tax liability.

Income taxes also have increased in complexity over the years. The person(s) responsible for taxes should prepare a tax calendar for a full year, specifying the due dates of all applicable tax payments. This function has responsibility for tax payments, tax planning and strategies, review of proposals to clients for tax issues, estimated tax payments, tax accruals, tax return filings, and tax examinations. Written policies and procedures regarding tax compliance are an important control requirement.

The penalties associated with late filing, failure to file, or incorrect tax payments are significant. Interest at the maximum rates allowed by law is also assessed. It is important to either have a tax professional in-house or use a knowledgeable, reputable, outside consultant.

§ 5.20 Invoicing and Collection

The profitability of a company is measured by the amount of net income shown on its profit-and-loss statement. The true financial condition of a company is measured by the health of its balance sheet. To maintain a healthy balance sheet, the company must turn profits into cash. That means controlling disbursements, billing clients, and collecting those bills in a timely fashion.

The invoicing and collection functions begin before the contract is signed, continue with the management of the contract, and are reinforced every time the design professional communicates with the client.

Clients must be assessed for risk. Statistics should be maintained on the payment performance of existing clients to help negotiate the terms on the next change order or contract with that client. New clients should be assessed for credit risk before responding to a request for proposal (REP). There are several sources available, with Dun & Bradstreet a popular choice. A banker is the most cost-effective credit source.

The terms of invoicing and payment should be clearly defined in the contract. Invoicing should be at least monthly, and a prepayment should be required whenever credit risk is too great. A copy of the firm's standard invoice should be attached to the proposed contract. Whenever possible, try to avoid creative invoice formats for clients. The invoicing process should be kept as simple and as standard as possible. Try to avoid situations in which the client wants status reports or manpower forecasts included with each invoice as a prerequisite for payment. The combination of the two can put an added burden on the project manager and biller, and invoices may be unnecessarily delayed. It should be agreed during negotiations that discrepancies or errors in the invoice should be deducted by the client and not delay payment of the portion of the invoice that is correct.

If the firm has the ability to issue letters of credit (LOC), be sure to negotiate them in lieu of retention whenever possible. The rates on an LOC are far lower than the cost of capital and are only costly when drawn by the client, usually for performance issues.

Invoicing should be consistent, timely, and accurate. Cumulative and current period information should be included on the invoice. This will help the client assess the total amount invoiced to date against the contract. Unpaid balances should be shown on the invoice as well. This will act as a monthly statement to remind the client of its unpaid obligation.

Never wait to send a first invoice because the dollars expended for a billing period were small. Early invoices of small dollar values can indicate the client's normal payment practices.

Accuracy in invoicing can and should be achieved before invoice preparation. Reports of costs incurred on all projects should be made available weekly. Project managers should review the charges for appropriateness at that time and not at billing time.

Project numbers should not be made available except to project managers and then only for their own projects. When project managers assign work they should provide the appropriate project numbers to charge along with a budget, so that the employees performing the work know their scope and how many hours they have to do the job. A listing of project numbers provided to all employees will cause unnecessary cost corrections and ultimately delays in invoicing.

Rotational billing should be employed when billing volume reaches a level at which the biller needs a full month to invoice all of the clients. Rotational billing is a concept whereby 25 percent of clients are billed in week one of the following month for costs incurred through the end of the preceding month, 25 percent are billed the second week for costs through the first week of the current month, and so forth. See **Table 5–11**. The

Table 5–11

Rotational Billing

	January				February				
	Wk1	Wk2	Wk3	Wk4	Wk1	Wk2	Wk3	Wk4	Total
Clients 1–25									
Costs	25	25	25	25	25	25	25	25	200
Invoice		25				100			125
Unbilled	25	25	50	75	100	25	50	75	75
Clients 26–50									
Costs	50	50	50	50	50	50	50	50	400
Invoice			100				200		300
Unbilled	50	100	50	100	150	200	50	100	100
Clients 51–75									
Costs	100	100	100	100	100	100	100	100	800
Invoice				300				400	700
Unbilled	100	200	300	100	200	300	400	100	100
Total									
Costs	175	175	175	175	175	175	175	175	1,400
Invoice		25	100	300		100	200	400	1,125
Unbilled	175	325	175	350	425	400	175	275	275

benefit of this system is in minimizing the amount of unbilled sales at the end of each month while employing the same level of billing staff.

After the invoice is sent, it is important to track its progress. Weekly accounts receivable aging reports should be provided to the project managers. Quality work and good client communications are the best ingredients for timely collection of invoices. There will, however, be times when payment is not so timely, and it is important to designate collection responsibility. Collection responsibility should be made clear in a written company policy. Making it part of the firm's compensation strategy is an effective policy reinforcement tool. Beginning with contract negotiations and continuing with each client communication, the client should know that payment is expected according to the terms of the contract.

Know the client's organization. Find out who receives and approves the invoice, who cuts the check, and at what stage each activity occurs. Project managers, or the designated collection person, should call the client weekly after an invoice ages 45 days. The following additional steps are recommended depending on the age of the invoice:

45–60 days	phone calls/visits
60 days	letter stating intentions if not paid
75 days	stop work/charge interest

To many design professionals (nonowners), invoicing and collection is a demeaning function not in line with their technical professional interests. To the design professional's clients, however, inconsistent, untimely, and inaccurate invoicing and lack of collection interest suggest that the firm is disorganized and unprofessional. It can only lead the client to wonder if the same lack of attention is paid to the design work in the contract.

§ 5.21 Reporting

Financial information provides business control. Most, if not all, issues that face a firm's management can be quantified and reported in financial terms. It is the financial manager's responsibility to determine management's information requirements to prevent events that could adversely impact the organization's fiscal health.

Management refers not only to the owners or principals of the firm, but also to each manager at every level of the organization. Each of these managers should receive financial information that quantifies their responsibilities through policies and procedures and targets or budgets. Placing controls at each level of the organization will, if properly managed, generate the desired fiscal results.

Beginning at the firm's lower level, the project manager charged with delivery of a contract must control project costs against the "as-sold" project budget. The project manager, or its designee(s) on large projects, should receive weekly reports that reflect all the costs charged against the project. See **Table 5–12**. This report allows the project manager to be sure that only costs attributable to that project were charged to it. The report also should provide the project manager with a comparison to the budget established for the project. If the contract is separated into multiple tasks, each task should be budgeted and a separate report produced. A weekly detail report also will give the project manager an opportunity to initiate timely cost corrections, a benefit to timely and accurate invoicing. This type of detail report also will satisfy the question always asked by external audit agencies: "How do you know the cost was charged to the correct contract?"

The project manager also should receive weekly summary reports that show how costs have accumulated for each task within the contract. See **Table 5–13**. This report helps the project manager assess the levels of costs expended against the estimated level of completion.

Proper management of invoicing is a necessary control. Clients want to have a single point of contact for all aspects of the project, including financial issues. In many organizations the project manager is the person responsible for reviewing invoices, making sure they are sent out on time, and making sure the client pays on time. To do this, the project manager must be aware of the amount of costs currently unbilled and the age of any unpaid invoices. It is recommended that the status of unbilled costs and

Table 5–12

Design Firm Sample Weekly Project Cost Report

Report For Period 01/01/91 To 01/07/91

Job Number
001234–001
Smithtown Town Hall

Job Manager Smith, John

Summary Status

	Current Budget	Expended This Period	Expended To Date	Remaining Budget
Labor Hours	12,616.0	96.5	8,617.0	3,999.0
Labor Dollars	372,264.00	2,774.86	185,562.30	186,701.70
Applied Overhead	632,848.80	4,717.26	315,455.91	317,392.89
Material Costs	65,150.00	1,154.17	43,126.52	22,023.48
Subcontract Costs	600,000.00	45,000.00	500,000.00	100,000.00
Consultant Costs	52,482.00	15,345.58	33,679.22	18,802.78
Total Cost	1,722,744.80	68,991.87	1,077,823.95	644,920.85

Labor Details This Period

Employee Number	Name	Hours	Dollars	Applied Overhead
1234	Apple, Tom	35.0		
4567	Brown, David	21.5		
8901	Smith, John	40.0		
Labor Total		96.5	2,774.86	4,717.26

Other Direct Cost Detail This Period

Cost Element	Reference Vendor #/Voucher	Cost Date	Description Invoice #/Vendor	Amount
2100	006543/000365	01/05/91	0134/Jones Supplies	249.52
2200	005365/000385	01/02/91	153675/Federal Express	9.50
2700	E0543	01/02/91	Smith, J Travel	895.15
	Subtotal Material Costs			1154.17
3200	000135/000426	01/06/91	0100/Acme Construction	45,000.00
	Subtotal Subcontract Costs			45,000.00
4165	095432/000565	01/04/91	645/Z-Labs	15,345.58
	Subtotal Consultant Costs			15,345.58
Total Other Direct Costs				107,653.92

Table 5–13

Design Firm Sample Weekly Contract Management Review

Week 01/01/91 - 01/07/91 Cum-to-Date Earliest - 01/07/91

Job # / Job Name / Job Manager	Period	Hours	Labor	Hrly Rate	Materials	Subs & Consult	Overhead	Total Cost	Revenue/ Funding	Last Inv Date/ A/R Unbill Sls
001234-001	Week	96.5	2,775	28.76	1,154	60,346	4,717	68,992		
Smithtown Town Hall	CTD	8,617.0	185,562	21.53	43,127	533,679	315,456	1,077,824		
Smith, John	Curr Est	12,616.0	372,264	29.51	65,150	652,482	632,849	1,722,745		
	% Comp	68.3%	49.8%	73.0%	66.2%	81.8%	49.8%	62.6%		
001234-002	Week	2,525.5	39,145	15.50	4,356	41,258	66,547	151,306		
Smithtown Library	CTD	4,512.0	75,576	16.75	10,652	153,263	128,479	367,970		
Johnson, Tom	Curr Est	10,350.5	170,783	16.50	35,252	359,699	290,332	856,066		
	% Comp	43.6%	44.3%	101.5%	30.2%	42.6%	44.3%	43.0%		
001234-003	Week	35.0	648	18.50	853	5,123	1,101	7,724		
Smithtown Police HQ	CTD	457.0	8,080	17.68	2,122	15,165	13,736	39,102		
Williams, Paul	Curr Est	8,250.0	134,063	16.25	25,000	350,000	227,906	736,969		
	% Comp	5.5%	6.0%	108.8%	8.5%	4.3%	6.0%	5.3%		
001234-004	Week	135.5	2,906	21.45	2,675	83,555	4,941	94,077		
Smithtown Town Offices	CTD	4,635.0	90,522	19.53	50,123	275,676	153,887	570,207		
Kramer, Robert	Curr Est	5,215.0	100,389	19.25	65,150	301,125	170,661	637,325		
	% Comp	88.9%	90.2%	101.5%	76.9%	91.5%	90.2%	89.5%		
Total Contract 001234	Week	2,792.5	45,474	16.28	9,038	190,282	77,306	322,100	354,310	01/05/91
Smithtown Rebuild	CTD	18,221.0	359,739	19.74	106,024	977,783	611,557	2,055,104	2,260,614	188,385
Evans, Paul	Curr Est	36,431.5	777,499	21.34	190,552	1,663,306	1,321,748	3,953,104	4,348,415	322,100
	% Comp	50.0%	46.3%	92.5%	55.6%	58.8%	46.3%	52.0%	52.0%	

unpaid invoices be reported to the project manager weekly. The importance of profitability is a given even to the project manager untrained in business matters. Weekly unbilled cost and unpaid invoice reports place the proper emphasis on cash flow.

Project managers also should be assigned to overload projects and receive the same types of reports as a project manager managing a client contract. These projects are specific proposals, selling efforts to specific clients, or projects associated with functions such as finance or human resources. One person should be responsible for the weekly review of costs.

The next level of the organization may be a principal, office manager, or product-line manager responsible for directing the project managers. This individual may be called the *P&L manager.* The P&L (profit-and-loss) manager typically would have full P&L responsibility with assigned new orders, sales, and profit targets, as well as asset management targets consistent with the firm's cash-flow plan.

At this level of the organization, different types of information are required. Although the P&L manager has project managers responsible for managing contracts, a report summarizing the current month, the fiscal year, and project-to-date revenues and costs, as well as billing and accounts receivable status, should be provided monthly. This report can be used to assess each project manager's performance.

The P&L manager should receive monthly reports that provide the status of actual performance against the targets assigned. The first of these reports would be a profit-and-loss statement (P&L). The P&L should be a one-page report that quickly alerts the P&L manager to the areas needing attention. **Table 5–14** is a sample P&L report for a design firm.

The components of the P&L that represent sales through gross margin are the individual contracts. Gross margin variances could represent a number of issues; however, they can be classified as either a rate variance or a volume variance. A *rate variance* is a variance caused by poor contract management, poor labor utilization, or too much "low margin" work. *Low margin work* is defined as work that was priced at profit margins below the firm's standards or plan. A *volume variance* is a variance caused by lack of work. The firm may not have achieved the level of anticipated new contract signings or was unable to hire employees to do the work it had.

The rate variance can be quantified by taking the multiplier variance and multiplying it by direct labor. The volume variance can be quantified by taking the direct labor variance and multiplying it by the plan multiplier less one (for example, plan multiplier of 2.85 – 1 = 1.85). See **Table 5–15.**

The rate variance can be further defined by identifying projects that generated losses or unusual gains, reserves for contracts anticipated to general losses or the reversal of prior reserves, or a greater degree of lower or higher-margin contracts than anticipated. The volume variance can be further analyzed by determining whether it was due to lower-than-plan

Table 5–14

Design Firm Sample Profit-and-Loss Report

Current Month				Year - To - Date			
Actual	Plan	Variance	Category	Actual	Plan	Variance	Formulas
50,000	40,000	10,000	New Orders	200,000	150,000	50,000	1*
550,000	0	550,000	Backlog	550,000	0	550,000	2**
250,000	260,000	(10,000)	Revenues	800,000	900,000	(100,000)	3
25,000	20,000	(5,000)	Subcontractor Costs	90,000	115,000	25,000	4
15,000	20,000	5,000	Direct Project Expenses	40,000	60,000	20,000	5
5,000	0	(5,000)	Contract Reserves	10,000	0	(10,000)	6
205,000	220,000	(15,000)	Net Revenues	660,000	725,000	(65,000)	3–4–5–6=7
65,000	70,000	5,000	Direct Labor	215,000	230,000	15,000	8
140,000	150,000	(10,000)	Gross Margin	445,000	495,000	(50,000)	7–8=9
			S,G & A Expenses:				
25,000	30,000	5,000	Indirect Labor	90,000	95,000	5,000	10
10,000	10,000	0	Compensated Absences	40,000	35,000	(5,000)	
15,000	18,000	3,000	Employee Benefits	60,000	60,000	0	
3,000	4,000	1,000	Travel & Entertainment	15,000	16,000	1,000	
4,000	3,500	(500)	Supplies & Postage	13,000	11,000	(2,000)	
2,500	2,500	0	Telephone Expenses	8,000	7,500	(500)	
2,500	1,000	(1,500)	Recruitment & Relocation	5,000	4,000	(1,000)	
1,500	2,000	500	Publ, Memb, & Training	5,000	6,000	1,000	
2,000	3,000	1,000	Promotional	10,000	9,000	(1,000)	
3,000	1,500	(1,500)	Outside Consultants	8,000	5,000	(3,000)	
2,000	0	(2,000)	Bad Debt Expense	6,000	0	(6,000)	

5,000	4,500	(500)	Computer Expenses	15,000	16,000	1,000	
3,500	3,500	0	Equipment Rental & Maint	10,000	11,000	1,000	
8,000	8,000	0	Insurance Expense	25,000	25,000	0	
10,000	11,000	1,000	Building Rent, Util & Maint	30,000	33,000	3,000	
12,000	12,000	0	Depreciation	35,000	35,000	0	
1,000	2,000	1,000	Other	4,000	8,000	4,000	
110,000	116,500	6,500	Total S, G & A	379,000	376,500	(2,500)	11
(5,000)	(4,000)	(1,000)	Interest Income/(Expense)	(12,000)	(16,000)	4,000	12
2,000	1,500	500	Other Income	8,000	6,000	2,000	
1,500	2,000	500	Other Expense	6,000	7,000	1,000	13
25,500	29,000	(3,500)	Income Before Taxes	56,000	101,500	(45,500)	9–11+12+13=14
1,275	1,450	175	State Taxes	2,800	5,075	2,275	15
5,500	9,625	4,125	Federal Taxes	18,620	33,749	15,129	16
18,725	17,925	800	Net Income	34,580	62,676	(28,096)	14–15–16=17

Ratios

3.15	3.14	0.01	Multiplier	3.07	3.15	(0.08)	7/8
72.2%	70.0%	2.2%	Utilization	70.5%	70.8%	–0.3%	8/(8+10)
173.5%	171.4%	–2.1%	Indirect Cost Rate	176.3%	163.7%	–12.6%	11/8
7.5%	6.9%	0.6%	Return On Sales	4.3%	7.0%	–2.6%	17/3
3,250	3,500	(250)	D.L.Per Day	3,359	3,594	(234)	8/Work Days

* Funded value of signed contracts.

** If using Percent Complete Method for revenue rcognition, then Backlog would be unrecognized revenue on contracts.

Table 5–15

Design Firm Gross Margin Variance Rate vs. Volume

Current Month Actual	Current Month Plan	Current Month Variance	Category	Year - To - Date Actual	Year - To - Date Plan	Year - To - Date Variance
50,000	40,000	10,000	New Orders	200,000	150,000	50,000
(200,000)	(750,000)	550,000	Backlog	(200,000)	(750,000)	550,000
250,000	260,000	(10,000)	Revenues	800,000	900,000	(100,000)
25,000	20,000	(5,000)	Subcontractor Costs	90,000	115,000	25,000
15,000	20,000	5,000	Direct Project Expenses	40,000	60,000	20,000
5,000	0	(5,000)	Contract Reserves	10,000	0	(10,000)
205,000	220,000	(15,000)	Net Revenues	660,000	725,000	(65,000)
65,000	70,000	5,000	Direct Labor	215,000	230,000	15,000
140,000	150,000	(10,000)	Gross Margin	445,000	495,000	(50,000)
3.15	3.14	0.01	Multiplier	3.07	3.15	(0.08)

Current Month Rate/Volume Variance Sample Calculation
Favorable/(Unfavorable)

Rate Variance

(Multplier Variance) X (Plan Direct Labor)

OR,

.01 X $70,000 = $700

Volume Variance

(Direct Labor Variance) X (Plan Multiplier Less 1)

OR,

($5,000) X (3.14 - 1.0) =($10,700)

Total Gross Margin Variance is $700 + ($10,700) = ($10,000)

utilization, below-plan sales on existing contracts, or delays in bringing in new contracts.

The selling, general, and administrative (SG&A) portion of the P&L represents the costs charged to bid and proposal activities, activities such as finance, legal expenses, and personnel, and overhead activities such as technical employee downtime or technology development. Similar to the way a contract summary report supports the gross margin of a P&L, detailed reports should be available to the P&L manager to support the SG&A costs. A detailed SG&A report identifying each cost element according to the SG&A categories should be produced and be similar in format to the P&L. **Table 5–16** is a sample SG&A report.

Bid and proposal and selling and marketing reports that identify current month and year-to-date costs against individual project budgets should be available on request. Labor utilization reports that present trends (that is, several weeks), current month, and year-to-date labor utilization against a target for each employee are an effective tool to identify indirect labor and gross margin volume variances.

Table 5–16

Design Firm Sample Selling, General, and Administrative Report

Last Month	Current Month Actual	Current Month Plan	Current Month Variance	Category	Year-to-Date Actual	Year-to-Date Plan	Year-to-Date Variance	Full Year Plan	% Expnd
				Indirect Labor					
12,000	11,000	15,000	4,000	Admin Labor	40,000	42,000	2,000	150,000	26.7%
9,000	8,000	8,000	0	Bid & Proposal Labor	28,000	30,000	2,000	120,000	23.3%
5,000	6,000	7,000	1,000	Selling & Mktng Labor	22,000	23,000	1,000	70,000	31.4%
26,000	25,000	30,000	5,000	Total Indirect Labor	90,000	95,000	5,000	340,000	26.5%
				Compensated Absences					
5,000	4,000	5,000	1,000	Vacation	16,000	15,000	(1,000)	45,000	35.6%
4,000	3,000	3,000	0	Holiday	12,000	12,000	0	36,000	33.3%
1,000	3,000	2,000	(1,000)	Sick	12,000	8,000	(4,000)	24,000	50.0%
10,000	10,000	10,000	0	Total Compensated Absences	40,000	35,000	(5,000)	105,000	38.1%
				Employee Benefits					
7,500	7,000	8,000	1,000	FICA	25,000	23,000	(2,000)	69,000	36.2%
700	600	500	(100)	FUTA	2,000	2,000	0	6,000	33.3%
1,000	900	1,000	100	SUTA	4,500	5,000	500	15,000	30.0%
5,000	4,000	5,000	1,000	Health Insurance	14,500	16,000	1,500	48,000	30.2%
2,000	2,000	2,000	0	Profit Sharing	8,000	8,000	0	24,000	33.3%
1,500	1,500	1,500	0	Bonus	6,000	6,000	0	18,000	33.3%
17,700	16,000	18,000	2,000	Total Employee Benefits	60,000	60,000	0	180,000	33.3%
				Travel & Entertainment					
3,000	1,200	2,000	800	Travel	9,000	10,000	1,000	30,000	30.0%
800	500	600	100	Meals	2,400	2,500	100	7,500	32.0%
200	800	500	(300)	Meetings	1,600	1,800	200	5,400	29.6%
1,000	500	900	400	Entertainment	2,000	1,700	(300)	5,100	39.2%
5,000	3,000	4,000	1,000	Total Travel & Entertainment	15,000	16,000	1,000	48,000	31.3%
				Supplies & Postage					
				etc...					

If the owner/president is comfortable with the control structure that is in place, it is possible to monitor the business with smaller quantities of information. A single sheet of paper analyzing key areas on which the owner/president should focus may be sufficient. Owners/presidents are interested in a consolidated P&L and a P&L for each of their P&L managers. From these, a president can call any manager and ask the questions that have surfaced on the P&L.

The owner also should be interested in a balance sheet, cash-flow statement, and forecasts. The balance sheet is best reported in comparative form to previous months and the previous fiscal year end. This format allows senior management quickly to identify unusual trends. A cash-flow statement shows how much cash was generated and how it was used during a period of time.

Forecasts should be done on both a short- and long-term basis. P&L and cash forecasts should be prepared monthly for the next three months and quarterly for a 12-month period. Forecasts are the best indicator of what will happen unless change is introduced. Projections should accompany the forecast to reflect impacts of events should they occur or not occur. It is extremely important in the organization to communicate to the people responsible the differences between a plan, a forecast, and a projection. A *plan* is a management budget and is based on the assumptions that steps will be taken to make events correspond to the plan. A *forecast* is a prediction of what will most likely happen and does not imply the forecaster will attempt to shape events to realize the forecast. A *projection* is an estimate of what will happen if various conditions or situations occur or do not occur.

§ 5.22 Audits

Audits come in many forms, shapes, and sizes and are commonplace for the design firm. Examples of typical audits include:

Contract audits (direct and indirect cost as stipulated in the contract)
Federal agency overhead or proposal audits
IRS audits
State tax audits
Sales tax audits
Insurance audits
Internal audits (financial and operational)
External audits (CPA firm)

The term *audit* automatically engenders unpleasantness. However, as long as the firm has documented policies and procedures and has an adequate accounting system, the audit should be nothing more than an administrative function. Nevertheless, do not take audits lightly; there may be severe consequences if the auditor is not satisfied with the provided documentation or justifications of cost. Without an adequate audit trail, there is the possibility that fines, penalties, and possible paybacks may occur. In addition, an unfavorable audit often requires the attention of executive level management. Their time can be better spent focusing on achieving the firm's business plan.

Following is a guideline for the types of documentation needed for audit purposes:

1. General ledger and chart of accounts
2. Financial statements (P&L and balance sheet)
3. Organizational charts (operational and legal entity)
4. Documentation of fringe and benefit plans
5. Documentation of policies and procedures
6. Detailed support for sales calculations
7. Sales by state
8. Payroll by state
9. Payroll by professional and clerical employees
10. Detail of labor costs (direct and indirect)
11. Original time sheets to support labor charges
12. Personnel and payroll records to support salary rates
13. Original approved vendor invoices that support payments to outside sources
14. Original contract documents, any change orders or amendments, and proposal data
15. Copies of invoices sent to the client
16. Detailed project cost reports
17. Documentation for competitive pricing or procured services
18. Purchase orders and subcontract/consulting agreements
19. Original employee expense reports
20. Cancelled checks
21. W2s, quarterly federal payroll tax returns (941s)

To properly respond to audits, it is imperative that there be an adequate records retention system in place. Regardless of the size of the firm, one person should be assigned the responsibility for records retention. There are no standard guidelines for exactly how long to retain records. Typically, the statute of limitations is considered the guideline; however, most states and regulatory agencies have varying requirements. In addition, there may be specific contract language dictating the period for records retention (such as three years after grant closeout), a situation over which the firm has no control. In any case, be certain the firm is in compliance with all record retention requirements before records are destroyed. However, records should not be kept for longer than the required retention period. Even if the required retention period has elapsed and the firm still has the documents, the firm is legally obligated to produce the records in a court case, a position that may not produce a favorable outcome.

CHAPTER 6

GENERAL LIABILITY FOR DESIGN PROFESSIONALS

David J. Dybdahl

David J. Dybdahl is managing director of environmental risk management services for the National Resource Division of Willis Corroon, an insurance brokerage firm. He serves as a corporate advisor to account executives who are designing and implementing risk management programs for clients. Mr. Dybdahl received his B.B.A. and M.B.A. degrees from the University of Wisconsin in risk management and insurance and risk management, insurance, and finance, respectively. He is an associate in risk management (ARM) and a chartered property and casualty underwriter (CPCU).

§ 6.1 Introduction

To understand the insurance coverage provided by the general liability policy, it is important to understand some of the basic principles of liability.

Laws have been created to protect the legal rights of others. There are three broad classes of legal wrongs: crime, breach of contract, and tort. Each is addressed by a different branch of the law.

Business entities and individuals can face potential liabilities from a number of different legal wrongs. In general, legal liability can be imposed either by common law (tort) or statute (civil). *Common law* consists of a body of principles and rules of conduct that have developed over the years. In the United States, the basis of the common law in most states is English common law. These rules have not been codified, and common law is often modified by the courts with the changes of society.

A *statute* consists of the written enactment of a law by a legislative body. A statute can amend the common law and create liabilities where liabilities did not exist under common law. For example, § 107 of the Comprehensive Environmental Response Compensation and Liability Act (CERCLA or Superfund)[1] created retroactive liability for waste generators, transporters, and site operators to pay for current and future cleanup costs at hazardous waste facilities. Under common law, only the site owners faced the potential liability for the cleanup of a site. Another example of a statute's superseding common law is the enactment of workers' compensation laws that compensate injured workers on a no-fault basis.

Workers compensation laws are a very significant departure from the principles of common law and deserve a separate discussion. Workers compensation laws have been passed in all 50 states to recognize that since society as a whole benefits from the production of goods and services, society as a whole should bear the burden of compensating injured workers. By imposing strict liability (liability without negligence) on the employer, workers compensation laws force the cost of industrial accidents to be incorporated into the costs of goods and services.

One of the fundamental principles behind workers compensation laws is that injured workers receive the benefit of being compensated for their injuries without a costly and lengthy legal proceeding. In exchange for quick and certain compensation, the worker trades his right to sue his employer directly for his damages under the law.

An injured worker is entitled to many benefits that are specifically provided for within the actual legislation. To be entitled to receive

---

[1] 42 U.S.C. § 9607 (1988).

benefits under the law, the injury must arise "out of and in the course of employment."

All state laws provide for the reimbursement of medical expenses, survivors death benefits, rehabilitation benefits, and compensation for various forms of disabilities. The actual amounts of these benefits vary a great deal state to state so an employer must be certain to have the appropriate workers compensation insurance in place.

All states require an employer to insure its obligations under the workers compensation statutes, either with commercial insurance, qualified self-insurance or the state fund. Failure to insure these obligations can leave the employer open to unlimited liability for medical expense and strict liability under tort for the injured worker's damages.

Early in the development of the common law, the courts decided that certain acts and/or omissions were offensive to the peace and continuity of the community. Such acts and/or omissions were designated as crimes. All states have codified their criminal law by enacting penal statutes setting forth the elements of each crime and prescribing the punishments that should be imposed.

The general rule is that when an employee commits a crime, even though it is in the course and scope of his employment, the employer is not criminally liable unless the employer aids, abets, or compels the commission of the crime, in which case the employer can be held responsible along with the perpetrator. A corporation cannot be imprisoned, but it can be fined or enjoined from committing illegal acts and/or be stripped of its license to do business. (However, in recent environmental cases senior management has, in fact, been imprisoned. See **Chapter 26**.)

In general, an insurance contract that purports to hold a criminal harmless from the consequences of his criminal acts is an illegal contract against public policy and, therefore, is void. A criminal act is a public wrong (that is, a violation of a duty owed to society as a whole) for which society seeks punishment of the perpetrator. Criminal acts also may have private or civil consequences. Only when this is true and monetary damages are awarded as remedies will criminal activities be the subject of general liability insurance.

Contractual agreements voluntarily entered into by entities or individuals create legal duties owed to the other contracting entities. Breach of a contractual agreement is a civil (versus public) wrong for which one possible remedy is a monetary award.

It is possible to assume the tort liability of another contracting party through the use of hold-harmless or indemnity agreements in contracts. These provisions are very common in construction and engineering service contracts. The general liability policy is structured to respond on behalf of the individual or entity who assumed the tort liability of another through a contractual provision, such as a hold-harmless or indemnity clause, providing the specific contract is not excluded by the definition of an insured contract within the policy form (see **§ 6.7**).

A *tort* is a wrongful act or omission, outside of a contract, that violates a person's legally protected right and for which the law provides a remedy in the form of an action for damages. In order for a tort to occur, there must be an unjustified breach of a legal duty causing direct damage to the injured party. The damages recoverable are those directly caused by the wrongful act. There must be an unbroken chain of causation from the act to the injury. Injuries that are not proximately caused by the wrongful act usually are not recoverable.

Torts can be divided into three groups according to their nature and origin: intentional torts, the tort of negligence, and strict liability. If a person intends the reasonable consequences of a tortious act, the tort is said to be intentional. The act does not necessarily have to be committed with malicious or hostile intent. If it is the result of a voluntary action, it will fall within this classification. Some intentional torts may be insured under the general liability policy. A few of these intentional torts are battery, false arrest, damage to property of others, disparagement of goods, defamation of character, invasion of privacy, assault, and malicious prosecution.

Negligence is a tort that is the main subject of general liability insurance. To maintain an action of negligence against a wrongdoer, the plaintiff must show the defendant owed a duty to the plaintiff to act or not to act as a reasonable and prudent person and that the defendant breached that duty. Claims for bodily injury and property damage arising out of negligence are the most common claims incurred under the general liability policy. Negligent acts are also a topic within the insuring agreements of many architects' and engineers' professional liability insurance policies. An in-depth discussion of professional liability is in **Chapter 7**.

Strict liability in tort is liability imposed by law without regard to negligence or intent. Activities that expose others to unreasonable harm may expose the person or entity conducting the activities to strict liability. Examples of activities that could lead to strict liability are the possession or maintenance of dangerous instrumentalities (such as dams, tigers, rocket fuel) or the conducting of ultrahazardous activities (such as blasting). Theoretically, the cleanup of toxic waste sites may, in fact, expose the engineer or contractor to liability for ultrahazardous activity that may be strict. See **Chapter 26**.

The important distinction between strict liability and negligence lies in the burden of proof required of the plaintiff. Under strict liability, the plaintiff only needs to prove damages that are a direct result of the activities of the defendant. The burden of proof then shifts to the defendant to prove that the plaintiff was not injured. The defendant cannot argue that he acted as a reasonable and prudent person (not negligent) to avoid liability.

In performing environmental cleanup services, the concept of strict liability becomes even more onerous. The plaintiff may only need to prove that he has been exposed to a toxic material, in many cases a minute amount, to show damages. Because there is often no direct cause and effect relationship between exposure to a toxic material and the manifestation of a disease, the defendant could find it impossible to show the plaintiff was not actually damaged, in which case the plaintiff could be awarded damages in the case, even if the defendant was not negligent.

The general liability insurance policy provides coverage for claims that allege strict liability. However, as might be expected, underwriters tend to shy away from insuring classes of businesses that may incur strict liabilities from their activities.

§ 6.2 General Liability Policy

The general liability insurance policy is the litigation insurance coverage purchased by the vast majority of businesses. In a general liability policy, the insurance company agrees to pay those sums that the insured becomes legally obligated to pay because of bodily injury or property damage claims brought against the insured by third parties.

The general liability policy provides the insured with protection against legal liability imposed by violations in tort. These may be violations of the insured, the insured's employees, or the violations of others that are assumed by the insured through contracts. In addition, the policy provides for the defense of legal action by others against the insured. In most general liability insurance contracts, the insurance company will pay the costs of investigation and defense in addition to the policy limits.

General liability insurance policies have been standardized in the insurance industry since 1940. The standardization of the policy form helped to alleviate many of the problems insurance buyers, agents, claims adjusters, and the courts were having in interpreting the various coverage forms. Quotes from different insurance companies became easier to compare, rate making became easier and more credible, and court interpretations of coverage issues could be applied unilaterally. The first standardized general liability policy was introduced in 1940. Revisions were made in 1943, 1955, 1966, and 1973, and finally, in 1986, the Insurance Services Office (ISO) produced the commercial general liability policy.[2]

[2] The Insurance Services Office is an insurance industry-sponsored organization that assists member companies with rate making and policy forms.

§ 6.3 Commercial General Liability

The commercial general liability (CGL) policy form was introduced in 1986. It is the successor to the previous comprehensive general liability policy form. Coverage under the new commercial general liability policy is essentially the same as that under the previous comprehensive general liability policy except that it includes some coverage extensions usually provided under the old policy by an endorsement known as the Broad Form Comprehensive General Liability Endorsement.

Because the broad form endorsement coverage extensions have already been incorporated within the commercial general liability policy, most underwriters are unwilling to attach the broad form endorsement to the new CGL because doing so would violate the filings the insurers have made with the state insurance commissioners. This can create problems for insureds when trying to certify general liability insurance with a broad form endorsement. Generally, contract specifications that require general liability insurance with the broad form endorsement are out of date. In most cases, an explanation from the insurance broker to the insured's client will result in the acceptance of the newer commercial general liability policy.

There are two versions of the commercial general liability policy: the *occurrence form* and the *claims-made form.* Coverage is identical under both policies. The difference is the triggering of coverage. The claims-made form only covers claims that are first made during the policy term. The occurrence form of the commercial general liability policy applies in the same manner as the old comprehensive general liability policy and only covers claims for injury or property damage that actually occur during the policy period, regardless of when the claim is reported.

Historically, the insurance industry has used the date of the injury or loss as the triggering event for general liability and umbrella liability insurance. This is known as an *occurrence* or *accident coverage trigger.* With an occurrence trigger, the insurance policy in effect at the time a covered bodily injury or property damage loss occurs responds to that loss regardless of when the insured learns about the occurrence or when a claim is filed against the insured. In other words, the insured is assured that liability insurance protection will be available for claims made at any time in the future if the bodily injury or property damage occurs during the policy period.

Some insurance buyers may find that only claims-made insurance is available to them. This is usually true in classes of businesses that either have a very short or undefined loss history (such as remedial contractors) or face loss exposures that may have long latency periods (such as chemical manufacturers).

Both claims-made and occurrence policy forms have positive and negative aspects. The advantages to the insured of the occurrence policy form are:

1. If the injury or damage occurs during the policy period, the coverage applies no matter when its resulting claims are made.
2. Cancellation or nonrenewal after the injury or damage occurs does not affect coverage for the resulting claims.
3. If the injury or damage is held to have occurred over several policy periods, all the policies in effect during these periods may be required to provide primary coverage for a single claim.

The disadvantages to the insured of an occurrence policy form are:

1. Claims for injury that occurred long ago will be assigned back to previous policies that may have inadequate limits and/or coverages.
2. Policy records may need to be kept open indefinitely for possible future claims.
3. Keeping limits current and adequate may be difficult.
4. Disputes and litigation may arise in determining when the injury occurred and which policy applies.

The claims-made policy form offers a few advantages to the insured and one major disadvantage. The advantages are:

1. Disputes over which policy applies will be reduced.
2. Limits can be kept current to reflect expected claims patterns.
3. Policy files need not be kept open indefinitely.

The major disadvantage of the claims-made policy form is that coverage must be kept in force during the entire loss exposure period. If a claims-made policy is not in force when a claim is actually made, there is no coverage available. This can create significant problems for the insurance buyer if the policy is not renewed, cancelled, or priced beyond the range of affordability. Buyers also have less flexibility to change insurance companies because of the need to maintain the original retroactive date of coverage.

When a policy has a claims-made trigger, the policy is triggered when the claim is made against the insured rather than when the covered injury or property damage occurs. **Table 6–1** illustrates the difference between claims-made and occurrence liability insurance:

Table 6–1

Claims-Made Versus Occurrence Insurance

Injury	Claim	Settlement
1986	1987	1988

Assume occurrence policy:	Assume claims-made policy:
The 1986 occurrence policy is triggered because the injury occurred during its policy period. The date of claim and settlement date have no bearing on which policy applies.	The 1987 claims-made policy is triggered because the claim was first made against the insured during its policy period. The date of injury and settlement date have no bearing on which policy applies.

Unless modified, a claims-made policy covers any injury or damage that occurred in the past as long as the claim is made during the current policy period. However, the insurer will normally want to limit the duration of prior acts' coverage to avoid overlaps with previous occurrence policies.

The underwriting tool that enables the insurer to limit the duration of coverage for prior injuries is the *retroactive date provision,* which is a provision in a claims-made policy that excludes any claims arising from injuries or damages that occurred before the retroactive date stated in the policy declarations.

It is important to remember that the imposition of a retroactive date is at the option of the underwriter. Ideally, an insured's claims-made policy will have no retroactive date, thus giving full coverage for claims made during the policy period regardless of when damage or injury occurred. However, if a retroactive date is used, it should be no later than the effective date of the first claims-made policy written for the insured, and the same retroactive date should be used for all subsequent claims-made policies.

As already noted, a claims-made policy only insures against claims made while the policy is in force or, in some cases, against claims made after policy expiration if the event for which the claim is made was reported to the insurer during the policy period. Because there is always a possibility that injuries have occurred but claims have not been made, this aspect of claims-made insurance can present substantial coverage gaps for an insured in certain circumstances. For example, each of the following incidents could result in some gap in coverage:

1. The insurer cancels or refuses to renew a claims-made policy and the insured cannot buy a replacement.
2. The insured cancels or does not renew and chooses not to buy a replacement policy.
3. The insured switches from a claims-made policy to an occurrence policy.

4. A claims-made policy is renewed subject to an advanced retroactive date.
5. The insurer attaches an exclusion for a product, accident, or location to a renewal claims-made policy.

An *extended reporting period (ERP) provision* is the most common safeguard against these types of coverage gaps. In general, an ERP causes the policy to respond to claims made after the policy is terminated (cancelled or not renewed) if the injury or damage for which the claims are made took place on or after the retroactive date and on or before the effective date of termination.

§ 6.4 Covered Loss Exposure

The commercial general liability policy provides insurance for claims arising out of the following risks or exposures:

1. **Premises and operations liability.** Coverage against claims arising out of premises owned, rented, leased, or used by the insured and for operations such as well-drilling work. However, coverage is excluded for liability claims arising out of the ownership, maintenance, or use of automobiles or aircraft by the insured. Coverage is afforded for liability claims arising out of the rental or use of nonowned watercraft under 26 feet long, not being used to carry persons or property for a charge. Coverage is not afforded for any owned watercraft regardless of length.
2. **Protective liability.** Coverage for claims made against a named insured arising out of operations performed by subcontractors and sub-subcontractors.
3. **Completed operations and products liability.** Insurance for claims for bodily injury and property damage that occur after the operations or work has been completed. Coverage against claims arising out of products manufactured, sold, or distributed by the named insured. Coverage does not extend to damage to the product itself or to the faulty work itself.
4. **Broad form property damage liability.** This coverage, previously added by endorsements, is incorporated in the commercial general liability policy. This modifies the old care, custody, or control exclusion and provides coverage in some instances for real property considered in the insured's care, custody, or control. Coverage is excluded, however, for personal property in the care, custody, or control of the insured.

5. **Fire legal liability.** Subject to the separate limit shown in the policy for this coverage, insurance is provided for damage by fire to premises rented to or leased to the insured if the fire damage results from the insured's negligence.
6. **Contractual liability.** Coverage against claims for liability of others for bodily injury or damage to property assumed by the insured under a written or oral contract. This includes liability of others assumed by the insured under indemnification or hold-harmless provisions of contracts. Other examples of agreements for which contractual liability insurance is afforded are lease agreements, easement agreements, and permits required by cities, counties, and other public entities.

   Contractual liability insurance is provided for liability assumed under contract by the insured for claims related to nonowned aircraft or watercraft. However, contractual liability insurance is not afforded to claims arising out of automobiles, which are covered under a business auto policy.

   The professional liability of architects and engineers receives special consideration in the contractual liability extension of the general liability policy. This liability is specifically excluded within the definition of an *insured contract.*
7. **Personal injury liability.** The policy also provides coverage for defined personal injury claims. *Personal injury claims* are defined in the policy as claims for false arrest, detention or imprisonment, malicious prosecution, wrongful entry or eviction, libel, slander, and oral or written publication of material that violates a person's right of privacy. If the insured assumes the personal injury liability of another under contract, coverage is not provided for such contractual liability.

§ 6.5 Limits of Liability

The commercial general liability policy has six different limits of liability:

1. **Each-occurrence limit.** The limit for all bodily injury, property damage, or medical expenses resulting from any one occurrence.
2. **Products-completed operations aggregate.** The maximum the insurance company will pay for the total of all bodily injury and property damage claims included in the products-completed operations hazard. Within the general liability policy, the insured's products include any goods or products manufactured, sold, handled, distributed, or disposed of by the insured; and completed operations include work performed by or on behalf of the named insured in connection with that work.

3. **General aggregate limit.** The total amount the insurance company will pay for all bodily injury and property damage (other than products-completed operations claims) and personal injury claims. This aggregate limit applies to the total of all claims.
4. **Personal and advertising injury limit.** Provides a per-person (or per-organization) limit of liability for claims involving covered personal injury and covered advertising injury. This coverage is also subject to the general policy aggregate.
5. **Fire damage limit.** Establishes a limit, subject to the each-occurrence limit, for damage arising out of any one fire. The coverage typically has a $50,000 limit. Increases beyond $50,000 must be negotiated with the insurer.

§ 6.6 Exclusions

Section I of the CGL coverage form contains the insuring agreement and related provisions for three coverages: coverage A, bodily injury and property damage liability; coverage B, personal and advertising injury liability; and coverage C, medical payments. Each coverage part has a group of exclusions that apply to that coverage.

Exclusions in insurance contracts usually appear for one of two reasons. First, the exposure may be uninsurable. Within the general liability policy, the pollution and property damage to one's own product are examples of this first type of exclusion. The second type of exclusion is used when the underwriter wants to eliminate loss exposures from the coverage that could be addressed more accurately in a separate insurance contract. For example, the general liability policy excludes thc maintenance, operation, or use of an automobile. This loss exposure should be covered under the business auto policy. Although both the general liability and auto liability policies cover bodily injury and property damage liability, the auto policy only applies to claims arising out of the maintenance, operation, or use of a covered auto. The exclusions in the general liability policy have been manuscripted to allow for (or force) the purchase of business automobile, workers' compensation, property, contractors' equipment, pollution liability, and professional liability insurance.

§ 6.7 —Coverage A: Bodily Injury and Property Damage Exclusions

In the general liability policy, coverage for bodily injury and property damage is defined by what is excluded as opposed to what activities are covered. Therefore, a good understanding of the exclusions is necessary to understand what is covered under the general liability policy.

The majority of the risk transfer provided in the general liability policy is found in coverage part A, bodily injury and property damage. This coverage part has its own set of exclusions, (a) through (n).

Exclusion (a)—Intentional Injury

Exclusion (a) of the 1986 CGL form applies to "bodily injury or property damage expected or intended from the standpoint of the insured." The exclusion does not to apply to "bodily injury resulting from the use of reasonable force to protect persons or property." This exclusion generally fits the uninsurable reasoning for an exclusion.

Exclusion (b)—Contractual Liability

Exclusion (b) excludes all contractual liability except that which is assumed under an "insured contract" or liability that would have been incurred by the insured in the absence of the contract.

For design professionals, the definition of *insured contract* has a great deal of importance. The definition is found within the conditions section of the general liability policy. An insured contract includes:

1. A lease agreement
2. A sidetrack agreement
3. Most easement agreements
4. Indemnification of a municipality
5. Certain other indemnification agreements in the course of the insured's business.

An insured contract *does not* include:

1. Any agreement for an insured to indemnify an architect or engineer for the architect's or engineer's professional liability
2. Any agreement, in which the insured is an architect or engineer, that indemnifies a third party for claims arising out of the professional services of the insured
3. Any agreement that indemnifies a third party for damage by fire of premises rented to the insured. (This exposure is addressed separately in the fire legal liability coverage.)

The resulting coverage embraces most indemnification agreements outside of professional liability for design professionals. This professional liability exposure is more appropriately insured under an architects' and engineers' errors and omissions policy. See **Chapter 7**.

Exclusion (c)—Alcoholic Beverages

This exclusion deletes coverage for liquor liability, but only for insureds that are in the business of manufacturing, distributing, selling, or serving alcoholic beverages. The effect of this exclusion is to force firms in those businesses to purchase special liquor liability policy forms.

Exclusions (d) and (e)—Workers' Compensation and Employers' Liability

These exclusions delete coverage under the general liability policy for workers' compensation and employers' liability claims. Both of these loss exposures should be insured under workers' compensation insurance policies. The exclusion not only deletes coverage for claims arising from the employee, but also excludes claims from a spouse, child, parent, brother, or sister of the employee. There is a specific exception to this exclusion for contractual liability protection under an insured contract.

Separate workers compensation insurance must be purchased to cover this loss exposure. All states require the purchase of insurance or formal self-insurance. The penalties for noncompliance are severe.

Exclusion (f)—Pollution

This exclusion has been designed to eliminate almost all general liability coverage for claims that arise from the release of pollutants. Although there is some coverage for the insured's products and completed operations that is not excluded, it is safer for the insurance buyer to assume the general liability policy will not respond to any claim for pollution liability.

In general, the exclusion deletes coverage for pollution claims that arise from the insured's:

1. Premises
2. A waste disposal site
3. A waste stream
4. Remedial actions or operations of a remedial action contractor.

Part 2 of the exclusion is designed to eliminate coverage for liabilities that may be incurred by the insured under the federal Superfund law.

The second part of the pollution exclusion has the potential to be onerous. This section eliminates "any loss, cost or expense arising out of any request, demand or order that any insured or others test for, monitor, clean up, remove, contain, treat, detoxify or neutralize or in any other way respond to or assess the effects of pollutants." As mentioned, this exclusion was designed to eliminate Superfund claims under the general liability policy. However, the assumably unintended effect of the exclusion, if read in its broadest sense, would be to eliminate all general liability insurance for any claims arising from work performed for any governmental agency under a remedial action contract because any loss, cost, or expense arising out of the scope of services could be excluded, not just claims arising from pollution. For a discussion of insurance coverage that may be obtained for environmental liabilities, see **Chapter 26**.

Design professionals performing environmental restoration services must be keenly aware of the effect of the pollution exclusion on their risk management programs. Although the general liability policy does not provide coverage for the professional liability of a design professional, it does apply to the contingent liability a design professional can incur through hiring subcontractors. If a subcontractor is performing operations at a waste disposal site, no general liability coverage for pollution losses would be in force. If the subcontractor has not specifically addressed the pollution liability exclusion in its liability insurance program through the purchase of the appropriate environmental impairment liability insurance, the entire operation would be uninsured for bodily injury and property damage liability claims arising from pollution releases.

Exclusion (g)—Aircraft, Autos, Watercraft

The general liability policy excludes claims arising out of the maintenance, operation, or use, including the loading or unloading, of aircraft, automobiles, and watercraft. These exposures are usually covered under separate insurance contracts outside of the general liability policy. The exclusion contains specific exceptions for:

1. Watercraft when on the insured's premises
2. A nonowned watercraft less than 26 feet in length and not being used to carry persons or cargo for a charge
3. Parking an auto on the insured's premises
4. Liability assumed under an insured contract but only for watercraft and aircraft.
5. Bodily injury and property damage arising out of the use of mobile equipment. *Mobile equipment* and *autos* have specific definitions in the general liability policy. Particular attention must be paid to these

to evaluate the amount of coverage provided within the general liability policy on any given piece of equipment.

Exclusion (h)—Mobile Equipment

The only coverage A exclusion directly applicable to mobile equipment is (h), which eliminates coverage for:

1. The transportation of "mobile equipment" by an "auto" owned or operated by or rented or loaned to any insured; or
2. The use of "mobile equipment" in or while in practice or preparation for, a pre-arranged racing, speed or demolition contest or in any stunting activity.

Part 1 of this exclusion is covered under the business auto policy. Part 2 would require the purchase of a specialty policy form to cover this exposure.

Exclusion (i)—War

This exclusion eliminates coverage for liability the insured has assumed under contract for bodily injury and property damage due to war, civil war, insurrection, rebellion, or revolution.

Exclusion (j)—Care, Custody, and Control

The essence of this exclusion is to prevent the insured from using the general liability policy to pay claims that should be covered under property or first-party insurance policies. The exclusion has six separate parts that delete coverage for property damage to:

1. Property the insured owns, rents, or occupies
2. Premises the insured sells, gives away, or abandons, if the property damage arises out of any part of those premises
3. Property loaned to the insured
4. Personal property in the care, custody, or control of the insured
5. That particular part of real property on which the insured or any contractors or subcontractors working directly or indirectly on the insured's behalf are performing operations, if the property damage arises out of those operations
6. That particular part of any property that must be restored, repaired, or replaced because the insured's work was incorrectly performed on it.

For design professionals performing design/build services, items 5 and 6 of this exclusion have important implications. To illustrate the effect of part 5 of this exclusion, assume that an electrical subcontractor working for a general contractor accidentally starts one of the builder's projects on fire while working on a transformer and the entire structure is burned down. If the owner of the project sues the general contractor for the loss, the care, custody, and control exclusion would apply only to "that particular part" of the structure on which the subcontractor was working. Thus, the named insured would be covered for damage to all parts of the building other than the transformer and all parts of the electrical system other than the particular part being worked on at the time of the loss. Part 6 of the exclusion is the faulty workmanship exclusion. It applies to any property (real or personal), whether on or away from the insured's premises, and contains an exception stating that it does not apply to property damage included in the products-completed operations hazard.

Exclusion (k)—Property Damage to Insured's Product

Insuring property damage to the insured's own product is generally thought to be a business risk that is uninsurable under a general liability policy. Because most design professionals do not manufacture or sell "products," this exclusion should not be of significant consequence.

Exclusion (l)—Damage to Insured's Work

In concept, this exclusion is designed to prevent the general liability policy from becoming a performance guarantee vehicle for the insured. The performance of a particular work product is generally thought to be a business risk and not insurable.

The exclusion deletes coverage for property damage to "your work" or any part of it. There is one exception to the exclusion. It "does not apply if the damaged work or the work out of which the damage arises was performed" on the insured's behalf by a subcontractor. The exception to the exclusion has particular importance if the design professional is performing design/build services and is acting in the role of a general contractor.

Exclusion (m)—Impaired Property

This exclusion eliminates coverage for property that has not been physically injured arising out of a defect, deficiency, or inadequacy in the insured's product or work, or a delay or failure to perform under a contract.

There is an exception to this exclusion. It does not apply if the loss of use of the other property is a result of the sudden and accidental physical injury to the insured's work or product after it has been put into its intended use.

Exclusion (n)—Sistership Liability

This is a continuation of the "business risk" exclusions. In essence, this exclusion deletes coverage for claims that are a result of the recall of the insured's products or work from the marketplace.

The last part of the coverage A exclusions deletes exclusions (c) through (n) to provide fire damage legal liability coverage. This coverage is subject to its own sublimit on the policy.

§ 6.8 —Coverage B: Personal and Advertising Liability Exclusions

Coverage part B of the general liability policy covers personal and advertising liability. The definitions of *advertising injury* and *personal injury* are of particular importance in understanding the coverage this section provides.

Advertising injury includes libel, slander, violation of rights of privacy, misappropriation of advertising ideas, and infringement of copyright, title, or slogan. *Personal injury* is defined to include injury other than bodily injury arising out of false arrest, detention or imprisonment, malicious prosecution, wrongful entry or eviction, libel, slander, and a violation of a person's right to privacy.

In order for coverage to apply, the personal injury must be caused by an offense arising out of the insured's business, but coverage does not include advertising, publishing, broadcasting, or telecasting done for the insured. The latter exposure must be insured separately. Advertising injury must be caused by an offense committed by the insured in the course of advertising its services, goods, or products.

Coverage part B has its own set of exclusions. Many separate causes of loss are addressed within exclusion (a):

1. Publication of written or oral material that the insured knew was false
2. Acts that took place before the coverage period of the policy
3. Losses that are a result of the willful violation of statute
4. Losses that have been assumed under contract.

Exclusion (b) deletes advertising injury arising out of:

1. A breach of contract other than misappropriation of advertising ideas
2. The failure of goods or services to conform with advertised quality or performance
3. The wrong description of price
4. Claims by an insured who is in the business of advertising, broadcasting, publishing, or telecasting.

§ 6.9 —Coverage C: Medical Payments Exclusions

The general liability policy will pay for bodily injury caused by an accident at the insured's premises or in the insured's operations, regardless of fault or liability. In order for coverage to apply, the accident must take place during the policy period, must be reported within one year, and the injured person must be willing to be examined by a physician of the insurer's choice.

Medical payments have a separate sublimit on the policy and are usually fairly low amounts of $5,000 to $10,000. A separate set of exclusions applies to the medical payments coverage part. The policy will not respond to claims for bodily injury:

1. To any insured
2. To a person hired by the insured
3. To a person who normally occupies that part of a premises
4. To a person eligible for workers' compensation benefits
5. To participants in athletics
6. To "products-completed operations" claims
7. To any claim that would be excluded under coverage A, bodily injury and property damage
8. Due to war. This goes beyond the war exclusion in coverage part A.

§ 6.10 Section II: Who Is an Insured

The commercial general liability policy has very broad provisions to extend coverages under the policy to the insured. *Insureds* include:

1. a. An individual and spouse for an owned business
   b. A partnership or joint venture
   c. Organizations other than a partnership or joint venture (such as corporations) and the directors, officers, and shareholders as respects their liability in those roles
2. a. Employees of the insured for acts within the scope of their employment. However, there are exclusions for bodily and personal injury to an employee or coemployee, medical malpractice, and property damage to property of an employee
   b. Persons acting as a real estate manager for the insured
   c. Persons having temporary custody of the insured's property
   d. The legal representative of a deceased insured.
3. The operators of "mobile equipment"
4. Newly acquired organizations, for 90 days.

§ 6.11 How Premiums Are Determined

The general liability premium for design professionals is computed using base rates published by the Insurance Services Office (ISO). The rates vary depending upon the classification code assigned to the various payroll streams inherent in the underwriting submission. Classification codes are standardized descriptions of the services provided by classes of employees. See **Table 6–2.**

For every general liability class code there is a corresponding workers compensation class code.

Premiums are actually computed by multiplying the rate times the exposure basis. In the case of design professionals, the *exposure basis* is the actual payroll of the various classifications.

Some general liability classifications are not given a suggested rate by ISO. These are "A"-rated classifications. The individual underwriter determines the rate and/or the premium based on the perceived exposure to loss the applicant may present. In general, much more pricing flexibility rests in the hands of the underwriter in "A"-rated classifications. However, these are usually under general home office underwriting guidelines to prevent wild deviations from one insured to another.

The proper rating of the submission is usually one of the most effective ways to reduce the premium paid for general liability and workers compensation insurance. To assure the most accurate rating of the submission, the insured must provide sufficient underwriting data on the payrolls in the applicable class codes. Without a breakdown of payroll, the natural tendency of most underwriters is to select a single class code, which is usually on the higher end of the possible choices of the rate scale. An insurance agent or broker who is knowledgeable in the writing of design professionals' insurance should be able to assist the applicant in selecting the appropriate class codes and completing the applications.

Table 6–2

Base Rates

Description	Code	Rate per $1000 payroll
Analytical chemist	91135	2.20
Draftsman	91805	.50
Drilling (no other classification)	92101	25.23
Engineer or architect	92663	8.10
Excavation	94007	78.75
Geophysical exploration	95359	10.90
Contractor executive supervisor	91580	34.50

To determine the final premium for the general liability policy, the underwriter computes the manual premium (rate x payroll) and then debits or credits the premium based on the insured's past loss record. In some cases, the underwriter can lower the final premium by applying credits for safety and loss control procedures or other factors that may lessen the perceived exposure to loss. In general, underwriters have less pricing flexibility in workers compensation insurance because the states determine the classifications, set the rates, and compute the experience modification factor.

§ 6.12 Other Underwriting Considerations for Design Professionals

As a general rule, design professionals should have a small exposure to loss under the general liability policy. Because there are usually no products or completed operations loss exposures and the primary "operations" loss exposure—professional liability—is almost always excluded by endorsement on the general liability policy, what is left is basically insurance for the insured's premises under coverage A, bodily injury and property damage, coverage B, personal and advertising injury, and coverage C, medical payments.

The potential to pay claims changes dramatically under the general liability policy when a design professional hires subcontractors to perform operations (such as well drilling or tank pulling) or goes one step further to provide design/build services. The general liability policy automatically covers the contingent liability loss exposures of the insured for the operations of subcontractors. Therefore, the design professional's loss exposure for general liability insurance rating purposes becomes that of a general contractor. This is usually a problem for underwriters because the distinction of the loss exposure between the engineering and the construction service becomes blurred, making it difficult to assess where one exposure ends and the other begins.

Underwriters have various tools to address this potential ambiguity in exposure. One of the easiest and most common underwriting guidelines is to not write any design professional business that has a general contracting exposure. Following are typical underwriting guidelines for architects and engineers:

ARCHITECTS AND ENGINEERS

Sample Underwriting Guidelines

DESCRIPTION The architects and engineers which should be targeted are those risks which are involved in the following activities: the writing of reports, preparing specification sheets, drawing up or examining plans and blueprints, creating layout or scale drawings and models, reviewing standards and rendering opinions, and developing manuals and preparing recommendations for use in construction/renovation projects.

EXPOSURES

There is an increased general liability off-premises exposure when architects or engineers visit construction or project sites. When off-premises work is done it must be only for construction observation on behalf of the architect's or engineer's clients. An additional premium charge is applied to the liability portion of the policy for the off-premises exposure. This is a charge per employee for anyone spending more than 10% of their work time away from the office.

ELIGIBILITY/UNDERWRITING REQUIREMENTS

Architects and engineers who are associated with the following are ineligible:

- those directly engaged in supervising or controlling any construction, manufacturing, or installation projects (design/building contractors);
- those who own interests in building, contracting, or developing companies; and
- any firm staffed to provide geotechnical engineering services.

Professional Liability Insurance is required. This eliminates the possibility of the general liability coverage being asked to respond to a claim resulting from design errors. The professional liability insurance carrier and policy number must be provided. The underwriting file must also contain documentation of the renewal of the professional coverages.

Of particular interest in these guidelines is the underwriter's desire to avoid the operations/completed operations and products liability loss exposures. Firms that have these exposures are ineligible for this particular underwriter. Another way for the underwriter to address these increases in exposure would be to make a premium charge in the general liability policy for those classifications. However, the majority of underwriters tend to shy away from the entire risk instead of trying to correct an ambiguous exposure through premium surcharges.

To further define the risk under the general liability policy, the underwriting guidelines require that professional liability insurance be maintained before the applicant will be eligible for the general liability insurance. This is a very common general liability underwriting guideline for design professionals. The logic behind this requirement is that in the absence of professional liability insurance, the general liability underwriter may face professional liability claims made against the general liability policy. The ISO manual rates for the various design professional class codes do not contemplate this additional exposure and, therefore, the underwriter tries to avoid this claims situation whenever possible.

In addition to requiring the purchaser of general liability insurance to purchase a separate professional liability insurance policy, most general liability underwriters will attach a separate exclusion for professional liability by endorsement, which excludes liability arising out of the provision of professional services including:

1. The preparing, approving, or failing to prepare or approve maps, drawings, opinions, reports, surveys, change orders, designs or specifications; and
2. Supervisory, inspection or engineering services.[3]

For firms that provide construction management services, it is common to see general liability underwriters attach a separate construction manager's errors and omissions exclusion by endorsement to the policy. This exclusion does not apply to "bodily injury" or "property damage" due to construction or demolition work done by you, your employees or your sub-contractors.[4]

§ 6.13 Environmental Restoration Work

Design professionals venturing into environmental restoration work face three significant problems within their insurance programs. First, environmental liabilities can be very severe, and only a few underwriters are willing to provide even limited insurance against them. Second, there is significant market pressure to force design professionals into a full-service or design/build mode to be competitive in the remedial action contracting marketplace. Third, the majority of underwriters shy away from environmental work and design/build work, even though there is a pollution exclusion on both the general liability and most professional liability policies. As

[3] Insurance Services Office, Inc., Commercial General Liability Coverage Form (1986).
[4] *Id.*

a result, a firm venturing into environmental work not only faces pollution exclusions on its liability insurance policies, but it also potentially faces the nonrenewal or mid-term cancellation of its entire casualty insurance program.

Specialty insurance markets have been developed to provide various forms of environmental liability insurance. In essence, there are three types of policies that can be used to address potential environmental liabilities:

1. Professional liability insurance without a pollution exclusion
2. Contractor's pollution liability, which provides bodily injury and property damage coverage for the insured's operations
3. Packages that provide either professional liability with limited contractor's pollution liability insurance or general liability with professional liability with limited pollution coverage for professional errors and omissions loss exposures.

In general, asbestos is treated as a separate item from other hazardous materials by the insurance industry. To cover the general liability exposure, there are specialty forms available which are basically a general liability policy with an amended pollution exclusion designed to provide coverage for asbestos claims. Professional liability coverage can often be obtained by endorsing this coverage onto the practice is professional liability coverage. Pollution and asbestos coverages vary a great deal. It is wise to obtain the professional advice of a specialized insurance broker before purchasing any type of coverage.

§ 6.14 Role of Insurance Broker

The insurance broker can play an important role in the overall risk management program of a firm. Some of the functions and services of the broker are:

1. Evaluating and accessing the marketplace
2. Checking market security
3. Keeping risk manager abreast of market conditions
4. Assisting in risk identification
5. Organizing the underwriting submission
6. Getting submission to underwriter on a timely basis
7. Assuring submission's completeness and accuracy
8. Providing creativity in program design and rating
9. Evaluating coverage needs

10. Negotiating rate, price, and coverage
11. Evaluating insurance specifications on contracts
12. Evaluating the quotation's strengths and weaknesses
13. Preparing the renewal presentation
14. Informing underwriters of results
15. Providing ongoing communication and service.

Some larger brokerage firms also offer their clients claims specialists, risk management consulting services, captive insurance company management, and other resources on a fee-for-service basis.

To objectively assess the capabilities and services of a broker, insurance buyers should evaluate:

1. The experience, educational background, and training of the broker
2. The resources available to the broker to service the account (such as specialists in the insured's industry)
3. The capabilities, educational background, and training of the account service team
4. The services provided by the brokerage firm
5. Referrals from other accounts the broker handles.

Most brokers will welcome the opportunity to compete in a broker selection process based on the broker's capabilities, which may include a conceptual proposal on how the broker would design the insurance program, market the insurance, and service the account in the future. In the long run, this type of broker selection should lead to superior results because the most qualified broker will be representing the insurance buyer in the insurance marketplace.

CHAPTER 7

RISK MANAGEMENT AND MALPRACTICE INSURANCE FOR DESIGN PROFESSIONALS

Michael G. Welbel
John S. Wersyn

Michael G. Welbel is assistant vice president and product manager for Shand, Morahan & Company's Architects and Engineers Professional Liability Program in Evanston, Illinois. He is a member of the Illinois and American Bar Associations. Mr. Welbel has extensive experience in handling claims against architects and engineers, lawyers, real estate agents and brokers, and insurance companies. He has authored a number of articles on matters affecting the design profession, has been involved in the drafting of a contracts law case book, and has lectured on insurance issues.

John S. Wersyn is an attorney and civil engineer with Shand, Morahan & Company in Evanston, Illinois. He handles malpractice claims against design professionals as a claims representative for the architects and engineers professional liability insurance programs underwritten by Shand Morahan. Mr. Wersyn specializes in regulatory, environmental, and design professional liability matters, and he has authored articles and lectured on various aspects of design professional loss control and risk management. He received a B.S. degree from the University of Illinois and a J.D. degree from DePaul University.

EVALUATING PROFESSIONAL LIABILITY RISKS

§ 7.1 Introduction

Today's design professionals who aspire to grow in knowledge, experience, and responsibility must master many aspects of both the design profession and running a business, including knowledge of rudimentary accounting and law, psychology, and employer/employee relations. Included in this spectrum are risk management and insurance.

This chapter focuses on risk management and the design professional's malpractice liability insurance considerations. Topics include identifying and understanding risks faced by the design professional firm, addressing and providing for such risks, minimizing the consequences of risk, and using insurance as a key tool for managing risks.

§ 7.2 Identifying the Risks

The individual undertaking the role of risk manager for a design firm might begin by identifying and categorizing the various risks to be addressed and managed. One approach is to focus on four broad categories, including business risk, risk of direct loss, risk of resource-draining disputes, and risk of liability.

Business Risk

In the broadest sense, the term *business risk* encompasses economic factors such as the general health of the national economy, interest rates, and market factors such as the labor market and competition. Other risks that can be included in the business risk category are risks associated with hiring and managing employees, maintaining social and political alliances, and other such broadly defined uncertainties of providing a professional service to the general public.

Usually, such broad types of risk cannot be controlled through techniques normally used to protect against risks of specific loss, but they can be addressed through the implementation of business philosophies, personnel philosophies and policies, and a well-planned marketing process including careful client and project selection. Techniques include diversification and networking to minimize the adverse effects of changes in politics, demographics, and business climate.

Risk of Direct Loss

Certain kinds of risk from loss are common to any business venture. The ability to define the risks, their causes, and consequences are factors that make them manageable. These risks include unexpected events' causing the loss of office space, equipment, key personnel, and other business essentials.

One risk that is easy to identify and protect against is the risk of losing facilities or equipment to severe weather, fire, theft, or vandalism. This risk is typically provided for through insurance. A different kind of risk is the risk of losing key personnel. This can become a serious problem for any service firm. Service organizations are highly dependent on their personnel, especially the highly skilled specialists who either market or deliver the service. Loss of key personnel can occur for various reasons. Some, such as the departure of key personnel to other firms, can only be protected against through work environment, compensation and incentive programs. The worst consequence of others, such as sickness or death, can be protected against through disability and life insurance programs that merely cushion the impact.

Risk of Dispute

The risk of becoming engaged in resource-draining disputes is another distinct hazard of providing a professional service. Recognizing this risk is essential to the well-being of any professional organization, in part because it is insurable only to some degree. Although out-of-pocket costs of disputes are often covered by insurance, lost production time and use of the firm's resources to address the dispute are not covered.

The design and construction of any project incorporates the efforts of many individuals who, given human nature, are likely to disagree. Accordingly, the risk of a dispute's arising during the design and construction process is high. Although insurance can be purchased to cover the cost of legal defense in a malpractice action, the cost of collecting fees, for example, is not insurable. Also, the time and manpower costs of addressing fee disputes and malpractice claims, whether they have merit or not, are not insurable and must be absorbed by the design firm as a cost of doing business.

The design professional generally plans the time needed for delivering the agreed-upon services for a project. The amount of time needed to perform the various planning, design, and construction-related functions can be estimated in advance. However, the risk of becoming involved in time- and resource-consuming disputes in connection with the contracted-for project services is difficult to predict. The potential loss of otherwise billable time and the expense of addressing disputes cannot be insured. It can, however, be provided for by factoring in a number of hours of "dispute management time" when calculating an appropriate fee to charge for a project.

Given the common interest in taking a project to a successful conclusion, many such disputes are resolved amicably and with a minimum investment of time and expense. Accordingly, even though the risk of dispute is a high probability, it often is one with minimal consequences. Nevertheless, certain disputes require formal intervention to facilitate a conclusion. Formal intervention is usually arbitration or litigation in court. The notorious costs and time consumption of litigation have created a market for a wide spectrum of alternative dispute resolution services. These services bridge the gap between informal negotiation of disputes and the highly formalized and expensive litigation process.

Regardless of how and in which forum the dispute is addressed, there is no question that the design firm faces increased costs and risk of loss when a dispute moves from voluntary dispute negotiations to dependence upon an intervening authority. The risk of becoming involved in a dispute in which time and expense will be spent conforming to the procedures of the intervening authority is just as real and potentially debilitating as the risk of making an error that leads to professional liability.

This risk of disputes and claims is, to a large extent, outside the design professional's control. No matter how carefully the service is performed, there will always be a client or other individual or entity affected by that service who will find it necessary or appropriate to begin a dispute, make a claim, or file a lawsuit. Once the process is launched, it is difficult to stop. Our legal system highly values each individual's right to have her day in court. Accordingly, often despite doubtful or unclear evidence as to the merits of the claim, the design professional finds it necessary to participate in the litigation process through refining pleadings, extensive discovery, and, occasionally, trial. This costly process represents a low-probability but high-loss risk for the design firm that should be provided for through some formal risk management technique. If it is not provided for, the losses associated with costly litigation can be fatal to the design firm.

The risk of disputes can be managed by the design firm through a combination of techniques, including errors and omissions (E&O) insurance for the out-of-pocket costs of litigation and a dispute management factor in the fee structure. This could be either a *risk-of-dispute premium,* sometimes referred to as a *contingency factor,* added to the gross fee or an additional risk-of-dispute component added to the hourly rate structure. One key to making this work is to actually place the money in the firm's dispute cost fund.

Risk of Liability

The design professional also faces the risk of liability, that is, the risk of being held accountable for damage caused to other parties by improper or negligent conduct in the performance of design services. Liability can be either general liability or professional liability.

General liability is common to all types of business. Liability can arise out of circumstances such as a hazardous condition at the office that causes injury to a visitor or a nonprofessional activity such as driving a vehicle that becomes involved in an accident. Such risks are provided for through the purchase of commercial general liability and vehicle insurance policies.

The design professional who provides planning, design, or construction-related services continuously faces the risk that during the performance of the services there will be one or more "acts, errors, or omissions" that result in injury or damage to the client or some third party, thus exposing the design professional to *professional liability.* The most common categories of consequences of such "acts, errors, or omissions" are discussed in §§ 7.5 through 7.8. Before discussing consequences, however, it is useful to identify and review several general concepts common to all professional liability situations.

§ 7.3 Professional Liability Issues

The risk of committing errors and omissions when providing services can be more clearly defined as the risk of departing from the professional standard of care in the performance of services. To establish professional liability, the claimant must be able to demonstrate that the service provided departed from the professional standard of care. The exercise is typically, but not necessarily, accomplished through expert testimony. The claimant's expert witness must testify that the service provided did not, in some way, meet the appropriate professional standard of care. Of course, the design professional's defense also can rely on expert testimony to establish that the professional standard of care was met. If the disputing parties cannot agree on whether the professional standard of care was met and cannot settle the dispute, then a jury decides which of the experts to believe.

Traditionally, the jury was intended to be a jury of peers. However, the design professional is not judged by design professional peers in a jury trial but by nontechnical individuals. Thus, the design professional should be wary of allowing professional liability disputes to reach the point at which a jury will be making key decisions.

Professional liability claims often originate with the client's project expectations, which may not be clear in the client's own mind. The client also may not clearly communicate those expectations. Often, the design professional with experience on similar projects may fill in the information gaps by interpreting the client's expectations. If the design professional's understanding of the client's expectations and the client's actual expectations differ, there is a risk of dispute, claims, and possible loss.

Sometimes failure to take into account a project owner's reasonable expectations will be viewed as an error and a departure from the professional standard of care. For example, when a client/owner retains a design professional to design a building, the unstated expectation is that the design professional will be aware of and will conform the design to the applicable building codes. If the owner insists on certain building features violating applicable building codes, the design professional's compliance with the owner's request in violation of the building codes that later become the source of a claim can be viewed as an error if the design professional fails to raise the building code constraints as an objection to the owner's design criteria.

The foregoing example of an error is a point on a spectrum that encompasses, at one end, errors in judgment, and, at the other end, errors and omissions in the highly technical or mechanical aspects of the service. Technical errors can include mathematical errors and drafting inconsistencies. Somewhere in between are errors such as failure to use certain techniques in making design decisions or inappropriate application or implementation of design techniques.

The design professional's decisions that lead to malpractice claims can be made at various levels of decision-making and range from poor judgment to errors and omissions. Therefore, controlling the risk of professional liability requires a broad range of risk management techniques.

§ 7.4 Specific Professional Liability Risks

Professional liability claims against design professionals, whether justified or not, arise out of several typical categories of loss: (1) construction site injuries, (2) delay/extra claims, or (3) defects in the completed project. **Sections 7.5** through **7.7** examine each of these potential consequences of a design professional's "act, error, or omission."

§ 7.5 —Construction Site Injuries

The construction site injury claim is one of the most frequent error and omission (E&O) claim situations for the design professional. Construction is generally a hazardous activity, and accidents lead to claims and lawsuits.

Construction workers and construction site visitors or bystanders can sustain injuries leading to allegations that the design professional's services contributed to the causes of those injuries. To those not familiar with construction contracts and law, the design professional's presence at the construction site can create the appearance that he or she was in charge and should be held responsible for any hazardous conditions and the accidents that result.

The most frequent injury claim involves construction workers who file suit against on-site entities other than their employer. The employer is often protected from suit by the workers' compensation statutes. The theory of liability against the design professional can be either statutory (safe workplace statutes, for example) or negligence.

In certain states, statutes may require the person "in charge" or the project "owner" and the owner's agents and representatives to provide a safe place for workers. When an injury-causing accident occurs, such statutes provide an avenue of attack against those project participants who either have or appear to have responsibility for maintaining a safe workplace.

In addition to the statutory basis for liability, the construction worker can allege that the design professional's negligent performance of construction site services was a contributing cause of the accident and injury. To pursue such a theory of liability, the construction worker must be able to demonstrate that the design professional, among others, owed a duty of care to the construction worker, that the design professional's actions breached that duty of care, that the breach of the duty of care caused the accident and injury, and that the amount of damages resulted from the negligent breach of the design professional's duty of care.

The duty of care can be established either through contract language[1] or, when that is impossible, through evidence of the design professional's activities at the construction site. Occasionally, design professionals provide construction site services under a contract that either creates or gives the appearance of creating a duty of care by defining the design professional's obligations at the site in broad terms. One example of such broad language is the contractual undertaking to "make sure that the work is properly done by the contractor" or the contractual designation of the design professional as the owner's representative with the authority to stop work. Under court interpretations, such authority can make the design professional "in charge" of the work and therefore responsible and legally liable for accidents.[2]

The preferred language, as has been incorporated into the standard American Institute of Architects (AIA) contract documents, is that the design professional's on-site responsibilities are to "visit the site at intervals appropriate to the stage of construction . . . to become generally familiar with the progress and quality of the Work and to determine in general if the Work is proceeding in accordance with the Contract Documents . . . the Architect shall not be required to make exhaustive or continuous on-site inspections to check the quality or quantity of the Work."[3] The agreements also contain disclaimers of responsibility for methods, means, and techniques of performing the work and for project safety.[4] Normally, these

---

[1] The duty of care is typically created through the contract description of the service to be performed combined with § 1.8.1 of AIA Document B141, which states: "The Architect shall perform Basic and Additional Services as expeditiously as is consistent with professional skill and care and the orderly progress of the Work."

[2] McGovern v. Standish, 65 Ill. 2d 54, 357 N.E.2d 1134 (1976).

[3] AIA B141-1977, § 1.5.4.

[4] *See id.* § 1.5.5. In Brown v. Gamble Constr., 537 S.W.2d 685 (Mo. 1976), the court decided that the architects were under no duty to supervise construction unless they expressly agreed to do so. *See also* Kreiger v. J.E. Greiner Co., 282 Md. 50, 382 A.2d 1069 (1978); Porter v. Stevens, 24 Wash. App. 624, 602 P.2d 1192 (1979); Wheeler & Lewis v. Slifer, 195 Colo. 291, 577 P.2d 1092 (1978); Reber v. Chandler High School Dist. No. 202, 13 Ariz. App. 133, 474 P.2d 852 (1970). Other cases, although not contradictory, have imposed liability because of assumption of responsibility or silence as to responsibility for construction activity. *See* Duncan v. Pennington County Housing Auth., 283 N.W.2d 546 (S.D. 1979); Cutlip v. Lucky Stores, 325 A.2d 432 (Md. 1974); Erhart v. Hummonds, 232 Ark. 133, 334 S.W.2d 869 (1960).

activities are viewed as the realm of the general contractor and subcontractors. Despite such language, project owners occasionally insist on the design professional's participation on safety committees. Owners may require the design professional to watch for and report contractor violations of project safety requirements. When the design professional becomes engaged in such activities, either as a result of contract provisions or informal on-site practices, the injured worker is provided the evidence necessary to argue fact issues regarding the design professional's role. When litigation begins, this evidence keeps the design professional involved as a defendant in the lawsuit. Alternatively, if the contract does not provide evidence of involvement in safety-related concerns and if the injured worker is unable to develop any evidence of the design professional's involvement in safety-related aspects of the construction, the design professional may be successful in securing an early summary dismissal from the lawsuit. Thus, the design professional has a degree of control over the risks associated with worker injury litigation through clear contract language and on-site activities conforming to that language.

Breach of duty is the second element of negligence needed to establish liability for a construction accident. The plaintiff must establish the breach of duty through expert testimony concluding that the defendant design professional's performance of services was below the appropriate standard of care. For example, the plaintiff's expert might testify that a design professional who had undertaken a duty (by contract) to participate in job safety meetings and to monitor safety aspects of the construction activity should have prepared a checklist of daily inspections to perform and, therefore, would not have overlooked the inadequate trench excavation shoring that led to the collapse. The testimony might be that after the design professional became involved in the safety aspects of construction, failure to follow an affirmative inspection plan was a breach of duty. Examples of breach of duty are numerous and can include such actions or inactions as noticing a dangerous condition and failing to report it or insisting on conformance to a schedule despite dangerous site conditions.

The third element in a negligence action is causation, that is, the breach of duty must have caused the accidental injury. This can be a problem in failure to act cases. To overcome this problem, the courts have developed active and passive theories of negligence. In *active negligence,* the activity of the design professional causes the accident. Because the design professional usually is not in charge at the site, active negligence is a less likely source of liability. More common is *passive negligence,* in which a design professional fails to stop some activity that leads to an accident.

The last and often disputed element in a negligence action is damages. Typically, damages include out-of-pocket medical expenses (both past and future), lost wages (past and future), and other less tangible losses (such as companionship and consortium). Although out-of-pocket losses are easily proven, future employability and future medical expenses usually are disputed.

The design professional also can become a defendant in a lawsuit arising out of injuries to a construction site bystander who may have been struck by a falling object or who became involved in a traffic accident as a result of allegedly inadequate barricades or signage. The theory of liability against the design professional is negligent performance of services.

There are similarities between worker injury litigation and lawsuits brought by injured construction site visitors or by-passers. Questions regarding the scope of the design professional's responsibilities and obligations, whether they were properly carried out, whether failure to carry them out properly caused the injury, and the extent of recoverable damages also are addressed in passerby claims.

Managing the risk of liability for construction site injuries follows the elements discussed. First, the design professional must be careful to carve out and exclude those activities and responsibilities over which the professional has little or no control. This addresses the question of whether a duty exists. To the extent that the design professional can explicitly and clearly demonstrate that she had no duty with respect to site safety, the risk of liability is reduced. Beyond the contractual limitation of duty is the need to perform consistently within the contractual obligations and standards of care. This requires understanding the standard of care through education and training, including appropriate procedures for delivering construction site services. The damages that are the consequence of a given on-site accident are usually beyond the design professional's control.

§ 7.6 —Delay/Extra Claims

The delay/extra claim illustrates another type of design professional malpractice consequence. When the design professional undertakes to provide design and/or construction administration services, the contractor may allege that those services were a factor in causing construction delays and extra costs. Key aspects of this type of claim are privity of contract and recoverability of damages.

Claims for additional compensation were traditionally directed by the contractor to the owner, who then sought recovery from the design professional either as a third-party defendant or in a separate claim or action. The process followed the lines of contract law obligations between the parties involved in the construction. More recently, however, contractors have been allowed in many jurisdictions to pursue delay/extra claims directly against design professionals by using negligence theories.[5] As with

---

[5] *See* Normoyle-Berg & Assoc. v. Village of Deer Creek, 39 Ill. App. 3d 744, 350 N.E.2d 559 (1976); Shoffner Indus. v. W.B. Lloyd Constr. Co., 42 N.C. App. 259, 257 S.E.2d 50 (1979).

negligence actions by injured construction workers, the contractor must be able to demonstrate that the design professional owed a duty of care to the contractor in preparing the plans and specifications and providing construction site services, that the duty of care was breached by performance departing from the appropriate standard of care, that the substandard performance caused the contractor's delay and extra losses, and the amount of damages. Under this theory, the contractor can be viewed as a third-party beneficiary of the design professional's contract with the project owner. The argument is that if the negligent performance of the design professional's obligations causes damages to a foreseeable third party, then that third party, the contractor, should be allowed to recover those damages.

Issues related to quantification of damages and the recoverability of certain types of damages are key and often hotly debated. They do not appear to be issues over which the design professional has a great deal of control. Such control is limited to recommending restrictive construction contract language governing the recoverability of delay/extra damages by the contractor. For example, AIA Document A201 states in § 12.3.1 that if the contractor wants to make a claim for an increase in the contract sum, he must give the architect written notice within 20 days of the event causing the claim. Article 12 of AIA Document A201 governs the change order procedure. Section 12.1.3 defines methods for determining the cost or credit of change orders. Section 12.1.4 addresses the possibility that none of the procedures in § 12.1.3 may be effective in resolving the cost issues and that, ultimately, the cost of the work will then be determined by the architect based on what it cost to perform the change.

Active management of the delay/extra claim risk requires design professional initiatives including precise definition of services to be provided, combined with disclaimers of responsibility for various results over which the design professional has no control. It also entails the careful definition and implementation of predesign, design, and construction site service procedures that minimize the chances of disrupting the contractor's (and owner's) schedules and project cost estimates. Services are defined in the design professional's agreement. Examples of clearly defined services are in AIA Document B141 (1977 edition), Article 1, and in the Engineers Joint Contract Documents Committee (EJCDC) Standard Form of Agreement No. 1910-1 (1984 edition). Implementation of the services in a manner least likely to adversely affect the contractor's work requires the establishment of procedures such as daily or weekly meetings to discuss obstacles and how they can be removed, the maintenance of project diaries, and definition of specific steps the contractor must take to keep the design professional's on-site representative informed of activity. Much of this is project communication procedure.

A number of specific aspects of project management can become factors in the delay/extra claim. These include adequacy of predesign investigation, clarity and understandability of plans and specifications, consistency between plans and specifications, and clear and enforced procedures for responding to contractor requests for clarification, as well as for processing shop drawing review requests. The predesign investigation must be sufficient to determine existing physical conditions as well as regulatory and other constraints. The plans and specifications must be understandable, clear, sufficiently specific but not overly restrictive, and consistent. The construction administration procedures must allow sufficient control without interfering with the contractor's ability to get the job done. Each of these aspects of the design professional's services has, at one time or another, been a factor in contractor delay/extra claims.

§ 7.7 —Defects in the Completed Project

The third possible consequence of design professional malpractice or, more specifically, errors and omissions in plans and specifications or providing construction-related services, is a project defect that leads to a claim. Examples might include injuries to a completed project user caused by inadequate safety features, improper or inadequate performance, such as leaky roofs or windows, an improperly functioning heating, ventilation, and air conditioning system (HVAC), waste water treatment facilities that do not produce an effluent conforming to regulatory constraints, and production facilities that fail to meet preestablished operating criteria.

There are often multiple causes of such project defects. They can include poorly thought-out design, construction defects for which the design professional can be partially held responsible, improperly selected equipment, equipment not conforming to performance specifications, improper maintenance by the owner, and many others.

Improper design can be a key factor in an ultimate project user's injury lawsuit. For example, failure to provide adequate site distances at an intersection, inadequate lighting of restaurant stairs, or inadequate barriers between a parking lot and an adjacent pond can become the source of liability exposure for a design professional. To control the risk of an ultimate user's injury lawsuit, the design professional must include ultimate user safety considerations in the design. Occasionally such decisions may include balancing costs against incremental safety improvements. When serious injuries are possible, the risk-aware design professional will be uncompromising on cost.

Improperly specified or accepted equipment can lead to unreliable or inadequate performance. Frequent examples of improper equipment selection are found in connection with HVAC systems. Inability to control temperature or humidity can lead to discomfort as well as damage to ceilings, walls, and floors. Occasionally, designs do not meet special requirements, such as those of a contact lens manufacturer, leading to claims and litigation.

Although the design professional is not responsible for the contractor's failure to construct and/or install in accordance with the plans and specifications, the construction site services portion of the design professional's agreement for services can create an obligation to guard the owner against nonconforming performance of the construction contract. Accordingly, when a project defect is later discovered, as happens in condominium projects, for example, the design professional becomes a defendant in the lawsuit by the condominium owners. The claimants argue that the design professional failed to perform the guarding functions adequately and thereby contributed to the loss. The design professional's exposure is aggravated when the developer or contractor primarily responsible for the defects is not financially viable.

Improper maintenance also can be a factor in project defect claims and disputes. Examples include failure to periodically apply sealant to concrete garages, failure to periodically clean and adjust HVAC systems, failure to clean leaves from gutters, thus allowing water and ice roof damage to occur, and many similar circumstances. Evidence of such factors can reduce the amount of damages the project owner is allowed to recover for defective design and/or construction.

The design professional can reduce and control the risk of project defect claims through the use of modern, quality design techniques and documentation. In years past, many design decisions were based on expense and rules of thumb. Modern techniques, such as computer simulation of water distribution or drainage systems or HVAC systems and materials testing techniques, allow much greater predictability of performance and reduce the probability of project defect claims.

However, the economics of using such techniques, in a competitive design service market where some design professionals are willing to take risks to save the client money, make it difficult for the conscientious and risk-wise design professional to compete for assignments. The design professional must take into account the crushing costs of claim litigation, including the loss of otherwise productive time, and ultimately higher malpractice insurance rates that result when design professionals try to cut corners.

In addition to strict adherence to the highest design standards, documentation of the design and construction process can reduce the risk of both cost and loss in addressing project defect claims. Proper documentation can be evidence that the appropriate techniques were used and can demonstrate the chronology of the evolution of a problem to help pinpoint the exact cause. Even when the design professional does make an error or omission, proper documentation can greatly reduce the cost of addressing the claim.

The end product of a designer's effort is a set of plans and specifications. Those plans and specifications reflect hundreds or thousands of decisions. A quality designer will document those decisions by maintaining design notebooks organized in such a way that someone reviewing the design will be able to find the rationale for sizing a component or selecting a given material. If discussions with a manufacturer or a regulatory agency took place in connection with a specific decision, notes of such discussions should be easy to locate. If others placed constraints on the design, those constraints should be documented in the notebook. If design options were identified and compared during the design process, then the entire exercise should be documented in the designer's notebook.

Similarly, the design professional's on-site representative should keep detailed logs and meeting notes. When problems arise, they should be noted in the log. Meeting notes should be written up and circulated to participants for their comment and decisions should be confirmed in writing.

The existence of such documentation is strong evidence that the design professional used a disciplined approach to the design and construction process. The absence of such a notebook leads to a suspicion that the process was undisciplined and perhaps unreliable.

Action-oriented individuals, as many in the construction business are, dislike paperwork. It is viewed as interfering with action, demonstrating mistrust, or reflecting a defensive attitude toward work. Yet the lack of clear and accurate records of the design and construction process probably adds millions of dollars annually to the cost of addressing and resolving disputes and claims. There is no question that proper record-keeping is an essential element in the design professional's goal of helping the client effectively and efficiently achieve project goals.

§ 7.8 —Risk of Liability for Others

The design professional also faces the risk of liability for the actions of others. The risk can arise from the activities of subconsultants and the operation of joint and several liability rules of law.

The design professional occasionally subcontracts certain services to subconsultants. If those subconsultants fail to perform adequately, the design professional can become vicariously liable for the deficiencies. This can be a serious problem if the subconsultant is uninsured or inadequately insured. These situations typically arise when the architect subcontracts for structural or HVAC engineering services. When a defect is discovered, the owner looks to the architect with whom it contracted for services. The architect then adds the subconsultant engineer to the dispute or suit as a third-party defendant. If the third-party defendant is financially responsible, the architect's loss may be limited to the costs of lost productive time and litigation. The actual liability can be passed through to the subconsultant.

Sometimes the agreement between the architect and the subconsultant contains indemnification language that requires the subconsultant to reimburse the architect for costs incurred in litigating the subconsultant's design error issues. However, as a practical matter, recovering the architect's costs of litigation, even with such indemnification language, can be difficult. One obstacle to enforcement of indemnification language is the need to conclusively demonstrate that the entire problem was exclusively caused by the subconsultant. Often, a sufficient argument can be made that the architect's actions or inaction sufficiently contributed to the problem to make the indemnification provision unenforceable.

The second source of risk for the architect is the subconsultant's potential lack of financial resources. If the subconsultant is uninsured or underinsured, the architect can be held vicariously liable for the acts, errors, and omissions of its subconsultant. One avenue for the owner who sustains the loss is to argue that the architect negligently selected a subconsultant to work on the project.

Liability for others also can arise by operation of law. Many states have joint and several liability laws. When the damage to the claimant is determined to be the result of multiple causes, including deficiencies in the design professional's services, the law may allow the damaged or injured party to collect the damages from any financially viable entity. On occasion, the contractor is uninsured for the particular problem, has inadequate financial resources, or is no longer in business. A design professional who has been allocated 5 percent or 10 percent of the damages by the court based on liability may end up paying the entire amount of the damages if none of the other parties can pay.

The risk of vicarious liability (liability for others) can be controlled through a number of techniques. These include careful screening of project participants, enforcement of contractual financial responsibility requirements (including insurance), and careful definition of responsibility for various aspects of a project.

MANAGING PROFESSIONAL LIABILITY RISKS

§ 7.9 Relationships

There are two aspects of relationships as a risk management tool. The first is creating a project team that minimizes the risk of dispute and poor performance, both factors in any cooperative project effort. The second is developing project management methods and techniques that foster good will and cooperation during the planning, design, and construction phases of the project.

The design and construction of a project is a complex matter requiring the cooperation of a number of participants. These participants form a team whose goal is to deliver a completed project meeting the owner's expectations. Only individuals with reputations for integrity, professionalism, and quality performance should be allowed on the project team. To the extent that the team can work together responsibly towards its objective, the risks of disputes, claims, accidents, delays and extras, project defects, and liability for others are substantially reduced.

Contracts and legal processes are available for defining relationships among the project team and resolving the disputes that arise from them. However, relying solely on contracts and legal procedures to make the project team reach its goal is foolhardy. The design professional should not become involved in a project where the participants are known to be antagonistic, quarrelsome, and opportunistic. If the personal chemistry of cooperation is not the basis upon which the project team functions, the likelihood of disputes, claims, and lawsuits is great, resulting in a substantial loss of time and money for all parties involved.

In addition to selecting the project team carefully, it is necessary to foster good will and cooperation during the progress of design and construction. Occasionally, there is a difficult gap between maintaining goodwill and enforcing contractual obligations and requirements. The design professional who bridges that gap can limit the risk of professional liability exposure.

§ 7.10 Contracts

The second major tool for managing risk of loss is the contract. The design professional generally has a contract with the project owner and often influences the owner's contract with the contractor. Input into the definition of these contractual relationships provides an opportunity to control the risk of loss. The contract performs the functions of (1) defining responsibilities, (2) allocating risks, (3) expressly limiting liabilities, (4) implicitly limiting liability, and (5) requiring other project participants to meet financial responsibility requirements, including maintenance of adequate insurance.

One key function of the contract is to define responsibilities for certain aspects of the work. The planning, design, and construction of a project involves many tasks. Prior experience, local custom, and many other considerations play a role in determining which project team member will be responsible for a given job. Tasks generally include obtaining adequate surveys and site inspection, regulatory approvals, and the owner's performance criteria, designing specific aspects of a project, and various aspects of construction administration, including scheduling, processing of contractor payments, and quality control. When responsibility for certain tasks is not clearly assigned through contract, a dispute and liability can result. The design professional and the client, the owner, take into account various considerations in defining the scope of the services to be performed. Considerations can include the size and complexity of the project, budgeting constraints, the owner's willingness to delegate broad responsibility to a single design professional, or the need to coordinate a number of specialized design professionals if the owner's in-house capability allows it. In addition to taking into account the owner's capabilities and desires, it is necessary to consider the design firm's capabilities and limitations.

Another function of the contract is risk allocation. Certain aspects of the design and construction process are inherently risky. Siting risks, including those associated with obtaining project approvals and geological uncertainties, should be allocated to the owner through contract provisions. The owner can limit the risk of site adequacy through thorough investigation.

Another category of project risk is the risk of construction site accidents. The contractor ultimately assumes the responsibility for delivering a project meeting specifications for a predetermined price. The means and methods used to accomplish this objective are under the contractor's control. Accordingly, it is appropriate to assign the risk of accidents associated with those means and methods to the contractor. This can be done by contract language consistent with this view. One example of such language might be a contract requirement that the contractor assume responsibility for establishing and maintaining safety procedures at the construction site.

The design professional also can insist upon other contract provisions that either reduce or allocate the risk of known uncertainties. For example, the construction contract may allocate the risk of weather, labor problems, construction loan interest rates, new technology, financing, or project safety either to the owner or the contractor. Contract language can be used further to expressly limit the parties' scope of liability exposure. For example, the design professional can insist on provisions limiting liability exposure to the amount of the fee paid in connection with that project. The effectiveness of such provisions should be evaluated in light of the law in the state where the contract is entered into and performed.

§ 7.11 —Implied Liability Limitations

The design professional's liability can be impliedly limited through specific and narrow definition of service obligations in the contract with the client/owner.

Design professionals sensitized to the risks of being in charge of construction activity are careful to contractually limit their on-site responsibilities to observation for the purpose of determining that the progress and quality of the work generally conforms to the intent of the design. Consistent with ent with this, the construction contract must specifically make the contractor responsible for the "means, methods and techniques of construction" and construction site safety.

With such contractual safeguards in place, the design professional often can escape liability for construction site injuries. Nevertheless, two aspects of this type of claim persist and cause problems for the design professional. The first is that the contract language cannot prevent the injured party from bringing the design professional into the suit, which necessitates the expenditure of time and money toward removal efforts. Sometimes the design professional can become disengaged from the litigation relatively inexpensively (if up to several thousand dollars can be viewed as inexpensive) through persuading the plaintiff to voluntarily dismiss the suit or through a motion for summary judgment. A series of such litigation "successes" can become a serious drain of resources for a small design firm. The second debilitating aspect of a construction site injury claim is that evidence of the design professional's activities inconsistent with the limiting contract language will defeat the effort to secure a summary dismissal and will necessitate the design professional's participation in the lawsuit through expensive and time-consuming discovery and probably through the trial itself. Once it becomes apparent that the design professional will not be removed from the lawsuit through a summary dismissal, the nuisance value of the claim (often used in evaluating an appropriate settlement contribution) increases substantially.

Evidence of inconsistencies with the contract language could be a worker's testimony that she saw the design professional at the site giving instructions to workers about how to build some aspect of the project; that despite contractual limitations, the design professional participated in job-site safety meetings; or that the design professional, despite the contract language, became involved in "means, methods and techniques" or project safety concerns.

The design professional with limited on-site responsibilities and on-site performance consistent with the contract does not face substantial liability exposure for construction site injuries. However, there are the costs of addressing such claims. Also, on occasion, when the primarily liable party cannot be held liable (perhaps because of protection by the workers' compensation statute) or is not financially responsible (bankrupt, out of business) and the plaintiff is able to articulate a plausible theory of liability against the design professional, substantial liability exposure can result.

§ 7.12 —Contractual Requirement of Contractor's Insurance

Another layer of protection for the design professional can be achieved through insistence on contractual financial responsibility requirements for the contractor, including performance bonds, commercial general liability insurance, and other forms of financial responsibility. For example, both the project owner and the design professional can require, through the construction contract, that they be listed as additional named insureds on the contractor's commercial general liability policy. If this provision is enforced and implemented and if the owner and design professional become defendants in a lawsuit arising exclusively out of the contractor's negligent activity, the contractor's insurer may be required to provide a defense for the owner and design professional. However, because such policies typically exclude coverage for liability arising out of professional activities, and because allegations against the design professional are typically professional negligence, such coverage can be of limited value.

A second option for protecting the design professional against defense and loss exposure in connection with the contractor's activity is to require either the owner or the general contractor to purchase owner's and contractor's protective (OCP) insurance coverage. The owner and potentially the owner's agents or representatives, such as the design firm, are covered for contingent liability for the contractor's activities. This type of protection should be discussed with an insurance broker knowledgeable in construction risk and insurance.

§ 7.13 Communication

The third tool for limiting the risks associated with design and construction-related services is communication. Communication as a risk management tool can be broken down into several components, including recognizing the appropriate people or entities (channels) with whom to communicate, creating specific procedures, and documenting meetings and decisions.

Channels. The project team must establish and maintain effective communication channels. Channels relate to the roles of the owner, design professional, and contractor and their representatives. When problems arise, proper communication channels can be crucial in controlling the situation and preventing it from deteriorating into a dispute or litigation. For example, the architect at the construction site, in the interest of "clarifying a construction drawing," may begin directing the construction workers on how to perform the work; the project engineer may direct a contractor regarding a sequence of work that turns out to be inconsistent with the contractor's work plan; or an informal comment by the project owner may get misinterpreted as an instruction to change the design. Using formalized communication channels can reduce the risk of misunderstanding.

Procedures. Creating and enforcing communication procedures also can be a factor in reducing the risk of disputes and claims. Weekly project meetings, monthly reports, and specific procedures for addressing certain predictable types of problems that arise during the design and construction process keep all the project team members informed and give them an opportunity to identify and address problems and issues at an early stage in the process. This can involve standardization of communications, similar to how airline pilots, law enforcement officers, or military people communicate. Developing and using precise, objective phrases and printed forms when delivering messages can prevent problems.

Documentation. The third important communication tool is documentation. Project meetings that are not documented by meeting notes exchanged later can become the source of miscommunication and misunderstanding. Similarly, meetings and decisions that are not confirmed in writing may not be implemented or may be implemented based upon the interpretation and understanding of one of the parties and inconsistent with the interpretation and understanding of another. Documentation also facilitates fact finding when a dispute develops. The cost of fact finding during litigation can become a major burden to the design professional.

§ 7.14 Quality Control

The fourth risk management tool can be viewed as the design professional's quality control system. To the extent that top quality design and construction-related services are provided, the design professional reduces the risk of liability exposure. Quality control can take the form of checklists, insistence on predesign and preconstruction site investigation, insistence on the use of certain design techniques, even if they may result in increased design costs for the owner, and review procedures.

INSURANCE AS RISK MANAGEMENT TECHNIQUE

§ 7.15 Errors and Omissions Insurance

The last tool for managing professional liability risks is insurance. Various forms of insurance coverage are available and routinely purchased by the design professional. The most prominent, and perhaps most important, to the design professional's practice is professional liability coverage, which is often referred to as *errors and omissions coverage,* or E&O. Professional liability coverage for design professionals generally has been available throughout the latter half of this century. It has developed from a somewhat exotic form of insurance coverage to one that is now routinely purchased.

Today, there are more than two dozen insurance companies providing E&O coverage for architects and engineers. It is important to recognize that there is no accepted industry coverage form, and terms and conditions of coverage vary with each company. **Sections 7.16** through **7.28** discuss the general approach to coverage taken by E&O insurers and some of the more important distinctions. The decision to purchase E&O coverage may have a significant impact on a design professional's practice. Likewise, the selection of an E&O insurer may determine whether or not a particular claim is covered and may have an impact on the design professional's day-to-day practice.

§ 7.16 —Claims-Made Provisions

To the authors' knowledge, all architects' and engineers' E&O policies are written on a *claims-made basis.* It is inaccurate, however, to assume that all claims-made policies operate in the same manner. A pure claims-made policy is one in which the event that triggers coverage occurs within the policy period. Some insurance companies require yet another event to occur before coverage is triggered: the reporting to the company of the claim within the policy period. This is often referred to as *claims-made and reported* coverage. Some insurance companies that impose the added reporting requirement allow the insured a grace period of 30 to 60 days after the expiration of the policy to report the claim to the company.

Claims-made and reported coverage is intended to assure prompt reporting of claims. During the design and construction phase of a building project, there may be a number of events that may be defined as a claim by a designer's E&O policy. The designer must be aware of when one of these events rises to the level of a claim to assure timely reporting to the insurance company. A danger exists when the designer fails to recognize that a claim, as defined by the policy, has been made. If the reporting occurs after the expiration of the policy and the applicable grace period, the designer will most likely be denied coverage. Therefore, on its face, claims-made and reported coverage is narrower than pure claims-made coverage because pure claims-made coverage does not have the reporting requirement as a condition precedent. Adding the reporting requirement to the claims-made provision became more popular in the latter half of the 1980s as insurance companies attempted to avoid surprises associated with late-reported claims. The insured must thoroughly examine the policy to determine the nature of its reporting provisions and the definition of a claim to assure timely notification.

The pure claims-made policy maintains a more traditional approach towards claims reporting, typically requiring either immediate written notice or notice provided as soon as practicable. Determining whether or not notice is timely will depend upon the facts of the situation and the applicable state law governing such provisions.

§ 7.17 —What Is a Claim?

What constitutes a claim can vary depends upon which insurance company is providing coverage. For example, one insurance company defines a claim as "a demand received by the insured for money or services, including the service of suit or institution of arbitration."[6] This is a rather straightforward approach, and many insurance companies adopt similar approaches to the definition of claim. Significant differences, however, exist. For example, another insurance company defines a claim as "the insured's receipt of a written demand and, including the service of process and the institution of arbitration proceeding, seeking money or the remedying of an alleged defect."[7] The distinction between the former and the latter definitions is that the latter company requires that the demand also be in writing.

Less subtle distinctions also can be found. Consider this definition: "Claim" means:

1. a demand for money or services, or the filing of a suit or institution of arbitration or mediation proceedings naming any insured and alleging an actual or alleged error, omission or negligent act arising out of the conduct of your professional practice; or
2. an actual event or alleged event which has resulted in damages and of which any insured has knowledge; or
3. an actual event or alleged event which may cause damage and of which any insured has knowledge.[8]

Given this definition of claim, the insured not only must notify the E&O insurance company of demands made, but also of circumstances that may give rise to such demands to assure timely notice.

Failure to understand the reporting requirements of an insured's policy may have disastrous results. Broader reporting requirements require greater care by the insured to comply with policy conditions. Consider the policy in which the definition of claim includes knowledge of an occurrence "which may result in damages." An insured may not recognize that mere knowledge of potential damages is cause to notify the insurer. Because insureds often change insurers, it is important to recognize that the new insurer may treat the definition of claim differently from the expiring carrier.

---

[6] Evanston Insurance Co. Architects and Engineers Professional Liability Policy, Doc. No. EIC 1101 (Jan. 1981).

[7] Homestead Insurance Co. Professional Liability Insurance Policy for Architects and Engineers, Doc. No. H A&E (Oct. 1987).

[8] DPIC Companies Professional Liability Policy, Doc. No. DP-6001-0 (Aug. 1986).

§ 7.18 —Discovery or Awareness Clauses

Some policies contain language providing coverage for claims made after the policy expires. These are usually identified as *discovery* or *awareness provisions.* Policies containing a discovery provision allow the insured to advise the insurer during the policy period of circumstances that would subsequently give rise to a claim against the insured by reason of an act, error, or omission for which coverage would otherwise be afforded. These provisions typically require written notice to be received before the expiration of coverage. Thus, if the policy has a discovery provision, coverage can be extended for claims made subsequent to the expiration of the policy.

It is important to keep in mind that not all policies allow the insured to establish coverage for later-made claims. E&O policies exclude coverage for claims arising out of circumstances known to the insured before inception of coverage, so the discovery provision plays an extremely important role. Without such a provision, an insured may be stuck with renewing the current carrier until all potential claims have either materialized into claims as defined in the policy or have otherwise been resolved.

Discovery provisions also should be examined carefully for subtle distinctions. One policy provision contains the following language: "If, in the opinion of the company, the information provided about such circumstances is inadequate, the company shall inform the insured that any claim made after the policy period will not be covered."[9] If an insured or counsel representing the insured faces such a provision, care must be exercised to satisfy its requirements.

The discovery provision must not be confused with what is known as an *extended reporting period,* which provides coverage for claims made subsequent to the expiration of the policy for a specified period of time, provided that the act, error, or omission occurred before the expiration of the policy. Although both the extended reporting and discovery provisions require that the act, error, or omission occur before the expiration of the policy, they operate in very different ways. A typical discovery provision requires notice of the potential claim before the expiration of coverage; however, coverage will be afforded for the claim should it occur any time thereafter. The extended reporting period is not designed to deal with potential claims; thus, notification before the expiration of the policy is not required. However, if coverage is to attach, a claim must occur within a specified period of time.

The duration of extended discovery provisions and their general availability tend to vary with market capacity. Currently, if an extended reporting

---

[9] Homestead Insurance Co. Professional Liability Insurance Policy for Architects and Engineers, Doc. No. Form H A&E (Feb. 1989).

period is available, the duration ranges between one and five years. It most likely will require an additional premium, and it is of greatest value to insureds who, for some reason, cease purchasing E&O coverage.

§ 7.19 —Typical Coverage

In addition to the claims-made requirements discussed in **§ 7.16**, the typical architects' and engineers' policy provides coverage in the following manner:

> The company will pay on behalf of the insured all sums in excess of the deductible amount stated in the Declarations, which the insured shall become legally obligated to pay as damages by reasons of any act, error or omission committed or alleged to have been committed by the insured, or any person or organization for whom the insured is legally liable, provided always that the insured's legal liability arises out of the performance of professional services as described in the Declarations, and the insured has no knowledge of such act, error or omission on the effective date of the policy.[10]

This type of coverage is essentially a broad form agreement subject to certain exclusions. Given this type of coverage, the company agrees to "pay on behalf of the insured." This is distinguished from an indemnity type coverage under which the insurer will only reimburse the insured. Although generally an exception, some E&O policies for design professionals are written on an indemnity basis. The central feature of this coverage is that the claim must arise out of professional services described in the declarations. Insureds or those counseling them must take care that the description of their professional services is complete and accurate.

§ 7.20 —Limits of Liability

Coverage for architects and engineers has changed considerably during the 1980s. Losses of the late 1970s and the early 1980s led to an industry response, which included changes in the treatment of limits of liability. Most architects' and engineers' E&O policies (except when prohibited by state regulation) provide *cost inclusive coverage.* Cost inclusive coverage is designed so that the limits of liability are reduced by defense expense payments. Therefore, if the policy has a $100,000 limit of liability and defense

---

[10] Evanston Insurance Co. Architects and Engineers Professional Liability Policy, Doc. No. EIC 1101 (Jan. 1981).

costs are $25,000, only $75,000 will be left to satisfy a judgment or settle the claim. Limits that operate in this fashion have a significant impact on the resolution of claims. Counsel representing an architect or engineer must immediately determine whether or not the limits of liability are cost inclusive to determine the appropriate strategy for resolving the claim. The limits available vary by insurance company but range from as low as $100,000 to as high as $15 million.

§ 7.21 —Deductibles

There are numerous ways in which a deductible may apply to a given claim. The amount of the deductible varies depending upon the size of the firm and is usually equal to 1 percent to 2 percent of the firm's gross revenues. A firm may be able to obtain a larger deductible, provided its financial condition satisfies the requirements of the company. A larger deductible will lower the premium. Likewise, should the insured firm seek a lower deductible, an increase in the premium usually will be required. The most common deductible is called *loss and expense,* which requires the insured to pay both loss and defense expenses as they are incurred up to the amount of the deductible.

In some instances, an insured might be able to purchase, at an additional premium, a *loss-only deductible,* which requires the insured to satisfy the deductible when and if a judgment is paid or payments made to settle the claim. Thus, no matter how much money was incurred to defend a claim, all defense expenses will be borne by the insurance company. This form of deductible option is quite favorable to the insured because it allows the insured to have significant latitude in defending a claim without incurring costs. However, this type of deductible may potentially discourage the prompt resolution of claims because it may operate as a financial disincentive to the insured to settle. If, however, the limits of liability of the coverage are reduced by defense costs, an insured may feel the need to preserve the limit, thus restricting this financial disincentive.

A variation of the loss-only deductible is the *defense cost sharing deductible.* With this type of deductible, the insurance company will pay a share of the defense costs, typically 75 percent to 80 percent, with the insured paying the balance of expenses incurred until the deductible is exhausted. This type of deductible option attempts to reduce the immediate impact of defense expenses on the insured, while maintaining an incentive for the insured to cost effectively resolve a claim.

Insurers are constantly coming up with innovative approaches to deductibles. For example, an *aggregate deductible* is another variation. Under this type of coverage, an insured must pay the deductible for each claim until a certain amount has been expended. This is typically two or three times the deductible amount. After that, the insured's deductible obligation may either be waived entirely or substantially reduced. Because the deductible selection may have a significant impact on risk management activities, architects and engineers should be aware of the available options.

§ 7.22 —Consent to Settle

The impact of deductible selection on settlement may be affected by a *consent to settle* feature. Typically, the policy provides that the insurance company will not settle any claim without the consent of the insured. However, should the insured refuse to consent to a recommended settlement by the company and elect to contest the claim or continue any legal proceedings in connection with the claim, then the company will limit the liability for the claim to the amount for which the claim could have been settled plus expenses incurred up to the date of the settlement.

§ 7.23 —Who Is an Insured?

The identity of the insured is usually contained in the declarations page. Therefore, care must be exercised to assure that all entities, corporations, proprietorships, and the like are properly listed. Further, other insureds may be added as additional named insureds or simply additional insureds. There is a distinction as to how coverage applies to these additional entities: an *additional named insured* is treated as an insured in the same fashion as the named insured; an *additional insured,* however, is typically only covered for claims arising out of activities by the additional insured on behalf of the named insured.

There is also a class of insureds who are insureds by definition. An *insured* is usually defined to include any partner, director, officer, or employee of the named insured while acting in the course of duties conducted by that person for and on behalf of the named insured solely in the professional capacity as described in the policy.

§ 7.24 —Single or Combination Claims

An issue that commonly arises is whether or not a particular claim is actually one claim or a combination of claims. This is critical because it may determine the number of policies involved and whether more than one limit or, perhaps, more than one deductible applies.

In § **7.17** a claim was defined as "the receipt of a demand for money or services." Often included is an additional definition entitled *single* claim, which has been defined in one policy as "two or more claims arising out of a single act, error or omission shall be treated as a single claim."[11] Thus, it is conceivable that one lawsuit will have a number of claims to which the same policy applies. Consider an action against an architect by a developer arising out of the design and construction of a housing development consisting of several independent structures. The developer may claim a design deficiency in the roof of one structure and, perhaps, a foundation deficiency in another. The developer claims damages arising out of these defects in one lawsuit. In this situation, the damages complained of do not appear to be related and should be treated as two single claims to which a single date claim made attaches. In this scenario, both claims would fall under the same policy; however, two deductibles would apply, as well as potentially two single-claim limits of liability if an aggregate limit were applicable to single limits.

Sometimes, a number of different lawsuits clearly concern a single claim. Consider a claim for bodily injuries arising out of a bleacher collapse. Although there may be a number of different lawsuits arising out of the event, all demands against the insured would be treated as a single claim. It is possible that the demands made against the insured would span more than one policy period. In that situation, all demands would relate back to the date when the first claim was made. Careful examination of the facts and how they apply to the policy is necessary to determine the applicable policy period, limits, and deductibles.

§ 7.25 —Exclusions

A typical E&O policy for design professionals provides for a broad form type of coverage, which is subject to various exclusions. A review of the many policies currently available indicates that the number of exclusions ranges from less than 10 to as many as 24. Of course, the number of exclusions without further analysis is not an accurate indication of the breadth of coverage.

Certain exclusions are common and found in nearly all policies, such as an exclusion regarding liabilities of others. This exclusion and its operation must be taken into account in connection with the insured's professional services agreement. These agreements routinely contain some form of indemnification agreement that may expose the designer to liability broader than the coverage.

---

[11] *Id.*

The effect of the contractual liability exclusion can be modified or eliminated by purchasing what is known as *contractual liability coverage.* Depending upon the insurance company involved, coverage under the E&O policy may be purchased for liability assumed by contract. This additional coverage is typically provided by an endorsement. Because the amount of coverage varies by insurance company, the endorsement should be examined carefully.

Asbestos and pollution exclusions are also common to all policies. These exclusions must be closely examined to determine what coverage, if any, the insured may have in connection with asbestos and pollution exposures.

It is also common for policies to exclude claims arising out of insolvency or bankruptcy, a claim by one insured against another, the ownership or operation of a watercraft or automobile, express warranties or cost estimates being exceeded, acts of discrimination, punitive damages, intentional acts and fraud, and claims by an employee arising out of the course of employment for which an insured may be liable under any workers' compensation law.

Although these exclusions commonly are encountered, it is a mistake to assume that all E&O policies are the same with regard to exclusions. One policy contains exclusions regarding certain types of projects. This exclusion applies to "claims arising out of operations in connection with bridges, tunnels or dams." This same policy also excludes, "claims arising out of activities at fairs or exhibitions unless the loss is related to a permanent structure."[12] This particular insurer is apparently responding to adverse claim results in connection with those types of projects. Similarly, another exclusion expressed the insurer's unwillingness to cover claims arising out of an insured's design/build activities.

These less common exclusions demonstrate the need for designers and those representing them to review the policy form. It is important to keep in mind that if during the course of a particular policy period the insured contemplates a change in activities, the policy should be reviewed to ascertain what coverage limitations may apply. Some policies exclude claims for damages arising out of bodily injury or property damage. This exclusion is most likely encountered when the architects' and engineers' liability coverage is written on a miscellaneous professional liability form.

[12] International Surplus Lines Insurance Co. Architects and Engineers Professional Liability Policy, Doc. No. ISLIC 112 (May 1978).

§ 7.26 Project and Practice Coverage

Practice coverage is typically an annual policy designed to cover claims arising out of the insured's practice in general. *Project coverage,* on the other hand, is designed to provide coverage for claims arising out of a specific project. Project coverage is primarily intended to satisfy the requirements of owners who want to be assured of a certain limit that will not be depleted by claims arising out of other projects. Another distinguishing feature of project coverage is that it is usually designed to cover the design team rather than a single insured. This simplifies the process of obtaining sufficient coverage for all design team members.

If a designer has project coverage on one or more projects, typically the practice policy will be amended to exclude coverage for claims arising out of a specific project. When this occurs, the premium for the practice coverage will be reduced to reflect the diminished exposure. Project coverage also makes it easier for the design professional to charge the appropriate cost of coverage to the specific project.

Some companies offer increased limits for a specific project. This coverage is appropriate for a designer who has practice coverage and is required to maintain a minimum limit of liability for a particular project that is higher than desired for the practice policy. For example, an insured who otherwise carries a limit of liability of $500,000 may be required to carry $1 million to secure a job in connection with a public project. If the designer is dealing with a company that offers this type of coverage, an additional $500,000 of coverage will be provided for the specific project. This type of coverage, in essence, provides excess coverage to build necessary limits but not a separate limit of liability.

§ 7.27 Wrap-Up Coverage

Increasingly, major construction projects have used what are sometimes referred to as wrap-up programs in an effort to provide all desired insurance coverages in a single program. *Wrap-up coverage* is an owner-controlled insurance program that can include workers' compensation and employers' liability, general liability, errors and omissions, and surety bonds, as well as automobile liability. The purpose of putting together a wrap-up program is to reduce costs and increase purchasing power. In addition, centralizing the purchase of coverage helps assure that adequate coverage is being obtained.

A wrap-up program is purchased by the owner and is comprised of a number of different policies, likely issued by a number of different insurers.

The wrap-up program is tailored to meet the insurance requirements of the owner on a given project, which might include professional and general liability coverage for the design team. This coverage would be written on a project basis and would only cover the design professional for claims in connection with the project. The design professional would, therefore, need to maintain independent coverage for the protection of the practice. The benefits to the designer of being an insured under a wrap-up program include clear allocation of insurance costs to a specific project that might enable passing insurance costs on to the owner as an additional project expense. To the extent specific projects are covered under wrap-up programs, the designer can reduce the cost of practice coverage.

E&O coverage for architects and engineers as discussed in this chapter can be provided in the context of a wrap-up program. In essence, the program would provide a project policy limited to claims arising out of the project, with all design professionals covered under the E&O portion of the policy.

§ 7.28 Related Coverage

In addition to E&O coverage, the design professional typically purchases and maintains general liability or comprehensive liability coverage. The purpose of this insurance is to provide coverage against claims for damages including bodily injury or property damage caused by an accident or occurrence arising out of specific hazards. Like the E&O coverage, the extent of coverage depends upon the insuring agreements, conditions, and exclusions. A typical exclusion for architects and engineers contained in the general liability policy is as follows:

> This insurance does not apply to "bodily injury," "property damage," "personal injury" or "advertising injury" arising out of the rendering or failure to render any professional services by or for you, including:
>
> 1. The preparing, approving, or failing to prepare or approve maps, drawings, opinions, reports, surveys, change orders, designs or specifications; and
> 2. Supervisory, inspection or engineering services.[13]

Thus, if a claim is made against a designer arising out of a construction-related accident and it is determined that this exclusion applies, coverage would not be available under the general liability policy. However, because the E&O policy provides coverage for bodily injury as well as property

[13] Copyright Insurance Services Office, Inc., Form CG 22 43 (11-85).

damage, it would be a source of coverage for this type of claim. The issue, however, of whether construction-related bodily injury necessarily arises out of professional services is not a clear one and has been treated differently in various jurisdictions.[14] Determining which policy applies to such a claim may have a significant impact on an insured.

---

[14] *See, e.g.,* Wheeler v. Aetna, 11 Ill. App. 3d 841, 298 N.E.2d 329 (1973), *aff'd,* 57 Ill. 2d 184, 311 N.E.2d 134 (1974). In *Wheeler,* the insured architect was issued a public liability insurance policy that included a professional liability exclusion applicable to architects similar to the one noted. The insured tendered the defense of a claim by an injured iron worker to Aetna, which denied coverage based on the exclusion. In finding for Aetna, the court held:

> [E]ven though the . . . complaint . . . expressly alleged that the architects themselves willfully failed to place the hoist properly, the court should have noticed what everyone else knows (i.e., that employees of contractors and subcontractors place and operate hoists and that architects and there employees never do so) . . . which would of course, put the duty to defend squarely on their Professional Liability carrier, not on their Public Liability carrier.

See also United States Fidelity & Guar. Co. v. Continental Casualty Co., 153 Ill. App. 3d 185, 505 N.E.2d 1072 (1987).

CHAPTER 8

INDEMNIFICATION

Walter H. Monroe III

Walter H. Monroe III is a partner with the law firm of Bradley, Arant, Rose & White in Birmingham, Alabama, where he specializes in representing design professionals and contractors in financing, negotiation, risk allocation, performance, administration and interpretation of contracts, subcontracts, and supply contracts for industrial and commercial facilities and the remediation of hazardous waste sites. He is a member of the Alabama bar and is admitted to practice before the United States Supreme Court. Mr. Monroe received a B.A. degree in political science from the University of Alabama and a J.D. from the Cumberland School of Law of Samford University. He is a member of the American Bar Association's Forum Committee on the Construction Industry and is chairman of the Planning Committee for the Southeastern Corporate Law Institute, an adjunct professor of law of Cumberland School of Law, and a member of the Construction Arbitration Panel of the American Arbitration Association.

§ 8.1 Introduction

This chapter addresses several common issues related to indemnity provisions that design professionals may be asked to accept in their contracts with owners or contractors or which they may obtain from an owner or a contractor. Also discussed are the unwritten indemnity obligations that may be faced by design professionals under varying circumstances, together with the limitations available, both legal and contractual, to check the application of written and unwritten indemnities.

The term *indemnity,* commonly used interchangeably with the term *hold harmless,* is usually viewed by design professionals as a means for owners to protect themselves from lawsuits arising from work on a construction project, particularly lawsuits brought by injured construction workers for whom workers' compensation recovery is not sufficient to cover damages sustained from work-related injuries. It is viewed as acceptable practice in the construction industry for the owner to obtain an indemnity from the contractor to cover the owner for such expenses, particularly when the injury was due to the negligence of the contractor or its subcontractors. Design professionals' organizations provide aids to owners in creating these indemnity obligations on the part of contractors through publication of standard contract forms, which not only protect the owner but also make the design professional a beneficiary to the contractor's indemnity obligation.[1] However, when owners incorporate indemnity clauses in contracts for design services that require the design professional to hold the owner harmless from liability or costs that might arise from the negligence of the design professional, these same professional societies hoist warning signals.[2] When design professionals are asked to indemnify the owner, they quickly learn to use very effectively some of the scurrilous adjectives generally used by contractors when referring to hold-harmless clauses. Owners, for their part, resist any attempts by contractors and design professionals to limit or modify contractual indemnity obligations.

This chapter first provides an overview of indemnification and reviews the various indemnification or hold-harmless clauses that may be included in design contracts. Under many such provisions, design professionals may assume far greater risks than they realize and may unknowingly undertake significantly greater obligations than the law would otherwise allocate in the absence of such contractual provisions. Additionally, design professionals have in numerous instances obtained indemnities in their favor from construction contractors through the mechanism of the owner's contract with the construction contractor, which indemnity obligations may prove to be unenforceable because of anti-indemnification statutes or court decisions of many states. The effect of these legal limitations, both statutory and case law, are discussed, together with contractual methods of limiting indemnity obligations. Common law principles of indemnity, which determine indemnification rights and obligations when no contractual provision

---

[1] *See* standard forms of agreement published by the American Institute of Architects and Engineers Joint Contract Documents Committee.

[2] Clark, *Indemnification by Engineers—A Warning,* Constr. Specifier, Sept. 1989.

exists, and the application of insurance coverage to indemnification obligations also are explored.

§ 8.2 Indemnity: Definition and Background

The term *indemnity* has been defined by the courts to mean an obligation to save harmless or secure against future loss or damage.[3] The word is used in two general senses: first, in the sense of giving security, and second, in the sense of compensation for actual damages.[4] These two concepts are historically viewed as "indemnity against liability," in the sense of giving security, which gives rise to a claim on its default, and "indemnity against loss," in the sense of compensation for actual damages, which can be enforced only after damages actually have been paid.[5] These concepts result in the shifting of financial and legal obligations from one party to another who may or may not otherwise be responsible for those obligations. Thus, the term indemnity means to secure against hurt, loss, or damage, and to make compensation to for incurred hurt, loss, or damage.[6]

The use of written indemnity provisions in contracts is not new. Courts have dealt with the enforceability and interpretation of contractual indemnity agreements from the earliest days of reported American law. Even oral agreements to indemnify another have been held enforceable unless they were agreements to answer for the debt of another.[7] The indemnity principle also was long recognized by the common law before indemnity provisions came into wide use in contracts. In tort law, a party is entitled to indemnity when it, although personally innocent of wrongdoing, is held legally responsible for the wrong of another and compensates that injured party for the harm. The party entitled to indemnity is entitled to recover the amount paid from the party truly responsible. The principle of *contribution* is analogous. It requires parties who are jointly and severally responsible for harm to reimburse their share of the harm to a fellow guilty party who has paid the entire loss. The result of the operation of the common law indemnity and contribution principles is to shift liability for payment of damages so that it matches responsibility for the damage.

Contracts between owners and their contractors also contain hold-harmless provisions designed to shift liability and to protect the owner (and usually the owner's design professional) from liability for property damage

---

[3] Ordinary v. Connolly, 75 N.J. Eq. 521, 72 A. 363 (1909).

[4] New York Cent. R.R. v. General Motors Corp., 182 F. Supp. 273 (N.D. Ohio 1960).

[5] Central Nat'l Bank v. McDaniel, 734 P.2d 1314 (Okla. Ct. App. 1986).

[6] Cunningham v. Government of Nashville, 476 S.W.2d 641, 643 (Tenn. 1972).

[7] Green v. Brookins, 23 Mich. 48 (1871); Morehouse v. Crangle, 36 Ohio St. 130 (1880); Kilbride v. Moss, 113 Cal. 432, 45 P. 812 (1896).

and bodily injury, particularly injuries to the contractor's employees incurred during the course of construction. Although the contractor is primarily liable for the injury because of the nature of workers' compensation laws, the employee's sole recourse against the employer is restricted to the amounts recoverable under the employer's workers' compensation insurance, which recovery is usually limited. Workers' compensation laws were introduced in the late nineteenth century in an attempt to compensate injured employees who were unable to sue and recover from their employers because of employer defenses such as assumption of risk, contributory negligence, and the fellow-servant doctrine.[8] These defenses made recovery by an employee from an employer virtually impossible even though the employer may have been negligent. Workers' compensation laws generally provide for recovery by the employee from the employer for job-related injuries, in a limited amount, without any proof of the employer's negligence. The employer is required by law to maintain insurance coverage for the amount due to the employee. In return, the employee waives any claim against the employer, including claims that the employer was negligent.

Because of limited recovery against the employer due to workers' compensation laws, attorneys representing injured employees, particularly those with crippling injuries that prevent further work and result in loss of income, bring actions against other parties who in some way caused or contributed to the employee's injury. Such actions are sometimes brought irrespective of the degree of negligence or culpability of the employee for the injury. Because workers' compensation laws place no limits or prohibitions on recovery from other parties (such as the owner or its design professional), if an injured employee convinces a court or jury that the owner or design professional was in some degree negligent and responsible for the injury, the employee may recover amounts far in excess of the amounts paid by workers' compensation insurance. The owner or design professional may claim indemnity from the employer if a written indemnity or a common law right of indemnity exists or if contribution is allowed, for all or part of the amount recovered by the injured employee. Whether a right to indemnity exists in a particular case is, however, based upon a determination of whether the owner or design professional has a legal or contractual basis for claiming indemnity.

This discussion illustrates several issues inherent in the operation of the principle of indemnity. Should an employer be held liable to indemnify another party (who may have, in fact, been the cause of the injury) and be obligated to pay more than workers' compensation? Is it acceptable public policy to enforce a clause in a contract that indemnifies one party against

[8] The fellow-servant doctrine precludes recovery from an employer for an injury suffered by an employee as a result of the negligence of a fellow worker engaged by the same employer. Parker v. Tharp, 409 N.W.2d 915 (Minn. Ct. App. 1987).

the results of its own negligence?[9] Many state laws limit contribution among parties jointly liable for an injury (commonly referred to as *joint tortfeasors*) and also limit the use of common law indemnity to circumstances in which the party who seeks to be indemnified is innocent of any wrongdoing. Because of these legal limitations, the use of contractual or *express indemnity* obligations is necessary. However, many states now also constrain the use of express indemnity provisions by court decision or statutes known as *anti-indemnification laws,* especially in contracts involving construction. Nevertheless, express indemnity provisions are enforced in numerous circumstances and it is important to understand the operation and nature of these clauses.

§ 8.3 Express or Contractual Indemnity Provisions

Contractual indemnity provisions used in the construction industry seek to reallocate damages among the participants in the construction process. Such provisions often apply to property damage, personal injury, wrongful death, and sometimes to claims regarding patent, copyright, or trademark infringement. To the extent that such clauses attempt to relieve a party of responsibility for its own negligence, they go beyond the rationale underlying common law indemnity, which places the risk of loss on the party responsible.

The language of an indemnity clause varies with each contract, although the clauses are similar. The American Institute of Architects' (AIA) Standard Form General Conditions provision provides a starting point for reviewing the potential range of indemnity obligations. The clause provides that the contractor shall indemnify the owner and the architect from claims arising out of the performance of the work, provided that any such claim:

> (1) is attributable to bodily injury, sickness, disease or death, or to injury to or destruction of tangible property (other than the Work itself) including the loss of use resulting therefrom, and (2) is caused in whole or in part by any negligent act or omission of the Contractor, any Subcontractor, anyone directly or indirectly employed by any of them or anyone for whose act any of them maybe liable, regardless of whether or not it is caused in part by a party indemnified hereunder.[10]

Paragraph 4.18.2 of the AIA Standard Form General Conditions provides that the obligation to indemnify shall not be limited to any restriction on the amount of damages payable under workers' compensation and other similar statutes.

---

[9] J. Acret, Architects and Engineers 275 (2d ed. 1984).

[10] *See* AIA A201-1976, para. 4.18.1.

The AIA clause addresses the relevant criteria: who is covered; the scope of the coverage with regard to claims and nature of damage; the nexus between the clause and the project; and any limitations. The clause covers the owner, the architect, and their employees and agents. It then addresses the nature of the claims covered and includes, by implication, the obligation to defend insofar as legal fees may be included in the expenses covered by the provisions. Other formulations require the contractor to defend and indemnify, making the contractor responsible for providing legal defense. The clause next addresses the kinds of damages covered: personal injury, including wrongful death, and property damage, other than damage to the work. It also addresses the necessary causation, that is, the harm must have been caused in whole or in part by the general contractor and those for whom it is responsible. Paragraph 4.18.1 also relieves the owner and the architect of responsibility for their own negligence if their negligence is part of the cause of the harm.

The contract provision creating the indemnity obligation will determine the scope and nature of the obligation and also will determine the degree, if any, to which the obligation will be legally enforced or construed. First, several factors are used by the courts in construing indemnity clauses. These factors include:

1. The clarity of the language (and thus the intent) of the indemnity clause
2. Whether the party being indemnified owes a special or public duty to the other contracting party
3. The relative bargaining power of the contracting parties
4. The extent to which enforcement of the indemnity clause is perceived as against "public policy"
5. Other legal prohibitions against the type of indemnity assumed.

It is a generally accepted principle that an agreement for indemnification against one's own negligent act must be clear, explicit, and unambiguous and will be construed strictly against the party seeking indemnity.[11] In many instances, the word *negligence* need not appear in the language of the clause for an obligation to indemnify to cover negligence, but the intention to do so must be clear from the wording of the instrument.[12] A provision in a contract between an owner and a contractor wherein the contractor agreed to save the owner harmless from "any and all claims . . . growing out of injury to . . . any of Contractor's employees . . . while on or about Owner's premises" was sufficient to impose liability upon the

[11] 41 Am. Jur. 2d *Indemnity* § 15 (1968).

[12] Georgia, Fla., Ala. Transp. Co. v. Deaton, Inc., 293 Ala. 359, 304 So. 2d 168, 170 (1974).

contractor for injuries to its employee caused by the owner's negligence.[13] However, in a similar case, the use of the general terms "indemnify against any and all claims" did not disclose an intention to indemnify for consequences arising solely from the negligence of the indemnitee.[14] Generally, the intent to indemnify the *indemnitee* (the party who benefits from the indemnity) for its own negligence must be specifically provided for in the indemnity agreement. In addition, there must be a substantial business reason for the indemnity clause and that reason must be reasonable in light of the transaction.[15]

If the indemnity clause is deemed to be legally enforceable, the scope of what is covered by the indemnity clause is usually determined from its terms. The indemnity clause may provide for indemnification against any or all of the following:

1. Losses, damages, or expenses
2. Legal liability of the indemnitee
3. Defense against claims, suits, or demands.

If the clause provides only for indemnification against loss, damages, or expenses, the obligation need not be honored until the actual loss, damage, or expense has been incurred by the indemnitee, which usually happens when the indemnitee makes a payment to the injured party. Therefore, until payment is made, no obligation of indemnity exists.[16] If the indemnity clause adds the obligation to indemnify against the legal liability of the indemnitee, the obligation to indemnify arises when the legal liability is established, such as when the judgment is entered. It is sufficient that the judgment has been made against the person to be indemnified even though the judgment remains unpaid.[17] If the obligation to defend against claims, suits, or demands is included in the indemnity clause, the *indemnitor* (the party assuming the indemnity obligation) is required to provide defense and hold the indemnitee harmless against any such claim, suit, or demand whether or not any legal liability has been determined or any payment made by the indemnitee.[18]

Finally, the terms of the indemnity clause also will determine the nature of the coverage. The indemnity clause can include property damage or personal injury, including death. It also can include other claims not resulting in property damage or personal injury such as "claims arising out of or

---

[13] Deel v. United States Steel Corp., 105 Ill. App. 2d 170, 245 N.E.2d 109 (1969).

[14] University Plaza Shopping Center, Inc. v. Stewart, 272 So. 2d 507 (Fla. 1973).

[15] Eley v. Brunner-Lay S. Corp., 289 Ala. 120, 266 So. 2d 276 (1972).

[16] 41 Am. Jur. 2d *Indemnity* §§ 28, 31 (1968).

[17] *Id.*

[18] Christy v. Menasha Corp., 297 Minn. 334, 211 N.W.2d 773 (1973).

resulting from the performance of the work." Such a broad provision could, however, make the indemnitor responsible for delays, disruptions, lost productivity, and other extras incurred by the indemnitee. The indemnity clause also may contain an obligation to pay expenses, including those of witnesses, experts, attorneys, and the like, incurred by the indemnitee. As a general matter, such fees, expenses, and costs must be reasonable and must have been incurred in defending against the claim.[19] In the absence of express contractual terms to the contrary, an indemnitee may not recover legal fees incurred in establishing the right to be indemnified.[20]

Contractual indemnity clauses are generally classified by the insurance industry, as a means for pricing premiums for contractual liability coverage, as *limited, intermediate,* or *broad* form clauses.[21]

Limited Form

In a limited form of indemnity, the party assuming the indemnity obligation (the *indemnitor*) holds someone harmless (the *indemnitee*) against claims due to the *sole* negligence of the *indemnitor.* Such a provision does not create any greater liability than that for which the indemnitor would be ordinarily liable: its negligent acts and those of its subcontractors. The common law indemnity would create the same obligation and also would achieve the same result. However, a common law indemnity (or an implied indemnity) would not provide for defense of the indemnitee, whereas the limited form of indemnity usually does. The following is an example of a limited indemnity provision:

> The Indemnitor agrees to indemnify, defend and save harmless the Indemnitee, its agents and employees, from and against all loss or expense (including costs and attorneys' fees) by reason of liability imposed by law upon the Indemnitee for damages because of bodily injury, including death at any time resulting therefrom, sustained by any person or persons or on account of damage to property, including loss of use thereof, arising out of or in consequence of the performance of this work, provided such injury to persons or damage to property is due or claimed to be due to the sole negligence of the Indemnitor, its subcontractors, employees or agents.

The limited form of indemnity creates an obligation for defense of the indemnitee if the indemnitee is sued or incurs expenses as a result of something the indemnitor did or should have done. With adequate insurance, "this substantially means payment of legal fees to bail out the others."[22]

---

[19] United Gen. Ins. Co. v. Crane Carrier Co., 695 P.2d 1334 (Okla. 1984).

[20] Jones v. Strom Constr. Co., 84 Wash. 2d 518, 527 P.2d 1115 (1974).

[21] W. Derk, Insurance for Contractors (5th ed. 1981).

[22] *Id.*

Intermediate Form

The intermediate form of indemnity not only provides for the payment of legal fees and a defense to a lawsuit, but also provides that the indemnitor pay for damages incurred when the indemnitor is only *in part* liable for the loss. An example of an intermediate form of indemnity is as follows:

> The Indemnitor agrees to indemnify, defend and save harmless the Indemnitee, its agents and employees, from and against all loss or expense (including costs and attorneys' fees) by reason of liability imposed by law upon the Indemnitee for damages because of bodily injury, including death at any time resulting therefrom sustained by any person or persons or on account of damage to property, including loss of use thereof, arising out of or in consequence of the performance of this work, whether such injuries to person or damage to property is due or claimed to be due in whole or in part to the negligence of the Indemnitor, its agents and employees, excepting only such injury or damage as shall have been occasioned by the sole negligence of the Indemnitee.

In the intermediate form of indemnity, the indemnitor agrees to be responsible for defense of the indemnitee and to waive any claim against the indemnitee that the indemnitee's partial negligence contributed to the loss, but does not waive a claim that the indemnitee's sole negligence caused the loss. In effect, the indemnitor agrees to pay for the loss as if it were fully responsible, and the only instance in which the indemnitor could avoid such an obligation would be to demonstrate that the indemnitee was solely the cause of the loss. In addition, the duty to defend the owner remains. It may be virtually impossible to provide a defense and at the same time attempt to establish the sole negligence of the party being defended. In such cases, two lawsuits are required: one to determine the obligation to indemnify and the second to defend against the loss if indemnity is required.

An additional problem exists in using the intermediate form of indemnity. The intermediate form does not apportion liability among the parties on the basis of their responsibility for the loss or their relative fault. The indemnitor is responsible for the entire loss provided the loss was due in any part to its negligent conduct, irrespective of the degree or extent of negligence of the indemnitee. The indemnitor is held to not be responsible only if the indemnitee is *solely* negligent. This literally means that if the indemnitor were only 1 percent responsible and the indemnitee were 99 percent responsible, the indemnitor nonetheless would be responsible for the full amount of the loss. Having been partially responsible for the loss, the indemnitor would be liable for the whole and would be absolved only if the loss were caused solely by the negligence of the indemnitee.[23] Because of

[23] Dozier v. J.A. Jones Constr. Co., 587 F. Supp. 289 (E.D. La. 1984).

this harsh result, many intermediate forms of indemnity clauses contain an apportionment based upon relative fault which requires the indemnitor to be responsible only for the degree of loss caused by its own degree of negligence. Many states create the same result through case decisions or legislation creating "comparative negligence" as a basis of determination of liability among jointly liable parties.

The Arkansas Supreme Court held that an indemnity agreement did not, with sufficient clarity, obligate the contractor to indemnify the owner for the owner's partial negligence in causing a worksite accident.[24] The agreement contained the following indemnity clause:

> To the extent that, in performance of this order, Seller shall do any work or cause any work to be done on any premises of the Buyer, then Seller shall indemnify and hold Buyer harmless against any and all liabilities or claims for injuries or damages to any person or property arising out of such work.[25]

The contractor's employee was injured on the job, and the employee sued the owner. The owner then brought an action against the contractor. The jury apportioned liability among the worker, the owner, and another contractor and found the contractor free of negligence. The court stated that although a contract of indemnity is to be interpreted in accordance with the rules for construction of contracts generally, an indemnitor's agreement to indemnify the indemnitee for the indemnitee's own negligence must be expressed in clear and unequivocal terms so that no other meaning can be ascribed. The clause in this contract did not spell out such a duty on the part of the indemnitor in unmistakable terms.

In a recent Illinois case in which an indemnity provision was enforced,[26] a subcontractor sued a prime contractor and its insurer, seeking a ruling that it was not required to reimburse the prime contractor and its insurer for repairs made to silos constructed by the subcontractor but which were damaged by the contractor. The prime contractor and its insurer filed counterclaims against the subcontractor, claiming that the subcontractor was obligated to indemnify them for their expenses in repairing the silos under the terms of an indemnification provision in the subcontract which required the subcontractor to indemnify the prime contractor "for property damage . . . caused, directly or indirectly by any act or omission . . . on the part of the subcontractor." The subcontractor argued that the provision was void under both Illinois's and Georgia's anti-indemnification statutes, which void all contracts requiring an indemnitor to indemnify an indemnitee for the indemnitee's own negligence. However, the court held that the

---

[24] Arkansas Kraft Corp. v. Boyed Sanders Constr. Co., 298 Ark. 36, 764 S.W.2d 452 (1989).

[25] 764 S.W.2d at 453.

[26] Venturi, Inc. v. Austin Co., 681 F. Supp. 584 (S.D. Ill. 1988).

language of the indemnification provision did not require indemnity for the prime contractor's sole negligence and the provision was thus enforceable against the subcontractor.

Broad Form

A broad form indemnity clause requires the indemnitor to pay for all claims even if due to the sole negligence of the indemnitee. A broad form indemnity clause might read:

> The Indemnitor agrees to indemnify, defend and save harmless the Indemnitee, its agents and employees, from and against all loss or expense (including costs and attorneys' fees) by reason of liability imposed by law upon the Indemnitee for damages because of bodily injury, including death at any time resulting therefrom, sustained by any person or persons or on account of damage to property, including loss of use thereof, arising out of or in consequence of the performance of the work, whether such injuries to persons or damage to property is due or claimed to be due, in whole or in part, by the negligence of Indemnitee, its agents or employees.

Courts strictly construe these types of clauses that "exculpate" an indemnitee from its own solely negligent conduct, and many states have passed legislation to limit the use of such clauses in connection with construction projects.[27] However, a clause that contains no reference at all to the negligence of the indemnitee may, in fact, create an obligation to indemnify against the sole negligent acts of the indemnitee, particularly if the language is clear, explicit, and unambiguous.[28] Insurance companies will base the premium charge for providing contractual liability insurance coverage for such a "silent" clause on the assumption that the clause requires indemnification of the indemnitee. Modification of such a clause (or one specifically requiring indemnification for the indemnitee's sole negligence) by the exclusion of the indemnitee's sole negligence could cut the premium in half for insurance to cover such a clause.[29]

A recent Texas case illustrates the difficulty inherent in construction of this type of indemnity clause. The indemnity clause in the contract stated:

> CONTRACTOR agrees to hold harmless and unconditionally indemnify COMPANY against and for all liability . . . arising from the work performed hereunder, including but not limited to any negligent act or omission of [Company], its officers, agents, or employees.[30]

---

[27] See summary of state anti-indemnification statutes and court decisions in § **8.8**.

[28] Deel v. United States Steel Corp., 105 Ill. App. 2d 170, 245 N.E.2d 109 (1969).

[29] W. Derk, Insurance for Contractors 24 (5th ed. 1981).

[30] Atlantic Richfield Co. v. Petroleum Personnel, Inc., 768 S.W.2d 724 (Tex. 1989).

The Texas court stated that this indemnity clause expressly called for the contractor to indemnify the owner for its "negligent act or omission" and it would be difficult for the contractor to argue that it was unaware of its obligations to indemnify the owner for the owner's own negligence. Indemnification would be required under such a clause for the owner's sole, joint, concurrent, or comparative negligence.[31] An earlier Texas court had stated that the failure to mention "gross" negligence of the owner meant that punitive damages were not subject to indemnification.[32] These cases point out the necessity for precision in drafting indemnity clauses so that the parties adequately and knowingly express their intent as to indemnity obligations.

§ 8.4 Common Law and Implied Indemnity

In addition to express indemnity obligations set forth in the contract, the duty to indemnify also may arise from "implied" agreements to indemnity or by operation of law, independent of contract, based upon the relationship of the parties.[33] This type of indemnification obligation is generally referred to as *common law indemnity* or, in some states, *implied indemnity.* When there is no express contractual provision for indemnification, a party's right to seek indemnity is often limited to rights and remedies afforded under common law.

Common Law Indemnity

The *Restatement (Second) of Torts* § 886 B describes the concept of common law indemnity as follows:

> (1) If two persons are liable in tort to a third person for the same harm and one of them discharges the liability of both, he is entitled to indemnity from the other if the other would be unjustly enriched at his expense by the discharge of the liability.
>
> (2) Instances in which indemnity is granted under this principle include the following: (a) The indemnitee was liable only vicariously for the conduct of the indemnitor; (b) The indemnitee acted pursuant to directions of the indemnitor and reasonably believed the directions to be lawful; (c) The indemnitee was induced to act by a misrepresentation on the part of the indemnitor, upon which he justifiably relied; (d) The indemnitor supplied a defective chattel or performed defective work upon land or buildings as a result of which both were liable to the third person, and the indemnitee innocently or

[31] *Id.*

[32] Crown Cent. Petroleum Corp. v. Jennings, 727 S.W.2d 739 (Tex. Ct. App. 1987).

[33] Ke-Wash v. Stauffer Chem. Co., 177 N.W.2d 5 (Iowa 1970).

negligently failed to discover the defect; (e) The indemnitor created a dangerous condition of land or chattels as a result of which both were liable to the third person, and the indemnitee innocently or negligently failed to discover the defect; (f) The indemnitor was under a duty to the indemnitee to protect him against the liability to the third person.

This right to common law indemnity arises when a party who is only "secondarily" or "passively" responsible (the indemnitee) pays an injured party for damages caused by a third party who is primarily responsible for such damages (the indemnitor). The indemnitee is entitled to recover the payment made to the injured party from the indemnitor.[34] For instance, a contractor may be primarily liable for injury to its employee, but because the employee is precluded from suing the employer due to the workers' compensation laws, the employee sues the owner and the design professional and recovers damages from them even though the owner and the design professional were only secondarily responsible for the injury to the contractor's employee. The owner and the design professional, in the absence of any legal prohibition, may seek recovery from the contractor for the contractor's conduct, which was the primary cause of the injury.[35] However, such a result is not always allowed. In the example noted, the contractor's employee was precluded from recovery due to workers' compensation laws. Such a prohibition against recovery from the employer has been extended by some courts to include any recovery from the employer, whether under a contractual indemnity or a common law indemnity, regardless of the degree of negligence or responsibility of the employer.[36]

Generally it is difficult to obtain indemnification based solely upon common law principles. For instance, a general contractor was not entitled to indemnity from a subcontractor for liability to an injured employee of the subcontractor regardless of the conduct of the subcontractor when the general contractor's negligence was "active or primary" rather than "passive or secondary."[37] An elevator company could not recover for common law indemnity arising out of a wrongful death action brought on behalf of a hotel employee who fell down an empty elevator shaft to his death because the record demonstrated the "active" negligence of the elevator company.[38] However, the liability of a general contractor and a subcontractor for the wrongful death of an employee of a second subcontractor who was killed

---

[34] 41 Am. Jur. 2d *Indemnity* § 19 (1968).

[35] Annotation, *Duty of Construction Contractor to Indemnify Contractee Held Liable for Injury to Third Person, in Absence of Express Contract for Indemnity,* 97 A.L.R.2d 616, 621–24 (1978).

[36] Paul Krebs & Assocs. v. Matthews & Fritts Constr. Co., 356 So. 2d 638 (Ala. 1978).

[37] Svenson v. Miller Builders, Inc., 74 Ill. App. 3d 75, 29 Ill. Dec. 931, 392 N.E.2d 628 (1979).

[38] Miami Elevator Co. v. La Concha Motor Inn, 462 So. 2d 511 (Fla. Dist. Ct. App. 1985).

when a load of concrete blocks fell while being lifted by the first subcontractor's crane was only "vicarious," and therefore the general contractor and the first subcontractor could seek indemnity against the second subcontractor after settling the wrongful death action against them arising out of the accident. The second subcontractor had accepted responsibility for keeping its workers from underneath the crane and had breached that duty, and the general contractor and the first subcontractor were deemed to be without fault.[39] In an action brought in Michigan for an employee's wrongful death as the result of a fall through a roof during the course of employment at a construction site, a contractor was determined to have no valid claim against a subcontractor for common law indemnity because the contractor had a duty to supply adequate safety devices and properly instruct the subcontractor concerning safety procedures. The contractor's failure to do so constituted an act of negligence on the part of the contractor, which precluded its right to indemnity.[40]

Implied Indemnity

The theory of implied indemnity applies to situations in which no express contractual indemnity exists in the contract, but because of a breach of an express affirmative duty in the contract damages are incurred.[41] For instance, a Massachusetts court determined that the owner of a ship who was sued by a worker injured by a defective hatch on the vessel was entitled to indemnity from a contractor who previously had been hired to replace the hatch cover.[42] The ship owner's right to indemnity was based upon the implied agreement to perform the work under the contract in a proper manner and to exercise due care to avoid injury to third parties. Failure to do so constituted a breach of the contract, which entitled the owner to indemnity from the contractor.[43] The implied right to indemnity requires that actual loss or damage be incurred and paid by the party seeking indemnity.[44] Therefore, if implied indemnity is sought, the indemnitee must wait until a judgment is rendered, must pay the judgment, and then seek recovery for the amount of the judgment from the implied indemnitor. No defense of the original action is available in such circumstances.

Several cases further illustrate the theory of implied indemnity. In New York, an engineer approved shop drawings for a hot water distribution

[39] Atlantic Coast Dev. Corp. v. Napoleon Steel Contractors, Inc., 385 So. 2d 676 (Fla. Dist. Ct. App. 1980).

[40] Hardy v. Monsanto Enviro-Chem Sys., Inc., 414 Mich. 29, 323 N.W.2d 270 (1982).

[41] 41 Am. Jur. 2d *Indemnity* §§ 7 to 8 (1968); Lipman v. Well-Mix Concrete, Inc., 138 N.Y.S.2d 316 (1954).

[42] Barker S.S. Lines, Inc. v. Quinn Bros., Inc., 104 F. Supp. 78 (D. Mass. 1952).

[43] D.M. Picton & Co. v. Eastes, 160 F.2d 189 (5th Cir.), *cert. denied,* 331 U.S. 859 (1947).

[44] Willey v. Minnesota Mining & Mfg. Co., 755 F.2d 315 (3d Cir. 1985).

system on a college campus. Serious leaks developed in the heat exchanger because of galvanic corrosion due to the use of dissimilar metals. The contractor made repairs and sued the university for compensation. The university filed suit against the engineer, claiming indemnity. The New York court required the engineer to indemnify the university because the engineer's duty to review and approve the shop drawings implied an obligation to insure that the correct metals were used.[45] In another New York case, the owner sued a contractor for using defective water pumps and the contractor filed a claim for indemnity against the engineer. The court determined that the contractor had a right to seek indemnity from the engineer regardless of whether the engineer owed a duty of care to the contractor. The court stated that the right of implied indemnity rests on a showing that the contractor "might" be held liable to the owner because of the engineer's negligence if the defects in the pumps could be shown to have been caused by improper engineering design.[46]

A Florida court ruled that an architect was entitled to full indemnity from an engineer who redesigned a loading dock to accommodate heavier traffic than originally anticipated. The dock failed, and in court the evidence showed that the architect relied on the engineer's expertise to design the dock in a structurally sound manner.[47] However, a different result was reached by a South Dakota court in determining that an engineer who designed an air-supported dome for a football field was not obligated to indemnify the architect when the dome failed.[48] The owner of the stadium sued the architect when the dome failed and recovered. The architect sought full indemnification from the engineer it had hired. The engineer had designed the only existing air-supported domes in the world. The court determined that the architect was contractually bound to the owner (a public body) to review the plans, including those of the engineer, and to affix its seal to all plans. The court found that the architect had a duty to review the plans to ensure they were sound, and if the architect did not feel it had the expertise to review the engineer's plans it should have withdrawn from the work. It may be possible to distinguish these two cases on the basis that one project was public and the other was private, or that in one case the architect was not "actively" negligent[49] and in the other the architect's nonfeasance negated its right to indemnity.[50]

All of these implied indemnity cases point out the necessity of obtaining a written indemnity clause when contracting a portion of work for which

---

[45] John Grace & Co. v. State Univ. Constr. Fund, 99 A.D.2d 860, 472 N.Y.S.2d 757 (1984).

[46] Irondequoit Bay Pure Water Dist. v. Nalews, Inc., 123 Misc. 2d 462, 472 N.Y.S.2d 842 (1984).

[47] Grossman v. Sea Air Towers, Ltd., 513 So. 2d 686 (Fla. Dist. Ct. App. 1987).

[48] South Dakota Bldg. Auth. v. Geiger-Berger Assocs., 414 N.W.2d 15 (S.D. 1987).

[49] Grossman v. Sea Air Towers Ltd., 513 So. 2d 686, 689 (Fla. Dist. Ct. App. 1987).

[50] South Dakota Bldg. Auth. v. Geiger-Berger Assocs., 414 N.W.2d 15, 23 (S.D. 1987).

one is otherwise responsible due to the conflicting nature of various state laws and court decisions. Reliance on an implied (or common law) indemnity right to be available is not recommended.

Equitable Indemnity

California also recognizes a concept of *equitable indemnity,* which is distinct from either common law or implied indemnity. This doctrine of equitable indemnity permits jointly negligent parties to apportion loss in proportion to each wrongdoer's relative culpability. Its purpose is to ameliorate the harsh effect of joint and several liability, in which one jointly negligent party pays for more than its share of damages. A developer sued by homeowners could seek equitable indemnification against the original owner who had graded the lots.[51] In finding that equitable indemnity applied to this fact situation, the court devised the following rule: any theory that would have been available to the homeowners against the grader is also available to the developer to pursue in an equitable indemnity action against the grader.

§ 8.5 Contribution among Joint Tortfeasors

As noted in § **8.4**, common law indemnity requires that the indemnitee be free of *active* negligence and implied indemnity requires that the indemnitee be owed a duty by the indemnitor. However, in the absence of an express indemnity or other contractual obligation, either express or implied, a party whose active negligence contributes to a loss is not, in most states, entitled to indemnity or *contribution* from another party who may be equally at fault.[52] A plaintiff who sued two or more parties could, if successful, pick and choose among the jointly responsible parties (the *joint tortfeasors*), obtain a judgment against one or all, and satisfy the judgment against any one of them. The party who ultimately paid the judgment would not be able to recover anything from the other joint tortfeasor. This general rule has been expressed by one court that stated that "joint tortfeasors are not entitled to indemnity or contribution."[53] When each tortfeasor is chargeable with active or affirmative negligence contributing to the injury for which recovery is had, neither is entitled to indemnity from the other. A person's rights to indemnification will be denied when his own wrongful act or omission

[51] People *ex rel.* Dept. of Transp. v. Superior Court, 26 Cal. 3d 814, 608 P.2d 673, 163 Cal. Rptr. 585 (1980).

[52] Newport News Shipbuilding & Drydock Co. v. United States, 226 F.2d 137 (4th Cir. 1955).

[53] Crigler v. Salac, 438 So. 2d 1375 (Ala. 1983).

proximately contributes to the injury complained of because, under the rule that no one should be permitted to found a cause of action on his own wrong, the courts will not aid one tortfeasor against another.[54]

However, some exceptions exist to the rule that indemnity will not be allowed among joint tortfeasors. A joint tortfeasor may claim indemnity when it has not been guilty of any fault, except technically or constructively, or when both parties are at fault, but the fault of the party from whom indemnity is claimed was the proximate or primary cause of the injury.[55] This concept is very close to common law indemnity. Because the right of indemnity shifts the risk from one party to another, a joint tortfeasor is not entitled to indemnity even if the degree of negligence of the other joint tortfeasor was greater.[56] The distinction between a right to indemnity and a denial of contribution is one of *active* or *passive* (*secondary*) negligence.[57] Indemnity among joint tortfeasors generally is not allowed, except if an express contract provision exists, or in situations involving vicarious liability and passive negligence. A contractor's employee was injured when his surveyor's rod came into the vicinity of a power company's uninsulated power lines while the employee was engaged in measuring the height from the power lines to a roadway constructed by the contractor. The roadway was built too high by the contractor and there was a question whether the power company knew about this condition. The power company would not be entitled to indemnity from the contractor if the trier of facts should determine that the power company was negligent because it had actual notice of the improper road elevation. If, however, the trier of facts should determine that the power company had no notice and was not negligent in respect to the employee's measurements, then the power company would be only passively negligent and would be entitled to indemnity because of the contractor's active negligence in elevating the road beyond contract specifications. The mere failure to discover an unsafe or dangerous condition created by a joint tortfeasor constitutes passive negligence which will not bar indemnity against the active tortfeasor whose primary negligence created the dangerous condition.[58]

This distinction is less important in those states that do not recognize the contribution rule or that have adopted comparative negligence systems of recovery to allocate recovery among joint tortfeasors.[59] The common law doctrine of indemnity among joint tortfeasors in negligence cases is abrogated by state statutes providing that contribution of joint tortfeasors is to

[54] Stuart v. Hertz Corp., 351 So. 2d 703 (Fla. 1977).

[55] *Id.*

[56] Crouch v. Tourtelot, 350 S.W.2d 799 (Mo. 1961).

[57] Svenson v. Miller Builders, Inc., 74 Ill. App. 3d 75, 392 N.E.2d 628 (1979).

[58] Florida Power Corp. v. Taylor, 332 So. 2d 687 (Fla. Dist. Ct. App. 1976).

[59] Associated Eng'rs, Inc. v. Job, 370 F.2d 633 (8th Cir. 1967).

be in proportion to the percentage of negligence attributable to each defendant.[60] However, a contract clause requiring indemnity still will overcome proportional responsibility. For example, an injured employee of a contractor sued the construction manager on the project, who then filed a claim against the contractor. The jury had found the construction manager 45 percent liable, the contractor 35 percent liable, and the employee 20 percent liable for the injuries. The indemnity provision in the contract between the contractor and the construction manager provided that the contractor would indemnify and hold the construction manager harmless against all personal injury claims arising out of the performance of the work, if the injury was caused in whole or in part by any negligent act or omission of the contractor, "regardless of whether or not it is caused in part by a party indemnified hereunder." The Minnesota Court of Appeals held that this language was sufficiently specific to require the contractor to indemnify the construction manager by paying the construction manager's share of the damages as well as its own.[61]

Because of the legal complexities inherent in depending upon a right of contribution, comparative negligence, or implied indemnity, it is understandable why parties to contracts seek to shift responsibility for risks or allocate risks among those best suited to manage them by including indemnity clauses in their contracts. In addition, it is also understandable why many states have adopted statutes that limit the application of indemnity clauses in contracts, particularly when such clauses attempt to circumvent case law by creating broad obligations to indemnify for matters not otherwise allowed by state law or public policy, such as an indemnity for one's own negligence.

§ 8.6 Limitations on Indemnity by State Law

Anti-Indemnification Statutes

The New Mexico Supreme Court has held that its state's anti-indemnity statute voids any indemnity agreement in the construction industry that attempts to release the indemnitee from the consequences of its own negligence.[62] The court stated that the New Mexico statute voids as against public policy any agreement in the construction industry whereby one party agrees to indemnify another from liability or damages "caused by, or resulting from, in whole or in part, the negligence of the indemnitee."[63] This

[60] New Terminal Warehouse Corp. v. Wilson, 589 S.W.2d 465 (Tex. Ct. App. 1979).

[61] Oster v. Medtronic, Inc., 428 N.W.2d 116 (Minn. Ct. App. 1988).

[62] Sierra v. Garcia, 106 N.M. 573, 746 P.2d 1105 (1987).

[63] N. M. Stat. Ann. § 56-7-1 (1978).

statute has been noted as unique in the United States because it deals with liability resulting from the indemnitee's negligence "in whole or in part," or an intermediate form of express indemnity. It would seem that the only type of indemnity agreement enforceable in New Mexico would be one wherein the indemnitor agreed to indemnify the indemnitee for the indemnitor's sole negligence (limited form of indemnity), which would generally be its obligation under the common law. It is possible that New Mexico has established a rule that a party who is 99 percent responsible for a claim can be completely exonerated of any liability. However, a recent New York case deals with a more specific application of an anti-indemnification statute.

A New York court determined that a subcontractor was contractually obligated to indemnify a general contractor irrespective of New York's anti-indemnity statute and even though the general contractor was the cause of the accident. Under New York law, contractual indemnification is precluded if the indemnitee's negligence contributed to the accident. In this case, the general contractor was strictly liable for the accident under the New York Scaffolding Act[64] without any proof of negligence. The subcontractor's employee was injured when the scaffolding on which he was working gave way. The employee sued the general contractor and the general contractor sought indemnification under the subcontract agreement from the subcontractor. The subcontract agreement provided a broad indemnity from any accident that occurred where the subcontractor worked. The subcontractor raised the New York anti-indemnity statute as a defense and the court agreed that, under the anti-indemnity statute, contractual indemnification was precluded if the general contractor had negligently contributed to the accident. However, the court ruled that the statute could not be raised when statutory liability was established without proof of negligence and, because the accident occurred in an area where the subcontractor was working, indemnification was appropriate under the terms of the subcontract.[65]

Florida's anti-indemnity statute contains a *specific consideration* requirement. Florida Statutes § 725.06 provides that any construction contract indemnification agreement that purports to provide indemnification for one party for the acts or omissions of that party shall be void and unenforceable unless: "(1) [t]he contract contains a monetary limitation on the extent of the indemnification and shall be a part of the project specifications or bid documents, or (2) [t]he person indemnified by the contract gives a specific consideration to the indemnitor for the indemnification that shall be provided for in his contract and section of the project specifications or bid documents, if any." Subsections (1) and (2) are presented in the disjunctive, that is, the satisfaction of either constitutes

[64] N.Y. Lab. Law § 240(1) (McKinney 1965).

[65] Walsh v. Morse Diesel, Inc., 143 A.D.2d 653, 533 N.Y.S.2d 80 (1988).

sufficient reason to render an otherwise invalid construction contract indemnification clause enforceable under the statute.[66] Consideration by payment of a percentage of a defined amount is valid under Florida law. The specific consideration required by Florida Statutes § 725.06(2) need not be a dollar amount. A recital of a specific percentage of the contract price for the indemnity provision may be found to represent a specific consideration given to a contractor within the meaning of Florida Statutes § 725.06(2).[67]

A subcontract that required the subcontractor to procure liability insurance on behalf of itself and of the general contractor was deemed by a Florida court to be a contract for insurance, not for indemnification. Thus, although a contract in Florida for indemnity will not be sustained when it purports to indemnify the indemnitee from liability resulting from its own negligence unless clearly so expressed and unless consideration is exchanged, when the subcontractor breached its contract by failing to make the general contractor a named insured under its policy, it was liable to the general contractor for all damages arising out of four personal injury suits directed against them, including that portion attributable to the general contractor's own negligence.[68]

California by statute invalidates for public policy reasons indemnity clauses in construction contracts that seek indemnification against liability for damages caused by the sole negligence of the indemnitee. However, an indemnity clause providing that the indemnitor would indemnify the indemnitee from any and all claims that may be made against the indemnitee by reason of injury or death to person or damage to property, however caused or alleged to have been caused and though claimed to be due to the negligence of the indemnitee, was not void under the statute. In construction contracts, the statute prevents indemnification for the indemnitee's sole negligence but does not prevent indemnification when there is concurrent negligence.[69]

Texas has adopted a statute declaring void agreements that purport to indemnify a registered architect or engineer from defects in plans, designs, or specifications prepared or used by the architect or engineer or for negligence in rendering professional services.[70]

---

[66] Westinghouse Elec. Corp. v. Turnberry Corp., 423 So. 2d 407 (Fla. Dist. Ct. App. 1983).

[67] Peoples Gas Sys., Inc. v. RSH Constructors, Inc., 563 So. 2d 107 (Fla. Dist. Ct. App. 1990).

[68] Cone Bros. Contracting Co. v. Ashland-Warren, Inc., 458 So. 2d 851 (Fla. Dist. Ct. App. 1984).

[69] Armco Steel Corp. v. Cox (Roy H.) Co., 103 Cal. App.3d 929, 163 Cal. Rptr. 330 (1980).

[70] Tex. Civ. Prac. & Rem. Code Ann. § 130 (Vernon 1991).

Court Decisions

When an owner's negligence was the sole cause of injury to an employee of the contractor, the contractor had no liability under a contract provision providing for indemnity to the owner "for injury to the contractor's employees in any way arising out of or connected with performance by the contractor," as the indemnity agreement did not provide for indemnification of the owner's negligence in the clear and unequivocal language required by Louisiana law.[71] In an action by an employee of a contractor resulting from injuries due solely to the owner's negligence, the contractor was not obligated to defend and indemnify the owner under a provision of the contract indicating that the contractor would indemnify and hold the owner harmless from liability "without limitation and irrespective of negligence," as such a provision was ambiguous and did not express a clear and unequivocal obligation required by Texas law.[72] Contracts will not be construed to indemnify a person against his own negligence unless such intention is expressed in unequivocal terms.[73]

An indemnitee cannot, in some jurisdictions, enforce its right to indemnity under an agreement in which the injured party is an employee of the indemnitor. This occurs because many states will not allow contribution—payment of all or a portion of a judgment or settlement from the employer when the employer (because of workers' compensation laws) has no independent liability to the employee. Adding to this seeming injustice in Alabama, the employer, or its insurance carrier, may recover from the design professional any money paid out in workers' compensation, despite any negligence on the part of the employer.[74] This result is not followed by all states. For example, the exclusive liability of an employer provision of the Alaska workers' compensation act did not render invalid an express indemnity agreement between a third-party tortfeasor and the employer of an employee who had been killed.[75] The exclusive remedy provision of Florida's workers' compensation act did not preclude a passively negligent third-party tortfeasor from being indemnified by an actively negligent employer, who had made payments of compensation and medical benefits to an injured employee, in a suit for damages by such employee against the third party, in which it was alleged in the claim for indemnity that the employer's act of negligence was primarily responsible for the injury.[76] An indemnity agreement based on a subcontract that contained the subcontractor's

[71] Smith v. Chevron Oil Co., 517 F.2d 1154 (5th Cir. 1975).

[72] Chevron Oil Co. v. E.D. Walton Constr. Co., 517 F.2d 1119 (5th Cir. 1975).

[73] Morgan v. Good Humor Corp., 54 A.D.2d 560, 386 N.Y.S.2d 888 (1976).

[74] Paul Krebs & Assocs. v. Matthews & Fritts Constr. Co., 356 So. 2d 638 (Ala. 1978).

[75] Manson-Osberg Co. v. State, 552 P.2d 654 (Alaska 1976).

[76] Trail Builders Supply Co. v. Reagan, 235 So. 2d 482 (Fla. 1970).

agreement to assume all obligations and responsibilities that the contractor had assumed pursuant to the prime contract with a town in construction project at a town school was enforceable against a subcontractor for the contractor's civil liability to a subcontractor's employee who was injured by falling off a ladder at a construction site, even though the subcontractor was immune from all tort claims of its employee under Massachusetts's workers' compensation statute.[77]

Texas rejected its clear and unequivocal test in favor of an "express negligence doctrine," under which a party seeking indemnification from the consequences of its own negligence must specifically state that intent within the four corners of the contract. In Texas, indemnitees seeking indemnity for the consequences of their own negligence that proximately causes injury jointly and concurrently with the indemnitor's negligence also must meet the express negligence test. Parties in Texas also may contract for comparative indemnity so long as they comply with the express negligence doctrine.[78]

The statutes and cases discussed present interesting contrasts in the ways in which various states deal with indemnity provisions in contracts. **Section 8.8** sets forth a state-by-state examination of decisions and statutes limiting the application for contractual indemnity provisions. Many of the anti-indemnification statutes and decisions noted apply only in the context of construction contracts and very few cases have been decided that construe these statutes in factual situations involving design professionals.

Statutes of Limitation

In any action for indemnification, whether based upon an express contractual provision, common law, or an implied obligation of indemnity, the application of statutes of limitation must be recognized. In one case, an architect sought indemnity from a contractor after the architect was sued by the owner. The Illinois court dismissed the architect's action for indemnity against the contractor on the ground that the action was barred by the five-year statute of limitations that began to run when the negligent act occurred, even though the architect and the owner had no knowledge of the negligent conduct of the contractor.[79] In another case in North Carolina, an architect was absolved of liability because the applicable statute of limitations provided that no action for contribution or indemnity for damages for wrongful death could be brought against any person furnishing design, plans, supervision of construction, or construction of improvements to real

[77] Whittle v. Pagani Bros. Constr. Co., 383 Mass. 796, 422 N.E.2d 779 (1981).

[78] Ethyl Corp. v. Daniel Constr. Co., 725 S.W.2d 705 (Tex. 1987).

[79] Board of Educ. v. Joseph J. Duffy Co., 97 Ill. App. 2d 158, 240 N.E.2d 5 (1968).

property more than six years after the service was performed.[80] In other instances, however, the statute of limitations in an indemnity action does not commence until the indemnitee pays the injured party.[81] A Washington developer's action against a general contractor and a mechanical subcontractor for indemnification for damages arising out of breach of an agreement to correct design defects in a swimming pool/bathhouse was barred by the terms of the contract between the developer and the operator of the recreational complex, which required that actions be brought within a reasonable period of time, because no claim in writing was presented until four years after the defects were first observed.[82] In Michigan, the six-year statute of limitations applicable to torts by architects governs claims for indemnity.[83]

§ 8.7 Limitations on Indemnity by Contract

A recent case illustrates the need to deal with indemnity issues in the contract between the parties. A Texas court determined that in the absence of specific language in the general contractor's contract with the owner, an architect was not entitled to rely upon the general contractor's agreement to indemnify the owner "and its agents" from any damages. The incident giving rise to the damages resulted in part from the failure of the architect to discover construction defects, even though the architect's contract with the owner expressly provided that the architect would "not be responsible for the Contractor's failure to carry out the work in accordance with the Contract Documents."[84] Despite this disclaimer, a jury found the architect was liable for not having discovered the construction defects and attempted to apply comparative fault principles, finding the architect 5 percent and the contractor 95 percent negligent. The Texas appellate court refused to allow the evaluation of the contractor's and the architect's comparative negligence and determined that the architect was not entitled to indemnity from the contractor. This case illustrates the necessity for a design professional to insure that its contract with the owner (and that of the owner with its contractors) contains adequate language delineating the scope of its responsibility and placing either a limitation upon its obligations to indemnify the owner or obligating the owner (or its contractor) to specifically indemnify the design professional.

---

[80] Lamb v. Wedgewood S. Corp., 55 N.C. App. 686, 286 S.E.2d 876 (1982).

[81] Owings v. Rose, 262 Or. 247, 497 P.2d 1183 (1972).

[82] Black Mountain Ranch v. Black Mountain Dev. Co., 29 Wash. App. 212, 627 P.2d 1006 (1981).

[83] United States v. Burton, 580 F. Supp. 660 (E.D. Mich. 1984).

[84] Hunt v. Ellisor & Tanner, Inc., 739 S.W.2d 933 (Tex. Ct. App. 1987).

The Engineers Joint Contract Documents Committee (EJCDC) has published two useful documents, one relating to the use of limitation of liability clauses in standard forms of agreement between engineers and owners for professional services and the other dealing with indemnification. The first document[85] contains an excellent exposition of the reasons why design professionals should obtain indemnity agreements from owners and otherwise limit their liability to the owner (and presumably to third parties by way of the owner's indemnity). The second document[86] states that the owner should not expect an unlimited or broad form indemnity from the design professional and provides the rationale why the owner should be willing to include the design professional in indemnity agreements obtained from contractors or be willing, under certain circumstances, to indemnify the design professional.[87]

It does make sense for a design professional to limit its liability to the owner for personal injury or property damage at the project site, because the owner or its contractor is in control of the project site and usually obtains insurance coverage for the project (which could include the interest of the design professional at little or no premium increase so long as the design professional's errors and omissions are excluded from coverage). Second, the design professional is responsible for performance of its work in accordance with a higher degree of skill and care than that used in determining ordinary negligence and such higher degree of care provides adequate protection to the owner and the general public, including the contractor's employees. Finally, the design professional cannot always obtain insurance for all the risk associated with contractual liability, particularly due to the design errors and omissions exclusions contained in general liability insurance policies. Design professionals who are able to obtain errors and omissions coverage endorsements to their policies usually find the coverage to be limited in dollar amount and scope. See **Chapter 7**. In some policies, the errors and omissions endorsement itself excludes liability assumed under contract. A design professional very likely will have little insurance coverage for liability for damages resulting from its design error or omission and no coverage for its indemnity obligations to the owner. Most often circumstances that give rise to an indemnity demand under an express contract clause (whether limited, intermediate, or broad) involve work-related injuries not caused by the design professional's design error or omission. The design professional should be able to persuade the owner not

---

[85] *See* Kennedy, *Limitation of Liability in Design Professional Contracts,* Engineers Joint Contract Documents Committee (1986).

[86] Clark, *Indemnification by Engineers—A Warning,* Constr. Specifier, Sept. 1989.

[87] These documents, together with the standard forms of limitation of liability published by EJCDC, are available from the National Society of Professional Engineers, P.O. Box 96163, Washington, D.C. 20090-6163.

to require an indemnity or, if one is required, to either limit the indemnity to the insurance coverage provided by the design professional or to place a cap on the liability assumed under the indemnity obligation at a fixed dollar amount.

Liability of a design professional may be limited in several ways, including:

1. Limitation of liability to the amount of compensation (or a percentage thereof) received from the owner
2. Limitation of liability to the amount of insurance coverage to be carried by the design professional pursuant to the contract. If no coverage is available, a specific dollar limitation should be included for uninsured claims
3. Limitation of liability to a specific dollar amount by use of a liquidated damages provision.[88]

Contract clauses that limit the liability of one party to another for its negligent acts are generally referred to as *exculpatory* clauses. The law does not favor contracts that exculpate or release a person from liability for future negligent acts; therefore, they are always strictly construed against the party seeking release from liability. However, these contracts are usually held valid if written in clear, explicit, and unequivocal language. It is said that the wording of such a clause must be so clear and understandable that an ordinarily prudent and knowledgeable party would know what it was contracting away.[89] Courts can, however, refuse to enforce these clauses, if under the circumstances of the case the contract is contrary to public policy.[90] As a general matter, circumstances in which a design professional's exculpatory contracts would offend public policy would be those involving the rendering of services to the general public or failure to perform a duty imposed by law.[91] If the exculpatory clause is unambiguous and not against public policy, and provided the parties to the contract freely negotiated the agreement and one side did not have a greater bargaining power than the other, the exculpatory clause will be allowed to have its intended effect. For instance, an exculpatory clause in a contract involving specialized services was not enforced because the services were not available from others and the party rendering the service insisted its contract form be signed before rendering the service.[92]

---

[88] Kennedy, *Limitation of Liability in Design Professional Contracts,* Engineers Joint Contract Documents Committee (1986).

[89] 57A Am. Jur. 2d *Negligence* §§ 49, 65 (1989).

[90] Motorists Mut. Ins. Co. v. Jones, 9 Ohio Misc. 113, 223 N.E.2d 381 (1966).

[91] 57A Am. Jur. 2d *Negligence* §§ 57, 58 (1989).

[92] Mohawk Drilling Co. v. McCullough Tool Co., 271 F.2d 627 (10th Cir. 1959).

However, in most instances exculpatory clauses are enforced by the courts. The following clause was upheld by a Florida court in a situation involving a power company and a well-known engineer in connection with the collapse of an embankment for a cooling water reservoir:

> Engineer's liability to Owner for any indemnity commitments or for any damages arising in any way out of the performance of this contract is limited to such insurance coverages and amounts [Previously set forth in the clause]. In no event shall Engineer be liable for any indirect, special or consequential loss or damage arising out of the performance of services hereunder including, but not limited to, loss of use, loss of profit, or business interruption whether caused by negligence of Engineer, or otherwise, and owner shall indemnify and hold Engineer harmless from any such damages or liability.[93]

The court ruled that the engineer's liability for its own negligence was limited to the insurance coverage provided and that the engineer was entitled to be indemnified by the owner from the damages noted in the clause. The court stated the language was clear and unequivocal in application and therefore served to limit the engineer's liability to the insurance coverage because an earlier provision of the clause allowed the owner to obtain, at its expense, increased insurance limits, which the owner declined to do.

An exculpatory clause will not limit a design professional's responsibility to a third party, but the design professional can seek to have the owner or its contractor agree to indemnify it from suits brought by third parties. However, such indemnity agreements are subject to the same limitations as noted in § **8.6** with respect to anti-indemnification statutes and decisions of some states, particularly with respect to the sole negligent acts of the design professional. In addition, exculpatory clauses that attempt to absolve a party from intentional torts, wanton or willful misconduct, or gross negligence are not allowed.[94]

In addition to limiting liability for damages arising out of negligent acts or performance of the work, it is common practice today for design professionals to include a "Waiver of Consequential Damages" clause in their contracts, limiting liability for loss of use of an owner's building or facility or for lost profits, and a provision requiring the owner to indemnify the design professional from loss associated with hazardous waste and asbestos.[95] A "Waiver of Subrogation" clause also will protect a design professional from claims made by an owner's (or its contractors') insurance carriers. As a general rule, an insurer is subrogated to its insured's right to recovery of losses from parties legally responsible for the loss. Most

---

[93] Florida Power & Light Co. v. Mid-Valley Inc., 763 F.2d 1316 (11th Cir. 1985).

[94] 57A Am. Jur. 2d *Negligence* § 55 (1989).

[95] For examples of these clauses, *see* Kennedy, *Limitation of Liability in Design Professional Contracts,* Engineers Joint Contract Documents Committee (1986).

insurance policies state that the insured will not take any action after an occurrence to prejudice the insurer's right of recovery against other parties liable for the loss. However, most insurers recognize (but do not like) the fact that the insured may legally waive a claim or right to claim in advance of a loss. Such a waiver is commonly referred to as a *waiver of subrogation* and can help a design professional limit recovery for losses for which the design professional may be legally responsible but for which the owner or the contractor's insurer has made payment.

§ 8.8 Anti-Indemnification Statutes and Decisions

Following is a state-by-state listing of anti-indemnification statutes and decisions:[96]

Alabama. Alabama common law permits indemnification agreements that clearly and specifically express the intent of the parties to the agreement. *Georgia, Florida, Alabama Transportation Co. v. Deaton,* 293 Ala. 359, 304 So. 2d 168 (1974), *Crigler v. Salac,* 438 So. 2d 1375 (Ala. 1983). No legislation regarding this issue has been passed.

Alaska. Agreements affecting construction contracts that indemnify one for his sole negligence or willful misconduct are void. Alaska Stat. § 45.45.900 (1975).

Arizona. Agreements affecting construction or "architect/engineer professional service contracts" that indemnify one for his sole negligence are void. Ariz. Rev. Stat. Ann. § 34-226 (1981). All indemnity clauses in contracts that predate this statute and that do not specifically define the intent of the indemnity clause are "general indemnity agreements." *Estes Co. v. Aztec Construction, Inc.,* 139 Ariz. 166, 677 P.2d 939 (Ct. App. 1983). These general indemnity agreements are effective for passive, but not active, negligence. *Id.*

Arkansas. Arkansas common law permits indemnification agreements that clearly and specifically express the intent of the parties to the agreement. *Hood v. Welch,* 249 Ark. 1159, 463 S.W.2d 362 (1971). One may not, however, be indemnified against his sole and exclusive negligence. *Pickens-Bond Construction Co. v. North Little Rock Electric Co.,* 249 Ark. 389, 459 S.W.2d 549 (1970).

---

[96] The author acknowledges the assistance of Paul D. Gilbert, an associate with the law firm of Bradley, Arant, Rose & White, Birmingham, Alabama, for his research and preparation of this section.

No statute specifically addressing indemnification agreements in the construction context has been enacted. Arkansas legislation does, however, provide that every corporation is liable to its employees injured during the course of employment resulting from the employer's negligence or that of its agents. Ark. Stat. Ann. § 11-8-103 (1987).

California. Agreements affecting construction contracts that indemnify one for his sole negligence or willful misconduct are void. Cal. Civil Code §§ 2782 and 2782.2 (West 1990). Professional engineers providing inspection services may, under certain circumstances, be exempt from these provisions. *Id.*

Colorado. Colorado common law permits indemnification agreements that clearly and specifically express the intent of the parties to the agreement. *Barker v. Colorado Regents Sports Car Club,* 35 Colo. App. 73, 532 P.2d 372 (1974). Colorado has not addressed this issue by statute.

Connecticut. Agreements to indemnify one for his sole negligence in connection with a contract relating to the construction, alteration, repair, or maintenance of any building, structure, or appurtenance thereto are void. Conn. Gen. Stat. (Civil Action) § 52-572(k) (1979). Architects and engineers are not specifically mentioned by this statute.

Delaware. Provisions in construction contracts purporting to indemnify the promisee for damages arising from liability for bodily injury or death to persons or damage to property caused partially or solely by negligence of the promisee are void. This statute applies to all phases of preconstruction, construction, repairs, and maintenance. Del. Code Ann. tit. 6, § 2704 (1988).

Florida. Architects and engineers are specifically mentioned in Florida's statute that voids indemnification agreements in construction contracts for damages caused in whole or in part by the indemnitee unless: "(1) [t]he contract contains a monetary limitation on the extent of the indemnification and shall be a part of the project specifications or bid documents, if any; or (2) The person indemnified by the contract gives a specific consideration to the indemnitor for the indemnification that should be provided for in his contract and section of the project specifications or bid documents, if any." Fla. Stat. § 725.06 (1972).

Georgia. Agreements to indemnify one for his sole negligence in connection with a contract relating to the construction, repair, or maintenance of a building, structure, appurtenance, or appliance, including moving, demolition, and excavation in connection therewith, are void. Ga. Code Ann.

§ 13-8-2 (1982). Architects and engineers are not specifically mentioned by this statute.

Hawaii. Agreements to indemnify one for his sole negligence in connection with a contract relating to the construction, repair, or maintenance of a building, structure, appurtenance, or appliance, including moving, demolition, and excavation in connection therewith, are void. Haw. Rev. Stat. §§ 431–453 (1975). Architects and engineers are not specifically mentioned by this statute.

Idaho. Agreements to indemnify one for his sole negligence in connection with a contract relating to the construction, repair, or maintenance of a building, structure, appurtenance, or appliance, including moving, demolition, and excavation in connection therewith, are void. Idaho Code § 29-114 (1971). Architects and engineers are not specifically mentioned by this statute.

Illinois. An agreement in a construction contract to indemnify another person for that person's own negligence is void as against public policy. Ill. Rev. Stat. ch. 29, para. 61 (1971). Architects and engineers are not specifically mentioned by this statute.

Indiana. Agreements affecting construction or design contracts, except those pertaining to highway contracts, that indemnify one for his sole negligence or willful misconduct are void unless liability insurance normally available within the United States at standard rates cannot be obtained for the facility being constructed or designed because it constitutes a dangerous instrumentality. Ind. Code Ann. §§ 26-2-5-1, 26-2-5-2 (1975).

Iowa. Iowa common law permits indemnification agreements that clearly and specifically express the intent of the parties to the agreement. *Evans v. Howard R. Green Co.,* 231 N.W.2d 907 (Iowa 1975). Iowa has not yet addressed this issue by statute.

Kansas. Kansas common law permits indemnification agreements that clearly and specifically express the intent of the parties to the agreement. *Bartlett v. Davis Corp.,* 219 Kan. 148, 547 P.2d 800 (1976). Kansas has not addressed this issue by statute.

Kentucky. Kentucky courts will enforce indemnification agreements, *Reynolds Metal Co. v. I.W. Schickli & Bros.,* 548 S.W.2d 841 (Ky. 1977), but not against active negligence. *Ohio River Pipeline Co. v. Landrum,* 580 S.W.2d 713 (Ky. Ct. App. 1979). Kentucky has not addressed this issue by statute.

Louisiana. Provisions in public contracts, other than insurance contracts, for contractors to indemnify a public body for damages arising out of injuries or property damage to third parties caused by the negligence of the public body are void. La. Rev. Stat. Ann. § 38:2216 (West 1980).

Maine. Maine common law permits indemnification agreements that clearly and specifically express the intent of the parties to the agreement. *Emery Waterhouse Co. v. Lea,* 467 A.2d 986 (Me. 1983). Maine has not addressed this issue by statute.

Maryland. Agreements to indemnify one for his sole negligence in connection with a contract relating to the construction, repair, or maintenance of a building, structure, appurtenance, or appliance, including moving, demolition, and excavation in connection therewith, are void. Md. Cts. & Jud. Proc. Code Ann. § 5-305 (1975). Architects and engineers are not specifically mentioned by this statute.

Massachusetts. Any indemnification agreement relative to the construction, reconstruction, alteration, remodeling, repair, or demolition of a building, structure, highway, appurtenance, or appliance is against public policy and is void and unenforceable. Mass. Ann. Laws ch. 149, § 29(c) (Law. Co-op. 1985).

Michigan. Agreements to indemnify one for his sole negligence in connection with a contract relating to the construction, repair, or maintenance of a building, structure, appurtenance, or appliance, including moving, demolition, and excavation in connection therewith, are void. Mich. Comp. Laws § 691.991 (1966).

Minnesota. An indemnification agreement contained in, or executed in connection with, a building and construction contract is unenforceable, except to the extent that the underlying injury or damage is attributable to the negligent or otherwise wrongful act or omission, including a breach of a specific contractual duty, of the promisor. Minn. Stat. §§ 337.01, 337.02 (1983).

Mississippi. Agreements in public or private construction contracts to indemnify another person from that person's own negligence are void as against public policy. Miss. Code Ann. § 31-5-41 (1972). Architects and engineers are not specifically mentioned in this statute.

Missouri. Missouri common law permits indemnification agreements that clearly and specifically express the intent of the parties to the agreement. *Asher v. Broadway-Valentine Center, Inc.,* 691 S.W.2d 478 (Mo. Ct. App. 1985). Missouri has not addressed this issue by statute.

Montana. Any indemnification agreement between a company and its employees or servants is void. Mont. Code Ann. § 39-2-705 (1989). Beyond this, specific and clear language is required by Montana courts before indemnification agreements will be enforced. *Sweet v. Colborn School Supply,* 39 Mont. 168, 639 P.2d 521 (1982).

Nebraska. Indemnity agreements relating to contracts for the construction, alteration, repair, or maintenance of a building, structure, highway bridge, viaduct, water, sewer, or gas distribution system, or other work dealing with construction, or for any moving, demolition, or excavation connected with such construction, that indemnify for one's own negligence are void. This statute does not apply to construction bonds or insurance contracts. Neb. Rev. Stat. § 25-21-187 (1979).

Nebraska courts will enforce indemnification agreements that clearly and specifically express the intent of the parties to the agreement. *Peter Kiewit Sons' Co. v. O'Keefe Elevator Co.,* 191 Neb. 50, 213 N.W.2d 731 (1974).

Nevada. Indemnity contracts and insurance contracts that purport to waive or modify the liability created by the state's workers' compensation statutes are void. This statute does not apply specifically to architects, engineers, or to construction contracts. Nev. Rev. Stat. § 616.265 (1947).

New Hampshire. "Any agreement or provision whereby an architect, engineer, surveyor or his agents or employees is sought to be held harmless or indemnified for damages and claims arising out of circumstances giving rise to legal liability by reason of negligence on the part of any said persons shall be against public policy, void and wholly unenforceable." N.H. Rev. Stat. Ann. § 338-A:1 (1973).

New Jersey. Provisions indemnifying architects, engineers, surveyors, or their agents for damages caused by or resulting from their sole negligence and arising out of (1) the preparation or approval by them of maps, drawings, opinions, reports, surveys, change orders, designs, or specifications; or (2) the giving of or failure to give directions or instructions by them when such giving or failure to give is the cause of the damage, are against public policy and void. N.J. Stat. Ann. § 2A:40A-1 (West 1983).

New Mexico. "In any agreement relating to the construction, installation, alteration, modification, repair, maintenance, servicing, demolition, excavation, drilling, reworking, grading, paving, clearing, site preparation or development, of any real property or any involvement of any kind whether on, above or under real property, including without limitation, agreements concerning buildings, shafts, wells and structures, which indemnifies one for liability arising out of (1) preparation or approval of maps, drawings, opinions, reports, surveys, change orders, designs or specifications, and (2) the giving of or failure to give directions or instructions, is void and unenforceable." N.M. Stat. Ann. §§ 56-7-1, 56-7-2 (1971).

New York. Agreements that indemnify architects, engineers, or surveyors from liability for bodily injury or property damage arising out of defects in maps, plans, designs, or specifications, prepared, acquired, or used by such architect, engineer, or surveyor or their agents, are void. N.Y. Gen. Oblig. Law § 5-324 (McKinney 1965).

North Carolina. Design services are specifically mentioned in North Carolina's statute that invalidates agreements indemnifying the promisee against liability proximately caused, in whole or in part, by negligence of the promisee or its agents. N.C. Gen. Stat. § 22B-1 (1979).

North Dakota. "Any provision in a construction contract which would make the contractor liable for the errors of the owner or his agents in the plans and specifications of such contract is against public policy and void." N.D. Cent. Code § 9-08-02.1 (1969).

Beyond this provision, North Dakota seems to allow indemnification agreements that are specific and clear. *Bridston v. Dover Corp.,* 352 N.W.2d 194 (N.D. 1984).

Ohio. Agreements to indemnify one for his sole negligence in connection with a contract relating to the construction, repair, or maintenance of a building, structure, appurtenance, or appliance, including moving, demolition, and excavation in connection therewith, are void. Ohio Rev. Code Ann. § 2305.31 (Anderson 1975).

Oklahoma. All contracts that exempt one for his own fraud, or willful injury to the person or property of another, whether willful or negligent, are void. Okl. Stat. Ann. tit. 15, § 212 (West 1981).

Oregon. Construction agreements requiring a person to indemnify another against liability for damage arising out of the indemnitee's negligence in the design or the indemnitee's sole negligence in the inspection of the work that is the subject of the agreement are enforceable only if the indemnitee secures or maintains insurance covering such risks. Any provision in a construction agreement that requires a person to indemnify another against liability for damage caused by the sole negligence of the indemnitee is void. Or. Rev. Stat. § 30.140 (1973).

Pennsylvania. Architects, engineers, and surveyors are specifically mentioned in a Pennsylvania statute that voids indemnification agreements seeking to protect these workers from damages arising out of (1) the preparation or approval of designs, specifications, surveys, change orders, etc., or

(2) the giving or failure to give directions or instructions when such giving or failure to give is the cause of the claim. Pa. Stat. Ann. tit. 68, § 491 (Purdon 1970).

Rhode Island. Agreements to indemnify one for his sole negligence in connection with a contract relating to the construction, repair, or maintenance of a building, structure, appurtenance, or appliance, including moving, demolition, and excavation in connection therewith, are void. R.I. Gen. Laws § 6-34-1 (1976). Design services are specifically mentioned by this statute.

South Carolina. Agreements in connection with the design, planning, alteration, repair, or maintenance of a building, structure, highway, road, appurtenance, or appliance purporting to indemnify the promisee against liability for damages caused by the promisee's sole negligence are against public policy and are unenforceable. S.C. Code Ann. § 32-2-10 (Law. Co-op. 1980). This statute further provides that "nothing contained in this section shall affect a promise or agreement whereby the promisor shall indemnify or hold harmless the promisee . . . against liability for damages resulting from the negligence, in whole or in part, of the promisor." *Id.*

South Dakota. Agreements in construction contracts that indemnify architects or engineers for liability arising out of (1) preparation or approval of maps, drawings, opinions, reports, surveys, change orders, designs, or specifications, and (2) the giving of or failure to give directions or instructions are unenforceable. Additionally, agreements to indemnify one for his sole negligence in connection with a contract relating to the construction, repair, or maintenance of a building, structure, appurtenance, or appliance, including moving, demolition, and excavation in connection therewith, are void. S.D. Codified Laws Ann. § 56-3-16 (1972).

Tennessee. Indemnity agreements in construction contracts that purport to protect the promisee against liability for damages caused by or resulting from the promisee's sole negligence are against public policy and are void. Tenn. Code Ann. § 62-6-123 (1976).

Texas. Any agreement whereby a registered architect or registered engineer is indemnified by the contractor from liability for injury caused by or resulting from (1) defects in plans, designs, or specifications prepared or used by the architect or engineer, or (2) negligence in rendering professional duties called for in the contract is void. Tex. Civ. Prac. & Rem. Code Ann. § 130 (Vernon 1991). This act does not apply to the contracts of insurance contractors, owners, architects, or engineers indemnifying them from liability for negligent acts other than those described above or for the negligent acts of contractors.

Utah. Agreements in construction contracts purporting to indemnify the promisee against liability for damages resulting from the promisee's sole negligence are against public policy and void. Utah Code Ann. § 13-8-1 (1969). Agreements that are clear and specific may be enforced if not otherwise prohibited by statute. *Shell Oil Co. v. Birnkerhoff-Signal Drilling Co.,* 658 P.2d 1187 (Utah 1983).

Vermont. Vermont has not enacted a statute against hold-harmless agreements, nor is there any case law restricting or prohibiting indemnification against one's own negligence.

Virginia. Construction contract provisions by which a contractor purports to indemnify another party to the contract against liability for damages resulting solely from the negligence of such other party are against public policy and are void. Va. Code Ann. § 11-4-1 (1974). This provision does not affect the validity of contracts entered into before July 1, 1973.

Washington. Agreements to indemnify one for his sole negligence in connection with a contract relating to the construction, repair, or maintenance of a building, structure, appurtenance, or appliance, including moving, demolition, and excavation in connection therewith, are void. Wash. Rev. Code Ann. § 4.24.115 (1986). Such contracts may be enforceable to the extent of the indemnitor's negligence and only if such is specifically provided therefor. In addition, the indemnitor's immunity may be waived under industrial insurance if the agreement specifically provides therefor and the waiver is mutually negotiated. These latter provisions only apply to agreements made after June 11, 1986.

West Virginia. Construction agreements purporting to indemnify against liability for damages resulting from the sole negligence of the indemnitee are against public policy and are void. W. Va. Code § 55-8-14 (1975).

Wisconsin. "Any provision to limit or eliminate tort liability as a part of or in connection with any contract, covenant or agreement relating to the construction, alteration, repair or maintenance of a building, structure, or other work related to construction, including any moving, demolition or excavation, is against public policy and void." Wis. Stat. § 895.49 (1977). This statute does not apply to any agreement entered into before July 1, 1978 and has been held inapplicable to indemnification agreements.

Wyoming. Wyoming common law permits indemnification agreements if the agreements clearly and specifically express the intent of the parties to the agreement. *Mountain Fuel Supply Co. v. Emerson,* 578 P.2d 1351 (Wyo. 1978).

PART III

BUSINESS DEVELOPMENT AND PROCUREMENT

CHAPTER 9

MARKETING DESIGN PROFESSIONAL SERVICES TO PRIVATE CLIENTS

A. Eugene Kohn

A. Eugene Kohn holds both bachelor's and master's degrees in architecture from the University of Pennsylvania. He is a partner in Kohn Pedersen Fox Associates P.C., in New York, New York, a firm of architects and planners that received the Architectural Firm of the Year award in 1990 and the Medal of Honor in 1989 from the American Institute of Architects (AIA). Mr. Kohn is a Fellow of the AIA and a member of the Royal Institute of British Architects, the New York Building Congress, the Urban Land Institute, and the Municipal Arts Society of New York. He is past president of AIA's New York chapter and has served on the board of directors for the Architectural League, the advisory board for the master of science degree in real estate development at Columbia University's Graduate School of Architecture and Planning, and the Yale University Committee on the Arts Gallery and British Arts Center.

§ 9.1 Introduction

Only since the 1960s has marketing become an acceptable and necessary part of running a design practice.[1] This trend developed significantly during the 1970s, as a result of the recession, inflation, and increased competition for a limited number of projects. For instance, the Society for Marketing Professional Services (SMPS) was founded in 1973 and now numbers over 2,500 members.[2]

Several factors have influenced the move toward marketing, most notably the "current information age," the 1980s boom economy in the United States that was dominated by service industries, and constantly increasing national and international competition for a smaller number of design jobs.[3] According to the 1982 edition of the *Architect's Handbook of Professional Practice:*

> The traditional practice of architecture has changed much since World War II. Earlier, in an age of simpler technology, a gentler legal climate and a less critical concern for getting the most value for each expended dollar, the architect in private practice was able to adequately cover most of the bases. No more. To survive and prosper in today's complicated and toughened practice climate, most firms have found that specialization among their staff is a necessity. . . . In addition to the traditional design and delineating functions, these areas include: marketing . . . marketing communications . . . programming . . . project management . . . practice management . . . specification

---

[1] For the oldest account of an effort to market design professional services, *see* Vitruvitus: The Ten Books on Architecture 35–36 (M. Hickey trans. 1960).

[2] The A/E Marketing Handbook: A User's Manual 5 (S. D'Elia, J. Ricereto, & M. Spaulding eds. 1984) [hereinafter Handbook].

[3] Dean, *Seventy-Five Turbulent Years of American Architecture,* Architecture, Dec. 1987, at 100.

> writing . . . estimating and cost control . . . construction contract administration . . . and other specialties.[4]

This statement reflects a significant change in attitude from one made in the 1917 edition, which made it clear that soliciting work was not acceptable, and that architects should wait to be contacted by prospective clients. This meant that most architects had to rely heavily on their personal contacts, many of which were developed either socially or during the course of their architectural education. However, things were changing by the 1950s. According to the 1958 handbook, written during a period when there was a great deal of work:

> Little that is useful can be written about securing a commission . . . . To impress the client with one's qualifications, the restraints of modesty should be observed, but favorable facts need not be withheld. Recently reported methods of explaining proposed architectural services include the use of: 1. photographs; 2. colored projection lantern slides; 3. exhibits; 4. a presentation book; 5. reprints of published articles; 6. scrap book; 7. motion pictures . . . . Brochures are used by many.

Advertising, however, was not allowed on the grounds that it was unethical; in the words of the handbook, "not merely on the basis of abstract ethical ideals, but also because it is not in the public interest."[5]

By 1980, advertising was accepted and even encouraged by the handbook:

> The architect advertises for one or more of the following reasons: To obtain leads to sources of work. To build up a mailing list. To build up an image with existing or past clients. To offer specialized services to clients or other design professionals. To become known (especially new firms or firms with new names). To reach large groups of similar clients requiring modest-scale services (e.g., residential or store-front remodeling) . . . . One rule of thumb is to advertise whenever the firm wants to bring out a single feature that makes it distinctive from competitors . . . . Another rule is to advertise when one wants to reach large numbers of readers with news of a low-cost service that requires a high volume of business.[6]

Today, most firms in the design disciplines support some type of marketing function, whether it is as large as an entire department, or just one person who maintains contacts and prepares proposals for new work. Printed materials, standard text, agency forms, graphic materials, slide presentations—all are more sophisticated than they were just a few years ago,

---

[4] Gordon, *The Evolution of Architectural Practice,* Architecture, Dec. 1987, at 122.

[5] *Id.* at 125.

[6] *Id.* at 126.

and all are continuing to become more sophisticated and streamlined as competition becomes stiffer and as professional staffs become more comfortable with new techniques and technologies for the production of graphics and other marketing materials.

§ 9.2 What Is Marketing?

According to the American Marketing Association, marketing is "the performance of business activities that direct the flow of goods and services from producer to consumer or user."[7] In the more specific context of the architectural profession, marketing is any activity that is related to getting new work. The range of activities necessarily varies from design firm to design firm, depending on each firm's goals, size, age, type of work, and a number of other factors. *The A/E Marketing Handbook: A User's Manual* defines marketing as "an umbrella that covers all the things that need to be done to close the sale or get the contract signed. The specific activities that marketing covers include: planning, research, developing strategies, implementing strategies, public relations, advertising, pricing, selling, producing the work, and evaluating results."[8]

Some of these activities are emphasized more in certain firms; some are not at all a part of the marketing process. For example, some firms elect to mount exhaustive public relations campaigns, while others choose not to use any public relations techniques or any advertising, relying instead on their planning, research, and work products to achieve results. (For more information on the detailed administrative aspects of a strong marketing effort, such as budget, the development of a firm-specific marketing plan, and how to set up a marketing department, consult *The A/E Marketing Handbook: A User's Manual,* widely accepted as the classic text on this subject. Also see the recommended reading list in **§ 9.21**.)

§ 9.3 Marketing versus Selling

Generally speaking, marketing is forward thinking, future oriented, long range, conceptual before specific, and encompasses a range of activities. Selling, on the other hand, is focused in the present and involves a specific product or service.

Certain design firms do not even use the word marketing. Their business development activities are very traditional in the sense that they identify a need for something they can provide, and then proceed to sell the firm and

---

[7] Handbook at 2.

[8] *Id.* at 3.

its product or service to the prospective buyer. This approach assumes that the buyer will be able to relate the firm's approach and previous experience to their current needs. A marketing approach allows for a response to the prospective client that is more tailored to the client's needs, based on research into the client, the project requirements, and the site and background of the project. Each of these approaches can be successful, depending on the character of the firm and the nature of the prospective client.

§ 9.4 The Private Sector

For purposes of this chapter, the private sector is defined as any nongovernmental, privately owned organization that contracts for professional design services. In general, private sector clients are corporations, institutions, or real estate developers, and themselves represent a variety of client types who require a wide range of building types, including commercial offices, research and development offices, and laboratories, industrial buildings, and retail facilities.

§ 9.5 The Firm

Before any marketing activities begin, crucial decisions must be made about the nature of the design firm itself. In the case of a new firm, the principals must decide what kind of firm they want to be: the types of work they want to pursue, the size of the firm, and whether the firm will be primarily local, regional, national, or international in scope. Specialization in a particular building type or approach to architectural projects must be decided on early in the process, although it can and will be reconsidered later as the firm grows. If the firm plans to provide more general services, they should be marketed accordingly. Once these basic decisions have been made, a marketing plan can be developed.

If the firm already exists, its strengths should be recognized. A firm that specializes in historic preservation work, for example, should not be submitting qualifications for high-tech laboratory work, unless it is teamed with another firm that has expertise in that area.

§ 9.6 Direct Marketing

Direct marketing comprises a variety of activities that lay the groundwork for obtaining a job. Again, there is a marked difference between marketing and selling professional services. Direct marketing activities are proactive in nature and, ideally, should be occurring in various stages at all times in an established firm. Activities required to obtain a client successfully include research, developing leads, courting prospective clients, presenting the firm, closing the contract, and evaluating the firm's entire marketing and presentation process for that project.[9]

§ 9.7 —Research

Webster's Dictionary defines research as "careful, patient, systematic, diligent inquiry or examination in some field of knowledge." Two types of research are crucial to any marketing effort, no matter how small or new a firm is. Market research should address the market for the building type and professional services that are the firm's area of expertise. This differs from lead research, which is the process of identifying potential clients and discovering whether there could be any future work.[10]

Before any market research can begin, of course, the firm must have identified its market type and the geographic area in which it intends to work. Ideally, this will have been done at the firm's outset. There are three major task areas to market research: talking directly with resource people, extensive reading in a variety of sources, and constantly evaluating and reevaluating the firm's abilities and goals.

Verbal research should be focused on a range of professional groups, including past clients, heads of organizations or corporations in the identified market, heads of trade associations such as the American Association of Law Schools or the American Library Association, editors of trade publications, key contact people in federal, state, and local agencies, any experts in the field, and other architects and engineers with whom relationships have been established. In fact, prospective clients can be approached as resource people who are experts in their fields; in this manner, a relationship is being established that is not specifically focused on an upcoming project.

Reading research can include general circulation newspapers, any of the financial newspapers periodicals (*The Wall Street Journal, The Financial Times of London, Barron's*), the professional journals appropriate to the firm's work (*Architectural Record, Progressive Architecture, Building Design and Construction, Architecture, ENR*), and professional journals for the client's discipline (*Connections,* the magazine for American law schools), as well as more specific material about the client and the project site.

Evaluating the firm requires identifying any key people on staff who have particular experience in the market being approached and who may know additional resource people to contact. These staff people, and other

---

[9] Handbook at 43.

[10] Handbook at 44.

members of the staff, also can provide information on various consultants and other design firms who have expertise in areas that the firm does not, and who can be invited to participate on teams when it is time to prepare a proposal for a particular job. It is also important to understand why the firm has been hired in the past, and to see if these reasons are transferable to the market or job in question.

§ 9.8 —Developing Leads

In the words of *The A/E Marketing Handbook,* "Developing leads is probably the single most important concern of a professional marketer. . . . Genuine leads meet certain criteria, including:

> The project is real and likely to go ahead.
> It is or can be funded.
> Your firm is qualified to provide services.
> No other firm has been selected."[11]

Similar to market research, leads can be developed by talking to professional contacts, subscribing to publications that list leads, and creating needs with clients.

Real estate agents, contractors, consultants, and colleagues who are friendly with the firm also should be approached. Once relationships have been developed with these resource people, it becomes much easier to interact in an informal way; eventually, both receiving and passing along leads will happen as a matter of course. Relationships that are developed for the purpose of finding leads should be initiated by a telephone call that is planned, asks specific questions, and takes place between equals, whether between two marketing directors or between the principals of the firm and the client firm or organization.[12]

Publications that are specifically related to unearthing leads include the federal government's *Commerce Business Daily, Dodge Reports, ENR* (formerly *Engineering News-Record),* newspapers of local communities, municipalities, and counties, and those of lead-finding services. In most cases, however, by the time a project appears in one of these publications, the process is so far along that it is too late to submit for the job. In ideal circumstances, a carefully developed network will have provided the information well in advance of its publication.

Creating leads with prospective clients can involve helping a client take ideas and develop specific projects from them or helping to assess sites or

---

[11] Handbook at 49.

[12] *Id.* at 50.

investments that the client owns. Presumably, with an established network in real estate, leasing groups, and various agencies, a project could be generated. This requires a significant investment of time and money on the part of the firm.

Once a lead has been developed, a "hand-off" should take place between the marketing professional and a member of the professional staff (a principal or project manager) who will make the prospective client the most comfortable and who will be able to run the project, should it turn into one. Throughout this process, the design professional should work closely with the marketing person to stay well informed.[13]

§ 9.9 —Courting Prospective Clients

Courting a client is part of the long-range marketing process, in which a relationship is developed and sustained over a long period of time. Ideally, client contact should be initiated just to establish the relationship, rather than to obtain a specific job. Courting requires the firm to maintain reasonably close contact with the client, providing updated information on the firm's activities and giving the client a chance to become familiar with professional staff people.

In addition to keeping the client informed through telephone contact, letters, and materials about the firm, some entertaining is generally considered necessary. Many marketing professionals use mealtimes as opportunities for better acquainting potential, current, or past clients with the firm and its work. This type of entertaining, however, is not an option with public sector clients.

After developing a lead, following through is probably the most important aspect of the direct marketing process. A successful follow-through process requires all parties involved to understand what roles the firm and its consultants should play. Issues that should be addressed include whether or not other leads can be derived from this one, consultant disciplines that must be covered for this client's projects, where the project or projects would be located, and how the firm can assist in the development stages of the project.

The next step is selling the firm's professional services to the client for a specific project. Ideally, by this point the client should be quite familiar with the firm, although the client still may have questions about its capabilities. Constant evaluation of the firm's strengths and adherence to the goals and directions that the firm is pursuing will help anticipate some of the client's doubts. Clients are most often concerned at this stage with experience in the project type, office location, appropriate consultants for the

---

[13] *Id.* at 53.

design team, cost and schedule control, technical capabilities, and quality assurance.

At a certain point the firm must decide whether or not to pursue a client. Although clients select the firms with whom they want to work, firms also must select their clients, which is part of the process of developing the firm's character and direction. Factors that are crucial to deciding whether or not a job should be pursued include the probability of selection, the relative experience of the firm, the competition (especially related to fee), and whether or not the project will be realized.[14]

§ 9.10 —Presenting the Firm

Presenting the firm's credentials to a client for a specific project normally follows a formalized process, but one that varies more in the private sector than in the public sector. In the private sector, the process can include some or all of the following steps: a letter introducing the firm's qualifications; a qualifications package that includes basic written information and graphic materials on the firm, often submitted in response to a request for qualifications (RFQ); a proposal that is generated in response to a request for proposal (RFP) for a specific project; a scope statement with a fee proposal (although often part of the proposal, this may be presented as a separate document); and an interview with the client.

Although each qualifications package and each proposal must be tailored to the requirements of the project in question, much of the information that must be submitted should be readily available in the firm's marketing files. Standard marketing materials include what is called *boilerplate,* or written text that generally describes all aspects of the firm's practice and professional services; reprints from publications that have featured the firm's work; brochures developed by the firm; photographs and slides of the firm's projects; and any other visual supporting materials, such as computer-generated site plans or facsimiles of awards received.

Written boilerplate materials include a background statement about the firm, its design philosophy, project descriptions, awards, professional resumes, and statements about other aspects of the practice that might address computer-aided design and drafting (CADD) capabilities, cost and schedule control, phasing, workload, quality control, energy conservation, security issues, and client references. Other materials are generated by the design and construction process itself, and completed projects may be presented for the client's review. All materials should reflect graphic excellence and the character of the firm, and they should be identified with an established firm logo.

---

[14] Handbook at 59.

"A proposal is the sales tool that can edge your firm past the competition."[15] If the qualifications statement has been successful, and the firm has been invited to respond to an RFP, a detailed proposal is the next step. In addition to the basic information about the firm that is usually requested, most RFPs ask for information generated by a list of stated selection criteria. The following list incorporates many of the most frequently used selection criteria:

1. Related experience

   How many projects of a similar nature has the firm worked on within the last 10 years?

   Is there a consistent trend in the experience?
2. Size of the firm

   Will the firm be able to handle the project with current or only slightly increased work force? Preferably, a single project should not occupy more than one-third of the staff.
3. Cost record of a typical completed project

   What were the project costs during planning, bidding, and at completion of construction?

   What is the attitude towards change orders?

   How are costs estimated?
4. Agency interaction

   Is the firm experienced in dealing with regulatory agencies?

   What is the firm's record?

   How does the firm intend to interact with agencies?
5. Understanding of project

   What does the firm see as major objectives of the project?

   What problems does the firm foresee?

   What is the firm's approach to construction implementation? (Construction management versus conventional lump-sum bid)
6. Project team

   All of the criteria should be met to a satisfactory degree not only by the firm in total, but also by the individuals in charge of the project. A comprehensive understanding is required on the part of one or two key members in the project team, who can then delegate specific tasks to the specialists on the team.

   How will the team work and have its members worked together before?

---

[15] Handbook at 64.

7. References
   Check references on completed projects and projects in progress
   How was the service?
   Do the references know the individuals proposed for the team?
   How have they handled problems?[16]

A successful proposal not only responds to the basic questions and to the identified selection criteria, but also anticipates the needs and wishes of the client. Again, the success of such a proposal is contingent on research, not only about the client, but also about the locale of the project, the history of the organization, and possibly even the history of the building type. During the production of the proposal, the marketing person should be planning for the interview, so that the necessary written materials, photos, graphics, and slides can be adapted for a live presentation.

The interview or presentation is a crucial part of the selection process. Handled well, the presentation itself is a powerful marketing tool. Usually the material presented in an interview is derived from the qualifications package and the proposal. Often, however, it is necessary to generate additional materials just for the presentation, such as slides, presentation boards, graphs, or charts.

The key members of the project team should lead the presentation. Excellent presentation skills are a real asset, and as many key persons in the firm as possible should develop them. Consultant firms may be included as part of the team, should the client require a total architect/engineer (A/E) team for consideration. In some cases, the client will limit the number of people who may attend the interview. The most successful presentations are made after some rehearsal, so enough time should be budgeted for both preparation and rehearsal. Intangible qualities such as personality, sense of humor, and "chemistry" between the design professional and client cannot be measured or planned, but are significant factors in the final selection. No matter how qualified a particular firm may be, a client will not hire someone with whom he or she is uncomfortable.

§ 9.11 —Closing the Contract

After the firm has been selected for the job, the relationship with the client must be firmed and a contract signed. Ideally, closing should "create an atmosphere for completing the selection in which the client's commitment

[16] Planning, Financing, and Constructing Health Care Facilities 313 (R. Cushman & S. Perry ed. 1983).

to [the firm] is seen as a perfectly natural step in the development of the relationship."[17] A principal of the firm should handle this step, negotiating compensation while maintaining the good relationship that has been painstakingly developed with the client.

§ 9.12 —Evaluating the Process

As marketing is a research activity, it also can be considered an activity of almost constant evaluation. The firm's principals and marketing professionals must be evaluating their efforts at every step of the process of getting a job. Initially, it is necessary to evaluate the firm itself, its strengths and weaknesses. As the process advances, marketing materials must be evaluated and updated or revised. Qualifications packages, proposals, and presentations always should be evaluated afterwards in terms of what worked and what did not. If the firm goes through the interview process and is not selected for the job, it is very important to discover the reasons; a post-interview review with input from the "lost" client is most valuable. This information adds to a growing knowledge base and allows the marketing effort to become increasingly effective and sophisticated.

§ 9.13 Indirect Marketing

Indirect marketing functions are those that ultimately draw clients to the firm and result in "referral, reputation, and repeat work."[18] These functions, which also can be viewed as public relations, vary widely from firm to firm, depending on the choices the principals make about expenditures of money and the time of marketing staff people. Publications, advertising, direct mail, professional awards, participation in design competitions, professional memberships, lectures, seminars, and entertaining are all possible approaches that fall into the category of indirect marketing.[19] Each of these should be evaluated carefully; any one of them, if not appropriate to the firm or if used unsuccessfully, can waste significant amounts of time and money. All of them have the potential to increase exposure to the firm in a positive way, and positive exposure of the firm, its people, and its work is the best way to build an excellent reputation and be considered for many important projects.

---

[17] Handbook at 81.

[18] Polites, *How Architects Market Themselves,* Architectural Rec., July 1990, at 27–28.

[19] Handbook at 86.

§ 9.14 —Publications

The most effective way for a firm's work to become known is through published articles. Trade publications (in design, engineering, and planning, and in the fields of prospective clients), local newspapers, and national newspapers and news magazines are the most immediately useful markets. Often resulting from pieces placed in these publications are referrals from other professionals, high-quality reprints to include among marketing materials, and the recruitment of new professionals for the staff. Other publications that are appropriate to the firm's type of work can be good vehicles for publicity as well, particularly if they are aware of the firm's interest in publishing an occasional article. Naturally, any in-house article should be written by the most senior person who is available and who is comfortable with technical language and editorial demands.

Press releases and press packets also can be used to generate publicity; however, these tools generally are used by larger firms with larger marketing staffs and substantial publishing networks.

§ 9.15 —Advertising

As discussed in **§ 9.1**, advertising was not allowed in the architectural profession until 1980. Most design firms still do not advertise directly; "advertising usually has less credibility than the same information presented in an article written by a third party, such as the magazine's editorial staff."[20]

§ 9.16 —Direct Mail

Along with published articles, direct mail campaigns are an extremely effective way to maintain contact with past, current, and prospective clients, as well as with a variety of publications. The quality of the mailing list is crucial to the success of such an effort; a substantial mailing list requires consistent maintenance and continuous updating and revision. Some of the materials distributed this way include firm brochures, announcements of moves, appointments to the firm, or new services; invitations to special events, such as holiday parties or exhibits of the firm's work; posters or seasonal greeting cards; and newsletters.

---

[20] Handbook at 97.

§ 9.17 —Awards Programs and Design Competitions

As with other aspects of marketing, submitting materials for various awards must be judiciously considered. Certain awards are more credible and carry more weight than others within the profession, and should be pursued if there is a reasonably good chance of winning one. They can then be incorporated into the firm's qualifications packages and formal proposals.

Likewise, entering design competitions entails significant investments of manpower and money. Although there is often a good deal of publicity associated with design competitions, the cost of participating usually far outweighs the compensation gained from clients. However, competitions are a good way to break into a new market area in which the firm has little or no previous experience.

§ 9.18 —Memberships

Memberships in organizations that can enhance the marketing network and result in work are worthwhile, particularly in those trade associations that attract professionals from the markets the firm has targeted. Involvement with the American Institute of Architects (AIA), by giving time and talent, helps the profession. However, one must weigh the time devoted to all memberships to be sure that leads are being produced and that the firm is ultimately benefiting from the absence of key staff members.

§ 9.19 —Speaking Engagements and Seminars

Speaking engagements and seminars, like any other type of exposure, can advance a firm's reputation. If there is a principal or associate of the firm who is an excellent public speaker, that person's appearances at various conferences can benefit the marketing effort, especially if the speeches are published subsequently. Seminars require more effort on the part of the marketing staff in terms of organization, planning, and selecting key people to make presentations and to be available to the seminar guests. Events like these provide a forum for demonstrating the firm's expertise in a given area.

§ 9.20 Marketing Staff

A firm's single most important resource in its marketing effort is its staff, both the people in the marketing department and the professional design staff. Marketing staffs vary widely in size and structure, depending on the size of the firm, the attitude of the principals toward marketing, the spoken and unspoken goals of the firm, and a number of other factors. One-person firms are their own one-person marketing departments, that also do the design work and oversee construction. Slightly larger firms may have one principal who makes the client contacts and who has some part-time assistance fulfilling the requirements for qualifications and proposal submittals. Large firms often have separate marketing or new business development departments, with a range of positions that cover the development of new leads and all written materials, including publishable articles, graphics, photograph and slide collections, and proposal preparation. A general rule is that for every 20 to 25 people in a large firm, there should be one full-time marketing person.[21] In all cases, there is at least one firm principal who is responsible for marketing and new business development.

In a firm that is large enough to support several people in a marketing department, responsibilities can be divided among them for more effective response. Communication among professional staff, among members of the marketing department, and between the professional staff and the marketing department is crucial to the success of any marketing effort. The marketing staff should be kept informed of any new leads obtained by others on the staff so they can be prepared to respond when the time comes. Conversely, it is the responsibility of the marketing staff to keep the principals and associates of the firm up to date on any new leads, proposals, or upcoming presentations for scheduling purposes.[22]

§ 9.21 Reading List

Following is a recommended reading list for marketers of design services:*

D. Cooper, *Architectural and Engineering Salesmanship* (John Wiley & Sons 1978).

W. Coxe, *Marketing Architectural and Engineering Services* (2d ed. 1983).

W. Coxe, *Success Strategies for Design Professionals* (1987).

---

[21] Handbook at 18.

[22] Kohn Pedersen Fox Associates offers full services in architecture, master planning, space planning, programming, and building analysis. Established in 1976, the firm has collaborated with some of the most significant developer, corporate, and institutional clients in the world on award-winning projects. Kohn Pedersen Fox received the 1990 Firm of the Year Award from the American Institute of Architects, the highest national honor to be given an architectural firm.

*Compiled by Gerre Jones and used with permission.

S. D'Elia, J. Ricereto, & M. Spaulding, eds., *The A/E Marketing Handbook: A User's Manual* (1984).

K. Delmar, *Winning Moves: The Body Language of Selling* (1984).

G. Jones, *How to Market Professional Design Services* (2d ed. 1983).

G. Jones, *Public Relations for the Design Professional* (1980).

G. Jones, *The No-Fear Guide to Public Speaking and Effective Presentations* (1987).

J. Morgan, *Marketing for Small Design Firms* (1984).

M. Spaulding & S. D'Elia, *Advanced Marketing Techniques for Architecture and Engineering Firms* (1989).

F. Stasiowski & D. Burstein, *Project Management for the Design Professional* (1982).

R. & A. Stewart, *Proposal Preparation* (John Wiley & Sons 1984).

F. Stitt, ed., *Design Office Management* (1986).

C. Thomsen, *CM: Developing, Marketing, and Delivering Construction Management Services* (1982).

J. Ullmann, ed., *Handbook of Engineering Management* (John Wiley & Sons 1984).

CHAPTER 10

MARKETING DESIGN PROFESSIONAL SERVICES TO PUBLIC CLIENTS

Philip D. Giantris
Lloyd F. Thompson

Philip D. Giantris has 25 years' experience with technical and marketing responsibilities in the engineering design profession. He holds a B.S. in civil engineering from Worcester Polytechnic Institute and an M.B.A. from Boston University in marketing and organizational development. He is president of Bird Environmental Systems and Services, in Norwood, Massachusetts. Previously he held the position of senior vice-president of marketing and corporate development for Metcalf & Eddy, Inc. Mr. Giantris is very active in the area of public-private partnerships as a means of providing public services.

Lloyd F. Thompson is president of Marketing Strategies Inc., a full-service marketing, advertising, and public relations firm headquartered in Rockland, Massachusetts. He earned his B.S. in public relations from Boston University, attended the graduate program at the George Washington University Sino-Soviet Institute, graduated from the management program at Bentley College, and has taken numerous courses/seminars at Lesley College, the Amos Tuck School at Dartmouth, the Sloane School at M.I.T., and the Harvard University Graduate School of Design. Mr. Thompson has been a member of the seminar faculty at Bentley College and a seminar leader for events sponsored by the Associated General Contractors and the Association for Continuing Higher Education. He is a member of the American Marketing Association.

§ 10.1 Introduction

For the design professional today, the public sector market is more significant than ever before. The growth in government over the years has generated the need to create and maintain facilities in support of new programs and services. In serving this need, the design professional has provided services ranging from feasibility and economic studies, through conceptual design, final design, management during construction, start-up services, and training.

This chapter addresses how the principles of marketing professional services can be successfully applied to the unique needs of the design professional who chooses to offer services to the public sector. It stresses the need to understand the client's specific needs and unique procurement framework. Building a sound selling plan and developing a proposal are discussed, along with price issues and the final interview that cements the design professional/client relationship.

§ 10.2 Who Is the Public Client?

At the highest and most visible level, the public client is the federal government acting through its numerous departments, including the Departments of Defense, Transportation, Housing, and Urban Development, and Energy, and administrations and agencies such as the Environmental Protection Agency and the General Services Administration.

Many of the federal government departments are mirrored at the state level because these state agencies often are the conduits for dispersing federal funds for various programs. For example, gasoline taxes that are paid at the pump carry both a state and federal tax component. The federal portion is reissued to the states to fund a wide range of transportation programs.

Below the state structure is a mosaic of public entities, each having various needs for design professional services and each with its own unique funding sources and procurement procedures. These include counties, towns, cities, and villages as well as special purpose government units such as sewerage, water, and solid waste districts and agencies, transportation authorities, and school districts.

A primary characteristic of these public clients is that the "buyer" will be a committee made up of paid public employees, elected or appointed public officials, or community volunteers. Such committees normally operate from a very structured format with criteria and rating systems, leaving the design professional little opportunity to "negotiate" a procurement. This structure challenges the design professional to operate outside the criteria to differentiate the offering. Many design professionals find such situations totally unacceptable and thus should avoid a major commitment to this market segment. However, for those who can adapt to the unique procurement procedures of the public sector, there is a vast opportunity to grow a practice and earn a fair return on the investment of resources.

§ 10.3 Marketing versus Selling

All too often, the words "marketing" and "selling" are used interchangeably and thus incorrectly. Although it has become fashionable to describe most sales activities as marketing, in reality each category has its own sets of rules, disciplines, and implementation strategies and tactics. Historically, design professionals have viewed sales activities as something less than professional, but when those activities are called marketing, they receive a stamp of approval. However, both are legitimate and vital business functions.

Marketing is the broad discipline involving strategic planning, market research and analysis, identifying client needs, positioning the firm and its specific service offering, developing key accounts, creating sales support literature, gathering competitive intelligence, assessing the impact of external forces, forming strategic partnerships, external communications, internal communications, marketing and sales training, and client service, retention, and follow-up strategies. Marketing should be one of the major management disciplines in a professional design firm and, as such, should be the responsibility of a principal officer.

Sales involves the direct interface with the customer, including service presentations, lead qualification, proposal management and presentation, contract negotiations, and the completion of the transaction or closing the sale. Effective selling includes consulting—research to determine the prospective client's situation and how the firm's services and experiences can fit those needs.

In traditional practice, sales is a marketing discipline, one of the many important activities used to acquire a client and to gather first-hand market and client intelligence. The information-gathering function of the sales force is as critical as its customer contact role. If the sales force does not understand the client's business and business environment, it has little chance of long-term success, and it is of only marginal value to the firm's overall marketing efforts. The overriding goal of both marketing and sales activities is to improve the effectiveness with which the firm responds to customer needs. As Dr. Denis Healy, a nationally recognized marketing consultant, comments on marketing effectiveness, "Effectiveness as a term is related to how well the match is made between the requirements of the marketplace and the capabilities of your organization. An effective relationship is one where both sides of the transaction achieve their objectives. Effective marketing programs are those that result in customers who are ready to buy."[1]

§ 10.4 Marketing Plan

The marketing plan is the end result of a process that involves:

Stating the firm's vision
Assessing strengths and weaknesses
Evaluating market segment opportunities
Defining targeted market(s)
Assessing the potential competition
Defining the client's buying behavior
Stating the factors leading to success
Stating the strategic selling approach
Describing the marketing communication objectives to support sales.

To develop a marketing plan, the design professional must identify the firm's niche and differentiate the service offering. The public sector market, as discussed in **§ 10.2**, is largely driven by federal and state regulations. The formulation of public policy and the passage of these regulations create the market. The ability of the design professional to anticipate changes, quantify their impact, and reshape the firm's services to meet these needs in a timely manner will differentiate a market leader from a follower.

---

[1] D. Healy, Marketing and Selling—Aren't They the Same? (May 1986) (unpublished paper).

To effectively apply marketing tools and techniques to professional design services, it is useful to appreciate the parallels between marketing *capital services* and marketing *capital goods*. For example, a high-tech capital goods marketing plan might include the following characteristics:

1. The product's development is generally the responsibility of top management.
2. Product development has a major capital impact on the company.
3. Changes in that product, or adding a new product, have a major capital impact on the company.
4. Product success depends heavily on a successful integration of research and development and engineering and manufacturing capabilities, as well as personnel, accounting, and marketing.
5. The seller has intimate details of the customer's product, manufacturing environment, and end-user needs.
6. The seller identifies the decision makers and the company's sale cycle.
7. Senior management makes go/no-go decisions with respect to the marketing/sales efforts on a prospect-by-prospect basis because the marketing/sales process is expensive and lengthy, often running from many months to more than one year.
8. Existing customers provide the most fertile marketing opportunities.
9. The buyer is usually an enterprise, not an individual.
10. The product is often very complex.
11. The sale usually involves extensive contractual arrangements.
12. There are numerous performance and liability issues associated with the product.
13. The purchase process is complex. Persons involved in the purchase decision must carefully consider the expenditure.
14. The buyer and seller deal with one another directly, often undertaking intense negotiations over a lengthy time period.
15. Quality control is vital to product performance and customer satisfaction.
16. The buyer's risk is in the performance of the product and in the service and technical support provided by the seller.

The parallel characteristics of a professional design services marketing plan might be:

1. Senior management is involved with the formulation and delivery of the service and with the addition or deletion of a service.

2. Each activity within the firm—project programming, design documents, construction administration—has a high dependence on the other activities and on other business functions such as accounting, personnel, and marketing.
3. A complex service is being marketed.
4. The seller gains significant knowledge about the prospective client's problem, who the decision makers are, and the timetable for selection.
5. Senior management makes go/no-go decisions with respect to the pursuit of projects.
6. The marketing/selection process requires a considerable investment, is lengthy, and can span several months to one year. In some cases, even a larger time frame is required.
7. The buyer of the service makes a considered judgment in selecting the design firm.
8. There are intense negotiations and complex contractual arrangements between buyer and seller.
9. There are numerous performance and liability issues associated with the services being offered.
10. The buyer and seller deal with one another during and after the transaction.
11. Quality control is a vital component of client satisfaction.
12. The buyer's risk is in the performance of the professional staff servicing the account.

Section 10.11 presents an excellent example of how a piece of legislation, in this case the federal Safe Drinking Water Act Amendments of 1986[2] created an opportunity for an aggressive, focused, professional design firm to create a marketing and sales strategy that took risks but ultimately delivered the desired results. The firm in this case, by anticipating the legislation, in effect defined the market in terms of how the clients saw their needs and, therefore, the firm became the obvious source for information.

Marketing must be a priority within an organization. Management must recognize that everything the firm does communicates something to the market. Therefore, every decision and every action of the firm should be made within the context of understanding the market and the specific sensitivities of clients and prospects.

---

[2] 42 U.S.C. §§ 330f–300j (1988).

§ 10.5 Sales Plan

The sales plan is the day-to-day execution of the in-market aspects of the marketing strategy. The people selected to assume sales responsibility for the firm must be self-starters who can identify all the issues affecting a project opportunity. The sales staff must be comfortable in dealing with the bureaucracy of the public sector market as well as the political consequences of a project.

The sales plan uses the marketing strategy as its "policy" and then probes the market to identify the opportunities that the marketing plan has defined as the targeted niche(s). Once the sales staff has determined an opportunity, it is critical that the management team use a *go/no-go* decision process before any significant resources are expended. Such a process integrates generalized criteria that the design professional believes are common and important to the client's decision, with a rating system that attempts to quantify the design professional's competitiveness on a project. **Section 10.12** presents one way to make that decision through a matrix process with a point system.

Design firms must be cautioned to set high standards in the conduct of their sales professionals. The public sector has implemented many laws recently to remove any appearance of impropriety by its employees. The simple "business lunch" has become illegal if the salesperson picks up the whole check.

As design professionals broaden their services to include project delivery and operations and management services, there also will be conflict-of-interest claims from those who feel the design professional is limiting competition on subsequent phases of a project. The design professional would be wise to clearly communicate to the client or prospective client from the outset the breadth of his service offering and the ability to make the transition to the next phase of implementation. The critical area of conflict results when a design professional is engaged to provide an independent recommendation for a subsequent phase and endeavors to recommend himself.

§ 10.6 Qualifications Statement

It is common within the public sector market to initiate the procurement process for design professional services with a formal request for qualifications (RFQ). This can be done through a preestablished mailing list solicitation or a notice in appropriate printed media such as newspapers or trade publications. An effective sales program for the targeted market should insure that the design firm stay well informed. The firm should know that an RFQ is to be issued before it is actually received and should automatically receive all RFQs in its targeted market.

The RFQ is a critical decision point for the design professional because it represents the beginning of the go/no-go process of determining resource allocations. It is important to apply the tools of the go/no-go process (discussed in **§ 10.5**) rigorously at this stage, so that the business focus is not lost as the activity moves from strategy to reality.

It may sound obvious, but the RFQ must be read in its entirety to insure that the client's intent and the basic ground rules for continuing in the procurement process are clearly understood. Critical factors to look for include:

1. When, where, and in what form must the response to the RFQ be received?
2. What special demonstrated capabilities and experience will be required of the design professional to continue in the procurement process?
3. What unique requirements will the design professional need to address that are specific to the client's procurement procedures (minority and/or women's business enterprise participation, local office requirements, business registration)?
4. What is the client's basis for evaluating the RFQ in order to arrive at a pass/fail decision?
5. What specific pieces of supporting documentation (financial history, employment policies and records, ownership information) will be required to be submitted with the RFQ?

After a thorough evaluation of the RFQ, the go/no-go decision must be made before any additional resources are committed to the specific opportunity. This decision is a routine procedure that should not require much time if the sales program has targeted the market correctly.

With a decision to "go," the firm must develop a response to the RFQ that clearly will pass this first procurement hurdle. The documentation must be clear and responsive to the RFQ while differentiating the firm's capabilities from others who are pursuing the opportunity. If the design professional has done the same type of project before, then the process of documenting capability and experience should be fairly straightforward. However, if this is not true, the design professional must demonstrate that elements of other projects, successfully completed, represent similar sets of skills and experience. The design professional's case can be strengthened through a conceptual approach to the client's project, which identifies the critical skills needed and how these skills have been documented in the response to the RFQ.

A critical decision at this point is whether it is desirable to team with another design professional to insure that all of the capabilities and experience issues have been addressed. When considering a team arrangement, be sure that:

The project is big enough to share

The added capabilities are actually a complement and not merely more of the same

The project can be divided easily either by phase or by discipline

The final team arrangement actually can execute the project

It is clear to the client that there is one person in charge with singular responsibility to the client.

Once the response to the RFQ has been submitted, a parallel action program must be implemented that reinforces the design professional's qualifications and builds a base of support among responsible public officials who may influence the selection process. Although design professionals may fear they are being self-laudatory, this is an important step in winning a project. The period between the RFQ submission and the issuance of the request for proposal (RFP) or the invitation for bid (IFB)[3] is also critical in influencing what goes into the RFP and how that will affect the design professional's ability to respond successfully.

The design professional deals in a service offering that often requires a degree of problem solving. As such, the scope of the work and the perceived needs cannot be precisely defined by the client. This reality allows for some collaboration with the client to influence the RFP that is finally issued. An old expression among design professionals in the public sector market is, "If you didn't write the RFP for the client, then your competitor did, and you shouldn't waste your time preparing a proposal." The objective is to point up items that the design professional feels are important to the successful execution of the assignment and, obviously, for which the design professional has a competitive or differentiated advantage.

Requirements typically found in an RFP include:

1. Conceptual layout of the proposed facility to illustrate how the design professional might address specific site conditions
2. Computer-generated task and schedule plan for the project showing resource allocations

[3] The request for proposal (RFP) and the invitation for bid (IFB) are essentially the same. Generally, an RFP is issued for professional services, whereas equipment and labor are purchased with an IFB.

3. Typical computer-based report generation to demonstrate the ability to provide overall program management
4. Specific examples in which a particular approach was successful
5. Forecast of the manpower loading by discipline over the life of the project.

The public sector client looking to procure design professional services is increasingly demanding that the design professional make his proposal more tangible so that the client has a better view of what he is getting before he commits to the professional services. This merely reflects the greater public scrutiny that these public agencies are receiving in the conduct of their duties.

§ 10.7 Proposal

The request for proposal (RFP), like the RFQ, represents a clear milestone in the go/no-go process of determining resource allocation. The decision at this point is far more important and equally more *difficult* to make.

This decision is important because it is at the proposal stage that the cost to pursue the project escalates rapidly and continues through final selection and contract negotiation. Resources committed will include significant hours of key personnel who are critical to the production of existing projects and the firm's profitability. Critical considerations at this point include:

1. Does the nature of the project still fit the market focus of the firm?
2. How many design professional firms have been qualified to make a proposal?
3. How competitive is the firm in that field?
4. Is there still an opportunity to form a joint venture with one or more firms from the qualified list to improve competitiveness?
5. How has the client finally structured the requested pricing of the proposal and how will it factor into the final selection process?
6. How much will it cost (labor and material expense) to stay in the competition?
7. What is the dollar value of the project and the probable margin?

The reason that the go/no-go decision is difficult to make at this point is a combination of human nature and market image. Once the firm has "qualified" for the project, it may be difficult to be objective about moving ahead. It is helpful to allow other professionals not directly involved in the project to review the opportunity. If a no-go decision is made at this point, the perception left with the potential client can be a problem if the potential client could be a continuing source of work. The best advice in such situations is to candidly share the no-go decision with the potential client, explaining how and why the decision was made. This tells the client the firm has thoroughly analyzed the situation, which builds market image. In turn, the client may share information about how the firm is viewed that could influence future projects.

Once the decision to go ahead has been confirmed and any team arrangements have been established, the proposal process takes on an increased level of focus. This focus starts with a clear understanding of who is singularly responsible for the proposal. This must be a senior manager in the firm with the authority to commit resources and make decisions.

The responsible design professional manager then must identify the client's risk concerns, including such issues as:

1. Technology risk associated with necessary state-of-the-art treatment processes
2. Public reaction risk due to the nature of the project or its location
3. Scheduling and completion risk to meet a regulatory deadline
4. Operational performance risk due to the lack of a skilled work force
5. Implementation funding risk due to bond capacities and taxing limitations.

It is around the risk issues that the design professional builds a winning proposal. Yet the common mistake many design professionals make is to use the proposal to tout their skills rather than communicate how they plan to minimize risk for the client. The responsible senior manager for the proposal must be the leader of this risk-oriented approach, communicating to the client during the proposal process how he is moving to address the client's concerns and how he has organized a team of professionals with the skills and experience to deliver a successful project. The goal, without being too presumptuous, is to start managing the project before it is awarded.

Another important part of the proposal process is to understand how the proposal will be evaluated. Most proposal review procedures use specific rating criteria with a weighted point system to assist the reviewers. These procedures are not always made available to the design professional with the RFP, but they should be requested.

It is critical to understand how much of the evaluation will be based on technical issues related to the project (technical approach, experience of professionals proposed, project schedule, management techniques) versus sociopolitical issues (where the work will be produced, percent of local or minority professional services involved, hiring practices to be used).

Price also plays a major role in the proposal evaluation. There are still design professionals who consider priced proposals as unethical, but such a view is naive and impractical in today's economic climate. There is a distinction, however, between bidding design work and submitting a priced proposal. To bid design work, the client is in a position to outline its exact needs and to provide fairly detailed technical data as a basis for the design work. This type of procurement leaves little room for creative problem solving and the normal collaboration with the client. This market is driven by defined standards, and some would not consider this type of work a professional service. In a priced proposal, the design professional lays out a process that will arrive at the final design. At the point of presentation, the design professional prices that process based on the various levels of effort needed to address each phase.

In dealing with the priced proposal, the design professional can write the proposal to help the potential client evaluate price in the context of the proposed scope of work. The scope of work should read like a series of building blocks, each of which is critical to achieve success. These building blocks, or work tasks, also should support the critical underlying proposal theme of minimizing risk to the client. The level of effort, normally expressed in work hours, is tied to each task so that the client begins to realize what is needed for a successful project. If this is well done, every other proposal will be tested against this model.

It is beyond the scope of this chapter to deal with the issue of pricing professional services. However, there are some simple truths about this subject:

1. Price will always be a selection criterion in the public sector market.
2. The uninformed or unsophisticated client will try to reduce his request to a bid even if he does not have the knowledge to detail his needs and provide sufficient technical data, as a way of avoiding an objective evaluation process and a public challenge to a selection.
3. A project/client opportunity that has passed rigorous criteria established in a go/no-go decision process for professional design services should prequalify those projects that will accommodate the concept of a priced proposal that is not necessarily the lowest bid.
4. A risk-oriented proposal strategy will be very effective in helping the client's review committee select a firm based on reasons other than the lowest price.

§ 10.8 Formal Interview

The formal interview is often misused by the potential client and misunderstood by the design professional. Frequently the client does not apply a rigorous, decision-making approach to the proposal review process and, therefore, all proposers are interviewed. This clearly is a waste of time and money for both parties. The process is misunderstood by the design professional, who believes that style is more important than substance.

For the design professional who has mapped out a sound strategy built on minimizing the client's perception of risk on the project, the interview is effectively the "closing argument" to present the reviewing body with the clear reasons for making the desired award. A design professional should consider the following points in preparing for a formal interview:

1. **Clearly state critical issues.** The issues are the client's risk considerations and resolving them is the project. For example, the project may be to build a waste treatment plant, but the issues are probably compliance schedule deadlines, contaminant level reductions, reliability and redundancy, life cycle costs, and other factors.
2. **Enlist partnership with the client.** Share the thought process used to develop the proposal solution to the client's risk issues, demonstrating empathy for the client. Never minimize the client's concerns.
3. **Solve each issue.** Show a solution path for each issue. This part of the interview process affords the design professional the opportunity to differentiate his firm or project team from the rest based on particular expertise or technical capability. For example, if one issue is security of a facility and the design professional firm has an advantage in this area, this is when to describe an award received or a recognized authority on staff.
4. **Allow time for questions.** Encourage the client's questions while there is sufficient time to respond to them. A good approach might be to say, "My sense is that there are some unanswered questions in your minds about __________, __________, and __________." If appropriate, recognize someone on the review committee to respond to the statement.
5. **Ask for the order.** Restate the issues, give a one-sentence reason why the design firm is best positioned to address them, ask for the order, and leave.

§ 10.9 Evaluation

Meeting with the client to evaluate why the design firm won or lost an assignment is important because:

1. It helps the firm see its flaws as others see them.
2. It helps refine strategy for future projects through the RFQ, RFP, and interview stages.

3. It can keep the firm from repeating the same mistakes.
4. It affords you the opportunity to build the relationship with the client.

Asking for and participating in an evaluation is more difficult when the firm has lost the assignment. Some points to keep in mind during this process are:

1. Treat it as a positive experience—the first step toward winning the next project.
2. Be organized.
3. Remember that the mission is to investigate, not to argue.
4. Thank the client for his candid views and encourage him to consider the firm for other projects.

§ 10.10 Selected Bibliography

Bell, *What Makes an Engineering Firm Grow?* Consulting Eng'r, Oct. 1986.

R. Connor & J. Davidson, Marketing Your Consulting and Professional Services (John Wiley & Sons 1985).

D. Healy, Marketing and Selling—Aren't They the Same? 3 (May 1986) (unpublished paper).

P. Kotler, Marketing Professional Services (1984).

P. Kotler & K. Cox, Marketing Management and Strategy (3d ed. 1984).

Smallowitz & Molyneux, *Engineering a Marketing Plan,* Civ. Eng'r, Aug. 1987.

Weil, *Marketing Professional Services, Consulting Eng'r,* Nov. 1984.

Weil, *Ten "Do's" and "Don'ts" for Marketing Success,* Consulting Specifying Eng'r, May 1987.

§ 10.11 Case Study

The following describes how a professional design services firm capitalized on the public sector market created by the Safe Drinking Water Act Amendments of 1986 (SDWA):

Problem: Revitalize a relatively small water quality strategic business unit. Overcome a lack of awareness or a hesitancy on the part of prospects to consider the firm for major water projects, due to an existing market perception that the firm lacked expertise in this particular environmental sector.

Opportunity: In June 1986, Congress enacted the Safe Drinking Water Act Amendments of 1986, one of the most comprehensive pieces of environmental legislation of the decade. The SDWA immediately affected thousands of water utilities nationwide, thus creating significant opportunities for environmental firms with water technology capabilities. The legislation, to be fully implemented in stages over a six-year period, generally broke down into the following segments: regulatory compliance, design and engineering, and construction of treatment facilities.

Strategy: Aggressively pursue strategies to effectively position the firm as an expert in issues resulting from the passage of the SDWA.

Market analysis showed that 58,000 public water utilities would be affected by the passage of the amendments. Within the firm's 21-state area of activity, there were approximately 12,000 water utilities, of which some 7,000 fit size and level-of-technical-complexity criteria established within the firm's marketing program.

A long-term marketing and communications program was prepared with these objectives:

1. Build an awareness of the firm's capabilities in the field of water technology, with particular emphasis on the compliance strategies required by utilities
2. Enlist the services of the firm's water quality experts to write articles, present papers and participate in seminars
3. Develop an internal awareness program of the SDWA program
4. Develop a high visibility communications program to generate prospect inquiries by offering useful, up-to-date information on the SDWA
5. Build a perceived expertise in water technology through a carefully planned program of technical and feature articles in publications reaching prime decision makers in water utilities within the identified market areas
6. Prepare and place full-color advertisements in key trade publications and offer SDWA information to respondents
7. Prepare a comprehensive information package in response to inquiries, including a printed copy of the legislation, highlighting changes to the Safe Drinking Water Act of 1974; a printed summary of the SDWA, explaining the regulations and how they would become effective during the implementation period; brochures describing the services of the firm; technical papers, technical articles, and a detailed compliance schedule chart for easy reference
8. Send information packages to existing clients
9. Send information packages to prospective clients

10. Develop an SDWA seminar program, to which clients and prospects would be invited
11. Reduce the cost of sales, through a high generation of market interest in the firm.

Results: In the first year of the program, 520 leads were generated from advertising and publicity. Seven feature articles, including four cover positions, resulted. Nine technical seminars were held. Sales revenues (in fees) rose from $5.5 million to $12 million.

In year two, 1,400 leads were generated. Four feature articles were published. Twenty-one technical seminars were conducted. The firm was invited to submit a significant number of proposals for services. Sales increased from $12 million to $24 million.

In year three, 500 additional leads were generated. Three feature articles were published. Proposal levels were above those of the previous year. Fifteen technical seminars were held. Sales rose from $24 to $34 million.

At the end of the third year of the program's life, more than 2,400 leads had been generated from the mix of communications and seminars (which had been attended by nearly 800 persons). The firm had achieved a strong market recognition as water quality experts, the cost of sales had been reduced by more than $1 million, and the water quality strategic business unit was a significant contributor to the overall performance of the firm. The SDWA strategic plan became a model for many other strategic programs within the firm. (Note: Sales figures represent increases in order of magnitude and are not actual figures.)

§ 10.12 Go/No-Go Decision Matrix

Table 10–1

Go/No-Go Decision Matrix

RATING CRITERIA	SUPERIOR (10-9)	ABOVE AVERAGE (8-7)	AVERAGE (6-5-4)	BELOW AVERAGE (3-2)	POOR (1-0)	RATING (10-0)
Client Relationship; Intelligence/Feed Back	Very close relationship; Personal relationship with 2 or more decision makers	Good relationship; Previous contact; Personal relationship with 1 decision maker	Good relationship; Know at least 1 decision maker	Minimum client contact-client knows Firm	No client contact or exposure to Firm	
Firm's Experience/ Project Team Qualifications	Meet all task descriptions; client knows Firm's key project personnel	Meet all task descriptions; client familiar with Firm's key project personnel	Meet all task descriptions; client does not know Firm's project personnel	Need subcontractors to meet task descriptions; client not familiar with Firm's project personnel	Cannot submit without subcontractors; client not familiar with Firm's project personnel	
Location of Project/ Client Office	Both project and client office within 25 miles of Firm's project office	Project location or client within 25 miles of Firm's project office	Project location or client within 50 miles of Firm's project office	Project location or project office more than 1 1/2 hours' travel	Project location or client office more than 2 1/2 hours' travel	
Time to Prepare Proposals/Gather Additional Info.	Sufficient time to obtain additional information; personnel available	Sufficient time to obtain back-up information and prepare proposal; adjust personnel schedules	Time available to review back-up information and prepare proposal for review on tight schedule	Rush proposal; no review; personnel pressured to complete on time	Rush proposal; no review; personnel must work overtime	
Cost to Prep. Proposal vs. Project Gross Margin	Less than 1.0%	1.0% to 2.0%	2.0% to 3.0%	3.0% to 5.0%	Over 5%	
Time to Execute Project; Scheduling Problems	Plenty of time; no special scheduling conflicts with other projects	Sufficient time to complete tasks; no rescheduling of personnel	Adequate time to complete tasks; some personnel adjustments needed	Very tight schedule; conflict with personnel and other projects	Extremely tight schedule; serious conflict with personnel and other projects	
Competition	Firm in #1 position technically and on price	Firm will be shortlisted with 2 other companies; Firm has technical or price advantage	Firm will be shortlisted with 6 or less companies	Firm will most likely make shortlist; estimate 10 other companies	Not sure if Firm will make shortlist	
Capability	Meet all project needs from Firm's project office	Req. subcontr. for less than 25% of project $	Req. subcontr. for less than 35% of project $	Req. subcontr. for 35% to 50% of project $	Req. subcontr. for more than 50% of project $	
Price	3.3 or greater multiplier on labor; and 20% mark-up on subcontractors	3.15 to 3.3 multiplier on labor; and 15% to 20% mark-up on subcontract	3.05 to 3.15 multiplier on labor; and 10% to 15% mark-up on subcontract	2.95 to 3.05 multiplier on labor; and 5% to 10% mark-up on subcontract	Less than 2.95 multiplier on labor; or less than 5% mark-up on subcontract	
Chance of Success	100%; no competition; equal to an add-on service	Only 2 or less competitors and est. 50% probability	Six (6) or less competitors and est. 25% probability or more	Ten (10) or less competitors and est. 25% probability or less	More than ten (10) competitors and est. 10% probability or less	

CHAPTER 11

FEDERAL GOVERNMENT CONTRACTING ISSUES

Michael R. Charness
Thomas C. Wheeler*

Michael R. Charness is a partner in the Washington, D.C., office of Howrey & Simon, where he specializes in government contract and construction claims and litigation. He received his undergraduate degree from the University of Pennsylvania and his law degree from Georgetown University. Mr. Charness is a member of the District of Columbia Bar and is active in a number of professional associations involving construction and government contract law. He also lectures and writes extensively on environmental, construction, and government contract issues.

Thomas C. Wheeler is a partner in the Washington, D.C., office of Pettit & Martin, specializing in government and construction contract claims and litigation. He received his undergraduate degree from Gettysburg College, Gettysburg, Pennsylvania, and his J.D. degree from the Georgetown University Law Center, Washington, D.C. Mr. Wheeler is a member of the District of Columbia Bar and is admitted to practice in the United States Supreme Court as well as many federal courts of appeal and district courts throughout the United States. He is a member of the American Bar Association and is active in the Public Contracts and Litigation Sections.

*The authors gratefully acknowledge the invaluable contribution to this chapter made by Benjamin Fishman, a law student at the UCLA School of Law.

§ 11.1 Introduction

Architect/engineer (A/E) services have become increasingly important in the federal procurement arena, most recently in the area of environmental cleanup projects. Federal government A/E services can include the creation of drafts and designs, the critique of specifications for the construction of a project, and the administration of the construction of that project. In part because A/E services are considered so vital, the government selection process for A/E firms is conducted in a manner that is very different from the traditional procurement selection process. Special noncompetitive selection procedures have been promulgated in the Brooks Act[1] to guarantee that A/E firms are selected based upon their qualifications and past performance and not upon whether they had the lowest bids.

The key to successful bidding and performance of government A/E contracts is regulatory awareness. The A/E contractor must be familiar with the Federal Acquisition Regulation (FAR), particularly FAR part 36 containing the special A/E selection procedures.[2] Further, many federal agencies have adopted FAR supplements that contain additional regulations. This chapter reviews the federal regulations and procedures that govern the bidding and performance of government A/E contracts. The administrative and judicial procedures used to resolve federal contract disputes also are outlined. With the proper awareness of the federal procurement system, A/E government contracting can be a smooth and profitable venture.

§ 11.2 Legislative and Regulatory Framework

Government A/E services and the procedures under which such services are procured have their origins in the Brooks Act.[3] The Brooks Act and all of its relevant amendments and revisions have now been incorporated into part 36 of FAR.[4] Part 36 also contains certain requirements and limitations that A/E contractors must comply with whenever entering into a contract with the government. Although the FAR contains most of the regulatory framework that applies to a potential A/E contract, each federal agency also has its own special regulatory supplement that should be consulted before bidding or negotiating for a particular project.

Although there are many agencies that contract for A/E services and a substantial number of government-sponsored projects that necessitate such services, one area may soon dominate the A/E market: environmental contracting. Specifically, the Resource Conservation and Recovery Act (RCRA)[5] and the Comprehensive Environmental Response Compensation

---

[1] Brooks Architect-Engineers Act, Pub. L. No. 92-582, 86 Stat. 1278 (codified as amended at 40 U.S.C. §§ 541–544 (1988)).

[2] 48 C.F.R. pt. 36 (1990).

[3] Brooks Architect-Engineers Act, Pub. L. No. 92-582, 86 Stat. 1278 (codified as amended at 40 U.S.C. §§ 541–544 (1988)).

[4] 48 C.F.R. pt. 36 (1990).

[5] Resource Conservation and Recovery Act of 1976, Pub. L. No. 94-580, 90 Stat. 2795 (codified at 42 U.S.C. §§ 6901–6992k (1988)).

and Liability Act (CERCLA/Superfund)[6] mandate the expenditure of substantial funds for environmental cleanup projects. These projects rely heavily on A/E firms to perform numerous services in the cleanup efforts, and the increasing number of these projects, in a period of budgetary cutbacks, merits particular attention in any discussion of government contract opportunities.

§ 11.3 —Brooks Act and Federal Acquisition Regulation

The traditional selection process for A/E contracts is quite different from procurement methods used in most government contracts because it is based primarily on a firm's past performance and qualifications rather than price. These A/E procurement principles originally were codified in the Brooks Act[7] and can be found in both 10 U.S.C. §§ 541 to 544 and FAR part 36.[8] The Brooks Act has remained essentially intact, but it was amended by the Business Opportunity Development Reform Act of 1988[9] to expand the discretion given to agency heads in applying these principles to unique procurement situations. The FAR also contains most of the required clauses that form the basis of the typical A/E contract. The "mandatory," "optional," and "required when applicable" clauses that pertain to A/E contracts are listed in the FAR part 52.3 solicitation provisions and contract clauses matrix[10] under a column titled "Architect-Engineering Contracts." Some of the "required when applicable" clauses are activated when a contract's value reaches a certain threshold amount, such as the provision mandating submission of cost or pricing data to the government in compliance with the Truth-in-Negotiations Act (TINA).[11] Other FAR provisions apply when the government uses a certain contract type, such as the FAR part 31 cost principles in cost-reimbursement contracts.[12] The FAR Council and the Office of Federal Procurement Policy (OFPP) are quite proficient at quickly

---

[6] Comprehensive Environmental Response, Compensation, and Liability Act of 1980, Pub. L. No. 96-510, 94 Stat. 2767 (codified at 42 U.S.C. §§ 9601–9675 (1988)).

[7] Pub. L. No. 92-582 (1972), 86 Stat. 1278 (codified as amended at 40 U.S.C. §§ 541–544 (1988)).

[8] 48 C.F.R. pt. 36 (1990).

[9] Pub. L. No. 100-656, 102 Stat. 3853 (1988) (codified in scattered sections of 15 U.S.C. and 40 U.S.C.).

[10] 48 C.F.R. § 52.301 (1990) (matrix).

[11] 10 U.S.C. § 2306 (1988).

[12] H. Blasky, R. Boyd, E. Crowell, H. Gold, P. Hutchinson, Jr., & L. Spiller, The Architect-Engineer Primer of Federal Government Contracting 6–7 (3d ed. 1983) [hereinafter Architect-Engineer Primer].

revising or amending the FAR to include newly enacted legislation. This means that every A/E firm considering government contract work must keep abreast of the latest FAR revisions. Moreover, no pre-bid effort is complete until the prospective A/E contractor reviews the FAR supplement of the particular agency contracting for the A/E work.

§ 11.4 —Special Agency Contracting Procedures

There are approximately 20 federal agencies that regularly contract for A/E services. Those agencies include the Agency for International Development, Department of Agriculture, Department of the Air Force, Department of the Army, Department of Commerce, Department of Defense, Department of Energy, Department of the Interior, Department of Justice, Department of the Navy, Department of State, Department of Transportation, Environmental Protection Agency, General Services Administration, National Aeronautics and Space Administration, Tennessee Valley Authority, United States Information Agency, United States Postal Service, and the Veterans Administration. Many of these federal agencies have supplemented the selection procedures, contract clauses, and provisions promulgated by the FAR, reflecting the special needs of each particular agency.

For example, the Department of Energy (DOE)'s FAR supplement provides for additional selection criteria geared toward the procurement of large-scale projects. These selection criteria focus on the adequacy of a firm's facilities, its previous experience, the quality of its past work, the proposed project organization, the availability of adequate personnel, and the volume of the firm's past work.[13] The DOE's special procedures also include the use of additional interviews to determine if an A/E firm has the capacity to handle a proposed project.[14] The DOE FAR supplement divides A/E services into four categories: (1) conceptual design (Title I: estimates, initial planning, and studies; Title II: complete design of work; and Title III: A/E supervision and inspection); (2) process design; (3) procurement of materials; and (4) a general category encompassing all other miscellaneous services. The DOE regulations call for the use of fixed-price contracts for as many of these categories as is possible for a given project.[15]

The DOE is not the only agency with special requirements. Many other agencies either supplement the FAR or urge the use of one of the optional FAR provisions and/or clauses. The Army supplements the FAR with provisions addressing the proper use of indefinite-delivery contracts for

---

[13] 48 C.F.R. § 936.602-70 (1990).

[14] *Id.* § 936.602-20.

[15] *Id.* § 936.602-20(a).

smaller acquisitions of A/E services.[16] Additionally, some agencies emphasize the inclusion of certain optional FAR clauses. For example, the Department of Transportation (DOT) supplement encourages the use of liquidated damages clauses whenever possible.[17]

Although there are almost 20 agencies that traditionally contract for A/E services, the most important four are the Department of Defense (DOD), the Department of Energy, the Department of Transportation, and the Environmental Protection Agency (EPA). The largest amount of A/E contracting historically has been done for the DOD (involving both the Corps of Engineers and the Naval Facilities Engineering Command), the DOE, and the DOT. However, it now appears that a larger percentage of total federal A/E contracting will be done by the EPA. This increase can be attributed to the significant funding that is, and will be, spent on environmental cleanup projects. The two main sources of appropriated environmental cleanup funds for the EPA are the Resource Conservation and Recovery Act (RCRA) and the Comprehensive Environmental Response Compensation and Liability Act (CERCLA/Superfund), described in §§ **11.5** and **11.6.**

§ 11.5 —Resource Conservation and Recovery Act

The Resource Conservation and Recovery Act (RCRA) was enacted in 1976[18] and amended by Public Law No. 96-510 in 1980 and Public Law No. 98-616 in 1984. RCRA supplemented the Clean Air Act[19] and the Clean Water Act[20] to empower EPA to regulate the removal of solid and hazardous waste materials from functioning facilities. The need for this Act arose from an EPA study concluding that nearly half of the municipal landfills operating in 1986 would be closed by 1991. The report stressed that a better alternative to incinerating the hazardous materials had to be implemented and that many environmental recovery actions also were needed.[21]

Congress enacted the Hazardous and Solid Waste Amendments to RCRA in 1984,[22] which mandated that EPA create regulations (by certain

---

[16] Army FAR Supplement § 36.602-90.

[17] 48 C.F.R. § 1236.206 (1989).

[18] Pub. L. No. 94-580, 90 Stat. 2795 (codified as amended at 42 U.S.C. § 6901 (1988)).

[19] Clean Air Act, ch. 360, 69 Stat. 322 (1955) (codified as amended in scattered sections of 42 U.S.C.).

[20] Federal Water Pollution Control Act, ch. 758, 62 Stat. 1155 (1948) (codified as amended in scattered sections of 33 U.S.C.).

[21] Congressional Research Service, Environmental Protection Legislation in the 101st Congress 1 (May 29, 1990).

[22] Pub. L. No. 98-616, 98 Stat. 3221 (codified as amended at 42 U.S.C. § 16901 (1988)).

deadlines) for a broad range of subjects, including identifying hazardous wastes and banning land disposal of most hazardous wastes that were left untreated. RCRA authorizes EPA to regulate the control of *solid wastes,* which are defined as:

> any garbage, refuse, sludge from a waste treatment plant, water supply treatment plant, or air pollution control facility and other discarded material, including solid, liquid, semi-solid, or contained gaseous material resulting from industrial, commercial, mining and agricultural operations, and from community activities, but does not include solid or dissolved materials in irrigation return flows or industrial discharges which are point sources subject to permits under Section 402 of the Federal Water Pollution Act as amended (86 Stat. 880), or source, special nuclear, or by-product material as defined by the Atomic Energy Act of 1954, as amended (68 Stat. 923).[23]

The main purpose of RCRA has been to regulate those solid wastes that are also hazardous. Hazardous solid wastes are defined as being those that, because of their quantity, concentration, or infectious characteristics (1) may cause or contribute to an increase in mortality or in the number of cases of irreversible and/or incapacitating diseases, or (2) pose a substantial hazard to human health or to the environment when improperly treated.[24] Additionally, RCRA authorizes EPA to conduct resource recovery and reuse programs. Other goals of the Act include promotion of solid waste management principles; separation, recovery, and recycling of solid wastes; and coordination of federal, state, local, and private waste management groups to improve the recovery of value materials and energy from solid wastes.[25]

The initial liability for improper hazardous waste management under RCRA's *cradle-to-grave* system lies with the generator of that waste.[26] The generator is responsible for determining if a produced waste is hazardous. If the waste is hazardous, the generator may not treat, store, dispose of, transport, or offer it for transportation without first obtaining an EPA identification number.[27] A generator is allowed to accumulate hazardous waste on-site for up to 90 days as long as it is placed in proper, well-labeled containers and provided that the generator has the necessary emergency plans and equipment in place.[28] RCRA also guides the regulation of

---

[23] 42 U.S.C. § 6903 (27).

[24] *Id.* at § 6903 (5).

[25] M. Charness & J. Dobbs, Government Environmental Contracting Course Manual A-38 (1990) [hereinafter Charness & Dobbs].

[26] 40 C.F.R. § 262.11 (1990).

[27] *Id.* § 262.12.

[28] *Id.* § 262.34.

hazardous waste interim shortage[29] and disposal facilities. In 1984, RCRA was expanded to include the regulation of underground storage tanks[30] and medical waste. The primary functions of an A/E firm under a RCRA-funded contract are (1) to analyze the hazardous waste storage problem of a generator, interim storage, or disposal site; (2) to design a safer, more conservation-oriented system; and (3) to work with the agency and construction contractor to administer the incorporation of that new system.[31] A/E firms will perform many of these same functions for EPA under Superfund contracts as well.

§ 11.6 —Comprehensive Environmental Response Compensation and Liability Act

Congress enacted the Comprehensive Environmental Response Compensation and Liability Act (CERCLA or Superfund) in 1980.[32] CERCLA authorized federal and state governments, and private parties in certain instances, to clean up hazardous substances and other toxic pollutants in the air, water, and on the land. The government cleanup response actions, directed mainly at inactive or abandoned sites, are financed from a "Superfund" created by a tax on the chemical and petroleum industries. CERCLA was aimed at creating a minimum of regulations and a maximum of voluntary cleanup performed by the private sector. Congress, frustrated by a lack of progress, enacted the Superfund Amendments and Reauthorization Act of 1986 (SARA).[33] SARA codified most of the concepts EPA created to induce the privatization of the recovery/cleanup efforts; increased the funding from $1.6 billion to $8.5 billion for five years; and imposed an ambitious and mandatory schedule for EPA to follow in the plan's implementation.[34]

Based upon CERCLA, the government is empowered to take remedial action to stop the release or significant threat of release of any hazardous substance or of "any pollutant or contaminant which may present an imminent and substantial danger to the public health or welfare."[35] CERCLA encourages the use of hazardous waste treatment over the land disposal method. CERCLA also includes remedial action standards that must be

---

[29] *Id.* § 265.1(b).

[30] 42 U.S.C. § 6901 (1988), *amended by* Pub. L. No. 98-616, 98 Stat. 3221 (1984).

[31] Medical Waste Tracking Act, Pub. L. No. 100-582, 102 Stat. 2950 (1988) and 42 U.S.C. § 6992c (1988).

[32] Pub. L. No. 96-510, 94 Stat. 2767 (1980) 42 U.S.C. § 9601 (1988).

[33] Pub. L. No. 99-499, 100 Stat. 1613 (1986) (codified in scattered sections of 10 U.S.C., 26 U.S.C., 29 U.S.C., 33 U.S.C., and 42 U.S.C.).

[34] Charness & Dobbs at A-63.

[35] 42 U.S.C. § 9604(a) (1988).

met in the cleanup of all Superfund sites.[36] Many of these standards are contained within the National Oil and Hazardous Substances Pollution Contingency Plan or National Contingency Plan (NCP), as it is informally known.[37]

Subpart E of the NCP separates hazardous substance response into seven phases: (1) discovery or notification; (2) removal site evaluation; (3) immediate removal action to mitigate significant risks of harm to human life or the environment; (4) remedial site evaluation; (5) establishing remedial priorities; (6) remedial investigation/feasibility study and selection of remedy; and (7) remedial design/remedial action, operation and maintenance.[38] The sites chosen to be cleaned up are selected from a National Priorities List (NPL) that EPA is required to create from a list of selection criteria, such as potential harm and cleanup costs.

Once a site is on the NPL, EPA will contract for A/E firms to conduct analysis and feasibility studies of the risk of removal and the potential harm from the hazardous waste on the site. EPA will then notify the site's owners if remedial actions are necessary. If voluntary cleanup cannot be induced, EPA can file suit under CERCLA § 7003 against the site's owners to pay for any needed remedial actions. In addition to the remedial actions undertaken on NPL sites, Title V of SARA established a $500 million trust fund to repair and clean up leaking underground storage tanks. The implementation of all Superfund remedial actions and coordination efforts with other agencies is handled by the office of the assistant administrator for solid waste and emergency response within EPA.

The most recent estimate of the Office of Technology Assessment places the expenditure for Superfund remedial actions at over $500 billion over the next 50 years (excluding the DOE cleanup costs).[39] With this level of appropriations in the works, A/E firms can be assured of a steady flow of environmental recovery contracting opportunities for the government. A/E services play an important role in the design of remedial actions and their support services. Some of these support services that require the use of A/E contractors are technical enforcement support contracts; technical assistance team contracts; field investigation team contracts; and Superfund innovative technologies evaluation contracts.[40] All of these contract types include A/E participation and supplement the main Alternative remedial contracts strategy (ARCs) provided for by the Superfund, under which selected A/E firms oversee the entire cleanup effort from initial site investigation to management of the cleanup itself. All of these programs

---

[36] *Id.* § 9621.

[37] *Id.* § 40 C.F.R. § 300 (1990).

[38] § 40 C.F.R. §§ 300.400–300.440 (1990).

[39] Charness & Dobbs at B-4.

[40] *Id.* at B-5, 6.

and resulting contracts are under the auspices of EPA, but the DOE, the Naval Facilities Engineering Command, and the Army Corps of Engineers all provide additional funds and contract opportunities for similar environmental cleanup work under their own programs.

§ 11.7 Source Selection under Brooks Act

In 1972, the Brooks Act[41] was established to codify source selection procedures for A/E contracting services. This Act promulgated a noncompetitive procurement process in which quality of work, past performance, and professional qualifications were the prime factors used to select which firms would then be given the opportunity to negotiate a "fair and reasonable" contract price with government agencies.

The need for this law arose after a 1965 United States General Accounting Office (GAO) report determined that the traditional A/E selection methods did not comply with the Federal Property and Administrative Services Act of 1949[42] because the A/E's fee was not used as a factor in the selection process.[43] Thus, Congress enacted the Brooks Act to provide the legal framework for "traditional" A/E procurement principles. During the House Committee on Government Operation's hearing on this subject, the comptroller general stated that the A/E selection process should include both performance and cost factors.[44] However, a majority of the committee believed that any savings gained as a result of the use of cost factors and low bids would be offset by a lowering in the overall quality of the completed projects. Therefore, the Brooks Act, encompassing a selection methodology based solely upon qualifications and experience, was enacted in 1972.

Despite the passage of the Brooks Act, the debate continues as to what role, if any, cost factors should play in the A/E procurement process. Free market advocates claim that price competition is a time-honored way in which to assure both quality and a reasonable price. These proponents of the use of cost factors have won several small victories, such as when Maryland enacted legislation that required price competition to be one of the

---

[41] Pub. L. No. 92-582, 86 Stat. 1278 (codified at 40 U.S.C. §§ 541–544 (1988)).

[42] Federal Property and Administrative Services Act of 1949, ch. 288, 63 Stat. 377 (1949) (codified as amended in scattered sections of 40 U.S.C., 41 U.S.C., 44 U.S.C., and 50 U.S.C. App.).

[43] Slawsky, *The Architect-Engineer Selection Process: To Bid or Not to Bid,* 11 Pub. Cont. L. J. 252 (1979).

[44] House Committee on Government Operations, Amending the Federal Property Administrative Services Act of 1949, H.R. Rep. No. 91-1445, 91st Cong., 2d Sess. 4-6, at 18 (1970).

selection criteria for all state A/E contracts.[45] However, the majority view, favoring noncompetitive procurement principles, still holds the upper hand and the Brooks Act not only remains in place, but recently was strengthened with an expansion of its scope.

The Brooks Act was intended to apply to all "A/E" government contracts, which it defined as: "Those professional services of an architectural or engineering nature as well as incidental services that members of those professions and those in their employ may logically or justifiably perform."[46] Each agency head was to determine when the Brooks Act should apply based upon a discretionary decision of whether or not a particular service was incidental to a traditional A/E project.[47] This interpretational framework changed when the Brooks Act was broadened by the Business Opportunity Development Reform Act of 1988.[48]

The new definition of A/E services now includes functions associated with research, planning, development, design, construction, and alteration or repair of real property.[49] This new definition, which has been incorporated into the FAR, also lists several specific services that now are to be considered A/E in nature, including studies, investigations, surveying and mapping, tests, evaluations, consultations, comprehensive planning, program management, conceptual designs, plans and specifications, value engineering, construction phase services, soil engineering, drawing reviews, preparation of operating and maintenance manuals, and other related services.[50] The Conference Report for Public Law No. 100-656 indicated that this new definition of A/E activities does not prevent an agency from obtaining any or all of the above services from a construction contractor, whose selection would not be governed by the Brooks Act.[51]

The comptroller general has held that the new test to determine if the Brooks Act applies, as mandated by the changes set forth in Public Law No. 100-656, is whether the service can be justifiably performed by an A/E firm because it is incidental to the nature of the profession, not whether it is incidental to a traditional A/E project. Thus, although more limited in nature, agency heads still have some discretion to determine if services, not associated with a particular project, are subject to the Brooks Act.

---

[45] S. Zemensky, M. Lunch, & P. Schnitzer, *Architect/Engineer Procurement—The Battle Goes On,* 19 Cont. Mgmt. 4–5 (Aug. 1979).

[46] Architect-Engineer Primer.

[47] *Change in Statutory Definition of A-E,* 31 Gov't Contractor ¶ 256 (1989).

[48] Pub. L. No. 100-656, 102 Stat. 3853 (codified in scattered sections of 15 U.S.C. and at 40 U.S.C. § 541 (1988)).

[49] M. Doke, Jr., K. Weinberg & S. Hinton, *1988 Procurement Review,* Briefing Papers No. 89-2, 1 Briefing Papers Collection 84 (1989).

[50] P. Lubka, Government Architect-Engineer Contracting Course Manual A-3 (1989).

[51] M. Doke, Jr., K. Weinberg & S. Hinton, *1988 Procurement Review,* Briefing Papers No. 89-2, 1 Briefing Papers Collection 5 (1989).

However, if an agency head abuses this discretion by not invoking the Brooks Act for a service that is clearly incidental to the A/E profession, the comptroller general will hold that person accountable for an act in bad faith.[52]

§ 11.8 Noncompetitive Selection Procedures

The Brooks Act was incorporated into FAR 36.6 to create a system for evaluating A/E firms on the basis of experience and quality of work rather than price. The selection process typically has three phases: the advertising phase, the evaluation phase, and the interview/negotiation phase.

Advertising. In the initial phase, all federal agencies must announce publicly their requirements for any needed A/E services. Agencies generally meet this obligation by publishing their advertisements in the Commerce Business Daily (CBD). To qualify to receive an A/E project, a prospective contractor should have on file with the agency a standard form (SF) 254, the United States Government Architect-Engineer Services Questionnaire. This form, which should be updated yearly and submitted to all applicable agencies, initially will be analyzed to classify an A/E contractor with respect to location, performance, specialized experience, professional capabilities, capacity to perform specific agency jobs, and performance on previous jobs. Potential A/E contractors also must fill out SF 255, Architect-Engineer and Related Services Questionnaire, for a specific project.[53] (Both forms are available from any government agency contracting for A/E work.) When a project is announced in the CBD, all A/Es responding to the advertisement will be evaluated to establish a preselection list to be given to an evaluation board. This initial prescreening will be based upon the two forms and any additional information provided to the agency, such as photographs of previous work.[54]

Evaluation. The intermediate phase begins once the evaluation board has been given the preselection list of potential contractors. Each agency is required by FAR 36.602-2(c) to have a permanent or ad hoc A/E evaluation board composed of persons experienced with A/E, construction, and government acquisition matters.[55] The board reviews preselected candidates

---

[52] *Change in Statutory Definition of A-Es,* 31 Gov't Contractor ¶ 256 (1989) (citing Forest Service, B-233987 (July 14, 1989), 89-2 CPD ¶ 47 (1989)).

[53] Architect-Engineer Primer at 9.

[54] *Id.* at 13–14.

[55] In a recent case, IDG Architects, B-235487 (Sept. 18, 1989), 89-2 CPD ¶ 236 (1989), the comptroller general ruled that no one member of these evaluation boards had to be either an architect or an engineer, they need only have experience in their fields.

based upon the following selection criteria: (1) professional qualifications; (2) capability of firm to sustain loss of key personnel and continue work; (3) ability of branch office to act independently of main office; (4) location; (5) professional quality and background of key employees; (6) specialization; (7) quality of past performance; and (8) the firm's ability to meet time and construction cost limitations.[56] These factors are similar to, but somewhat more in-depth than, the preselection criteria used to reduce the original number of prospective candidates.

Interview/negotiation. Using the selection elements described, the evaluation board chooses and ranks at least three firms that fared best in meeting all of the test criteria. The board then initiates the final phase of the procurement process—price negotiations with the highest-ranked firm. The A/E firm and the contracting agency discuss the required scope of the project and the contractor then gives price, cost, and fee presentations in an effort to reach the "fair and reasonable" price requirement of the Brooks Act. If a "fair and reasonable" price cannot be agreed upon by the two parties, the agency will conduct negotiations with the second highest-ranked firm and will continue negotiations with subsequent firms until an agreement is reached.

When determining the fair and reasonable price, a contractor may be required to certify all of its pricing by submitting cost or pricing data under the Truth-in-Negotiations Act (TINA). This data will be used by the agency to help formulate a fair price. However, under any circumstances there is a statutory limitation that the A/E contract price or estimated cost and fee cannot exceed 6 percent of the estimated construction cost.[57] Although previous categories of allowable costs, such as soil studies and surveys, were exempted from this fee limitation, the new definition of A/E services substantially shortened the list of exceptions. However, travel and per diem allowances, special consulting services not traditionally available in A/E firms, and costs for reproduction of approved designs or models still remain free from the fee limitation.[58]

§ 11.9 Bid Protests

There are three sources of bid protests in traditional procurement procedures: (1) defects in solicitation, rendering it impossible for a contractor to submit a proper proposal; (2) mistakes made by the bidder in creating its

---

Architect Need Not Be Included on All A-E Evaluation Boards, 31 Gov't Contractor ¶ 395 (1989).

[56] P. Lubka, Government Architect-Engineer Contracting Course Manual A-9-ID (1989).

[57] 48 C.F.R. § 15.903 (1990) (cited in *id.* at A-22).

[58] P. Lubka, Government Architect-Engineer Contracting Course Manual A-22 (1989).

proposal; and (3) deficiencies in the evaluation of a proposal that prevent the contractor from being awarded a project. In A/E government contracting, due to the Brooks Act selection procedures, the largest number of bid protests comes from contractors who were not awarded a project. These protests generally fall into the third category and take the form of a challenge to the agency's decision-making process. A protesting contractor has three options: it can file a protest with the contracting agency or the GAO, or it can file suit in federal court.

Protest to Contracting Agency

In challenging a procurement decision by an agency, a protesting contractor must demonstrate that the agency abused the discretionary power afforded by the Brooks Act. An abuse of discretionary power generally takes the form of an irrational decision, such as leaving a deserving contractor off one of the preselection or final candidate lists or not awarding the contract to the best prospective firm. Although agency discretion under the Brooks Act has been interpreted to be broadly based, the agency must remain fundamentally fair.[59]

FAR 33.103 provides the procedural framework for protesting directly to the contracting agency.[60] The protester must establish that the agency's procurement actions violated the selection criteria and policy requirements of the Brooks Act. If the protest is based upon the exclusion of the contractor from a preselection or final candidate list and the contract has not yet been awarded, the agency is generally prohibited from making an award until the matter has been resolved. However, if a prompt award would be advantageous to the government, then the agency will not be restricted from making an award before the resolution of the protest. If an award already has been made before the filing of the protest, it is unusual for performance of that contract to be suspended in an agency protest unless the agency is convinced by the protester's allegations that the award almost certainly will be overturned. If it appears that an award will be invalidated due to a strong bid protest, the contracting officer is required to seek a mutual agreement with the contractor who had been awarded the project to suspend performance.[61]

---

[59] Nash, *Source Selection: A Discretionary Decision,* 2 Nash & Cibinic Report No. 10 ¶ 62, at 153 (1988).

[60] Charness & Dobbs at C-73.

[61] *Id.*

Protest to General Accounting Office

The Competition in Contracting Act[62] codified the comptroller general's jurisdiction to decide bid protests concerning alleged violations of procurement statutes such as the Brooks Act.[63]

A protest will be filed timely if the GAO receives it within 10 working days (Saturdays, Sundays, and holidays are excluded) of when the contractor knew, or should have known, of the grounds of the protest. If a contractor knows the basis of a protest before the date for submission of its proposal or bid, then it must protest before the due date for the proposal or bid. If an award has been made and the GAO receives a protest within 10 calendar days after award (Saturdays, Sundays, and holidays included), then the contract award will be suspended pending an outcome of the protest. If the protest was filed with and denied by the contracting agency, the protest must be received by the GAO no later than 10 working days after the contractor knew, or should have known, that the agency had acted adversely to its protest.[64]

A protest to the GAO must clearly detail the legal and factual grounds of the complaint and specify the particular type of relief requested.[65] If a protester is unable to provide a detailed statement of its complaint, but still believes there is a basis for it, the contractor may request a debriefing with the contracting agency. At this meeting, the agency must reveal any perceived weak or deficient factors in the contractor's proposal or qualifications. The contractor will have 10 working days to file its protest if it obtains information forming the basis of its protest at this debriefing.

The agency must respond to the protest within 25 working days of notice of the protest. This report not only must comment on the protest, but also must include any pertinent documents relating to the protest. The protester then has 10 working days to comment on the report.

At the discretion of the GAO, fact-finding conferences also may be scheduled to resolve factual disputes on the written record.[66] These conferences can be either formal or informal. If such an informal conference is held, the protester has seven days from the conference to comment on the conference and the agency report. A decision must be rendered within 90 days of the filing of the protest. In requesting relief in a protest, it should be noted that the GAO, in addition to other remedies, is empowered to grant

---

[62] Competition in Contracting Act, Pub. L. No. 98-369, 98 Stat. 1175, 31 U.S.C. § 3552 (1982 & Supp. III 1985).

[63] 4 C.F.R. § 21.2(a)1, 2 (1991); *id.* § 21.4(b).

[64] *Id.* § 21.2(1) (3).

[65] *Id.* § 21.1(c).

[66] *Id.* § 21.5(b).

monetary relief for bid and proposal development costs and for costs incurred as a result of the protest, including attorneys' fees.[67]

Bid Protest in Federal Court

A bid protest injunction action can be filed in certain circumstances in the United States Claims Court or in a United States district court. A contractor can bring a protest in a district court if the claim is based upon an alleged violation of a statute or regulation, or abuse of agency discretion. Most of the A/E bid protests in district courts are filed after a contract award has been made and are based upon both a violation of the selection criteria requirements in the Brooks Act and an abuse of discretionary power by an agency head or evaluation board.

If a bid protest is filed before the award of a contract, the protester can obtain a temporary restraining order (TRO) that would block an agency from making an award until the protest has been resolved. Previously, a TRO or other form of declaratory relief was available only in the district courts. However, the Federal Courts Improvement Act of 1982[68] empowered the Claims Court to grant declaratory and injunctive relief in pre-award protests.[69] Since the passage of this Act, it has become increasingly doubtful that pre-award relief will be available in the district courts. If a contract award has been made, a protester can only obtain a TRO in district court.

In order to obtain injunctive relief from either court, the contractor must prove that (1) it will sustain irreparable harm without an injunction; (2) neither the government nor the public interest would be substantially harmed if an injunction is granted; and (3) there is a substantial likelihood that the contractor will prevail on the merits of its case.[70] If a contractor wins on the merits in Claims Court, the agency must correct the cited discrepancy and generally restart the procurement process. If a contractor wins on the merits of a post-award protest in district court, then a preliminary injunction will become permanent and the contract award will be invalidated.[71] It is much easier to overturn an agency decision and to prove no harm to the public interest if start-up costs have not yet been incurred from the initial performance of an awarded contract.

---

[67] *Id.* § 21.6(d). *See* Tandem Computers, B-221333 (Apr. 14, 1968), 86-1 CPD ¶ 362 (1986), *modified on other grounds,* 86-2 CPD ¶ 315 (1986).

[68] Pub. L. No. 97-164, 96 Stat. 25 (1982) (codified in scattered sections of various U.S.C. titles).

[69] Charness & Dobbs at C-74.

[70] *See* Virginia Petroleum Jobbers Ass'n v. Federal Power Comm'n, 259 F.2d 921 (D.C. Cir. 1958).

[71] Charness & Dobbs at C-77.

§ 11.10 Types of Contracts

There are two main categories of contracts used for government projects that employ A/E services: cost-reimbursement contracts and fixed-price contracts.[72] Most A/E contracts are fixed-price awards with reimbursement for some specific costs incurred, such as travel, reproduction costs, or the use of consultants.[73] However, in some cases, cost-type contracts are used for A/E services.

Cost-reimbursement contracts. There are three types of cost-reimbursement contracts commonly used by the government: (1) cost-plus fixed fee; (2) cost-plus incentive fee; and (3) cost-plus award fee. The FAR limits the use of these contracts to negotiated procurements, such as for A/E services procured under the Brooks Act.[74] The *cost-plus fixed fee* contract is the most commonly used of the cost-reimbursement contract types, but also provides the least incentive for a contractor to complete performance in a cost-efficient manner. The contractor receives a set fee and recovers all allowed costs up to an estimated cost ceiling.[75] The *cost-plus incentive fee* is an attempt to increase the contractor's incentive to perform efficiently. The contractor's fee is tied directly to how completely and efficiently it performs its services.[76] In a *cost-plus award fee* contract, the fee is divided into two parts: (1) a fixed fee; and (2) an award fee that varies with the effectiveness and quality of the contractor's performance. The amount and criteria for the award fee are preset within the terms of the contract.[77]

Fixed-price contracts. There are three types of fixed-price contracts generally used by the government: (1) firm-fixed price; (2) fixed-price with economic price adjustment; and (3) fixed-price incentive contracts. The *firm-fixed price* contract is most favored by the government because it sets one lump sum to be paid for the successful completion of a project and thus places the maximum potential risk on the contractor, who may have to spend its own funds to finance any cost overruns.[78] The *fixed-price with economic price adjustment* contracts are frequently used in periods of high inflation and normally are not desired by the government because of their tendency to escalate costs. This type of contract provides for an upward price adjustment based upon an agreed-upon index of up to 10 percent

---

[72] 48 C.F.R. § 16.101(a), (b) (1990).

[73] P. Lubka, Government Architect-Engineer Contracting Course Manual B-1 (1989).

[74] Charness & Dobbs at C-84.

[75] 48 C.F.R. § 16.306 (1990).

[76] *Id.* § 16.304.

[77] *Id.* § 16.305.

[78] *Id.* § 16.202-2.

and for an unlimited downward price adjustment for any unexpected economic contingencies that might occur during performance of the project.[79] The final type, *fixed-price incentive contracts,* contains a preset contract price; however, the contractor's profit may be adjusted based on an agreed-upon sharing ratio of cost overruns or underruns with the government.[80] For A/E contractors, their estimated cost-plus fee under this contract is automatically capped at 6 percent of the estimated construction costs.

§ 11.11 Performance-Related Clauses

The responsibility of an A/E contractor lies on two different planes: one for its own work and one for the construction work already performed. In addition to having to meet the requirements of the various "boilerplate" FAR clauses discussed in § **11.3**, an A/E firm is responsible for the "professional quality, the technical accuracy, and the coordination of all designs, drawings, specifications, and other services furnished by the contractor under this contract."[81] This clause is implemented by the FAR and requires an A/E firm to uphold its status as a "professional" firm by fulfilling the obligations and accepting the liability of the various clauses that must be included in any A/E contract.

§ 11.12 —Redesign Responsibility for Design Errors Clause

The first potential liability of an A/E contractor is defined by the *redesign responsibility for design errors clause,* as described in FAR 36.609-2 and implemented in A/E contracts by FAR 52.236-23. The clause states that any corrections to the A/E's work must be done at no cost to the government "when the designs, drawings, specifications, or other items or services furnished contain any errors, deficiencies, or inadequacies."[82] If the government does not require such corrections from the A/E firm free of charge, the contracting officer must submit a written justification.[83]

As further prescribed by FAR 36.609-2, the *responsibility of the architect/engineer contractor clause*[84] should be inserted in all A/E contracts. This clause provides that an A/E firm is liable for all damages caused by its

[79] *Id.* § 16.203.

[80] *Id.* § 16.403.

[81] 48 C.F.R. § 52.236-23 (1990).

[82] 48 C.F.R. § 36.609-2(a) (1990).

[83] *Id.*

[84] *Id.* § 52.236-23.

negligent performance of the contract work. If the contractor(s) are involved in a joint venture, each entity will be jointly and severally liable. This clause creates both a professional standard of negligence as well as the more traditional breach of contract standard. Although it is possible to breach one of these standards without violating the other,[85] it is far more common to breach both simultaneously. Although an A/E's responsibility under the "professional" standard may go beyond meeting the requirements of the contract, "liability rests only on unskillfulness or negligence and not upon mere errors of judgment."[86] When determining if the professional standard of negligence has been breached, the evaluation board will use a case-by-case evaluation[87] and will determine if the A/E firm's actions were the proximate cause of the damages.[88] If an A/E firm was guilty of negligence and either the construction contractor or the government was simultaneously negligent, then the board will reduce the damages proportionately to the A/E firm's responsibility.[89]

§ 11.13 —Changes Clause

There are two forms of changes that an A/E firm may encounter during the course of its contract performance: formal changes and constructive changes. *Formal changes* generally are revisions to the scope of the contract requested by the government in writing and are covered by the FAR changes clause:[90] one for cost-reimbursement contracts and one for fixed-price contracts (alternate III of the fixed-price changes clause applies to A/E services). *Constructive changes* are those in which the government orders no revisions to the contract work scope; however, certain government actions or inactions have the effect of causing the contractor to perform differently than anticipated.

Formal Changes

The changes clause found in government contracts allows the government to direct the contractor to perform any change it desires, as long as the change falls within the scope of the contract and the direction is made in writing.[91]

---

[85] *See* Leo A. Daly Co., Eng BCA No. 4463, 85-1 B.C.A. (CCH) ¶ 17,740, at 88,592 (1984).

[86] *Id.* at 88,591.

[87] *See* Heimsath & Assoc., NASA BCA No. 180-1, 83-1 B.C.A. (CCH) ¶ 16,133 (1982).

[88] *See* Swan Wooster Eng'g, AGBCA Nos. 83-104-1, 83-124-1, 87-2 B.C.A. (CCH) ¶ 19,894 (1987).

[89] *See* Heimsath & Assoc., NASA BCA No. 180-1, 83-1 B.C.A. (CCH) ¶ 16,133 (1982).

[90] 48 C.F.R. § 52.243 (1990).

[91] *Id.*

Both clauses allow a contractor 30 days in which to assert its right to an "equitable" adjustment in the contract price and/or schedule.[92] In some cases, the 30-day notice provision is waived, if the contractor's delay in asserting the right to an equitable adjustment would not prejudice the government.[93] The changes clause allows a contracting officer to make changes within the general scope of the contract. Examples of changes might include (1) changes in the manner in which the work is performed; (2) changes in government-provided equipment, facilities, services, materials, or site location; and (3) changes for the purpose of delaying or accelerating the work.[94]

The primary difference between the changes clause found in fixed-price and cost-reimbursement contracts is that in a cost-reimbursement contract, a contractor need only work until the allotted funds have been exhausted. The contractor is under no obligation to provide further services until the government provides more funds pursuant to the limitation of cost clause.[95] Conversely, a contractor operating under a fixed-price contract must continue performance and wait for compensation until its equitable adjustment request has been approved. However, both types of changes clause require a contractor to proceed with the contract as changed while any disputes are resolved. A contractor's failure or refusal to proceed with the changed work may lead to a termination for default of the contract.[96]

Alternate III of the fixed-price changes clause applies to all fixed-price A/E services and provides: "No changes for which an additional cost or fee will be charged by the Contractor shall be furnished without the prior written authorization of the contracting officer."[97] This additional restriction could limit the circumstances in which an A/E firm could recover extra expenses. The government could argue that any extra work performed without authorization is voluntary and therefore not compensable. The alternate III restriction was added because of the difficulty encountered in defining what constitutes additional work under the scope of an A/E contract.[98]

Constructive Changes

The Boards developed the concept of constructive changes to deal with situations in which no formal change order was issued, but the contractor relied on an action or inaction of the government to perform differently than it had reasonably anticipated. There is no specific time limit in which a contractor must provide the government with notice of a constructive

---

[92] *Id.* § 52.243-1, -2.

[93] *See* Etowah Mfg. Co., ASBCA No. 23521, 80-1 B.C.A. (CCH) ¶ 14,438 (1980).

[94] 48 C.F.R. § 52.243-1-4 (1990).

[95] *Id.* § 52.243-2(e).

[96] *Id.* §§ 52.243-1(e), 52.243-2(d).

[97] *Id.* § 52.243-1 (alternate III (f)).

[98] P. Lubka, Government Architect-Engineer Contracting Course Manual D-13 (1989).

change, unless the contract contains a separate clause (such as the notification of changes clause) requiring such notice. Constructive changes often arise from disagreements between the parties on the proper interpretation of the contract specifications. If a contracting officer mistakenly refuses to order a formal change because the officer believes the work is required by the contract, a contractor's performance of that work will be considered a constructive change entitling the contractor to recover any increased costs attributable to the changed work.[99] The contractor also may be entitled to a time extension for completion of the work.

Constructive Acceleration

Constructive acceleration may result from an act or order by the contracting officer that requires the contractor to complete work earlier than it would have been completed if the contract schedule had been properly adjusted to reflect any "excusable" causes of delays. *Excusable delays* are delays that are beyond the control and without the fault or negligence of the contractor or its subcontractors. It may include both government-caused and nongovernment-caused delays, such as strikes, embargoes, or unusually severe weather. This theory is based on the concept that with every excusable delay, a contractor is entitled to an extension of the contract schedule. If a contracting officer ignores the contractor's request for a schedule extension due to excusable delays and requires a contractor to adhere to the original schedule, the contractor will be awarded an equitable adjustment of the contract schedule and possibly additional compensation (if the government caused the delay).[100]

§ 11.14 —Value Engineering Clause

The government relies upon the A/E firm's ability to develop professional designs for particular projects. If, after the award of a contract, the A/E firm further discovers an innovative design approach that would reduce the contract price, it is bound by the *value engineering clause*[101] (if included in the contract) to alert the contracting officer and to implement those changes (if accepted). The value engineering clause stipulates that:

> The contractor shall (1) perform value engineering (VE) services and submit progress reports as specified in the Schedule; and (2) submit to the Contracting Officer any resulting value engineering proposals (VEPs). Value

---

[99] *See* Blake Constr. Co., GSBCA No. 2477, 71-1 B.C.A. (CCH) ¶ 8,870 (1971).

[100] *See* Electronic & Missile Facilities, Inc., ASBCA No. 9031, 1964 B.C.A. (CCH) ¶ 4,338 (1964).

[101] 48 C.F.R. § 52.248-1 (1990).

> engineering activities shall be performed concurrently with, and without delay to, the schedule set forth in the contract. . . . The contractor shall be paid as the contract specifies for this effort, but shall not share in savings which may result from acceptance and use of VEPs by the Government.[102]

Thus, unlike the normal fixed-price supply contract, an A/E firm normally does not share in the savings from value engineering. However, the A/E firm is still responsible for conducting this value engineering.

§ 11.15 —Suspension-of-Work Clauses

As prescribed by FAR 12.505(a), a *suspension-of-work clause* is to be inserted in all A/E contracts. The first paragraph of the suspension-of-work clause provides: "(a) The Contracting Officer may order the Contractor, in writing, to suspend, delay or interrupt all or any part of the work of this contract for the period of time that the Contracting Officer determines appropriate for the convenience of the Government."[103] The use of this provision is relatively rare because suspension-of-work orders are seldom issued by a contracting officer. There is also a provision for equitable adjustment (without profit) for increased costs due to an unreasonable suspension or delay of work.[104] A claim must be made before incurring costs beyond 20 days after receiving the contracting officer's notice of suspension of work.[105] The only limit to recoverable costs, other than the exclusion of profit, is that a contractor must be able to prove that such costs would not have been incurred but for the suspension order.[106] The equitable adjustment could include such costs as overhead, idle time, increases in the costs of labor and materials, or the loss of efficiency.

The suspension-of-work clause is more commonly used by contractors seeking an equitable adjustment for "constructive" suspensions of work. The second paragraph of the suspension-of-work clause provides relief for constructive suspensions so long as no remedies are available under other clauses and provisions of the contract. A constructive suspension of work is one in which the A/E firm relied on or was induced to suspend performance based upon an act or omission by the government but was not formally directed by the government to suspend work.[107] The same notice and

---

[102] *Id.* § 52.248-2(a).

[103] 48 C.F.R. § 52.212-12(c) (1990).

[104] *Id.* § 52.212-12(a).

[105] *Id.*

[106] R.C. Hedreen Co., ASBCA No. 20599, 77-1 B.C.A. (CCH) ¶ 12,328 (1977) and Joseph Pickard's Sons Co., ASBCA Nos. 13585, 15537, 73-1 B.C.A. (CCH) ¶ 10,026 (1973).

[107] 48 C.F.R. § 52.212-12(b) (1990).

proof requirements exist for both constructive and actual suspensions of work.

An A/E contract also may contain a *stop work order clause.*[108] This clause allows a contracting officer to order that a portion of the A/E work be stopped for a period of up to 90 days. This time limit may be extended by agreement between the A/E firm and the contracting officer. The clause also provides that a contractor can file a claim for equitable adjustment of increased costs caused by the stoppage if it files within 30 days of the stop work order.[109]

§ 11.16 —Performance Evaluations

The FAR requires that the contracting officer conduct performance evaluation reports on standard form 1421 for all A/E contracts with a value greater than $25,000.[110] At the contracting officer's discretion, these reports also may be filed for contracts that are less than $25,000. The reports are prepared at the time of final acceptance of the work, when the contract is terminated, or at any other time dictated by specific agency procedures. The person who performs the evaluation also must be the person responsible for monitoring the contract performance.[111] All reports must be reviewed for accuracy by an official with knowledge of the project and who is at "an organizational level above that of the evaluating official."[112] Each report is distributed according to agency procedure, with copies sent to offices or boards of other agencies to update the shared pool of qualifications data for A/E firms. Each report will be included in the contract file and will be retained for at least six years after its completion.[113] The importance of these reports should not be underestimated because it is largely through these evaluations that agency evaluation boards determine an A/E firm's qualification and capabilities, the two main elements in the noncompetitive selection process promulgated by the Brooks Act.

§ 11.17 —Design-Within-Funding Clause

Another unique A/E clause is the *design-within-funding clause,* which is described in FAR 36.609-1 and implemented by FAR 52.236-22. This clause

---

[108] *Id.* 52.212-13.

[109] *Id.* § 52.212-13(b)(2).

[110] 48 C.F.R. § 36.604(a) (1990).

[111] *Id.* § 36.604(b).

[112] *Id.*

[113] *Id.* § 36.604(c).

allows the government to dictate that a project will be designed so that its construction cost will remain within a stated limit. If the specifications and estimated cost indicate that the construction price will exceed this limit, the government can require the A/E firm to redesign the project so that it will remain within the funding limit. Furthermore, this redesign work must be done at no additional cost to the government. However, if the construction cost increase was caused by uncontrollable events or by government delays, the A/E firm may charge the government for the costs of the redesign.[114]

The estimated construction price generally is used as the funding limitation, but it does not include allowances for government supervision, overhead, or funds earmarked for contingencies. The government is required to disclose all information to the A/E firm that was used as the basis for its construction estimate, as well as any subsequent information that affects construction costs.[115] For its part, the A/E firm is responsible for notifying the government when it believes that the designed project will exceed the funding limitation or if it is unable to design a functioning facility within the preset price limit. In some instances, the government might then direct a reduction in the scope of the project. If an agency head believes that performance goals are more important than cost limitations and that excess funding likely will be needed, the design-within-funding clause can be waived.[116] Still, an A/E firm should not rely on such a waiver and should be well aware of the funding limit when performing or designing a project for the government.

§ 11.18 —Termination Clauses

The basic *termination clauses* promulgated by the FAR and applicable to A/E contracts include provisions that allow the government to (1) terminate the contract for default if the contractor fails to perform as required; or (2) terminate the contract, in whole or in part, for its own convenience subject to an equitable adjustment, which will not include an allowance for anticipated profit or unperformed services.[117] These termination clauses must be included in all A/E contracts, but even if they are omitted, the courts have held that the clauses are incorporated by operation of law, and therefore the government still has the right to terminate the project.[118]

---

[114] 48 C.F.R. § 52.236-22(a) (1990).

[115] *Id.* § 52.236-22(b).

[116] *Id.*

[117] 48 C.F.R. § 52.249-7 (1990).

[118] *See* United States v. Corliss-Steam Engine Co., 91 U.S. 321 (1876).

Terminations for Default

There are four principal grounds for a default termination: (1) failure to deliver on time; (2) failure to comply with the specifications; (3) failure to make progress; and (4) failure to meet any other material term of the contract. Additionally, a contractor may face default if it fails to give the government adequate assurances of timely performance following receipt of a *cure notice.*[119] The government is required to give the contractor a written notice, in which 10 days are allotted to try to effect a cure before the government can issue a default termination for failure to make progress or failure to meet a material term of the contract.[120] This notice must be specific enough to allow a contractor reasonable opportunity to cure the problem.[121]

The procurement regulations specify a series of determinations that a contracting officer must make before issuing a default termination. The determinations include: (1) verification of the delay; (2) evaluation of the probability that the contractor will try to correct the problem causing delay; (3) an analysis of the government's need of the services in question; (4) an analysis of the liquidated damage clauses or other remedy clauses in the contract; (5) the issuance of a cure notice; and (6) the issuance of a default termination if the contractor fails to respond adequately or timely to the cure notice.[122]

The two main defenses available to a contractor who wishes to challenge a default termination are *excusable delay* and *waiver.* To successfully use an excusable delay defense, a contractor must prove lack of fault and demonstrate that it took some steps to mitigate or prevent the delay.[123] A second contractor defense to a default termination can be used when the government waived the contract delivery date by failing to terminate when the delivery date came due, and then failing to establish a new one. The government's election to allow performance to continue without a new delivery date may defeat an attempt to issue a default termination. This defense can be used even before the delivery date when the contractor informs the government that it will not meet the upcoming delivery date.[124] It is essential to this defense that the contractor be able to prove reliance on the waiver through continued performance, or that some other factor made reliance

---

[119] *See* Discount Co. v. United States, 213 Ct. Cl. 567, 554 F.2d 435, *cert. denied,* 434 U.S. 938 (1977).

[120] 48 C.F.R. § 52.249-8(a)(2) (1990).

[121] *See* Valley Contractors, ASBCA No. 9397, 1964 B.C.A. (CCH) ¶ 4,071 (1964).

[122] 48 C.F.R. §§ 49.504(a)1, 52.249-8 (1990).

[123] *Id.* § 52.249-8(c), (d).

[124] *See* Precision Prod., Inc., ASBCA No. 14284, 70-2 B.C.A. (CCH) ¶ 8,447 (1970) and Phil Rich Fan Mfg. Co., ASBCA No. 12770, 71-1 B.C.A. (CCH) ¶ 8,694 (1971).

unnecessary.[125] If the contractor accepts the default termination, the government is entitled to damages in the amount of any excess costs of reprocuring the contracted services.[126]

Terminations for Convenience

If the government decides that it is in its "best interests" to discontinue performance of a contract, the government has the right to terminate it for its convenience. If a contract is terminated for convenience, the contractor is entitled to all reasonable and allocable costs associated with performance and to a reasonable profit on those costs.[127] The termination for convenience of the government clause provides that the government can invoke this clause at any time when it is in its best interests, except it cannot do so if such action will constitute bad faith or an abuse of discretion.[128]

Paragraph (B) of the clause provides a checklist of steps to be taken by a contractor after receipt of notice of termination, including ceasing work, canceling subcontracts, and mitigating losses by selling termination inventory.[129] Usually, a contractor's termination claim, which must be submitted on standard form (SF) 1435 or 1436 to the contracting officer within one year of the effective date of termination, is settled by a negotiated settlement.[130] If no settlement can be reached or if SF 1435 or 1436 is not timely submitted, the contracting officer may make a unilateral determination of the amount due, subject to appeal under the contract's disputes clause.[131] Two types of post-termination expenses may be recoverable: (1) those that cannot be immediately stopped, despite a contractor's best efforts; and (2) legal, clerical, and other settlement expenses incurred in preparing, presenting, and negotiating the settlement claim.[132] Finally, the termination for convenience of the government clause requires a contractor to retain and make available to the contracting officer all books, records, documents, and other evidence for a period of three years after a final settlement.[133]

---

[125] *See* Electro Optics, Inc., ASBCA Nos. 24235, 24390, 81-2 B.C.A. (CCH) ¶ 15,181 (1981).

[126] 48 C.F.R. § 52.249-8(b) (1990).

[127] *Id.* § 52.249-1, -2.

[128] *Id.* § 52.249-1.

[129] *Id.*

[130] *Id.* at paras. (d), (e).

[131] *Id.* at para. (f).

[132] 48 C.F.R. § 31.205-42(b), (g) (1990).

[133] *Id.* at para. (m).

§ 11.19 Federal Acquisition Regulation Part 31 Cost Principles

FAR part 31 contains cost principles that govern the allowability and recovery of costs under various scenarios, including (1) terminations for the convenience of the government; (2) contract modifications; and (3) cost-type contracts. In order to determine the allowability (and, therefore, recoverability) of a particular cost, five factors are considered by the government: (1) reasonableness; (2) allocability; (3) terms of the contract; (4) all limitations stated within the cost principles; and (5) cost accounting standards (CAS) promulgated by the Cost Accounting Standards Board (CASB), if applicable, otherwise, generally accepted cost accounting standards appropriate to the circumstances.[134]

Reasonableness

In the past, the government had the legal burden of proving that a particular cost incurred by the contractor was unreasonable, either in amount or type, and therefore unallowable. However, under the Defense Authorization Act of 1986, this rule was changed to provide in the FAR that a contractor now has the burden of proving the reasonableness of its incurred costs:[135]

> A cost is reasonable if, in its nature and amount, it does not exceed that which would be incurred by a prudent person in the conduct of competitive business . . . no presumption of reasonableness shall be attached to the incurrence of costs by a contractor, and upon challenge of a specific cost by the contracting officer, the burden of proof shall be upon the contractor to establish that such cost is reasonable.[136]

Although this change may appear to be relatively harmless on its face, it has had a material effect on the government auditors' review of cost allowability. Formerly, most auditors would challenge the reasonableness of a particular cost only when it was a fairly clear case of what they considered abuse. Otherwise, they had an almost insurmountable burden of showing that the contractor unreasonably incurred a particular cost. Now that the burden has shifted, auditors have felt more free to challenge cost reasonableness, recognizing that a contractor must come forward with evidence of its cost reasonableness.

---

[134] 48 C.F.R. § 31.201-2 (1990).

[135] Title IX is Defense Procurement Improvement Act of 1985, Pub. L. No. 99-145, 99 Stat. 682 (1985), 10 U.S.C. § 2324 (repealed by Pub. L. No. 100-370 § 1(f)(3)(B), 102 Stat. 846 (1988)).

[136] 48 C.F.R. § 31.203-3(a) (1990).

Allocability

An *allocable cost* is one that is "assignable or chargeable to one or more cost objectives on the basis of relative benefits or other equitable relationship."[137] In order to be allocable, a cost must satisfy one of three criteria promulgated in FAR part 31. The cost is allocable if it (1) is incurred directly for the project; (2) benefits both the project work and other services and can be allocated among these items in reasonable proportion to the benefits received; or (3) is essential to the general operation of the firm, despite the lack of a direct link to a particular contract.[138]

Terms of Contract and Cost Principle Limitations

In addition to any limitations on the allowability of a particular type of cost set forth within a particular contract, an A/E contractor must take into account the limitations mandated by FAR 31.205. FAR 31.205 discusses approximately 50 selected costs and the circumstances under which these costs are allowable or unallowable. A partial list of costs that are generally unallowable according to this part includes general advertising, donations, entertainment expenses, interest on loans, organizational expenses, attorney and accounting fees incurred in a claim against or by the government, first-class air fare, certain relocation expenses, alcoholic beverages, certain legislative lobbying, goodwill, most fines and penalties, losses on other contracts, and bad debts.[139]

One example of the type of cost made unallowable in a particular contract arises from the transfer of a contract from one entity to another due to a merger or acquisition known as a *novation.* A novation agreement typically provides that the government will not pay for any rise in cost directly or indirectly stemming from the transfer. A novation agreement frequently has been used to stop the transferee (the new contractor) from recovering increased depreciation costs[140] or fees for overhead services paid to the new parent corporation.[141]

Cost Accounting Standards

The last factor that must be evaluated in determining the allowability of a particular cost item is the applicability of the cost accounting standards

---

[137] *Id.* § 31.201-4.

[138] *Id.*

[139] *Id.* § 31.205.

[140] *See* Sundstrand Turbo v. United States, 182 Ct. Cl. 31, 389 F.2d 406 (1968).

[141] *See* ITT Gilfillon v. United States, 200 Ct. Cl. 367, 471 F.2d 1382 (1973).

(CAS) or, in the alternative, generally accepted cost accounting principles. The CAS consists of 19 standards promulgated by the Cost Accounting Standards Board (CASB) governing a contractor's cost accounting practices under negotiated "national defense" A/E contracts or subcontracts worth more than $100,000. In order to be subject to CAS for contracts over $100,000, the contractor must first receive a contract worth $500,000 or more subject to CAS. "National defense" contracts include some NASA and DOE contracts because the category covers contracts in any program for military or atomic energy production, foreign military assistance, or space. Under a recent amendment to be implemented sometime in 1991, CAS will apply to nondefense contracts to the same extent as defense contracts, and CAS will apply only to contracts over $500,00.

If CAS does not apply, a contractor's accounting system must be consistent with generally accepted principles and practices. There is no set definition as to what constitutes a generally accepted practice, so a contractor must use reasonable judgment in either maintaining consistency or in following the methods currently in use in the industry. If a system is used consistently and is not unfair to the government, it probably will be accepted.

Congress established the CASB in 1970[142] to create consistency within the various defense contractors' accounting methods. The board regulations required contractors to disclose, in writing, their cost accounting practices and to be subject to downward price adjustments for any failure to meet the generally accepted cost accounting procedures or the promulgated CAS. Although the CASB was essentially eliminated in 1980 when Congress withheld its funding, it was reinstituted in 1984 and its regulations were incorporated into FAR part 30. The CASB consists of five members: the Office of Federal Procurement Policy (OFPP) administrator, Department of Defense (DOD) and General Services Administration (GSA) representatives, and two private sector members—usually one accounting expert and one industry representative. The board can make, amend, or rescind any CAS but it has no power over the FAR part 31 cost principles.[143]

The cost accounting standards clause requires contractors to:

> (1) disclose, in writing, its cost accounting practices; (2) follow consistently the cost accounting practices which are disclosed; (3) comply with all standards in effect on the date of award of the contract, subject to the Act's requirements, and any subsequent standard; and (4) agree to appropriate price adjustments which may be necessitated by changes in the contractor's disclosed cost accounting practices.[144]

[142] Pub. L. No. 91-379, 84 Stat. 796 (1970), 50 U.S.C. § 2168 (repealed by 100-679, 1025 Stat. 4063 (1988)), (current version at 41 U.S.C. § 401 (1988)).

[143] Charness & Dobbs at D-22.

[144] 48 C.F.R. § 30.303-2 (1990).

Once a contractor has received a single "covered" contract of $500,000 or more, the board has the power to grant exemptions for any contract or subcontract of less than $500,000. Additionally, exemptions may be gained if the price of the contract is based upon an established catalog or market price of commercial items sold in substantial quantities or for a price set by law or regulation.[145] These exemptions are very similar to those under the Truth-in-Negotiations Act, discussed further in § **11.20**.

Finally, the board adopted a modified coverage plan for companies that receive less than $10 million annually in awards of covered contracts or in instances in which covered contracts are less than 10 percent of their total annual sales. Modified contract coverage consists of CAS 401 and 402, a modified CAS clause, and, if necessary, a statement of disclosure.[146] Formal disclosure statements of a contractor's cost accounting practices must be submitted by any contractors awarded a total of $10 million or more in covered contracts over the previous year.

Currently, there are 19 CAS as promulgated by the CASB:

1. CAS 401: Requires consistency in estimating, proposing, and reporting costs
2. CAS 402: Requires costs to be uniformly accounted for, as direct or indirect, if incurred by the same business unit for the same purpose
3. CAS 403: Provides for methods of allocation of expenses from the home office to segmented units on a causal basis
4. CAS 404: Provides criteria for the capitalization of tangible assets, which relates to the acquisition cost or service life of the asset
5. CAS 405: Requires that unallowable costs be excluded from all claims or billings
6. CAS 406: Provides that a contractor will use the measurement of its fiscal year to account for costs
7. CAS 407: Provides standard costs for direct material but doesn't apply to A/E contractors
8. CAS 408: Provides rules for accounting of severance and sick leave compensation
9. CAS 409: Provides methods to account for the depreciation of the service life of an asset
10. CAS 410: Provides definition of general and administrative expenses and describes the allocation bases available to contractors
11. CAS 411: Pertains to material costs and the use of inventory pricing methods

---

[145] 4 C.F.R. § 331.30 (1991).

[146] *Id.* §§ 331.30(b), 30.301(b).

12. CAS 412 and 413: Relate to pension costs and the use of actuarial gains and losses
13. CAS 414 and 417: Relate to secretary-of-the treasury-determined interest rates to be applied to facilities capital and to costs of investments of partially constructed assets
14. CAS 415: Relates to deferred compensation
15. CAS 416: Pertains to insurance costs
16. CAS 418: Requires written classification of indirect and direct costs and provides factors to determine the allowability of average labor rates (CAS 419 was withdrawn)
17. CAS 420: Relates to practices and standards involving bid and proposal (B&P) and independent research and development (IR&D) expenses.[147]

§ 11.20 Complying with the Truth-in-Negotiations Act

Typically, under the Brooks Act there is no price competition during the negotiation of an A/E contract. The government, therefore, attempts to gather as much information about the contractor's cost and pricing data as it can pursuant to the Truth-in-Negotiations Act. Unless an exemption applies, a contractor generally must disclose accurate, current, and complete cost and pricing information in support of, and together with, its proposal on standard form (SF) 1411 for any negotiated prime contract over $100,000 (for defense contracts, over $500,000). A subcontractor also must provide cost or pricing data for any subcontract over $100,000 (for defense contracts, over $500,000). Moreover, even if a contractor or subcontractor is not required to provide cost or pricing data in connection with a contract award, it must do so in connection with a modification proposal over $100,000 (for defense contracts, over $500,000). If the cost or pricing data are not accurate, current, and complete, the government, among other things, can reduce the contract price.

Cost or Pricing Data Defined

Cost or pricing data are defined by FAR 15.801 as: "All facts as of the time of price agreement that prudent buyers and sellers would reasonably expect to affect price negotiations significantly. Cost or pricing data are factual, not judgmental and therefore verifiable."[148] Some examples of cost or

[147] This list of cost accounting standards was derived from similar summaries contained in P. Lubka, Government Architect-Engineer Contracting Course Manual F-5 to F-8 (1990).

[148] 48 C.F.R. § 15.801 (1990).

pricing data listed in the FAR are vendor quotations; nonrecurring cost data; information on changes in purchasing volume, unit cost trends, and make-versus-purchase decisions; and information on management decisions that could significantly affect costs.[149]

Several questions have arisen regarding the definition of cost or pricing data contained within TINA and the FAR. The first point of confusion centers on the "fact" versus "judgment" debate. *Facts* are defined by FAR 15.801 and interpreted by the administrative boards and the courts to be any current or historical data as well as any projections or estimates formulated from this data. Although judgmental information need not be submitted as cost or pricing data,[150] the factual information upon which any judgmental data are based does require disclosure and certification.[151]

The second point of confusion about the definition of cost or pricing data arises over the meaning of "significant effect on price negotiations" mentioned in TINA and the FAR. Generally, the administrative boards and the courts have interpreted this phrase to have a broad scope. The effect of this interpretation has been that almost any amount, no matter how small, can be considered "significant." This "de minimus" concept allows the government to reduce the contract price for almost any "error" that would affect the price.[152] However, most defective pricing claims are not issued unless they can be combined or are big enough themselves to warrant government action.

Cost or Pricing Data Disclosure

It is not enough to submit cost or pricing data; the disclosed information also must be in a form that is easy for the government to understand and evaluate. Although it generally has been held that a contractor must analyze and explain to the government which elements of the disclosed cost or pricing data are relevant to a particular contract,[153] the recent trend has moved away from this principle. As long as the government is capable of correctly interpreting the data, a contractor is generally under no further obligation to analyze or interpret the cost or pricing data: "We do not believe that TINA requires a contractor to lead the Government by the hand, forcing it to analyze relevant data, properly submitted, but which the Government

---

[149] *Id.*

[150] *Id.* § 15.801(g).

[151] *See* PAE Int'l, ASBCA No. 20595, 76-2 B.C.A. (CCH) ¶ 12,044 (1976).

[152] *See* Sylvania Elec. Prod., Inc., ASBCA No. 13622, 70-2 B.C.A. (CCH) ¶ 8,387 (1970), *aff'd,* Sylvania Elec. Prod., Inc. v. United States, 202 Ct. Cl. 16, 479 F.2d 1342 (1973).

[153] *See* M-R-S Mfg. Co. v. United States, 203 Ct. Cl. 551, 492 F.2d 835 (1974) *aff'g* 71-1 B.C.A. (CCH) ¶ 8,821 (ABSCA 1971) and Sylvania Elec. Prod., Inc., 202 Ct. Cl. 16, 479 F.2d 1342 (1973), *aff'g* 70-2 B.C.A. (CCH) ¶ 8,387 (ASBCA 1970).

chooses or happens to ignore."[154] However, even if a contractor is not obligated to analyze data for the government, it still must submit the cost or pricing data in a form that the government is capable of analyzing itself.

Cost or Pricing Data Certification

As soon as possible after the parties agree on price, a contractor must submit a certificate of current cost or pricing data. This certificate states that the contractor has complied with TINA and that the disclosed cost or pricing data are accurate, current, and complete.[155] FAR 15.804-4 gives an example of a typical certificate.

The phrase "time of agreement on price," which appears in the certificate, has been interpreted to mean that significant new or changed facts occurring after the "shake-hands" date on price agreement need not be submitted, either before or after the execution of the certificate itself. However, a distinction must be drawn between informing the government of new facts and updating already disclosed cost or pricing data. To best avoid liability, a contractor should submit cost or pricing data updates throughout the negotiation period.[156] Generally, a contractor will not be liable for defective pricing if the data could not be updated due to an unreasonable time constraint.[157] However, the urgency of a procurement solicitation is not a defense against a defective pricing claim.[158]

Exemptions from Cost or Pricing Requirements

A contractor can claim an exemption from having to submit certified cost or pricing data if the negotiated price is (1) based upon adequate price competition; (2) based upon established catalog or market prices of commercial items sold in substantial quantities to the general public; (3) set by law or regulation; or (4) in exceptional cases, when an agency head waives the requirements and submits a written justification for the decision.[159] Adequate price competition exists if two or more competitive, independent, and qualified offers are submitted in response to the government's solicitation and the most qualified one (as determined by the Brooks Act

[154] *See* American Mach. & Foundry Co., ASBCA No. 15037, 74-1 B.C.A. (CCH) ¶ 10,409, at 49,173 (1973).

[155] 48 C.F.R. ¶ 14.804-4 (1990).

[156] *See* Lambert Eng'g Co., ASBCA No. 13338, 69-1 B.C.A. (CCH) ¶ 7,663 (1969).

[157] *See* Central Navigation & Trading Co., S.A., ASBCA No. 23946, 82-2 B.C.A. (CCH) ¶ 16,074 (1982).

[158] *See* Baldwin Elec., Inc., ASBCA No. 19683, 76-2 B.C.A. (CCH) ¶ 12,199, at 58,737 (1976).

[159] 48 C.F.R. § 15.804-3 (1990).

procedures) is selected.[160] The other exemptions have little, if any, bearing on A/E contractors. The final exemption to the requirements of TINA, secretarial waiver by an agency head, is rarely invoked and should not be relied upon by an A/E contractor.[161]

Defective Pricing and Fraud Implications

The key limiting provision in TINA for contractors is the required inclusion into all applicable contracts of a price reduction for defective cost or pricing data clause. There are price reduction clauses for contracts requiring cost or pricing data as part of negotiations and for contracts requiring cost or pricing only for modifications. Once the certification requirements of TINA are triggered, the government agencies, either themselves, or with the aid of the Defense Contract Audit Agency (DCAA), will conduct audits. These audits may be conducted on either a prime contractor or on any covered subcontractor for which the prime contractor is responsible. If an agency was overcharged because of defective cost or pricing data, the contractor is liable for the amount of the overpayment and the interest on that overpayment[162] as determined by the current rate presented by the secretary of the treasury.[163]

If the defective pricing of the cost or pricing data was done intentionally, the contracting officer can contact the United States Department of Justice, which can take action against the contractor under either the Criminal False Statements Act[164] or the False Claims Act,[165] which has both criminal and civil liability sections. Anyone convicted of intentionally falsifying cost or pricing data under the False Statements Act is subject to a fine of up to $10,000 and/or five years' imprisonment. Under the Criminal False Claims Act, a convicted party may face a maximum penalty of $1 million and/or five years' imprisonment. Additionally, a party may be civilly responsible for $5,000 to $10,000 for each false claim, treble damages, and a forfeiture of the claim.[166] For cases of fraud not exceeding $150,000, an administrative penalty of $5,000 for each false claim may be imposed on each party involved in the falsifying of the cost or pricing data. Finally, the "qui tam" provision of the False Claims Act allows private individuals with evidence

---

[160] *Id.* § 15.804-3(b).

[161] *Id.* § 15.804-3(c).

[162] 10 U.S.C. § 2306(e)(1)(B) (1988).

[163] I.R.C. § 6621 (1987).

[164] 18 U.S.C. § 1001 (1982 & Supp. VI 1988).

[165] 18 U.S.C. § 287 (1982 & Supp. VI 1988) (criminal); and 31 U.S.C. § 3728 (1982 & Supp. V 1987) (civil).

[166] *Id.*

of fraud to file a false claim on behalf of themselves and the government and to keep a percentage of any monetary recovery.[167]

§ 11.21 Limitation-of-Cost Clause

Under a cost-type contract, an A/E firm's reimbursement of costs may be directly affected by the limitation-of-cost clause (LOCC) required in all such contracts. The LOCC is included to aid in the enforcement of the Anti-Deficiency Act, which prohibits government expenditures or agreements in excess of appropriated amounts.[168] The clause mandates that a contractor give notice to the government of any potential overrun of the estimated costs to complete a project. The government may respond by either (1) increasing funding; (2) decreasing contract performance; (3) stopping performance; or (4) terminating the contract. By requiring notice, it is hoped that neither the contractor nor the government will be unknowingly responsible for any unexpected additional costs. It should be noted that the limitation-of-funding clause (LOFC) serves the same purpose as the LOCC for incrementally funded contracts.

The FAR requires the use of LOCC in all fully funded cost-reimbursement supply contracts. The purpose of the LOCC is to "prevent overruns of expenditures on contracts, maintain budget controls and eliminate one cause of deficiency appropriations."[169] Neither the LOCC nor the LOFC applies to the contractor's recovery of its fee. The clause only requires contractors to give notice of expected overrun of estimated costs, not fees.[170]

The LOCC requires a contractor to give notice to the government at any point at which it believes that (1) the cumulative performance costs are expected to surpass 75 percent of the total estimated contract cost at any point within the next 60 days; or (2) the total costs (excluding the fee) will be greater or substantially less than the total estimated cost of the project.[171] The LOCC creates the affirmative duty for the contractor to use its best efforts to either stay within its total estimate or to provide the government with adequate written notice. To be adequate, the written notification must be as specific as possible. Although no particular form is required, proper notification must (1) mention that, pursuant to its LOCC obligations, notice is being given of an impending cost overrun; and

---

[167] *Id.*

[168] 31 U.S.C. § 665(a) (1982 & Supp. VI 1988).

[169] *See* ITT Defense Communications Div., ASBCA No. 14270, 70-2 B.C.A. (CCH) ¶ 8,370 at 38,920 (1970).

[170] Charness & Dobbs at D-14.

[171] 48 C.F.R. § 52.232-20(b) (1990).

(2) include a new estimated cost of completion. This notification should be sent to the contracting officer; however, if it is too vague or does not include the new estimated cost of completion, it will be ruled to be an inadequate notification.[172] If notice is ruled inadequate or if a contractor does not attempt to provide it, the government will not reimburse any cost overruns.[173]

There are three main exceptions to the LOCC that allow a contractor to be reimbursed for a cost overrun without having submitted notification. The first notice exception is that the contracting officer had sufficient knowledge of the financial condition of the project to have known (or should have known) that a cost overrun would occur.[174] However, the boards of contract appeals have not been too receptive to this argument and have held that the government is under no affirmative duty to audit a contractor's financial status to determine whether or not a cost overrun is likely.[175] The board in *Hughes Aircraft Corp.*[176] established the criteria that must be met for a contractor to gain this exception to the LOCC notice requirement:

1. The government must know of the overrun
2. The government must intend that the conduct alleged to have induced continued performance will be acted on, or the contractor has a right to believe the conduct in question was intended to induce performance
3. The contractor must not be aware of the facts, that is, no implied funding of the overrun was intended by the contract
4. The contractor must rely on the government's conduct to its detriment.

The second exception to the LOCC notice requirement is easier to attain than the first. If an impossible situation prevents providing notice, such as when a contractor, through no fault of its own, has no reason to believe an overrun will happen during contract performance, then a contractor may still be able to be reimbursed for the additional costs.[177] This exception has developed into a foreseeability test. If the board believes the contractor knew or should have known of a cost overrun, no exception to the notification

[172] *See* Falcon Research & Dev. Co., ASBCA No. 26853, 87-1 B.C.A. (CCH) ¶ 19,458 (1986).

[173] *See* Varigas Research, Inc., ASBCA No. 28610, 84-1 B.C.A. (CCH) ¶ 17,154 (1984); Kirschner Assocs., Inc., ASBCA No. 24958, 81-1 B.C.A. (CCH) ¶ 14,834 (1980) and City of Wichita Falls, HUD BCA No. 76-13, 77-2 B.C.A. (CCH) ¶ 12,764 (1977).

[174] *See* Consulting Serv. Corp., ASBCA No. 20288, 76-2 B.C.A. (CCH) ¶ 12,124 (1976).

[175] Optonetics, Inc., ASBCA No. 17015, 73-2 B.C.A. (CCH) ¶ 10,173, at 47,897 (1973).

[176] ASBCA No. 24601, 83-1 B.C.A. (CCH) ¶ 16,396, at 81,516-17 (1983).

[177] *See* General Elec. Corp. v. United States, 194 Ct. Cl. 678, 440 F.2d 420 (1971).

requirement will be allowed.[178] The burden of proof for this foreseeability test is upon the contractor.[179] The foreseeability test is composed of two parts: (1) the adequacy of the contractor's accounting system; and (2) the accuracy of its business projections. If a contractor keeps an inadequate accounting system, it cannot satisfy its burden of proof that it could not foresee the potential cost overrun. This type of self-imposed ignorance of foreseeability will not warrant an exception to the LOCC notification requirement.[180] Generally, a contractor also will not satisfy the foreseeability test by claiming that expected business did not materialize, resulting in higher overhead and indirect costs than were expected.[181] However, if the contractor's inaccurate business projections are based upon reasonable data and assumptions, the failure to give notice may be excused.[182]

The final exception to the LOCC's notice requirement involves proving that the lack of notification was due to the fault or negligence of the government. For example, if the government fails to conduct an audit that it has promised to perform, and as a result of this failure the contractor could not foresee the cost overrun, the contractor may be excused from the notification requirement.[183] However, if a contractor could have learned from its own accounting system that an overrun would occur because its actual overhead was exceeding its provisional overhead (even if the final rate could not be determined until after a government audit), the contractor will not get an exception to the LOCC and, thus, will get no compensation.[184] Therefore, in order to comply with the LOCC and to assure full reimbursement, an A/E contractor, whenever possible, always should notify the government of even the most remote likelihood of a cost overrun.

§ 11.22 Avoiding Conflicts of Interest

In light of recent investigations of improprieties in the procurement community, there has been a rash of legislation and regulations designed to curtail unlawful and unethical practices. A prime concern of many of the new restrictive measures is to eliminate the vast number of actual or potential conflicts of interest that arise from the movement of personnel between the government agencies and the firms that contract and subcontract with

---

[178] *See* Stanwick Corp., ASBCA No. 14905, 71-1 B.C.A. (CCH) ¶ 8,777 (1971).

[179] *See* General Time Corp., ASBCA No. 18962, 75-2 B.C.A. (CCH) ¶ 11,462 (1975).

[180] Optonetics, Inc., ASBCA No. 17015, 73-2 B.C.A. (CCH) ¶ 10,173, at 47,899 (1973).

[181] *See* Kirschner Assoc., Inc., ASBCA No. 24958, 81-1 B.C.A. (CCH) ¶ 14,834 (1980) and Inter-National Research Inst., ASBCA No. 24212, 80-1 B.C.A. (CCH) ¶ 14,345 (1980).

[182] *See* Bissett-Berman Corp., NASA No. 1270-19, 73-2 B.C.A. (CCH) ¶ 10,346 (1973).

[183] *See* Scherr & McDermott, Inc. v. United States, 175 Ct. Cl. 440, 360 F.2d 966 (1966).

[184] *See* Dynadyne, Inc., IBCA No. 1329-1-80, 81-1 B.C.A. (CCH) ¶ 15,054 (1981).

them. Potential conflict of interest problems can be broken down into three categories: (1) unlawful payments to lobbyists and/or consultants; (2) personal conflicts of interest; and (3) organizational conflicts of interest. In addition to the measures promulgated in the FAR, many agencies require the inclusion of supplemental anti-conflict-of-interest clauses into their contracts, such as EPA's limitation-of-future-contracting clause. Thus, during this period of heightened scrutiny, it becomes especially important to both understand what constitutes a conflict of interest and to know how to avoid one.

§ 11.23 —Restrictions on Use of Lobbyists and Consultants

On December 23, 1989, the Byrd amendment to the 1990 Department of the Interior and Related Agencies Appropriations Act took effect.[185] In essence, the Byrd amendment states that all those who receive appropriated federal funds, including contractors, are prohibited from using those funds to "pay any person for influencing or attempting to influence an officer or employee of any agency, a member of Congress, or an employee of a member of Congress in connection" with the awarding, renewal, or modification of any contract with the government.[186] However, a contractor is not prohibited from paying for its lobbying costs from (1) the portion of its government funds that represents profit; (2) monies acquired from a claim or settlement against the government; or (3) any nongovernmental funds.[187]

There are several exceptions contained within the Byrd amendment that allow a contractor to use appropriated funds for lobbying; however, the restrictions against using these funds for consultants are harder to waive. It is allowable to use appropriated funds for "agency and legislative liaison activities" that are not directly related to a particular contract.[188] This exception only applies if the payment is made to a regular worker who has been with the employer for at least 130 days of the previous year before the payment.[189]

Another exception to the Byrd amendment applies to consultants. After a solicitation has been issued, a contractor may use appropriated funds for "professional or technical services" that are required as a result of an

---

[185] Pub. L. No. 101-121, § 319, 103 Stat. 701, 750 (codified at 31 U.S.C. § 1352 (1989)).

[186] Pushkar & Stoughton, *Restrictions on Consultant Services,* Briefing Papers No. 90-6, May 1990, at 8–9.

[187] H.R. Conf. Rep. No. 264, 101st Cong., 1st Sess. 97 (1989), 135 Cong. Rec. H. 6385 (daily ed. Oct. 2, 1989).

[188] Pushkar & Stoughton, *Restrictions on Consultant Services,* Briefing Papers No. 90-6, May 1990, at 8.

[189] 31 U.S.C. § 1352(h)(8)–(10) (1982 & Supp. IV 1988).

obligation or condition created by the contract. For example, technical advice from an engineer used directly in the performance of a contract is an allowable cost. However, in the case of this hypothetical engineer, the stated exception is significantly self-limited by the declaration that:

> Communications with the intent to influence made by an engineer providing an engineering analysis prior to the preparation and submission of a bid or proposal are not allowable under this section since the engineer is providing technical services but not directly in the preparation, submission or negotiation of a covered Federal action.[190]

The Office of Management and Budget (OMB) recently issued a guidance to clarify the "professional or technical services" exception to the Byrd amendment: "Professional or technical services shall be advice and analysis directly applying any professional or technical expertise."[191]

The Byrd amendment states that if a contract is subject to full cost accounting standards (CAS) coverage, then accounting for lobbying activities as unallowable costs under CAS 405 will satisfy the requirement. If unallowable costs are not segregated, a contractor must provide some means of proving that no appropriated funds were used for lobbying. In either case, certification is required that no payment will be made in violation of the Byrd amendment and that all monies spent on influencing executive or legislative branch officers in connection with a contract will be disclosed.[192]

These declarations concerning any payments made with unappropriated funds must include the following information: (1) the name and address of the person paid; (2) the name and address of each individual performing services; (3) the amount of the payments; (4) the manner in which the person is paid; and (5) the activity for which the person has been paid. This certificate must be filed with every submission that initiates a procurement consideration by an agency; upon receipt of a federal contract; and at each calendar quarter in which a material change has occurred that alters the accuracy of the last declaration. A material change is a payment increase of at least $25,000 or a change in the person being paid. The Byrd amendment provides for from $10,000 to $100,000 in civil penalties for a violation of its restrictions and requirements as well as potential criminal liability for false declarations.[193]

In addition to the Byrd amendment, on December 18, 1989, the Office of Federal Procurement Policy (OFPP) published a policy letter that mandated certification requirements for contractors who use consultants in

---

[190] 48 C.F.R. § 3802(c)(2)ii (1990).

[191] *OMB Clarifies Byrd Amendment,* 53 Fed. Cont. Rep. (BNA) No. 25, at 837 (June 18, 1990).

[192] *Id.* at 9.

[193] *Id.* at 11.

connection with procurement activities. Prime contractors who have hired marketing consultants to aid in a government acquisition exceeding $200,000 must certify the following information: (1) the name of the agency and its solicitation; (2) the name(s) of the consultant(s) and anyone with knowledge of services provided to aid in that contract; (3) a description of the services obtained; (4) a list of other clients whom the consultant(s) has aided on the same subject; (5) a statement of the consultant's awareness of the OFPP policy; and (6) the signature and titles of the contractor's and consultant's certifying official.[194] In addition, all contractors that provide the government advisory or assistance services must certify this same information for contracts worth $25,000 or more.[195]

§ 11.24 —Personal Conflicts of Interest: Revolving Door Provisions

A personal conflict of interest is defined as a relationship of an employee, subcontractor employee, or consultant with any person or group that could impede the objective performance of a contract.[196] The *"revolving door" provisions*[197] of the conflict-of-interest laws were passed to combat these potential personal conflicts of interest.

The revolving door provisions of the conflict-of-interest laws govern the activities of persons who leave federal government employment for jobs in the private sector. Any violation of the revolving door statute could result in a maximum fine of $10,000, two years' imprisonment, or both.[198]

The revolving door statute provides that no former executive branch employee can ever work for any party other than the United States in matters in which the government interest is substantial and in which the employee personally and significantly participated.[199] Furthermore, no executive branch employee may appear before any tribunal or agency for two years after leaving the government with regard to matters that were within the employee's official duty. This restriction applies to all such matters that were pending in the last year of the worker's government service, regardless of whether the employee personally handled the matter.[200] The revolving door statute also prohibits senior government employees who now work with a private body at least 60 days per calendar year from communicating

---

[194] Charness & Dobbs at D-193.

[195] *Id.* at D-194.

[196] 48 C.F.R. § 1552.209-73(a) (1989).

[197] 18 U.S.C. § 207 (1982 & Supp. VI 1988).

[198] *Id.* § 207(a).

[199] *Id.*

[200] *Id.* § 207(b); 5 C.F.R. § 737.7 (1990).

with their former employing agency for one year on any matter in which the agency has a "direct and substantial" interest.[201]

The Office of Federal Procurement Policy Act Amendments of 1988 included both contractual and civil penalties for violations of the revolving door rules that affect government procurement officials. During the procurement process, no such official is allowed to discuss future employment or business opportunities with any contractor or with any of its competitors. Certification that there is no information on any violation of this rule is required for all contracts worth more than $100,000.[202] False certifications will be subject to prosecution under the Federal Criminal False Statements Statute.[203] Furthermore, penalties for the willful violation of these requirements include (1) the dismissal of the government procurement officer; (2) forfeiture of profit under the contract; (3) contract default; (4) suspension or debarment of contractor; and (5) civil fines of $100,000 per involved party and $1 million for the contractor.[204]

§ 11.25 —Organizational Conflicts of Interest

An organizational conflict of interest exists when the type of work performed under contract may, without some restriction on future activities, result in an unfair competitive advantage or in an impairment to the contractor's objective performance of the work.[205] The government established regulations in FAR part 9.5 designed to deter organizational conflicts of interest. Although an agency head has the authority to waive the limitation on future activities of a contractor,[206] it is highly unlikely that this would occur very often with an A/E contractor.

The few areas in which conflicts of interest generally arise and that are subject to limitations on future activities as promulgated by the FAR are (1) systems engineering and technical direction; (2) development of specifications or work statements; (3) technical evaluations or consulting services; and (4) access to proprietary information.[207] Many of these activities often are performed by A/E contractors.

---

[201] *Id.* § 207(c); 5 C.F.R. § 737.11 (1990).

[202] Pub. L. No. 100-679, 102 Stat. 4055 (1988) (amending Office of Federal Procurement Policy Act, Pub. L. No. 93-400, 88 Stat. 796 (1974) and codified as amended at 41 U.S.C. § 401 (1988)).

[203] 18 U.S.C. § 1001 (1982 & Supp. VI 1988).

[204] Darley, *New "Revolving Door" Issues for Federal Officials under the OFPP Policy Act Amendments of 1988: A Quick Overview,* 18 Pub. Cont. L. J. (1989).

[205] 48 C.F.R. § 9.501 (1990).

[206] *Id.* § 9.503.

[207] *Id.* § 9.505.

Systems engineering and technical direction. If a contractor is responsible for systems engineering and technical direction, but not for the system's development, assembly, integration, or checkout, it cannot (1) be a consultant or subcontractor to a supplier of the system or any of its major components, or (2) be awarded a contract to supply the system or any of its major components.[208]

Development of specifications or work statements. If a contractor produces all specifications covering nondevelopmental items to be used in a competitive procurement, it cannot provide those items, either as a prime contractor or as a subcontractor, for a reasonable period of time. This time frame must last for at least the duration of the initial award.[209] An exception exists if the contractor furnishes specifications or data at the request of the government or in the capacity of an industry representative that is aiding the government to revise or prepare the specifications.[210] Furthermore, if a contractor creates a work statement for a competitive procurement, it cannot supply the product. However, this limitation will not apply if the contractor (1) is the sole source of the product; (2) aided in the development or design preparation; or (3) was not the only contractor involved in providing the work statement.[211]

Technical evaluation services. Projects involving technical evaluation of other contractor's offers, products, or consulting services will not be awarded to a contractor if the contractor would be required to advise the government about its capabilities or those of its competitors. However, if proper safety measures to guarantee the contractor's objectivity and to protect the government's interest can be established, this limit will not apply.[212]

Access to proprietary information. If a contractor gains access to a competitor's proprietary data while providing a consulting service to the government, that contractor must agree to protect the information from unauthorized use or disclosure and to avoid using the information for any reason other than that for which it was provided originally.[213]

---

[208] *Id.* § 9.505-1(a).

[209] *Id.* § 9.505-2(a)(1).

[210] *Id.* § 9.505-2(a)(1)i.

[211] 48 C.F.R. § 9.505-2(b)(1) (1990).

[212] *Id.* § 9.505-3.

[213] *Id.* § 9.505-4(a).

§ 11.26 —Anti-Conflict-of-Interest Regulations on the Agency Level: Environmental Protection Agency's Response

In addition to the four general sources of organizational conflicts of interest that are subject to limitations in the FAR, each agency has promulgated regulations of its own to address conflict-of-interest problems that pertain specifically to that agency. Before entering into any project, a potential A/E contractor should consider any limitations on its future contracting that would apply if it worked for a particular agency. For instance, the acquisition regulations for the Department of Energy (DOE), the Environmental Protection Agency (EPA), and the Department of Defense (DOD) all have supplemented the FAR with additional disclosure requirements and special anti-conflict-of-interest contract clauses. Because of the substantial number of A/E environmental contracting opportunities, EPA's acquisition regulations are examined here.

Conflicts of interest have been a source of much debate and concern within the EPA. In a report published by the congressional Office of Technology Assessment (OTA), EPA was criticized for depending too heavily upon outside consultants and contractors for assistance in creating policies for the Superfund program. In April of 1990, in an effort to curb this perceived trend and to crack down on these potential conflicts of interest, EPA issued proposed regulations concerning conflicts of interest of contractors and consultants for the Superfund program.[214]

The purpose of the proposed regulations is to prevent contractors from entering into outside contracts that might result in "actual, apparent or potential" conflicts of interest both before and after the contract has been completed, and to ensure that Superfund contractors identify and report all personal and organizational conflicts of interest to the EPA contracting officer. The new regulations include strict notification and certification requirements and the use of limitation-of-future-contracting clauses.

Once the regulations are enacted, A/E contractors for EPA will have to notify the agency of all actual, apparent, or potential conflicts of interest.[215] The EPA acquisition regulations (EPAAR) have been amended to require that notification of any organizational or personal conflict of interest be made to the appropriate contracting officer before the commencement of any project.[216] In emergency situations, the project may be started, but notification must be given within five working days. This disclosure requirement also applies to all subcontractors and consultants, unless they

[214] Charness & Dobbs at D-189.

[215] 48 C.F.R. § 1552.209-71(a) (1989).

[216] *Id.* § 1552.209-71(c).

deal with well-drilling, fence erecting, plumbing, utility backups, security guard services, or electrical services.[217]

Under the proposed regulations, Superfund contractors also will have to certify annually that all conflicts of interest have been reported to the EPA. Furthermore, the contractor will be obligated to obtain confidentiality agreements from all employees, subcontractors, and consultants working on the project that will be valid for the life of the contract plus a period of five years after completion. Contractors also will be required to keep records of previously performed and future planned work that might pose a conflict-of-interest problem.[218] However, cost increases resulting from the added record keeping may be an allowable cost that can be charged to the government.

The provision that promises to affect EPA A/E contractors the most is the use of one of eight versions of a limitation-of-future-contracting clause. The basic limitation clause applies to all alternative remedial contracts strategy (ARCS) and remedial (REM) solicitations and consultants of the prime contractor. A key provision of this clause states:

> The contractor, during the life of the work assignment and for a period of five years after the completion of the work assignment, agrees not to enter into a contract with or to represent any party with respect to any work relating to CERCLA enforcement actions, pertaining to a site where contractor previously performed work for the EPA.[219]

An exemption to this limitation can be gained with the prior written approval of the cognizant EPA contracting officer. However, the government will not be liable for any expenses incurred in the creation of bids or proposals that require prior written approval when such approval was not obtained, regardless of whether or not approval is ever granted. Finally, the clause prohibits any proprietary or confidential method from being disclosed or used competitively.

There are seven alternatives to the limitation clause that apply to different types of EPA A/E contracting services. Alternatives I and II govern emergency response cleanup services (ERCS) and technical assistance team activities (TAT) contracts, respectively, and prohibit those working on one of these types of contracts from engaging in the other type of service within the contract-covered area. Alternative III applies to field investigative team (FIT) contracts and calls for only a three-year limitation period upon completion of the project. Alternatives IV, V, and VI apply to environmental services assistance team (ESAT) contracts with minor contextual changes of the base clause; technical enforcement support (TES) contracts contain a

[217] *Id.* § 1552.508(c)(2).

[218] *Id.* §§ 1552.210-78, .212-71.

[219] *Id.* § 1552.209-74(a)(2).

version of the clause with a seven-year limitation period; and Superfund headquarters support contracts have a clause prohibiting the contractor from engaging in any type of response action work. Finally, alternative VII restricts any contractor with a site-specific solicitation and/or contract from accepting a TAT contract until five years after the completion of the original project.[220]

The overall effect of the proposed certification, notification, and limitation regulations upon EPA A/E contractors is to compound the importance of properly evaluating a prospective contract, not only for its current economic feasibility, but also for its potential to block other EPA contractual work for up to seven years. Significantly, current EPA contractors are not exempt from these anti-conflict-of-interest regulations. The EPA has included an incorporation clause, covering all contracts in progress before the effective date of these regulations, which mandates that each contracting officer negotiate substantially similar clauses as those contained within these suggested regulations.

EPA's proposed regulations are some of the most extensive and burdensome of all the agencies and have prompted many different organizations to submit comments in response to them. One of the most frequent criticisms of the proposed regulations was that they would reduce competition because fewer contractors would be willing (or eligible) to risk their future contracting status for one contract. Additionally, in a study completed by the Hazardous Waste Action Coalition, it was determined that between 1986 and June of 1990 there were no cases of conflicts of interest pending at EPA.[221] Thus, the new regulations were as unnecessary as they were expensive—an estimated cost of almost $18 million that probably would be paid for by EPA.[222] Furthermore, the inclusion of the personal conflict-of-interest requirements might force contractors to develop and maintain recording systems on certain individuals. Industry representatives complained that these recording efforts, as promulgated by the Privacy Act of 1974, would be in place solely to perform an agency function and would result in added notification requirements and other expenses.[223]

The American Bar Association Section of Public Contract Law declared that the limitation-of-future-contracting clause is an automatic restriction that might be too arbitrary to solve conflict-of-interest problems that are best judged on a case-by-case basis.[224] However, in spite of these and other

---

[220] *Id.* § 1552.209-74.

[221] Gleason, Hazardous Waste Action Coalition's Comments on EPA's April 26, 1990 Proposed Rule Concerning Conflicts of Interest 2 (June 25, 1990) [hereinafter Gleason].

[222] EPA's Information Collection Request No. 1550 (filed with OMB) 8–9 (1990).

[223] Gleason at 6.

[224] Gavin, American Bar Association Section of Public Contract Law's Comments on EPA's April 26, 1990 Proposed Rule Concerning Conflicts of Interest 12 (June 28, 1990).

perceived problems of the proposed regulations, it appears that they will be fully implemented, in approximately the form that they are now in, sometime in 1991. Thus, in light of these proposals and the regulations and limitations of all the other agencies, careful record keeping and an effective analysis of future work plans will become crucial to the economic success of an A/E firm.

§ 11.27 Contract Disputes and Remedies

Any A/E firm that wishes to file a claim against the government must adhere to the rules and restrictions of both the disputes clause[225] contained in every government contract and the Contract Disputes Act of 1978.[226] The FAR defines what may constitute a claim and requires that a contractor must certify the accuracy and validity of its claim if it is seeking more than $50,000. Furthermore, a decision must be made by the contracting officer before any appeal outside of the agency. However, upon receiving an unfavorable decision, a contractor may file an appeal with the appropriate board of contract appeals (BCA) or with the United States Claims Court. Finally, a contractor may opt to use some form of alternative dispute resolution. Some types of alternative dispute resolution are provided for under the Contract Disputes Act.

§ 11.28 —Disputes Clause

The disputes clause is included in all A/E government contracts, and it specifically provides that all contractor "claims" must be submitted to the contracting officer for a final decision. The disputes clause defines a claim as: "A written demand or written assertion by one of the contracting parties seeking, as a matter of right, the payment of money in a sum certain, the adjustment or interpretation of contract terms, or other relief arising under or related to the contract."[227] The definition also distinguishes a routine invoice or voucher from a claim. If an invoice or other routine request for payment is not in dispute at the time of its submission, then it is not a claim. However, pursuant to the disputes clause definition, such a payment request can be converted into a claim if it has not been paid within a certain period of time and proper written notice is provided to the contracting officer.[228]

---

[225] 48 C.F.R § 52.233-1 (1990).

[226] 41 U.S.C. § 601 (1988).

[227] 48 C.F.R. § 52.233-1(c) (1990).

[228] *Id.*

Before initiating the first step of a claim—submission to the contracting officer—an A/E firm should weigh the size and importance of its dispute. Because the selection process under the Brooks Act is partially determined by a firm's professional demeanor, many A/E firms are reluctant to file claims against the government. If the claim is sufficiently large and valid, then there should be no hesitation in pursuing the matter. However, if the claim is a smaller one and/or on tenuous legal ground, an A/E firm should consider the potentially unfavorable impact that the claim might have on its future business opportunities.[229]

If an A/E contractor decides to pursue a claim, it must be filed in writing to the contracting officer. Similarly, a government claim against the contractor must be submitted in writing to the contractor.[230] The Contract Disputes Act requires that a contractor certify any claim seeking more than $50,000. The certification should be signed by a senior company official in charge of the contractor's facility/plant or one having overall responsibility for the contractor's affairs. This required submission must certify that: "(i) The claim is made in good faith; (ii) supporting data are accurate and complete to the best of the contractor's knowledge and belief; and (iii) the amount requested accurately reflects the contract adjustment for which the contractor believes the Government is liable."[231]

Although there is no required claim format (other than the written requirement), all pertinent factual and legal supporting arguments should be included as part of the claim submission. Gathering and organizing the necessary backup materials to support a claim may well make the difference in obtaining a favorable decision from the contracting officer. These backup materials may include (1) a daily project log; (2) memoranda of meetings with government representatives, inspectors, and subcontractors; (3) all written correspondence applicable to the disputed contract; (4) statements from key involved personnel; and (5) all cost accounting records.[232] A crucial element in the success of any claim is being able to describe the facts and the development of costs in enough detail to establish entitlement to additional funds based upon the costs incurred.

The boards of contract appeals (BCAs) have recognized many methods by which to prove additional costs. The most common methods are (1) the direct cost method; (2) the total cost method; (3) the modified total cost method; and (4) the jury verdict method. The *direct cost method* is most preferred by the BCAs and involves claiming additional costs based upon actual cost records. The *total cost method* is least preferred by the BCAs and involves a calculation of the additional costs based upon the difference

---

[229] P. Lubka, Architect-Engineer Government Contracting Course Manual H-8 (1989).

[230] 48 C.F.R. § 52.233-1(d)(1) (1990).

[231] *Id.* § 52.233-1(d)(2)i–iii.

[232] Charness & Dobbs at E-9 to E-11.

between the bid price and the costs incurred. This method assumes that the costs incurred should have been the contract price and that the government is responsible for all cost overruns. With the *modified total cost method,* the contractor modifies its bid price and total costs incurred to account for underestimating its bid in some respects and for contractor-caused cost increases during performance. The *jury verdict method* is a combination of the other three methods in which the court or BCA simply decides on its own the amount of recovery due the contractor based on all of the cost submissions provided by the two sides during litigation.[233]

If the claim is for $50,000 or less, the contracting officer must render a decision within 60 days of receipt of the claim if the contractor specifically notifies the contracting officer of this obligation. If the claim is for more than $50,000, the contracting officer must, within 60 days, either render a decision or notify the contractor of a date when the decision will be made.[234] If the contracting officer takes an unreasonable amount of time to issue a decision, a contractor may appeal to the appropriate BCA to obtain an order requiring a decision by a particular date. Failure to issue a decision will be interpreted as an automatic denial of a contractor's claim.[235]

The final decision must include a justification for the decision and notice to the contractor of its right to appeal an adverse finding under the Contract Disputes Act. However, the decision does not have to include specific findings of fact. If a contracting officer rules in favor of the contractor, the Contract Disputes Act provides that interest on the amount owed to the contractor shall be paid (based upon the fluctuating rate set by the secretary of the treasury) for the period between the receipt of the certified claim and the time of the decision. If the contractor pursues an appeal of an adverse final decision and is successful at the BCA or Claims Court, interest is paid from receipt of the certified claim until actual payment by the government.[236]

§ 11.29 —Appealing Contracting Officer's Decision

The Contract Disputes Act provides that an appeal of a contracting officer's decision may be taken either to the United States Claims Court or to the appropriate agency's board of contract appeals (BCA). Further appeals from either of these forums can be taken to the United States Court of Appeals for the Federal Circuit. If the contracting officer's decision is not

---

[233] *Id.* at E-14.

[234] 48 C.F.R. § 52.233-1(2)(e) (1990).

[235] P. Lubka, Architect-Engineer Government Contracting Course Manual H-10 (1989).

[236] 41 U.S.C. § 611 (1988).

appealed to either forum within the prescribed time limits, the decision will become final and thereafter unappealable.

Appealing to Board of Contract Appeals

There are 12 BCAs, each of which has jurisdiction over a particular agency or entity therein. For example, the EPA uses the Department of Interior BCA, the Corps of Engineers uses the Corps of Engineers BCA, and all other military contracts are handled by the Armed Services BCA. Although the boards were created to administer cases quickly and inexpensively, they still permit full procedural due process. A contractor has 90 days in which to appeal an unfavorable decision by the contracting officer to the appropriate BCA. If the ninetieth day falls upon a Saturday, Sunday, or holiday, the deadline will be extended to the next working day. The preliminary step is for the contractor to submit a notice of appeal to the BCA and the contracting officer that indicates the amount in controversy and the objections to the contracting officer's decision. After receiving a docketing notice of the case from the BCA, a contractor has 30 days in which to file a complaint. Upon receipt of the complaint, the government will have 30 days to submit an answer.[237]

The boards generally follow the Federal Rules of Civil Procedure in matters of discovery, interrogatories, requests for production of documents, and requests for admissions and depositions. Unless requested, no hearing will be conducted and the case will be considered on the record. There is no deadline for a decision unless the claim is for less than $50,000, in which case a contractor may request in writing within 10 days after receipt of the notice of appeal the use of the accelerated procedure. Under the accelerated procedure, if possible, the board must render a decision within 180 days. If the claim is for less than $10,000, procedures exist to encourage the board, again if possible, to render a decision within 120 days. However, before opting to use either procedure, a contractor should be aware that these processes give the contractor less time to obtain evidence to support its case.

Appealing to United States Claims Court

The Federal Courts Improvement Act of 1982 created the United States Claims Court and empowered 16 judges to make dispositive rulings on contractor claims.[238] The Claims Court replaced, and adopted the precedents of, the United States Court of Claims and is governed by the Federal Rules of Evidence. Although the Claims Court uses the Federal Rules of

---

[237] 41 U.S.C. § 606 (1988).

[238] Pub. L. No. 97-164, 96 Stat. 25 (1982).

Civil Procedure, it is not bound by them. A contractor has 12 months after the receipt of an adverse contracting officer's decision in which to file a complaint with the Claims Court. The Claims Court often uses pretrial procedures to narrow and focus the issues involved in a case and to attempt to reach an agreement between the parties. The basic procedures are essentially like those of any federal district court (without a jury), with the full complement of motions available. Parties file post-trial briefs and the court then will render a decision. There is no set time limit for the issuance of the court's decision. Appeals of Claims Court decisions may be brought to the Federal Circuit Court of Appeals within 60 days of an adverse decision.[239]

In choosing between bringing its claim in either the Claims Court or the BCA, a contractor should evaluate carefully the relevant differences between the two forums. Traditionally, the BCA judges rarely overrule precedent, so if a claim is contrary to existing law, it might be better received in the Claims Court where the authority is less uniform and overrulings are more common. Furthermore, the case law in both forums may not be exactly the same and an analysis might reveal that one is preferable for a particular set of facts over the other. Finally, a contractor may wish to use the more relaxed and simplified measures of the BCA over the more formal procedures of the Claims Court.

§ 11.30 —Alternative Dispute Resolution

In addition to the alternative dispute paths in the Contract Disputes Act that allow a contracting officer and a contractor to settle their differences outside the court, there are several other viable alternative dispute options. These methods can be used even after a contractor has filed an appeal of an adverse contracting officer's decision. Alternative dispute resolution (ADR) generally consists of binding or nonbinding arbitration, mediation, minitrials, settlement judgments, and fact finding. Almost any type of ADR can be binding and is designed both to bring the parties together and to foreshadow what final decisions are likely to be reached. Many agencies, especially the Navy, have been intent upon increasing the use of ADR.[240] Furthermore, in General Order No. 13 dated April 15, 1987, the United States Claims Court advocated the use, whenever appropriate, of both settlement judges and minitrials. Given the potential savings possible by a successful ADR, an A/E contractor should always keep these inexpensive, informative procedures in mind when deciding whether or not to appeal a claim.

---

[239] 28 U.S.C. § 1295(a)(3) (1988), (codified in scattered sections of various U.S.C. titles).

[240] P. Lubka, Architect-Engineer Government Contracting Course Manual H-16 (1989).

PART IV

CONTRACT DOCUMENTATION AND ADMINISTRATION

CHAPTER 12

PREPARING ARCHITECT/ENGINEER CONTRACTS WITH CLIENTS

Gerald Gamliel Weisbach

Gerald Gamliel Weisbach practiced and taught architecture in California for over 25 years and has practiced law since 1978 as a partner in the law firm of Natkin Weisbach Higginbotham, San Francisco and Santa Ana, California. He earned his degree in architecture from the University of California at Berkeley and his J.D. from Hastings College, University of California. He has taught on the faculties of the University of California at Berkeley and the London University and was associate dean for architecture at the University of Southern California. He is a nationally recognized expert on the legal aspects of architecture, engineering, and construction practice. Mr. Weisbach is a licensed architect and is a Fellow of the American Institute of Architects.

§ 12.1 Introduction

Preparing agreements for professional services is all too often, in the excitement of starting a new project, given little time or attention. The result is often a misunderstanding of the obligations and rights of the parties, leading to dissatisfaction with performance and subsequent disputes because of unfulfilled expectations.

The negotiation and formation of the contract provide an opportunity to arrive at a meeting of the minds, an understanding of who does what, and an agreement about when the project should be completed and how much and when compensation is payable.

§ 12.2 Professional Organization Forms

Professional organization forms are often "sold" on the basis of being consensus forms. They are also intended to provide a certain sense of security as to their meaning, the argument being that they have been construed by the courts and therefore one can count on the meaning of the language. What is often not stated is that certain industry bias has crept into the agreements and that because of their general nature, they rarely accommodate the specifics of a project without a good deal of tailoring.

One need only recognize that not all projects are of the same type, size, or complexity, nor do they all require the same level of services, nor do they all have the same expectation as to timely performance, nor are they all governed by the same codes or laws. If there is no such thing as a standard project, then it is difficult to conceive of a standard contract that will accommodate all projects.

All contracts require careful analysis, review, and tailoring to the specifics of the project, its size, its complexity, the nature of the services desired by the owner, and the abilities and willingness of the design team to provide such services.

It is also important to recognize that there will be more than one contract related to any specific project. In most instances, there will be subconsultant agreements as well as construction agreements. All agreements must be similarly constructed to avoid ambiguities and the arguments that arise from them.

Although a professional organization form may be an appropriate starting point for the development of a contract, rarely will the agreement, as it is printed, serve the interests of the design professional, the owner, and the contractor. It should be noted that in certain industry form contracts, provisions that may be important to the architect but contrary to the interests of contractors or owners have been omitted. This is all in the interest of "consensus." Although the standard forms of agreement published by the American Institute of Architects (AIA) are presented as agreements arrived at by consensus of the major participants in the construction industry, they are often regarded by attorneys and developers as having an architect bias. Architects similarly expect that the agreements published by "their" association will adequately protect them in all instances. Both views are less than correct, emphasizing the need for careful negotiation and formation of each agreement between architect/engineer and client.[1]

§ 12.3 Changes to Protect Architect

Many factors dictate what changes to standard forms are necessary to protect the architect. For example, are the parties using a standard form of agreement or one generated by the owner? Who is the client? Is the client a sophisticated developer or a builder of a single-family residence? What is the scope of services? What is the project type? What is the project schedule? Will the construction contract be competitively bid or negotiated? Is the project fast track? Will there be separate bid packages? Are there any hazardous materials at the project site? All these factors and many more may necessitate changes to the architect/client agreement.

For purposes of discussion, we will assume that the agreement is the 1987 AIA Document B141, Agreement Between Owner and Architect. Although generated by an association of architects, AIA Document B141 attempts to represent fairly the interests of the architect, owner, and contractor. The AIA's drafting process is intended to provide the construction industry with a family of consensus documents.

Because of its universality, however, B141 does not aggressively protect or insulate the architect from exposure to liability or losses, nor does it clearly define the parties' rights and obligations in nonstandard situations. As a result, the B141 form should be modified both to specifically protect the architect's interests and account for project idiosyncrasies. Architects also must be prepared to respond to typical owner-requested changes.

One benefit of using an AIA family of documents is that the documents are integrated and coordinated with one another. A problem can arise, however, when a change is made in one document but not integrated into the others. For example, if an architect and owner using the 1987 version of

---

[1] *See* J. Stephenson, Alternative Clauses to Standard Construction Contracts (John Wiley & Sons 1990) and J. Sweet, Sweet on Construction Industry Contracts (John Wiley & Sons 1987 & Supp. 1990).

B141 agree that the architect's drawings, specifications, and other documents become the client's property upon project completion and full payment, subparagraphs 6.1 and 6.2 in B141 would need to be modified, as well as subparagraphs 6.1 and 6.4 in Document C141. Because the architect's consultant's drawings would be required to complete portions of the project, the architect would be unable to provide the owner with a complete set of documents in accordance with the terms of the revised owner-architect agreement if the B141 and C141 agreements were not coordinated. Subparagraph 1.3.1 in Document A201 also would need modification if the architect gave up ownership of its documents.

The following review discusses selected provisions of the 1987 version of Document B141 in terms of issues that are typically significant to architects and their attorneys. This discussion follows the paragraph format of B141.

A. Title Page: Description of Project

The owner and architect should define the scope of the project (such as the description of the project's location, intended use, square footage) to the greatest extent possible because this description might later determine whether the architect is entitled to additional compensation for owner-requested changes to the project.

B. Article 2: Scope of Architect's Basic Services

Subparagraph 2.1.1. A comprehensive and well-articulated description of the scope of the architect's professional services is essential. It is extremely important to express the parties' understandings and expectations, particularly in the construction setting in which owners are often inexperienced and have unrealistic expectations of the architect. A well-defined scope of services provision also facilitates evaluation of the risks involved in a particular project by the parties, their counsel, and their insurers and may aid in avoiding disputes, particularly if the architect claims compensation for "additional services." It should be noted that B141, as a generic document, may not set forth the complete intent of the parties; therefore, architects should review B141 with an eye to conforming the document to the parties' actual understanding, expectations, and agreement.

Paragraph 2.6. Paragraph 2.6, which contains 19 subprovisions, sets forth the architect's basic services during the "construction phase" of the project. During this phase, the architect provides services necessary to administer the construction contract. Such services include visits to the site by the architect to become familiar with the progress and quality of the work and the review of specific contractor submittals such as shop drawings.

The architect's potential liability exposure is greatest during the construction phase of the project because most claims against architects result either from technical defects in the architect's plans and specifications that manifest themselves during construction or from misinterpretations of the architect's plans and specifications by others. Very few claims result from the visual or aesthetic aspects of the architect's design. If the architect provides the full scope of services set forth in paragraph 2.6, the architect partially mitigates exposure during construction of the project. When the architect does provide construction phase administration, the language of AIA Document B141, paragraph 2.6.6, should be used. This paragraph makes it clear that the architect does not have control over or charge of construction means, methods, techniques, sequences, procedures, safety precautions, or programs. Unfortunately, in attempting to reduce project costs, many owners do not retain the architect to provide complete construction phase services. If the architect is unavailable during this critical phase to clarify the work product and identify and/or correct errors, the likelihood of misinterpretation and miscommunication in implementing the architect's plans and specifications is increased. In fact, most professional liability insurance carriers discourage architects from entering into agreements in which the architect does not provide complete administration of the construction phase.

An architect's exposure can be reduced by negotiating indemnification from the owner when the architect does not provide complete construction phase services.

Although a carefully drafted indemnification provision can help shield the architect from liability exposure, it is not a panacea and is only as good as the owner's ability to back it up. It is wise to secure financial evidence supporting the owner's ability to stand behind an indemnification provision.

Subparagraph 2.6.5. Perhaps no other provision in B141 engenders more discussion and misinterpretation than subparagraph 2.6.5. Many owners assume that site visits will prevent all defects in the work, but such is not the case. The architect's role as a design professional during construction is to visit the site at periodic intervals to determine in general if the work is being performed in accordance with the construction documents. These visits are typically of a limited duration and are not intended to be a complete inspection of the work or the work in progress. By the nature of such visits, the architect is rarely in the position of uncovering anything other than gross visual errors in the work. Unfortunately, this reality often runs contradictory to the owner's expectations.

Subparagraph 2.6.5 states that the architect "shall endeavor to guard the Owner against defects and deficiencies in the Work." Unfortunately, such "endeavor to guard" language is rarely read in context with the architect's obligations during site visits and fosters unreal expectations on the part of the owner. Subparagraph 2.6.5 should therefore be modified as follows:

> On the basis of on-site observations as an architect, the Architect shall keep the Owner informed of the progress and quality of the Work. (More extensive site representation may be agreed to as an additional service, as described in paragraph 3.2.)

Similar "endeavor to guard" language also must be deleted from subparagraph 3.2.3.

Subparagraph 2.6.12. Shop drawings are drawings, diagrams, schedules, and other data specially prepared for the work by the contractor or any subcontractor, manufacturer, supplier, or distributor to illustrate some portion of the work. The architect's obligations as to shop drawings, as well as product data and samples, must be clearly stated, otherwise the architect could be responsible for services not originally contemplated. For example, the descriptions of "contractor submittals" and "information given" in subparagraph 2.6.12 are open-ended and could unnecessarily increase the architect's workload and liability exposure. "Contractor submittals" should be restricted to those required by the contract documents. "Information given" could be construed to obligate the architect to cross-reference and confirm the accuracy of the contractor submittals with the information given in the drawings and specifications—a gargantuan task and one fraught with potential liability.

Subparagraph 3.1.1. Language in subparagraph 3.1.1 may be construed to require the architect, when authorized by the owner, to provide any of the additional services described under paragraphs 3.2 and 3.4. An architect should reserve the right to refuse to perform certain additional services. For example, subparagraph 3.4.4, which states that special surveys, environmental studies, and submissions required for approvals of government authorities or others having jurisdiction over the project are additional services, could be construed to mean that an architect must prepare an environmental impact report when requested by the owner. An architect may not have the resources or qualifications to prepare such a study. Thus, the words "shall only" in the sixth line should be replaced by the word "may."

Subparagraph 3.4.16. This provision states that the architect may, as an "optional additional service," prepare "a set of reproducible record drawings showing significant changes in the Work made during construction based on marked-up prints, drawings and other data furnished by the Contractor to the Architect." Because record drawings are prepared on the basis of information furnished by others that is impossible or impractical for an architect to verify, they potentially expose an architect to serious professional liability. In the absence of contractual language recognizing the potential for inaccuracies, the architect could be held responsible for errors or omissions in the record drawings regardless of the source of the information relied upon by the architect. An architect can be protected by insuring that the owner thoroughly understands the limitations on an architect's ability to control the accuracy of the record drawings. It is, therefore, strongly recommended that the general contractor be made responsible for preparing these drawings and documents, as it is only the general contractor who has access to all of the day-to-day field changes and modifications to location of utilities and services.

C. Article 6: Use of Architect's Drawings, Specifications, and Other Documents

Paragraph 6.1. The "instruments of service" language in the third line is intended to clarify that the architect's plans and specifications are not products. Any attempt to remove this language should be vigorously resisted by the architect because the architect may be held to an inappropriate standard of care if the drawings contain errors or omissions (that is, strict products liability as opposed to a negligence standard).

Owners often insist upon ownership of the architect's plans and specifications. Corporations may do so for proprietary reasons, although public officials often do so in the belief that the public is entitled to the architect's work product because it has paid for the architect's services. Transferring ownership creates the possibility that plans and specifications may be revised or reused without the architect's knowledge, exposing the architect to claims of professional liability.

An architect can attempt to retain ownership and avoid that exposure by arguing that the client paid for unique professional services and that the plans and specifications are simply instruments of that service, not independent products subject to sale or transfer. If the owner insists upon ownership, an indemnity provision is appropriate to protect the architect from liability created by any reuse of the documents.

D. Article 7: Arbitration

Paragraph 7.1. Architects should carefully consider whether such a mandatory arbitration provision is advantageous. Although many participants in the construction industry support arbitration because arbitrators are generally knowledgeable about construction, others claim that not all types of construction disputes lend themselves to arbitration. Arguments against arbitration include the following: (1) the American Arbitration Association rules do not provide for discovery proceedings that may be necessary to adequately defend an architect; (2) improper decisions of law or erroneous determinations of fact are not appealable except in limited circumstances such as fraud, bias, or prejudice; (3) arbitration is not always speedier or less costly than litigation, especially when there are multiple issues or multiple parties. The architect's insurance carrier, if any, should be consulted to determine the carrier's dispute resolution preference.

One common solution to the arbitration question is for the parties to agree to discretionary rather than mandatory arbitration. The parties can thus evaluate whether a claim lends itself to arbitration based on the nature of the dispute. An agreement alternatively could provide for other dispute resolution mechanisms such as mediation. It should be noted, however, that any modification to paragraph 7.1 will have an impact upon subparagraph 2.6.19.

The preceding represents some of the issues an architect must consider when reviewing or negotiating the 1987 version of AIA Document B141. As is the case with most agreements, however, what is omitted from an agreement can be just as important as what is included. The following discusses "other conditions or services" that architects should consider adding to B141 by including them in Article 12, which is left blank in the B141 form for that purpose.

E. Article 12: Other Conditions or Services

1. Attorneys' fees. Because a lawsuit is often the only means for an architect to collect fees owed pursuant to an agreement, and because the cost of litigation may be prohibitive relative to the amount owed, an attorneys' fees provision may be desirable.

2. Limitation of liability. When an architect's exposure to risk could result in losses significantly greater than is justified by the architect's fees, a provision limiting the architect's liability for services performed should be considered. In the past there was some concern about the effectiveness of limitation-of-liability provisions. Recent case law, however, has upheld contract provisions that limit a design professional's liability to the value of services rendered.[2] The cases have not discussed a specific measure, but it is not unreasonable to assume that a limitation of liability in any amount agreed upon between the owner and architect would be upheld.

3. Indemnification. As discussed with respect to specific subparagraphs of B141, indemnification may be appropriate in many circumstances, such as when the architect's services are prematurely terminated, when the contract requires less than complete construction phase administration services, or when the owner is retaining ownership of the architect's drawings, specifications, or other documents.

---

[2] Markborough Cal., Inc. v. Superior Court, 91 C.D.O.S. 1165 (1991).

§ 12.4 Liability/Insurance

Most clients have become sophisticated enough to understand that professional liability insurance is an important aspect of the financial ability of an architect to meet any liability claims. As a consequence, clients have become more concerned with contractual provisions regarding insurance.

Because clients rarely understand what a professional liability policy covers, their demands are often excessive and, in many instances, undeliverable. It should be noted that a policy of professional liability insurance covers the negligent acts, errors, and omissions of the architect and is basically intended to protect the architect from financial exposure. Because all policies vary somewhat, it is important for the insured as well as the client who seeks protection under an insurance policy to understand what is covered and what is excluded.

In drafting a contract insurance provision, it should be recognized that at the present time all policies of professional liability insurance are written on a claims-made basis. This essentially means that in order for there to be insurance coverage, a claim for damages must be made within the policy period. This raises a question. If at the time the contract is entered into a policy is in effect, is the named insured protected? The answer requires another question and that is, was the policy in effect at the time the claim was made? It is not inconceivable that a claim will be made as much as 10 years after the contract is entered into or the initial policy is secured. At that time, coverage may not be available. It is important to understand this concept and to provide for continuity of insurance to the extent that such continuity is available. In the past the insurance market has, from time to time, "dried up" and professional liability insurance was not available, or only available at premiums so high that it was financially impossible for a design professional to continue a policy. Thus, it is not unreasonable for a client to require continuity of insurance. However, it is important to frame such a requirement in relation to the economic feasibility of maintaining such insurance.

Project policies that insure a project team and a specific project for the design period and a three- to five-year discovery period after completion of construction are available and assure that insurance will be available throughout the most critical time frame of a project.

In structuring the insurance requirements in a contract, it is appropriate to note the limits. In some instances, clients will ask that the deductible be stated to ascertain that the deductible is within reasonable limits. This is also a consideration to the insurance carrier, and in most instances insurance companies have performed their own financial investigations of their insureds to ascertain that the insured can indeed cover the deductible. As to the limits, they are stated in the aggregate and it is conceivable that the limits may not be available in any particular instance due to prior claims against the policy. This is often the reason for clients' requesting extremely high limits or limits dedicated to their particular project. When clients insist on dedication of limits to their project, it is appropriate to suggest a project policy.

§ 12.5 Scope of Work

One of the problems generated by professional organization standard form agreements is the misleading signal given to architects by the small amount of space provided in these contracts for describing the scope of the work. These contracts often assume a "standard" scope of work. That standard does not, in fact, exist.

Contrary to popular belief within the legal community, this author believes the scope of work should not only state what is included, but also what is not included. The reason for this is that clients are often unsophisticated in their understanding of the role of the architect or engineer and expect a level of performance that is not intended by the architect and often not even possible. Standard language that says the architect will include all services ordinarily provided assumes that there is a single standard in the industry. This is misleading and generates unreasonable expectations.

Without a clear definition of the scope of work, the resolution of misunderstandings as to what is in the contract and what is out and what constitutes extra services is difficult and often leads to litigation. An effective way to avoid such conflict is to append to the contract a scope-of-work statement that carefully and completely establishes the parameters of the project as well as the services that the architect is prepared to provide. It is important to review such document against what the standard form agreement calls for, if such an agreement is being used. Should there be a need to interpret or determine the actual "scope of work" in the face of an ambiguity, it should be understood that such interpretation will be guided by standards in the industry. Because the standards vary so greatly from office to office and from locality to locality, resolution of such ambiguities is difficult and generally costly.

§ 12.6 Owner's Responsibility

Because each new project may be considered a "prototype," there is a close relationship between the design professional's performance and the owner's participation in the process. Contracts must make the owner's responsibilities clear and must impress upon the owner the importance of participation. This participation includes not only meeting the owner's financial obligations to the design professional, but also providing an appropriate program definition complete with information on special needs and necessary supporting equipment. In order for the design professional to appropriately address the owner's program needs in the form of a completed project, a budget must be established by the owner in consultation with the architect. The architect or design professional must have access to all accurate site information and project constraints.

Because the design process generally involves alternative solutions to the owner's program needs, the owner must play an active role in making decisions as to these alternatives, and these decisions must be made in a timely manner to avoid undue delay or adverse effects on the efficient decision making of the design professional.

Because each project can be expected to be quite unique, special support is often necessary. Such support may consist of special consultants such as those for acoustics, food service, and security. Such consultants must be provided in a timely manner. Often accounting or financial questions will be raised and the owner must be prepared to provide expert counseling. In almost all projects, the owner will be asked to make decisions that are in essence legal decisions, and the owner should be prepared to engage legal counsel when necessary.

The owner's role in any construction project requires ongoing and active participation. Contracts should make this responsibility clear.

§ 12.7 Standard of Care

In providing design services, an architect is obligated to use the care ordinarily exercised by reputable members of the profession practicing in the same community. When entering into an owner/architect agreement, particular care should be taken that the provisions of the agreement do not alter the architect's standard of care. In the absence of any contractual language altering the architect's standard of care, negligence must be proven to impose liability for damages. A finding of negligence would result from a showing that the architect had failed to exercise ordinary and reasonable skill in providing professional services, in other words, that the architect had breached the standard of care.

Owners and their attorneys frequently draft agreements that, either knowingly or unknowingly, alter the architect's standard of care. Often this arises out of the owner's misunderstanding of the architect's role and responsibilities in the construction process. Owners are frequently willing to modify language that increases the architect's standard of care after the architect explains any concerns. If language increasing the standard of care cannot be negotiated out of an agreement, an architect should seriously consider walking away from the project. So long as architects agree to enter into contracts that impose greater liability than required by law, owners will continue to try to obtain this additional benefit.

Although the architect's standard of care is imposed by law, the architect can increase or lower that standard of care by contract. Increasing the standard of care can have serious consequences for the architect. It may impose upon the architect increased or even strict liability. Further, an architect's errors and omissions insurance covers only negligent acts. Agreeing to a higher standard of care can make the architect's insurance coverage questionable or inapplicable as to a resulting claim.

When entering into a contract, the architect should be particularly concerned with the inclusion of phrases such as "highest standards of professional practice." Such a standard can never be met, and this language may allow an owner to obtain a judgment against the architect even if the architect used due care in providing professional services.[3]

Ambiguous contract language that may impose a stricter standard of care upon the architect also should be avoided. Extreme words such as "guarantee," "warrantee," "insure," "achieve," "accomplish," and "comply with" may result in the architect's unintentionally assuming a higher standard of care.

To clarify that the architect is performing only to the standard of care imposed by law and to avoid any unintentional increase in that standard, an architect may insert a general contract provision that sets out the standard of care. Such language as "notwithstanding any provisions to the contrary in this agreement, the architect shall provide services using the skill and care ordinarily exercised by reputable members of the profession" can prevent subsequent claims that the architect agreed to a higher standard of care.

Sometimes it may be appropriate for the architect to request that the owner lower the architect's standard of care. This may be appropriate when an owner has requested the use of unproven technologies or materials. The architect also might request that the standard of care be lowered when the owner insists on a unique and innovative design that has no precedent. A general contract provision stating that the architect shall only be liable to the owner for "gross negligence" would lower the architect's standard of care. Of course, a contract provision that imposes liability for gross negligence applies only to the owner's claims and does not alter the architect's standard of care with regard to third-party claims, including contractors' claims.

---

[3] *See* J. Stephenson, Alternative Clauses to Standard Construction Contracts (John Wiley & Sons 1990) and J. Sweet, Sweet on Construction Industry Contracts (John Wiley & Sons 1987 & Supp. 1990). For a case holding the architect to a higher standard of care, *see* Tamarac Dev. Co. v. Delamater, Freund & Assocs., P.A., 234 Kan. 618, 675 P.2d 361 (1984) (work of an architect is an exact science).

§ 12.8 Implied Warranty and Adequacy of Design

A common question arises in a construction case as to whether or not the design professional has impliedly warranted the adequacy of the project plans or specifications. Currently, there is a split of authority throughout the United States on this issue. The courts have compared the services of an architect or engineer to those provided by various other professionals when determining whether design professionals are subject to liability under an implied warranty theory.

In California, builders and sellers of new construction (developers) impliedly warrant that the completed structure was designed and constructed in a reasonably workmanlike manner.[4] This implied warranty applies only to new residential construction, and the courts have refused to extend this rule to owner-builders who are not in the business of commercial development.[5]

The California courts have routinely held that when the primary objective of the transaction is to obtain services, the doctrines of implied warranty and strict liability do not apply.[6] Simply stated, the services of design professionals are sought because they have special skills.

Design professionals have a duty to exercise ordinary skill and competence of members of their profession, and a failure to discharge that duty will subject them to negligence. Those who hire design professionals cannot expect infallibility. Rather, they can expect the design professional to act with reasonable care and competence. They purchase services and not insurance. Thus, California follows the rule that a developer of new residential construction can be held liable for the breach of implied warranty whereas the design professional cannot.[7]

The South Carolina Supreme Court has held that when a person holds himself out as specially qualified to perform work of a particular character, there is an implied warranty that the work that he undertakes shall be of proper workmanship and reasonable fitness for its intended use.[8] If a party

---

[4] East Hilton Dr. v. Western Real Estate, 136 Cal. App. 3d 631, 632, 186 Cal. Rptr. 267, 268 (1982); Pollard v. Sacks & Yolles Dev. Co., 12 Cal. 3d 374, 380, 525 P.2d 88, 115 Cal. Rptr. 648, 651 (1974).

[5] Sefton v. Pasadena Waldorf School, 219 Cal. App. 3d 359, 268 Cal. Rptr. 335, 343 (1990); Siders v. Schloo, 188 Cal. App. 3d 1217, 1221, 233 Cal. Rptr. 906, 908 (1987).

[6] Pierce v. Pacific Gas & Elec. Co., 166 Cal. App. 3d 75, 79, 212 Cal. Rptr. 283, 288 (1985); Allied Properties v. John A. Blume & Assoc., Eng'rs, 25 Cal. App. 3d 848, 102 Cal. Rptr. 259 (1972).

[7] La Jolla Homeowners v. Superior Court, 212 Cal. App. 3d 1131, 261 Cal. Rptr. 146 (1989); Allied Properties v. John A. Blume & Assoc., Eng'rs, 25 Cal. App. 3d 848, 855, 102 Cal. Rptr. 259, 264 (1972); Gagne v. Bertran, 43 Cal. 2d 481, 489, 275 P.2d 15, 21 (1954).

[8] Kennedy v. Columbia Lumber & Mfg. Co., 299 S.C. 335, 384 S.E.2d 730 (1988); Hill v. Polar Pantries, 219 S.C. 263, 64 S.E.2d 885 (1951).

furnishes plans and specifications for a contractor to follow in a construction job, he thereby impliedly warrants their sufficiency for the intended purpose.[9] The rule followed by South Carolina courts appears to be the minority rule.[10]

Finally, the Kansas Supreme Court has recently held that certain professionals such as doctors and lawyers are not subject to an implied warranty. However, the work of architects and engineers is subject to an implied warranty.[11] The work performed by architects and engineers is an exact science, while that performed by doctors and lawyers is not. A person who contracts with an architect or engineer for a building of a certain size and elevation has a right to expect an exact result.

Because of the difference in attitudes of the courts in the various jurisdictions, it is important for the design professional to carefully consider contractual standard-of-care language.

§ 12.9 Termination

It is not unusual for the work of the design professional to be terminated before completion of a project. Such termination can occur at any stage of the design construction document or construction administration phase and may be the decision of either of the parties, depending on the contract termination provisions.

Contracts may be terminated for the client's convenience when the client changes plans, abandons the project, or suspends the project for a prolonged period of time. Such termination also may occur because of a client's dissatisfaction with the design professional's services. If such dissatisfaction occurs because of default by the design professional, it may be based on principles of breach of contract.

Architects may choose to include a termination-for-convenience provision including any concern regarding the ability of the architect or engineer to satisfactorily work with the client. Clearly, mutual respect between a client and design professional is essential if a project is to be completed successfully.

Termination provisions also should be considered for dealing with the default of one or more of the parties in meeting their contract obligations. This may occur through the design professional's not meeting

---

[9] Hill v. Polar Pantries, 219 S.C. 263 (1951).

[10] Allied Properties v. John A. Blume & Assoc., Eng'rs, 25 Cal. App. 3d 848, 855–56, 102 Cal. Rptr. 259, 264 (1972); J. Sweet, Legal Aspects of Architecture, Engineering and the Construction Process § 17.07 (4th ed. 1989).

[11] Tamarac Dev. Co. v. Delamater Freund & Assocs., P.A., 234 Kan. 618, 675 P.2d 361 (1984).

contract-established time limits or the owner's not meeting its contract payment obligations.

It is possible for projects to be reinstated after termination with subsequent work's being completed by someone other than the original design consultants. In such an instance, it is necessary to protect the original design professional from liability exposure as well as to protect the original design professional's economic value in the design. In such instance, it would be appropriate to include an indemnity provision wherein the client agrees to indemnify the design professional for any liability arising out of any subsequent use of the documents if either the documents have not been 100 percent completed or the services anticipated under contract (including construction administration phase services) have not been completed. Such a provision also may be triggered by any change in the extent of services required of the architect, that is, when the owner chooses to cut out any previously agreed-upon services. Clearly, such a cutback can increase the architect's liability exposure. Therefore, it is not inappropriate for the design professional to have further protection in the form of an indemnity provision.

§ 12.10 Shop Drawing Review

To fully appreciate the importance of contract language as it relates to shop drawing review, one should carefully evaluate the purpose of shop drawings.

The AIA defines shop drawings as drawings, diagrams, schedules, and other data specially prepared for the work by the contractor or any subcontractor, manufacturer, supplier, or distributor to illustrate some portion of the work.

Historically, shop drawings were required under the technical section of the specifications for particular trades. These were trades in which the coordination between two or more trades or the interface between two or more pieces of equipment or products was critical, and therefore the architect would require submission of the shop drawings to ascertain that the work, when installed, would comply with the *design intent.* Design intent was generally understood to be the visual aspect of design. Contractors at that time would invariably complain and state "the drawings are complete enough, we don't need any shop drawings." Over the years, however, architects have relied on shop drawings to cover areas that were incomplete in their own construction documents, and contractors realized the advantage of having the architect further check the contractor's or its subcontractor's work. The result has been an increase in the number and complexity of documents submitted to the design professional for review. These documents all are lumped into the category of "shop drawings."

Contractual language has attempted to reduce the exposure of the architect by either omitting the word "approval" or "approved" or by defining the review of the shop drawings for limited purposes. Short of language that limits the responsibility of the architect, it would not be unreasonable for the owner and contractors to expect that any error in the shop drawings would be caught by the architect, and that short of the architect's doing such a complete job, the architect may be held responsible for such errors if they are incorporated into the work.

This author believes it is unnecessary for most shop drawings to be reviewed by the design professional and that the contract documents should make clear what shop drawings, if any, are to be required and to what extent and for what purposes they will be reviewed.

§ 12.11 "Or Equal" Clause

The "or equal" clause, which is required in most public and used in many private construction contracts, is fraught with pitfalls for the design professional. Whenever it appears, the design professional must exercise caution throughout all phases of a project to protect both the owner and himself.

The "or equal" clause is designed primarily to prevent bid irregularities that can arise under "sole source" product specifications. Typically, specifications will call for two or more specific models or items, followed by the phrase "or equal." The clause is designed to permit sophisticated contractors to prepare and submit bids using nonspecified (and usually less costly) items. However, use of the "or equal" clause creates numerous problems for the design professional.

First, the design professional may be required to "approve" substitutions of nonspecified items that a bidder claims are equal to the specified items. When passing on a proposed substitution, the conscientious design professional must be prepared to defend his decision in the face of a protest (or worse yet, a lawsuit) from a disgruntled bidder. The additional time burden on the architect to adequately evaluate the acceptability of substitutions should be considered in the fee proposal.

When a contractor proposes a substitution, the design professional must be prepared to defend his own decision. The design professional must be prepared to satisfy the owner that a less costly item is not "equal," or to demonstrate that the substitution was "equal" when faced by a claim that the substitution was inappropriate or inadequate.

Despite attempts to disclaim responsibility for determining whether a nonspecified model or item is an equal (for example, by noting "no exception taken" or similar language to a proposed substitution), unless a proposed substitution is rejected as not equal, the design professional may have, in effect, "approved" the substitution.

To avoid being coerced into approving an inadequate substitution, the design professional should require a bidder or contractor to substantiate a claim that the proposed substitution is equal. Often, however, the design professional must assume the responsibility (and consequent expense) of determining the adequacy of the substitution. The design professional should anticipate such burden and require reimbursement from the owner for all such costs as part of the initial contract fee proposal.

In addition, the design professional should insist on a rational schedule for submittals of proposed substitutions. Such schedules reduce the cost to the owner for the design professional's time in reviewing proposals. They should be structured to allow the design professional to account for earlier substitutions in reviewing later proposals.

Finally, the design professional must remain cognizant that ever-increasing liability insurance premiums are directly related to soaring construction costs, which in turn tempt owners and contractors to use the "or equal" clause to approve or propose substitutions of less adequate materials or systems. By insisting on both a rational review process and compensation for participation in that process, the design professional can avoid many of the pitfalls that the "or equal" clause presents.

§ 12.12 Arbitration

Arbitration is generally regarded as a speedier, informal, and less costly form of dispute resolution than litigation. Consequently, trade organizations include an arbitration provision in their standard form agreements. By including an arbitration clause in a contract, the parties agree to voluntarily submit future disputes that may arise between them to a disinterested arbitrator for a binding determination.[12]

Typically, the arbitration process is administered by the American Arbitration Association (AAA), a nationwide not-for-profit organization that maintains panels from which arbitrators may be chosen. Alternatively, the parties may agree by contract to privately arbitrate future disputes pursuant to any provision upon which they can agree. An AAA-administered arbitration is governed in accordance with the parties' agreement and AAA's Construction Industry Arbitration Rules.

Either party to a contract containing an arbitration provision may initiate the arbitration process by filing notification of its intent to arbitrate with the other party and the AAA. This demand should contain a statement of the dispute, the damages or amount at issue, and the requested relief.

[12] For a sample binding arbitration provision, *see* AIA B141-19, Art. 7. *See also* M. Callahan, Arbitration of Construction Disputes (John Wiley & Sons 1990).

The party upon whom the demand is made may file a written answer or counterclaim.

The parties may mutually agree to the location of the arbitration. If one party selects a certain location and the other party fails to object, the location is set as requested. If a party files an objection, the AAA will make a binding decision on the location. If no preference is stated, the arbitrator will determine the time and location of the arbitration.

Administrative fees are advanced by the parties with the filing of the demand and answer. The fee schedule is based upon the amount of the claim and is subject to apportionment by the arbitrator in the award. The parties must bear the expenses associated with their own witnesses. All other expenses, including the arbitrator's fee are borne equally by the parties unless agreed otherwise or assessed differently in the award.

If the parties have not otherwise selected or agreed upon a method for selecting an arbitrator, the AAA submits to the parties a list of persons chosen from its panel of qualified individuals. Each party may strike any name from the list. If the parties cannot agree on an arbitrator, one will be appointed from the panel without the parties' consent. If the parties' agreement does not specify the number of arbitrators, only one will be appointed unless the AAA determines a greater number is appropriate.

Some agreements permit each party to select an arbitrator who in turn jointly appoint a third neutral arbitrator. Difficulties can arise with this type of arrangement when the two party-appointed arbitrators cannot agree on the third. It is also difficult at the contract stage, when problems have not yet arisen, to determine whether the particular dispute would best be resolved by a single or multiple arbitrators. The size of the contract and the complexity and inherent risks associated with the particular project should be considered in drafting any arbitration clause. Consequently, the architect or engineer may wish to consider language that permits the parties to decide on the number of arbitrators after the dispute arises. If one party wishes the services of multiple arbitrators and the other does not, the party seeking multiple arbitrators can assume the expense of the additional panel members.

What many view as the primary advantage of arbitration over litigation is the cost and time savings associated with the discovery process. Discovery is a time consuming and expensive fact-finding investigation during the litigation process. Arbitration rules preclude the various methods of formal discovery absent an agreement to the contrary. This limitation, however, may result in a "trial by ambush" because parties are unaware what evidence the other side may produce at the arbitration. The rules of discovery in litigation are designed to avoid such surprise. To prevent this possibility, parties often agree to an informal exchange of documents limited in scope.

Although arbitrator(s) are authorized to subpoena witnesses or documents upon a party's request or on their own initiative, they are not bound by the rules of evidence in conducting the arbitration. Under the AAA rules, the arbitrator is the sole judge of the relevance and materiality of the evidence offered. Although this may result in a more informal and perhaps speedier proceeding, it can also work a severe disadvantage. Evidence that would be excluded under the rules of evidence in a court or other legal proceeding may well be permitted by an arbitrator who is empowered to render an equitable result. One method of addressing this concern is to provide in the arbitration clause that the jurisdiction's evidentiary rules must be followed.

The arbitrator is directed to "promptly" make an award, no later than 30 days after the closure of the hearings unless otherwise agreed by the parties. The award must be in writing signed by the sole arbitrator or a majority of a multiarbitrator panel. Under AAA's Construction Industry Arbitration Rules, the arbitrator may grant any "relief that is just, equitable, and within the terms of the agreement of the parties."[13] The arbitrator is also directed to allocate the arbitration fees and expenses among the parties.[14]

When drafting a professional services agreement, the architect or engineer should seriously weigh the advantages and disadvantages of the arbitration process. If the parties' agreement contained an arbitration clause, it is unlikely that the parties can agree to mutually waive the provision. Although it is possible to draft an arbitration clause that reserves the option to arbitrate or to arbitrate specific types of disputes under a certain dollar limit, these provisions give rise to a host of additional questions and uncertainty.

Perhaps the single most problematic aspect of arbitration is also one of the factors that contributes to its desirability—the fact that the arbitrator is not "constrained" by the law in reaching an equitable result. Moreover, except for limited grounds involving the procurement of the award by fraud or corruption, or misconduct by the arbitrator including an abuse of the arbitrator's powers, an arbitrator's decision is final, despite an error of law or fact.

Another potential disadvantage is that with litigation, a party suing an architect or engineer has the burden of establishing that the design professional's work fell below the applicable standard of care before liability for professional negligence may be imposed. In a multiparty dispute, arbitrators are often tempted to simply apportion damages among the various parties in an effort to reach an "equitable" result, and the issue of whether a design professional's conduct fell below the applicable standard is overlooked.

---

[13] American Arbitration Association Construction Industry Arbitration Rules, Rule 43 (amended Jan. 1, 1991).

[14] *Id.*

§ 12.13 Inspection Services

Many owners mistakenly assume that the purpose of a design professional's site visits is to make inspections of the work. Owners often expect that such inspections will uncover building and other code violations and errors in the work and prevent all defects. Such assumptions and expectations can expose the design professional to liability unless the scope of the design professional's duties is clarified at the outset of the project when the agreement is negotiated with the owner.

In reality, the design professional's site visits are typically of a limited duration and are not intended to be a complete inspection of the work or the work in progress. The design professional's role during construction is to visit the site at periodic intervals to determine in general if the work is being performed in accordance with the construction documents. By the nature of such visits, the design professional is rarely in the position of uncovering anything other than gross visual errors in the work. Faulty workmanship, procedures, or methods used by the contractor cannot be avoided by the design professional's simply making site visits.

This view of the design professional's role during construction is generally consistent with the AIA documents. Although the word "inspect" does appear in parts of the AIA documents and should be changed, the overall language attempts to make it clear that the purpose of the site visits is only to make the architect generally familiar with the progress and quality of the work.

If an owner requires thorough inspection services, the owner should hire a qualified inspector to perform continuous on-site inspections. A design professional should avoid contracting directly with such an inspector so that no responsibility for the actions or inactions of the inspector will be assumed.

If the owner insists that the design professional retain an inspector, the design professional should consider increasing his fee, requesting that the owner procure and pay for insurance covering such activities and requiring indemnification from the owner, contractor, and inspector. These costs should be borne by the contractor.

A design professional who agrees to make site visits cannot close his eyes on the construction site and refrain from making any observations whatsoever. The duty to make visits to the site does not, however, include the duty to make exhaustive, continuous on-site inspections.

It is important that the design professional make clear to the client at the contract formation stage that the design professional's site visits will not guarantee error-free work of the contractor. To the extent it is possible to define the precise intent of such site visits as to any specific project, it is wise to do so.

§ 12.14 Liquidated Damages Provision

The purpose of a liquidated damages provision in a construction contract ordinarily is to establish, in advance of contract performance, an amount of damages to be assessed by the owner against a party if the completion of the project is delayed beyond the promised completion date. The amount of liquidated damages is an estimate of the cost of delay to the owner based upon factors known at the time of contract formation.

Liquidated damages provisions are most often found in owner/contractor agreements. On occasion, however, a design professional who is dealing with an unsophisticated client or attorney may be asked to agree to a liquidated damages provision.

It is not appropriate to include a liquidated damages provision in the design professional's agreement and it is unreasonable for an owner to ask a design professional to agree to such a provision.

In an owner/contractor agreement, a liquidated damages provision may be an appropriate means for the owner to induce timely performance by the contractor. By imposing liquidated damages for each day's delay, the owner is assured that the contractor will coordinate and manage its work forces and do everything within its powers to complete the project by the date originally promised and agreed upon.

The design professional usually has no control over the contractor's work forces, nor does the design professional normally control the actions of the owner or public building officials who must approve portions or phases of the project at intervals. Under such circumstances, a design professional could not completely control the progress of the construction or of the completion of the construction document phase through issuance of permits. It is, therefore, unreasonable for the design professional to assume such liability for delay in completion of its work.

CHAPTER 13

PREPARATION OF CONSTRUCTION CONTRACT BY DESIGN PROFESSIONAL

William Shields

William Shields is a trial partner in Day, Berry & Howard's Boston office and leads the firm's construction practice group. He specializes in representing design professionals, devoting a significant portion of his practice to construction litigation and municipal law. He holds a B.A. from Yale College and an LL.B. from Harvard Law School. Mr. Shields was a United States Navy JAG and has been town counsel for Hamilton, Massachusetts for 15 years. He is admitted to practice law in Massachusetts, New York, and the District of Columbia and is a member of the Massachusetts, Boston, and American Bar Associations. He is also vice-chairman of the Boston Bar Association Committee on Construction Litigation.

§ 13.1 Introduction

The construction contract is the central document in establishing the legal relationships among owner, contractor, and designer that govern the construction process. It is consulted with regularity by parties, subcontractors, subconsultants, developers, lenders, sureties, program managers, insurers, lawyers, and judges. Thus, whether the construction contract is in simple form or highly detailed and technical, it is the starting point for any problem solving during a construction project.

This chapter is a nontechnical survey of issues contained in the construction contract and its surrounding legal landscape, presented to familiarize the design professional (also referred to interchangeably as architect, engineer, or A/E) with the whole contracting process. It assumes a traditional construction setting (owner-designer-contractor) but references some of the newer forms of contractual arrangements for the building project. It identifies the parties and their concerns and examines the key elements defining their relationship. It considers the use of forms and their relative merits. It focuses on the pivotal provisions for protection of the owner and the design consultant. And, finally, it examines the process of contract interpretation.

§ 13.2 Contract Functions

The construction contract performs a multitude of functions. It identifies the parties, what is to be done, where it is to be done, and what the contract documents are; divides responsibility; states when the work is scheduled for completion, how long the parties are to be bound in contract, and under what circumstances those relationships can be terminated; outlines whether the term of the agreement can be extended; states the price to be paid, in what increments, and with what modifications; names who has intracontractual authority to make decisions and settle disputes and what extracontractual mechanism will be consulted for ultimate resolution; represents the premises of the contract award and what warranties are to be given; allocates risk, stipulating what happens to time and price in the event of contingencies and who is to purchase insurance, provide indemnity, and defend.

Although the successful project involves a joint effort by the participants, the tension in negotiating the construction contract comes from the parties' divergent objectives.

Through the contract the owner, and by extension the owner's representative, the designer, wants to say to the construction contractor:

> I want this job built the way it was designed. I've had the plans and specifications prepared and here they are. I want quality workmanship. I want it built on time, and I want it to cost what I have budgeted.
>
> I want you to build it, or if not you, I want to approve your replacement.
>
> I don't want to argue with you about extras or delays; I don't want any liens on my property; I don't want to hear about claims of subcontractors, third

> parties, or passersby. I certainly don't want to have any lawsuits on my hands.
>
> You have control over the premises. During construction you're responsible for protection of life, limb, and the work itself. I want you to insure against virtually all risks and hold me harmless against loss.
>
> I want you to warrant the work. If you foul up, I want someone else to step in, and I don't expect to pay more or to delay progress. To that end, I want bonds, the right to take over the work myself, and the right to suspend and terminate.

On the other hand, the contractor wants to say to the owner:

> I want to build this job the way I bid it (see my detailed estimate or statement of contract sum). I want to make a reasonable profit. I don't want any surprises (novel interpretations) along the way. I don't want to be told later that I should have "reasonably inferred" something from the drawings or the specs.
>
> I'm not responsible for the design's compliance with applicable laws—that's the owner's job—and I'm not doing any "secondary design reviews" here. That's what the architect gets paid for.
>
> I don't want anyone telling me how to schedule this job or how to divide the work among my subs. I'll draft the scopes and get the work done.
>
> I don't want a lot of retainage. I want an indemnification against problems created by the owner, the owner's representative, or other contractors for whom I am not responsible.
>
> The owner should deal with hazardous waste and other hidden conditions.
>
> I want to know who I'm taking orders from. If I'm held up, delayed, or disrupted I want to get paid. I've done a reasonable investigation of the site and I've used my expertise. If there's something that gets in my way or hinders my progress, then I don't want to suffer while someone figures out what to do.
>
> When I buy material, I want to get paid for it; when I do work, I want to get paid for it. I want to be sure that the owner has the wherewithal to pay me, and that means I want to know about the owner's bank account and lender.
>
> And I don't want anyone looking over my shoulder.

§ 13.3 Who Prepares the Contract

Who prepares the construction contract largely depends on the sophistication of the owner. A first-time, one-project owner with little experience in construction is likely to rely on the design professional from inception to completion. The designer will assume responsibility for a study or report, an estimate, preliminary design, perhaps financing advice, governmental permitting, final design, preparing a bid package, assisting in the bid or award process, recommending the contractor, and construction services including arbitration of disputes.

Not only does the architect/engineer (A/E) have the expertise on which the owner will rely, but the A/E is the first on the scene. Due to the sequential nature of traditional construction, it is the designer who will be the first party to establish contractual ties with the owner. Only after the planning effort is complete does the construction contractor step in.

Historically, the designer has assumed a special, complex, and quasi-fiduciary role in relation to the client, the owner. The design professional owes the client a clear duty to exercise professional judgment in a manner that produces the best project for the most reasonable price. Because the design professional is uniquely situated to coordinate design intent with owner objectives and constraints, the A/E often has a major role in preparing the construction contract.

That is not to say that the designer *should* control the contracting process. In fact, the designer would be well advised to step away from the process to let other fiduciaries, such as the lawyer and the accountant, take on nondesigner duties. Both the American Institute of Architects (AIA) and Engineers Joint Contract Documents Committee (EJCDC) standard forms of construction agreement warn that the contract "has important legal consequences" and that an attorney should be consulted. Nevertheless, even the standard forms contemplate the designer's involvement in preparing contract documents.

The AIA Standard Form of Agreement between Owner and Architect, Document B141, says that the architect will prepare drawings and specifications,[1] as well as "the necessary bidding information, bidding forms, the Conditions of the Contract, and the form of Agreement between the Owner and Contractor."[2] The architect then assists in obtaining bids, negotiating proposals and award, and preparing contracts for construction.[3]

Standard engineering practice, in EJCDC Document 1910-1, is for the engineer to:

> Prepare for review and approval by Owner, its legal counsel and other advisors contract agreement forms, general conditions, and supplementary conditions, and (where appropriate) bid forms, invitations to bidders (all of which shall be consistent with the forms and pertinent guide sheets prepared by the Engineers Joint Contract Documents Committee) and assist in the preparation of other related documents.[4]

---

[1] AIA B141-1987, subpara. 2.4.1.

[2] *Id.* subpara. 2.4.2.

[3] *Id.* subpara. 2.5.1.

[4] EJCDC 1910-1 (1983), subpara. 1.4.4.

The more standardized the form, and the less inclined the owner is to spend money for legal help, the more central is the role of the design professional in preparing the construction contract.

By way of contrast, the developer or sophisticated owner stands on different footing. A public owner or an owner with its own A/E department may seek the assistance of an outside design consultant only as an independent contractor, rather than as a fiduciary or agent. Because of in-house familiarity with codes, choices, building practices, and specialty construction, there will be little reliance on the designer to prepare the construction contract.

§ 13.4 Using Standard Forms

The fundamental choice in preparing construction contracts is the degree of commitment to forms. An off-the-shelf set of documents, bearing the familiar logo of the AIA, EJCDC, Associated General Contractors (AGC), or Construction Management Association of America (CMAA), like an off-the-rack suit of clothes by a famous maker, may give the comfort of the familiar and even the assurance of durability, but all too often at the expense of a good fit. The forms also may come from the owner's "shelf" or the design professional's formbook. Because every building project is not a replica of another, however, tailoring forms to the specific project and the specific needs of the parties becomes the principal challenge of a construction contract negotiation.

As a starting point, professionals typically turn to their own industry forms—the architect to the AIA, the engineer to the EJCDC, the contractor to the AGC, and the construction manager to the CMAA. Most consultants have worked those industry forms into their own mold and can produce them on their word processors in seconds. Standard industry forms come with handbooks, guides, explanations, and even legal citations, providing a body of ready and written advice.

Other sources of forms are public and corporate forms; numerous standard texts and services; materials developed and published for seminars; regional versions of standard forms; and the files of professionals.

Factors favoring the use of standard forms include:

Complexity. Developing a viable set of construction contract documents is not simple.

Completeness. In all likelihood, the forms will address the issues needed for a complete project. There is little chance that subjects will be left out.

Consistency. The package put forward has been worked and reworked (in the case of the AIA, for more than a century). There is little chance of inconsistency.

Cash. Money need not be spent to "reinvent the wheel" while drafts are traded back and forth.

Choices. For those who hate to make hard decisions, the standard forms present a body of choices and trade-offs already made.

Courts. The standard forms are familiar and accepted by the courts.

Factors weighing against the use of standard forms include:

Project size. The parties may consider the job too big or too small for a set of packaged, standardized material.

Project complexity. Although the drafting committees would argue to the contrary, parties might well avoid standard forms in contracting for a project that presses into areas of new or innovative technology, establishes complex performance criteria, or involves parties beyond the traditional triangular model.

Power. The powerful owner may not favor industry documents that are drafted with a sense of equilibrium or that give the designer or contractor an advantage.

Precedent. It may not be standard in a particular industry, region, or sector to use the forms.

Perceptions. The owner may feel that the forms are not well suited to its particular concerns.

Whether a standard form is selected or not, there is danger in mixing different types. A well-intentioned but unskilled assemblage of clauses from a variety of forms will certainly lead to inconsistency and perhaps chaos.

The primary goal of the designer who drafts the construction contract is the protection of the client. Protection of the owner will protect the designer as well. The drafter should strive for fairness. One often encounters the punitive contract of adhesion, but if the real goal is trust and confidence in a mutual undertaking, then the "stacked deck" may be counterproductive. An adverse tone will permeate the job, and the contractor will work to the rule instead of showing flexibility. In short, the contract should be responsive to all the parties' needs. Clarity of definition, crisp delineation of responsibility, and spelled-out consequences will go far to avoid problems. Accuracy also is essential in the contract documents. The drafter should use design and contract review procedures to insure "buildability" (the documents must lead to a complete project) and "biddability" (the documents should not lead to wildly divergent bids).

Accountability is based upon a clear delineation of responsibility and consequence.

§ 13.5 Elements of Contract

The construction contract documents are a composite of materials, written and graphic, that owner, designer, and contractor intend as a code of governance for completion of the construction project. The contract between the design professional and the owner is a separate agreement and is not considered a part of the construction contract documents.

The owner/contractor agreement is the centerpiece of the contract documents. Typically, it is the only document signed by both owner and contractor and, through incorporation, it ties the other documents together. If typical standard forms are used, in all likelihood the contract documents will include an owner/contractor agreement, conditions of contract (general, special, or supplementary, and other), drawings, specifications, and various amendments or addenda. To this list also may be included the bid documents. The AIA takes the position that bidding procedures are pre-agreement; the bid documentation may conflict with the integrated agreement. The EJCDC incorporates the contractor's bid and any post-bid documentation submitted before the notice of award. It also includes bonds.

The owner/contractor agreement and the general conditions are bound to each other by "incorporation" and address many of the same subjects. They are generally separated into two documents, but only the owner/contractor agreement is executed.

There is no magic to this "two-document" model of the EJCDC and the AIA, but it does have historical acceptance. The owner/contractor agreement and the general conditions have long served as a formula for organization, but there is no compelling reason that the two agreements cannot be merged into one.

The reasons behind the practice of using two documents are essentially those of sequence and confidentiality. First, due to the sequential nature of the design and construction process, the bid package is prepared before the contractor is on the scene. When ready for distribution, the package will include a set of proposed general conditions formulated by the owner and designer. The contractor's bid or proposal then keys on the general conditions, just as it does on the design. Only after award or negotiation are the blanks in the agreement filled and the document signed. Thus, the agreement contains "the business terms": price; form of contract, (fixed price or cost plus a fee or other); and retainage. The general conditions are "the construction terms" providing a detailed exposition of the standard conditions, undertakings, and responsibilities of the parties. Second, the agreement need not be shown to subcontractors or others in the contractor's line of authority, and that confidentiality may be important to the parties.

Over time, those in the construction field have developed familiarity with the two-document model. Users know where to look in the documentation for specific provisions and answers to questions. The phrase "general conditions" has even achieved a price connotation, as in a contractor's claim for "extra work plus general conditions." It may be troublesome to work through a new form or a single document that merges the familiar structure.

In the two-document model, the typical owner/contractor agreement, such as AIA Document A101, contains:

Date, identity of project, and parties, including architect
Article 1: The Contract Documents
Article 2: The Work of This Contract
Article 3: Date of Commencement and Substantial Completion
Article 4: Contract Sum
Article 5: Progress Payments
Article 6: Final Payment
Article 7: Miscellaneous Provisions
Article 8: Termination of Suspension
Article 9: Enumeration of Contract Documents

The captions highlight the three principal elements of the construction contract: work, time, and money.

The premises and promises of the owner/contractor agreement are that the owner pays money; the contractor builds the work to plan and specifications; and the project is complete within a given time. These elements are woven into the construction contract. Even a rudimentary construction contract covers the following:

1. **Parties.** Identification of the key players of owner, contractor, and A/E is accomplished as the first order of business in the Standard Forms of Agreement Between Owner and Contractor (AIA Documents A101 and A111 and EJCDC 1910-8-A-1 and 1910-8-A-2) and in virtually every other form of construction contract. The contract then details the rights and responsibilities of each.
2. **Work.** The contractor is engaged to complete the work, which may be a part or the whole of the project.[5] In standard forms, the work is to be specified in the contract documents.[6]

The identification of the work can be a source of tension. The owner wants an expansive interpretation to avoid paying extras for work "outside

[5] EJCDC 8-A-1 (1983), Art. 1; AIA A101-1987, Art. 2.

[6] There is a difference between the AIA's and the EJCDC's formulation. Without further definition or elucidation, the EJCDC's definition is broader by virtue of the word "indicated." That word connotes judgment on the part of the reader of the contract documents and is preferable when dealing with a contractor seeking to claim countless extras.

the scope." The owner will press for an addition to the description of the work to include work "reasonably inferable by the Contractor as necessary to produce the results intended by the Contract Documents." The contractor, on the other hand, wants protection against incomplete or unfinished drawings. The contractor does not want to be told after the fact that it should have carried something in its bid because the work was readily inferable.

3. **Time.** The number of days within which or the date by which the work is to be substantially completed, the date when the contract is deemed to begin, the measure of substantial completion, together with concepts of suspension, delay, acceleration, and even termination are the very core of the construction contract. These definitions are critical to determining compliance by the contractor and the triggering of remedies such as liquidated damages.
4. **Price.** The contract sum or contract price provisions set the monetary basis of the agreement. Whether stipulated sum,[7] stipulated price,[8] cost-of-the-work-plus a fee,[9] cost-plus with or without a guaranteed maximum price,[10] or one of a myriad other forms of compensation, the construction contract addresses dollars and cents and then determines when there will be entitlement to payments. The contract typically addresses such issues as unit pricing, progress payments, final payment, change of contract price, materials escalation, retainage, and release of retainage.

   In a cost-plus format, definitions must be scrutinized to determine reimbursables, approved accounting procedures, and values scheduled.
5. **Changes.** Changes to the work, whether expected or intended, whether additive or deductive, must be addressed in the construction contract. Changes seem to come at the project from all directions. The owner may have a change of heart (or funding). The contractor may encounter bedrock where only "cobbles" were foreseen. The architect, or more likely the contractor, may uncover a design omission. A desirable process or product also may become available during the term of the contract.

   Changes may lead to extra work or to a credit due the owner. If the changes are material and outside the scope of the contract, the more unsettling question may arise as to whether the contractor is even bound to perform. There is also the "constructive change" in which

---

[7] AIA A101-1987.

[8] EJCDC 1910-8-A-1 (1983).

[9] AIA A111-1987.

[10] EJCDC 1910-8-A-2 (1983).

the parties have divergent views as to whether the work has been changed.

6. **Suspension or termination.** The ultimate change to the work is the owner's right to suspend the work or to terminate the work altogether for cause or convenience. Rights and remedies are typically spelled out in the general conditions.[11]
7. **Other.** Other provisions may be required in a given jurisdiction or type of contract. Public bidding requirements generate documentation and contract requirements. Compliance may entail inclusion of specific clauses.

§ 13.6 Key Provisions for Protecting Owner and Designer

There are certain provisions that the designer must raise with the owner/client for its, and perhaps their mutual, protection. The clauses fall into logical categories: assurance that the work will be completed and the contractor will perform; flexibility of contract for the owner; protection of the owner and designer from third-party claims and actions; limitation of liability; designation of remedies; and establishment of lines of authority.

Nonassignment of Work or Monies

The owner contracts with a contractor, an entity in which the owner places trust and confidence. The contractor runs a service business that depends upon workmanship and reputation. As with any personal services contract, the purchaser of services wants assurances that the entity she hires is the entity to perform.

On the other side of the ledger, the owner will likely want the right to assign its interest or ownership in the project free from any complaints of the contractor. To restrict assignability and to further its stated goals, the owner will want a clause declaring that the contractor will not:

Assign the contract
Subcontract the contract
Assign monies due or to be due the contractor without prior written approval of the owner.

A simple way of accomplishing this is to state that "Contractor shall not assign, subcontract or encumber this Contract, in whole or in part, without

[11] *See* AIA A201-1987, Art. 14, and EJCDC 1910-8 (1983), Art. 15.

prior written consent of the owner." A more neutral clause would state that the agreement is binding upon successors and assigns and that neither party may assign, subcontract, or transfer an interest in the agreement without written consent of the other.

Assignment by Owner

While holding a strict rein on the contractor, the owner wants to reserve the right to assign or sell the project and to be relieved of responsibility thereafter. The owner will want language stating:

Owner reserves the right to assign the contract to an entity of its choosing

Owner reserves the right to sell the project

In the event of sale or assignment, owner will be relieved of, or cease to have, obligations under the contract.

Often the owner will insist on the right to assign the contract to a limited universe, such as a parent, subsidiary, or affiliate, to a purchaser of the project, to its lender, or to the purchaser of the owner's business. Finally, the owner should clarify by express language that an entity succeeding the owner is positioned and authorized to enforce the owner's rights in the construction contract.

Indemnity

This is the battleground. The owner and A/E want full protection. The contractor wants to limit liability to that which the law would require anyway. With the caveat that state law, statutory and decisional, must be examined to determine what effect will be given to these clauses, the contract preparer must provide a tight, enforceable indemnification clause. For the most impact, it should provide for defense and indemnification, and by separate covenant the contractor should be obligated to buy contractual liability insurance covering the specific undertaking. Certificates of insurance should be obtained and policies should be monitored for lapse.

The elements of an indemnity clause favoring the owner are:

The contractor's agreement to indemnify, hold harmless, and defend the owner and the architect/engineer, their parents, subsidiaries, and affiliates, and their agents, employees, consultants, and independent contractors

That obligation to extend to the widest range of "imaginables," that is, liability for any damage or cost arising out of, resulting from, or relating to the work

The contractor's obligation to provide contractual liability insurance covering the liability assumed under the indemnification clause. Such a clause is usually found under the insurance provision and requires the contractor to buy and keep in force "contractual liability insurance covering the liability assumed by the contractor under section ______ of this agreement."

The objective of the owner and the design professional is to be in the strongest position to hand off or "tender" the defense of any claim to the contractor, and to make sure that the contractor's obligation is backed by insurance.

The designer may be considered a third-party beneficiary of this clause, and that is certainly the designer's intent. In jurisdictions that curtail the right of a third-party beneficiary to enforce contractual provisions, there is often an exception relating to insurance provisions, hence the desirability of the clause requiring contractual liability insurance.

The contractor will resist the breadth of this arrangement, seeking to limit its exposure to indemnification (without defense), to its own negligent acts (as opposed to any cause arising out of the work), and to personal injury or property damage (as opposed to economic loss).

A standard concession to the contractor is that it will not be required to indemnify against damages and costs occasioned *solely* by acts or omissions of the owner or the owner's representative.

Insurance and Bonds

As part of the program of protecting the owner and the project, the designer should consider bond alternatives and insurance coverages. A discussion of bonding is beyond the scope of this chapter. The more common types of insurance to be considered for inclusion[12] in the contract documents are:

Workers' compensation
Employer's liability
Automobile
Comprehensive general liability
Bodily injury protection
Property damage protection
Completed operations and products liability
Contractual liability
Builder's risk
Umbrella: all operations

---

[12] *See generally* AIA A201-1987, Art. 11.

Operations and premises liability (including elevator liability)
Independent contractor's protective liability
Explosion, collapse, and underground damage liability
Pollution liability

Policy periods, limits, and deductibles also should be considered and waivers of liability reviewed. The relative merits of waivers of subrogation must be weighed and it should be determined if the owner and A/E need additional protections such as professional liability insurance and loss of use, boiler, and machinery coverage.

Warranty or Guarantee

The construction contract should include a warranty or guarantee provision requiring the contractor to stand behind its workmanship and materials. The warranty is for a stated period, usually a year, from acceptance of the work or a portion thereof. The warranty is not intended to provide a one-year insurance policy for the project, but only to provide a remedy against noncomplying performance.

The contractor is usually called on to "unconditionally" warrant and guarantee labor and material and to make good any defects appearing during the guarantee period to the satisfaction of the owner and the designer. The architect/engineer is usually the arbiter of imperfect workmanship, and the contract should include a provision that, as required by the designer, the contractor is obligated to furnish satisfactory evidence as to the kind and quality of materials and equipment. If the work is deemed defective and the contractor refuses to perform, the owner will be best served by a clause retaining the right to repair, remedy, and replace at the expense of the contractor. Amounts retained by the owner are an important source of this expense.

Uncovering and Correcting Work

If any work is covered contrary to the written request of the engineer, it must, upon request, be uncovered for observation and then replaced at the contractor's expense without contract extension. In any event, the owner retains the right to demand uncovering for observation, testing, or inspection. If work is properly covered, then uncovered, and the work turns out to be defective, the contractor will bear the cost. If not defective, the contractor is entitled to compensation for an extra and perhaps an extension of time.[13]

---

[13] *See* extensive uncovering and correction provisions of AIA A201-1987, Art. 12.

Note that the owner usually retains other options, such as the right to perform corrective work itself and the right to accept defective work and make a deductive change order.

Stopping Work

If the contractor fails to correct defective work as required or fails to perform the work in accordance with the contract documents in any material respect, the contract may provide that the owner, in addition to its other remedies, by an order in writing may order the contractor to stop the work, or any portion thereof, until further notice.

Work by Owner or Separate Contractors

The owner may want to control the project as a whole and retain the ability to parcel work among its own forces and others. A clause such as the following would accomplish this purpose:

> The Owner reserves the right to perform work related to the Project with his own forces and to award separate contracts in connection with other portions of the project or other work on the site on the following conditions.
>
> The Owner reserves the right to require that certain work related to construction of . . . . be eliminated from the Work . . . and/or added back after elimination.

Liens

The owner should require the contractor to maintain a lien-free environment. The contract should contain a covenant by the contractor to keep the owner's property free and clear of all liens and charges arising out of the work. Further, the contractor should be obligated to provide prompt notice of actual and prospective claims of liens and charges. The contractor's obligation is to satisfy or discharge the lien at its expense, whether by payment, bond, or otherwise. An owner and designer are well served by an additional clause requiring the contractor to indemnify and defend them against liens and claims.

Waiver of Liens

The contractor is usually required to furnish the owner and designer such partial releases and waivers of lien from materialmen and creditors as may be requested. The contractor should provide final releases and waivers of lien at the time of final payment.

Lines of Authority

It is critical to the job that clear lines of authority be established and adhered to. All parties benefit.

The owner's representative is the entity designated in writing by the owner from time to time. Whenever action is to be taken or agreement or approval is required, those terms will only be deemed satisfied if performance is by the owner's representative.

Likewise, the contractor must designate an official representative to deal with the owner.

Subcontracts

The owner normally retains the right to object to subcontractors.[14] The owner also may propose a clause directing the contractor "to subcontract such portions of the Work as the Owner in its sole discretion may deem appropriate."

Further, the owner will want the benefit of a flow-down of contractual obligations, requiring that the contractor insert in its subcontracts that subcontractors agree to be bound by the terms of the owner/contractor agreement.

Time Clauses

Time is critical to the parties and the project. Three fundamental concepts for owner protection are as follows:

1. **Time of the essence.** The owner's concern with time is underscored by a time of the essence clause. The contractor, by signing a contract containing such a clause, recognizes that concern and recognizes further its obligation to perform continuously and expeditiously. Failure to make progress to the satisfaction of the architect/engineer is cause for termination.
2. **Liquidated damages.** The construction contract often contains a liquidated damages clause to the effect that if substantial completion is not attained by a date certain, the owner is entitled to a specified sum per day for delay. The effort to identify and quantify damages at the construction contract stage is obviously anticipatory, that is, construction has not begun and completion may be years away. The parties therefore agree that in the face of imprecision and uncertainty, they

[14] *See* AIA A201-1987, subpara. 5.2.

will strike a bargain as to the amount of liquidated damages. In most jurisdictions, liquidated damages clauses will be enforced unless a court is persuaded that the amount is a penalty (arbitrarily high or punitive) and is set without regard to a reasonable assessment of real damages.

3. **No damage for delay.** A no damage for delay clause is self-explanatory. The contractor will not be able to claim damages if its work is delayed by any cause (or by specified causes). The contractor's sole remedy will be an extension of the completion date of the contract and consequent relief from the liquidated damages clause. The harshness of such a clause has led to a significant amount of litigation, and one should consult local statutes and case law to determine enforceability. The owner should recognize that a no damage for delay clause may substantially increase the bid range, as contractors are likely to seek a measure of protection in their price.

Nonwaiver Clauses

The owner wants assurances that being magnanimous in one instance will not backfire as the project progresses. Therefore, a nonwaiver clause is typically included in the construction contract to say that no action or failure to act by the owner or its architect or engineer will constitute a waiver of all other or subsequent contract requirements, or be considered an approval of any breach or relieve the contractor of any contractual duties.

Dispute Resolution

In deciding upon a forum for dispute resolution, whether it be arbitration or litigation, the owner should consider the following factors:

Who has the deep pocket to fund the process?

Who has the staying power?

Is speed of the essence? (consider docket backlogs in courts)

Scheduling ease (arbitrators conform to reasonable desires of the parties; courts do not)

Discovery (limited in arbitration)

Joinder of parties or consolidation of claims among different parties (permitted under rules of civil procedure; no joinder or consolidation in arbitration without consent)

"Split the difference" mentality prevails in arbitration, as opposed to "all or nothing," usually demanded by a party

Arbitrators' compromises often waive less "equitable" claims, such as interest and lost profit

Rules of evidence applicable in each forum
Arbitration panels may be drawn from the construction industry, which means that less alignment with the Owner is likely.

If the choice is arbitration, consider:

Requiring a consolidation-of-arbitration provision in subcontracts
Choosing location and type of arbitration
Agreeing to limited discovery (jurisdiction dependent).

Termination Clauses

Termination clauses spell out the circumstances in which the contract may be terminated by the owner. A termination for *cause* contemplates a breach or other unsatisfactory performance by the contractor. The clause identifies the right, the method, and the consequences. A termination for *convenience* clause, on the other hand, posits the right of the owner to stop the job for any cause or for no cause. If the owner wants to maintain the prerogative to change its mind, such a clause should be included in the construction contract. Public contracts often contain termination for convenience clauses to protect against inadequacy of funding or changes of political wind.

Miscellaneous

The drafter will consider whether to include a *representation* clause, that is, the contractor being called upon to represent and warrant something to the owner. For example, the contractor may be asked to warrant its financial condition and the financial condition of subcontractors, its experience and competence in a particular area of construction, and that it is licensed. Importantly, the contractor often will be asked to acknowledge its familiarity with the site and its opportunity to perform investigations and review specified materials. Representation clauses are an affirmation of the parties' expectations. They serve notice that certain conduct is contemplated and expected. They can be mere window dressing or of pivotal importance. For example, a battle about whether a site condition was foreseen or foreseeable will focus on a warranty of familiarity with the site, and its interpretation may be central to the outcome of a claim.

§ 13.7 Contract Interpretation

As noted in § **13.1**, the construction contract will be consulted over the course of the project and beyond by those charged with project administration and those charged with resolving disputes.

Although it is important to develop the most clear and complete contract documents possible, it is equally important to have a sense of the rules that will apply in the event of a dispute. The rules of contract interpretation and construction may vary from jurisdiction to jurisdiction, but there is a body of generally accepted principles that will be applied by all courts and some arbitrators.

The first step in the process is to have full grasp of the dispute and the context of the dispute. The positions of the parties must be heard and understood. The contract documents must be consulted in an effort to understand the meaning of the words and their application to the issue at hand. If the meaning of the contract is plain and unambiguous, the contract likely will be considered conclusive. This formulation is generally referred to as the *plain meaning rule.*

However, despite plain and unambiguous meaning, the dispute may not end there. A party may attempt to raise matters outside the four corners of the document to cast doubt on or to contradict the written terms. That leads to the concept of *integration,* which considers whether the contract constitutes the final and complete expression of the agreement.[15] Normally the parties deal with the issue in an *integration clause* in the contract.[16]

If the contract is deemed integrated, a court will not look to earlier agreements, understandings, or statements that conflict with the final, integrated agreement. The concept is carried forward in the *parol evidence rule* which, invoked in a forum in which the rules of evidence are applied, excludes evidence of prior understandings to contradict the final agreement.

If, however, there is ambiguity in an agreement, whether the agreement is integrated or not, then parol evidence may be considered to resolve or clarify the ambiguity. The concept is that parol evidence is not being used to contradict or vary the terms of the written agreement, but only to explain it.[17]

The concepts of integration and parol evidence do not mean that the parties cannot contemporaneously or subsequently modify the construction contract. Typically, modification is, itself, a term of the contract.[18]

Interpreting the construction contract is an exercise in finding its meaning. The written contract, even an integrated contract, may not end the inquiry as to what the parties intended. It is that mutual intent, or meeting

---

[15] *See* Restatement (Second) of Contracts § 209 (1981).

[16] *See, e.g.,* AIA A201-1987, subpara. 1.1.2.

[17] *See* Restatement (Second) of Contracts § 214 (1981).

[18] *See, e.g.,* AIA A201-1987, subpara. 1.1.2., which provides, "The Contract may be amended or modified only by a Modification," earlier defined as a written amendment, change order, directive, or written order.

of the minds, that is the quest of the fact finder. In that effort, the fact finder is aided by certain precepts or rules of construction, including:

1. **Ordinary meaning.** The ordinary meaning of words and expressions throughout the country is given to words unless circumstances show that a different meaning was applicable.
2. **The whole.** The contract is to be interpreted as a whole and its terms and separate parts are to be given consistent interpretation.
3. **Specific terms.** Specific terms take precedence over general terms.
4. **Writings.** Handwriting prevails over typewriting, and both prevail over the printed form.
5. **Expresio unius est exclusio alterius.** To express one is to exclude another. To address certain items typically classified together is to exclude the others. That is why drafters often include the catchall phrase "including without limitation."
6. **Contra proferentem.** Literally "against the profferor" or selector of language, or ambiguous terms are construed against the party drafting it. In an attempt to avoid this canon of construction, consider the following clause, "Although drawn by ______, this agreement shall, in the event of any dispute as to meaning or application, be interpreted fairly and reasonably, and neither more strongly for or against either party."

Finally, the court or arbitrator may rely on terms not expressly within the contract.

There is also the matter of custom of trade, usage, and course of dealing. Prior dealings between these parties or dealings between parties of this type may be examined to supply a missing term or to interpret a contract.[19]

Terms and duties of implication are considered as well. In most jurisdictions, courts find that there is a duty of good faith dealing in all commercial relationships. In construction contracts, implied duties include the duty of cooperation and noninterference; the duty of coordination; the duty to provide timely and complete information; and the *Spearin* doctrine,[20] an implied covenant that the plans and specifications, properly followed, will lead to a satisfactory result.

---

[19] *See* Restatement (Second) of Contracts §§ 222, 223 (1981).

[20] United States v. Spearin, 248 U.S. 142 (1918).

CHAPTER 14

LIABILITY UNDER TURNKEY CONTRACTS

Mark S. Strukelj

Mark S. Strukelj is senior counsel in the law department of Fluor Daniel, Inc., an international engineering and construction company in Irvine, California. He advises Fluor Daniel in all aspects of engineering and construction contract law, project financed transactions, and related matters. Mr. Strukelj previously practiced general business law, primarily in the areas of tax and real estate. He obtained his undergraduate degrees at Loyola Marymount University and his law degree at Loyola Law School. He is a member of the California Bar Association.

§ 14.1 Introduction

Turnkey contracting, sometimes called *design/build* construction, offers an alternative to the traditional project development profile in which responsibility is shared among the design professional,[1] the contractor, and, often, a project manager. Turnkey contracting combines the design professional's and contractor's roles, raising issues about liabilities, costs, and conflicts of interests that do not usually arise with the traditional approach.

Design professionals and construction contractors accept the risks inherent in providing services under a traditional project structure, in which services are performed pursuant to a direct contract with the project owner. Under that structure, the design professional and construction contractor understand what steps must be followed to satisfy the various regulatory and licensing requirements, which have been adopted by all states to ensure that minimum levels of skill are maintained. Further, the design professional and construction contractor have accepted the proposition that so long as services are performed in a competent manner, consistent with customary "professional standards," legal liability will not result.

However, when services are to be performed under a turnkey contract, the contractor must reevaluate the risks to be assumed and the potential liability that may result. Because the design component is only one part of the turnkey contract whole, the scope of services to be performed will extend far beyond that which the design professional has traditionally accepted. Further, the independence of the design professional may be overshadowed by the judgment of the general contractor. To the extent different liability standards apply to a general contractor, those standards also may apply when responsibility is assessed for damages resulting from the combined acts or omissions of the designers and the constructors. The distinction between the design professional and the construction contractor becomes blurred.

---

[1] This chapter concerns professionals in the construction industry referred to generally as *design professionals,* including engineers, architects, and other construction professionals. References to "engineer" or "architect," particularly in quoted materials, apply equally to either design professional.

§ 14.2 Historical Perspective

The design professional's role in the building process historically has vacillated between mere engineering and design to actual participation in the construction of the building, often as an owner's representative or in an oversight role. The traditional structure for construction projects (illustrated in **Figure 14–1**) consists of separate entities that design and then construct the project. Standardized contract forms have formalized these distinct relationships.[2] Under the traditional approach, the design professional had no privity of contract with the contractor and vice versa.

The traditional structure continues as the predominant form of engineering and design practice today in most industries. The design professional creates design documents (the drawings and specifications) and coordinates the building design and construction.

The design professional's responsibilities also may include observation or supervision at the construction site to verify that the actual construction complies with the design documents. However, "supervision" by the design professional may result in the imposition of liability for improper

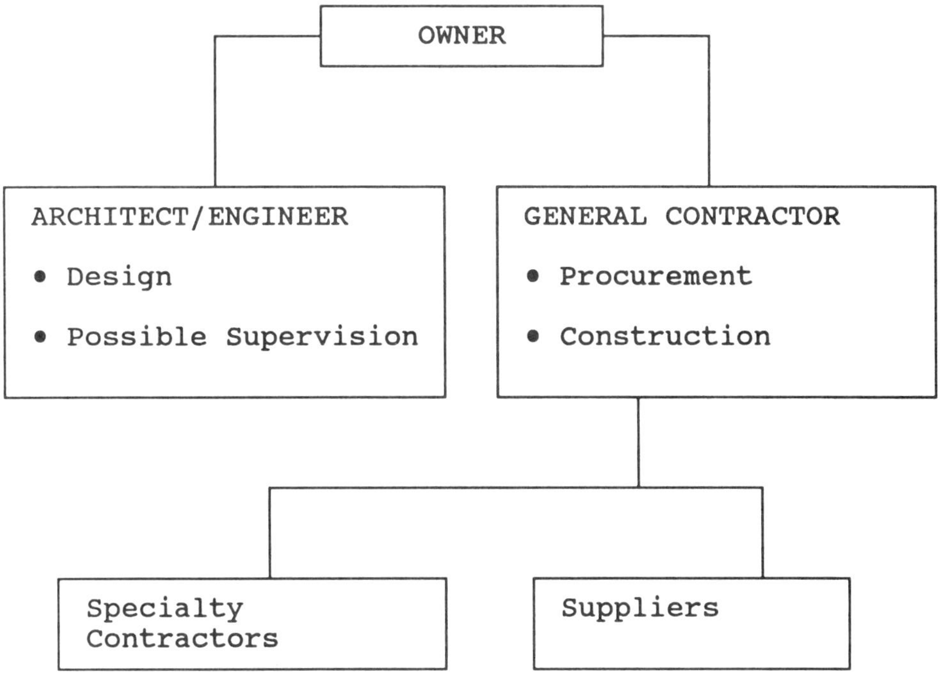

Figure 14–1. Traditional contract structure.

[2] *See, e.g.*, the American Institute of Architects Standard Forms of Agreement Between Owner and Architect (B141), Owner and Contractor (A101), and General Conditions of the Contract for Construction (A201).

construction work and, accordingly, many engineers performing in this capacity go to some lengths to downplay their authority at the construction site. If the design professional can exert control by stopping work for noncompliance with the design documents, or intervening to ensure compliance, that involvement may impose a responsibility on the design professional to insure the safe progress of the project.

§ 14.3 Turnkey Contracting

An alternative to this traditional contract structure has evolved into a form commonly referred to as the *turnkey construction contract.* In theory, a turnkey construction contract involves an owner who provides the parameters of the project to be designed and built, with the owner playing a lesser role in the process until the contractor has completed the project for the owner to "turn the key."[3]

Generally, the turnkey contract embodies the structure of a design/build contract and, as mentioned, sometimes those descriptions are used interchangeably. The turnkey contract has as its essential element the design and build feature, so that the design professional's role is merged with that of the construction contractor. **Figure 14–2** illustrates a typical turnkey contract structure.

The turnkey contract allows for a single source of responsibility and expertise for all aspects of engineering, design, procurement, and construction. The potential benefits derived from centralized management include a shortened design and construction schedule due to close coordination among the project participants, reduced project costs through elimination

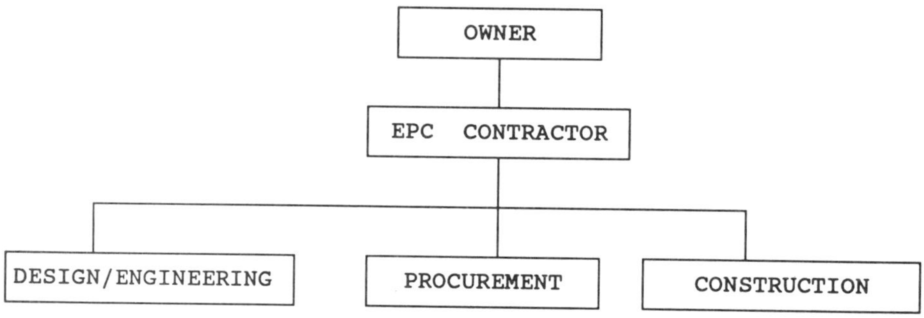

Figure 14–2. Turnkey contract structure.

[3] *See* Glassman Constr. Co. v. Maryland City Plaza, Inc., 371 F. Supp. 1154 (D. Md. 1974). Although turnkey contracting has been described to include the acquisition and ownership by the contractor of the land upon which the project is to be built, as well as the project's financing by the contractor, those activities are commonly performed by the project owner.

of unnecessary redundancies and duplicative administrative overhead, and avoidance of the inevitable finger pointing that might otherwise take place if problems develop.

However, single-source responsibility has its negative points. Without separate interests, it is much more difficult to maintain the traditional "checks and balances" between the designer and the construction contractor. Also, as a result of the consolidation of roles, the owner loses the independent consultant who would otherwise be available to assist in monitoring project costs, schedule, and other performance obligations.

Arguably, retention by the owner of an independent design professional may contribute to the best possible result. An unsophisticated owner may lack the expertise to evaluate whether the construction contractor is performing the project as promised and in accordance with the design of the independent engineer. Also, when the construction component is independently performed, the designer's work product, in turn, may be questioned and corrected as necessary during the construction phase. However, this lack of checks and balances can be overcome in a turnkey contract setting, so long as the owner has the resources or obtains independent design and supervision expertise. The owner can then independently evaluate the design and construction functions of the turnkey contractor.

Turnkey contracts may provide for design and construction at fixed prices, with guaranteed schedules and performance guarantees. As a result, they are an attractive alternative for specialized facilities, such as a power plant constructed on a project financed basis. Generally, project financing involves the development of a project with limited funds, typically from a third-party lender, which gives rise to schedule and performance guarantees to ensure an expected rate of return.

§ 14.4 Licensing Issues

The regulation and licensing of design professionals and construction contractors is a public safety measure undertaken to protect the public and promote consistency within those professions.[4] Licensing statutes enacted by every state and the District of Columbia establish the requirements for certification, restrict practice to only those individuals who are certified, and establish penalties for noncompliance.[5]

State licensing and registration laws may affect the manner in which design services are performed under a turnkey contract. As a general rule, a

---

[4] Regarding design professionals, *see* Seaview Hosp., Inc. v. Medicenters of Am., Inc., 570 S.W.2d 35 (Tex. Civ. App. 1978).

[5] A detailed discussion of the licensing requirements of the design professional is beyond the scope of this chapter.

licensed design professional must design the project. Therefore, a general contractor who is not licensed to practice architecture or engineering cannot itself perform those services. That contractor must use the services of a qualified design professional to ensure compliance with the law and enforceability of its contract with the owner.

However, contracting to perform those activities does not constitute the practice of architecture or engineering. As a result, a turnkey contractor may contract with or procure architecture or engineering services from a licensed design professional, and such activity does not constitute the practice of that profession.[6]

The performance of engineering and design services through a turnkey contract takes one of three forms: (1) a contractor performs the services through an employee who is a licensed professional, (2) a contractor enters into the turnkey contract and subcontracts the design services to a specialty subcontractor licensed to perform such services, or (3) a construction contractor and design professional form a joint venture, which then performs such services.

If a turnkey contractor that is not itself a design professional desires to design and construct a project under a turnkey contract structure, that contractor can employ licensed design professionals to perform related design services. However, in that situation, all plans, specifications, and other qualified design services must be prepared or performed in the design professional's name. The design professional's signature and seal may not be affixed to any work product that person did not perform or supervise.[7]

The use of in-house design staff typically overcomes licensing requirements. However, when the design professional is an employee of the turnkey contractor, conflicts of interest may arise. For example, the resolution of a design issue may conflict with the turnkey contractor's concerns regarding the costs of construction and the schedule for completion.[8] Notwithstanding that conflict, employees who are registered architects or

---

[6] *See* Seaview Hosp., Inc. v. Medicenters of Am., Inc., 570 S.W.2d 35 (Tex. Civ. App. 1978).

[7] *See* Markel v. Florida State Bd. of Architecture, 268 So. 2d 374 (Fla. 1972). *See also* Cal. Bus. & Prof. Code § 5582.1 (West 1985).

[8] *See* Charlebois v. J.M. Weller Assocs., Inc., 72 N.Y.2d 587, 531 N.E.2d 1288, 535 N.Y.S.2d 356 (1988), where in the dissenting opinion, the judges state, "[i]t is unrealistic to assume that the head of a construction company who, in managing that company's construction contract, must be concerned with time and cost restraints, allocation of resources and profit margins, will somehow remain unaffected by these concerns simply by donning his other hat and assuming the role of professional engineer. Indeed, the interrelated nature of the 'design-build' contract at issue makes this kind of distancing impossible."

engineers have an ethical responsibility to the public and are expected to perform their services with independent judgment.

Performing a turnkey contract through a joint venture may mitigate the conflicts of interest created through the employer/employee relationship. Although each joint venture's economic interest may be similar, depending upon the structure of the joint venture, each entity continues to be operated as a separate and independent organization.

However, a joint venture structure may create licensing problems as well as pose additional liability risks. As most states require construction contractors to be licensed, the design professional may have to obtain a contractor's license. If the design professional cannot hold a concurrent license (the registered professional can only engage in the profession for which he or she is licensed), entering into a turnkey construction contract as a joint venture participant may not be possible.

§ 14.5 Enforceability

Along with concerns relating to "professional responsibility," the turnkey contractor must comply with licensing requirements to ensure enforceability of the turnkey contract. The validity of a turnkey contract has been questioned when the design services to be performed by the turnkey contractor were executed by unlicensed or out-of-state designers.

Generally, courts have upheld the validity of turnkey contracts.[9] A determinative factor is whether the turnkey contract requires the use of independent design professionals to perform related professional services, rather than the nonprofessional contractor agreeing to render such services. Some courts have concluded that, under certain circumstances, turnkey contracts are invalid and unenforceable.[10] In those cases, contractors either agreed to perform design services without the assistance of a licensed design professional or used a design professional who was unlicensed within the state where the construction was performed.

Although licensing issues must be addressed and dealt with by the contractor who participates in a turnkey project, those issues can be overcome with a thorough understanding of the particular licensing requirements of the state in which the design services will be performed. The design professional should consult with legal counsel to identify applicable licensing regulations and ensure compliance.

---

[9] *See* Barondon Corp. v. Kunika Nakawatase, 196 Cal. App. 2d 392, 16 Cal. Rptr. 472 (1961); Charlebois v. J.M. Weller Assocs., Inc., 72 N.Y.2d 587, 531 N.E.2d 1288, 535 N.Y.S.2d 356 (1988).

[10] *See* Arkansas State Bd. of Architects v. Bank Bldg. & Equip. Corp. of Am., 225 Ark. 889, 286 S.W.2d 323 (1956).

§ 14.6 Tax Considerations

Combining the services of the design professional and the general contractor under one turnkey contract might give rise to tax liability that would not otherwise exist when such services are performed by separate contractors (or possibly under separate contracts). Additional tax exposure arises when a state or county imposes a tax on either the design professional's or the general contractor's services, but does not impose the same tax on both.

For example, some counties impose a tax on a contractor who performs construction services within the jurisdiction of the county based on the gross receipts of the contractor.[11] Although the tax is intended only to apply to construction services, if the taxing statute does not differentiate between design, procurement, and construction activities, the taxing authority may assert that the tax should be based upon the value of the entire turnkey contract. If that were the case, the design and procurement portions of the turnkey contract would be taxed in the same manner as the construction services.

To avoid the unintended application of such tax, the turnkey contractor must from the outset be knowledgeable of the tax statutes applicable to the particular project. With that understanding, the consequences of those statutes can then be addressed and factored into negotiations with the taxing authorities to minimize potential tax liability. Further, alternate contracting structures can be entertained and an increase to the turnkey contract price can be negotiated to avoid unintended consequences.

§ 14.7 Liability of Design Professional

Generally, the theories that give rise to liability for damages resulting from defective performance of design services originate either in common law (tort law) or contract law. Under principles of tort law, a turnkey contractor and the design professional individually[12] may be liable to the owner and others for damages arising from the negligent acts or omissions, misrepresentations, or intentional acts as respects design of the facility. The turnkey contractor also may be liable to the owner and, in certain cases, others[13] for damages as a result of obligations assumed under its contract with the

[11] *See generally* Va. Code Ann. § 58.1-3703 (1990); and Hanover County Code, Bldg. & Constr. Regulations § 6-31 (1990).

[12] Although design professionals may be liable under principles of common law for damages caused to another, quite often employers indemnify those professionals from damages arising from their professional acts or omissions.

[13] Under certain circumstances, the contractual obligations of the contractor may give rise to liability to parties who do not directly contract with the contractor, under a "third-party beneficiary" theory.

owner. Primarily, those obligations fall within two categories: warranty and indemnity.

§ 14.8 —Negligence and the Reasonable Professional Standard

Under the common law tort theory of negligence,[14] the design professional traditionally has been held to a "reasonable professional" standard when determining liability for defects in the performance of services. The design professional represents he possesses the skill and ability to perform the required services reasonably well, with reasonable judgment and without neglect. However, in exercising that judgment, the design professional does not warrant or guarantee a result. Instead, the design professional is expected to exercise reasonable care and competence.[15]

Most courts focus on the design professional's status when determining the liability standard to be applied. The professional standard of care requires an evaluation of the acceptable level of conduct as respects that particular professional.[16] The criteria to develop a professional standard are the customary standards applied to other professionals within the industry.

If the design professional performs his services negligently and causes another to be injured or damaged, the injured or damaged party is entitled to recover all reasonably foreseeable damages. The nature of those damages may include direct damages (for example, the actual costs to replace damaged property) as well as consequential or indirect damages (for example, loss of profits associated with downtime to an operating facility).

When a turnkey contractor undertakes design services pursuant to a turnkey contract, the standard to be applied in determining legal liability may change. The criteria applied in evaluating the "reasonable design professional" may be quite different from that applied to the "reasonable turnkey contractor." This is because the scope of the turnkey contractor's design services only forms one part of the turnkey contractor's overall

---

[14] The Restatement (Second) of Torts § 281 (1965) sets forth the following elements for a cause of action in negligence:

> The actor is liable for an invasion of an interest of another, if:
>
> (a) the interest invaded is protected against unintentional invasion, and
>
> (b) the conduct of the actor is negligent with respect to the other, or a class of persons within which he is included, and
>
> (c) the actor's conduct is a legal cause of the invasion, and
>
> (d) the other has not so conducted himself as to disable himself from bringing an action for such invasion.

[15] *See* Gagne v. Bertran, 43 Cal. 2d 481, 275 P.2d 15 (1954).

[16] *See* Huber, Hunt & Nichols v. Moore, 67 Cal. App. 3d 278, 136 Cal. Rptr. 603 (1977).

responsibility. Because the contractor's involvement under a turnkey contract does not stop with delivery of final drawings, likewise the turnkey contractor's duty to exercise reasonable care and judgment regarding design services does not cease.

Further, the turnkey contractor's risks and potential liability under a turnkey contract have increased, because the duty to others extends far beyond an obligation to exercise reasonable care and judgment in the preparation of drawings and specifications. Although the risks inherent in the production of design specifications and drawings can be significant, those risks are somewhat manageable. The contractor under a turnkey contract assumes many other risks inherent in the construction, in particular, those risks specifically related to field construction. Because the turnkey contractor, as defined, is responsible for engineering, procurement, and construction, parties available to assume those risks (for example, the independent design professional under the traditional structure) have been effectively eliminated.

§ 14.9 —Implied Warranty

Liability also may be imposed against the turnkey contractor under a common law theory of implied warranty. Most courts have refused to increase the standard of liability for the design professional from negligence to an implied warranty or strict liability standard. In the case of implied warranty, courts have held that the indeterminate factors that design professionals routinely manipulate make it impossible for them to guarantee a result.[17] In refusing to apply implied warranty standards to design professionals, courts have reasoned that the design professional makes representations regarding its services with the understanding those representations should not be interpreted as extending beyond the level of competence of the profession as a whole. Only when the design professional expressly guarantees the result should that level of understanding be imposed.[18]

[17] *See* City of Mounds View v. Walijarvi, 263 N.W.2d 420 (Minn. 1978).

[18] In Audlane Lumber & Builders Supply, Inc. v. D.E. Britt Assocs., Inc., 168 So. 2d 333, 335 (Fla. Dist. Ct. App. 1964), the court held an implied warranty of fitness should not be applied and stated:

> [A] professional does not "warrant" his service or the tangible evidence of his skill to be "merchantable" or "fit for an intended use." These are the terms uniquely applicable to goods. Rather, in the preparation of design and specifications as the basis of construction, the . . . architect "warrants" that he will or has exercised his skill according to a certain standard of care, that he acted reasonably and without neglect. Breach of this "warranty" occurs if he was negligent. . . . Any reliance, therefore, by the consumer on representations which exceed this implied understanding are found to be unreasonable unless the professional expressly and unequivocally warranted a specific result.

The courts also have hesitated to impose upon a design professional implied warranties that may apply to contractors.[19] This reluctance to imply warranties is due in part to the fact that design professionals, more so than contractors, clearly provide services rather than a product.[20] The court in *Ryan v. Morgan Spear Associates, Inc.* stated:

> It is a well settled rule that an architect must use the skill and care in the performance of his duties commensurate with the requirements of his profession, and he is liable in damages if he is negligent in performing such duties. . . . The Architect, by his contract, implies his profession of ordinary good taste, skill and ability, and a promise to exercise them reasonably, without neglect, and with a certain exactness of performance, in seeing that the work is properly done. The degree of skill required is such as would produce, if followed, a building of the kind called for, without marked defects in character, strength or appearance. . . . In the absence of special agreement, an architect is not liable for faults in construction resulting from defects in the plans, as his undertaking does not imply or guarantee a perfect plan or a satisfactory result, . . . Thus, the architect is only liable for a failure to exercise reasonable care and skill.[21]

Although it is the majority view that implied warranties will not be imposed upon design professionals, some courts have held that a design professional is responsible for the sufficiency of the overall construction plan.[22] Those courts suggest the design professional impliedly warrants general fitness of design, and fitness for the particular purpose the building is to serve.[23] A minority of courts have concluded that when a design professional holds himself out as an expert, it is not unreasonable to expect that professional to guarantee the results of his services will be satisfactory and sufficient for their intended purpose.[24]

However, when a contractor performs design services under a turnkey contract, the justification for not imposing an implied warranty is questioned. Courts are reexamining the rationale for not asserting implied warranties in the case of the turnkey contractor who performs design services, and there appears to be a trend toward imposing such a standard.

---

[19] *See* Ryan v. Morgan Spear Assocs., Inc., 546 S.W.2d 678, 681–82 (Tex. Civ. App. 1977).

[20] *See* Huang v. Garner, 157 Cal. App. 3d 404, 412, 203 Cal. Rptr. 800, 804 (1984), in which the court held, "where the primary objective of the transaction is to obtain services, the doctrines of implied warranty and strict liability do not apply."

[21] 546 S.W.2d 678, 681–82 (Tex. Civ. App. 1977).

[22] *See* Hill v. Polar Pantries, 219 S.C. 263, 64 S.E.2d 885 (1951) and Niver v. Nash, 7 Wash. 558, 35 P. 380 (1893).

[23] Because of the potential liability for implied warranties, design professionals typically disclaim such warranties within their express contract with the owner. See § **14.11**.

[24] *See* Broyles v. Brown Eng'g Co., 275 Ala. 35, 151 So. 2d 767 (1963); Federal Mogul Corp. v. Universal Constr. Co., 376 So. 2d 716 (Ala. Civ. App. 1979).

When the design professional performs services under a turnkey contract structure, a clear bifurcation between the professional services of the designer and the construction of the project to which the design relates is lost. In the turnkey contract structure, the owner executes a single contract with the contractor for both the design and construction of the project. The turnkey contract places responsibility for design, procurement, and construction on the contractor.

Numerous courts have applied an implied warranty of fitness to the design and build contractor.[25] In *Robertson Lumber v. Stephen Farmers Cooperative Elevator Co.,*[26] the court determined an implied warranty may be imposed if: (1) the contractor holds him or herself out as competent, (2) the owner has no particular expertise in design and construction, (3) the owner provides no plans or specifications, (4) the owner relies on the skill and expertise of the contractor, and (5) the contractor is aware of the intended purpose of the structure to be built.

§ 14.10 —Strict Liability

Thus far, the courts have refrained from subjecting the design professional to strict liability in tort.[27] As a general rule, strict liability deals with the condition of an object, whereas negligence deals with the actions of the "reasonable man." Strict liability avoids the issue of fault because an injured party does not have to prove fault to recover.

Strict liability in tort is commonly asserted against manufacturers of products under the assumption that the manufacturer is in a better position to control and spread the damages that may be sustained by an

---

[25] *See* Robertson Lumber Co. v. Stephen Farmers Coop. Elevator Co., 274 Minn. 17, 143 N.W.2d 622 (1966); Kennedy v. Bowling, 319 Mo. 401, 4 S.W.2d 438 (1928); and Kellogg Bridge Co. v. Hamilton, 110 U.S. 108, 3 S. Ct. 537 (1884).

[26] 274 Minn. 17, 143 N.W.2d 622 (1966).

[27] The Restatement (Second) of Torts § 402 A (1965) states:

Special Liability of Seller of Product of Physical Harm to User or Consumer

(1) One who sells any product in a defective condition and reasonably dangerous to the user or consumer or to his property is subject to liability for physical harm thereby caused to the ultimate user, consumer, or to his property if

(a) the seller is engaged in the business of selling such a product, and

(b) it is expected to, and does reach the user or consumer without substantial change in the condition in which it is sold.

(2) The rule stated in subsection (1) applies although

(a) the seller has exercised all possible care in the preparation and sale of his product, and

(b) the user or consumer has not bought the product from or entered into any contractual relation with the seller.

injured party. The courts have refused to extend strict liability in tort to design professionals and turnkey contractors because the underlying theory for strict liability does not apply. However, it can be argued that the turnkey contractor, who is responsible for the design, construction, and startup of a project, exhibits the characteristics of a manufacturer. This approach has been applied in the case of design/builders who mass-produce homes.[28]

The factors that influence application of the strict liability theory revolve around the level of control over the entire project from acquisition of land, financing, and design, through construction and startup. Whether a successful argument can be made that a contractor under a turnkey construction contract is liable under strict liability in tort may depend upon that level of involvement and control the turnkey contractor exerts in the entire project, as well as the performance of services.

§ 14.11 Warranty of Design Services under Contract

In addition to remedies available to an owner under relevant common law theories, liability can be imposed from obligations assumed by the contractor under its contract. Further, although common law remedies are theoretically available to an owner, they can be effectively restricted or limited by contract.

The parties to a turnkey construction contract retain a basic freedom to contract, and express warranties are generally enforced by the courts. Limited warranties have gained increased importance in the construction industry due to the high costs and enormous potential for losses arising from defective design and construction services. Because design and construction often involve significant risk and potential liability, the allocation and shifting of that risk among the owner, the turnkey contractor, and other interested parties, such as subcontractors, is essential.

Generally, a warranty is described as an assurance by one party pursuant to an agreement of the existence of a fact upon which another party may rely.[29] A warranty can be viewed as an understanding between the parties that an express promise will be achieved. That express promise is absolute, and a determination of a party's negligence is irrelevant in deciding whether a warranty has been breached.

[28] *See* Schipper v. Levitt & Sons, Inc., 44 N.J. 70, 207 A.2d 314 (1965); Kriegler v. Eichler Homes, Inc., 269 Cal. App. 2d 224, 74 Cal. Rptr. 749 (1969); Stuart v. Crestview Mut. Water Co., 34 Cal. App. 3d 802, 110 Cal. Rptr. 543 (1973); Weeks v. Slavik Builders, Inc., 384 Mich. 257, 181 N.W.2d 271 (1970).

[29] *See* Dale Constr. Co. v. United States, 168 Ct. Cl. 692 (1964).

It is often more expedient to recover on a warranty theory rather than on the basis of negligence, which requires a demonstration of a failure to exercise reasonable care. To recover under a warranty claim, the owner must establish the existence of the warranty, that it was breached, and that damages resulted from that breach.

Warranties may be either express or implied. An express warranty may derive from a written or oral representation by the turnkey contractor regarding services to be performed. Under the traditional structure, the typical contract between the design professional and the owner contained few, if any, express warranties.[30] As a result, the owner's warranty claim would be based upon some theory of implied warranty. However, when the design professional extends an express warranty as to a certain result, he is liable to the owner for damages if the result is not achieved.[31]

The principles of express warranty and a design professional's responsibility thereunder become clouded when services are to be performed under a turnkey contract. Because an owner typically requires an all-encompassing warranty to cover all services to be performed pursuant to the contract, design services of the turnkey contractor, related warranty standards, and the remedies made available to the owner should be distinguished from those offered by the traditional construction contractor.

Most standard form owner-contractor agreements contain express warranties regarding the quality of the contractor's work. For example, the warranty standard in the American Institute of Architects (AIA) Document A201 (1987 edition), which is a contract intended to be used under a traditional structure in which an owner has independently employed the architect, provides:

> The Contractor warrants to the Owner and Architect that materials and equipment furnished under the Contract will be of good quality and new unless otherwise required or permitted by the Contract Documents, that the Work will be free from defects not inherent in the quality required or permitted, and that the Work will conform with the requirements of the Contract Documents.

To the design professional, the standard referred to in this clause is overly broad, because it expands the standard otherwise applied to a design professional from a reasonable design professional standard to a standard of absolute liability (free from defects). To accommodate for the distinction between design services and construction services when both services are performed by one contractor pursuant to one contract, standard forms have adopted warranty language that avoids an absolute standard.[32]

---

[30] *See* AIA B141-1987.

[31] *See* Klein v. Catalano, 386 Mass. 701, 437 N.E.2d 514 (1982) and Swett v. Gribaldo, Jones & Assocs., 40 Cal. App. 3d 573, 576, 115 Cal. Rptr. 99 (1974).

[32] *See* AGC Document No. 415 and AIA A191-1987.

For example, the warranty standard that might be applied to services performed pursuant to a design/build contract is as follows:

> The Designer/Builder warrants to the Owner that all materials and equipment furnished under this Agreement will be new, unless otherwise specified, and that all construction work will be of good quality, free from improper workmanship and defective materials. . . . The foregoing warranties are in lieu of all other warranties express or implied, including but not limited to, the implied warranties of merchantability and fitness for purpose.[33]

Although this warranty does not specifically express a warranty for design services, it expressly excludes all other warranties, express or implied. An affirmative exclusion that disclaims all implied warranties must be explicit to limit the scope and duration of the express warranty because the existence of an express warranty does not, by implication, render null any implied warranties.[34]

It is common for an owner to insist upon a standard of performance regarding design services. The nature and scope of that standard will depend upon that which is negotiated among the parties. Without a standard for design services, an owner may refuse to exclude all implied warranties. In this situation, the turnkey contractor should propose a design standard consistent with the standard that would otherwise apply under law, namely, the "reasonable professional" standard.

Following is an example of a warranty standard that accommodates both design and construction:

> Contractor warrants (1) it will perform its services in a professional manner in keeping with generally accepted industry standards, (2) all materials and equipment furnished under the Agreement will be of good quality and new, unless otherwise required or permitted, and (3) all materials and workmanship will be free from defects.

In addition to the warranty standard, the turnkey contractor should focus on the remedies available to the owner and how those remedies can be enforced if it is determined the turnkey contractor has not complied with the express warranty standard.

The nature of available remedies is particularly important in the case of the warranty for design services because the potential liability resulting from deficient performance of design services could be greatly disproportionate to the value of the services rendered. For example, faulty design could lead to significant reperformance of field construction substantially complete before the identification of the design defect. Also, the time period

---

[33] *See* Scott, *Design/Build Agreements,* Construction Industry Forms (John Wiley & Sons 1988).

[34] *See* Hoagland v. Celebrity Homes, Inc., 40 Colo. App. 215, 572 P.2d 493 (1972) and Tibbits v. Openshaw, 18 Utah 2d 442, 425 P.2d 160 (1967).

in which an owner might make a claim is important, because the time period for claims relating to latent defects is significantly longer than the period an owner would agree to under contract.[35]

Generally, a provision in a contract that provides for an exclusive remedy is enforceable. A turnkey contractor can limit its potential liability to a time period shorter than that which is otherwise provided by law for breach of contract.[36] Further, an express provision that limits an owner's related remedies to those specified pursuant to a warranty is enforceable.

For example, an express provision limiting an owner's right to "repair or replacement" precludes the owner from recovering any other damages.[37] Also, an unambiguous provision stating that liability for defects arising from faulty materials and workmanship is limited to the period expressed in the warranty generally will protect the contractor from liability for defects appearing after that period.[38]

The following warranty language is an example of an express warranty period and exclusive remedy for nonconforming design services and would be used with the express warranty standard discussed:

> If within the 12-month period following completion of its services, or termination of this agreement, whichever comes first, Owner informs Contractor in writing that any part of the services fails to meet the standard set forth in the preceding sentence, Contractor will reperform such part of its services within its scope of work that is deficient. The foregoing is Contractor's sole warranty and Owner's exclusive remedy in respect of the quality of the services, and implied warranties, including but not limited to implied warranties of merchantability and fitness for a particular purpose, are expressly disclaimed and waived.

§ 14.12 Application of Uniform Commercial Code

Generally, the courts have been reluctant to apply the provisions of the Uniform Commercial Code (UCC) to the design professional and the turnkey contractor. By its terms, Article 2 of the UCC applies only to commercial

---

[35] Various states have different statutes of limitation and repose. California: four-year limitation for patent defects and ten-year limitation for latent defects; Illinois: four-year limitation period for architects and engineers; ten-year statute of repose; Massachusetts: six-year limitation period; New York: No separate statute for design professionals, but a general malpractice law applied to cut off actions against design professionals on contract claims after six years following issuance of certificate of completion; Texas: ten-year limitation period.

[36] *See* Independent Consol. School Dist. No. 24 v. Carlstrom, 277 Minn. 117, 151 N.W.2d 784 (1967).

[37] *See* A-Larms, Inc. v. Alarms Device Mfg. Co., 165 Ga. App. 382, 300 S.E.2d 311 (1983).

[38] *See* Independent Consol. School Dist. No. 24 v. Carlstrom, 277 Minn. 117, 151 N.W.2d 784 (1967).

contracts for the sale of "goods."[39] Because construction contracts and the design services associated therewith typically involve the performance of services, those services would appear to be excluded from application of the UCC.

However, some courts have looked beyond the traditional classification of construction contracts as service contracts and have focused upon the nature of the goods and services provided. In evaluating this issue, the courts look to the predominant factor for the contract, namely, whether the purpose of the contract is the rendition of services, with goods incidentally involved, or whether the transaction is a sale of goods, with labor incidentally involved.[40]

The courts have enumerated several factors to be applied when evaluating whether a contract comes under the purview of the UCC. The language of the contract is critical. For example, use of "services" versus "goods" and "contractor" versus "seller" as descriptions of the nature of the business and the provider of the service (or, for example, a "builder" versus an "equipment manufacturer/installer") are important criteria.[41]

Application of the UCC to the turnkey contractor would subject it to various UCC principles, including the implied warranties of merchantability and fitness for a particular purpose. However, as in contractual warranties, a seller under the UCC can limit the available remedies of the buyer of the goods, although it is generally more difficult to disclaim UCC express warranties.

Thus far, turnkey contractors have resisted direct application of the UCC to their services contracts. Nevertheless, the courts are frequently applying the principles of the UCC (for example, course of dealing and usage of trade) to resolve disputes among the contracting parties. This unintended consequence is yet another good reason for careful and thorough drafting of the turnkey contract, anticipating disputes and providing clear resolutions.

§ 14.13 Fiduciary Duty

As discussed, the turnkey contractor has overall responsibility for the design and construction of the facility to be built. Because of the breadth of that service and the turnkey contractor's "special knowledge" of the owner's requirements and objectives, an assertion may be made that the turnkey contractor's responsibility extends beyond mere design and construction of the facility, and into the realm of its commercial practicability and economic feasibility. To the extent the turnkey contractor assumes

---

[39] *See* U.C.C. § 2-105 (1952).

[40] *See* Bonebrake v. Cox, 499 F.2d 951 (8th Cir. 1974).

[41] *See* Bob Neiner Farms, Inc. v. Hendrix, 141 Ill. App. 3d 499, 490 N.E.2d 257 (1986) and Ranger Constr. Co. v. Dixie Floor Co., 433 F. Supp. 442 (D.S.C. 1977).

that relationship, it accepts responsibility and potential liability beyond the scope of the traditional design/build contractor.

For example, the owner under a turnkey contract structure may insist that the turnkey contractor represent it is experienced and competent in the services to be performed, that it is aware of the requirements of the owner respecting the nature and quality of the facility to be designed and built, and that the owner is relying upon the experience and expertise of the contractor. Under those circumstances, can the owner assert the contractor has a duty to advise the owner whether or not to proceed with or discontinue a project due to commercial impracticability or economic infeasibility?

That responsibility is typically not assumed intentionally by the turnkey contractor. However, the contractor, by making representations within the turnkey contract suggesting such a relationship, may unintentionally assume a fiduciary responsibility. As a consequence, the nature and scope of its warranties and guarantees under the contract may be expanded and the threshold for legal liability under the theories of negligence and implied warranties may be reduced.

§ 14.14 Indemnification Obligations

The concept of indemnification is frequently encountered in the construction industry and is particularly important to the turnkey contractor. Indemnification is when one party (the indemnifying party) agrees (or is compelled by law) to hold the other person (the indemnified party) harmless and reimburse the indemnified party for loss or damage that the indemnified party has incurred or may incur as a result of certain acts or omissions of the indemnifying party. Indemnification can shift liability from one party to another. Therefore, depending upon the nature of the liability assumed, the financial effect of that obligation can be significant.

An obligation to indemnify can be implied by law or expressed by contract. Express indemnification agreements serve several important functions. First, they allow the parties to the contract control over allocation of risk of loss. The contracting parties can apportion the potential damages that may arise from the turnkey contract and the turnkey contractor's acts or omissions, thereby insuring that risks are appropriately allocated in relation to the reward anticipated by each party.

Second, indemnification agreements can establish each party's liability exposure. Understanding that exposure, the turnkey contractor can consciously accept risks or cover risks through insurance. When an indemnity obligation protects the indemnified party against "loss," actual loss must be shown before there is an obligation to indemnify. However, when the indemnity obligation protects the indemnified party against "liability," then an obligation exists as soon as liability is either alleged or imposed.

An agreement to indemnify has been held to be valid and enforceable provided it is not against public policy. An agreement to indemnify, which sets no time period for the obligation, is terminable at will. However, when the obligation is in connection with a construction contract, the obligation extends for a reasonable period of time and at least until the contract is completed.[42]

Many states have adopted statutes regulating the circumstances under which express indemnification is enforceable, and in certain circumstances, broad indemnities are unenforceable.[43] Before such legislation, contractors routinely were required to indemnify others (including design professionals) from their negligent acts because the damages were caused in part by the acts of the contractor. Although those statutes provide some relief from broad, open-ended indemnities, generally an owner may continue to be indemnified from damages arising from the acts or omissions of the contractor, even when the owner is partially responsible for those damages.

When a turnkey contractor assumes risks through an indemnification agreement, ideally those risks are covered by insurance. Insurance coverage is also important from the indemnified party's point of view. The allocation and shifting of risks is only effective if the indemnifying party has adequate financial resources to cover the liability arising from the indemnity obligation.

Many forms of insurance allow the contractor to assume, by contract, liability it ordinarily has under common law. However, because typical professional liability insurance[44] only covers damages arising from the negligent performance of design services, it is essential that a contractor only indemnify the owner for damages arising from its negligent acts or omissions. Broad obligations, such as an indemnification against "any acts, errors, or omissions," should be avoided.

§ 14.15 Mitigating Liability Risks

Although the turnkey contractor is exposed to varying degrees of risks and liability, those risks can be mitigated and potential liability reduced or eliminated under certain circumstances. One vehicle used by turnkey contractors to minimize liability is the corporate structure. The overwhelming reason for selecting that form of entity is the turnkey contractor's desire to

---

[42] *See* Employers Liab. Assurance Corp. v. Tebbs, 137 F. Supp. 869 (D. Wyo. 1956).

[43] A majority of states have enacted some type of "anti-indemnity" legislation. Those statutes can be classified into three basic categories: (1) statutes that bar indemnification for unlawful acts, (2) statutes that bar indemnification for "sole" negligence or "willful misconduct," and (3) statutes that bar indemnification for "negligence."

[44] See § **14.20**.

shield the owners from unlimited liability. However, a design professional operating in a corporate structure remains accountable and may be held personally liable with the corporation for acts or omissions.[45]

It may be advantageous for the design professional to associate in corporate form. The majority of states allow a design professional to limit liability regarding the malpractice of others or for nonprofessional, service-related obligations, although the design professional continues to be personally liable for his own acts.

§ 14.16 —Contractual Limitations of Liability

By contract, the turnkey contractor may expressly limit or avoid liability arising from contractually assumed obligations and its performance or failure to perform its design responsibilities. Limitations and exclusions of liability are commonly incorporated in indemnification provisions, exculpatory clauses, and liquidated damage provisions.[46]

Limitation of liability provisions are particularly important to the contractor performing design services because the fees earned in or allocated to the performance of those services are far less than the potential liability that may arise for costs associated with structural failures. Further, it is difficult, if not impossible, to obtain adequate professional liability (errors and omissions) insurance to cover those risks.

Of particular importance to the turnkey contractor is the potential liability for consequential damages (for example, lost profits, lost revenues, or loss of use of the owner's existing facilities or the facilities to be constructed). As with all construction projects, the contractor must evaluate the risks to be assumed in relation to the reward to be received. Because the amount of damages that may be assessed almost always will be disproportionate to the fee that may be earned, the turnkey contractor should always seek a contractual exclusion of that risk.

In certain jurisdictions, limitation of liability provisions are enforceable.[47] In other cases, the limitation of liability provisions have been upheld to the extent of insurance maintained by the party charged.[48] Further, some

---

[45] *See generally* American Ins. Group v. McCowin, 7 Ohio App. 2d 62, 218 N.E.2d 746 (1966).

[46] *See* Village of Rosemont v. Lentin Lumber Co., 144 Ill. App. 3d 651, 494 N.E.2d 592 (1986).

[47] *See* Farris Eng'g Corp. v. Service Bureau Corp., 406 F.2d 519 (3d Cir. 1969); Baird v. Chesapeake & Potomac Tel. Co., 208 Md. 245, 117 A.2d 873 (1955); Primrose v. Western Union Tel. Co., 154 U.S. 1, 14 S. Ct. 1098 (1894).

[48] *See* Florida Power & Light Co. v. Mid-Valley, Inc., 763 F.2d 1316 (11th Cir. 1985); Long Island Lighting Co. v. IMO Delaval, Inc., 668 F. Supp. 237 (S.D.N.Y. 1987).

courts have held such clauses are unenforceable.[49] Generally, however, within the context of the typical turnkey construction project, the courts have allowed limitation of liability provisions, so long as the limitations are reasonable and not, on their face, violative of applicable law.[50]

Although the turnkey contractor may have to assume risks arising from design services that would not otherwise exist if those services were performed under the traditional structure, those risks can be mitigated through the careful drafting of contractual provisions that limit the contractor's liability. At best, the potential liability that may arise from the combined efforts of design and construction services are outweighed by the reward received from that combination. In addition, the turnkey contractor can turn to insurance as a hedge against potential liability.

§ 14.17 Using Insurance to Cover Anticipated Risk

The turnkey contractor may cover various risks and potential liability with insurance. Through the use of insurance, the turnkey contractor is better able to quantify those risks.

As discussed in **§ 14.14**, indemnification is the allocation of liability among those who will share responsibility for the loss. A contract for insurance is a form of contractual indemnification, but instead of risks being shared between the turnkey contractor and the owner, the allocation of liability is made between the turnkey contractor and its insurance carrier.

Only "insurable interest" can be covered under insurance. An insurable interest is something of value an insured possesses that may be lost or damaged, or a financial loss the insured may otherwise incur if a peril identified in the insurance policy occurs. Generally, the insured can collect only the amount of the loss up to the amount named as the policy limit.

When insurance coverage protects against loss, actual loss must be established as a condition precedent to recovery under the policy. When insurance coverage indemnifies against liability, then the policy is effective as soon as liability is either alleged or imposed, whether or not there is an actual loss to the insured.

Generally, a turnkey contractor is asked to maintain the following types of insurance:

---

[49] *See* White Constr. Co. v. Commonwealth, 11 Mass. App. Ct. 640, 418 N.E.2d 357 (1981); W. William Graham, Inc. v. City of Cave City, 289 Ark. 105, 709 S.W.2d 94 (1986); Mohawk Drilling Co. v. McCullough Tool Co., 271 F.2d 627 (10th Cir. 1959); Lane v. New York Tel. Co., 7 A.D.2d 702, 179 N.Y.S.2d 536 (1958).

[50] The turnkey contract should always contain express language explicitly stating that the parties intend the releases or limitations agreed to among them will apply in all events, including a party's negligence or other fault.

1. Workers' compensation and employer's liability insurance
2. Comprehensive general liability insurance
3. Automobile liability insurance
4. Builder's all-risk insurance
5. Professional liability (errors and omissions) insurance.

Of those traditional categories of insurance, three have particular significance to design services: (1) comprehensive general liability insurance, (2) builders' all-risk insurance, and (3) professional liability (errors and omissions) insurance.

§ 14.18 —Comprehensive General Liability Insurance

A turnkey contractor maintains comprehensive general liability (CGL) insurance to cover possible injuries or damages suffered by third parties. Generally, coverage under a standard CGL insurance policy extends to losses that the insured shall become legally obligated to pay arising from bodily injury or property damage to which the insurance applies and which is caused by an occurrence described within the policy.[51]

The scope of coverage will depend upon the terms and exclusions of the insurance policy. As a result, the turnkey contractor may not have coverage under a CGL policy for all potential legal liabilities that may arise from performance of services under a turnkey contract.

Bodily injury loss includes bodily injury, sickness, or disease sustained by a person that occurs during the policy period and death resulting therefrom. Property damage includes physical injury to or destruction of tangible property that occurs during the policy period, including loss of use therefrom and loss of use of tangible property caused by an occurrence described in the policy. Generally, economic losses, such as loss of profits, are not covered by CGL insurance.

Although initially the scope of CGL coverage appears broad, various exclusions significantly limit the application of the policy when losses arise from acts of architects or engineers. Those exclusions include contractual liability, work-in-progress damages, and professional liability. Generally, coverage for the risks excluded under a standard CGL policy can be obtained through endorsements to the CGL policy or through additional insurance policies pertaining to the excluded risks.

For example, a contractual liability endorsement extends coverage under the policy to liability an insured assumes under any contract or agreement

---

[51] *See* Insurance Services Office, Comprehensive General Liability Policy, Insuring Agreement.

relating to the conduct of the named insured's business.[52] As a result, the turnkey contractor's liability assumed under its contract with the owner is covered, subject to specific exclusions. The endorsement, however, is intended only to cover liability incurred when the insured promises to indemnify or hold harmless another, rather than liability arising from breach of contract. The contractual liability endorsement also does not extend to certain events, including bodily injury or property damage arising from an insured's failure to render professional services, if the insured is an architect, engineer, or surveyor.[53]

Two particular exclusions relate specifically to design services performed by the turnkey contractor. Construction work-in-progress is not covered under the standard CGL policy[54] (although work-in-progress coverage can be obtained through builder's all-risk insurance), and professional liability is excluded from the standard CGL policy.

Liability arising from design services may be covered under two types of insurance. A turnkey contractor may be covered under professional liability insurance for third-party damages resulting from the negligence of the design professional in the rendering of professional services. Also, the turnkey contractor may maintain general liability insurance to cover liability arising from "nonprofessional" liability.

§ 14.19 —Builder's All-Risk Insurance

Builder's all-risk insurance is a property insurance policy that covers losses resulting from damage to or loss of construction work-in-progress. "All-risk" provides coverage for most common perils.[55] The standard builder's risk policy has a broad exclusion for damages arising from design and workmanship. Builder's all-risk coverage does not extend to faulty, inadequate, or defective design, specifications, workmanship, and construction. However, it does extend to the damage resulting from faulty, inadequate, or defective services.

§ 14.20 —Professional Liability Insurance

A turnkey contractor's liability for professional errors or omissions is typically excluded from a standard CGL policy. As a result, many of those who

---

[52] *See* Insurance Services Office, Standard Contractual Liability Endorsement.

[53] *Id.*

[54] *See* Comprehensive General Liability Policy, Exclusion J.

[55] *See* Insurance Services Office, Builder's Risk Policy. Although builder's all-risk coverage is a broad form of property insurance, certain exclusions do apply, which could limit recovery in certain circumstances (for example, acts or decisions of governmental bodies).

perform design services maintain professional liability insurance (also commonly referred to as errors and omissions insurance) to cover that liability.

Professional liability insurance only covers damages arising from the professional negligence of the provider of the design services. Professional liability insurance covers losses that the turnkey contractor becomes legally obligated to pay as a result of liability arising from the performance of services in a professional capacity as an architect or engineer, when the liability is caused by a negligent act, error, or omission of that professional.

Most professional liability policies do not cover guarantees or warranties made by the provider of the design services. As discussed, under common law, the design professional is not the guarantor of a result. The design professional is only under a duty to render services in accordance with applicable professional standards. Therefore, the liability resulting from express warranties or guarantees made by the turnkey contractor is outside the coverage of professional liability insurance.[56] Also, professional liability insurance may not cover indemnification agreements because there is the potential that the indemnity agreement may expand the turnkey contractor's liability beyond what that contractor would otherwise have under law.

In the case of the turnkey contract, it may be prudent for the contractor to maintain professional liability insurance to cover liability arising from design errors. However, that coverage may only be available if the design work is performed by in-house design professionals.[57] When the turnkey contractor retains an outside design professional to perform design services, the contractor should cover its risk through a direct indemnification from that outside professional, with a requirement that adequate professional liability insurance be maintained, if financial credit support is necessary.

Although professional liability insurance generally is available to cover liability arising from professional negligence, in many cases that insurance is impractical or unavailable. Insurance companies may not cover the limits requested by the owner or the risk inherent in the nature of the services to be performed. Also, because of the high cost of such insurance (based upon the amount of the premium and the level of the deductible), self insurance may be the only practical solution. Under those circumstances, the importance of limiting liability through carefully drafted warranty and indemnity clauses again becomes critical.

---

[56] *See* Bates & Rogers Constr. v. North Shore Sanitary Dist., 92 Ill. App. 3d 90, 414 N.E.2d 1274 (1980) and City of Mounds View v. Walijarvi, 263 N.W.2d 420 (Minn. 1978).

[57] *See* Underwriters at Lloyds of London, Contractors Design Professional Liability Insuring Agreements.

CHAPTER 15

PREPARING SUBCONTRACTS WITH ARCHITECTS, ENGINEERS, AND CONSULTANTS

Dorn C. McGrath III
Mark W. Pritchard
Harold I. Rosen

Dorn C. McGrath III, a partner in the law firm of Zorc, Rissetto, Weaver & Rosen in Washington, D.C., has had extensive experience in the negotiation and litigation of construction claims involving major projects such as water treatment plants and military facilities. He is the author or coauthor of a variety of publications on construction matters and government procurement. Mr. McGrath graduated from Davidson College and received his law degree from the George Washington University National Law Center. He is a member of the American Bar Association Forum Committee on the Construction Industry and Public Contract Law Section.

Mark W. Pritchard is an associate with the law firm of Zorc, Rissetto, Weaver & Rosen. He is a licensed professional engineer in five states. He also is a graduate of the George Washington University National Law Center. His legal career has been primarily focused on construction law and government contracts. Mr. Pritchard currently serves on the American Bar Association's Public Contract Law Section's Superfund Procurement Committee and Construction Committee, and he is a member of the National Society of Professional Engineers and the American Society of Civil Engineers.

Harold I. Rosen is a partner in the Washington, D.C. law firm of Zorc, Rissetto, Weaver & Rosen. He has represented construction contractors and engineers in claims, litigation, and contract administration for many years. In addition, he has served as counsel to the Associated General Contractors of America and to the Society of American Military Engineers in contract matters. He is associate counsel to the Society of American Military Engineers and is a fellow of that organization.

§ 15.1 Introduction

Architects and engineers are called upon to provide a wide variety of design services. The Federal Property and Administrative Services Act, for example, lists the following as the

> professional services . . . which members of the architectural and engineering professions . . . logically and justifiably perform . . . studies, investigations, surveying and mapping, tests, evaluations, consultations, comprehensive planning, program management, conceptual designs, plans and specifications, value engineering, construction phase services, soils engineering, drawing reviews, preparation of operating and maintenance manuals, and other related services.[1]

Architects and engineers (A/Es) may perform all the work necessary for a contract in-house or may employ other design professionals to assist in

[1] 40 U.S.C. § 541 (1988); *see* Federal Property and Administrative Services Act, 40 U.S.C. §§ 470–475, 541–544 (1988), 41 U.S.C. §§ 251–255 (1988). *See also* the Armed Services Procurement Act, 10 U.S.C. §§ 2301–2330 (1988).

performing the services required for a project. At any given time, entering into a subcontract with other professionals may be necessary to obtain special expertise, or simply to provide additional staff to perform the work. A growing number of A/E firms are using the subcontracting process to better manage professional liability.

This chapter provides an overview of the considerations involved in A/E subcontracting. The recommended terms and conditions for subcontracts with architects, engineers, and consultants are discussed. Issues likely to arise involving A/E subcontractors in the administration of a project are also noted. Finally, there are particular aspects of geotechnical and structural services that merit special attention in the preparation of A/E subcontracts.

§ 15.2 Standard Form Contracts

Although in one sense an A/E selects other architects, engineers, and consultants for a team effort to complete a project, there are legal considerations that will govern the relationships among the parties and the responsibility for their work. Typically, an A/E engages other design professionals as independent contractors and maintains that relationship throughout the course of the project. The parties usually do not wish to be considered joint venturers, employer-employee, or each other's agents, insofar as these various relationships result in different legal consequences. Under the terms of its contract with the owner, the A/E may be liable for the acts of other design professionals it retains. However, when other architects, engineers, or consultants are retained as independent contractors, the liability attributable solely to their negligence can be limited.[2]

The language of an agreement between the A/E and other design professionals sets the legal standards of performance and liability. Fortunately, there are at least three carefully drafted and well-tested sets of forms to consider when preparing an A/E subcontract. Although these forms differ in certain respects, each covers key provisions that should be included in any subcontract.

The Engineers Joint Contract Documents Committee (EJCDC) is an important source of construction-related documents.[3] The EJCDC standard

[2] *See generally* Note, *Contracts: Liability of Architect to Owner for Defects in Plans Furnished by a Consultant,* 48 Calif. L. Rev. 151 (1960). *But see* Johnson v. Salem Title Co., 246 Or. 409, 425 P.2d 519 (1967) (A/E remains liable for "non-delegable duties," such as statutory requirements or inherently dangerous conditions); South Dakota Bldg. Auth. v. Geiger-Berger Assocs., 414 N.W.2d 15 (S.D. 1987) (A/E held liable for actions of consulting engineer because it fixed its seal to the consultant's drawings).

[3] EJCDC documents are available through the National Society of Professional Engineers (NSPE), P.O. Box 96163, Washington, D.C. 20090-6163.

forms are issued and published jointly by the National Society of Professional Engineers, the Consulting Engineers Council, the American Society of Civil Engineers, and, recently, the Construction Specifications Institute.[4] The following EJCDC documents are available for A/E subcontracting:

Standard Form of Agreement Between Engineer and Architect for Professional Services, 1910-10 (1985)

Standard Form of Agreement Between Engineer and Associate Engineer for Professional Services, 1910-13 (1985)

Standard Form of Agreement Between Engineer and Consultant for Professional Services, 1910-14 (1985)

Standard Form of Agreement Between Engineer and Geotechnical Engineer for Professional Services, 1910-27-B (1986)

The American Institute of Architects (AIA) also has produced a set of subcontract documents that are in wide use.[5] The AIA documents are issued in an A Series (owner-contractor), B Series (owner-architect), C Series (architect-consultant), D Series (architect-industry), F Series (accounting forms), and G Series (office and project forms). The following C Series documents are drafted for A/E subcontracting:

Standard Form of Agreement Between Architect and Consultant, C141-1987

Abbreviated Form of Agreement Between Architect and Consultant, C142-1987

Standard Form of Agreement Between Architect and Consultant for Designated Services, C161-1979

Standard Form of Agreement Between Architect and Consultant for Special Services, C727-1982

A third source of A/E subcontracting documents is the Associated General Contractors (AGC). AGC's standard form documents include:[6]

---

[4] EJCDC also provides useful commentaries on the standard form documents, as well as guidelines for their use with updates to explain any significant changes in revised editions of the documents. *See, e.g.,* Clark, *Commentary on Agreements for Engineering Services and Construction Related Documents,* EJCDC 1910-9 (1985).

[5] AIA documents may be obtained from your local authorized AIA Documents distributor, or AIA's Order Department, 9 Jay Gould Court, P.O. Box 753, Waldorf, MD 20604 (1-800-242-4140).

[6] AGC documents may be ordered from its Publications Department, Associated General Contractors of America, 1957 E St., N.W., Washington, D.C. 20006.

Standard Design-Build Subcontract Agreement with Subcontractor Providing Design, No. 450-1 (1986)

Conditions Between Contractor and Subcontractor for Design-Build, No. 430 (1982)

Standard Form of Agreement Between Contractor and Architect, No. 420 (1979)

As with any well-drafted subcontracts, these forms are derived from the applicable prime contracts. For example, the EJCDC subcontract documents refer to the Standard Form of Agreement Between Owner and Engineer for Professional Services, EJCDC 1910-1, and the AIA subcontract documents relate to the Standard Form of Agreement Between Owner and Architect, AIA Document B141.[7] It is good practice to incorporate the pertinent portions of the applicable prime contract into the subcontract, recognizing that the subcontractor is bound to perform services for the prime contractor which, in turn, the prime contractor is bound to perform for the owner. The prime contract and subcontract documents, therefore, must be closely coordinated.

The most direct method to ensure that a subcontract accurately reflects the work required is to physically incorporate the pertinent sections of the prime contract into the subcontract. For example, EJCDC 1910-10 states: "A copy of all portions of the Prime Agreement pertinent to [the A/E subcontractor's] responsibilities, compensation and timing of services hereunder is attached, made a part hereof and marked Exhibit A-A."[8]

It is legally no less effective, and sometimes more convenient when several different documents are involved, to provide that they are "incorporated by reference" into the subcontract. Incorporation by reference means that documents, such as prime contract provisions, specifications, and drawings, or industry technical standards, are as much a part of the subcontract as if they were set forth therein.[9] Although it is not necessary to use any particular language to incorporate portions of a prime contract into a subcontract, the references should be plainly stated and the documents should be readily available.[10]

The basic services or statement of work in the EJCDC documents are divided into phases: study and report, preliminary design, final design, bidding or negotiating, and construction. AIA Document C141 provides a

---

[7] *See also* AIA B141/CM-19, B151-19, B181-19, and B727-19, as possible prime contracts. AGC Nos. 410 and 415 (1986) are the designated standard forms of design-build agreements and general conditions between an owner and contractor.

[8] EJCDC 1910-10 (1985) at 1.

[9] Rosco, Inc., ASBCA No. 32102, 88-1 B.C.A. (CCH) ¶ 20,489 at 103,640 (1987).

[10] *See, e.g.,* Maryland Nat'l Capital Park & Planning Comm'n v. Lynn, 514 F.2d 829 (D.C. Cir. 1975); United States Fidelity & Guar. Co. v. Long, 214 F. Supp. 307 (D. Or. 1963).

similar breakdown of work, with a detailed approach to the construction phase-administration of the construction contract.

Notwithstanding the EJCDC or AIA description of the work, the subcontractor also must be required to perform work resulting from *changes* in "the general scope, extent or character of [the project] or its design including, but not limited to, changes in size, complexity, OWNER's schedule, or character of construction or method of financing."[11] The AGC language similarly provides that the "Contractor, without invalidating the Contract, may order Changes in the Work within the general scope of the Subcontract consisting of additions, deletions or other revisions."[12]

The terms of payment contained in the subcontract must be coordinated with the timing and method (or methods) of payment in the prime contract. The EJCDC documents offer five alternatives.[13] The first two are widely accepted for most public and private projects: lump sum, in which the project can be adequately defined in advance, and cost-plus fixed fee, in which a definite scope of services cannot be determined at the time of initial negotiations. Of more limited application, but still viable for appropriate circumstances, are payment provisions based on a percentage of cost (the total prime contract or subcontract work accomplished) and direct labor cost (multiplied by a factor) or a percentage of cost and salary costs (multiplied by a factor).[14] Similar payment options appear in the AIA and AGC documents.[15] Payments can be further classified in accordance with the AIA publication, *Compensation Guidelines for Architectural/Engineering Services.*[16] In any case, when a subcontractor's compensation is based on costs incurred, it is advisable to obtain an estimate in advance and provide for limitations on cost overruns.[17]

Regarding the timing of payments to an A/E subcontractor, the EJCDC documents suggest a "pay-when-paid" provision that states as follows:[18]

> ENGINEER shall bill OWNER monthly on account of [ARCHITECT/ENGINEER's] services and expenses and shall pay [ARCHITECT/ENGINEER] within fourteen days of the time ENGINEER receives payment

---

[11] EJCDC 1910-10 and 1910-13 (1985), ¶ 2.1.3. *See also* AIA C141-19, ¶ 3.3.2, Additional Services.

[12] AGC No. 430 (1986), ¶ 13.1.2.

[13] *See generally* § 5 of EJCDC 1910-10, 1910-13, and 1910-14 (1985).

[14] Percentage of costs and multipliers are prohibited or restricted in many public contracts. *See, e.g.,* EPA State and Local Assistance Regulations, 40 C.F.R. pt. 35, subpt. E, App. D (1990).

[15] *See* AIA C141-19, Payments to the Consultant, Art. 10, and Basis of Compensation, Art. 11. *See also* AGC No. 430 (1986), Payments and Completion, Art. 10.

[16] AIA F Series.

[17] *See, e.g.,* EJCDC 1910-10 and 1910-13 (1985), ¶ 5.1.1.

[18] EJCDC 1910-10 and 1910-13 (1985), ¶ 5.2.2.

> from OWNER on account thereof. It is intended that payments to [ARCHITECT/ENGINEER] will be made as ENGINEER is paid by OWNER under the Prime Agreement and that ENGINEER shall exert reasonable and diligent efforts to collect prompt payment from OWNER. However, whether or not OWNER pays ENGINEER in full, ENGINEER shall pay all amounts due [ARCHITECT/ENGINEER] within a reasonable time after completion of [ARCHITECT/ENGINEER's] services under the Prime Agreement.

The AIA version requires "prompt" payment in proportion to payments received, thus leaving some leeway. The provision states:[19]

> Payments to the Consultant will be made promptly after the Architect is paid by the Owner under the Prime Agreement. The Architect shall exert reasonable and diligent efforts to collect prompt payment from the Owner. The Architect shall pay the Consultant in proportion to amounts received from the Owner which are attributable to the Consultant's services rendered.

By contrast, one suggested AGC clause simply states that an agreed-upon percentage will be paid upon receipt of payment from the owner:[20]

> The Contractor agrees to pay to the Subcontractor for the satisfactory completion of subcontractor's work the Contract Sum of ________ ($________) in monthly payments of ______ percent of the work performed in any preceding month, in accordance with estimates prepared by the Subcontractor and approved by the Contractor. Payment of the approved portion of the Subcontractor's monthly estimate and final payment shall be conditioned upon receipt by the Contractor of his payment from the Owner.

Because the terms of payment are a central concern in drafting a subcontract, A/Es are encouraged to carefully consider the matter, including the issue of whether the A/E's subcontractor receives full payment if the A/E does not. To this end, the AIA documents recommend that users identify and insert any "provisions as to conditions, contingencies . . . and other particulars concerning payments."[21]

An A/E subcontract should require firm assurances that subcontracted services will be forthcoming in accordance with the A/E's time schedule for the project. For example, the EJCDC subcontract forms emphasize, in the schedule provisions, that the subcontractor's services "have been agreed to in anticipation of the orderly and continuous progress" of the work.[22] Moreover, the subcontract must anticipate the possibility that a project schedule

---

[19] AIA C141-19, ¶ 10.3.6.

[20] AGC No. 450-1 (1986), ¶ 5.1.

[21] AIA C141-19, ¶ 11.4.3. *See also Commentary on AIA C141,* EJCDC 1910-25 (1985).

[22] EJCDC 1910-10 and 1910-13 (1985), ¶ 4.1.

may be extended. If scheduled dates are exceeded through no fault of the subcontractor, an equitable adjustment of the subcontract schedule, and in some cases price, may be necessary.[23] The EJCDC documents suggest a breakdown setting dates to cover the different phases of the services to be provided.[24]

In addition to a comprehensive schedule, the subcontract should include a termination provision keyed not only to the subcontractor's performance, but also to any termination of the prime contract.[25]

As to the reuse of documents, the EJCDC and AGC forms provide that drawings and specifications are "instruments of service" for which the subcontractor retains a property interest whether or not the project is completed, while the prime contractor has the limited but continuing right to use the same documents for information and reference purposes.[26] The AIA documents recently have been revised to adopt this approach, whereby the subcontractor is said to "retain all common law, statutory and other reserved rights."[27] The EJCDC and AIA documents seek to protect the A/E subcontractor from subsequent use of the documents for other projects, both in terms of reserving a right to additional compensation and a disclaimer of liability for unauthorized use.[28]

Finally, A/Es are frequently required to maintain professional liability insurance. All subcontractors should likewise be required to maintain equivalent coverage. If an A/E subcontractor itself obtains outside services, then insurance coverage must be obtained for all respective professional services rendered in connection with the project. If the insurance required is in excess of what the subcontractor normally carries, additional cost reimbursement is both necessary and appropriate, particularly when the prime contractor is likewise reimbursed by the owner.[29]

---

[23] An *equitable adjustment* is a term of art defining compensation as the difference in the reasonable time and cost to perform the work as originally required and the reasonable time and cost to perform the work as changed, including an allowance for profit on work actually done. *See* Pacific Architects & Eng'rs, Inc. v. United States, 491 F.2d 734 (Ct. Cl. 1974).

[24] EJCDC 1910-10 (1985), Exhibit A-B.

[25] *See* EJCDC 1910-10 and 1910-13 (1985), ¶ 7.1, EJCDC 1910-14 (1985), ¶ 6.1; AIA C141-19, Art. 8, AIA C161-19, Art. 10; AGC No. 420 (1986), Art. 7, AGC No. 430 (1986), Art. 15.

[26] EJCDC 1910-10 and 1910-13 (1985), ¶ 7.2; AGC No. 420 (1986), Ownership and Use of Documents, Art. 6.

[27] AIA C141-19, ¶ 6.1.

[28] *Id.;* EJCDC 1910-10 (1985), ¶ 7.2.

[29] *See* EJCDC 1910-10 (1985) Guide Sheet, para. 13, at iii, for a discussion of extending insurance coverage to cover the joint and several liability of all design professionals associated with a project. *See also* AIA C141-19, Insurance ¶ 10.6, and Insurance Coverages, ¶ 11.5. For additional discussion of liability insurance for design professionals, see **Ch. 6**.

An AGC form adds an indemnity clause in conjunction with insurance coverage, requiring that the A/E subcontractor provide indemnification for "all claims and losses arising from negligent acts, errors or omissions of the [A/E subcontractor] in the performance of professional services."[30] The A/E subcontractor is given the option of assuming the legal defense of such claims.

The possibilities for the *disputes* provision of a subcontract, including arbitration, require separate consideration. **Section 15.5** suggests several approaches for handling subcontractor disputes. No subcontract is complete without an effective disputes provision.

§ 15.3 Federal Government Contracts and Subcontracts

Federal government contracts are written under the authority of the federal procurement laws. These statutes fall into two major categories. The first group relates to the procedures for enhancing competition and awarding contracts for civilian and military supplies or services, with A/E services being largely governed by the Brooks Act.[31] The second group comprises more than a dozen civil and criminal statutes for investigating and punishing what has come to be known as "fraud, waste and abuse" in government contracting.[32] Certain statutes, such as the Anti-Kickback Act, specifically address the role or actions of subcontractors on a project.[33] Given a perceived lack of integrity in federal procurement, all contractors should be aware of these laws and potential penalties to ensure compliance.

The Federal Acquisition Regulation (FAR) sets forth the government's standard form provisions for prime contracts. In government contracting, subcontracts (and lower-tier subcontracts) are also required to include

---

[30] AGC No. 420 (1986), Indemnity, Art. 9.

[31] 40 U.S.C. §§ 541–544 (1988). Among other things, the Brooks Act prohibits competition for A/E services based on price, but also limits fees for certain public works or utility projects to 6% of the estimated project cost, as further detailed in 48 C.F.R. § 15.903 (1990). The limitation applies to the A/E contract price, including cost and profit.

[32] *See, e.g.*, False Claims Acts (Criminal and Civil), 18 U.S.C. § 287 (1988); 31 U.S.C. §§ 3729–3733 (1988); False Statement Act, 18 U.S.C. § 1001 (1988); Program Fraud Civil Remedies Act, 31 U.S.C. §§ 3801–3812 (1988); Mail and Wire Fraud Acts, 18 U.S.C. §§ 1341 and 1343 (1988); Major Fraud Act, 18 U.S.C. § 1031 (1988); Bribery and Gratuities, 18 U.S.C. §§ 201(b) and (c) (1988); Anti-Kickback Enforcement Act, 41 U.S.C. §§ 51–54 (1988); Conspiracy, 18 U.S.C. § 371 (1988); Racketeer Influenced and Corrupt Organizations (RICO), 18 U.S.C. §§ 1961–1968 (1988); Drug-Free Workplace Act, 41 U.S.C. §§ 701–707 (1988); Obstruction of a Federal Audit, 18 U.S.C. § 1516 (1988); Ethics in Government Act, 18 U.S.C. § 207 (1988); and Immigration Reform and Control Act, 8 U.S.C. § 1324a-b (1988).

[33] 41 U.S.C. § 53 (1988).

certain FAR terms and conditions. These are the so-called mandatory *flow-down* clauses. Other nonmandatory terms of the prime contract often should be included in the subcontract as well. The result is that, in addition to the pertinent technical specifications and drawings, the general and special provisions of an A/E subcontract on a government project are, to a large extent, the same as those in the prime contract. Furthermore, under an A/E prime contract, government consent to subcontracts for A/E services is required at the outset and before making any substitution of A/E subcontractors or consultants.[34]

The mandatory flow-down clauses generally constitute those contract provisions that implement a significant government policy or protect the government's interests. The following list is not comprehensive, but it gives an indication of the nature and scope of the mandatory flow-down clauses:[35]

Title	C.F.R. Citation
Subcontractor Cost and Pricing Data	48 C.F.R. § 52.215-24 (1990)
Examination of Records by Comptroller General	48 C.F.R. § 52.215-1 (1990)
Small Business and Small Disadvantaged Business Subcontracting Plan	48 C.F.R. § 52.219-9 (1990)
Labor Surplus and Area Subcontracting Program	48 C.F.R. § 52.220-4 (1990)
Equal Opportunity	48 C.F.R. § 52.222-26 (1990)
Clean Air and Water	48 C.F.R. § 52.223-2 (1990)
Cost Accounting Standards	48 C.F.R. § 52.230-3 (1990)
Value Engineering	48 C.F.R. § 52.248-1 (1990)[36]

[34] *See* 48 C.F.R. §§ 44.201-3, 44.204(d), and 52.244-4 (1990).

[35] Different government agencies, particularly the Department of Defense and the National Aeronautical and Space Administration (NASA), have additional mandatory flow-down clauses.

[36] Other mandatory flow-down clauses (from the 1990 C.F.R.) include: Restrictions on Subcontractor Sales to the Government (48 C.F.R. § 52.203-5), Security Requirements (48 C.F.R. § 52.204-2), Required Sources for Jewel Bearings and Related Items (48 C.F.R. § 52.208-1), Audit-Sealed Bidding (48 C.F.R. § 52.214-26), Subcontractor Cost or Pricing Data-Modifications-Sealed Bidding (48 C.F.R. § 52.214-28), Audit-Negotiation (48 C.F.R. § 52.215-2), Subcontractor Cost and Pricing Data Modifications (48 C.F.R. § 52.215-25), Integrity of Unit Prices (48 C.F.R. § 52.215-26), Price Redetermination-Prospective (48 C.F.R. § 52.216-5), Price Redetermination-Retroactive (48 C.F.R. § 52.216-6), Incentive Price Revision-Firm Target (48 C.F.R. § 52.216-16), Incentive Price Revision-Successive Targets (48 C.F.R. § 52.216-17), Notice to the Government of Labor Disputes (48 C.F.R. § 52.222-1), Contract Work Hours and Safety Standards Act Overtime Compensation (48 C.F.R. § 52.222-4), Affirmative Action for Special Disabled and Vietnam Era Veterans (48 C.F.R. § 52.222-35), Employment Reports on Special Disabled and Veterans of the Vietnam Era (48 C.F.R. § 52.222-37), Clean Air and Water Certification (48 C.F.R. § 52.223-1), Hazardous Material Identification and Material Safety Data

Even if not required by law, government prime contractors are best advised to incorporate most, if not all, of the applicable FAR provisions into subcontracts. For one reason, a prime contractor is required to give specific certifications and indemnifications to the government throughout the course of project work, and will want a supporting certification from a subcontractor.[37] Secondly, the subcontractor should be working under the same basic conditions as the prime. The following clauses, although not mandatory, are among those that are a practical necessity for a prime contractor's A/E subcontract administration:

Title	C.F.R. Citation
Gratuities	48 C.F.R. § 52.203-3 (1990)
Covenant Against Contingent Fees	48 C.F.R. § 52.203-5 (1990)
Price Reduction for Defective Cost or Pricing Data	48 C.F.R. § 52.215-22 (1990)
Changes	48 C.F.R. § 52.243 (1990)
Terminations (Convenience or Default)	48 C.F.R. § 52.249 (1990)
Suspension of Work	48 C.F.R. § 52.249-10 (1990)[38]

(48 C.F.R. § 52.223-3), Privacy Act (48 C.F.R. § 52.224-2), Duty-Free Entry (48 C.F.R. § 52.225-10), Certain Communist Areas (48 C.F.R. § 52.225-11), Authorization and Consent (48 C.F.R. § 52.227-1), Notice and Assistance Regarding Patent and Copyright Infringement (48 C.F.R. § 52.227-2), Reporting of Royalties (Foreign) (48 C.F.R. § 52.227-8), Refund of Royalties (48 C.F.R. § 52.227-9), Filing of Patent Applications-Classified Subject Matter (48 C.F.R. § 52.227-10), Patent Rights-Retention by the Contractor (48 C.F.R. § 52.227-11, 12), Patent Rights-Acquisition by the Government (48 C.F.R. § 52.227-13), Workers' Compensation Insurance-Defense Base Act (48 C.F.R. § 52.228-3), Insurance-Work on a Government Installation (48 C.F.R. § 52.228-5), North Carolina State and Local Sales and Use Tax (48 C.F.R. § 52.229-2), Administration of Cost Accounting Standards (48 C.F.R. § 52.230-4), Disclosure and Consistency of Cost Accounting Practices (48 C.F.R. § 52.230-5), Progress Payments (48 C.F.R. § 52.232-16), Subcontracts-Cost-Reimbursement and Letter Contracts (48 C.F.R. § 52. 244-2), Special Tooling (48 C.F.R. § 52.245-17), Limitation of Liability (48 C.F.R. § 52.246-23, -24, -25).

[37] An A/E subcontract under a government contract should contain a separate section setting forth the required "Representations and Certifications," which are to be made by a subcontractor representative with adequate authority. At a minimum, *reps and certs* should be obtained to cover persons authorized to conduct negotiations; equal employment opportunity; labor utilization; corporate affiliations; contingent fees; federal, state, and local taxes; foreign content represented in subcontract price; cost accounting standards; clean air and water; nonsegregated facilities; independent price determination; previous government contracts and compliance reports. Any claim under the Contract Disputes Act will require a separate certification at the time it is submitted.

[38] Other recommended flow-down clauses (from the 1990 C.F.R.): New Material (48 C.F.R. § 52.210-5), Defense Priority Allocation Requirements (48 C.F.R. § 52.212-8), Stop Work Order (48 C.F.R. § 52.212-13, -14), Price Reduction for Defective Cost or Pricing Data (48 C.F.R. §§ 52.214-27, -28, 52.215-22, -23), Allowable Cost and Payment (48 C.F.R. § 52.216-7), Utilization of Small Business Concerns and Small Disadvantaged Business Concerns (48 C.F.R. § 52.219-8), Utilization of Labor Surplus Area

FAR 52.236-23 sets forth a "Responsibility of the Architect-Engineer Contractor" clause, and it is of potential importance to an A/E subcontract. This clause states that an A/E will be responsible for the professional quality, technical accuracy, and coordination of the work done under the contract. The A/E is obliged to correct or revise any errors or omissions without charge. The A/E will be liable to the government for all damages caused by its negligence, even after the government reviews, approves, accepts, and pays for the work. Therefore, when preparing an A/E subcontract, this same provision should be included therein:

> RESPONSIBILITY OF THE ARCHITECT-ENGINEER CONTRACTOR (APR 1984)
>
> (a) The Contractor shall be responsible for the professional quality, technical accuracy, and the coordination of all designs, drawings, specifications, and other services furnished by the Contractor under this contract. The Contractor shall, without additional compensation, correct or revise any errors or deficiencies in its designs, drawings, specifications, and other services.
>
> (b) Neither the Government's review, approval or acceptance of, nor payment for, the services required under this contract shall be construed to operate as a waiver of any rights under this contract or of any cause of action arising out of the performance of this contract, and the Contractor shall be and remain liable to the Government in accordance with applicable law for all damages to the Government caused by the Contractor's negligent performance of any of the services furnished under this contract.

Regarding the right to reuse documents, if a government A/E contract's (and related subcontract's) purpose is the performance of experimental, developmental, or research work, or involves the design of a government facility and equipment, a clause will be included in the prime contract to give the government patent rights.[39] The government also may acquire rights in data if produced or furnished under an A/E contract.[40] The patent and data rights policies and procedures apply to all subcontracts at any tier.[41] Hence, an A/E prime contractor must be aware of the government's rights and obtain from its subcontractors all similar rights necessary to

Concerns (48 C.F.R. § 52.220-3), Davis-Bacon Act (48 C.F.R. § 52.222-6 to -17), Walsh-Healy Public Contracts Act (48 C.F.R. § 52.222-20), Buy American Act (48 C.F.R. § 52.225-3), Balance of Payments Program (48 C.F.R. § 52.225-10), Patent Indemnity (48 C.F.R. § 52.227-3), Rights in Data (48 C.F.R. § 52.227-14, -16 to -23), Protest After Award (48 C.F.R. § 52.233-3), Government Property (48 C.F.R. § 52.245-2, -5), Inspection (48 C.F.R. § 52.246-2, -3, -6), Preference for United States Flag Carriers (48 C.F.R. § 52.247-63), Indemnification Under Public Law 85-804 (48 C.F.R. § 52.250-1).

[39] 48 C.F.R. § 27.304-3 (1990).

[40] *Id.* §§ 27.409(a)(1)(iv), 52.227-17.

[41] *Id.* §§ 27.304-4(a), 52.227-17(e).

fulfill the A/E's obligation to the government. If a subcontractor refuses to accept terms affording the government such rights, the prime contractor should bring it to the attention of the government before proceeding further with the subcontract award.[42] Of course, from an A/E's viewpoint, it will be important to protect proprietary rights when appropriate. In one court case, an A/E subcontractor was deemed to have given a prime shipbuilding contractor authority to sell plans at the cost of reproduction to other contractors. The subcontract contained no restrictions pertaining to reuse of the plans, and the prime contract gave the government the right to disseminate the plans.[43] The court held that had the subcontract contained clearly stated limitations and restrictions, they would have been upheld.[44]

Finally, when drafting a subcontract under a government prime contract, an A/E is well advised to resist the temptation to use a name modification clause such as: "Whenever necessary to make the context of FAR clauses applicable to this subcontract, the word 'Government' means the 'Architect/Engineer' etc." This type of all-purpose clause can lead to unnecessary confusion that can be avoided by retyping the applicable FAR provisions and making the necessary name changes in each clause.[45] By contrast, EJCDC, AIA, and AGC provide their standard form subcontracts cross-referenced and ready for use, and generally these should not be modified.

§ 15.4 Subcontract Award Controversies

Once the A/E subcontract documents are prepared, the next step is the subcontract award. Commercial or other private owners awarding contracts have wide discretion in choosing contractors. Federal, state, or local authorities, on the other hand, must comply with procedural requirements for awarding public contracts to promote competition.

On many public projects, A/Es are selected without emphasis on price competition. Federal government policy, for example, is to "publicly announce all requirements for architectural and engineering services, and to negotiate contracts for architectural and engineering services on the basis of demonstrated competence and qualification . . . at fair and reasonable prices."[46] Similar considerations are often the basis for state and local A/E

---

[42] For additional discussion of patents, copyrights, and other provisions governing the ownership and reuse of an A/E's work product, see **Ch. 17**.

[43] J.J. Henry Co. v. United States, 411 F.2d 1246 (Ct. Cl. 1969).

[44] *Id.* at 1250.

[45] There is no set format for A/E subcontracts, but it makes practical sense to follow the established uniform government contract format described in FAR pt. 15.406.

[46] 40 U.S.C. § 542 (1988).

contracting.[47] Therefore, A/Es eligible for the award of a public contract stay current on public projects and procurement actions, including the announcement of requirements, the selection criteria, the source selection personnel, appraisal of A/E qualifications, the selection and ranking of firms, and the negotiations ultimately leading to the contract award.[48] Taking the federal government again as an example, at any point in the selection process, A/E prime contractors may file protests with a government agency, the General Accounting Office (GAO), or possibly in federal court.[49]

Unlike prime contractors, A/E subcontractors on public projects usually do not have rights to protest procurement actions. Largely because subcontractors do not enter into a contract with the government, and therefore are said to lack "contractual privity" with the government, federal agencies, the GAO, and the courts are not willing to review subcontract award controversies.[50]

However, the GAO has identified five possible exceptions under which it will consider subcontract award protests. The GAO may review a subcontractor protest when:

1. A prime contractor acts as a "purchasing agent" of the government
2. There is government participation in the subcontractor selection such that it controlled the selection or significantly limited subcontract sources
3. There is fraud or bad faith in government approval of the subcontract award
4. The prime contractor makes a contract award "for" an agency of the government or
5. There are questions concerning the award of subcontracts submitted by government officials entitled to advance decisions from the comptroller general.[51]

---

[47] The American Consulting Engineers Council (ACEC) maintains a general listing of state A/E procurement laws. Currently 34 states have A/E procurement laws similar to Brooks Act procedures. However, there are exceptions and the applicable state law should be consulted. *See, e.g.,* Texas Professional Services Procurement Act, Tex. Rev. Civ. Stat. Ann. art. 664-4.3 (Vernon 1964).

[48] *See, e.g.,* FAR subpt. 36.6, Architect-Engineer Services.

[49] *See, e.g.,* 48 C.F.R. § 33.103 (1990) (protests to an agency); Randolph Eng'g, Inc., B-192375, 79-1 C.P.D. ¶ 465 (1979); Scanwell Laboratories, Inc. v. Shaffer, 424 F.2d 859 (D.C. Cir. 1970). *But see* American Consulting Eng'g Council v. Lewis, No. 82-1715, slip op. (D.D.C. July 15, 1982) (regarding standing of A/E firms to protest procurements). For additional discussion of contract award problems, see **Ch. 20**.

[50] *See, e.g.,* Rubber Millers, Inc. v. United States, 596 F. Supp. 210 (D.D.C. 1984). *See also* Annotation, *Standing of Unsuccessful Bidder for Federal Procurement Contract to Seek Judicial Review of Award,* 23 A.L.R. Fed. 301 (1975).

[51] Optimum Sys., Inc., B-183039, 75-1 C.P.D. ¶ 166, at 7-8 (1975).

It is not often that an A/E subcontractor will be able to persuade a public authority to consider a protest even under the exceptions noted. In some circumstances, a prime contractor may have an interest in issues that are related to an A/E subcontractor's complaint, and in such case may agree to assert the protest. Aside from this possibility, there occasionally is a federal, state, or local regulation that, in the interest of promoting competition, permits subcontractor protests. The Environmental Protection Agency (EPA) regulations have extended the scope of protests in this manner for procurements under assistance agreements.[52]

§ 15.5 Subcontract Performance Disputes

The disputes provision of an A/E subcontract will very often determine the difference between an orderly resolution of disputes and time-consuming, expensive litigation. Because the prime contractor will be caught in the middle of any dispute, it is important that the terms of the subcontract define the A/E subcontractor's rights as appropriate for the nature of the work.

A general reference in the A/E subcontract to the disputes clause in the prime contract will not suffice. For example, in one court case, a subcontractor brought suit against its prime contractor and, as a defense, the prime contractor argued that the subcontractor was bound by the disputes procedure that the prime followed under its contract with the owner. The court held that, absent clear contractual language, the subcontract had not incorporated the prime's disputes procedure. The subcontractor was free to bring suit against the prime contractor, regardless of the status of the claims or issues that the prime was pursuing against the owner.[53] As mentioned in **§ 15.4** in connection with subcontractor bid protests, even if the subcontractor is disposed to proceed directly against the owner, the lack of a contractual relationship between the subcontractor and the owner will prevent most such actions.

The preferable method, from the prime contractor's perspective, is to place the A/E subcontractor in the same position as the prime for disputes that ultimately are caused by the owner. Rather than bearing responsibility for an owner's actions, the prime can effectively require the subcontractor to seek any recovery exclusively from the owner.

[52] *See, e.g.*, CCTW&M v. United States Envtl. Protection Agency, 452 F. Supp. 69 (D.N.J. 1978) (construing 40 C.F.R. § 35.939).

[53] Washington Metro. Area Transit Auth. v. Norair Eng'g Corp., 553 F.2d 233 (D.C. Cir. 1977). *See also* W. Wright, Inc. v. Korshoj Corp., 197 Neb. 692, 250 N.W.2d 894 (1977) (incorporation of the entire prime contract into the subcontract does not give the subcontractor a right to recover from the prime for everything that gave the prime rights against the owner). *Compare* Seal & Co. v. A.S. McGaughan Co., 907 F.2d 450 (4th Cir. 1990) (subcontractor bound by disputes procedure in prime contract).

The procedure generally used is to provide for the prime's sponsorship of the subcontractor's claim. The subcontractor prepares and prosecutes the claim in the name of the prime, and with the approval of the prime, even though the subcontractor is the immediate party in interest. The prime may take an active part in the claim if its basis is related to other important issues under the prime contract. The FAR expressly recognizes the subcontractor sponsorship procedure for government contracts.[54] Significantly, the prime need not pay the subcontractor before proceeding with a claim, "[i]t is sufficient that the prime contractor acknowledge that he will be liable to the subcontractor if the Government is liable to him."[55] Subcontractor claims and privity requirements vary under state law, and are sometimes addressed by statute.[56]

The arrangement for handling an A/E subcontractor claim can be detailed in a written "Claims Handling and Liquidating Agreement." A basic disputes provision contemplating this procedure under a government contract might read as follows:

> Recognizing that this is a Subcontract under a Government prime contract, the final decision of the Government Contracting Officer relating to this Subcontract or the [A/E Subcontractor's] performance hereunder shall be conclusive and binding upon the [A/E Subcontractor], provided that the [A/E Subcontractor], in the sole discretion of the prime contractor, is given the opportunity to appeal such decision, in the name of the prime contractor, pursuant to the Contract Disputes Act of 1978, 41 U.S.C. §§ 601–613, and fails to do so. The prime contractor shall notify the [A/E Subcontractor] of any final decision within fifteen days of prime contractor's receipt thereof.

A similar contractual agreement is possible for projects not involving the federal government. The primary purpose of any such disputes clause will be to direct an A/E subcontractor's right of recourse for claims caused by the owner. In those cases in which either by agreement with the Owner, or for other reasons, the prime contractor intends to limit or prevent any subcontractor involvement in actions against the owner, the prime may include other language in the subcontract. One alternative is arbitration pursuant to the Construction Industry Arbitration Rules.[57] If an arbitration provision is included in a contract (or subcontract), it is binding and mandatory in most states and under the Federal Arbitration Act.[58] Certain states

---

[54] 48 C.F.R. § 44.203(c) (1990).

[55] TRW, Inc., ASBCA No. 11373, 66-2 B.C.A. (CCH) ¶ 5882, at 27,296 (1966).

[56] *See, e.g.,* APAC-Va. v. Department of Highways & Transp., 9 Va. 450, 388 S.E.2d 841 (1990); Corpus Christi v. Acme Mechanical Constr., Inc., 736 S.W.2d 894 (Tex. 1987); ABC Plumbing & Heating, Inc. v. Dick Corp., 684 S.W.2d 84 (Tenn. 1985).

[57] Available from and administered by the American Arbitration Association, 140 W. 51st St., New York, NY 10020.

[58] 9 U.S.C. §§ 10–11 (1988).

require notifications regarding arbitration provisions, such as a specific statement appearing on the face of the contract documents.[59] The EJCDC, AIA, and AGC documents all make allowance for including arbitration provisions in subcontracts.[60]

§ 15.6 Engineering During Construction

One of the significant factors determining the total cost of A/E professional services to be furnished during the construction phase of a project is the duration of the construction activities requiring those services. Regardless of whether the prime contract is based on a cost-reimbursement or a firm fixed-price form of payment, the anticipated period of performance should be clearly defined. The appropriate period of time for subcontracted A/E services during construction likewise should be clearly defined in the subcontract.

A contract or subcontract simply stating that services are to be furnished "during the construction period" is problematic. At least one A/E was unable to recover an additional fee for inspection services when construction work extended beyond the scheduled date for completion because there was no agreement providing for additional compensation in such an event.[61] Citing cases involving similar contractual language, the United States Department of Transportation Contract Appeals Board held: "the most reasonable reading of the contract is that the architect undertook an obligation to provide services to oversee the construction of the project to its actual completion without regard to the date of that event's occurrence."[62]

An A/E thus should neither automatically rely on the owner to pay for extended inspection services, nor place an A/E subcontractor in the position of absorbing the costs of the extended services.

Another area of legal exposure for A/Es subcontracting construction phase services is the assumption of greater responsibility in practice than is allocated in the contract or subcontract. The standard form contracts for construction are closely coordinated to clearly define the duties and authority of the parties on a construction project.[63] And A/E subcontractor adds

---

[59] *See, e.g.,* Tex. Rev. Civ. Stat. Ann. art. 224–249 (Vernon 1973).

[60] *See, e.g.,* EJCDC 1910-10 (19), ¶ 7.7; AIA C141-19, Art. 7; AGC No. 430 (19), ¶ 8.8.

[61] Perry, Dean, Hepburn & Stewart, DOTCAB Nos. 67-24C, 67-24D, 70-1 B.C.A. (CCH) ¶ 8293, at 38,536–37 (1970). *Accord* Ricciuti Assocs., AGBCA No. 289, 73-2 B.C.A. (CCH) ¶ 10,133, at 10,133–34 (1973), discussing similar cases.

[62] Perry, Dean, Hepburn & Stewart, DOTCAB Nos. 67-24C, 67-24D, 70-1 B.C.A. (CCH) ¶ 8293, at 38,537 (1970).

[63] *See e.g., Suggested Listing of Duties, Responsibilities and Limitations of Authority of Resident Project Representative,* EJCDC 1910-1-A (1983).

yet another party whose duties and authority must be defined. If the A/E prime or subcontractor exercises control over a contractor's means, methods, and procedures of construction, such actions may give rise to liability for negligently exercising that control. Accordingly, it is important to carefully define the lines of authority at the outset and adhere to them throughout the course of the project. Moreover, the A/E should request notification from the owner or construction contractor in the event the A/E's subcontractor acts in a manner inconsistent with that stated in the subcontract.

If an A/E has the contractual right to stop the work upon discovering defective performance or a safety problem, then the A/E also may have a duty to stop the work. The failure to do so could impose liability on the A/E and on the subcontractor for consequent damages or injuries.[64] Likewise, assigning the A/E subcontractor supervisory powers carries the potential for liability.[65] Courts consider this as a matter of the degree of contractual authority over the work performed:

> As a general rule it has been said that the general duty to "supervise the work" merely creates a duty to see that the building when constructed meets the plans and specifications contracted for . . . . In the present case, however, . . . we believe that under the terms of the contracts the architects had the right to interfere and even stop the work if the contractor began to shore in an unsafe and hazardous manner in violation of its contract with the owner.[66]

The courts have further held that "there is no point in calling upon the architect . . . to inspect the progress . . . if the architect may, without incurring any liability, do that work incompetently or not at all."[67] Subcontract language can limit an A/E's supervisory responsibilities by avoiding the use of terms such as "inspect," or "supervise," which imply a detailed

---

[64] Miller v. DeWitt, 37 Ill.2d 273, 226 N.E.2d 630 (1960). *See also* Annotation, *Liability to One Injured in Course of Construction Based upon Architect's Alleged Failure to Carry Out Supervisory Responsibilities,* 59 A.L.R.3d 869 (1974); and Annotation, *Tort Liability of Project Architect for Economic Damages Suffered by Contractor,* 65 A.L.R.3d 249 (1975).

[65] *See, e.g.,* Associated Eng'rs, Inc. v. Job, 370 F.2d 633 (8th Cir. 1966), *cert. denied,* 389 U.S. 823 (1967); and C.W. Regan, Inc. v. Parsons, Brinkerhoff, Quade & Douglas, 411 F.2d 1379 (4th Cir. 1969).

[66] Miller v. DeWitt, 37 Ill.2d 273, 226 N.E.2d 630, 638 (1960) (citing Clinton v. Boehm, 139 A.D. 73, 124 N.Y.S. 789 (1910); Garden City Floral Co. v. Hunt, 126 Mont. 537, 255 P.2d 352 (1953); and Day v. National United States Radiator Corp., 241 La. 288, 128 So. 2d 660 (1961).

[67] White Constr. Co. v. Commonwealth, 11 Mass. App. Ct. 640, 418 N.E.2d 357, 361 (1981), *aff'd,* 385 Mass. 1005, 432 N.E.2d 104 (1982). *See also* Watson, Watson, Rutland/Architects, Inc. v. Montgomery County Bd. of Educ., 559 So. 2d 168 (Ala. 1990) (A/E under a duty to notify owner of known defects).

review of the work. A better approach defines the A/E subcontractor's role as limited to providing assurances that the project will conform with the design intent embodied in the plans and specifications. Similar issues of authority and responsibility often involve the applicability of the state statutes governing A/E liability for structural and other work.[68] These statutes should be carefully evaluated in all jurisdictions where an A/E performs or subcontracts work.

§ 15.7 Exculpatory Clauses

Contract and subcontract documents often attempt to limit liability by exculpatory disclaimer language. As a general rule, overly broad exculpatory language will not be enforced.[69] The basic objective in drafting valid and enforceable exculpatory language is to tailor the language to the subject matter of the particular contract, keeping it as narrow as possible to achieve the desired protection.[70] The level of protection should be reasonable under the circumstances, and the contract negotiations should address the disclaimer.

One example of exculpatory language would be that used by the A/E subcontractor furnishing on-site project representation services during construction. The subcontractor may attempt to disclaim responsibility for the construction contractor's means, methods, and procedures of construction, and for jobsite safety. In either event, no matter how carefully drafted the language may be, to the extent the subcontractor takes actions whereby it in fact assumes responsibility for means, methods, and procedures of construction, or for jobsite safety, disclaimers may be unenforceable.

§ 15.8 Geotechnical Services

Geotechnical engineering and testing services are used by A/Es during planning, designing, and project construction. From a geotechnical subcontractor's perspective, the nature of the work is different when performed for an A/E than for a construction contractor. The areas of focus for contractors can include excavation methods, excavation support, dewatering, and others, all of which constitute the construction contractor's

---

[68] *See, e.g.,* Kleb v. Wendling, 67 Ill. App. 3d 1016, 385 N.E.2d 346 (1979); and Ill. Rev. Stat. ch. 48, paras. 60 and 69 (1985) (statute providing for protection and safety of persons in and about the construction, alteration, or removal of structures).

[69] *See, e.g.,* United Contractors v. United States, 368 F.2d 585 (Ct. Cl. 1966).

[70] *See, e.g.,* P.J. Maffei Bldg. Wrecking Corp. v. United States, 732 F.2d 913 (Fed. Cir. 1984); E.H. Morrill Co. v. State, 65 Cal. 2d 787, 423 P.2d 551 (1967).

methods and procedures of construction, which are not addressed by the plans and specifications. The nature of the geotechnical services rendered will primarily be professional advice.[71]

By contrast, geotechnical engineering and testing services furnished to an A/E frequently involve subsurface exploration for purposes of furnishing subsurface data to a geotechnical engineer for evaluation. A relatively small percentage of the total dollar value of such subcontracts involves the furnishing of professional services, yet there are the attendant risks of performance, including ground water contamination and other environmental concerns. There is no sure way to eliminate or even minimize the exposure to such open-ended risks, but a preferred approach may be to have the geotechnical engineering services performed under a separate prime contract directly with the owner.[72] Before the geotechnical work is undertaken, or even afterwards in some cases, the A/E may insist that the owner deal directly with the geotechnical consultant. The A/E thereafter would only use the data and recommendations furnished by the geotechnical engineer to the owner. Not only does this approach reduce environmental and other unforeseen liabilities, but it obviates the need for the A/E to administer a subcontract.

§ 15.9 Structural Engineering

Perhaps no engineering issue in recent years has received more publicity than the 1981 Hyatt Regency disaster in Kansas City, Missouri. See **Chapter 2**. More than 100 lawsuits subsequently were filed, naming the several A/Es involved as defendants.[73] As a separate but not unrelated result, some A/E firms have dismantled in-house structural engineering departments and now subcontract for these services. By subcontracting the structural engineering work, the A/E has an independent design professional to look to for professional liability and contractual indemnification. Nonetheless, A/Es are still called upon to exercise particular care and judgment in the selection of their consultants and review of the work in this respect.[74]

---

[71] For a related discussion involving soils registration laws, see **Ch. 2**.

[72] EJCDC 1910-27B (19) is available as an agreement between the A/E and geotechnical engineer if required by the owner on a project.

[73] *See* Duncan v. Missouri Bd. for Architects, 744 S.W.2d 524 (Mo. Ct. App. 1988).

[74] *See* Victor, *The Hyatt Collapse—A Post Mortem,* 10 Constr. Law. 7 (1990). *See also* Kahn, *Introduction: The Changing Role of the Architect,* 23 St. Louis U.L.J. 216 (1979).

CHAPTER 16

PREPARING JOINT VENTURE AGREEMENTS

Roger S. Mertz

Roger S. Mertz is a member of the San Francisco law firm of Severson & Werson. His practice includes advising businesses, including architects and engineers, on a wide variety of transactional matters. Mr. Mertz has extensive experience in negotiating domestic and international joint ventures. He is a graduate of Stanford University and the University of Southern California Law Center.

§ 16.1 Introduction

Independent businesses, for many reasons, agree to combine their separate assets, skills, or knowledge to carry out a single business enterprise loosely referred to as a *joint venture.* Documenting a joint venture begins with a thorough analysis of these reasons, because what is called a joint venture in business may take one of many legal forms.

Despite attempts by courts and commentators to create an independent business entity known as a joint venture, having clearly defined and predictable internal and external legal relationships, no such legal entity exists. The frustration of these attempts was expressed well by Judge Learned Hand, who characterized a joint venture as "one of the most obscure and unsatisfactory of legal concepts."[1] Businesses described as joint ventures always take on the legal attributes of the underlying legal entities they most resemble. Differences in the attributes can result in significant differences in external and internal legal consequences. For example, if structured as a partnership, the joint venturers will have unlimited liabilities to third parties; if structured as a corporation, those liabilities ordinarily will be limited. Left ambiguous, the parties risk interpretations most adverse to their interests.

Although the most common form of joint venture is the partnership,[2] before documenting a joint venture it is useful to consider whether some other form of business relationship may be more appropriate. After analysis, many parties find their needs best suited by a jointly owned corporation[3] or a lesser relationship such as a limited partnership,[4] a subcontract, a seconding of employees, a license, or a sale of technology. On the other hand, the parties' needs may be met best by a greater relationship, such as a merger.

Because considering alternative forms of business is so necessary, standard forms of joint venture agreements, such as the American Institute of Architects (AIA) Document C801, Joint Venture Agreement for Professional Services, can provide helpful frameworks for certain types of transactions.

---

[1] National Comics Publications v. Fawcett Publications, 191 F.2d 594, 599 (2d Cir. 1951).

[2] Structuring a joint venture as a partnership "for a specific purpose" or "for a fixed period of time" does not lessen the applicability of partnership rules generally. *See* Bank of Cal. v. Connolly, 36 Cal. App. 3d 350, 364, 111 Cal. Rptr. 468 (1973).

[3] The use of the term *joint venture corporation* may expose the parties to claims that partnership rules should apply to a joint venture operated in the corporate form. *See, e.g.,* Foster v. Keating, 120 Cal. App. 2d 435, 445, 261 P.2d 529 (1953); Elsbach v. Mulligan, 58 Cal. App. 2d 354, 368, 136 P.2d 651 (1943); *but see* Jackson v. Hooper, 76 N.J. Eq. 592, 75 A. 569 (1910).

[4] A limited partner will lose his status as a limited partner and become a general partner vis-à-vis third parties if he participates in the control and management of the partnership. *See, e.g.,* Cal. Corp. Code § 15507(a) (West Supp. 1991), which is identical to Unif. Partnership Act § 7, 6 U.L.A. 38 (1969).

However, such forms should not be used as substitutes for a careful selection of an appropriate relationship for the parties.[5]

In general, when the parties have not made more specific agreements, a relationship denominated a joint venture normally will be treated as a partnership.[6] Joint ventures in the partnership form have many advantages, including the right of joint management and control, ease and minimal expense of organization, flexibility in allocating profits or losses other than in accordance with capital contributions,[7] freedom from fixed corporate governance rules, and the ability to make frequent modifications. Among a number of disadvantages, the most important are the unlimited liability of the joint venturers for the liabilities of the business,[8] the lack of centralized management, and limited transferability of interests.

Businesses contemplating the formation of a joint venture or a lesser relationship should be aware of the inadvertent joint venture. It is possible that loosely structured or preliminary activities may be considered to create a joint venture. This is because a joint venture relationship need not be created in writing, but rather may be implied and inferred, in whole or in part, from the conduct of parties. Courts regularly find joint ventures when there exists (1) a community of interest, that is, a joint interest in a common business undertaking, (2) an understanding as to the sharing of profits and losses, and (3) a right of joint control.[9]

Businesses commonly contribute small amounts of capital or resources to a prospective business. Absent proper documentation, the parties risk that the relationship will be deemed to be a joint venture with the consequences of unlimited liabilities to third parties, fiduciary duties, and a commingling of property. Even though the parties believe that their preliminary efforts have not created a legal relationship, courts regularly find that the relationship is not so indefinite as to preclude the existence of a joint venture.[10]

---

[5] For other forms of joint venture agreements, *see* 3 A. Dib, Forms and Agreements for Architects, Engineers and Contractors, ch. 14 (1989), and Transnational Joint Ventures 1001–1012 (P. Fitzpatrick ed. 1989).

[6] In California, it has been held that the relations of joint venturers as between themselves and as to third parties are generally the same as those of partners, and to the extent they are the same are governed by the same law as partnerships. Orlopp v. Willardson Co., 232 Cal. App. 2d 750, 754, 43 Cal. Rptr. 125 (1965).

[7] Subject to the requirement, for federal income tax purposes, that the allocation must have a "substantial economic effect" independent of income tax consequences or it will be disregarded. I.R.C. § 704(b)(2) (1989).

[8] As in the case of partnerships, liability for the negligent acts of the ventures is joint and several. Lemming v. Oilfields Trucking Co., 44 Cal. 2d 343, 350, 282 P.2d 23 (1955). As a result, a claimant may elect to claim against any one of the members and sue him alone.

[9] Holtz v. United Plumbing & Heating Co., 49 Cal. 2d 501, 506–07, 319 P.2d 617 (1957).

[10] *See, e.g.*, Mason v. Rose, 176 F.2d 486 (2d Cir. 1949).

§ 16.2 Structuring a Joint Venture

Objectives. The documentation of a joint venture relationship cannot commence until the objectives of the parties are identified. The formation of a joint venture usually begins with a party's desire to enter a new business or a new market. The parties must ask many questions of themselves, such as, "Why not go it alone?" The answer may be the risks are too great, or the party does not have the resources to enter the business alone, or has only the technology without the marketing relationships. Is one party or the other looking for a permanent relationship, or is there just one project in mind? Is a party looking for a short-term relationship with the objective of "going it alone" after learning as much as it can from the other joint venturer? For foreign or out-of-territory projects, is it necessary to have a local partner who knows the laws, customs, and prospective local clients? Do the parties have to demonstrate multiple disciplines to compete with others who have such skills? Do you want a horizontal relationship, such as between an architect and an engineer, or a vertical relationship, such as between an architect/engineer and an owner? Short-term and long-term objectives and needs should be identified. Are there conflicting objectives? Are there tax considerations?

Strengths. It is also important to determine the respective strengths of the prospective joint venturers. Do you have technology, capital, business relationships, geographic experience, complementary skills, or other resources? Also determine the weaknesses or vulnerabilities of the parties. If the joint venture business is likely to be capital intensive, will you have the resources to put up additional capital if it is needed? If you are to supply services, can you supply them in a timely, professionally competent manner, consistent with your other business obligations?

Business plan. Having in hand the business and financial plan for the joint venture also will be helpful to the drafting process. Depending on the nature of the project, such a plan will involve the financial projections, staffing needs, capital requirements, and general operating plan.

Negotiation. Finally, the drafting process can be facilitated if the parties have developed an intelligent negotiation plan. Such a plan involves identifying prenegotiation issues, possibly drafting a letter of intent,[11] preparing

---

[11] Considerable care must be exercised in preparing letters of intent. For a discussion of the current status of the law with regard to letters of intent, *see* Temken, *When Does the "Fat Lady" Sing?: An Analysis of Agreements in Principle in Corporate Acquisitions,* 55 Fordham L. Rev. 125 (1986), and Comment, *Devil's Advocate: Salvaging the Letter of Intent,* 37 Emory L.J. 139 (1988). For a model letter of intent to create a joint venture in the corporate form, *see* Transnational Joint Ventures 1001 (P. Fitzpatrick ed. 1989).

and implementing a due diligence plan, establishing a schedule, and assembling an appropriate negotiation and due diligence team. When confidential information is being exchanged before the joint venture's formation, the parties will want to enter into confidentiality agreements to preserve the integrity and confidentiality of the information being exchanged and to insure return if the joint venture is not formed.

§ 16.3 Alternative Structures

Regardless of the legal form of the joint venture, the main variables of any structure will be (1) the duration of the joint venture, (2) the degree of risk undertaken by the partners, and (3) the degree of interrelationship between the businesses of the venturers and the business of the joint venture. A short time frame for the venture suggests a partnership form; a more permanent business suggests a corporate form. A less permanent form is suggested when the venture is nonintegrated, that is, when the venturers' activities are to be closely tied in with the joint venture. A more permanent form is suggested when the venture is integrated, or when all of the business will be conducted by the joint venture.

After the essential information has been collected and analyzed, the actual drafting of the agreements can begin. The documentation for a traditional joint venture with internal and external partnership legal consequences normally consists of a joint venture agreement. If the arrangement is project specific, AIA Document C801 can serve as a basic framework. Conventional partnership agreements also can serve as basic frameworks for such an arrangement. If a party will be providing the joint venture with intellectual property, for example, computer software, trademarks, know-how, or other technology, a separate license agreement should be prepared. If a party is supplying professional services, a separate services agreement should be prepared. Both agreements should contain the usual and customary terms appropriate for such relationships. These agreements can serve as mechanisms for allocating the risks of the business on a basis other than in accordance with the agreed-upon allocation of profits and losses.

The documentation of a joint venture in corporate form typically requires a series of documents, beginning with a preincorporation or shareholders' agreement (commonly denominated "Shareholders' Agreement," "Joint Venture Agreement," or "Joint Venture Company Agreement"). This agreement obligates the parties to form and capitalize the jointly owned company, and it establishes the parties' duties to each other and to the joint venture. Usual shareholder agreement concepts apply to the formation and operation of a joint venture. The shareholders' agreement provides for a series of subsidiary agreements, such as the articles of incorporation and bylaws of the company. Because of the nature of corporate law, these documents spell out the basic understandings of the parties regarding structure, capitalization, control, and corporate governance.

As with a joint venture operated in partnership form, the shareholders' agreement ordinarily provides for subsidiary agreements with respect to intellectual property, services, supplies, subleases, and other similar relationships.

§ 16.4 Drafting a Joint Venture Agreement

Following is a review of the principal issues that should be considered in drafting a joint venture agreement:

Choice of entity. The first issue that must be addressed is the legal relationship under local law that will govern the relationship between the joint venturers with respect to both internal and external legal issues. Some of the factors influencing such a decision are described in **§ 16.2**. Although the following discussion assumes that the form of the transaction will be either a partnership or a corporation, many issues apply to other legal forms as well.

Parties. It may seem obvious, but the parties to the joint venture should be identified at the beginning of the contract. In addition, consider making your affiliates[12] and the affiliates of your joint venturer beneficiaries of the agreement and bound by it. For example, if the agreement provides for confidentiality of information or for noncompetition, it is appropriate for the joint venturers' affiliates to be bound by, or for the joint venturers to cause them to be bound by, the terms of the agreement.

Scope. The scope of the joint venture should be specified in detail. The more specific the scope, the greater is the likelihood that the parties have reached a common understanding as to the joint venture's proposed business. AIA Document C801 provides for the scope of the joint venture to be project specific. However, if the joint venturers intend to be engaged in business for more than one project, a more general scope should be specified. Although possible, having a series of project-specific agreements is not recommended.

The scope section is an appropriate place to set forth the geographic territory of the joint venture's activities and the type of services to be provided. The form of business should be specified, of course. The scope section also

[12] The term *affiliate* should be defined in the agreement. A commonly used definition is "a person controlling, controlled by or under common control with another person." Investment Company Act of 1940, 15 U.S.C.A. § 80a-2(3)(C) (1981).

is an appropriate place in the agreement to set forth any limitations on the parties' rights to act on behalf of the joint venture. Absent such limitations, under normal rules applicable to partnerships, each joint venturer has the power to bind the joint venture with respect to matters within the scope of the venture's activities.[13] A carefully drafted scope also will state that the scope will not be changed without agreement of both joint venturers. A limited scope also will lessen the fiduciary duties owed by the joint venturers with respect to corporate opportunities.[14]

Name. Problems with proposed names may arise early and may have legal implications beyond the pride of the respective parties. The name under which the joint venture will operate should be agreed upon early. The availability of the name under trademark laws or corporate or partnership registration statutes should be ascertained before marketing and other brochures are prepared. In addition, many states have limitations on the names that may be used by certain design professionals.[15]

Term. The term of the joint venture should be specified. If the purpose of the joint venture is the completion of a specific project, the completion of the project should be the termination date. However, provision should be made for the joint venture to continue for such time as may be necessary to satisfy obligations that remain after completion of the project, such as post-completion assistance, claims, and the normal steps necessary to wind up and dissolve a business. Whether the joint venture is operated as a partnership or as a corporation, absent a contrary provision, the parties will have broad rights to dissolve the business.[16] For example, a joint venturer may cause the dissolution of the joint venture upon the giving of notice in the manner similar to a partnership. Similarly, under corporate law shareholders are given broad rights to cause the dissolution of the corporation, particularly in cases of deadlock and fraud.[17]

---

[13] It is customary to provide that the joint venturers must indemnify the joint venture and the other joint venturers from unauthorized acts.

[14] "The officer and directors who occupy the dual positions are fiduciaries to both companies and owe a duty of loyalty to each. Thus, they cannot favor the interest of one corporation while sacrificing or betraying those of the other." Western Pa. R.R. Corp. v. Western Pa. R.R. Co., 192 F.2d 994, 1000 (9th Cir. 1951), *rev'd on other grounds,* 345 U.S. 247 (1953).

[15] *See, e.g.,* Cal. Bus. & Prof. Code § 6738(a)(3) (West Supp. 1991).

[16] Cal. Corp. Code §§ 15029–15032 (West 1977 & Supp. 1991); Del. Code Ann. tit. 6, §§ 1529–1532 (1990) (dissolution of partnerships); Cal. Corp. Code §§ 1800–1809, 1900–1907 (West 1990); Del. Code Ann. tit. 8, §§ 273–285 (1990) (dissolution of corporations).

[17] Normally, such rights exist only when the shares of the corporation are owned 50/50 by the parties. Some statutes permit shareholders holding small amounts of stock to request a judicially supervised dissolution. See Cal. Corp. Code § 1800 (West 1990).

In the case of a corporation, which ordinarily will have perpetual existence, absent a contrary provision in the articles of incorporation, the shareholders' agreement should provide the date for the shareholders to agree to wind up and dissolve the corporation. At the same time, it is appropriate in the shareholders' agreement to require the shareholders not to petition the courts for a premature liquidation of the corporation before the completion of its agreed-upon term.[18]

The agreement also should provide for return of confidential information, post-termination confidentiality of such information, payment of debts and taxes, completion of outstanding contracts, indemnity, noncompetition, and distribution of remaining assets.

§ 16.5 —Capital Contributions

Initial and subsequent. The joint venture agreement, most importantly, must provide for the capital contributions to be made by the joint venturers. The agreement should set forth the amount, nature, and time of payment of the capital contributions. Both the initial contributions and subsequent contributions, if any, should be provided for.

Default provisions. Provisions must be included to deal with situations in which a joint venturer fails to honor a promise to make a subsequent capital contribution. AIA Document C801 provides for a defaulting party's distributions to be held in an escrow.[19] Other alternatives include diluting the defaulting venturer's interest based on a formula, or granting the other joint venturer the right to make the contribution, with such payment to be a lien on the interest of the defaulting party repayable, with interest, from the share of the defaulting party. In other cases, particularly when there is a fundamental disagreement over the direction and future of the joint venture's business, the agreement will provide for termination of the joint venture or a right on the part of the other joint venturer to buy out the interest of the noncontributing joint venturer. Some care is necessary to draft the provisions in a way that does not encourage a party to use the procedures as a way to buy out the other partner in a successful joint venture.

---

[18] To avoid problems, it is wise to include in the joint venture agreement, following whatever provisions are agreed upon with respect to liquidation, a clause similar to the following: "The parties agree that the sole procedure for dissolution of the Joint Venture shall be the foregoing; and the parties specifically agree not to exercise any rights they might have under applicable law for the involuntary winding up and dissolution of the Joint Venture."

[19] *See* AIA C801-1979, Art. 21.2.2.

Guarantees. Joint venturers frequently agree to guarantee loans, leases, or other obligations of the joint venture. Such venturers should consider an agreement stating that the repayment of any such guarantees is ahead of any joint venture repayments of capital or distributions of profits. Also, a guaranteeing joint venturer should consider taking a security interest in the joint venture's assets to secure its obligations under the guarantee.

Title to property. The general confusion that exists over the legal status of joint ventures has affected the law applicable to title to property. The joint venture agreement should provide how title to property is to be held. Historically, property held by a joint venture was held in the names of the joint venturers as tenants in common or in the name of one of the joint venturers as an implied or expressed trustee for the other joint venturers. However, because of the possibility of such property being attached by the title-holding joint venturer's creditors, such a method is undesirable. A better course is for the joint venture's property to be held in the name of the joint venture. However, these issues are governed by the law of the jurisdiction where the property is located, and such law should be consulted before title is taken to any property.

§ 16.6 —Management

The sharing of management and control of the business is characteristic of any joint venture. Structuring the sharing relationship requires a delicate balance between fair participation by venturers, on one hand, and unified, unambiguous direction and control on the other. No single management structure works for all joint ventures, but rather, various elements must be combined to design the optimum structure suitable to the duration of the venture, subject matters, risks, and relationships of the venturers.

Most joint ventures, whether partnerships or corporations, have some form of policy board or board of directors. The role of this board is to establish overall direction and policy for the venture. The representatives on this board have the dual roles of representing their own party's interest while making sure these interests are reconciled with the interests of the venture and of the other parties.[20] The structuring of this board is probably

[20] "The officer and directors who occupy the dual positions are fiduciaries to both companies and owe a duty of loyalty to each. Thus, they cannot favor the interest of one corporation while sacrificing or betraying those of the other." Western Pa. R.R. v. Western Pa. R.R., 192 F.2d 994, 1000 (9th Cir. 1951), *rev'd on other grounds,* 345 U.S. 247 (1953).

the most important way a joint venturer can exercise control over the management of the joint venture.[21]

The most common form of express control is for the board to be composed of an equal number of representatives from each joint venturer. The effect of such a structure is to give each joint venturer a veto power over the affairs of the joint venture. To maintain voting equality, the agreement should obligate the parties to elect the other's nominees, because if a director resigns or dies, the other party, under conventional corporate law principles, will have the right to elect a replacement.

A clause similar to the following should be included in the joint venture agreement:

> At any meeting of shareholders at which members of the board of directors are to be elected, the joint venturers shall vote their respective shares in favor of the other party's nominees in order to assure the election of such nominees.

In some instances it may not be possible to keep the board equally divided. It may be desirable to include on the board a person unaffiliated with either party, but who can make a contribution to the board's work. Typically, this might be the chief executive of the joint venture. Also, there may be instances in which one or more of the directors may be unable to attend a meeting. Such an event will result in shifting the majority to one side or the other.

To preserve the veto power, it may be appropriate to create certain supermajority issues in which the consent of both parties is required to approve a particular matter. Local law will determine whether the provisions should be in the joint venture agreement, the articles of incorporation, or bylaws of the joint venture. Typical supermajority decisions include the contribution of additional capital, the admission of new joint venturers, the authorization of major contracts and bids, the changing of the scope of the joint venture, the payment of dividends and distributions, the authorization of borrowings, the establishment of pricing, and the selection of operating management. Probably the most important supermajority right for a joint venturer is the right to approve an annual business plan or budget, because without such approval the joint venture's business cannot proceed.

Control can be exercised in a number of ways other than through voting rights. For example, one joint venturer may be granted the right to select or supply certain executive officers of the venture. If one venturer is supplying technology and the other marketing, it may make sense for the technology

---

[21] A party at risk ordinarily will want a say in the management of the venture. However, it is possible to delegate all of the operations of the joint venture to one party. This is commonly referred to as the *sponsor method* of joint venture management. Before adopting such a structure, both parties should seriously consider whether some other form of structure is more appropriate.

partner to select the joint venture's chief technical officer and the marketing partner to select the joint venture's chief marketing officer. Some joint venturers find the most effective way to have a say in the joint venture is to have the right to select the joint venture's chief financial officer. A joint venturer can exercise control by being contractually responsible for marketing, for controlling technology, or for providing technical assistance. Other control mechanisms include having voting and nonvoting stock, rotating chairmanships, and classified boards of directors (boards with two or more classes of directors, such as one class elected by common shareholders and another elected by preferred shareholders).[22]

When the venture is a corporation, local laws governing the entity must be carefully checked. In many domestic jurisdictions and foreign countries, even minority shareholders have substantial powers to direct or cause dissolution and other doomsday remedies. It is common for the parties to covenant not to exercise their rights under such statutes.[23]

Ordinarily in structuring corporations or partnerships, the positions and duties of the executive management will be left to the discretion of the board. In a joint venture, these positions are established in the joint venture agreement. In particular, the duties of the managing partner or president should be spelled out. As noted, one of the parties may be granted the right to appoint particular officers of the joint venture.

Any structure that provides for the right of venturers to veto some or all management decisions leads to the possibility of deadlock. Consequently, it is necessary to consider creating mechanisms to deal with this possibility.

There may be some instances in which the disagreements between the parties are so fundamental that a mechanism to break the deadlock serves no purpose. In such cases, some other procedure, such as dissolution, or a right for one party to buy out the other may be the only sensible solution. Under one commonly used arrangement, each of the parties is given the right to make an offer to the other to purchase its interest. The party receiving the offer is then given the choice to either buy the offering venturer's interest or to sell its interest to the offering venturer, in each case at the price set forth in the initial offer. Such a procedure, however, can put a cash-poor venturer at a disadvantage because it is unable to purchase and can only sell.

---

[22] For other methods of structuring a board of directors and other methods of exercising control, see Comment, *Protecting the Entrepreneur: Concerns for International Joint Venture Contracts,* 14 U.C. Davis L. Rev. 1001 (1981).

[23] To avoid problems, it is wise to include in the joint venture agreement, following whatever provisions are agreed upon with respect to liquidation, a clause similar to the following: "The parties agree that the sole procedure for the dissolution of the Joint Venture shall be the foregoing; and the parties specifically agree not to exercise any rights they might have under applicable law for the involuntary winding up and dissolution of the Joint Venture."

In other cases, the issues may not be fundamental and a deadlock-breaking mechanism may be useful. Already noted was the possibility of having a neutral party on the board of directors. Other possibilities include granting to one of the parties or to the operating management the right to make decisions with respect to specific types of matters.

When the issues are of a fundamental nature, as a last resort, the parties may wish to submit their dispute to arbitration or to the courts.[24]

§ 16.7 —Compensation

Indirect compensation. In establishing a joint venture, the parties should consider and agree upon possible forms of indirect compensation. Such indirect compensation can be part of the allocation of profits of the joint venture. For example, a joint venturer may bargain for royalties on technology licensed to the joint venture. Similarly, if the joint venturers are supplying services or goods to the joint venture, agreements should be reached in advance on pricing, including levels of overhead and profit, if any.[25]

Direct compensation. In the most simple partnership, a joint venturer's direct compensation will be its percentage interest in the joint venture's profits and losses. In the corporate context, a joint venturer's compensation will be its percentage interest in the dividends declared and paid by the corporation. An infinite variety of other methods of compensation also can be agreed upon. AIA Document C801 sets forth two commonly used methods of compensation in project-specific joint ventures. The so-called *division of profits/losses* method allocates profits and losses based on percentage interests fixed in advance. The alternative *division of compensation* method divides profits based on the amount of value or services to be provided to the joint venture by the party. Using this formula, a party providing 90 percent, by value, of services to the project would receive 90 percent of the profits or losses.

Allocation of cash flow. Actual profits and losses of the joint venture may not match cash flow. For example, if the joint venture accounts for profits and losses on an accrual basis, revenue may be realized and recognized long before the cash from the collection of accounts receivable is received. As a result, it is also desirable to agree on how and when cash is to be distributed from the joint venture in the form of profit distributions or dividends.

---

[24] For a discussion of mechanisms for dealing with deadlock, *see* Note, *Joint Venture Corporations: Drafting the Corporate Papers,* 78 Harv. L. Rev. 393, 398–401 (1964).

[25] *See, e.g.,* the treatment of this problem in AIA C801-1979, Reimbursements, § 21.5.

Financial issues. Several financial issues must be addressed in the joint venture agreement. The first is what accounting principles will be used in accounting for the joint venture's business. These include simple concepts, such as income and expense recognition (usually cash versus accrual), and more complex issues, such as methods of depreciation. A fiscal year should be agreed upon. This may have importance to the venturers if they have different fiscal years. Whether or not the joint venture's accounts will be audited and by whom should be addressed. There should also be an obligation on the part of the joint venture to provide the joint venturers with periodic financial statements and other requested information.

§ 16.8 —Allocation of Liability and Risk

The providing of professional services in the context of a joint venture entails complex risks and liabilities to clients, third parties, and to coventurers. The joint venture agreement must create a framework for the allocation of these risks. However, no agreement between the joint venturers will limit the liabilities of a party to clients and third parties under statutory and common law. It is also important to distinguish the various types of obligations that may arise. Different treatment may be appropriate for different liabilities. For example, the parties may agree to obligate themselves for bank borrowings in accordance with their respective interests in profits and losses, whereas liabilities for professional errors and omissions may be allocated 100 percent to the party committing the error.

When the joint venture is structured in a partnership form, the allocation of liabilities will depend on whether the arrangement is nonintegrated or integrated. If nonintegrated, the agreement normally will provide for each party to be responsible for losses and claims arising out of its work. To reflect this allocation, the joint venture agreement should provide for the indemnifying party to indemnify the joint venture and the other joint venturers for all losses and claims arising out of the indemnifying party's work.

A short-form cross-indemnity clause is as follows:

> To the extent permitted by law, each Party agrees to indemnify and hold harmless the other Party and the Joint Venture against all loss, damage, liability, claim or suit (including related expenses and attorneys' fees), resulting from injury to any person or damage to any property in any way connected with the performance of services by such Party pursuant to this Agreement whether in contract, indemnity, tort (including negligence, whether active, passive, or any other kind) or otherwise. The provisions of this paragraph shall survive the termination or cancellation of this Agreement, or the completion of the services performed hereunder.

The agreement also should deal with the situation in which the indemnifying party is, for example, 95 percent responsible and the other joint venturer is 5 percent responsible. Indemnifying joint venturers should consider whether their indemnity obligations are broader than their professional liability insurance. Generally, most professional and general liability insurance policies exclude liabilities that are created by contract, and as a result, to the extent a party agrees to indemnify another for liabilities beyond those owed by the party under common law, there may be no insurance to back up the indemnity.

When the joint venture is structured in a partnership form but operated as an *integrated venture,* or when the joint venture is structured as a corporation, the joint venture will bear risks and liabilities and the parties will bear such losses in accordance with the agreement's profit allocation formula. In such case, it is important for the joint venture to have its own insurance.

The parties also should keep in mind the subsidiary agreements in terms of liability and allocation of risk. As noted, the joint venturers may enter into a variety of agreements with the joint venture to provide technology, services, products, space, computer services, and the like. Absent contractual limitations, the supplier will have common law duties to the joint venture. In some cases, these duties may be appropriate. For example, if computer programs are being licensed, it is appropriate for the licensor to be fully responsible for infringement claims. In other cases, the duties may be inappropriate, such as when employees are being "loaned" to the joint venture.

Careful attention must be paid to employee liabilities. The agreement should provide for the employing joint venturer to be responsible for all compensation and fringe benefits of the "borrowed" employees.

§ 16.9 —Confidentiality

Joint venturers frequently contribute to the joint venture information they believe to be confidential and proprietary. Such information ranges from marketing information to computer programs. The contributing joint venturer wants the information to remain confidential. Accordingly, the joint venture agreement should contain a confidentiality provision. Such a provision typically obligates the joint venture and the other joint venturer to maintain the confidentiality of the information and to return all such information at the termination of the joint venture. So there is no dispute over what is confidential and what is not, the agreement should carefully describe the information considered to be confidential or require the disclosing party to identify in advance and mark the information deemed by it to be confidential. Typically, the confidentiality agreement would exclude information that is in the public domain or that the promising party learns about through some other means.

A typical short-form confidentiality clause reads as follows:

> All information disclosed by either Party to the other Party or to the Joint Venture in pursuance of this Agreement and declared in writing to be confidential by the party making such disclosure (the "Confidential Information") shall, during the continuance of this Agreement and for two years after its expiration or termination, be kept confidential, and the Joint Venture and/or party to which the same has been disclosed shall take all necessary precautions to prevent its disclosure to third parties. The Parties shall have the right to disclose the Confidential Information to any of their Affiliates, provided such Affiliates receiving the Confidential Information shall agree to be bound by the provisions of this paragraph, and provided further, that the disclosing Party agrees to be responsible for the actions of its Affiliates.
>
> Notwithstanding the foregoing, the provisions of the foregoing paragraph shall not apply to: (i) any such information which at any time after its disclosure by one Party to the other or to the Joint Venture falls into the public domain, except as a result of the fault of the Joint Venture or of the Party to which it was disclosed; (ii) any such information which at the time of its disclosure was known to the Joint Venture or to the Party to which it was disclosed, as evidenced by written records; or (iii) any information that regulatory bodies request be disclosed to them, provided that the Joint Venture shall use its best efforts to cause said regulatory bodies to agree to hold such information confidential.

To fulfill its confidentiality obligations, the joint venture and the other joint venturer should make sure its employees are aware of the confidentiality agreement. They can do this by having their employees enter into confidentiality agreements that incorporate the confidentiality obligations.[26]

§ 16.10 —Exclusivity and Noncompetition

In many instances, it will be appropriate for the joint venturers to agree to certain exclusivity for the joint venture. Exclusivity can apply to geographic area or line of business or be client specific. Such an arrangement, for example, might provide for the joint venturers to engage exclusively through the joint venture in the field of chemical plant design and construction. These provisions may raise issues under the antitrust laws. When large companies with significant market shares and strength combine in some common undertaking, antitrust considerations become very important.

[26] For a selection of confidentiality agreements used in architectural and engineering practice, *see* 3 A. Dib, Forms and Agreements for Architects, Engineers and Contractors, ch. 12 (1989).

When smaller entities who are not competitors combine, generally there should be no antitrust problems. There are few situations in which architects and engineers with complementary skills cannot combine in a joint venture.[27]

§ 16.11 —Representations and Warranties

It may be desirable for the joint venture agreement to provide for specific representations and warranties when those are important to the joint venture. Beyond common representations regarding the authority of the parties to enter into the contract, the due execution and delivery, and the absence of conflicting agreements, a joint venture partner may want to consider representations from the other party regarding professional licensing, qualification to do business, capabilities, and title to property.

§ 16.12 —Transferability of Interests, Withdrawal, and Removal

Because joint ventures generally require continuing contributions from the venturers, the joint venture agreement normally restricts the ability of venturers to transfer or assign their interests.

It is important not to allow transferability to be governed by statutory or common law. If the agreement is structured as a partnership, under general principles of partnership law a substitution of a new partner without the consent of the other is impossible, although a partner may assign the economic benefit of its interest without approval of the other partner.[28] When the joint venture is structured as a corporation, stock will be issued, and absent restrictions, the shares will be freely transferable.[29]

If restrictions on transfer cannot be agreed upon, the interests of the nontransferring joint venture may be protected by having the transferring joint venturer contractually bound to provide the joint venture with those items of property, skill, or knowledge that are expected of it.

The harshest form of restriction is an absolute prohibition on transfer, but it is unlikely that such a provision will be enforced in most jurisdictions

---

[27] The leading case with respect to these issues is United States v. Penn-Olin Chem. Co., 38 U.S. 158 (1964). For a discussion of these issues, *see* Pitofsky, *Joint Ventures under the Antitrust Laws,* 82 Harv. L. Rev. 1007 (1968); J. von Kalinowski, Antitrust Laws and Trade Regulation Desk Edition § 2.05 (1990); and T. Vakerics, Antitrust Basics, ch. 10 (1990).

[28] A conveyance by a partner does not entitle the assignee to interfere in the management of the business, but merely entitles the assignee to receive the profits to which the assigning partner would otherwise be entitled. Cal. Corp. Code § 15027 (West 1977).

[29] Subject to such restrictions that may exist under federal and state securities laws.

because of public policies favoring the free alienability of property. However, such provisions probably will be enforced if they are limited in time. Such an arrangement may assure the nontransferring venturer that the joint venture will receive what the transferring venturer promised at the outset of the business. It is common, but not necessary, for the agreement to exclude transfers to affiliates from the restrictions on transfer.[30] The interests of the parties may be protected by allowing shares to be transferred, but only with the prior consent of the nontransferring party.

Other possibilities include a right of first refusal and event-oriented options. For example, if a transferring party desires to transfer its interest, the nontransferring party is given a right to purchase the interest at the price and on the terms being offered by the third party. Alternatively, the purchase price can be a formula agreed upon in advance. It also is possible to give the parties rights to acquire the other party's interest in the event of a change in control of a party, following the passage of time, or in the event of insolvency, bankruptcy, or breach of the agreement.

When more than two parties are involved, it may be desirable to provide for circumstances under which a joint venturer may withdraw, as well as for circumstances under which a joint venturer may be forced from the joint venture. Breach of obligations under the agreement, bankruptcy, and insolvency are events that typically allow the other joint venturer to withdraw from or terminate the joint venture.

§ 16.13 —Dispute Resolution

Because the parties may disagree over a wide variety of issues, it is appropriate for the joint venture agreement to provide for multiple mechanisms to resolve these disputes. It is not necessarily appropriate for the parties to seek third-party arbitration of every dispute. Routine disputes can and should be dealt with using the management mechanisms described.

Because of the cooperative nature of joint ventures, it is common for arbitration to be the preferred mechanism for resolving major disputes. This is particularly so in connection with multinational arrangements. Before including an arbitration clause, consider the usefulness of such a procedure to the particular situation. Beyond the issues of cost, time, and lack of appeal, which may not favor arbitration over conventional litigation, there are other issues that may make arbitration less than satisfactory or that require the arbitration clause to be custom-drafted for the transaction. For example, many experts believe arbitration to be undesirable when professional negligence is at issue because of the tendency of arbitrators to "split the baby." Also, parties contemplating the use of arbitration should make

---

[30] See § **16.4**.

sure that injunctions and other interim remedies are not precluded by the form of arbitration clause.

A form of arbitration clause providing for arbitration under American Arbitration Association rules in California is as follows:

Arbitration. Any controversy between the parties involving enforcement, construction, or application of this Agreement, shall be submitted to binding and final arbitration in accordance with the rules of the American Arbitration Association, which arbitration shall comply with and be governed by the provisions of the California Arbitration Act, presently codified at California Code of Civil Procedure, section 1280 through 1294.2. The provisions of California Code of Civil Procedure section 1203.05 are incorporated into and may be applicable to this Agreement. The arbitration panel shall consist of three members, unless the parties are able to agree on one arbitrator. If the parties are unable to agree on one arbitrator then each party shall select one arbitrator. Those two arbitrators together shall appoint a third arbitrator. If the two arbitrators are unable to agree to a third arbitrator within ten days, then one or both of them immediately shall apply to the Presiding Judge of the San Francisco County Superior Court for appointment of a neutral, third arbitrator. Once selected, these three arbitrators shall constitute the panel and any decision by a majority of them shall be binding upon the parties. Judgment on any award entered by the arbitration panel pursuant to this Agreement may be entered by any court having jurisdiction. The arbitration shall take place in San Francisco, California and shall be in English.

The parties understand and agree the arbitration will be their exclusive form of resolving disputes between them regarding the issues covered by this Agreement. BOTH PARTIES EXPRESSLY WAIVE THEIR ENTITLEMENT, IF ANY, TO HAVE CONTROVERSIES BETWEEN THEM DECIDED BY A JURY OR COURT OF LAW.

Whether disputes are resolved by arbitration or otherwise, the agreement should include a forum or place for dispute resolution, as well as a governing law.

§ 16.14 —Fiduciary Duties

The relationship between the parties as joint venturers creates substantial fiduciary duties of the parties to each other. The relationship also creates substantial fiduciary duties of the parties' representatives to the joint venture and to the other joint venturer. Three duties come into play in the typical joint venture: (1) the duty of disclosure, (2) the obligation against self-dealing, and (3) the duty not to take personal advantage of corporate opportunities.

Under the duty of disclosure, a fiduciary is obligated to disclose to the joint venture all of the information within its knowledge relevant to the joint venture's business. Conflict arises when disclosure of the information will benefit the joint venture at the expense of the disclosing party. Conflicts also arise when a joint venturer is dealing with the joint venture. If the joint venturer gets the better of the deal at the expense of the joint venture, the self-dealing party is exposed to a claim by the other joint venturer that the transaction was unfair and constituted a breach of the joint venture agreement with regard to the allocation of profits and losses. The fiduciary duty with regard to corporate opportunities requires the fiduciary to offer to the joint venture all business opportunities reasonably related to its contemplated business. Conflict arises when the joint venturer prefers to take advantage of the opportunity for its own benefit.

There is a legal issue as to whether these fiduciary duties survive incorporation of the business. There is some authority that the fiduciary duties and the relationship of trust and confidence that precede the incorporation of the joint venture do not survive such incorporation.[31] The reason appears to be that the limited liabilities of shareholders under corporate law cut off any preexisting duty. It is clear, however, that courts enforce fiduciary duties between parties that engage in unincorporated joint ventures. It is equally clear that the representative directors of each of the parties have fiduciary duties to the joint venture and to its shareholder-joint venturers. The fact that such representatives have conflicting duties, on one hand to the joint venture and on the other hand to their employers, does not immunize them against claims. One cannot fulfill one fiduciary duty by breaching another.[32]

Accordingly, it is appropriate in a well-drafted joint venture agreement to deal with these issues as completely as possible. With regard to the duty of disclosure, the parties should carefully describe the types of information they are obligated to disclose to the joint venture and negate the obligation to disclose any other types of information.

Corporate opportunity duties can be dealt with in several ways. The first is by a narrow drafting of the scope of the joint venture. The second is by including a specific disclaimer.

A clause similar to the following may be included in the agreement:

Corporate Opportunities. The parties shall be obligated to present business opportunities to the Joint Venture if such opportunities relate to [describe field of business with respect to which opportunities must be disclosed]. Otherwise, the parties shall not be obligated to present any particular business

---

[31] Jackson v. Hooper, 76 N.J. Eq. 592, 75 A. 568 (1910).

[32] "The officer and directors who occupy the dual positions are fiduciaries to both companies and owe a duty of loyalty to each. Thus, they cannot favor the interest of one corporation while sacrificing or betraying those of the other." Western Pa. R.R. v. Western Pa. R.R., 192 F.2d 994, 1000 (9th Cir. 1951), *rev'd on other grounds,* 345 U.S. 247 (1953) [add city to jury instruction].

opportunity to the Joint Venture, even if the opportunity is of a character that, if presented to the Joint Venture, could be taken by the Joint Venture, and such party shall have the right to take for its own account.

The agreement also can include a provision to protect the officers who serve both the joint venture and a joint venturer.

The following can be used for this purpose:

> The Joint Venture's officers and directors may hold positions as officers and directors of other businesses and the effort to further the interests of such businesses in serving in such positions will not constitute a breach of their fiduciary duty to the Joint Venture.

§ 16.15 —Time Schedule

The joint venture agreement should set forth a time schedule for organizing the joint venture corporation or partnership, contributing the agreed-upon capital and other property to the joint venture, obtaining governmental and other approvals, and commencing business. This section of the agreement also can provide for an allocation of responsibilities between the joint venturers for completing all of the tasks and conditions necessary to commence business. Attorneys generally believe it advantageous to have drafting responsibilities, and this section may provide for an allocation of this task.

§ 16.16 —Conditions Precedent

The commencement of the joint venture business and the obligations of the parties to contribute capital ordinarily are subject to a number of conditions. Common conditions precedent include getting approval of the joint venturers' boards of directors (and sometimes shareholders), governmental approval, obtaining insurance, obtaining professional licenses, delivery of documents, and payment of the initial capitalization.

CHAPTER 17

CONTRACT PROVISIONS LIMITING LIABILITY

Robert E. Kerrigan, Jr.
Victor E. Stilwell, Jr.

Robert Emmett Kerrigan, Jr., is a partner in the law firm of Deutsch, Kerrigan & Stiles in New Orleans, Louisiana. His practice includes general aviation, securities, commercial, product defect, toxic waste and environmental litigation, professional liability defense, and personal injury litigation. He received an A.B. from Spring Hill College and a J.D. from Tulane University. Mr. Kerrigan is an Active Master of the Bench of the Tulane Law School American Inn of Court, a member of the International Association of Insurance Counsel, the American Board of Trial Advocates, and is a member of the House of Delegates, Louisiana State Bar Association. He is also a member of the New Orleans and American Bar Associations. He has lectured at numerous litigation and legal education seminars and has written articles relating to advocacy.

Victor E. Stilwell, Jr., is a partner in the law firm of Deutsch, Kerrigan & Stiles in New Orleans, and primarily represents design professionals and the construction industry. He holds a degree from the Tulane University School of Architecture, a graduate degree from the Princeton University School of Architecture, and received his legal education at Loyola Law School. Mr. Stilwell is a member of the American Bar Association, the Public Contract Law and Litigation Sections of the ABA, the ABA Forum Committee on the Construction Industry, Louisiana State Bar Association, American Institute of Architects, and the Louisiana Architects Association.

§ 17.1 Introduction

Design professionals must be concerned with much more than their scope of services and fees when executing contracts.

Project owners, usually with the stronger bargaining position, typically insist that design professionals assume risks attendant to their services that far outstrip the potential rewards. For example, owners require certifications from their design professionals that run in favor of third parties, such as regulatory agencies and lenders. They often require design professionals to waive or subordinate lien rights and to relinquish ownership of drawings and specifications. Increasingly, owners also impose confidentiality requirements on business information design professionals use. The list goes on and on.

Design professionals must understand the potential liabilities attendant to contract terms imposed by owners, and be aware of how those liabilities can be limited or shifted by appropriate contract terms that run in their favor. They must understand their lien rights and know how to protect themselves, their work product, and their designs.

§ 17.2 Limiting Liability

American society has become increasingly litigious in the last several decades, burdening the economy with the increased expense of rising insurance premiums, legal fees, and payment of judgments. The construction industry has suffered on this account as much as any segment of the economy.

Parties to construction contracts have sought to protect themselves from problems by contracting them away, that is, imposing contract conditions requiring other parties to bear the risks and costs.

Clauses that accomplish this fall into two general categories: those that eliminate or limit in advance a party's liability for its own negligence, and those in which one of the parties agrees to indemnify and hold the others harmless against such liability.

As a general proposition, there is no public policy that "opposes private voluntary transactions in which one party, for a consideration, agrees to shoulder a risk which the law would otherwise have placed on the other party."[1] This is particularly true when the parties are commercial entities of equal bargaining power.[2]

However, some jurisdictions have expressed hostility to such clauses, particularly when the public interest is involved, based on the notion that courts ought not enforce contracts that tend to be injurious to the public interests, or contrary to the public good.[3] Indeed, some states have statutes that prohibit the use of such clauses, and there are some prohibitions specifically directed at construction contracts.[4]

However, such agreements are strictly construed,[5] and to be valid and enforceable, they "must be clear, unambiguous, and explicit in expressing the intent of the parties."[6]

Nonlawyers should not attempt to draft such clauses, particularly not as an integral part of a conscious risk allocation program in a contract negotiating process, without the assistance of legal counsel. The enforceability of particular clauses or provisions varies from state to state, and the law is constantly evolving. A clause good when written might be rendered obsolete within a few years by legislative or judicial action.

---

[1] Madison v. Superior Court (Sulejmanagic), 203 Cal. App. 3d 589, 250 Cal. Rptr. 299 (1988) (court approved advance release of liability in favor of YMCA and swimming instructor, required of student before taking scuba diving course); Kurashige v. Indian Dunes, Inc., 200 Cal. App. 3d 606, 246 Cal. Rptr. 310 (1988) (court approved advance broad general release by dirt bike rider, relieving dirt bike track owner of all liability for injury to rider).

[2] Commercial entities, such as airlines and airplane manufacturers, are entitled to contract to limit the liability of one to the other, or otherwise allocate the risk of doing business. Philippines Airlines v. McDonnell Douglas, 189 Cal. App. 3d 234, 234 Cal. Rptr. 423, 424 (1987) (dismissing third-party demand by airline against airplane manufacturer for indemnity or contribution on claims brought by airplane passengers following airplane accident); Schrier v. Beltway Alarm Co., 73 Md. App. 281, 533 A.2d 1316 (1987) (approving limitation of liability clause in contract between liquor store and burglar alarm company, in suit brought by liquor store manager for damages resulting from a robbery).

[3] Walker v. American Family Mut. Ins. Co., 340 N.W.2d 599, 601 (Iowa 1983).

[4] Because the law in this area is constantly evolving, it is inadvisable to attempt to give here a definitive list of states with such prohibitions, or the nature of the prohibitions. Local counsel should be consulted with respect to prohibitions in a particular jurisdiction.

[5] Philippines Airlines v. McDonnell Douglas, 189 Cal. App. 3d 234, 234 Cal. Rptr. 423 (Cal. Ct. App. 1987).

[6] Madison v. Superior Court (Sulejmanagic), 203 Cal. App. 3d 589, 250 Cal. Rptr. 299 (1988). Whether such language is to be considered sufficiently clear is usually a question of law and not of fact and, therefore, decided by judges, not juries. *Id.*

It should be remembered that such clauses are limited in effect to claims between the contracting parties.[7] As noted, there is some hostility to these clauses, particularly when the public interest is affected, which has resulted in statutes and case law prohibiting such clauses. For example, California has a statute prohibiting contracts exempting people from liability for their own fraud, willful injury to persons or property of others, or violation of the law, whether willful or negligent.[8] From that statute arose a leading case on this point, *Tunkl v. Regents of University of California.*[9] Despite the statute, the defendant medical center required patient Tunkl, as a condition of admission, to sign a release of the hospital "from any and all liability for negligent or wrongful acts or omissions of its employees, if the hospital has used due care in selecting its employees."

After discussing the troubled history and the interpretation of the statute,[10] the court cut through subtleties of interpretation, noted that exculpatory provisions previously had been approved only when they did not involve "the public interest" of the state, and observed there was no single test as to what constituted the public interest. The court enumerated several tests, notable of which were that the service performed under the contract was one of an "essential nature," the economic setting of the transaction, and any superior bargaining advantage by one party against any member of the public who sought its services.[11] The court voided the medical center's

---

[7] Burns & Roe, Inc. v. Central Maine Power Co., 659 F. Supp. 141, 144 (D. Me. 1987).

[8] Cal. Civ. Code § 1668 (West 1956) provides: "All contracts which have for their object, directly or indirectly, to exempt anyone from responsibility for his own fraud, or willful injury to the person or property of another, or violation of law, whether willful or negligent, are against the policy of the law."

[9] 60 Cal. 2d 92, 383 P.2d 441, 32 Cal. Rptr. 33 (1963).

[10] The court pointed out that some cases interpreting the statute had held that it covered only violations of statutory law; still other cases held that the statute referred only to gross negligence; and other cases forbid exemption from active negligence, but not passive negligence. 383 P.2d 441, 442–43.

[11] At greater length, the court defined the test as:

> It concerns a business of a type generally thought suitable for public regulation. The party seeking exculpation is engaged in performing a service of great importance to the public, which is often a matter of practical necessity for some members of the public. The party holds himself out as willing to perform this service to any member of the public who seeks it, or at least to any member coming within certain established standards. As a result of the essential nature of the service, in the economic setting of the transaction, the party invoking exculpation possesses a decisive advantage of bargaining strength against any member of the public who seeks his services. In exercising a superior bargaining power, the party confronts the public with a standardized adhesion contract of exculpation, and makes no provision whereby a purchaser may pay additional reasonable fees and obtain protection against negligence. Finally, as a result of the transaction, the person or property of the purchaser is placed under the control of the seller, subject to the risk of carelessness by the seller or his agent. 383 P.2d 441, 445–46.

release, because the hospital patient's contract fell within the category of agreements affecting the public interest.[12]

Other jurisdictions have voided similar releases. The Tennessee Supreme Court voided a release for future negligence in favor of an osteopathic surgeon. Although acknowledging that there were general rules permitting risk allocation among parties, it observed that such rules:

> do not afford a satisfactory solution in a case involving a professional person operating in an area of public interest and pursuing a profession subject to licensure by the state. The rules that govern tradesmen in the marketplace are of little relevancy in dealing with professional persons who hold themselves out as experts, and whose practice is regulated by the state.[13]

Other states have reached the same result as the *Tunkl* case, but with less extensive theoretical analysis, simply noting that the offending clause violated public policy or affected an important public interest, or that there was something in the relationship of the parties, such as unequal bargaining power, that tainted the transaction.[14]

One need not be a lawyer to see the possible applicability of these principles to construction industry contracts, and that the same policy considerations could void such a clause in favor of a design professional.

The practices of engineering and architecture are regulated everywhere to some degree. Most, if not all, states require registration, and most states affirmatively regulate the practice of those professions. More important, design professionals provide services absolutely necessary for construction of a project of any consequence; building permits cannot, as a practical matter, be obtained without benefit of professional seals.

The remaining *Tunkl* criteria deal with disparity in the bargaining positions of the parties. These apply less to most design professional contracts than to doctor/patient relationships. Owners often will bargain with design professionals and accept reductions in fees for errors and omissions that may occur. In other contexts, the courts have enforced exculpatory or limiting clauses in similar circumstances, particularly when the releasing party

---

[12] Other jurisdictions have followed this lead, virtually eliminating exculpatory clauses for health care professionals. *See* Annotation, *Validity and Construction of Contract Exempting Hospital or Doctor from Liability for Negligence to Patient,* 6 A.L.R.3d 704–07 (1966).

[13] Olsen v. Molzen, 558 S.W.2d 429, 430 (Tenn. 1977). It should be noted that, following *Tunkl,* most cases involving exculpatory contracts for health care professionals have violated the clause. *See* Annotation, *Validity and Construction of Contract Exempting Hospital or Doctor from Liability for Negligence to Patient,* 6 A.L.R.3d 704–07 (1966).

[14] *See, e.g.,* W.H. Lyman Constr. Co. v. Village of Gurnee, 84 Ill. App. 3d 28, 403 N.E.2d 1325 (1980); Warren City Lines, Inc. v. United Ref. Co., 220 Pa. Super. 308, 287 A.2d 149 (1971).

received demonstrable benefit by relinquishment of future claims,[15] or there was a quid pro quo for the limitation.[16]

Mention should be made here of clauses that do not exculpate or release a design professional for future negligence, but that contractually limit liability to the owner to a set amount, such as the amount of the design professional's fee or insurance coverage.

These clauses are, like the exculpatory clauses, limited in effect between the contracting parties. A third party injured by a design professional's negligence is not bound by the limitation in any claim against the design professional. The limitation clauses, versus exculpatory clauses, probably will prove easier to get past the public policy challenge, particularly when it can be shown that the releasing party received some economic benefit, such as reduction of the design professional's fee by the cost of purchasing insurance to cover against the full risk. Drafters of such clauses should include the consideration received in return for the limitation.

Finally, there is another public policy argument against such clauses. Some courts have held that it is a violation of public interest, and therefore public policy, to permit a party to exculpate itself in advance from liability for violating a regulation or statute enacted to protect human life. In a Pennsylvania case,[17] the defendant, a bulk distributor of products, leased to the plaintiff, a retail distributor, the equipment used to dispense defendant's products. As part of the lease, the defendant obtained a prior exculpation for any liability arising out of the use or maintenance of the leased equipment. Plaintiff's facility was destroyed when the equipment exploded while being serviced. Plaintiff sued the defendant for the property damage, alleging, among other things, that the equipment and its installation violated a number of regulations promulgated by the fire marshal.

---

[15] For example, in Laverty, Inc. v. Mel Jarvis Constr. Co., 513 F.2d 1307 (8th Cir. 1975), such a clause was enforced against an owner who had been allowed to occupy part of the project before it was completed. Likewise, in 80-82 Greene St. Corp. v. AFA Protective Sys., Inc., 100 Misc. 2d 334, 418 N.Y.S.2d 971 (Sup. Ct. 1979), an exculpatory clause in a fire sprinkler contract was enforced against the owner, when the insulation contract showed that the owner could, by paying a higher fee, have had the exculpatory clause removed. Presumably, with the additional fee, the contractor would have insured against such claims. Some A/E exculpatory clauses specifically provide that the A/E will assume full liability for an additional fee, which usually is related to the cost of buying the additional insurance to cover that risk.

[16] Long Island Lighting Co. v. Imo Delaval, Inc., 668 F. Supp. 237 (S.D.N.Y. 1987). The court approved clause requiring engineer to purchase liability insurance in specified limits, limited engineer's liability to the amount of insurance, and permitted owner to require contractor to purchase additional insurance, presumably at owner's expense.

[17] Warren City Lines, Inc. v. United Ref. Corp., 220 Pa. Super. 308, 287 A.2d 149 (Pa. 1971).

The Pennsylvania court overruled defendant's preliminary motion to dismiss based on the exculpatory clause, holding it against public policy to permit prior exculpation for violation of regulations enacted to protect human life or safety.[18]

The implications of the rule are clear: few professions or occupations are more intertwined with enforcement of, and adherence to, a variety of statutes, codes, and regulations enacted to protect human life and limb than architects and engineers. Usually, any claim against a design professional involves at least one colorable claim that the design professional violated some building code, statute, or regulation that was imposed to protect human safety.

Some courts have refused to enforce the exculpatory clauses in cases alleging intentional acts or gross negligence.[19] Although true cases of gross negligence or willful injury by design professionals rarely materialize, plaintiffs do not hesitate to allege them to prevent early dismissal of claims. The defendant design professional is then exposed to the long and expensive proposition of discovery, and sometimes to trial.

Finally, in specific cases involving design professionals, courts have tended to construe such clauses very strictly, tending to deny the protection in close cases.[20]

In signing the various agreements, owners and design professionals also should be conscious of the distinction between exculpatory clauses among themselves and others with whom they contract. An architect might have no exculpatory or limitation clause in a contract with the owner, but be confronted with a limitation of the structural consultant's liability in the subcontract. In such a situation, the architect might be exposed to all damage, while potential contribution from the consultant would be limited.

Aside from possible personal expense of the architect, such a situation might impinge on the architect's insurance coverage. Most professional

---

[18] The court conceded that the claim was only for property damage, but refused to diminish the deterrent effect of possible tort liability by limiting the liability to damages for personal injury or death. *Id.*

[19] Shelby Mut. Ins. Co. v. City of Grand Rapids, 6 Mich. App. 95, 148 N.W.2d 260 (1967); Third Swansea Properties, Inc. v. Ockalund Constr. Co., 41 Ill. App. 3d 894, 354 N.E.2d 148 (1976).

[20] Burns & Roe, Inc. v. Central Maine Power Co., 659 F. Supp. 141 (D. Me. 1987); W. William Graham, Inc. v. City of Cave City, 289 Ark. 105, 709 S.W.2d 94 (1986) (limitation of engineer's liability for "negligent acts, errors or omissions" to amount of fee, held not to protect engineer from breach of contract claim for loss of federal funding due to engineer's tardy delivery of project plans); White Constr. Co. v. Commonwealth, 11 Mass. App. Ct. 640, 418 N.E.2d 357 (1981) (complete exculpation to engineer on acceptance of payment of conclusion of design, in contract drafted entirely by owner, held unenforceable because it would exonerate engineer for improper performance of statutorily required contract administration duties).

liability insurance policies subrogate the insurer to any rights that the design professional might have against third parties. Many insurers specifically require that they be subrogated to the rights of the design professional against any other persons or organizations who might be liable.[21] The general rule is, even without a policy clause, the insurer is subrogated by operation of law, unless the policy specifically provides otherwise, or some public policy prevents subrogation.[22] There have not been extensive decisions on this point, but there is authority for the proposition that an insured who by contract destroys the subrogation rights of the insurer before loss may lose coverage.[23]

It is important to note that, generally speaking, the courts recognize the distinction between exculpatory and limitation clauses on the one hand, and on the other those clauses by which parties agree that one will buy insurance to cover an anticipated risk, which insurance will indemnify the others against their own negligence. The latter clauses are generally enforced, even with approbation, as sensible business measures whereby parties shift anticipated risk to insurance, the cost of which is part of the project.[24] Good examples are clauses in construction contracts that require a party, usually the owner, to buy fire insurance or builder's risk insurance covering the project, and naming the contractor, subcontractors, and others as insureds, with all parties waiving subrogation against each other.[25] Indeed, even when the construction contract has required such blanket insurance naming all parties as insureds, without specifically requiring a waiver of claims, the owner or subrogated insurer is effectively barred from pursuing negligent contractors or subcontractors.[26]

---

[21] Typical subrogation language found in professional liability policies is as follows:

> In the event of any payment under this policy, the Company shall be subrogated to all the "Insured's" rights of recovery thereof against any person or organization, other than an employee of the "Insured," and the "Insured" shall execute and deliver instruments and papers and do whatever else is necessary to secure such rights. The "Insured" shall do nothing after loss to prejudice such rights.

[22] The general rules regarding subrogation in casualty insurance are discussed at length in 8B Appleman Insurance Law and Practice §§ 4941–4946 (1981).

[23] *See* Liberty Mut. Ins. Co. v. Altfillisch Constr. Co., 70 Cal. App. 3d 789, 139 Cal. Rptr. 91 (1977). The *Altfillisch* case did not arise in the context of an A/E contract; however, it does point out the potential problem. An opposite result was reached in Insurance Co. of N. Am. v. Universal Mortgage Corp. of Wis., 82 Wis. 2d 170, 262 N.W.2d 92 (1978).

[24] South Tippecanoe School Bldg. Corp. v. Shambaugh & Son, Inc., 182 Ind. App. 350, 395 N.E.2d 320 (Ct. App. 1979). Tuxedo Plumbing & Heating Co., Inc. v. Lie Neilson, 245 Ga. 27, 262 S.E.2d 794 (1980).

[25] South Tippecanoe School Bldg. Corp. v. Shambaugh & Son, Inc., 182 Ind. App. 350, 395 N.E.2d 320 (Ct. App. 1979). Tuxedo Plumbing & Heating Co., Inc. v. Lie Neilson, 245 Ga. 27, 262 S.E.2d 794 (1980).

[26]
> It has been recognized by numerous authorities that where parties to a business transaction mutually agree that insurance will be provided as part of the bargain,

Indemnity agreements are also important tools for limiting liability of the design professional. "Indemnity may be defined as the obligation resting on one party to make good on loss or damage another party has incurred."[27] As used in this context, it refers to a contractual promise by a party other than the design professional, such as the contractor or the owner, to protect the design professional from any claims that may be brought against it arising out of the project.

One of the best known indemnity provisions is found in subparagraph 3.18.1 of American Institute of Architects (AIA) Document A201, General Conditions of the Contract for Construction, which provides:

> [T]he Contractor shall indemnify . . . the Owner, Architect, Architect's consultants, . . . of them from and against claims, damages, losses and expenses, . . . but only to the extent caused in whole or in part by negligent acts or omissions of the Contractor, . . . regardless of whether or not such claim, damage, loss or expense is caused in part by a party indemnified hereunder.

Note that this particular clause is limited to claims attributable to bodily injury or property damage (as opposed to delayed completion of the contract, for example), and is conditioned on the damage having been caused entirely, or at least in part, by the negligence of the contractor or subcontractor. This clause, to which enormous creative thought has been given, is crafted as it is for a reason.

First, there is considerable hostility to such indemnity agreements. Most states look with disfavor upon clauses to indemnify a party for damages incurred due to the indemnitee's own negligence, and courts construe them strictly against reaching such an interpretation;[28] where that rule obtains, usually "anything less than an explicit statement clearly manifesting an intent to indemnify against the indemnitee's own negligence will not be sufficient to create an obligation to do so."[29]

However, even that is not enough in many jurisdictions. A number of jurisdictions prohibit absolutely a clause that will indemnify a party for damage caused *solely* by the indemnitee's negligence.[30]

> such agreement must be construed as providing mutual exculpation to the bargaining parties who must be deemed to have agreed to look solely to the insurance in the event of loss and not to liability on the part of the opposing party.

Tuxedo Plumbing & Heating Co., Inc. v. Lie Neilson, 245 Ga. 27, 262 S.E.2d 794, 795 (1980); Board of Educ. v. Valden Assocs., Inc., 46 N.Y.2d 653, 389 N.E.2d 798 (1979).

[27] Rossmoor Sanitation, Inc. v. Pylon, Inc., 13 Cal. 3d 622, 628, 119 Cal. Rptr. 449 (1975).

[28] Emery Waterhouse Co. v. Lea, 467 A.2d 986, 993 (Me. 1983).

[29] Burns & Roe, Inc. v. Central Maine Power Co., 659 F. Supp. 141, 144 (D. Me. 1987).

[30] A comprehensive survey of the state of such statutes is found in *Anti-Indemnification Statutes,* 19 Guidelines for Improving Practice, No. 8 (1989).

Still other states proscribe indemnification agreements in favor of design professionals for their own negligence, regardless of whether it is the only negligence that caused the damage.[31]

The general hostility to such agreements, particularly in favor of the design professional, is well demonstrated. For example, in *Burns & Roe, Inc. v. Central Maine Power Co.*,[32] the engineer on a construction project sued the owner for a declaratory judgment that the owner owed it a defense and indemnity against a lawsuit brought against the engineer and owner by a contractor. The engineer's contract provided indemnity for damages and expenses including legal fees, "but not including losses, damages and expenses due to the negligence or wrongful acts" of certain of the engineer's named employees. The court held that the clause did not "contain any clear and unequivocal statement that [owner] will indemnify [engineer] for damages arising out of [engineer's] own negligence. In fact, it specifically excludes any indemnification for expenses arising out of negligence on the part of named employees of [engineer]."[33]

Some states will enforce indemnity agreements when the requirements laid down by statute and/or case law are met.[34]

§ 17.3 Confidentiality and Nondisclosure

Design professionals and contractors often receive project information from owners that is proprietary and confidential. Information of this nature may take on the proportion of trade secrets.

A *trade secret* is generally defined as any formula, device, or compilation of information used in one's business that gives the proprietor an advantage over competitors. A trade secret need not be completely novel or unique, as in the case of a patent, but it must be secret.[35] Matters of public knowledge cannot be appropriated as a trade secret.

In the construction setting, knowledge of trade secrets may be necessary to design and build the owner's project. Because disclosure destroys the secrecy of the information, the owner must take steps to control the release of information by limiting disclosure to only those persons who need to know it and by making them aware that the information is to remain confidential.

---

[31] *Id.* It is inadvisable to include here a state-by-state review of anti-indemnity statutes because of their impermanent nature.

[32] 659 F. Supp. 141 (D. Me. 1987).

[33] *Id.* at 144.

[34] *See, e.g.*, Florida Power & Light Co. v. Mid-Valley, Inc., 763 F.2d 1316 (11th Cir. 1985).

[35] Henry Hope X-Ray Prods., Inc. v. Marron Carrel, 674 F.2d 1336 (9th Cir. 1982); Gilson v. Republic of Ireland, 606 F. Supp. 38 (D.D.C. 1984), *aff'd*, 787 F.2d 655 (D.C. Cir. 1986).

This is commonly accomplished by requiring persons receiving the information to sign a separate confidentiality agreement or to agree to a confidentiality provision in their contracts.[36] None of the standard AIA or Engineers Joint Contract Documents Committee (EJCDC) contracts currently contain confidentiality or nondisclosure provisions. Although such provisions cannot stop a person intent on breaching a confidence, they may prevent unintentional disclosure. Confidentiality and nondisclosure agreements basically create a positive duty not to divulge the subject information to other persons.

Trade secret protection exists whether or not a confidentiality or nondisclosure agreement is entered. The *Restatement of Torts* contains the following considerations for determination of trade secret status:

1. The extent to which the information is known outside of the owner's business
2. The extent to which it is known by employees and others involved in the business
3. The extent of measures taken by the owner to guard the secrecy of the information
4. The value of the information to the owner and competitors
5. The amount of effort or money expended by the owner in developing the information
6. The ease or difficulty with which the information could be properly acquired or duplicated by others.[37]

Additionally, the circumstances surrounding disclosure may imply a promise not to divulge the information. For example, if the person to whom disclosure is made is aware that the information is not generally known in the industry, a confidential relationship is likely to be presumed.

Because the proprietor's ultimate goal is to retain secrecy, the preferred remedy in cases of wrongful disclosure, or potential wrongful disclosure, is to enjoin further releases of the information. However, in situations in which injunctive relief is not appropriate, or is too late, damages may be awarded.

Trade secret protection also may be appropriate for information that design professionals use in their business. Design professionals can extract confidentiality agreements from their clients and other third parties to whom disclosure is made. Design professionals commonly extract

[36] Samples of confidentiality agreements can be found in 1A J. Rablein & M. Johnson, Current Legal Forms, Forms 3.38, 3.39 and 3.40 (1990), and 1 S. Stein, Construction Law, ch. 5 app. (1990).

[37] Restatement of Torts § 757 comment b.

confidentiality agreements from their own employees in case they leave their employment. Although covenants not to compete in employment contracts are generally looked on unfavorably as restraints on free trade, agreements not to disclose trade secrets are generally enforceable.[38]

There are other needs for confidentiality in the construction setting. Design professionals' agreements typically require owners to furnish evidence of their ability to satisfy professional fees and construction costs.[39] An example is contractors' bid workpapers, which reveal the process by which bid prices are determined. Because common law trade secret protection may not be available for this information, provisions preserving confidentiality should be inserted into the contracts if this information must be disclosed. Courts generally will enforce nondisclosure agreements even though the information does not have "trade secret" status.[40]

§ 17.4 Freedom of Information Act and Business Information

When contracting with the government, design professionals often must divulge sensitive business information that they do not want disclosed to competitors. Design professionals should know their rights to prevent such disclosure.

The federal Freedom of Information Act (FOIA)[41] requires all government agencies to make certain information available for public inspection. Disclosure is the rule, unless the information falls within one of nine exemptions. The exemption of particular concern to government contractors is that for: "(4) trade secrets and commercial or financial information obtained from a person and privileged or confidential."[42] This exemption is intended to encourage individuals to provide these kinds of confidential information to the government, and it must be read narrowly in accordance with that purpose.[43]

To qualify for exemption, the information must be (1) commercial or financial, (2) obtained from a person, and (3) privileged and confidential.[44] Commercial or financial matters are confidential for purposes of

---

[38] Federal Screw Works v. Interface Sys., Inc., 569 F. Supp. 1562 (E.D. Mich. 1983); NCH Corp. v. Broyles, 563 F. Supp. 142 (E.D. La. 1983).

[39] AIA B141-1987, para. 4.3; AIA A201-1987, subpara. 2.2.1.

[40] Modern Controls, Inc. v. Andreadakis, 578 F.2d 1264 (8th Cir. 1978); NCH Corp. v. Broyles, 563 F. Supp. 142 (E.D. La. 1983).

[41] 5 U.S.C. § 552 (1976).

[42] *Id.* § 552(b)(4).

[43] Soucie v. David, 448 F.2d 1067, 1078 (D.C. Cir. 1971).

[44] National Parks & Conservation Ass'n v. Morton, 498 F.2d 765, 766 (D.C. Cir. 1974).

the exemption if disclosure is likely to either (1) impair the government's ability to obtain necessary information in the future, or (2) cause substantial harm to the competitive position of the person from whom the information was obtained.[45]

Design professionals contracting with the government have both pre-award and post-award measures to avoid a competitor's access to such information.[46] Under § 15.413 of the Federal Acquisition Regulations (FAR), there are two prescribed alternatives for avoiding disclosure before the award. Under Alternative I, design professionals can attempt to protect proprietary information by inserting a restrictive legend on the title page of the proposal. Section 52.215-12 of the FAR sets forth a restrictive legend informing the government agency that the design professional does not want the data disclosed or used for any purpose other than evaluation. It provides: "This proposal or quotation includes data that shall not be disclosed outside the Government and shall not be duplicated, used, or disclosed—in whole or in part—for any purpose other than to evaluate this proposal or quotation."[47]

The design professional lists on the legend those pages containing confidential information and marks each of these pages individually. Marking the data with the proprietary legend does not in and of itself defeat the right of disclosure under the FOIA. Because the FOIA protects both the interests of the design professional and the government, the data still must meet the requirements of the Act.[48]

Section 15.413 of the FAR sets forth an alternative procedure for protecting proprietary information. Under Alternative II, the government agency may provide that information contained in the proposals will be used for evaluation purposes only and that disclosure outside the agency will be permitted only to the extent authorized by law. However, the agency also may provide that it assumes no liability for the use or disclosure of information not identified by the restrictive legend set forth under FAR 52.215-12.[49] Alternative II also gives the design professional providing the information an opportunity to take appropriate action before release of any information pursuant to a request under the FOIA.

After award of a contract, both the successful and unsuccessful offerors are protected by FAR 15.1001 and 15.1002. FAR 15.1001 requires the government to send each unsuccessful offeror a post-award notice containing

---

[45] National Parks & Conservation Ass'n v. Klepp, 547 F.2d 673, 677–78 (D.C. Cir. 1976); National Parks & Conservation Ass'n v. Morton, 498 F.2d 765, 770; Westinghouse Elec. Corp. v. Brown, 443 F. Supp. 1225, 1228–29 (E.D. Va. 1977).

[46] *See* Dobkin & Dempsey, *Protection of Corporate Secrets in Government Contract Proposals and Bids,* 15 Pub. Cont. L.J. 46 (1984).

[47] 48 C.F.R. § 52.215-12 (1990).

[48] Petkas v. Staats, 501 F.2d 887, 889 (D.C. Cir. 1974).

[49] 48 C.F.R. § 15.413-2(b) (1990).

such information as the number of offerors solicited, the number of proposals received, the name and address of each offeror receiving an award, the items, quantities, and unit prices of each award, and the reasons why the offeror's proposal was not accepted. However, in no event shall the post-award notice reveal any information that is not releasable under the FOIA.[50] Neither may proprietary information be revealed in debriefing.[51]

Business information is considerably more protected in the context of a negotiated procurement than in that of a formally advertised procurement,[52] because claims of confidentiality often directly conflict with the public bid opening requirements. In several cases, the General Accounting Office (GAO) held that bids containing proprietary legends were nonresponsive for failure to conform to the public opening requirement of formally advertised procurements.[53] FAR 14.404-4 provides: "The restriction renders the bid nonresponsive if it prohibits the disclosure of sufficient information to permit competing bidders to know the essential nature and type of the products offered or those elements of the bid that relate to quantity, price, and delivery terms." Unless the confidential information is the type that must be disclosed, it will not render the bid nonresponsive because the public opening requirement does not require public disclosure of all information.[54]

If the government agency intends to release proprietary data, the design professional may bring a "reverse FOIA" suit to prevent the agency from releasing the information.[55] In such an action, the design professional must show cause why the information should not be available under the FOIA.

§ 17.5 Copyrights and Patents

Design professionals historically have given little thought to copyrights because their work product enjoyed only partial protection. They have instead had to rely upon provisions in their contracts to preserve ownership of their documents and the rights in the intellectual property contained therein.

In November 1988, Congress amended the copyright laws, found at 17 U.S.C.A. §§ 101–103, 106, 120 (1990). On December 1, 1990, Congress enacted the Architectural Works Copyright Protection Act,[56] which now

---

[50] *Id.* § 15.1001(c).

[51] *Id.* § 15.1003(b).

[52] *See generally* Dobkin & Dempsey, *Protection of Corporate Secrets in Government Contract Proposals and Bids,* 15 Pub. Cont. L.J. 46, 51–52 (1984).

[53] *See, e.g.,* Computer Network Corp., 55 Comp. Gen. 445, 75-2 C.P.D. ¶ 297 (1975); IFR, Inc., B-203391.4, 82-1 C.P.D. ¶ 292, at 11–12 (Apr. 1, 1982).

[54] *See* Computer Network Corp., 55 Comp. Gen. at 452.

[55] *See* Planning Research Corp. v. Federal Power Comm'n, 555 F.2d 970 (D.C. Cir. 1977).

[56] 17 U.S.C.A. §§ 101–103, 106, 120 (1990).

prevents unauthorized construction of buildings from copyrighted drawings, no matter how they have been obtained.

Standard form agreements between design professionals and owners typically provide that drawings, specifications, and other documents prepared by the design professional are instruments of service and that the design professional is deemed author of the documents and vested with all common law, statutory, and other reserved rights including copyrights.[57] These same provisions are generally found in standard form general conditions, which are normally binding on the contractor and all subcontractors.[58]

The new legislation notwithstanding, contractual provisions that protect design professionals' ownership of their documents remain important. These provisions secure underlying creative integrity, protect the design professional's economic interests, and address potential liability concerns. Contract provisions also can protect design professionals from liability attendant to unauthorized modification and use of their documents.

The right to construct buildings from copyrighted documents is part of the economic value of the documents.[59] When a property owner retains a design professional to prepare drawings and specifications, in the absence of contractual language to the contrary, that owner also generally acquires the right to execute the drawings and specifications on one occasion only.[60] If owners or others who come into possession of drawings and specifications were free to build repeatedly from that set of documents, design professionals would have less incentive to do creative work, and the diversity of expression that is the hallmark of all copyright markets would effectively be discouraged. In addition, such infringement could damage a design professional's reputation and create potential liability if reuse of the documents bearing the design professional's name and professional seal proved to be improper or unsafe.

Unless relinquished by contract, ownership of copyrights in works related to architecture and engineering, as in all copyrighted works, vests in the author. In practice, the author is generally an architectural or engineering firm acting as the employer for hire of the architects, engineers, draftsmen, and technicians who actually create the drawings and specifications. It is well settled that owners of real property who commission the creation of works related to architecture and engineering are neither authors as commissioners of certain works made for hire nor coauthors with their design professionals.[61]

---

[57] AIA B141-1987, para. 6.1.

[58] AIA A201-1987, subpara. 1.3.1.

[59] Brainard, *Innovation and Implementation: Artistic Advance and the Legal Protection of Architectural Works,* 70 Cornell L. Rev. 81 (1984).

[60] Aitken, Hazen, Hoffman, Miller, P.C. v. Empire Constr. Co., 542 F.2d 252, 260 (D. Neb. 1982) [hereinafter Aitken].

[61] AIA B141-1987, para. 6.1; AIA A201-1987, subpara. 1.31.

Design professionals use and rely upon contracts that specify, in substantial detail, the allocation of rights in their work product between themselves, their clients, and contractors.[62] This system of contract protection has worked reasonably well, given the paucity of disputes among design professionals and their clients over ownership of drawings and specifications. However, contractual reservations of ownership rights have not been effective when enforcement was difficult or impossible.

In practical terms, design professionals' reserved rights have historically been diminished or effectively mooted. For example, there have been countless situations in which a client whose building was under construction was adjudicated a bankrupt and, thereafter, a lending institution undertook to complete construction of the building without the services of the design professional who prepared the drawings and specifications.[63] Under prior law, the design professional could not obtain an injunction against or damages from the lender, who realized a substantial benefit from the design professional's work without compensation therefor. With the enactment of the Architectural Works Copyright Protection Act, the ability of third parties to reduce design professionals' income from and control over execution of the drawings and specifications is effectively curtailed.

Under prior law, the building design was not entitled to copyright protection, but the drawings for the building were.[64] Before the passage of the Architectural Works Copyright Protection Act,[65] a person could not, by copyrighting drawings, prevent the construction of an identical building to that detailed in the copyrighted drawings. The new legislation offers copyright protection for the building design.

Design patent protection, which is rarely sought by design professionals, has been found applicable to building components but not to buildings themselves. Decisions on patent protection in favor of design professionals are sparse and relatively old.[66] Patent protection for design professionals in the construction industry remains obscure and rarely useful.

Unauthorized reproduction of a design professional's drawings for use on a subsequent project has been held to be a copyright infringement and unfair use.[67] Historically, recovery by design professionals in copyright

---

[62] General J. Shaw v. Williamsville Manor, Inc., 38 A.D.2d 442, 174 U.S.P.Q. (BNA) 277 (N.Y. 1972).

[63] Nucor Corp. v. Tennessee Forging Steel Servs., Inc., 476 F.2d 386, 390 (8th Cir. 1973).

[64] *See* Demetriades v. Kaufman, No. 88 Civ. 0848 (S.D.N.Y. Mar. 8, 1988). *But cf.* Herman Frankel Org. v. Wolfe, 184 U.S.P.Q. (BNA) 819 (E.D. Mich. 1974).

[65] 17 U.S.C.A. §§ 101–103, 106, 120 (1990).

[66] Aitken, 542 F.2d 252, 260 (D. Neb. 1982).

[67] *See* Robert R. Jones Assocs. v. Hino Homes, Corp. L. Rep. (CCH) 26,165 (E.D. Mich. 1987); Arthur Rettenberg Corp. v. Dawney, 647 F. Supp. 1214 (M.D. Fla. 1986); Aitken, 542 F.2d 252, 260 (D. Neb. 1982).

infringement suits has been essentially restricted to monetary damages, although injunctions have been awarded in a few cases.[68] The Architectural Works Copyright Protection Act now enables design professionals to seek injunctions to halt construction or to obtain court orders to demolish or even seize buildings if the infringement is so egregious as to warrant such action. Actual damages have been and probably will continue to be determined based on the fair market value of drawings that have been copied and reused without the consent of the authors.[69] When no ready market exists, courts have used the original value of the drawings as the benchmark.[70]

In addition to actual damages, design professionals are entitled to "any profits of the infringer that are attributable to the infringement and not taken into account in computing the actual damages."[71] Further, "[i]n establishing the infringer's profits, the copyright owner is required to present only the infringer's gross revenues, and the infringer is required to provide his or her deductible expenses and the element of profit attributed to factors other than copyrighted work."[72] Overhead expenses that assist in preparing an infringing work are deductible from the gross profit of the infringer.[73] Full costs of an infringement action, including attorneys' fees, can be awarded to the successful plaintiff.[74]

§ 17.6 Liens

Mechanic's liens are creatures of late eighteenth century development.[75] The common law evolved the possessory lien, similar to the artisan's and worker's privilege in civil law, which provided protection to craftsmen, but was of no value to one who furnished labor or materials for immovable construction.[76] There was no need for this protection because slave labor, feudal serfs, or labor furnished from monasteries built the edifices, which were chiefly public or semipublic in character.

---

[68] Aitken, 542 F.2d 252, 260 (D. Neb. 1982); Schuchart & Assocs., Professional Eng'rs, Inc. v. Solo Serv. Corp., 220 U.S.P.Q. (BNA) 170 (W.D. Tex. 1983).

[69] Aitken, 542 F.2d 252, 260 (D. Neb. 1982).

[70] 17 U.S.C.A. § 504(b) (1976).

[71] *Id.;* Riter-Conely Mfg. Co. v. Aiken, 203 F. 699, 702 (3d Cir. 1913); *Ex parte* Foshay, 7 U.S.P.Q. (BNA) 121 (1930).

[72] Smith v. Little Brown & Co., 273 F. Supp. 870, 874 (S.D.N.Y. 1967), *aff'd,* 396 F.2d 150 (2d Cir. 1968).

[73] 17 U.S.C.A. § 505 (1976).

[74] *Id.*

[75] IX Sanborn, Encyclopedia of Social Science, 456, 458 (1933) [hereinafter Sanborn].

[76] 20 American & English Encyclopedia of Law 269.

The need for the protection of free labor arose in continental Europe with the rise of the guilds. The civil law developed its own patterns of protection in the form of privileges against real property.[77] The British did not supply equivalents,[78] but early in American history, the mechanic's lien was invented.[79]

The first mechanic's lien law was enacted in Maryland in 1791.[80] Its immediate purpose was to expedite the construction of the national capital.[81] Mechanic's liens soon were made law by statute in all the states, and the legislation spread into Canada[82] out of a broader purpose to prevent unjust enrichment by leaving workers without protection.[83]

---

[77] I Domat, The Civil Law in Its Natural Order, arts. 1742–1745 (1853). Sanborn at 458.

[78] 20 American & English Encyclopedia of Law 271.

[79] Sanborn at 459.

[80] Act of General Assembly of Maryland, passed Dec. 19, 1791, *reported in* 2 Kitty, Laws of Maryland, 1791, ch. XLV, § 5.

[81] *Id.*

[82] Alabama: Ala. Code § 35-11-210 (1975); Alaska: Alaska Stat. § 34.35.050 *et seq.;* Arizona: Ariz. Rev. Stat. Ann. § 33-981 *et seq.;* Arkansas: Ark. Stat. Ann. § 51-601 *et seq.;* California: Cal. Civ. Code § 3082 *et seq.* (West); Colorado: Colo. Rev. Stat. § 38-22-101 *et seq.;* Connecticut: Conn. Gen. Stat. Ann. § 49-33 *et seq.* (West); Delaware: Del. Code Ann. tit. 25, § 2701 *et seq.;* District of Columbia: D.C. Code Ann. § 38-101 *et seq.* (1981); Florida: Fla. Stat. Ann. § 713.01 *et seq.* (West); Georgia: Ga. Code Ann. § 67-1701 *et seq.;* Hawaii: Haw. Rev. Stat. § 507-41 *et seq.;* Idaho: Idaho Code § 45-501 *et seq.;* Illinois: Ill. Rev. Stat. ch. 82, para. 1 *et seq.* (1979); Indiana: Ind. Code § 32-8-3-1 *et seq.;* Iowa: Iowa Code Ann. § 572.1 *et seq.* (West); Kansas: Kan. Stat. Ann. § 60-1101 *et seq.;* Kentucky: Ky. Rev. Stat. Ann. § 376.101 *et seq.* (Baldwin); Louisiana: La. Rev. Stat. Ann. § 9:4801 *et seq.* (West); Maine: Me. Rev. Stat. Ann. tit. 10, § 3251 *et seq.;* Maryland: Md. Real Prop. Code Ann. § 9-101 *et seq.;* Massachusetts: Mass. Gen. Laws Ann. ch. 254, § 1 *et seq.* (West); Michigan: Mich. Comp. Laws Ann. § 570.1 *et seq.* (West); Minnesota: Minn. Stat. Ann. § 514.01 *et seq.* (West); Mississippi: Miss. Code Ann. § 85-7-131 *et seq.* (1972); Missouri: Mo. Ann. Stat. § 429.010 *et seq.* (Vernon); Montana: Mont. Code Ann. § 71-3-501 *et seq.;* Nebraska: Neb. Rev. Stat. § 52-125 *et seq.;* Nevada: Nev. Rev. Stat. § 108.221 *et seq.;* New Hampshire: N.H. Rev. Stat. Ann. § 447:1 *et seq.;* New Jersey: N.J. Stat. Ann. § 48-2-1 *et seq.* (West 1978); New York: N.Y. Lien Law § 1 *et seq.* (McKinney 19); North Carolina: N.C. Gen. Stat. § 44A-1 *et seq.;* Ohio: Ohio Rev. Code Ann. § 1311.01 *et seq.;* Oklahoma: Okla. Stat. tit. 42, § 141 *et seq.* (1981); Oregon: Or. Rev. Stat. § 87.001 *et seq.;* Pennsylvania: 49 Pa. Cons. Stat. § 1101 *et seq.;* Rhode Island: R.I. Gen. Laws § 34-28-1 *et seq.* (1956); South Carolina: S.C. Code Ann. § 29-5-10 *et seq.* (Law. Co-op. 1976); South Dakota: S.D. Codified Laws Ann. § 44-9-1 *et seq.;* Tennessee: Tenn. Code Ann. § 66-11-101 *et seq.;* Texas: Tex. Prop. Code Ann. § 53.001 *et seq.* (Vernon); Utah: Utah Code Ann. § 38-1-1 *et seq.* (1953); Vermont: Vt. Stat. Ann. tit. 9, § 1921 *et seq.;* Virginia: Va. Code Ann. § 43-1 *et seq.* (1950); Washington: Wash. Rev. Code Ann. § 60.04.010 *et seq.;* West Virginia: W. Va. Code § 38-2-1 *et seq.;* Wisconsin: Wis. Stat. Ann. § 779.01 *et seq.* (West); Wyoming: Wyo. Stat. § 29-1-301 *et seq.* (1977).

[83] *See, e.g.,* Restatement of Restitution § 162 comment a (1936); 20 American & English Encyclopedia of Law 268; United States v. Albert Holman Lumber Co., 206 F.2d 685,

With the development of the contract system of construction, the mechanic's lien was legislated to attach to the res, or corpus of land, regardless of ownership. The effect of this arrangement was to make the owner the surety of the contractor to the extent the property was given as a guarantee that the laborers and materialmen would be paid.

Because of the diversity that exists among the various states' statutory schemes, generalizations are difficult. However, mechanic's liens fall into two general types. The first, known as the *New York system,* entitles a lienholder to recover only the amount currently due the contractor from the owner. The lien is to that extent derivative of the contractor's claim against the owner for payment. The owner has a defense to any asserted lien by making payment to the contractor, regardless of whether the contractor in turn pays the workers, subcontractors, or suppliers.

In contrast, the *Pennsylvania system* entitles a lienholder to assert a lien directly against the owner's property for the full amount of the claim, regardless of the owner's payments to the contractor. Thus, an owner may be forced to satisfy claims exceeding the price of the contract with the contractor.[84] Reference to the particular state's statutory scheme is necessary to determine the amount covered by the lien.

Lienholders typically include contractors, subcontractors, and their laborers and suppliers. Approximately 25 states have enacted mechanic's lien laws that either expressly include architects, engineers, and surveyors who have contracts with the owner in their definition of lienholder, or that define services protected by a lien to include those furnished by design professionals.[85] Of those 25 states, some have restricted claims for payment of architectural or engineering fees to those design professionals who have contracts directly with the owners. Other states have expanded lien rights to architects and engineers who have contracts with either the owner or the general contractor.[86] Under some schemes, architects, engineers, and surveyors must be registered professionals in order to have lien rights.[87]

In states that have not specifically included architects, engineers, or surveyors within the purview of their mechanic's lien statutes, the courts have nonetheless interpreted architects and engineers as "laborers and workmen" to bring them within the class of persons entitled to assert a lien.

690, *reaff'd on rehearing,* 208 F.2d 113 (5th Cir. 1953); *In re* Taylorcraft Aviation Corp., 168 F.2d 808, 811 (6th Cir. 1948); United States v. Griffin-Moore Lumber Co., 62 So. 2d 589, 590 (Fla. 1953).

[84] For general discussion of these two types of systems, *see* 53 Am. Jur. 2d *Mechanic's Liens* § 8 (1970); 57 C.J.S. *Mechanic's Liens* §§ 105–6 (1948).

[85] *See, e.g.,* Ind. Code § 32-8-25-1.

[86] *See, e.g.,* La. Rev. Stat. Ann. § 9:4802(5).

[87] Branecky v. Seaman, 688 S.W.2d 117 (Tex. Ct. App. 1984); Torkko/Korman/Eng'rs v. Penland Ventures, 673 P.2d 769 (Alaska 1983).

The owner's interest in the property is, of course, subject to a mechanic's lien. It typically includes any interest that is assignable, transferable, or conveyable.[88] Property subject to a lien also may include a lessee's leasehold interest,[89] which is important for design professionals engaged by lessees.

What constitutes a building or structure subject to a lien depends on the specific statutory language. Permanent buildings or improvements attached to the land or real property, including streets, curbs, sewer lines, gas and other utility lines, generally are held to be subject to a lien.[90]

In some statutes, the lien attaches only to materials that are physically incorporated into the building or improvement.[91] Other statutes allow the lien to attach to materials delivered to the jobsite even though not physically incorporated into the building.[92]

Most mechanic's lien statutes have technical requirements regarding notice and filing. Examination of each statute is essential. Failure to comply with notice and filing requirements may result in an unenforceable lien or extinguishment of an otherwise valid claim.

Most statutes require the lienholder to give written notice of a claim to the owner before filing the lien.[93] Some statutes may require notices to be sent at regular intervals throughout the project,[94] or within a certain time from the date services or materials are last furnished.[95]

Depending upon the particular statutory scheme, the lien becomes effective either from the date the work commences[96] or the date the lien is filed.[97] In Louisiana, if the notice of the contract between the owner and the contractor is properly filed, the lien (called a *privilege*) is effective as to third persons from the date of filing.[98]

---

[88] Hill Behan Lumber Co. v. American Nat'l Bank & Trust Co., 101 Ill. App. 3d 268, 427 N.E.2d 1325 (1981).

[89] *See, e.g.*, Ill. Rev. Stat. 9:4806; *In re* California Steel Co., 21 Bankr. 383 (N.D. Ill. 1983).

[90] *See* W.L. Dev. Corp. v. Triford Realty, Inc., 484 N.Y.2d 29, 370 N.E.2d 969, 406 N.Y.S.2d 437 (1978).

[91] Henry & John Assocs. v. Demmilo Constr. Corp., 137 Misc. 2d 354, 520 N.Y.S.2d 340 (1987).

[92] *See* Contract Steel Sales, Inc. v. Freedom Constr. Co., 321 N.C. 215, 362 S.E.2d 547 (1987).

[93] *See, e.g.*, Tex. Prop. Code Ann. § 53.001 *et seq.* (Vernon Supp. 1989).

[94] *Id.* (sub-subcontractors are required to send out notices at approximate 30-day intervals).

[95] Mechanic's Lien Act, ch. 82, § 24; La. Rev. Stat. Ann. (within 30 or 60 days from filing the notice of termination of the work or completion or abandonment of the work).

[96] Hickey v. Polachack, 63 Or. App. 784, 666 P.2d 294 (1983); Weather Eng'g & Mfg. v. Piron Springs Condominiums, Inc., 192 Colo. 495, 563 P.2d 346 (1977).

[97] Residential & Indus. Loan Co. v. Weinberg, 279 Md. 43, 369 A.2d 563, *cert. denied,* 434 U.S. 876 (1977).

[98] La. Rev. Stat. Ann. § 9:4820A (West).

A lienholder is free not to exercise lien rights if so desired. A lienholder also may agree in advance to waive lien rights, and such agreements, known as *waivers,* are generally enforceable.[99] A waiver is a knowing and voluntary act. It may be expressed in a written document, or implied from acts, conduct, or a course of dealing between the parties[100] indicating a clear intention to waive.[101]

Express waivers may be written into the contract between the owner and the contractor, who purports to waive the rights of employees, or in the contract between the contractor and subcontractors, materialmen, and suppliers. Not all states will enforce a contract provision between the owner and contractor that purports to waive the lien rights of laborers, suppliers, and subcontractors. In those jurisdictions that do give such provisions effect, the contractor is prohibited from waiving the lien rights of others after executing the contract with the owner or after the lien rights have attached. Moreover, waivers in contracts between the owner and the prime contractor are not binding on laborers and suppliers unless they have actual notice of the waiver at the time they furnish the labor or materials.[102] Reference to the state's statutory law and jurisprudence should be made before incorporating such a clause in a construction contract.

Standard form agreements between design professionals and their clients normally do not provide for lien rights, which are statutory in nature and exist by operation of law. Two standard clauses promulgated by the American Institute of Architects in Document A201, General Conditions of the Contract for Construction, relate to lien rights of others. Both have the intention and effect of requiring the contractor to pay subcontractors and suppliers timely in order to receive payment from the owner, but they do not purport to waive the lien rights of others. They represent an attempt to strike a balance between the rights of lienholders to timely payment and protection of the owner's property from liens that might upset financing.

Subparagraph 9.3.3 of AIA Document A201 obligates the contractor to warrant that the portion of the work for which application for payment is submitted will pass to the owner "free and clear of liens, claims, security interests, or encumbrances in favor of the contractor, subcontractors, materials suppliers, or other persons or entities making a claim by reason of having provided labor, materials and equipment related to the Work." A violation of this warrant will constitute a breach of the contractor's agreement, and will authorize the design professional, pursuant to subparagraph

---

[99] *See, e.g.,* Pero Bldg. Co. v. Smith, 6 Conn. App. 180, 504 A.2d 524 (1986); Greenfield Erectors & Builders, Inc. v. Feleure, 443 N.E.2d 87 (Ind. Ct. App. 1983); Formigli Corp. v. Fox, 348 F. Supp. 629 (E.D. Pa. 1972).

[100] 57 C.J.S. *Mechanic's Liens* § 223 (1948).

[101] *Id.,* § 224, at 795; *see also* 53 Am. Jur. 2d *Mechanic's Liens* § 292, at 827 (1970).

[102] 57 C.J.S. *Mechanic's Liens* § 222, at 793 (1948).

9.5.1, to withhold certification or, "because of subsequently discovered evidence or subsequent observations," entitle the design professional to nullify the payment certificate(s) previously issued.[103]

The second clause, contained in paragraph 9.10.2, concerns the contractor's right to final payment and release of retainage. Under this clause, the owner has no obligation to make final payment or release the retainage until the contractor submits evidence that all bills have been paid and "if required by the owner, other data establishing payment or satisfaction of obligation such as receipts, releases and waivers of liens, claims, security interests or encumbrances arising out of the Contract, to the extent and in such form as may be designated by the Owner."

If the subcontractor or supplier refuses to execute a waiver, the clause obligates the contractor to execute a release of the lien bond, indemnifying the owner's property, or refund to the owner all money that the owner may be compelled to pay to satisfy the lien, including costs and reasonable attorneys' fees.

These clauses create significant economic incentive for the contractor to pay workers and subcontractors without waiving their lien rights, and represent a reasonable means of protecting both the owner's property from lien encumbrances and laborers, subcontractors, and suppliers from nonpayment. Even in those states that enforce written waivers, these clauses should be considered as reasonable and workable alternatives.

§ 17.7 Payment and Completion Certificates

Contract administration duties normally include certification of contractor payment applications and substantial completion to client-owners. Such certifications go to the progress and quality of the work, measured against the requirements of the contract documents.

Third-party completion certificates, running in favor of project lenders, regulatory agencies, sureties, and investors, are now commonplace. These certifications are often done as an accommodation to the owner, and fall outside the design professional's normal contract obligations. Design professionals incur potential liability for third-party certifications, even in the absence of contracts with these parties.

With respect to contractor payment applications, design professionals essentially certify that the work has been performed in accordance with the contract documents and that the contractor is entitled to the payment for which application is made. Typical language outlining these duties can be found in AIA documents, including those relating to the agreement

[103] AIA A201-1987, para. 9.5.1. *See* Federal Ins. Co. v. Community State Bank, 905 F.2d 112 (5th Cir. 1990).

between owner and architect[104] and general conditions of owner-contractor agreements.[105]

Standard form payment applications normally contain dual certifications by the contractor and design professional. From the design professional's standpoint, it is essential that the wording of the certification echo that found in the underlying agreement with the owner, including all qualifying and protective language.[106]

Irrespective of the qualifying language in such payment applications, contracts, or general conditions, owners pay contractors in reliance on the certifications by their design professionals. When a certification is erroneous and the owner pays to his or her detriment, the liability implications for the design professional are clear and direct.

Design professionals should be aware of and insist on language in their contracts by which payment certifications can be declined and limited without undue risk of exposure to the contractor. An example of such language is found in AIA standard form general conditions.[107]

The design professional's underlying obligation to protect the owner is ineluctable and normally will eclipse most defenses the design professional may raise to claims of miscertification or overcertification. Certifications should, therefore, only be made upon careful investigation and verification of the facts.

Design professionals should avoid making any certifications directly to or for the benefit of third parties whenever possible. Certifications made to governmental and regulatory agencies, sureties, insurers, and lenders create additional potential tort liability for the design professional beyond the liability already assumed by contract with their clients. In the all too frequent situation of a contractor default or inability to complete a project, miscertification or overcertification of contractor payment applications that expose contractor sureties or project lenders to financial loss almost always will result in a claim against the design professional.

Regulatory agencies and lenders often have their own certification forms that project owners are required to submit to obtain financing and use and occupancy permits. Their forms normally contain strong, unqualified statements that the work was constructed in strict accordance with the contract documents and that the work meets all laws, codes, and standards. Sureties regularly ask design professionals to answer questionnaires about progress and status of the work. When certifications and responses are overstated and/or erroneous, and the intended recipient can show detrimental reliance thereon, the design professional is potentially exposed to claims

[104] AIA B141-1987, subpara. 2.6.10.

[105] AIA A201-1987, subpara. 9.4.2.

[106] AIA G702-1983.

[107] AIA A201-1987, subpara. 9.5.1.

of negligence, misrepresentation, breach of warranty or guarantee, or even fraud.

Design professionals can take measures to limit or spread the potential liability for certifications. In the case of payment certifications, which are virtually unavoidable when performing contract administration, design professionals should insist upon language in their owner contracts and the project general conditions similar to that quoted. Design professionals also can request that their clients and their clients' lenders engage their own inspectors or construction managers for independent verification and certification of payment requests.

Third-party certifications present unique problems, as owners frequently are unaware of their requirements at the time of contracting with their design professional. Standard form contracts do not normally obligate design professionals to make third-party certifications. In situations in which the design professional is requested to undertake third-party certifications not required by the contract, the design professional can always refuse. This approach has risks and may expose the design professional to economic pressure by the owner and threats of a claim for business interference. In the end, the design professional usually capitulates. A better approach may be to use a contract provision to the effect that any certifications required of the design professional, other than for contractor payment or substantial completion, shall only be in such form as agreed by the design professional. Again, there may be problems when the owner is confronted with statutorily mandated certifications that cannot be altered by private contract.

Third-party certifications must be approached on a case-by-case basis, based on the facts and circumstances of each situation. Certifications of matters beyond or inconsistent with the design professional's engagement must be avoided. Broad and unqualified statements should be avoided, such as "the project conforms to all laws, building codes, and standards." Express assumption of responsibility for a public duty should be avoided, as should express guarantees or warranties. In addition, when completed construction is involved, design professionals should attempt to condition their certification on similar certification from the contractor. A general working example of a third-party certification is as follows:

> I hereby certify that, to the best of my knowledge, information and belief, the work performed by (insert name of contractor) pursuant to Building Permit Number (   ), dated (   ) and issued by (   ), for (project description) located at (address) was substantially complete on (date), and that the work generally conforms to the requirements of the drawings and specifications upon which said building permit was issued.
>
> This certification is based upon and limited to observations made during periodic on-site visits of the work made by (design professional) and does not constitute a guarantee or warranty of the work by (contractor), (who/

> which) was solely responsible for all construction means, methods, techniques, sequences and procedures and (who/which) was solely responsible for performing the work in accordance with the drawings and specifications on which said building permit was issued.
>
> This certification is conditioned upon and subject to (contractor) making a similar certification, absent which this certification shall be without effect.

The risks of third-party certifications are obvious, but should be manageable with careful forethought and assistance from legal counsel.

§ 17.8 Preventing Unauthorized Use or Reuse of Contract Documents

Control over contract documents is warranted when confidential and proprietary subject matter is involved, and as a means of avoiding potential liability.

Public owners commonly want to own the contract documents and require specific contract provisions designating the documents as "works made for hire" and deleting all reference to the documents as "instruments of the design professional's service." In such instances, a contract provision is suggested that enables the design professional to remove title blocks and professional seals from the documents before delivery to the owner. Alternatively, a contract provision is suggested that prohibits the owner's reuse of the documents without the design professional's prior written consent and appropriate compensation, and which obligates the owner to hold harmless, indemnify, and defend the design professional in the event of claims arising from unauthorized reuse.

Owners also may seek to limit circulation of copies of the drawings and specifications. For example, commercial banks often insist upon closely controlled circulation of floor plans, wall sections, and material specifications of vault areas. In the case of custom or monumental projects, owners and design professionals alike have an interest in controlling circulation of the documents to deter replication.

Although absolute control over circulation of contract documents is a practical impossibility, protective measures can be taken.

Language addressing ownership and permissible use or reuse of contract documents should be incorporated in the design professional's agreement with the owner and the general conditions of the agreement between the owner and contractor.[108] Similar protective language also can be included or incorporated by reference in subcontracts and in all agreements between the design professional and its consultants.

---

[108] AIA A201-1987, subpara. 1.3.1.

Control over copies of the contract documents is possible through a log and numbering system maintained by the design professional, to account for each original copy made from the drawings and specifications. Design professionals ordinarily employ such a system for bid sets, requiring deposits from bidders as an inducement for the return of all sets taken by unsuccessful bidders. By suitable language in the construction contract, subcontracts, and agreements between the design professional and its consultants, the return of all original copies can be mandated. However, retention of record sets by contractors and design professionals is a normal practice. See § **17.9**.

Another measure is the use of a stamp on all original copies made of the drawings and specifications, containing restrictive wording similar to that quoted. The wording of the stamp should conform to the provisions on use and ownership of contract documents found in the design professional's agreement, the contractor's agreement, and the general conditions.

Design professionals now have copyright protection of drawings and specifications by law, and in some instances can secure patent protection for their work product, as discussed in § **17.5**.

By using the protective measures discussed, circulation and unauthorized use or reuse of contract documents can be controlled, and design professionals can reduce or avoid potential liability.

§ 17.9 Record Set Documents

Design professionals always should maintain a complete set of the contract documents for record purposes. The record set should be on a reproducible medium, in case additional copies are ever needed. Even when the owner contracts for and the design professional relinquishes ownership of the contract documents, the contract should contain an exception permitting the design professional to retain a record set.

Record documents serve two important purposes. First, in the event of claims against the design professional arising out of the design and/or construction, complete records are essential for defense. Second, when future renovations or additions are anticipated, original drawings and specifications are helpful.

§ 17.10 Approval of Shop Drawings and Other Documents

Contract administration services normally include review and approval of shop drawings, product data, and samples, which will be referred to collectively as *shop drawings*. Careful shop drawing review is critical to successful project completion. Careless review and approval of shop drawings is a frequent source of claims against design professionals.

Shop drawings are essentially an intermediate step between the contract documents and the fabrication and installation of materials and equipment. Contract drawings tend to be schematic and only show design intent, and are not ordinarily of sufficient detail for fabrication and installation of materials and equipment. Shop drawings, which are prepared by contractors, fabricators, and manufacturers, are typically large-scale, detailed representations of what is called for in the contract documents, for the purpose of fabrication and installation.

Although not normally part of the defined contract documents, shop drawings arguably supersede contract drawings and specifications to the extent that contractors are required to undertake the work only from approved shop drawings. Although the contractor is normally obligated to review and approve shop drawings before submission to the design professional, final approval normally lies with the design professional.

The very best contract documents are of little value if the flawed shop drawings are carelessly approved by the design professional. Potentially, the design professional faces sole responsibility for work performed pursuant to flawed shop drawings. At best, the design professional faces shared responsibility with the contractor for damages from deficient shop drawings.

Clear contract language is important to define the respective shop drawing responsibilities of the contractor and design professional.

Obligations normally placed upon the contractor found in the AIA general conditions speak to timely submittals, unnecessary submittals, verification, checking, coordination, deviations, and errors and omissions.[109] Most important is the requirement that the contractor approve shop drawings before submission to the design professional. Notwithstanding the obligations placed on the contractor, design professionals are not relieved of responsibility for shop drawing errors so long as they participate in the review and approval process.

It is also important, through supplemental general conditions, to require specific wording for an approval stamp to be used by the contractor on all shop drawing submittals. The wording should mirror the contractor's shop drawing obligations found in the general conditions. Design professionals are encouraged to rigorously follow the submittal procedure outlined in the general conditions, and not accept submittals that lack the contractor's stamp indicating review and approval. Submittals made without a contractor's stamp should be returned without any action taken. By accepting unapproved shop drawings from a contractor, the design professional may assume total liability for errors.

[109] AIA A201-1987, subparas. 3.12.5, 3.12.7, and 3.12.8.

The design professional's responsibilities for shop drawings should be set out in both the owner-design professional agreement and the general conditions. Typical language may be found in the AIA agreement between owners and design professionals.[110] The limitations and qualifications placed on shop drawing review found in most standard form agreements may give the design professional a false sense of security. Often-used limitations of the design professional's review and approval to "conformance with information given" or "design concept" may confuse a lay judge or jury asked to decide a matter involving shop drawing errors. Further, the attempted limitation of the design professional's review by excluding details such as dimensions, quantities, or substantiation of instruction for installation or performance, may be illusory. What happens if the design professional checks and notes selected dimensional or detail errors, and not others? If details are excluded, what is the design professional really reviewing and approving? Can't the contractor rely upon the design professional's approval? Although qualifications and limitations are appropriate, design professionals should not allow their contract provisions to become a disincentive for careful review and approval. The intended purpose of double review and approval of shop drawings (by the contractor and design professional) is to decrease the chance for errors and increase the prospect for a problem-free project.

The wording of contractors' and design professionals' shop drawing stamps is important. To the extent that the contract documents require both contractor and design professional to "review and approve" shop drawings, terms such as "not rejected," "accepted," "furnish as noted," "examined," or "no exception taken" generally will be ignored and courts likely will follow the underlying obligations found in contractors' and design professionals' agreements, and in the general conditions.

Design professionals are cautioned against specifying unnecessary shop drawings, and against reviewing and approving shop drawings that were not specified. Needless requirements for shop drawings only increase the chance for error and potential liability of the design professional. When shop drawings are specified but not submitted, the design professional is cautioned against allowing the work to proceed. Standard form general conditions normally include a provision mandating that work not proceed unless done from approved shop drawings.[111]

Design professionals should use care in contracting with their professional consultants, and bind their consultants to the same shop drawing and approval requirements placed on them. Consultants' contracts also should include requirements for shop drawing approval stamps, along the lines mentioned. For example, an architect who contracts with a structural

---

[110] AIA B141-1987, subpara. 2.6.12; AIA A201-1987, subpara. 4.2.7.

[111] AIA A201-1987, subpara. 3.12.6.

engineer should require the engineer to undertake review and approval of all structural shop drawings. Were the architect to undertake review and approval of this work, the architect would likely assume full liability for damages resulting from fabrication and installation errors.

The responsibility and procedures for correction and resubmission of rejected shop drawings also should be clearly established in the general conditions. Shop drawings often require correction and resubmission. Rather than requiring the contractor to correct and resubmit, design professionals often undertake the corrections themselves and approve the shop drawings on an "as noted" basis. This practice is dangerous because the design professional could be colored as the author or coauthor of shop drawings that may ultimately prove deficient. The safer procedure, albeit longer, is to require the contractor to resubmit shop drawings until all corrections have been made. Considering that shop drawings for manufactured items normally are very specialized and often employ graphic conventions with which the design professional may be unfamiliar, it is preferable that all changes and corrections be made by the contractor, supplier, or manufacturer who is the original author.

When corrections are necessary, it is also important that the design professional compare resubmissions with prior submissions to determine that no changes other than the noted corrections were made. Standard form language requiring contractors to point out deviations in shop drawings from the requirements of contract documents does not go far enough. The general conditions also should contain provisions mandating that all changes from previously submitted shop drawings be called to the design professional's attention. To facilitate comparative reviews with prior submittals, design professionals should maintain record copies of each shop drawing submission.

Design professionals have a tendency to place less importance on shop drawing review than on basic design and specification, and to use lower paid and less experienced personnel for these tasks. Ideally, the project designer and specifier, who are most familiar with the contract requirements, should review and approve shop drawings. If draftspersons or other nonregistered professionals are used for shop drawing review, their work should be done under the close and direct personal supervision of the project designer or specifier.

Design professionals would be better served by devoting their efforts to careful shop drawing review and avoiding construction problems, rather than trying to craft contract provisions that purportedly disclaim or shift shop drawing responsibility to contractors and consultants. The walkway collapse at the Kansas City Hyatt remains a painful testament to the importance of careful shop drawing review and approval.

CHAPTER 18

CONTRACT AND PROJECT ADMINISTRATION

Neil F. Katz
Frederic Z. Samelian
R. Burton Ward

Neil F. Katz is a civil engineer and an attorney with 23 years' experience in construction changes, claims, and disputes. He has served as a consultant on projects including warehouse, highway, bridge, and airport terminal construction. In his present position as a senior vice president for Hill International, Inc. in Irvine, California, he has been responsible for the evaluation of over $2 billion of construction disputes, most alleging design deficiencies. Mr. Katz is a practicing trial attorney, licensed in New Jersey and Pennsylvania, and is a member of the patent bar. He has presented in-house seminars to various clients and professional organizations and published articles on matters related to construction law and disputes.

Frederic Z. Samelian is president, western region, for Hill International, Inc. in Irvine, California. He has broad engineering and construction industry experience both in the United States and abroad. Mr. Samelian is project executive on several of Hill's major projects, including the Los Angeles Metro Rail Project for the United States Department of Transportation. He has been asked to speak internationally on subjects relating to trends in the construction industry and has authored articles and papers on the challenges facing managers of professional services organizations.

R. Burton Ward is a senior consultant for Hill International, Inc.'s western region. A graduate of Stanford University, he holds advanced degrees in civil engineering and architecture from the University of California at Berkeley. He also holds a J.D. from Whittier College. Mr. Ward applies his prior experience as an engineer and licensed architect to the investigation and resolution of construction claims relating to large-scale public works and commercial projects.

---

§ 18.1 Introduction

As a necessary consequence of providing design services to clients, architect/engineers (A/Es) find themselves administering the construction contracts that implement their designs. This chapter defines the scope of the liabilities that flow from the tasks a design professional may be called upon to perform during the administration of a construction contract. The design professional may be perceived as uniquely equipped to administer the construction contract by virtue of his knowledge of the design, his involvement in the preparation of the plans and specifications, and his professional skills. However, during construction administration, the A/E must deal with attacks on his design and his role as impartial interpreter of contract documents and arbitrator of disputes. The design professional can best limit construction administration risks and liabilities by means of carefully drafted service and construction contracts.

Contract administration responsibility poses professional and economic risks to A/Es through interpretation of contract documents, construction supervision, inspection, review of submittals, issuance of change orders, schedule control, cost control, payment certification, and the resolution of construction disputes.[1] The design professional must examine the scope of each specific responsibility and its associated risks in light of the particular type of contract employed by the owner for construction of the project.

Although the design professions have become increasingly aware of their vulnerability to malpractice liability in construction contract administration, courts are expanding the reach of that liability. Moreover, gaps sometimes develop between prudent professional practice and actual performance in the field. The design professional should provide the personnel, training, and document control necessary to minimize the risks for his client and himself.

§ 18.2 Contracts Allocate Risks and Responsibilities

The roles of the participants in a construction project vary with the type of construction contract. Contracts function to allocate risks and responsibilities among the parties. Selection of the appropriate type of contract and the choices as to pricing, scheduling, and organization of construction are a function of the owner's objectives and available resources. The particular contract chosen will determine the role the design professional will play and the risks and liabilities to be assumed. Construction contracts can be classified three different ways: by the method of fixing the price, by the method of designing the project, or by the method of managing construction.

§ 18.3 —Contracts Classified by Method of Fixing Price

Lump-Sum or Fixed-Price Contract

In a lump-sum or fixed-price contract, the contractor typically agrees to perform a specified scope of work for a fixed dollar amount. This type of construction contract works best for well-defined projects in which all participants have successful experience in similar projects. The owner seeks to

[1] AIA B141-1987, Standard Form of Agreement Between Owner and Architect.

minimize risks by fixing the scope of work through the design professional's preparation of a complete and accurate set of plans and specifications. Performance risks, such as cost and schedule control, are placed on the contractor. In practice, the scope of work may require adjustment to accommodate differing site conditions, design or specification shortcomings, and owner's revisions. Costs arising from perceived changes in the nature or scope of work, as well as delays and disruption, become sources of litigation.

The design professional's liabilities arise out of the design contract with the owner, which sets out the general responsibilities of the architect or engineer during contract administration. The design professional's role is limited by the design services agreement, and usually acknowledged in the construction contract, to be that of agent for the owner in the administration of the contract, and that of a quasi-judicial officer for resolving disputes between the owner and the contractor.[2] If the design professional uses one of the standard professional association service contracts, exculpatory language in the contract can effectively narrow responsibilities and isolate the architect or engineer from significant areas of malpractice liability that may arise during construction contract administration.[3]

Unit-Price Contract

In a unit-price contract, the contractor agrees, for a fixed price per unit of work, to perform work whose scope can only be estimated. A unit-price contract presupposes repetitive units of work, for which unit costs can be established. The owner and contractor agree to shift the economic risk of an uncertain total price from contractor to owner. In a unit-price contract, the contractor has based its unit contract prices upon estimated quantities furnished by the owner[4] and developed by the design professional.

Administration of a unit-price construction contract means added responsibility for the design professional in certifying or estimating quantities of work performed for purposes of progress payments to the contractor during the course of the work. Owners may make construction administration claims against design professionals for inaccurate quantity estimates.[5]

Any unbalanced bid pricing in the contract increases the incentives for fraud and collusion in the estimation of quantities of work during

[2] J. Acret, Attorney's Guide to California Construction Contracts and Disputes 474 (2d ed. 1990).

[3] Waggoner v. W&W Steel Co., 657 P.2d 147 (Okla. 1982).

[4] Peter Kiewit Sons' Co. v. United States, 109 Ct. Cl. 517, 74 F. Supp. 165 (1947).

[5] Newton Inv. Co. v. Bernard & Burk, Inc., 220 So. 2d 822 (Miss. 1969).

construction administration.[6] Contractor efforts to increase more profitable work and decrease less profitable work can interfere with the timely completion of the project.

Cost-Plus Contract

An owner may choose to contract on a cost-plus or a time and materials basis, if the scope of work, the means and methods of construction, or final cost are not clear before execution of the contract. Such contracts might include projects involving innovative designs or technologies, new or unusual materials, unusual sites, or incomplete designs and details.

The design professional owes heightened construction administration duties to the owner in a cost-plus or cost-reimbursable contract.[7] These contracts create a fiduciary relationship in which both the contractor[8] and the design professional[9] have a duty to protect the owner from excessive costs. At a minimum, the design professional has an implied duty to keep the owner informed of the costs of construction. Cost-plus contracts create a disincentive for the contractor to control construction costs; the contractor's profit increases as costs increase. For this reason, these contracts may have special provisions that attempt to control the amount paid to the contractor, or to provide incentives to the contractor to control costs.

The design professional is exposed to liability in administering the cost-plus contract if he fails to monitor cost increases and keep the owner informed. In *Williams Engineering, Inc. v. Goodyear, Inc.*,[10] for example, an engineer was retained to design a recreational water slide. The engineer suggested contracting for construction on a cost-plus basis. Upon completion of the design phase, the design engineer indicated the estimated construction price to be $409,000. Three days before the projected opening of the water slide, the cost was estimated at $409,000. Twenty days after the slide opened, the owner was billed for $880,000 in construction costs; the project was indicated to be only 82 percent complete and final costs were estimated to be approximately $1 million. The court denied the engineer additional fees sought from the owner and held him liable to the owner for $205,000 of excess construction costs for his negligent failure to reveal the approximate cost of the construction to the owner until near completion.

---

[6] Boenning v. Brick Township Mun. Utils. Auth., 150 N.J. Super. 32, 374 A.2d 1214 (1977).

[7] First Nat'l Bank v. Cann, 503 F. Supp. 419 (N.D. Ohio 1980), *aff'd*, 669 F.2d 415 (6th Cir. 1982).

[8] Jones v. J.H. Hiser Constr. Co., 60 Md. App. 671, 484 A.2d 302 (1984).

[9] Williams Eng'g, Inc. v. Goodyear, Inc., 496 So. 2d 1012 (La. 1986).

[10] *Id.*

§ 18.4 —Contracts Classified by Design Process

Single-Prime Contract

The single-prime or design-award-build contract is the traditional building contract and requires complete plans and specifications before the construction contract is awarded. The single-prime contract gives the contractor, who may subcontract portions of the work, full construction responsibility, while the owner retains responsibility for the design. The owner impliedly warrants to the contractor that the plans and specifications are free from defects and the project can be built from the plans and specifications. The owner therefore relies upon the design professional to provide complete and accurate contract plans and specifications.[11] If the contractor can prove the plans and specifications defective, then the contractor may be able to recover the costs of the extra work necessary to overcome the defects.[12]

Design-Build Contract

In a design-build contract,[13] the contractor assumes responsibility for design, or the designer assumes responsibility for construction. This type of contract enables the owner to hold the contractor/designer solely responsible for completing a project that meets the performance criteria, at the specified time, and at the agreed price.

An *outline specification* sets out in general terms the scope and quality of the finished work. It is prepared by a design professional before entering into the design-build contract and mitigates risks to the owner associated with the undefined scope of work. The owner has the right to insist upon the right to review complete plans before the contractor begins construction.[14]

Phased-Construction (Fast-Track) Contract

In a phased-construction or fast-track project, construction and design phases overlap, and construction proceeds before design is complete. An incomplete design results in an incomplete definition of the scope and cost

---

[11] United States v. Spearin, 248 U.S. 132 (1918).

[12] The ability of the contractor to recover damages has been subject to limitations. In particular, the liability of public entities under the theory of implied warranty may be limited by statute and common law particular to each jurisdiction. Jasper Constr., Inc. v. Foothill Junior College Dist., 91 Cal. App. 3d 1, 153 Cal. Rptr. 767 (1979).

[13] *See* J. Acret, California Construction Contracts and Disputes 63–66 (2d ed. 1990).

[14] Romala Corp. v. United States, 20 Cl. Ct. 435 (1990).

of the work. Unless a design-build type contract can be combined with a phased-construction contract to establish a fixed or lump-sum price, the contract necessarily requires a unit price or cost-plus price.

The promised advantages of a phased-construction contract relate to time savings: earlier start of construction, earlier completion, and earlier financial commitments to construction, occupancy, or ownership. To realize the promised time savings, however, design and construction processes require close coordination and the A/E must meet design schedule commitments. The fast-track contract is a high-risk proposition for both design professional and owner. Potential problems that could be otherwise controlled and managed in other types of contracts may create financial catastrophe in fast-track construction projects. Beyond certain stages of construction, further evolution of the project design may force the owner to abandon guaranteed maximum construction cost constraints to finish the project and recover construction funds already spent.

The time pressures inherent in a fast-track construction contract can force interdependent portions of the project to be designed concurrently, which complicates design and specification coordination. Improper design coordination before initiation of construction may produce field changes and construction claims, which may be attributed to the A/E. The size of construction delay claims can approach or exceed the original estimated construction cost of a project.[15] Because the starting point of a phased-construction contract is incomplete design, the potential claims are likely to be large and design related. Therefore, phased construction exposes the design professional to substantial liability risks during construction administration.

§ 18.5 —Contracts Classified by Construction Management Authority

Single-Prime Contract

This traditional contract choice offers the owner the most control over the construction process. The design clearly establishes the scope of work before the execution of the construction contract. The design professional observes construction to verify conformance with the plans and specifications and to ensure the quality of the work. The contractor manages the construction process and answers for the quality of the construction product. The architect or engineer has responsibility for certifying contractor entitlement to payment as well as monitoring the schedule and cost.

[15] Williams Eng'g, Inc. v. Goodyear, Inc., 496 So. 2d 1012 (La. 1986).

Construction Management Contract

In a construction management contract, a party other than the general contractor or the design professional is given management authority over the construction process. The authority of the construction manager varies considerably from project to project. In theory, the construction manager brings a detached, independent, experienced person onto the jobsite to increase the efficiency of construction and to safeguard the owner's interests. The construction manager also can supply valuable experience in cost and schedule control systems. The legal definitions of the rights, duties, and liabilities of the construction manager vis-à-vis the owner, design professional, and contractor, however, seldom are clear, because of a general lack of consensus in the industry.[16] To the extent the owner delegates to the construction manager construction administration duties that would otherwise be the responsibility of the design professional, the liability of the A/E would appear to be reduced; but in practice, the construction manager becomes just one more party with interests that may be adverse to the design professional. At a minimum, the introduction of a construction manager breaks the direct communication links that otherwise exist between the design professional and the owner, between the owner and the contractor, and between the design professional and the contractor. Furthermore, the introduction of a construction manager fragments accountability for completion of the construction product: responsibility for the management of construction is separated from the responsibility for the quality of the construction product.

Multiple-Prime Contract

In a multiple-prime construction contract, the owner contracts directly with different prime contractors to provide different portions of the work. In the absence of any contractual language delegating the supervisory authority to another party, the owner retains control over construction management. The leading case dealing with authority to manage construction on a multiple-prime construction contract is *Broadway Maintenance Corp. v. Rutgers.*[17] In that case, contracts conflicted as to who was to exercise supervisory control over construction. Project completion was delayed. Construction control was fractionized. Liability for delay was seen to follow control of construction, and the major participants in the project were disclaiming supervisory control to escape liability. In *Rutgers,* the university engaged an architect for contract administration of multiple-prime contracts for the construction of a medical school. Two of the contractors

[16] J. Sweet, Legal Aspects of Architecture, Engineering, and the Construction Process 387 (4th ed. 1989).

[17] 90 N.J. 253, 447 A.2d 906 (1982).

brought suit against the university for delay damages flowing from alleged breaches of contract. The issue was whether the university retained supervisory authority. The court stated that authority to supervise the work would "be found in the contract language illuminated by surrounding circumstances." In a multiple-prime construction contract, the owner has the implied duty to coordinate and control the work in the absence of the contractual delegation of the supervisory authority to one of the contractors, or a third party. Rutgers had intended to exculpate itself from liability for supervision of the work, but to whom the supervisory authority was delegated was unclear, because the university had delegated authority to several parties: one of the contractors, a scheduling consultant, and an architect. The court ultimately held that each of the contractors could maintain suit against a fellow contractor, who was a wrongdoer on a third-party beneficiary theory for damages. The design professional escaped liability despite contractual language that the architect was to:

> "supervise the construction of work by periodic inspections sufficient to verify the quality of construction and the conformity of the construction to the plans and specifications . . . and by which supervision the architect shall coordinate the work of the various contractors and expedite the construction of the Project." If a contractor were delayed in completing the work whether due to the owner, any other contractor, the architect, or other causes beyond the contractor's control, the architect alone was authorized to determine extensions of time to which a prime contractor would be entitled. In this respect the trial court found that the architect acted as a an impartial and independent umpire, and as such was not the agent of either Rutgers or the contractor.[18]

The architect and engineer must take particular care in preparing construction documents to delineate and allocate responsibilities for construction, supervision of the work, and contract administration. The multiple-prime contract's usefulness lies in the ability of the owner to retain close control over the various trade contracts. However, if the owner lacks the expertise, experience, and capacity to effectively manage the construction, the multiple-prime contract can produce severe management difficulties during construction.

§ 18.6 Contract Administration: Conventional View

Although traditionally the A/E may have taken an important part in the general supervision of construction work,[19] in recent decades the American

---

[18] 447 A.2d at 913.

[19] Only since 1961 has the AIA changed its standard contracts to exclude general supervision of the work.

Institute of Architects (AIA) standard design services agreement has attempted to insulate the architect from liability to owners, contractors, and third parties for administration of the construction contract. The AIA standard design services contract[20] divides design services into *basic services* and *additional services.* The AIA apportions basic services into five phases:[21]

Phase 1. Schematic Design
Phase 2. Design Development
Phase 3. Preparation of Construction Documents
Phase 4. Bidding or Negotiation
Phase 5. Construction Administration

This discussion focuses exclusively on phase 5, construction administration. The administration of the construction contract commences with the award of the contract for construction and terminates with the issuance of the final certificate for payment or 60 days after the date of substantial completion.[22]

In recent years,[23] the AIA standard design services contract has narrowly defined the range of contract administration services to be provided as part of the basic services. Basic services require the architect to:

1. Visit the site at appropriate intervals for observation of completed work
2. Check conformance with the contract plans
3. Review and certify the contractor's applications for payment
4. Reject work not in conformance with contract plans
5. Review and approve submittals
6. Prepare change orders
7. Approve minor changes in the work
8. Conduct inspections to determine substantial and final completion
9. Issue final certificate of payment
10. Render final decisions on matters relating to aesthetic effect
11. Render written decisions on claims, disputes, or other matters.

---

[20] AIA B141-1987, Standard Form of Agreement Between Owner and Architect.

[21] AIA B141-1977, Standard Form of Agreement Between Owner and Architect.

[22] AIA B141-1987, Standard Form of Agreement Between Owner and Architect.

[23] The AIA's 1958 *Standard Documents* listed no description of additional services. AIA B141-1987, Standard Form of Agreement Between Owner and Architect, lists nine "contingent additional services" and twenty "optional additional services."

The language of the AIA design services contract specifically excludes the architect from supervisory control in an effort to avoid professional liability arising from negligent supervision of the construction work, site conditions, operations, equipment, personnel, and safety.[24]

The intended result of this delineation of construction contract administration services in the AIA standard design services agreement is to substitute a narrow *observation standard* for measuring the architect's performance of construction contract administration responsibilities for the wider, more inclusive, *supervision standard.*

Underlying the AIA's effort to move the architect's contract administration role away from supervision toward observation is the basic legal liability principle that responsibility follows control. Control has two aspects: authority and skill. The responsibility for a construction defect runs to that participant in the construction process who represented himself to have the necessary authority and skill to make the construction decision. Thus, when a reputedly skilled design professional has been retained by the owner, not only to design the project but also to supervise construction, the design professional necessarily assumes responsibility for the construction work he supervises. In contrast, however, a design professional who is retained by the owner only to observe the work lacks the critical authority to control the construction work and, therefore, in theory incurs no liability for negligent performance of the construction work.

In practice, however, the design professional's exposure to liability for negligent construction work is not so easily eliminated. Pressures and realities of the construction process operate to expand the design professional's responsibilities beyond mere observation. The owner's use of nontraditional forms of construction contracts, the technical complexity of construction plans and specifications, and a lack of qualified construction personnel, skilled labor, and proper materials complicate the issue.

The observation standard of performance can best be applied only to an A/E administering the construction on a traditional lump-sum, single-prime construction contract with the general contractor managing construction. If the client elects to use another type of construction contract, the A/E is forced to move beyond the limits of mere observation.

The technical complexity of construction plans and specifications requires meticulous design detailing; however, the owner's design budget and construction schedule impose limits on the quality of design and detailing achievable on a set of construction plans and specifications.

Inadequate, incomplete, or inaccurate details and specifications force the design professional administering the contract into field redesign during construction. The A/E has a duty to report and correct design errors and

---

[24] J. Sweet, Legal Aspects of Architecture, Engineering, and the Construction Process 231 (4th ed. 1989).

omissions before completion of construction.[25] The A/E does not warrant the plans and specifications to be free of defects.[26] The AIA design services agreement does not explicitly address the architect's duty to correct design deficiencies during construction, but rather requires that the architect "shall endeavor to guard the Owner against defects and deficiencies in the Work."[27] The design professional's conduct in responding to the exigencies, problems, and pressures that develop during construction modifies the contractually defined scope of professional liability. The A/E's field representatives, who attempt to expedite completion and assure the best possible quality of construction, may be induced to go beyond the limits of mere observation in rendering assistance.

The cyclical economic nature of the construction industry also creates reoccurring shortages of qualified supervisory personnel, labor, and materials for construction projects, which necessarily result in portions of the work failing to conform to contract plans and specifications.

The end result of these forces is schedule delays, change orders, conflicts in design philosophy between owner, architect, and engineer, and ultimately contractor claims. In such an environment, the design professional becomes a participant rather than an observer.

§ 18.7 Contract Administration: Expanded View

Owners, contractors, and third-party claimants have enjoyed success in holding the design professional to a wider range of responsibility than the observation standard defined by the language of AIA's standard contract for design services. The courts generally have held that liability flows from responsibility or control. In the resolution of the scope of the design professional's responsibilities or control during contract administration, courts focus on three issues:

What are the design professional's contractual obligations?

Should the A/E's duty be measured by a supervision standard or an observation standard?

Has the A/E altered his obligations by his conduct?[28]

---

[25] Comptroller *ex rel.* VMI v. King, 217 Va. 751, 232 S.E.2d 895 (1977).

[26] "In the absence of an express contractual agreement to the contrary, an architect's obligation does not imply or guarantee a perfect plan." Frischertz Elec. Co. v. Housing Auth., 534 So. 2d 1310 (La. Ct. App. 1988).

[27] AIA B141-1987, Standard Form of Agreement Between Owner and Architect § 2.6.5.

[28] J. Sweet, Legal Aspects of Architecture, Engineering, and the Construction Process 232 (4th ed. 1989).

The standard design services agreement sets contractual limits on the duties and responsibilities of the design professional. Under the standard contracts,[29] the client engages the design professional to design the project, observe construction, interpret plans and specifications, and decide contract disputes. The design professional within this contract format is limited in his authority to act as an agent to bind the owner. It is important to note, however, that contractual limits on the design professional's authority can be modified by the A/E's conduct or course of dealing on a particular project. Owners who have relied upon design professionals for administration of construction contracts and who have experienced difficulties during construction have sought to expand A/E liability, so as to hold the design professional responsible for a wide range of problems that tend to arise during contract administration.

In the course of construction, parties may dispense with the formal contractual relationships, ostensibly to further the best interests of the project. If the design professional wishes to continue to rely upon the contract's formal requirements, he must notify others of his wish not to waive the formal procedures and documentation set forth in the contract. The observation standard of performance set forth under the AIA standard documents can be expanded to a supervisory standard by the conduct of the design professional in administering the contract, by apparent delegation of authority by the owner, or by owner ratification of the professional's conduct. Owners and contractors welcome, maybe even invite, the design professional's representative to relieve them of their contractual obligations, responsibilities, and ultimately liability. The A/E may willingly, or unwittingly, accommodate this expansion of its exposure to risk.

§ 18.8 Authority to Bind Owner

Distinctions must be made among the various actions of the design professional that operate to bind the owner in contract administration. First, the A/E can make decisions as an interpreter of contract documents. Second, the A/E can make decisions as to the performance of the contractor. Finally, the A/E can act as an agent for the owner. The decision-making responsibilities of the design professional are discussed in **§§ 18.9** through **18.15**. The focus in this section is upon the A/E's authority to act as an agent of the owner.

In contrast to the common law, the AIA standard agreement for design services limits the authority of the architect to act on behalf of the owner to

[29] Under both EJCDC and AIA standard general conditions, EJCDC 1910-8 (1983) and AIA A201-1987, the owner and contractor agree in advance to abide by the A/E's award issued after a hearing at which both parties have an opportunity to be heard.

the express delegations contained in the agreement and allows modifications of that authority only by written agreement. The architect is denied authority to modify the contract, other than to make "minor changes" that do not involve a change in contract price or time.[30]

Common law vests the design professional with inherent authority, albeit limited, to act as an agent for the owner, even in the absence of any express delegations of authority.[31] Although the design professional is an agent of the owner, his authority to act for the owner is limited to doing only what it is reasonable to believe the owner wants done. However, this is a difficult standard to apply in the field. For those acts not necessary or incidental to accomplishing an agent's primary responsibilities, the agent should seek authorization of the principal. Although third parties must exercise a degree of reasonableness and diligence in dealing with agents, if the owner has created the appearance of authority around the A/E, and the design professional exercises that apparent authority, liability may be imposed upon the owner for acts of the professional. To the extent that the A/E has exceeded the limits of his authority, the A/E is held responsible to the owner for the consequences.

§ 18.9 Construction Administration: Compliance with Contract

Construction projects can be complex undertakings. Although plans and specifications attempt to prescribe the desired construction in a precise manner, a certain degree of ambiguity is inherent. The more experience the project participants have with a particular construction system, its technical terms, and its trade customs, the less ambiguous the plans and specifications become. Even in a well-prepared set of plans and specifications, conflicts and inconsistencies in interpretation may arise. At least one court has seen that it is necessary to imply terms to construction plans.[32]

As the interpreter of contract plans and specifications,[33] the architect or engineer is given broad power over payment to the contractor. The common law requires performance of services to precede an obligation of payment.[34] This means that the obligation of the owner to pay the contractor for performance of work under a construction contract is conditioned upon the architect's decision that the work complies with the contract. Contractors

[30] AIA B141-1987, Standard Form of Agreement Between Owner and Architect § 2.6.13.

[31] Lundgren v. Freeman, 307 F.2d 104 (9th Cir. 1962).

[32] Fifteenth Ave. Christian Church v. Moline Heating & Constr. Co., 131 Ill. App. 2d 766, 265 N.E.2d 405 (1970).

[33] AIA A201-1987, General Conditions of the Contract for Construction § 4.2.11.

[34] Kingston v. Preston, Lofft 194, 2 Doug. 684 (K.B. 1773).

have successfully attacked the conditioning of payment upon a design professional's judgment as to the conformance of work to the contract. Courts have held the condition excused if the architect or engineer is unavailable or unable to interpret the contract or judge performance,[35] if the design professional refuses,[36] if there is collusion,[37] or if the condition is waived by the owner.[38] Note that the architect or engineer's authority to interpret the contract plans and specifications is vested personally in the individual principal of the firm with design responsibility for the project and may be challenged if this authority is delegated.[39]

Courts put limits on the power of the design professional to interpret the plans and specifications. The court in *Northwestern Marble & Tile Co. v. Megrath*[40] stated that the design professional does not have the authority to alter the plans and specifications. If rules of contract interpretation have been provided in the terms of the construction contract, they must be adhered to. As to ambiguities, courts require that an objective standard be applied to the interpretation of contract documents, which gives no weight to the owner's or the design professional's intentions.[41] When the traditional single-prime construction contract is used, this standard requires judgment from the perspective of an "honest contractor examining them before the bid or negotiation."[42] Unless the contractor could have reasonably been expected to notice and investigate the ambiguity, the ambiguity must be resolved in favor of the contractor.[43]

Courts have invoked a two-step analysis, the *doctrine of patent ambiguity,* to establish reasonableness. If a patent ambiguity is found in the plans and specifications, the contractor has a duty to inquire of the contracting officer as to the correct meaning.[44] First, it must be determined if the ambiguity is so glaring as to have raised a duty to inquire. Second, only if

---

[35] Grenier v. Compratt Constr. Co., 189 Conn. 144, 454 A.2d 1289 (1983).

[36] Anderson-Ross Floors, Inc. v. Scherrer Constr. Co., 62 Ill. App. 3d 713, 379 N.E.2d 786 (1978).

[37] Metropolitan Sanitary Dist. v. Anthony Pontarelli & Sons, Inc., 7 Ill. App. 3d 829, 288 N.E.2d 905 (1972).

[38] Steffek v. Wichers, 211 Kan. 342, 507 P.2d 274 (1973).

[39] J. Sweet, Legal Aspects of Architecture, Engineering, and the Construction Process 661 (4th ed. 1989) (citing Huggin v. Atlanta Tile & Marble Co., 98 Ga. App. 597, 106 S.E.2d 191 (1958)).

[40] 72 Wash. 441, 130 P. 484 (1913).

[41] J. Sweet, Legal Aspects of Architecture, Engineering, and the Construction Process 663 (4th ed. 1989) (citing Alabama Soc'y for Crippled Children & Adults, Inc. v. Still Constr. Co., 309 So. 2d 102 (Ala. Civ. App. 1975)).

[42] *Id.* at 664 (citing N.E. Redlon Co. v. Franklin Square Corp., 89 N.H. 137, 195 A. 348 (1937)).

[43] N.E. Redlon Co. v. Franklin Square Corp., 89 N.H. 137, 195 A. 348 (1937).

[44] Beacon Constr. Co. v. United States, 161 Ct. Cl. 1, 314 F.2d 501 (1963).

the ambiguity is not patent can a decision be made as to reasonableness of the contractor's alleged interpretation.[45]

In *Cofell's Plumbing & Heating, Inc. v. Stumpf,*[46] the court dealt with the reasons why the owner and/or the contractor accept the architect's interpretations of plans and specifications. The court emphasized the difference between disputes during construction regarding plans, specifications, and performance, which require immediate resolution, and disputes relating to other contractual matters, which do not require immediate resolution, such as matters relating to payment amounts, methods, and adjustments. In similar fashion, the AIA standard documents distinguish between an architect's authority to interpret contract documents for determining compliance of the work[47] and an architect's authority to resolve construction claims and disputes.[48]

The standard AIA General Conditions of the Contract for Construction advise the contractor first, that work specified by one document is required even if that work is apparently omitted from other documents, and, second, that work necessary to produce the intended results is required, even if that work is apparently omitted from other documents.[49] This provision has been effective to shift the burden to the contractor for additional work that may have been omitted from a particular plan or specification due to poor or incomplete drafting by the design professional.

If the contractor and the subcontractors refuse to yield to the interpretation of the architect, the process breaks down, and the architect may be subject to liability for delay. The architect in *E.C. Ernst v. Manhattan Construction Co.*[50] ran up against an electrical subcontractor who did not yield. The electrical subcontractor was unsuccessful in maintaining actions against the owner[51] and general contractor[52] but was successful in an action against the architect. The court found the architect negligent for creating an impasse on electrical submittals by repeatedly denying approval over the course of a year. Thus, although the design professional may be given authority to interpret the plans and specifications and may

---

[45] Mountain Home Contractors v. United States, 192 Ct. Cl. 16, 425 F.2d 1263 (1970).

[46] 290 N.W.2d 230 (N.D. 1980).

[47] AIA A201-1987, General Conditions of the Contract for Construction §§ 4.2.6, .11, .12, .13.

[48] *Id.* §§ 4.3, .4.

[49] *Id.* § 1.2.3.

[50] 551 F.2d 1026 (5th Cir. 1977).

[51] The subcontractor could not bring an action against the owner because it was not an intended third-party beneficiary of the owner's construction contract, and because a "no damages for delay" clause was enforceable.

[52] The subcontractor could not recover against the general contractor because the subcontract contained a "no damages for delay clause" which barred the action.

not be held liable under the terms of the contract for decisions in good faith, if he fails to adequately and fully document the basis for his decisions and fails to be prompt in rendering those decisions, this authority may be an ineffective defense against delay claims by contractors and subcontractors.

§ 18.10 —Testing and Inspection

The central duties of the design professional in construction administration relate to the A/E's contractual responsibility to the owner to monitor the progress of the work and general conformance to the plans and specifications. To meet these obligations, the architect or engineer is expected to visit the site and observe the work in progress. The design professional visits the site as the owner's representative to keep the project under general observation to protect and guard the owner's interests. The site visits and observation allow the design professional to ascertain the general quantity and quality of the work. These on-site observations provide the basis for the issuance of certificates of payment as the work progresses, and the rejection of observed defective work.

The design professional has a duty to the owner to reject defective work. Failure to do so has been held to be a breach of contract, under which the owner may be able to claim an offset against the design professional's fees for service[53] or claim reimbursement for the costs of correcting the defective work.

In *First National Bank v. Cann,*[54] granite panels on the exterior wall of a multistory bank building became unstable seven years after installation. Moisture had entered through the joints between the granite panels, which led to the subsequent formation of ice in cold weather, which dislodged the panels. In addition, the underlying steel structure supporting the panels had been improperly cut and welded during erection. The owner removed the granite panels and reconstructed the exterior granite wall to correct the problems. Investigation revealed the project had not been built in conformance to the plans and specifications. The court established that the architect had failed to visit the construction site to inspect the work under construction. The court held that although the architect was not required to have provided continuous, exhaustive, on-site inspection of the work, periodic visits to observe and inspect the work in progress would have revealed that the work was not in conformance with the plans and specifications. The architect's failure to provide reasonable inspection constituted a material

[53] Dan Cowling & Assocs. v. Board of Educ., 273 Ark. 214, 618 S.W.2d 158 (1981).

[54] 503 F. Supp. 419 (N.D. Ohio 1980), *aff'd,* 669 F.2d 415 (6th Cir. 1982).

breach of the design services contract,[55] in which the architect warranted, in certificates for payment which he had issued, that work had been consistent with the plans and specifications, to the best of his knowledge, information, and belief. The architect was liable for the cost of the corrective work for breach of this warranty.

If the design professional provides reasonable inspection of the site, he is not held to a strict warranty standard that the work conforms to the contract. Instead, under standard AIA and EJCDC general conditions,[56] it is the contractor who expressly warrants that the work be of good quality, free from defects, and in conformance with the plans and specifications. Furthermore, these standard general conditions explicitly obligate the contractor to correct discovered defects within one year of substantial completion.[57] The architect is thus relieved from a duty to discover nonobvious or latent defects in the work. The standard of care to which the design professional is held by the courts in the performance of on-site inspection is that of reasonable care. In the case of *City of Mounds View v. Walijarvi,*[58] the court stated the standard of care for site inspection for a design professional: "One who undertakes to render professional service is under a duty to the person for whom the service is to be performed to exercise such care, skill, and diligence as men in that profession ordinarily exercise under like circumstances."[59]

Although the architect is not required to discover defective work, but only to exercise ordinary care, once defective work has been discovered the architect has a duty to the owner to see that the defects are corrected. In *Roland A. Wilson & Associates v. Forty-O-Four Grand Corp.,*[60] the architect ordered caulking to correct a leaking problem in windows during construction, but failed to water-test the windows to ascertain whether the caulking had stopped the leaks. The architect was held negligent and liable to the owner.

Once a contractual administration duty is undertaken, the design professional is obligated to have performed the duty in a reasonable manner without negligence. In *Walnut Creek Aggregate Co. v. Testing Engineers, Inc.,*[61] an engineer employed by the school district to furnish continuous batch

---

[55] In *Cann,* the architect had used the 1963 editions of standard AIA contract documents: the owner-architect agreement, AIA Document B131, and the general conditions to the contract, AIA Document A201.

[56] AIA A201-1987, General Conditions of the Contract for Construction § 13.5, and EJCDC No. 1910-8 (1983), Standard General Conditions of the Construction Contract.

[57] AIA A201-1987, General Conditions of the Contract for Construction § 12.2.2.

[58] 263 N.W.2d 420 (Minn. 1978).

[59] Quoting City of Eveleth v. Ruble, 302 Minn. 249, 225 N.W.2d 521 (1974).

[60] 246 N.W.2d 922 (Iowa 1976).

[61] 248 Cal. App. 2d 690, 56 Cal. Rptr. 700 (1967).

plant inspection of concrete assisted employees of the subcontractor in mixing the concrete. The wrong admixture was used. The court held that the engineer voluntarily assumed a relationship to the subcontractor that allowed the maintenance of a suit for negligent inspection.

The design professional who is responsible for testing and inspection has been held liable to the contractor for failure to reject defective work in a timely manner.[62] In *United States ex rel. Los Angeles Testing Laboratory v. Rogers & Rogers,*[63] the contractor incorporated defective concrete precast structural elements into a building. Tests indicated the concrete was defective. Because the architect had not exercised due care in interpreting tests relating to the precast concrete, the prime contractor was able to maintain an action against the architect to recover the costs incurred in replacing the defective structural elements. In essence, the contractor was able to charge the architect with the costs of the subcontractor's mistake.

Under the AIA standard general conditions,[64] if the architect determines the need for special testing beyond what the contract documents require, the contractor bears the cost for tests that reveal a failure to comply with the contract; otherwise, the costs are borne by the owner. The architect must review the tests in a timely manner to avoid delaying the work and to keep the owner apprised of any deficiencies in the work disclosed by the special testing. One option to be considered by the architect or engineer is the election to conduct tests to insure compliance. Because the owner will bear the cost of performing the successful tests, it is recommended that the design professional consult the owner before requesting special testing and document the owner's reasons for refusal to authorize the testing program.

The design professional must disclose the basis of any refusal to approve a contractor's work. In *Hartford Electric Applicators of Thermalux, Inc. v. Alden,*[65] the court held that the architect owes a duty to specify corrections necessary to secure approval of a subcontractor's work found to be unsatisfactory upon inspection.

Delays associated with work stoppages can injure both the owner and the contractor on a project. The contract may or may not give the architect or engineer the authority to stop the work.[66] However, the authority to stop the work is sometimes necessary for the design professional to properly discharge testing and inspection duties and to protect third-party construction

---

[62] 161 F. Supp. 132 (S.D. Cal. 1958).

[63] *Id.*

[64] AIA A201-1987, General Conditions of the Contract for Construction § 13.5.

[65] 169 Conn. 177, 363 A.2d 185 (1980).

[66] AIA B141-1987, Standard Form of Agreement Between Owner and Architect, and AIA A201-1987, General Conditions of the Contract for Construction, do not give the architect the authority to stop the work.

workers from injury. In *Parks v. Atkinson,*[67] an architect had stopped the contractor's work twice because it failed to conform to contract documents. A construction worker injured after falling from scaffolding was not permitted to maintain an action against the architect because stoppage of work to maintain compliance to the contract was held not to be sufficient control of the work to hold the architect accountable for safety of third-party construction workers.[68]

Courts have held in some jurisdictions that the design professional's responsibilities for inspection extend beyond the immediate participants in the construction project to remote future owners and to the public. In these states, foreseeability of the harm sets the duty for inspection and testing, rather than the terms of the construction contract. In *Navajo Circle, Inc. v. Development Concepts,*[69] architects were held to owe a duty to remote condominium owners for the inspection of roof repairs on a project. An engineer who inspected a building and determined there existed an imminent danger of serious injury to the occupants had a duty to warn the occupants of that danger, despite an obligation to his client/owner to treat the information as confidential.[70]

§ 18.11 —Submittal Approval

The design professional who approves submittals may be subject to claims and liability for allegedly negligent review of submittals. If the contract documents provide that the design professional's standard of responsibility for submittal approvals is limited to observation, courts will limit the design professional's duty in the review of submittals to a review "only for conformance with the design concept of the project and with the information given in the Contract Documents."[71] Therefore, the architect will not incur liability for the means, methods, and sequence of construction, or installation of equipment referred to in the submittal.[72] Under the AIA standard contract documents[73] submittals are not contract documents, but

---

[67] 19 Ariz. 111, 505 P.2d 279 (1973).

[68] Caldwell v. Bechtel, Inc., 631 F.2d 989 (D.C. Cir. 1980); A.R. Moyer, Inc. v. Graham, 285 So. 2d 397 (Fla. 1973); Emberton v. State Farm Mut. Auto Ins. Co., 71 Ill. 2d 111, 373 N.E.2d 1348 (1978).

[69] 373 So. 2d 689 (Fla. Dist. Ct. App. 1979).

[70] Cal. Op. Att'y Gen. No. 85-208 (1985).

[71] Waggoner v. W&W Steel Co., 657 P.2d 147 (Okla. 1982).

[72] Day v. National United States Radiator Corp., 241 La. 288, 128 So. 2d 660 (1961).

[73] AIA B141-1987, Standard Form of Agreement Between Owner and Architect, and AIA A201-1987, General Conditions of the Contract for Construction.

merely serve to illustrate how the contractor proposes to conform the work to the design concept.

The design professional retains liability for negligent review of submittals and shop drawings in two important respects. Should the architect or engineer fail to approve submittals or shop drawings in a timely manner, or should he negligently approve a submittal or shop drawing that fails to conform to the requirements of the contract, the architect or engineer will be liable. In *E.C. Ernst, Inc. v. Manhattan Construction Co.,*[74] the architect was held liable for unreasonable delay in processing electrical submittals. In *Alabama Society for Crippled Children & Adults, Inc. v. Still Construction Co.,*[75] an architect approved incorrect shop drawings for the installation of windows and failed to catch the error until after the contractor had installed them. The court held that the contractor was entitled to claim the extra cost necessary to replace the incorrect windows. In *Duncan v. Missouri Board for Architects, Professional Engineers, & Land Surveyors,*[76] an engineer approved shop drawings from a steel fabricator that failed to meet building code structural requirements. As a result of the engineer's error, a pedestrian bridge in a crowded hotel lobby collapsed, killing 114 people and injuring 186. A state commission found the engineer negligent and revoked his license to practice. Upon appeal, a court upheld the finding of negligence and the license revocation.

The design professional should take care to insure that a *deviation clause*[77] is included in the contract documents. Courts will enforce this clause, which precludes the contractor from asserting approval of submittals or shop drawings that deviate from the contract documents without specific written notice of the deviation to the architect at the time of submittal.[78]

§ 18.12 —Change Orders

The design professional is commonly given the responsibility of administering change orders. For example, under the standard AIA contract documents,[79] the architect is delegated the duty of preparing change orders for approval and execution by the primary parties involved in the work: owner, contractor, and architect.

[74] 551 F.2d 1026 (5th Cir. 1977).

[75] 54 Ala. App. 390, 309 So. 2d 102 (1975).

[76] 744 S.W.2d 524 (Mo. Ct. App. 1988).

[77] AIA A201-1987, General Conditions of the Contract for Construction § 3.12.8.

[78] Creswell Iron Works v. Camden Hous. Auth., 449 F.2d 557 (3d Cir. 1971).

[79] AIA B141-1987, Standard Form of Agreement Between Owner and Architect § 2.6.13 and AIA A201-1987, General Conditions of the Contract for Construction, Art. 7.

The standard AIA contract documents, as well as many other construction contracts, give the owner the unilateral power to make changes in the work. The AIA documents define a change order that lacks the approval of the contractor to be a "construction change directive."[80] The architect has the responsibility to determine the adjustment in the contract price (including reasonable overhead and profit for the contractor) and time of performance, and to require an itemized accounting of the work done when contractor and owner cannot agree on the adjustments to contract price and contract time.[81]

The standard AIA contract documents give the architect authority to make only minor changes in the work that do not affect contract price or the time of performance.[82] However, the architect lacks the authority to make unilateral material changes in the work from that required by the contract documents. Courts have held that the design professional has no inherent authority to order or approve changes in the work which vary from that required by the contract documents.[83] Even if the design professional has been given authority to make minor changes that do not affect contract price or time of performance, the definition of "minor change" is not clear. In *Whitfield Construction Co. v. Commercial Development Corp.*,[84] the contractor requested the architect to make a change in the framing of a wall. The contractor contended that the architect had the authority to make the "minor change" because it involved neither a change in contract price or time. The court disagreed and stated that a structural change in a wall was a major change. Furthermore, if the design professional misrepresents that he has been authorized to order the change in the work, the contractor may be able to recover the cost of performing the unauthorized work from the architect or engineer.[85]

As the interpreter of contract documents, the design professional must render decisions as to whether the performance of disputed work entitles the contractor to a change order that adjusts the contract time and/or price. The general rule is that work required in the course of performance of the construction contract does not warrant a change order.[86] In *R&R Construction v. Junior College District No. 529*,[87] the court set out conditions under which extra work performed by the contractor warranted the issuance of a change order: (1) the work was outside the scope of the contract; (2) the

[80] AIA A201-1987, General Conditions of the Contract for Construction § 7.3.2.

[81] *Id.* §§ 7.3.6, .8.

[82] *Id.* § 7.4.1.

[83] Creswell Iron Works v. Camden Hous. Auth., 449 F.2d 557 (3d Cir. 1971).

[84] 392 F. Supp. 982 (V.I. 1975).

[85] Brown v. Maryland Casualty Co., 246 Ark. 1074, 442 S.W.2d 187 (1969).

[86] Obray v. Mitchell, 98 Idaho 533, 567 P.2d 1284 (1977).

[87] 55 Ill. App. 3d 115, 370 N.E.2d 599 (1977).

extra work was ordered by the owner, or the owner agreed, by words or conduct, to pay extra for the work; (3) the facts showed the work was not furnished voluntarily by the contractor; (4) the extra work was not made necessary by the fault of the contractor.

The design professional's conduct in administering the change order process will influence how a court treats the formalities required by the contract regarding changes. In *Huber, Hunt, & Nichols, Inc. v. Moore,*[88] a contractor sought negligence damages from architects who prepared the plans and specifications for a convention center and who administered the construction contract. The contractor suffered damages because the architects had delayed approving change orders. The court held that the architects were the agents of the owner in the administration of the contract, and conduct of the architects in delaying approval of the change orders would be attributed to the owner. In *Wyman v. Hooker,*[89] the owner was held to have waived the formal requirement of written change orders by approving change order work performed by the contractor without benefit of formal written change orders. Therefore, the design professional must not permit the contractor to proceed on change order work until the formalities of the contract are met. Failure to do so may make the formalities unenforceable. Furthermore, liability for delay may be imposed upon the design professional if he fails to exercise good faith or to act reasonably promptly in the issuance of change orders.[90]

§ 18.13 —Arbitration of Disputes

Most construction contracts require that the contractor continue with performance of the contract and the owner continue with payments to the contractor pending final resolution of claims.[91] Disputes arising during construction are divided into those that require immediate resolution so that the progress of construction is not unduly delayed, and those disputes whose resolution can be delayed. The parties to the construction contract typically give the design professional wide decision-making power to decide disputes requiring immediate resolution.

During the construction process, if performance of the owner or contractor is conditioned upon the rendering of a decision by the design professional, the condition may be excused if the parties so agree, or if the party for whose benefit the condition exists waives the condition. In *Steffek v.*

[88] 67 Cal. App. 3d 278, 136 Cal. Rptr. 603 (1977).

[89] 2 Cal. App. 36, 83 P. 79 (1905).

[90] Huber, Hunt, & Nichols, Inc. v. Moore, 67 Cal. App. 3d 278, 136 Cal. Rptr. 603 (1977).

[91] AIA A201-1987, General Conditions of the Contract for Construction § 4.3.4.

Wichers,[92] the owner was held to have waived the condition that final payment was to be made only upon the final inspection and approval of completion by the architect. The owner moved into the building and had delayed calling upon the architect to make the final inspection. If the design professional is unavailable, unable, or unwilling, to render the decision, contractual conditions also may be excused. An engineer's approval was excused in *Grenier v. Compratt Construction Co.*[93] when development of a road was conditioned upon the approval of the city engineer who refused to act. In *Hartford Electric Applicators of Thermalux, Inc. v. Alden,*[94] the condition that payment was due only upon the issuance of a certificate for payment by the architect was excused because the architect failed to reinspect the work.

The finality of decisions made by the design professional may be subject to challenge later for a variety of reasons. In *Laurel Race Course, Inc. v. Regal Construction Co.,*[95] the contractor challenged the authority of the engineer who had recommended withholding final payment because the race track failed to conform to specifications. The court stated the general rule that if the engineer's certification was a condition precedent to the liability of the owner for final payment, absent excuse of the condition, bad faith, collusion, waiver, or estoppel, the decision of the design professional as to interpretation of the plans and specifications and pertaining to the performance and execution of the work is final and binding upon the parties.

The design professional is not liable for decisions made in good faith,[96] but the A/E is required to render decisions promptly. Design professionals have been held liable for delay in rendering decisions. In *E.C. Ernst, Inc. v. Manhattan Construction Co.,*[97] an electrical subcontractor brought an action for damages caused by the architect's delay in rendering decisions. The court held that although the design professional may enjoy a limited immunity in the interpretation of contract documents, such immunity does not apply to an unjustified failure to render a decision.

The format of the decision may affect the finality of the decision. In *Zurn Engineers v. State Department of Water Resources,*[98] the court overturned the state engineer's decision regarding the requirements of the plans and specifications because the basis for the decision was not properly disclosed. The court reasoned that a party to the dispute must have

---

[92] 211 Kan. 342, 507 P.2d 274 (1973).

[93] 189 Conn. 144, 454 A.2d 1289 (1983).

[94] 169 Conn. 177, 363 A.2d 185 (1980).

[95] 274 Md. 142, 333 A.2d 319 (1975).

[96] AIA B141-1987, Standard Form of Agreement Between Owner and Architect § 4.2.6.

[97] 51 F.2d 1026 (5th Cir. 1977).

[98] 69 Cal. App. 3d 798, 138 Cal. Rptr. 478 (1977).

the opportunity to refute the material that forms the basis for the design professional's decision.

§ 18.14 —Payment Certification

Generally, construction contracts require certification for payment to the contractor by the design professional administering the contract.[99] In such contracts, the design professional owes a duty to the owner to perform the services required in a professional manner, and the architect or engineer is liable for damages incurred by the owner should he fail to do so. In *First National Bank v. Cann,*[100] the court stated that when a design professional issues a certificate of payment, he expressly warrants the work had progressed to the point indicated and that the work is to the best of his knowledge, information, and belief, consistent with the plans. The architect failed in his duty under the design services contract[101] to visit the site to become generally familiar with the progress and quality of the work. The court found breach of contract and held the design professional liable for the costs to reconstruct the work to comply with the contract. The standard to which a design professional is held in determining the progress and quality of the work is the professional negligence standard: exercise of ordinary care of similar professionals performing similar duties. He is not held to guarantee the work is in conformance, but only that he has exercised reasonable care to establish that to the best of his knowledge, skill, and belief the work conforms to the contract.

Respecting certification of payments, courts have found the architect acts as an agent for the owner, so the architect's negligent conduct in certification of payments may be attributed to the owner. In *Hall v. Union Indemnity Co.,*[102] the contract called for the architect to certify payments upon presentation of invoices. The architect had not demanded invoices and instead based the certification upon contractor estimates. The contractor subsequently defaulted on the construction contract and the owner brought an action against the contractor's surety. The surety's successful defense against the owner was based upon the negligence of the owner's architect. In *Fuchs v. Parsons Construction Co.,*[103] the architect certified the final payment, which under the terms of contract operated as owner's acceptance. The owner brought an action against the contractor when the

---

[99] AIA B141-1987, Standard Form of Agreement Between Owner and Architect § 2.6.10 and AIA A201-1987, General Conditions of the Contract for Construction § 9.4.

[100] 503 F. Supp. 419 (N.D. Ohio 1980), *aff'd,* 669 F.2d 415 (6th Cir. 1982).

[101] AIA B131-1967, Standard Form of Agreement Between Owner and Architect § 2.6.5.

[102] 61 F.2d 85 (8th Cir. 1975).

[103] 172 Neb. 719, 111 N.W.2d 727 (1961).

building was severely damaged by settlement several months later. The court held that the architect's certificate for final payment established that the contractor complied with the contract documents in the absence of a showing of bad faith on the part of the design professional.

Jurisdictions that do not limit the design professional's duty by privity of contract hold the design professional liable for foreseeable harm to third parties for the issuance of a certificate of payment. A design professional may be liable to contractors for negligent certification. The court in *Magnolia Construction Co. v. Mississippi Gulf South Engineers, Inc.*,[104] held that a contractor could maintain an action for final payment for work that failed to conform to plans and specifications, by virtue of reliance upon the prior negligent payment certifications by the engineer. The architect was held liable to a contractor's surety in *Aetna Insurance Co. v. Helmuth, Obata, & Kassabaum, Inc.*[105] The court found negligence and held the architect liable to the surety for continuing to certify progress payments despite knowledge that the contractor's subcontractors and suppliers were unpaid. Real estate lenders have been successful in holding design professionals liable for negligent certification. In *Browning v. Maurice B. Levien & Co.*,[106] the court held that an architect who contracts to certify payments is liable to anyone who might reasonably rely upon the certifications. In this case, the real estate lender relied upon the certification in making disbursements on the construction loan.

§ 18.15 —Completion and Acceptance

Completion and acceptance marks an important point in the construction process when rights, duties, and liabilities of the participants shift. The contractor on a project looks forward to the time when the owner accepts the project as complete.

The design professional plays a significant role in the completion and acceptance process, which occurs as two steps. First, the design professional is responsible for issuing a *certification of substantial completion* when the project is ready for occupancy or for its intended use. Minor defects still may require correction by the contractor, and portions of the work still may be incomplete. The *final certificate for payment* is issued by the design professional when the work is complete according to the plans and specifications. The design professional can incur liability for negligent acceptance of defective work and the negligent issuance of the final certificate for payment.

---

[104] 518 So. 2d 1194 (Miss. 1988).

[105] 392 F.2d 472 (8th Cir. 1968).

[106] 44 N.C. App. 701, 262 S.E.2d 355 (1980).

Claims for defective work pose the lesser threat to the design professional. Unless the owner manifests a clear intention to waive claims on known or obvious defects,[107] generally the owner's right to make claims for defective work is not waived for two reasons. First, warranty clauses in construction documents typically provide remedies for owners for defective work. Second, the law permits claims for latent or undiscoverable defects against the contractor.[108]

In the issuance of the final certificate of payment, the design professional should take care to identify areas of the work that remain incomplete for withholding of payment.[109] Care should be taken to advise the owner to examine the need to preserve any claims against the contractor arising from the construction of the project. Final payment may operate as a waiver of particular rights of the owner.[110] As part of this process, the contractor's application for final payment should be scrutinized by the owner for the possibility of future claims by the contractor, because the contractor must clearly reserve his rights to maintain later claims under the terms of the standard AIA contract and general conditions.[111]

---

[107] A.H. Sollinger Constr. Co. v. Illinois Bldg. Auth., 5 Ill. App. 3d 554, 283 N.E.2d 508 (1972).

[108] Saldal v. Jacobsen, 154 Iowa 630, 135 N.W. 18 (1912); Grass Range High School Dist. v. Wallace Diteman, Inc., 155 Mont. 10, 465 P.2d 814 (1970); Cantrell v. Woodhill Enter., Inc., 273 N.C. 490, 160 S.E.2d 476 (1968).

[109] City of Midland v. Waller, 430 S.W.2d 473 (Tex. 1968).

[110] AIA A201-1987, General Conditions of the Contract for Construction § 4.3.5.

[111] *Id.* § 9.10.4.

CHAPTER 19

USING COMPUTER-AIDED DESIGN SYSTEMS

James J. Myers

James J. Myers is a partner in the Boston, Massachusetts, and Washington, D.C., law firm of Gadsby & Hannah. Mr. Myers specializes in construction and procurement law, including dispute resolution through litigation and arbitration. He represents construction industry clients in public and private construction contracting. He is a graduate of the University of Pennsylvania and Boston University School of Law. Mr. Myers is a member of the bars of Massachusetts and the District of Columbia and the American and International Bar Associations. He is an adjunct lecturer at the International Law Institute, Georgetown University, and a member of the United Nations Commission on International Trade Law and of the National Panel of Arbitrators of the American Arbitration Association.

§ 19.1 Introduction

Computer-aided design (CAD) is a creature of the 1980s. It represents an enormous technological advance for all design professionals and their employers. Because the technology is so new, there is no law on using CAD equipment and software. Indeed, there may never be any "CAD law" per se.

The advantages of CAD are obvious to every design professional: speed, efficiency, standardization, more design work produced by lower-paid draftsmen, and the ability to readily use past design products in new applications.

The disadvantages of CAD systems, however, are that they are relatively new, they rely on the computer software program to perform traditional architect/engineer (A/E) design work, and the legal implications of CAD mistakes are not yet well defined.

Most of the commentators who have examined liability implications involved in the use of CAD concern themselves with the standard of care and precautions that design professionals should take when using the technology. This analysis views CAD in the same manner as other design tools used by A/Es in rendering professional services. Because few court decisions have been reported that would give design professionals or their legal counsel clear guidelines to follow, most commentators counsel A/Es to exercise the same degree of skill and care in using CAD technology as they do in using other design tools.

Indeed, most of the advice to CAD users in the liability area has been general in nature and oriented towards the duties of responsible care that design professionals owe to owners and third parties. Yet the technology itself has many contexts, and each context raises different questions. Some software is developed in-house. Other software is purchased from well-established vendors. Some owners insist that their design professionals have CAD capacity in-house. Some A/Es pool their software, but other A/Es are only concerned with desk-top computers used by project personnel. The industry is employing a new and developing collection of tools that have many applications in all areas of the design professional's business.

This chapter explores potential areas of liability to which an A/E may be exposed when using, or electing not to use, CAD. Traditional areas of A/E liability are reviewed to explain how they may be applied to the CAD user. Also discussed are aspects of CAD technology that may expose A/Es to legal issues with which they have not concerned themselves in the past.

§ 19.2 A/E Liability Traditionally

American law distinguishes between liability in tort for negligence and liability for breach of contract. The breach of a general duty that the law imposes on one party towards another, such as the duty to act with due care, is called a *tort.* Judicial construction of most agreements between owners and A/Es, however, has blurred the distinction between tort and breach of contract. Because such agreements generally address only those services that the A/E is specifically required to provide to the owner, contracts between an owner and an A/E are said to imply a duty of ordinary care and skill owed by the A/E when performing these services. An A/E's failure to provide services in accordance with this implied contractual duty of care has been held to be both a breach of contract and negligence, sometimes called *professional malpractice.*

A growing number of disputes between owners and A/Es concern the A/E's liability for additional construction costs paid by owners to third parties, allegedly resulting from the A/E's negligence or breach of contract. Some of these disputes arise from "risk-shifting" clauses found in most A/E owner contracts, under which the A/E assumes liability for damages and loss incurred by the owner and/or contractors resulting from defective specifications. If an A/E negligently designs or supervises a project and such negligence causes damage to the contractor or third parties, the A/E will be responsible at law for such damage. Such liability is often termed *negligence* or *malpractice.*

The law in this area has been described in general terms by the courts:

> Architects, doctors, A/E's, attorneys and others deal in somewhat inexact sciences and are continually called upon to exercise their skilled judgment in order to anticipate and provide for random factors which are incapable of precise measurement. The indeterminable nature of these factors makes it impossible for professional service people to gauge them with complete accuracy in every instance. . . . Because of the inescapable possibility of error which inheres in these services, the law has traditionally required, not perfect results, but rather *the exercise of that skill and judgment which can be reasonably expected from similarly situated professionals.*[1]

> The law imposes upon every person who enters upon an active course of conduct the positive duty to use ordinary care so as to protect others from harm. A violation of that duty is negligence. It is immaterial whether the person acts in his own behalf or under contract with another.[2]

---

[1] City of Mounds View v. Walijarvi, 263 N.W.2d 420, 424 (Minn. 1978) (emphasis added).

[2] Shoffner Indus., Inc. v. W.B. Lloyd Constr. Co., 42 N.C. App. 259, 265, 257 S.E.2d 50, 55 (1979).

> One who undertakes to render professional services is under a duty to the person for whom the service is to be performed to exercise such care, skill, and diligence as men in that profession ordinarily exercise under like circumstances.
>
> The circumstances to be considered in determining the standard of care, skill and diligence to be required in this case include the terms of the employment agreement, the nature of the problem which the supplier of the service represented himself as being competent to solve, and the effect reasonably to be anticipated from the proposed remedies upon the balance of the system.[3]
>
> It is the general rule that the employment of an architect is a matter of contract, and consequently, he is responsible for all the duties enumerated within the contract of employment. . . . An architect, as a professional, is required to perform his services with reasonable care and competence and will be liable in damages for any failure to do so.[4]

In essence, an A/E who designs a project owes a duty of care to any person who *foreseeably* and with *reasonable certainty* may be injured or damaged by the A/E's failure to exercise reasonable care.[5] American courts have found the contractor to be such a foreseeable party and have permitted recovery not only for resulting personal injuries, but for economic loss as well.[6]

The past 20 years have seen tremendous expansion of liability of design professionals to employers, contractors, and third parties. The entire construction industry is watching in anticipation to see how far this expansion will extend and how it will affect the relationships among the traditional parties to construction projects. It is likely that this expansion will include liability for failure to use CAD or for the improper use of CAD.

§ 19.3 Liability and Privity of Contract

The fifth edition of *Black's Law Dictionary* defines *breach of contract* as:

> Failure, without legal excuse, to perform any promise which forms the whole or part of a contract. Prevention or hindrance by a party to a contract of any occurrence or performance requisite under the contract for the creation or

[3] City of Eveleth v. Ruble, 302 Minn. 249, 253, 225 N.W.2d 521, 524 (1974).

[4] Moundsview Indep. School Dist. v. Buetow & Assoc., 253 N.W.2d 836, 839 (Minn. 1977).

[5] Inman v. Binghamton Hous. Auth., 3 N.Y.2d 137, 143 N.E.2d 895, 164 N.Y.S.2d 699 (1957).

[6] Davidson & Jones, Inc. v. County of New Hanover, 41 N.C. App. 661, 255 S.E.2d 580, *cert. denied,* 298 N.C. 293, 259 S.E.2d 911 (1979); W.H. Lyman Constr. Co. v. Village of Gurnee, 84 Ill. App. 3d 28, 403 N.E.2d 1325 (1980).

continuance of a right in favor of the other party or the discharge of a duty by him. Unequivocable, distinct and absolute refusal to perform agreement.[7]

An A/E's potential liability for breach of contract is well known to most design professionals. If an A/E fails to provide satisfactorily the services agreed upon in a contract with an employer, the A/E will be liable for such failure under a breach of contract theory of law.

Liability for breach of contract has many applications with regard to CAD technology. For instance, if an A/E is required to use CAD hardware or software as part of the design process and fails to do so, the A/E will be liable for breach of contract. Similarly, an A/E may be found liable for breach of contract if the A/E is unable to perform or is late in completing contract work because CAD equipment is inadequate or defective.

A new development in the design field is the requirement that design professionals develop CAD software packages themselves. With increasing frequency, owners require A/Es to develop software packages or programs that can be used for maintenance or expansion of a project. For instance, A/Es who design transportation networks are commonly asked to produce a software package that can be used by the owner to maintain the system. The A/E who fails to produce a workable software package will then be liable for breach of contract. Additionally, if the software program fails to satisfy the owner's specifications and requirements, the A/E may face any express or implied warranty problems that arise later.

The issues surrounding a transaction involving the exchange of a software package or computer program, including the question of whether such an exchange constitutes the sale of "goods" or "services," are discussed in § **19.9**. Design professionals should be aware, however, that failure to satisfy contract specifications for software packages can constitute breach of contract. A design professional also may have legal exposure for malpractice when acting simply as a professional computer programmer.

Another aspect of A/E-owner agreements with which A/Es are regularly concerned is the numerous risk-shifting provisions that assign responsibility for contract losses among the parties in advance of performance. Several risk-shifting provisions addressing CAD technology can be imagined that may have implications in the design field.

For instance, an A/E who produces a software package for an owner may be required to provide an express warranty concerning the quality or function of the software as part of the contract with an owner. Such warranties may be deemed to be in addition to implied warranties assumed by the design professional in producing the software package. Such warranties often go beyond simply indemnifying the owner against potential loss or damage incurred by the owner as a result of defects in the software. If an A/E purchases a software or hardware package from a company specializing in

---

[7] Black's Law Dictionary 171 (5th ed. 1979).

producing computer products for design professionals, the A/E should consider the implications of indemnity provisions in the contract with the supplier. Moreover, the design professional who produces a design software package that is released to the owner should consider including an exculpatory provision in the contract with the owner as protection from potential liability if the software package proves defective.

§ 19.4 Negligence

A/E liability to third parties has expanded in recent years. The theory of liability that third parties have used with the most success to recover against design professionals is negligence. Although few, if any, reported negligence cases involve CAD, it is foreseeable that the basic elements of a negligence claim will be applied to the use of CAD technology. They are:

1. The A/E owed the contractor a duty of care in the performance of contracted-for services (that is, the contractor's [or other third parties'] reliance on the A/E's work product was foreseeable)
2. The A/E breached the duty of care
3. The breach caused the contractor damage
4. The A/E's breach was the proximate cause of the contractor's damage.[8]

A claim against an A/E for negligence is remarkably similar to one for malpractice. For instance, the standard "duty of care" that an A/E must satisfy to avoid liability for negligence has been stated as follows: "An architect's efficiency in preparing plans and specifications is tested by the rule of ordinary and reasonable skill usually exercised by one of that profession. [I]n the absence of a special agreement he does not imply or guaranty a perfect plan or satisfactory result."[9]

It has become increasingly easy for third parties to recover from A/Es for negligence. Indeed, many states have eliminated the requirement of privity all together. For example, in a Massachusetts decision, *Craig v. Everett M.*

---

[8] Detweiler Bros., Inc. v. John Graham & Co., 412 F. Supp. 416 (E.D. Wash. 1976). *See also* Gravely v. Providence Partnership, 549 F.2d 958 (4th Cir. 1977); Prosser, Law of Torts § 30 (4th ed. 1971).

[9] Mississippi Meadows, Inc. v. Hodson, 13 Ill. App. 3d 24, 26, 299 N.E.2d 359 (1973). This standard was stated a bit differently in Shoffner Indus., Inc. v. W.B. Lloyd Constr. Co., 42 N.C. App. 259, 257 S.E.2d 50, 55 (1979):

> [T]he law imposes upon every person who enters upon an active course of conduct the positive duty to use ordinary care so as to protect others from harm. A violation of that duty is negligence. It is immaterial whether a person acts in his own behalf or under contract with another . . . . An act is negligent if the actor intentionally creates a situation which he knows, or should realize, is likely to cause a third person to act in such a manner as to create an unreasonable risk of harm to another.

Brooks,[10] a contractor brought suit against an A/E for erroneously locating certain stakes needed to direct construction. In addressing the A/E's liability to a third-party contractor for negligently locating the stakes, the court stated:

> The requirement for a contractual relationship for injury to the person due to negligent performance of a contractual duty was done away with in [a previous case]. In the case at bar, where the defendant was under a contract with the owner to perform professional services, where the plaintiff was under another contract with the owner which contemplated reliance on those services, where the identity of the only possible plaintiff and the extent of his reliance were known to the defendant, and where damages are not remote, it is reasonable to reach an analogous result.[11]

In light of this case and others, it will not be surprising if negligence emerges as the predominant theory of A/E liability for using CAD technology. It is plain that an A/E's failure to exercise reasonable care in using CAD will expose the A/E to claims for negligence as well as breach of express contract requirements (defective specifications, design defects, express warranties) and professional malpractice. For instance, an A/E may be liable for the negligent use of CAD in any of the following situations:

1. The A/E fails to select the proper computer or software package to perform necessary tasks
2. A computer is used to perform a complex calculation and the A/E fails to select the proper formula(ae) and/or assumption(s) for properly completing this task
3. The A/E fails to accurately assess and consider the margin of error inherent in the task the computer is asked to perform
4. The A/E does not obtain adequate training in the use of computers before incorporating CAD technology into a project
5. The A/E employs an unqualified computer operator or programmer
6. Improper data is entered into the computer for any of a number of reasons, including the following:
   a. The data is gathered improperly
   b. The A/E fails to verify the data before entering it into the computer
   c. The A/E fails to review and verify the data after it has been entered into the computer.
7. The A/E uses the computer to perform a task that is properly performed by other means

---

[10] 351 Mass. 497, 222 N.E.2d 752 (1967).

[11] *Id.* at 501, 222 N.E.2d at 755.

8. The A/E fails to detect errors in the program or software package used in performing the design work.

This is not an inclusive list of situations in which design professionals could be found liable for negligent use of CAD. It demonstrates, however, the importance of exercising reasonable care when using CAD technology to avoid liability for negligence.

A/Es are not the only ones who are potentially liable for design defects resulting from the use of CAD. Item 8 gives a situation in which an action may be appropriate against the programmer personally for negligence. This is especially true if it is assumed that a computer programmer is a professional for purposes of malpractice liability. Additionally, if the program or software package was obtained from an outside software design firm (a company that designs computer programs or software packages for design professionals to use in rendering professional services), the outside source ultimately may be liable for losses resulting from defects in the software package under a number of theories, including negligence, indemnity, implied and express warranties, or tortious interference with contractual relations. Most software design companies are aware of this potential and include exculpatory and/or "hold harmless" provisions in their contracts to limit their exposure to such claims. The design professional likewise should consider including such provisions in any contracts involving the use of CAD.

§ 19.5 Third-Party Beneficiary

Another theory under which third parties have achieved limited success in recovering losses against design professionals is as a third-party beneficiary of the contract between an owner and the A/E. In general, a third party must show it is a specifically *intended* beneficiary of the A/E's contract to be successful under this theory. Generally, contractors are considered only incidental beneficiaries of such contracts. Therefore, many of these claims have failed.

For instance, in *A.P. Moyer, Inc. v. Graham,* [12] the Supreme Court of Florida held that a third-party beneficiary relationship does not exist unless specific contract language expresses that a specific third party is the intended beneficiary of the contract between the A/E and the owner. Courts in other states have reached the same conclusion. In *Peter Kiewit Sons' Co. v. Iowa Southern Utilities Co.,* [13] the United States District Court for the Southern District of Iowa rejected a contractor's argument that portions of

[12] 285 So. 2d 397, 65 A.L.R.3d 238 (Fla. 1973).

[13] 355 F. Supp. 376, 392–94 (S.D. Iowa 1973).

an A/E-owner contract requiring the A/E to perform "in accordance with the highest standards of the engineering profession" were sufficient to establish a third-party beneficiary claim because the contractor was not specifically named as the intended beneficiary of the contract.[14]

The potential liability to third parties arising out of the use of CAD can be demonstrated by a hypothetical scenario. Assume that an owner contracts with an A/E to design a structure that is unique, requires the A/E to implement an innovative and technically complex idea, or necessitates the use of highly complex calculations. To design this structure properly, the A/E must incorporate CAD into the design plan.

Assume further that the A/E enters into a subcontract with a software design firm to provide a software package to perform these difficult tasks. If the software package produced by the subcontractor is defective and directly or proximately causes errors in the A/E's design, the software contractor may find itself liable to third parties, including the owner, contractor, and any subcontractors, who are damaged as a result. This probability is increased if the contract between the A/E and the software subcontractor specifically references and incorporates the owner's requirements or names the owner as an intended beneficiary.

If the A/E has an in-house programmer who is responsible for using an existing software package to develop a specific design, the software contractor may be successful in claiming the programmer's activities shielded the company from liability. Moreover, if the A/E's in-house programmer is not a professional, the A/E may bear full liability for the programmer's mistakes. If the programmer is unlicensed in the profession and is unable to check the programs as written, there even may be a question of unauthorized practice by the programmer, not to mention malpractice by the A/E. This is especially true if the alleged design defect was caused by the in-house programmer or the in-house programmer should have discovered the error during the course of the design process.

§ 19.6 Indemnification

In situations in which a contractor is held vicariously liable for the negligent acts of an A/E, the law may imply an obligation on the part of the A/E to indemnify the contractor from liability. (This principle also may apply when an owner is held vicariously liable for the A/E's negligence.) Under such circumstances, it is not always necessary that the A/E's duty to indemnify be derived from contract provisions; it may be implied by law even when the contractor is negligent.

---

[14] *See also* C.H. Leavell & Co. v. Glantz Contracting Corp., 322 F. Supp. 779, 783–84 (E.D. La. 1971).

For example, in *McCloskey & Co. v. Wright,*[15] the United States District Court for the Eastern District of Virginia held that a contractor's claim alleging that an A/E's negligent supervision and directives to the contractor during construction constituted "active" negligence by the A/E and stated a valid cause of action for indemnification even though the contractor was "passively" negligent himself. To date, the indemnification theory advanced in *McCloskey* has not been widely reported in the United States. Nevertheless, the *McCloskey* decision could have a significant future impact on A/E liability.

The utility of the indemnification theory is demonstrated in *Fidelity & Casualty Co. v. J.A. Jones Construction Co.*[16] In this case, the A/E's insurer sought indemnity from a contractor for a judgment awarded against an A/E and a contractor for negligence arising out of injury to the contractor's employees during a cave-in at the work site. The court noted that there was no express contract right requiring the A/E to indemnify the contractor because there was no privity of contract between them. Additionally, the court found that no common law right to indemnity existed. Because both the A/E and the contractor were "actively" negligent, neither had a right to be indemnified by the other.

It is interesting to observe that had the 1987 edition of the American Institute of Architects' (AIA) Owner/Contractor Agreement been used in the previous case, the A/E would have succeeded in its indemnification claim. The AIA's Owner/Contractor Agreement is generally used in conjunction with the standard AIA General Conditions of the Contract for Construction, Document A201. The 1987 version of Document A201 provides both the owner and A/E with an express contractual right to indemnification from the contractor for any bodily injury or property damage caused, in whole or in part, by a negligent act of the contractor. This type of clause has been construed to provide for indemnity by the contractor even when the A/E participates in the negligent act or acts that create liability.[17]

The hypothetical scenario in **§ 19.5**, setting forth the A/E's potential liability to third parties, also illustrates potential indemnity obligations arising from the use of CAD. For example, if the software subcontractor discussed in the scenario fails to provide a product that is adequate for the design of a particular project, it may be liable to the A/E for contractual or common law indemnity if the A/E is found liable to the owner for a design error caused by the defective software. Likewise, if an A/E creates an in-house program that is defective or negligently uses CAD in designing the project and thereby exposes the owner to liability to a contractor or other third party, the owner may have the right to indemnification from the A/E.

---

[15] 363 F. Supp. 223 (E.D. Va. 1973).

[16] 325 F.2d 605 (8th Cir. 1963).

[17] *See, e.g.,* Shea v. Bay State Gas Co., 383 Mass. 218, 418 N.E.2d 597 (1981).

An A/E also may be liable under the theory of indemnity if the A/E produces a software package that is released to the owner. If there are defects in the software package that cause the owner to incur liability to third parties when the owner subsequently uses the software, the owner may seek indemnification from the A/E for such losses.

§ 19.7 Tortious Interference with Contractual Relations

A new and potentially dangerous development for A/Es is the increasing frequency with which claims have been brought by contractors alleging that an A/E's interpretation of contract documents constitutes an intentional, tortious interference with the contractor's contractual relationship with the owner.

For example, in *Waldinger Corp. v. Ashbrook-Simon-Hartley, Inc.*,[18] a federal judge held an A/E liable in tort for the extra costs a contractor incurred to install substitute mechanical equipment in an Environmental Protection Agency (EPA)-funded sewer project. The court held that the A/E was liable for tortiously interfering with the contractor's agreement with the owner because the A/E wrote anticompetitive and restrictive specifications for the equipment and refused to accept substitute equipment without adequate justification.

The United States Court of Appeals for the Seventh Circuit heard the case on appeal.[19] In its decision, the circuit court recognized that an A/E possesses a conditional privilege to interfere with a contractor-owner agreement in its fiduciary capacity to the owner. Nevertheless, the court affirmed the district court's award of damages under the theory of intentional interference with contract. In reaching this decision the court stated:

> Where a conditional privilege exists, the plaintiff, to succeed on a claim for tortious interference with contract, must allege and prove that the agent's intentional acts were not taken to further its principal's best interests, but to further its personal goals or to injure the other party to the contract.[20]

The court further stated:

> The plaintiff may defeat the privilege by establishing that the defendant was acting other than in accord with his contractual obligations to his principal. Where an architect's action in enforcing literal compliance with contract

---

[18] 564 F. Supp. 970 (C.D. Ill. 1983).

[19] Waldinger v. CRS Group Eng'rs, Inc., 775 F.2d 781 (7th Cir. 1985).

[20] *Id.* at 790 (citing George A. Fuller Co. v. Chicago College of Osteopathic Medicine, 719 F.2d 1326, 1335 (7th Cir. 1983)).

> specifications was not justifiable in that it was not necessary to protect his principal's conflicting interests, but rather was taken with an intent to further his personal goals or to injure the party which is thereby forced to breach its contract with the plaintiff, the element of actual malice exists and the architect is liable for tortious interference.[21]

The decision and rationale used in *Waldinger* is likely to give rise to additional claims against A/Es under similar circumstances. Such circumstances may arise from the use of CAD.

Assume an A/E enters into a contract with an owner. The owner, in turn, enters into a contract for construction with a prime contractor. The A/E includes certain invalid assumptions in a computer program used in the design of the project, the invalidity stemming from the designer's desire to include a specific manufacturer's product in the structure. As a result of this error, the contractor installs improper material into the project. If the error is later discovered and the contractor is forced to remove and replace the inadequate material, the contractor may be able to recover directly against the A/E. This will be considered the "equitable" result because the designer's actions caused the defective material to be installed. Of course, it is also possible that the contractor could recover its losses directly from the owner. In that situation, the A/E may be required to indemnify the owner for such losses.

The foregoing hypothetical can be taken one step further to illustrate a more remote possibility of liability. Assume that there are multiple prime contractors involved in the project. Assume further that the prime contractor who must remove and replace the inadequate material, Contractor A, is delayed in completing its contract because of this error. A parallel prime contractor, Contractor B, is also delayed by this error because it cannot proceed with its work until Contractor A has completed performance. Because Contractor B's delay was caused by the A/E's negligence, the A/E may be liable for tortiously interfering with Contractor B's contract.

§ 19.8 Implied Warranty

A few courts have held that an A/E impliedly warrants that its work is fit for its intended purpose.[22] Some courts have limited such warranties to situations involving routine work similar to that involved in the mass production of consumer goods.[23]

---

[21] *Id.* at 790–91.

[22] *See, e.g.*, Hill v. Polar Pantries, 219 S.C. 263, 64 S.E.2d 885, 25 A.L.R.2d 1080 (1951).

[23] *See* Schipper v. Levitt & Sons, Inc., 44 N.J. 70, 82, 90, 92, 207 A.2d 314, 325–29 (1975); *cf.* Broyles v. Brown Eng'g Co., 275 Ala. 35, 40, 151 So. 2d 767 (1963).

A recent Minnesota case declined to follow that approach. The court stated:

> The finder of fact will be forced in every case to determine, as a preliminary matter, whether the alleged architectural error was made in the performance of a sufficiently simplistic task. Defects which are found to be more esoteric would presumably continue to be tried under the traditional [negligence] rule. It seems apparent, however, that the making of any such threshold determination would require the taking of expert testimony and necessitate an inquiry strikingly similar to that which is presently made under the prevailing negligence standard. We think that the net effect would be the injection of substantive ambiguity into the law of professional malpractice without a favorable trade-off in procedural expedience.[24]

In other circumstances, the courts have said that warranty claims are so similar to actions in tort that they are subject to the same statutes that expressly govern tort claims.[25]

In what appears to be an implied warranty decision, a court held that a contractor may sue an A/E directly for foreseeable economic loss resulting from the breach of an A/E's duty of reasonable care in the performance of the A/E's contract with the owner.[26] Because of the peculiarities of North Carolina law, the court held that neither the contractor nor subcontractors had a good cause of action against the A/E based upon the negligent performance of the A/E's contract with the owner.

A number of courts have, however, expressly rejected implied contract theory. For example, in *C.H. Leavell & Co. v. Glantz Contracting Corp.*,[27] a contractor argued that provisions in his contract with an owner that referred to the A/E's authority over the work also established implied contractual duties on the part of the A/E towards the contractor. The court held that the A/E was not a party to the contractor/owner agreement and dismissed the contractor's claim. This appears to be the likely result for implied contract claims involving the use of CAD. The example in **§ 19.5** used to illustrate potential liability of a software contractor to third-party beneficiaries also can be used to illustrate the potential liability of the software contractor under an implied warranty theory. For instance, if the software contractor (or the A/E) tailors a new program for a specific project, or advertises that the program or software package will perform a

---

[24] City of Mounds View v. Walijarvi, 263 N.W.2d 420, 425 (Minn. 1978).

[25] *See, e.g.,* Wolfe v. Ford Motor Co., 386 Mass. 95, 98–99, 434 N.E.2d 1008 (1982) (implied warranty); Salem Orthopedic Surgeons, Inc. v. Quinn, 377 Mass. 514, 386 N.E.2d 1268 (1978) (express warranty).

[26] Davidson & Jones, Inc. v. County of New Hanover, 41 N.C. App. 661, 255 S.E.2d 580, *cert. denied,* 298 N.C. 293, 259 S.E.2d 911 (1979).

[27] 322 F. Supp. 779 (E.D. La. 1971).

specific task inherent in the type of work performed, an implied warranty may be created. An A/E's liability for such warranties, both express and implied, is discussed in more detail in § **19.10**.

§ 19.9 Liability of Software Designer for Defective Computer Software

The analysis of a computer software designer's potential liability in the construction design area can be divided into two segments. First, software vendors face potential liability to software users with whom the vendor has a written contract. The contract generally governs the rights and liabilities between the contracting parties. Second, the software supplier may be obligated to third parties who are injured as a result of the use of defective computer software the supplier produces. In both situations, the injuries that may arise are not strictly economic or monetary. Physical damage to property or injury to persons can result from design defects. The type of injury involved is important because it may govern or limit the vendor's potential liability.

Virtually all computer software contracts include provisions that limit the vendor's liabilities and the buyer's remedies. These clauses include disclaimers that attempt to shield the vendor from all warranty claims except those expressly included by the parties to the agreement. Limitation of remedies clauses include provisions that limit the user's remedies to repair or replacement of defective software. Additionally, software vendors commonly include provisions in their agreements that preclude the buyer from enforcing claims for consequential or special damages. These clauses, coupled with the *integration clause,* which provides that the written contract constitutes the entire agreement between the parties, are used throughout the computer industry to protect software vendors from future claims.

Several factors determine the effectiveness of such provisions. Perhaps the most important factor is whether the transaction is considered the sale or licensing of "goods," thereby subjecting the transaction to the requirements of the Uniform Commercial Code (UCC), or "services," which are outside the scope of the UCC. A/Es are generally familiar with the sale of services, the product design professionals usually provide. Most design professionals, however, have little experience with the sale of goods or the legal implications involved in such transactions. Therefore, the proper classification of a transaction involving the exchange of software raises significant implications that A/Es generally have not had to consider in the past.

Most states have statutes very similar to the UCC that create implied warranties that attach to the sale of goods. Such warranties generally will be effective unless disclaimed in writing in accordance with the statute. No implied warranty implications attach to service contracts.

Courts traditionally have had difficulty applying legal concepts to computers and properly characterizing computer services. Although computer hardware resembles many other manufacturers' products from a legal standpoint, software is more complicated. Most courts have held that a contract involving the exchange of software alone is a sale of goods that falls within the scope of the UCC.[28] Indeed, software may appear to be more like a manufactured product when brought to market. Matters become more confusing when hardware and software make up varying degrees of a computer package.

The difficulty in properly defining a software package as a "good" or a "service" has led most courts to determine the applicability of the UCC to a contract for computer programs on a case-by-case basis. The court must examine the elements of the computer package to determine whether the sale or service aspects of the transaction predominate. For instance, the sale of computer hardware is almost always defined as a contract for the sale of goods under the UCC.[29] On the other hand, an agreement solely to perform data processing services is almost always considered a service that is outside the scope of the UCC. If a software package includes elements of both goods and services, courts generally look to "the essence of the agreement" to make a determination. For instance, when a sale of goods predominates, incidental services provided do not alter the basic transaction.[30]

In one decision, a computer data processing services company brought an action under a state statute prohibiting companies engaged in the selling of "goods or commodities" from participating in a monopoly. The plaintiff alleged that a software package provided by defendant was governed by the statute because the package not only included services such as computerized data processing, record keeping, and billing, but also goods such as printed records of fiscal conditions, statements of account, statistical reports, management reports, accounts receivable reports, and billing reports.

The court rejected this argument and found that although tangible goods were involved in the product produced by the defendant, "rarely is an intangible service performed without the involvement of some tangible."[31] The court also found that "the analysis and processing of customers records are the heart of the matter, the reports rendered to the customers being the

---

[28] *See generally* Rodau, *Computer Software: Does Article 2 of the Uniform Commercial Code Apply?,* 35 Emory L.J. 853 (1986).

[29] *See* Triangle Underwriters, Inc. v. Honeywell, Inc., 604 F.2d 737 (2d Cir. 1979).

[30] *See* R.R.X. Indus., Inc. v. Lab-Con Inc., 772 F.2d 543, 546 (9th Cir. 1985).

[31] SDK Medical Computers Servs. Corp. v. Professional Operating Management Group, Inc., 371 Mass. 117, 354 N.E.2d 852, 858 (1978).

embodiment of the services."[32] This analysis has been followed in some courts.[33]

Other courts have declined to follow this rationale. For instance, the United States Court of Appeals for the Second Circuit has held that a contract involving the exchange of a software package consisting of both hardware and software was a contract for the sale of goods as a matter of law.[34] In this decision, rather than holding that the sale of goods was incidental to the services provided, the court determined that the services were merely incidental to the sale of goods.[35]

Triangle Underwriters, Inc. v. Honeywell, Inc.[36] involved a defendant who was contractually obligated to develop and deliver a completed computer system for the plaintiff to operate. Defendant was not obligated to actually run a data processing service for the plaintiff. Moreover, defendant's compensation was limited to the purchase price for the hardware. Defendant did not bill for the services before, during, or after installation. The court believed that these were recognized conditions of a contract for the sale of goods, and not the rendition of professional services.[37]

From a computer software supply company's perspective, the Second Circuit's decision in *Triangle* may be disturbing. Software manufacturers generally limit their services to providing software or software packages that are used by consumers on an independent basis. The manufacturer's obligations, both before and after the sale, are generally limited to training the buyer's personnel in use of the system and routine upkeep and maintenance. Nevertheless, the law in this area is far from clear. For instance, courts often draw analogies to the typical A/E contract as an example of a contract for services. A/E services are generally limited to design and construction services and A/E work product is virtually always considered a service. This is true even in the government contract context in which the A/E only produces drawings, plans, and specifications.

If an A/E produces a software package that is released to the owner, he may face UCC problems. See § **19.10**. Obviously, the A/E's design effort is considered a service and is outside the scope of the UCC. Nevertheless, an

---

[32] 354 N.E.2d at 858.

[33] *See, e.g.*, Computer Servicenters, Inc. v. Beacon Mfg. Co., 328 F. Supp. 753 (D.S.C. 1970), *aff'd*, 443 F.2d 906 (4th Cir. 1971) (data processing services were held not to be the sale of goods because the contemplated payment was for the analysis, collection, storage, and reporting of certain data supplied to the plaintiff by the defendant).

[34] Triangle Underwriters, Inc. v. Honeywell, Inc., 604 F.2d 737 (2d Cir. 1979).

[35] *Id.* at 742 (citing Dynamics Corp. of Am. v. International Harvester Co., 429 F. Supp. 341, 347 (S.D.N.Y. 1977)).

[36] 604 F.2d 737 (2d Cir. 1979).

[37] *See also* Chatlos Sys., Inc. v. National Cash Register Corp., 479 F. Supp. 738 (D.N.J. 1979), *aff'd*, 635 F.2d 1081 (3d Cir. 1980).

A/E is potentially obligated to provide UCC-type warranties with regard to the software package actually released. Although this potential may be less than that faced by software design companies, the A/E should be aware of UCC implications inherent in such an exchange and attempt to limit exposure through exculpatory provisions.

The United States District Court for the District of New Jersey's decision in *Chatlos Systems, Inc. v. National Cash Register Corp.*[38] demonstrates the importance of classifying a transaction as the sale of goods or the sale of services. The court, after finding the contract in question was for the sale of goods, held the defendant liable for violations of both express and implied warranty provisions. Because the UCC remedies were applicable, the defendant was liable for breach of warranty damages equal to the difference between the value of the goods accepted and the value of the goods had they performed as warranted.[39] If the contract had been viewed as one for services, the court would have limited the plaintiff's remedies to those found in traditional contract law.

§ 19.10 UCC Problems Facing Software Dealers

Once a transaction is found to be a sale of goods under the UCC, the seller should consider its UCC rights and obligations. Through careful planning and foresight, a seller can avoid many of the UCC's problem areas.

1. **Express warranties.** One of the most important problems facing vendors is the creation of warranties under the UCC. Indeed, many software dealers create express warranties without even knowing it. UCC § 2-313 provides that an express warranty may be created orally or in writing. Even general statements regarding performance level or product demonstrations have been held to constitute express warranties.[40] Vendors should be aware that advertisements, product documentation, and employee statements also may constitute express warranties.[41] Therefore, vendors should review their product literature and instruct their employees to avoid responsibility for unlimited warranties.

   Perhaps the best way to avoid express warranties liability is to address the issue in the contract itself. The seller should avoid generalized and ambiguous statements and provide clear specifications

---

[38] *Id.*

[39] 479 F. Supp. at 744; U.C.C. § 2-714(2), (3) (1987).

[40] *See, e.g.,* Sierra Diesel Injection Serv., Inc. v. Burroughs Corp., Inc., 874 F.2d 653, 657 (9th Cir. 1989).

[41] Overstreet v. Norden Laboratories, Inc., 669 F.2d 1286, 1290 (6th Cir. 1982).

concerning the functioning of the software. Contractual provisions limiting warranties to specifically identified functions in clear and concise statements are helpful. Use of words such as "defects" or "errors" should be avoided. Provisions that limit the buyer's remedies and/or time within which the buyer must bring an action also should be included in the software contract.

2. **Implied warranties**. The UCC creates two implied warranties that attach to the sale of goods. An implied warranty of merchantability, which requires that goods be fit for the ordinary purpose for which they are used, is created by UCC § 2-314(2). An implied warranty of fitness for an intended purpose is created by UCC § 2-315. When a seller has reason to know that the buyer will use the goods for a particular purpose, and the buyer relies on the seller's opinion that the goods will be adequate for that purpose, the latter warranty will be implied.[42]

   Both implied warranties may be disclaimed through careful contract language.[43] Because contractual ambiguities are generally resolved against the warrantor, disclaimers should be clear, conspicuous, and unambiguous. They should not be lost in the fine print of a contract document.

3. **Limitation on remedy provisions**. Software manufacturers may be able to limit their UCC liability by including remedy limitation provisions in their contracts. Typical remedies included in such clauses include repair or replacement of specifically designated items. The UCC permits modification and limitation of remedies provided the seller makes it clear such remedies are exclusive.[44] Consequential damages also may be excluded provided such limitations are not unconscionable.[45] Nevertheless, when contractual remedies fail their "essential purpose," the buyer may be able to obtain excluded UCC remedies.[46]

§ 19.11 Software Manufacturer's Exposure to Professional Malpractice Liability

Two questions arise when analyzing the liability and malpractice implications facing a software manufacturer. First, is a computer programmer a professional for the purposes of malpractice liability? Second, if the

---

[42] *Id.*

[43] U.C.C. § 2-316 (1987).

[44] *Id.* § 2-719.

[45] *Id.* § 2-719(3).

[46] *Id.* § 2-719(2).

programmer is considered a professional, how does this status affect the manufacturer's liability for negligent preparation of software?

The courts have recognized the computer programmer's duty to exercise reasonable skill and care in using computers. Nevertheless, the determination of whether a programmer should be treated as a professional for purposes of liability is not clear. Indeed, the distinction between professional and nonprofessional services traditionally has been vague.[47]

The issue of whether a computer programmer is considered a professional when programming services are rendered in the design and engineering field is not yet clear either. The issue has been addressed, however, by the courts for the purpose of determining whether programmers are professionals as defined in the Fair Labor Standards Act (FLSA). In *Pezzillo v. General Telephone & Electric Information Systems, Inc.*,[48] the court found that computer programmers were not professionals with regard to the FLSA's provisions concerning exemptions from overtime requirements. To be included within the definition of "professional capacity" under the FLSA, the employee's work must require "the constant exercise of discretion and judgment in its performance." The court held that programmers are not professionals under this standard because 100 percent of their time is involved in purely mechanical and highly skilled work that does not require the use of discretion or the exercise of independent judgment.[49]

It is interesting that the court in *Pezzillo* drew an analogy to the A/E field to explain its decision. The court likened the duties of a programmer to those performed by a draftsman working for an architect. The court noted that both draftsmen and programmers generally perform mechanical functions while architects and computer analysts act as professionals. This distinction may be carried over to the malpractice area. If this type of distinction is raised, it would appear that the "exercise of discretion and skilled judgment" would be the determining factor in assessing whether a programmer or software developer is considered a professional. Of course, this analysis still leaves confusion because many persons employed by design firms are assigned hybrid duties including both mechanical and discretionary functions.

Perhaps it is this ambiguity that has led some courts to reject the concept of "computer malpractice" altogether. For instance, the United States District Court for the District of New Jersey addressed the issue of computer malpractice as follows:

> The novel concept of a new tort called "computer malpractice" is premised upon a theory of elevated responsibility on the part of those who render

---

[47] *See* Pezzillo v. General Tel. & Elec. Information Sys., Inc., 414 F. Supp. 1257 (M.D. Tenn. 1976), *aff'd per curiam,* 572 F.2d 1189 (6th Cir. 1978).

[48] 414 F. Supp. 1257 (M.D. Tenn. 1976).

[49] *Id.* at 1270.

> computer sales and service. Plaintiff equates the sale and servicing of computer systems with established theories of professional malpractice. Simply because an activity is technically complex and important to the business community does not mean that greater potential liability must attach. In the absence of sound precedential authority, the Court declines the invitation to create a new tort.[50]

Another distinction that may affect liability is whether errors in the computer software are substantive or merely mechanical. *Substantive errors* are errors in the instructions or advice normally given by professionals with respect to matters with which professionals deal. For example, in an Internal Revenue Service (IRS) ruling, a developer of a computer program for use in preparing income tax returns was found to be potentially responsible for errors in the tax law that were incorporated into the program.[51] Computer programs that incorporate substantive guidance based on human judgment from disciplines as diverse as medicine, law, accounting, engineering, and architecture may have liability beyond mere arithmetic or mechanical calculations in the computer software programs. Design professionals should take note of this development in implementing CAD technology or creating software packages to be turned over to owners.

Potential liability for errors in substantive guidance increases the legal exposure for software developers. Several tort theories may be available to impose liability for damages caused by substantive errors in computer software programs. These include negligence, misrepresentation, and product liability. If a computer program incorporates substantive engineering or architectural guidance, then the established legal standards of care applicable to the engineering and architectural communities may be applicable to the software program. If the substantive guidance does not measure up to the required standard of care, then the logical rule will be that the computer software developer may sustain liability not unlike that for professional negligence on the part of an architect or engineer. Therefore, the design professional should exercise reasonable care when using or developing software in the design process.

§ 19.12 Protecting Intellectual Property

The increasing frequency with which A/Es have been developing custom software in connection with construction and engineering projects creates additional legal considerations for the design professional. Because custom software has potential commercial applications in other projects, the

[50] Chatlos Sys., Inc. v. National Cash Register Corp., 479 F. Supp. 738 (D.N.J. 1979), *aff'd,* 635 F.2d 1081 (3d Cir. 1980).

[51] Rev. Rul. 85-189, 1985-2 C.B. 341.

developers must decide whether the software provides their companies with any competitive advantage in the marketplace, and if so, how the companies can best protect that advantage. Today, more than ever, software designers seek innovative methods to protect vital intellectual property. *Intellectual property* has been defined to include processes and methods used in business, including software, firmware, and hardware products.

Sections 19.13 through **19.15** summarize the methods available to protect intellectual property, with an emphasis on computer software. Discussed are three of the principal methods used by businesses to protect core technology:

1. Patent protection under federal law
2. Copyright protection under federal law
3. Trade secret protection under state law.

The form of protection that best suits the design professional will depend upon the nature of the technology being protected, the A/E's needs, the method and extent of the software's distribution, and the nature of the industry for which the software is developed. A single software program may be protected by patent, copyright, or trade secret. Conceivably, a software package could be protected by a combination of all three. Design professionals should consider the implications of each method in determining how to protect their software technology.

§ 19.13 —Patent Protection

Patent protection is available to anything that is of patentable subject matter, such as a process, machine, manufacture, or composition of matter, which meets the requirements of (1) novelty, (2) utility, and (3) nonobviousness. In the United States, a patent application must be filed within one year of the first publication or commercialization of the technology that the developer seeks to protect to avoid becoming statutorily barred from receiving patent protection. Laws of nature, formulae, and algorithms are not patentable subject matter. The grant of a patent provides the holder with a legally sanctioned monopoly in the process or product for a period of 17 years. Therefore, a design professional can prevent software packages from being used by others for 17 years by obtaining a patent.

It should be noted that the patent holder enjoys the right not only to prevent others from making, using, or selling a product that is in violation of the patent, but also allows the holder to prevent independent development or reverse engineering of the process or product by others.

After the grant of a patent, the holder must defend against infringement of the patent or patent rights may be forfeited. The grant of a patent merely allows its holder access to federal court to enforce the patent. Defense of the patent ordinarily involves proof in court of the same requirements shown to the Patent Office: that the program is patentable subject matter, novel, useful, and not obvious. If the court fails to agree with the patent examiner's initial determination that the program meets all necessary requirements to obtain a patent, the patent may be lost.

Initially, the Patent Office refused to grant patents to software because algorithms used in developing software are too similar to mathematical formulae or the "laws of nature" to be the proper subject matter for patent protection. This would appear to be a logical conclusion because the United States Supreme Court had defined *algorithm* as a "procedure for solving a given type of mathematical problem."[52] Although the Patent Office still maintains that algorithms in and of themselves are not patentable subject matter, the Supreme Court has held that patent protection is available for certain processes performed by the formula or algorithm.[53] This extension of patent protection has been used with limited effectiveness to obtain patents for computer programs.

Although the protection offered by patent law is broad, the time and expense involved in prosecuting a patent claim are substantial. Because many software programs have relatively short lifespans, particularly in the rapidly changing personal computer environment, the use of patents has been limited. Additionally, because the patent process requires complete disclosure of the process being protected, the use of patent protection generally precludes concurrent use of trade secret protection. However, patents have been used to protect firmware, unique aspects of operating systems, and processes incorporated in software programs that likely will outlive the program itself.

§ 19.14 —Copyright Protection

The Federal Copyright Act extends federal copyright protection to "original works of authorship fixed in any tangible medium of expression."[54] The Act specifically encompasses "literary works," which include computer programs and databases. Copyright protection extends to the expression of ideas, but does not protect the idea itself. This "expression/idea dichotomy" was described by the United States Supreme Court in *Baker v. Selden,*[55] and later became codified in the Copyright Act at 17 U.S.C. § 102 (1976).

---

[52] Gottschalk v. Benson, 409 U.S. 63 (1972).

[53] Diamond v. Diehr, 450 U.S. 175, 101 S. Ct. 1048 (1981).

[54] 17 U.S.C. §§ 101–118 (1976 & Supp. I 1988).

[55] 101 U.S. 99 (1879).

A discussion of this dichotomy in the software context is found in *Apple Computer, Inc. v. Formula International, Inc.*[56]

In the last several years, courts have been asked to extend the scope of copyright protection to the "structure, sequence and operation" of a software program, commonly referred to in the industry as the "look and feel" of the program.[57] It is still unclear how far the courts will extend copyright protection in the software area. Nevertheless, this may be an important area for the design professional. Lawsuits such as (1) the action brought in United States District Court for the District of Massachusetts by Lotus Development Corporation, alleging a violation of the copyright for Lotus 1-2-3;[58] (2) the action brought by Apple Computer against Microsoft Corporation and Hewlett-Packard alleging violation of Apple's copyright in the Macintosh operation system;[59] and (3) the recent action by Xerox against Apple for aspects of the Macintosh interface that allegedly were developed at Xerox's Palo Alto Research Center, are receiving close attention.

The procedures for obtaining and registering a copyright are simple and relatively inexpensive. At the time software is first published, a notice of copyright (commonly referred to as the *legend*) should be affixed to the work. Although the Berne Convention Implementation Act of 1988 makes the affixation of this notice voluntary, affixing the proper legend provides important benefits to the author under new subsections of the Copyright Act addressing instances of "innocent" infringement. The legend should be affixed in such a manner as to give "reasonable notice of the claim" and should include, at a minimum, the following: (1) the © symbol or the word "copyright," (2) the name of the author, and (3) the year the work was first published.

Although registration is not required to establish a copyright, registration has significant advantages. Registration of the work allows the owner of the copyright (1) access to federal court to enforce the copyright, (2) statutory damages, (3) statutory entitlement to costs and attorneys' fees, (4) criminal penalties, and (5) fines.

Of importance to the design professional is the issue of who possesses the rights to a copyrighted program as between an employer and employee. If the program is created by an employee during the ordinary course of employment, the program may fall within the "work for hire" doctrine. Under

---

[56] 562 F. Supp. 775, 783 (C.D. Cal. 1983).

[57] *See* Whelan Assocs., Inc. v. Jaslow Dental Laboratory, 797 F.2d 1222 (3d Cir. 1986), *cert. denied,* 479 U.S. 1031 (1987).

[58] Lotus Dev. Corp. v. Paperback Software Int'l, 740 F. Supp. 37 (D. Mass. 1990).

[59] Apple Computer, Inc. v. Microsoft Corp., 709 F. Supp. 925 (N.D. Cal.) *summary judgment granted in part,* 717 F. Supp. 1428 (N.D. Cal. 1989).

this doctrine, employers are granted copyright protection in works prepared by their employees during the ordinary course of business.[60]

In 1988, Congress amended the Copyright Act by passing the Berne Convention Implementation Act.[61] The 1988 Act incorporates the provisions of the Berne Convention including: (1) establishing the duration of the copyright for the life of the author plus 50 years, (2) providing the author of the work with the right to authorize translations, adaptations, and derivative works, and (3) giving the author greater control over the reproduction of copyrighted works, however accomplished.

§ 19.15 —Trade Secret Protection

Trade secret protection is a creature of state law, and is founded more on principles of business ethics than property law. The principle is simple: businesses should not be allowed to profit from proprietary information of another business that has been improperly acquired or disclosed. Accordingly, most states afford trade secret protection if: (1) information is maintained by a business as secret (not generally known in the trade or industry), (2) the owner has taken reasonable measures to insure the confidential nature of the information, and (3) the information provides the owner with a competitive advantage in the marketplace.

In order for a company to protect information as a trade secret, it must adopt and rigidly adhere to a program designed to prevent disclosure of the information. If the information is not afforded this protection and is "leaked" into the public domain, trade secret protection is lost. Moreover, because trade secret protection is not really a property right, the protections afforded do not prevent another company from developing the same product independently or through reverse engineering. Accordingly, it is advisable for A/Es who license software that is subject to trade secret protection to include provisions in the license prohibiting reverse engineering.

---

[60] *See* 17 U.S.C. § 101 (1976 & Supp. I 1988).

[61] Pub. L. No. 100-568, 102 Stat. 2853 (1988) (codified at 17 U.S.C. §§ 101, 116A, 116, 405, 406, 411 (1976 & Supp. I 1988)).

PART V

CONTRACT PERFORMANCE AND COLLECTION

CHAPTER 20

BIDDING

Steven J. Comen

Steven J. Comen is a partner in the Boston, Massachusetts, law firm of Hinckley, Allen, Snyder & Comen. He is a graduate of the University of Michigan Law School and a former law clerk for a United States district court judge. He has represented clients in state and federal courts, arbitration proceedings, boards of contract appeals, and before administrative agencies throughout New England, New York, Michigan, Puerto Rico, and the Virgin Islands. Mr. Comen has lectured extensively to professional groups of lawyers, contractors, architects, engineers, and others associated with the construction industry. He has spoken for seminars sponsored by *Engineering News Record,* Associated General Contractors, the Engineering Societies of New England, the Construction Industries of Massachusetts, and Continuing Legal Education of New England.

§ 20.1 Role of Design Professional in Bid Phase

Competitive bidding is intended to ensure fairness and maximize the return for the public dollar. It is instituted by an extensive statutory and regulatory scheme designed to award contracts to the lowest responsive and responsible bidder.[1] The statutes and regulations ensure that common standards for both responsiveness and responsibility are employed so that price comparisons are meaningful. This is done by a variety of measures, such as requiring the invitation for bids to describe work with clarity and definiteness, requiring the bidder to promise to do exactly what the invitation for bid requests, and requiring the bidder to have minimal financial standing, reputation, experience, resources, facilities, judgment, and efficiency.

The process of obtaining bids and awarding a contract takes place during what is known as the *bid phase.* It typically begins after the owner approves the drawings and specifications prepared by the design professional. During the bid phase, the owner prepares the necessary bidding information and forms, solicits bids, receives the bids, holds a bid opening, evaluates the bids, makes an award (or rejects the bids), and notifies the bidders. However, more often than not it is the design professional, not the owner, who performs the bulk of these tasks. This is often a result of necessity: usually the design professional, not the owner, has the necessary experience, manpower, and expertise.

In the American Institute of Architects (AIA) Standard Form Agreement Between Owner and Architect, Document B141, the role of the design professional in the bid phase is spelled out. Article 2.4.2 provides that the architect shall "assist" in the preparation of the bid documents: "The Architect shall assist the Owner in the preparation of the necessary bidding information, bidding forms, the Conditions of the Contract, and the form of Agreement between the Owner and the Contractor." Article 2.5.1. provides that the architect shall "assist" in obtaining bids and awarding the contract: "The Architect, following the Owner's approval of the Construction Documents and of the latest preliminary estimate of Construction Cost, shall assist the Owner in obtaining bids or negotiated proposals and assist in awarding and preparing contracts for construction."

The preparation of bid information and the selection of the lowest responsive and responsible bidder are often the source of claims by both disappointed and successful bidders. This chapter discusses these issues, along with suggestions on what the design professional can do to minimize such claims.

§ 20.2 Liability for Defective Bid Information

The information given to bidders usually consists of the invitation for bids (IFB), instruction to bidders, bid forms, contract forms, conditions of the

[1] All executive agencies of the federal government must follow the bidding procedures set forth in the Federal Acquisition Regulation (FAR). In addition, each executive agency has developed its own acquisition regulations that implement or supplement the FAR.

contract, plans, drawings and specifications. The bid information often provides that the plans and drawings are available for inspection at the office of the design professional. The same arrangement is usually made for the results of soil tests and subsurface investigations.

It is very important that the information given to bidders be as detailed and accurate as possible. This is particularly true for the plans and specifications (including subsurface data). Vague or inaccurate plans and specifications may discourage prospective bidders from submitting bids. Moreover, they may provide a basis for future claims by the contractor against the owner.

It is well established that the owner impliedly warrants the adequacy of the plans and specifications. The seminal case is *United States v. Spearin,*[2] which held that the contractor, who is bound to build according to the plans and specifications, is not responsible for the consequences of defects in those plans and specifications.[3] On the contrary, the owner must compensate the contractor for any additional costs caused by the defects.[4] In addition to the breach of warranty, the owner may be liable to the contractor for misrepresentation. As a general rule, "a contractor of public work who, acting reasonably, is misled by incorrect plans and specifications . . . and who, as a result, submits a bid which is lower than he would have otherwise made, may recover for extra work or expenses necessitated by the conditions being other than originally represented."[5] Of course, such claims may be legitimate when the defect or inadequacy is hidden. However, all too often the defect or inadequacy is known by an unscrupulous bidder who, as a result, bids unreasonably low in hope of winning the award and recouping any losses through claims for extras.

Potential liability does not stop with the owner. The design professional also may be liable to the contractor. Liability may exist for negligence,[6]

Most state governments also have developed statutory and regulatory procedures requiring that public contacts be awarded to the lowest responsive and responsible bidder.

[2] 248 U.S. 132, 136, 39 S. Ct. 59 (1918).

[3] *See also* J.L. Simmons Co. v. United States, 412 F.2d 1360, 188 Ct. Cl. 684 (1969); J.D. Hedin Constr. Co. v. United States, 347 F.2d 235, 171 Ct. Cl. 70 (1965). *But see* Emerald Forest Util. Dist. v. Simonsen Constr. Co., 679 S.W.2d 51 (Tex. Ct. App. 1984); Town of Urania v. M.P. Dumesnil Constr. Co., 492 So. 2d 888 (La. 1986).

[4] *See, e.g.,* Pine Bluff Hotel Co. v. Monk & Ritchie, 122 Ark. 308, 183 S.W. 761 (1916); Sandy Hites Co. v. State Highway Comm'n, 347 Mo. 954, 149 S.W.2d 828 (1941); Mayor of Columbus v. Clark-Dietz & Assocs. Eng'rs, 550 F. Supp. 610, 625 (N.D. Miss. 1982).

[5] Jasper Constr., Inc. v. Foothill Jr. College Dist., 91 Cal. App. 3d 1, 8, 153 Cal. Rptr. 767, 770 (1979).

[6] *See, e.g.,* Donnelly Constr. Co. v. Oberg/Hunt/Gilleland, 139 Ariz. 184, 677 P.2d 1292, 1295 (1984). To maintain an action for professional negligence requires proof that (1) the architect breached his duty of care, (2) the breach proximately caused an injury resulting in damages, and (3) the plaintiff and the risk were reasonably foreseeable.

misrepresentation,[7] or under a third-party beneficiary theory.[8] The design professional also may be liable to the owner for breach of express[9] or implied[10] performance warranties.

§ 20.3 Avoiding Liability for Defective Bid Information

The best way the design professional can avoid liability is to provide detailed and accurate plans and specifications. However, there are other precautions as well.

Bidders should be given ample opportunity to study the plans and specifications so they can discover any defects or ambiguities. They should be required to visit and inspect the site and given ample opportunity to perform tests.

The information to bidders should state that if the bidder believes that an ambiguity exists in the bid documents, the bidder must submit a request for clarification in writing before the award. In some jurisdictions, this duty to investigate is implied.[11] The implied duty arises with respect to "patent" ambiguities, that is, omissions, inconsistencies, or discrepancies that are apparent.[12] The duty can be satisfied simply by requesting the owner or design professional to clarify the perceived ambiguity. However, not all bidders may be aware of this duty. To make them aware, the duty should be spelled out clearly in the bid information.

---

[7] Guardian Constr. Co. v. Tetra Tech Richardson, Inc., 583 A.2d 1378 (Del. 1990).

[8] To be successful on a third-party beneficiary claim, the claimant must show that it was an "intended" rather than an "incidental" beneficiary. *See* Restatement (Second) of Contracts § 302(2) (1982) (an incidental beneficiary is a beneficiary who is not an intended beneficiary); *id.* § 315 (an incidental beneficiary acquires by virtue of the promise no right against the promisor or the promissee); *see also* Renel Constr. Inc. v. Brooklyn Coop. Meat Distrib. Center, 59 A.D.2d 391, 399 N.Y.S.2d 429 (1977) (incidental beneficiary has no right to enforce contract); E.C. Ernst, Inc. v. Manhattan Constr. Co., 551 F.2d 1026, 1031 (5th Cir. 1977) (same).

[9] The architect often makes express warranties as to the performance of his work. For example, Article 1.1.2 of AIA B141-1987 provides in part: "The Architect's services shall be performed as expeditiously as is consistent with professional skill and care and orderly progress of the work."

[10] *See, e.g.,* Surf Realty Corp. v. Standing, 195 Va. 431, 443, 78 S.E.2d 901, 907 (1953) (architect impliedly warrants to owner that he possesses and exercises "the care of those ordinarily skilled in the business").

[11] *See, e.g.,* John F. Miller Co. v. George Fichera Constr. Corp., 7 Mass. App. Ct. 494, 388 N.E.2d 1201 (1979).

[12] *Id.*

If requests for clarification are received, the design professional should provide written clarification to all bidders before the award. If the clarification is issued to fewer than all bidders, an unsuccessful bidder might protest the award on the basis that the successful bidder obtained an unfair advantage. If the clarification is issued orally, the successful bidder might later dispute the adequacy of the clarification and file a claim for extra compensation. Such problems frequently occur at pre-bid meetings. These simple precautions can do much to alleviate them.

The information to bidders also may contain disclaimer clauses. Such clauses are often used to attempt to shift to the contractor the risk for unknown subsurface conditions. The most common disclaimer is that subsurface data are furnished for informational purposes only and do not purport to represent existing field conditions.[13] Disclaimer clauses are generally effective. However, there are a number of exceptions.

The seminal case with respect to disclaimer clauses is *Hollerbach v. United States,*[14] which involved a contract to repair a dam. In its specifications, the government stated that the dam was backed mostly with broken stone and sediment. As the contractor proceeded, it was discovered that the backing of the dam was composed mostly of soft, slushy sediment which made performance of the contract substantially more difficult. The contract contained the following disclaimers:

> It is understood and agreed that the quantities given are approximate only, and that no claim shall be made against the United States on account of any excess or deficiency, absolute or relative, in the same. Bidders, or their authorized agents, are expected to examine the maps and drawings in this office, which are open to inspection, to visit the locality of the work, and to make their own estimates of the facilities and difficulties attending the execution of the proposed contract, including local conditions, uncertainty of weather, and all other contingencies.[15]

In spite of the government's attempt to make the contractor responsible for investigation of the site, the Supreme Court upheld the contractor's claim for extra compensation:

> [T]he specifications assured them of the character of the material, a matter concerning which the Government might be presumed to speak with knowledge and authority. We think this positive statement of the specifications must be taken as true and binding upon the Government, and that upon it rather than upon the claimants must fall the loss resulting from such

[13] Raymond Int'l, Inc. v. Baltimore County, 45 Md. App. 247, 412 A.2d 1296, 1300 (1980).

[14] 233 U.S. 165, 34 S. Ct. 553 (1914).

[15] 233 U.S. at 167–68, 34 S. Ct. at 554.

> mistaken representations. We think it would be going quite too far to interpret the general language of the other paragraphs as requiring independent investigation of facts which the specifications furnished by the Government as a basis of the contract left no doubt.[16]

Thus, specific and positive representations as to work conditions in a contract must override general language in the contract requiring pre-bid site investigations by the contractor. Subsequent to *Hollerbach,* the courts have attached significance to positive representations coupled with the presence of a changed conditions clause in the contract.[17]

Another exception is when the contractor cannot reasonably verify the representations made by the owner. Thus, when the pre-bid period is too short to permit adequate verification or when verification would be inordinately expensive or difficult, the disclaimer clause will be ineffective.[18]

A last exception to the validity of disclaimers is when the owner acts in bad faith. Such cases generally involve situations in which the owner conceals or withholds material facts unknown to the contractor.[19] A number of courts have held that the exception is inapplicable when the information is equally available to the contractor and the owner.[20] Courts also have held the exception inapplicable when the undisclosed information would have been of little use to the contractor.[21]

These cases show that one must look beyond the language of the disclaimer clauses to determine whether such clauses will be effective. However, a more basic inquiry is whether such clauses should be used at all. It

---

[16] 233 U.S. at 167–68; *see also* E.H. Morrill Co. v. State, 65 Cal. 2d 787, 423 P.2d 551, 56 Cal. Rptr. 479 (1967).

[17] *See, e.g.,* Foster Constr. C.A. v. United States, 435 F.2d 873, 193 Ct. Cl. 587 (1970). In *Foster,* the court explained that the two elements work together. "Bidders are given information on which they may rely in making their bids, and are at the same time promised an equitable adjustment under the changed condition clause if subsurface conditions turn out to be materially different than those indicated in the logs." 435 F.2d at 887. *See also* Al Johnson Constr. Co. v. Missouri Pac. Ry, 426 F. Supp. 639, 647 (E.D. Ark. 1976).

[18] *See, e.g.,* A.E. Ottaviano, Inc. v. State, 202 Misc. 532, 110 N.Y.S.2d 99 (1952) (two-week bid period); Alpert v. Commonwealth, 357 Mass. 306, 285 N.E.2d 755 (1970) (21-day bid period and 2- to 3-month period required for making adequate soil analysis); County Asphalt, Inc. v. State, 40 A.D.2d 26, 337 N.Y.S.2d 415 (1972) (three-week bid period).

[19] *See, e.g.,* Bernard McMenamy Contractors, Inc. v. Missouri State Highway Comm'n, 582 S.W.2d 305 (Mo. Ct. App. 1979); Jacksonville Port Auth. v. Parkhill-Goodloe Co., 362 So. 2d 1009 (Fla. Dist. Ct. App. 1978); Pennsylvania Dept. of Transp. v. Cumberland Constr. Co., 90 Pa. Commw. 273, 494 A.2d 520 (1985).

[20] *See, e.g.,* J.A. Thompson & Son, Inc. v. State, 51 Haw. 529, 672, 465 P.2d 148 (1970); State Highway Comm'n v. DeLong Corp., 9 Or. App. 550, 495 P.2d 1215 (1972).

[21] *See, e.g.,* Dravo Corp. v. Kentucky Dept. of Highways, 564 S.W.2d 16 (Ky. Ct. App. 1977).

may be less expensive for the owner to supply one set of subsurface data rather than have each bidder go to the expense of making independent tests not knowing whether it will be awarded the contract. Requiring each and every contractor to incur such an expense or to assume the risk of meeting unexpected subsurface conditions may only increase the bids and, in the end, create greater expense for the owner.

The owner or design professional also may employ other standard exculpatory clauses. For example, many owner-contractor agreements contain a *no damage for delay clause* that insulates the owner from liability to the contractor for delay.[22] Most agreements also contain a *changes clause* that requires the contractor to submit to the owner its claim for additional costs within a specific time period. Such clauses may be used by the owner as a defense to breach of warranty or contract claims.[23]

§ 20.4 Right to Reject All Bids

The awarding authority has considerable discretion to reject all bids. For federal contracts, federal statutes provide that all bids may be rejected when the agency head determines that it is in the public interest.[24] Standard Form 22, Instructions to Bidders (Construction Contract), expressly reserves the right to reject any and all bids in a clause providing that "[t]he government may, when in its interest, reject any and all bids or waive any informality in bids received." However, if the bids have been opened and each bidder's competitive position has been exposed, rejection of all bids should occur only for cogent or compelling reasons.[25]

---

[22] *See, e.g.*, E.C. Ernst, Inc. v. Manhattan Constr. Co., 551 F.2d 1026, 1029 (5th Cir. 1977) (no damages for delay cause).

[23] *See, e.g.*, S&M Constr., Inc. v. City of Columbus, 70 Ohio St. 2d 69, 434 N.E.2d 1349 (1982); Sasso Contracting Co. v. State, 173 N.J. Super. 486, 414 A.2d 603 (1980); Eastern Tunneling Corp. v. Southgate Sanitation Dist., 487 F. Supp. 109 (D. Colo. 1980).

[24] *See, e.g.*, 41 U.S.C. § 253b(b) (1989).

[25] Massman Constr. Co. v. United States, 60 F. Supp. 635, 643 (Ct. Cl.), *cert. denied,* 325 U.S. 866 (1945); *see also* Kinetic Structures Corp. v. United States, 6 Cl. Ct. 387, 395 (1984) (to preserve integrity of competitive bidding process and to prevent misapplication of public funds, the rejection of all submitted bids after opening is strongly discouraged). According to 48 C.F.R. § 14.404-1(c), the following are adequate grounds for rejection of bids after opening: (1) the advertised specifications are inadequate, ambiguous, or otherwise deficient; (2) the supplies or services are no longer required; (3) the IFB did not include all of the intended evaluation factors; (4) bids received indicate that the government's quality requirements were overstated; (5) the prices on all otherwise acceptable bids are unreasonable; (6) the bids were not independently arrived at in open competition, were collusive, or were submitted in bad faith; (7) the bids received did not provide sufficient competition to ensure adequate price.

As to state contracts, the provisions of a state constitution, city or county charter, or statute or ordinance frequently give the public authorities the express right to reject "any and all" bids or "any or all" bids. The right is usually given effect by the courts.[26] If there is no constitutional or legislative provision for the right to reject all bids, the courts usually recognize the right when there is an express reservation in the invitation for bids.[27] However, a number of courts have held that the right cannot be exercised arbitrarily[28] or in bad faith.[29]

§ 20.5 Requirement of Responsiveness

Individual bids may not be rejected arbitrarily. They may only be rejected for good cause, such as nonresponsiveness of the bid or nonresponsibility of the bidder.

The purpose of the requirement of responsiveness is to ensure that all bidders stand on an equal footing and the integrity of the formal advertising system is maintained.[30] For a bid to be responsive, it must constitute a definite and unqualified offer to meet the material terms of the IFB. *Material terms* are those that (1) could affect price, quantity, quality, or delivery,

---

[26] *See, e.g.*, John J. Brennan Constr. Corp. v. Shelton, 187 Conn. 695, 448 A.2d 180, 185 (1982) (law evinced a strong policy favoring the right of a municipality to exercise its right reserved in the city charter to reject all bids, absent fraud or corruption); Dickinson Co. v. Des Moines, 347 N.W.2d 436, 440 (Iowa 1984) (statute gave city the authority to reject all bids notwithstanding requirement to award to lowest responsible bidder); J.L. Manta, Inc. v. Braun, 393 N.W.2d 490, 493 (Minn. 1986) (state has statutory right to reject any or all bids for good and sufficient cause, including abandonment of project or insufficient funds).

[27] *See, e.g.*, R.S. Noonan, Inc. v. School Dist., 400 Pa. 391, 162 A.2d 623, 626 (1960) (because IFB included reservation of right to reject any or all bids, all bidders were on notice that their bids might be rejected; school district was empowered to reject all bids); Straw v. Williamsport, 286 Pa. 41, 132 A. 804 (1926) (reservation of right in advertisement gave city discretionary power to reject all bids for paving and sewer project).

[28] *See, e.g.*, Funderburg Builders, Inc. v. Abbeville County Memorial Hosp., 467 F. Supp. 821 (D.S.C. 1979) (bid may not be rejected even with such right reserved in the IFB unless bid fails to include required data, is incomplete or irregular, is unreasonable, or is submitted by unreasonable bidder); Housing Auth. v. Pittman Constr. Co., 264 F.2d 695, 703 (5th Cir. 1959) (in exercising discretion in awarding contract for construction of public works, awarding authority has the right to be dead wrong, but not unfairly or arbitrarily wrong).

[29] *See, e.g.*, Marshall Constr. Co. v. Bigelow, 29 Haw. 641, 655 (1927); La Mar Constr. Co. v. Holt County Region II School Dist., 542 S.W.2d 568, 571 (Mo. Ct. App. 1976). Other courts have held that motive is immaterial. *See, e.g.*, Shay v. McCormack, 167 A.D. 854, 153 N.Y.S. 808, 810 (1915). *See generally* Annotation, *Public Contracts: Authority of State or its Subdivision to Reject All Bids*, 52 A.L.R. 4th 186 (1987).

[30] P. Shnitzer, Government Contract Bidding 237 (1976).

or (2) are clearly identified by the IFB and which, for reasons of public policy, must be complied with at the risk of bid rejection.[31]

The causes that make a bid unresponsive may be placed into one of three categories: (1) reservation of rights, (2) "two bites at the apple," and (3) failure to meet specified requirements.

A *reservation of rights* is a bidder's reservation to change some material response to the IFB. For example, a bid submitted reserving the right to negotiate the terms of a warranty after bid opening is unresponsive,[32] even if after the bid opening the bidder can demonstrate that the change will not be made. The government must have an unqualified right to the bidder's performance in strict accordance with the IFB based on the form of the bid at the time of the bid opening.[33]

The prohibition against affording bidders *two bites at the apple* is based on the concept of full and fair competition. The purpose is to avoid giving any bidder the option after the bid opening, when all bids have been made public, to take any action that would either (1) qualify him for award or (2) disqualify him because it would give him an unfair second chance to decide whether or on what terms he wished the contract.[34] This rule is so rigid that it is sometimes necessary to reject a bid even though there is only a theoretical possibility that the bidder will obtain an unfair advantage.

Following are specific causes that will make a bid unresponsive and therefore require its rejection:

1. Offering less than the minimum time the IFB requires bids to remain open[35]
2. A bid submitted in the name of nonexisting corporation[36]
3. Unsigned bid[37]
4. Signer lacks authority[38]

---

[31] *See, e.g., In re* Contract for Route 280 Section 7U Exit Project, 179 N.J. Super. 280, 431 A.2d 848, 849–50 (1981); King v. Alaska Hous. Auth., 512 P.2d 887, 892 (Alaska 1973); Shannon Holloway Constr. Co. v. Louisville & Jefferson County Metro. Sewer Dist., 674 S.W.2d 523 (Ky. Ct. App. 1983).

[32] Secretary of the Navy, 42 Comp. Gen. 96 (1962).

[33] *See, e.g.,* Coller v. St. Paul, 223 Minn. 376, 26 N.W.2d 835 (1947); Albert Elia Co. v. Sioux City, 418 F. Supp. 176 (D. Iowa 1976) (responsiveness of bid on wastewater treatment plant is to be determined from face of the bid).

[34] *See, e.g.,* Grade-way Constr. v. United States, 7 Cl. Ct. 263 (1985) (bidder should not be able to turn an otherwise unresponsive bid into a responsive bid by electing to act, after bid openings, so as to come into compliance with amendments to IFB).

[35] *See* Admiral H. Arnold Karo, 39 Comp. Gen. 779, 780 (1960).

[36] Martin Co., Comp. Gen. B-178540 (May 8, 1974).

[37] Churchill Chem. Corp. v. United States, 602 F.2d 358 (Ct. Cl. 1979).

[38] Cool-Rite Corp., 48 Comp. Gen. 369 (1968).

5. Failure of the bid to provide a firm offer at a specific price[39]
6. Price conditioned on the award to the bidder of a contract under another IFB (tie-in bids)[40]
7. Unbalanced bids[41]
8. Any qualification that reduces the bidder's legal liability or increases the government's responsibility[42]
9. Failure on the part of a bidder to acknowledge in a timely manner receipt of amendment that could affect price, quantity, quality, or delivery.[43]

Although a contract is to be awarded only to a bidder who fully responds to the IFB, if the defect or omission in the bid is trivial or a matter of a mere formality, the bid need not be rejected. The bidder may be given an opportunity to cure the defect or the government may waive those terms to which the bid did not respond.[44]

§ 20.6 Requirement of Responsibility

A bid that is the lowest responsive bid still may be rejected if the bidder is not responsible. A *responsible bidder* is one who can or will be able to perform as promised.[45] An evaluation of responsibility is limited to a consideration of a bidder's financial standing, reputation, experience, resources, facilities, judgment, and efficiency.[46] The contracting officer has

---

[39] Secretary of the Army, 37 Comp. Gen. 780 (1958) ("approximate" prices).

[40] Secretary of Commerce, 37 Comp. Gen. 186, 1987 (1957).

[41] *Unbalanced bids* are bids that offer an unreasonably low price on some items and compensate for them by unreasonably high prices on other items. Such bids may be rejected unless it is reasonably certain it will result in the lowest cost to the government. Landis, Cohen, Singman and Rauh, Comp. Gen. B-172789 (July 19, 1971).

[42] *See, e.g.,* J.M. Thomson, Jr., 39 Comp. Gen. 259 (1959) (bid that deletes from IFB a provision making bidder liable for unexplained default of bidder's subcontractor).

[43] *See, e.g.,* Charles N. White Constr. Co. v. Department of Labor, 476 F. Supp. 862 (S.D. Miss. 1979).

[44] Grade-way Constr. v. United States, 7 Cl. Ct. 263 (1985); Northeast Constr. Co. v. Romney, 485 F.2d 752 (D.C. Cir. 1973) (failure to furnish required information concerning number of employees at time of bid is "minor formality").

[45] City of Rochester v. EPA, 496 F. Supp. 751, 756 (D. Minn. 1980).

[46] *See* Pearlman v. Pittsburg, 304 Pa. 25, 155 A. 118 (1931); *see also* O'Brien v. Carney, 6 F. Supp. 761 (D. Mass. 1925) (to determine responsibility it is necessary to consider judgment, skill, integrity, financial resources, fitness, and ability to fulfill successfully the requirements of the contract).

wide discretion in determining whether a bidder is responsible.[47] However, the consideration must be fair and impartial.[48]

Generally, information pertinent to responsibility may be provided after the bid opening and before the award.[49] A determination of responsiveness, however, generally may not be based upon information submitted after the bid opening.[50]

One of the principal considerations in assessing responsibility is the bidder's prior performance.[51] Other important considerations are the bidder's integrity[52] and financial condition.[53]

§ 20.7 Mistakes in Bids

The bidding process is highly conducive to making mistakes in bids. Bidders are often given only a few weeks to review the bid documents, inspect

---

[47] John Carlo, Inc. v. Corps of Eng'rs, 539 F. Supp. 1075 (N.D. Tex. 1982) (contracting officer's determination of nonresponsibility will only be set aside upon a clear showing of a lack of reasonable basis); Malan Constr. Corp. v. Board of County Comm'rs, 187 F. Supp. 937 (E.D. Mich. 1960) (county has right to investigate bidders after opening of bids and to adopt bid found to be in best interest of county, even if it is not the low bid).

[48] Housing Auth. v. Pittman Constr. Co., 264 F.2d 695 (5th Cir. 1959) (rejection of bid based on rumor without a hearing was abuse of discretion).

[49] Stewart Petroleum Co. v. United States, 438 F. Supp. 527 (D.D.C. 1977).

[50] City of Rochester v. EPA, 496 F. Supp. 751, 756 (D. Minn. 1980).

[51] When there is a logical relationship between a poor past performance record and the requirements of the contract being sought, the poor performance will be taken into account in determining responsibility. *See, e.g.,* PNM Constr. Inc. v. United States, 13 Cl. Ct. 745 (1987) (prior history of poor quality workmanship and tardiness as basis for determination of nonresponsibility); Rayco Constr. Co. v. Vorsanger, 397 F. Supp. 1105 (E.D. Ark. 1975). The experience and responsibility of the firm's principal officers may be considered in deciding its responsibility. Unpublished opinion of Comp. Gen. B-158543 (Apr. 23, 1966); unpublished opinion of Compt. Gen. B-160758 (May 15, 1967).

[52] Usually the issue of integrity arises because of criminal indictment of the bidder or one of its officials for an offense directly related to the manner in which the firm conducts its business. A conviction for a crime relating to government contracting or reflecting adversely on the bidder's business integrity can justify rejection of the bid for nonresponsibility. *See, e.g.,* Johnson, Drake & Piper, Inc., 39 Comp. Gen. 468 (1959) (bid properly rejected on ground that president and principal stockholder of one of joint venturers submitting bid was convicted for evading the federal income tax law). However, the government's rejection of a bid on the basis of lack of integrity implicates due process liberty rights granted by the Fifth and Fourteenth Amendments. Old Dominion Dairy Prods., Inc. v. Secretary of Defense, 631 F.2d 953, 962 (D.C. Cir. 1980). When there is a determination that the contractor lacks integrity and the government has not acted to invoke formal suspension or disbarment procedures, the contractor must be given notice of the charges and an opportunity to rebut them. *Id.* at 968.

[53] A bidder's bankruptcy may result in a finding of nonresponsibility. Dynamics Corp. of Am., 52 Comp. Gen. 372 (1972).

the site, estimate the work, obtain sub-bids, and complete the bid forms. Bids are therefore prepared in a hurried fashion with little time for scrutiny.

Relief from bid mistakes is governed by statutes or provisions in the invitation for bids. Usually, these statutes or bid documents contain provisions prohibiting the withdrawal of bids for a specified period of time absent the consent of the awarding authority. In many states, however, the courts of equity have intervened to afford relief to the erring bidder. The relief provided—rescission (withdrawing the bid) and reformation (rewriting the bid)—is equitable in nature and is founded on the court's inherent power to do equity.

Bid mistakes may be categorized into mistakes of fact, mistakes of law, and mistakes of judgment. A *mistake of fact* is a "state of mind or belief that is not in accord with the facts."[54] The term includes "an erroneous belief that the calculations upon which a bid was based are mathematically accurate, or that the bid was based upon all cost figures which the bidder had intended to use as the basis for his calculations."[55] Mistakes of fact are typically clerical errors, such as incorrectly adding or transposing numbers or inadvertently omitting numbers from the bid.

A *mistake of law* is a misrepresentation of the bid documents.[56] This typically involves the misinterpretation of the bid specifications.

A *mistake in judgment* is an inaccurate prediction as to matters known to be variables.[57] Examples of mistakes of judgment are inaccurate predictions as to weather conditions or the future cost of goods to be acquired for use in performance of the contract.[58]

In most jurisdictions, a bidder may be entitled to relief from a bid based on a mistake of fact.[59] In some jurisdictions, a bidder also may be entitled to relief for a bid based on a mistake of law.[60] The granting of relief in such instances is more likely if the mistake can be objectively proven.[61] However, mistakes in bids that are purely judgmental "never entitle the bidder to

---

[54] 2 A.L.R. 4th 991, 995 n.6 (1980).

[55] *Id.*

[56] *Id.*

[57] *Id.*

[58] *Id.*

[59] *See, e.g.,* Syracuse v. Sarkisian Bros., Inc., 87 A.D.2d 984, 451 N.Y.S.2d 945 (1982) (clerical mistake); State Highway Comm'n v. Canion, 250 S.W.2d 439 (Tex. Civ. App. 1952) (same); *see generally* Fields, *Relief from Mistakes in Bids,* 32 Ins. Couns. J. 259 (1965).

[60] *See, e.g.,* Peter Kiewit Sons' Co. v. Washington State Dept. of Transp., 30 Wash. App. 424, 635 P.2d 740, 744 (1981); Carrier Corp. v. United States, 6 Cl. Ct. 169, 175 (1984).

[61] Balaban-Gordon Co. v. Brighton Sewer Dist., 41 A.D.2d 246, 342 N.Y.S.2d 435 (1973) (misinterpretation of bid specifications concerning equipment to be provided).

equitable relief."[62] The principle underlying the denial of relief for such mistakes is that mistakes of judgment are inherent business risks that contractors must assume in formulating their bids.[63]

There is considerable diversity in the criteria applied by the courts in determining whether to grant rescission. The decision is usually made on a case-by-case basis. The following factors are usually considered:

Materiality. The bid mistake must relate to a "material" aspect of the contract. Although some decisions have treated this as a separate factor, it may be considered part of the factor of "unconscionability." A bid mistake that is so great as to render its enforcement unconscionable is necessarily one that is material.[64]

Unconscionability. The mistake must render enforcement of the contract unconscionable. A main consideration is the relative size of the bid error. Enforcement of a bid having an error constituting only 2.5 percent of the total bid price has been held not to be unconscionable.[65] Bid errors held to be unconscionable have ranged from 3.5 percent to nearly 100 percent of the bid price.[66]

Other considerations also may bear upon the question of unconscionability. When enforcement of the contract would put the contractor into bankruptcy or cause him to become insolvent, enforcement would be unconscionable.[67]

Unconscionability also may be established when it is shown that the bidder would lose money if forced to perform the contract at the bid price. In fact, some courts have held that when the plaintiff fails to prove that he could not have performed at the bid price without sustaining a loss,

---

[62] Peter Kiewit Sons' Co. v. Washington State Dept. of Transp., 30 Wash. App. 424, 635 P.2d 740, 744 (1981) ("guessed-at" costs of certain items of work mistakingly included in bid do not entitle bidder to relief); *see also* State *ex rel.* Mo. State Highway Comm'n v. Hensel Phelps Constr. Co., 634 S.W.2d 168 (Mo. 1982) (en banc) (bidder's mistaken presumption that his purchases would be exempt under state sales tax do not entitle him to relief).

[63] Balaban-Gordon Co. v. Brighton Sewer Dist., 41 A.D.2d 246, 342 N.Y.S.2d 435 (1973).

[64] D. Reimer & D. Shipman, *Mistakes or Errors in Bids,* in Construction Bidding Law 96 (R.F. Cushman ed. John Wiley & Sons 1990) (citing Alaska Int'l Constr. Inc. v. Earth Movers, 697 P.2d 626 (Alaska 1985).

[65] *Id.* (citing Alaska Int'l Constr., Inc. v. Earth Movers, 697 P.2d at 630 n.8).

[66] *Id.*

[67] Baltimore v. DeLuca Davis Constr. Co., 210 Md. 518, 124 A.2d 557 (1955). However, bankruptcy or insolvency is not a prerequisite to finding unconscionability. Baltimore County v. John K. Ruff, Inc., 281 Md. 62, 375 A.2d 237 (1977).

rescission will not be provided.[68] Finally, some courts have focused on the disparity between the bid price and that of the second lowest bidder. When the disparity is sufficiently great, it may be a basis for a finding of unconscionability.[69]

Reasonable care. The bidder must exercise reasonable care. However, what is reasonable is not considered in a vacuum. It is viewed in the context in which the mistake is made with due regard to the time pressures usually present in the bid formulation and submission process.[70] Arithmetical or computational errors are usually not viewed as the result of unreasonable care,[71] nor are transpositional errors.[72] However, in some instances the courts have held such errors to be the result of negligence. This occurred, for example, when the bidder made numerous omissions in the same bid.[73] It also occurred when it was the practice in the industry to cross-check bid figures and the bidder failed to do this.[74] One court has held that when the error was due to some dereliction on the part of the contractor himself, rather than his employee, relief for the mistake was improper.[75]

Prejudice. The plaintiff must show that the awarding authority will not suffer substantial prejudice if the inaccurate bid is withdrawn. Generally,

---

[68] *See, e.g.,* Glamorgan Pipe & Foundry Co. v. Washington Suburban Sanitary Comm'n, 183 F. Supp. 840 (D. Md. 1960); *see also* Board of Water & Sewer Comm'rs v. Spriggs, 274 Ala. 155, 146 So. 2d 872 (1962) (no relief where plaintiff fails to show what his reasonable cost of the work would be.)

[69] *See, e.g.,* Bethel Plumbing & Heating Co. v. General State Auth., 81 Dauph Co. 173 (Pa. 1963) (where plaintiff's bid was $13,873 and next lowest bidder's was $79,376, plaintiff was entitled to return of its bid bond).

[70] *See, e.g.,* R.O. Bromagin & Co. v. Bloomington, 84 N.E. 700 (Ill. 1908) (mistake not a result of negligence in view of great haste that was necessary in order to meet deadline for submission of bids).

[71] *See, e.g.,* State Bd. of Control v. Clutter Constr. Corp., 139 So. 2d 153 (Fla. Dist. Ct. App. 1962) (computation error); People *ex rel.* Dep't of Pub. Works & Bldgs. v. Southeast Nat'l Bank, 226 N.E.2d 778 (Ill. 1971) (adding machine tabulation error).

[72] *See, e.g.,* State Bldg. Comm'n v. Becknell Constr., Inc., 329 So. 2d 57 (Miss. 1976) (erroneous transposition of figures from worksheet in bid form); Jordan v. City of Beaumont, 337 S.W.2d 115 (Tex. Ct. App. 1960) (same); *but see* Dierks Heating Co. v. Egan, 115 A.D.2d 836, 496 N.Y.S.2d 97 (1985) (error due to omission rather than to arithmetic mistake in computation was unreasonable).

[73] *See* Nelson Inc. v. Sewerage Comm'n, 72 Wis. 2d 400, 241 N.W.2d 390 (1976) (five omissions).

[74] *See* Community Consol. School Dist. v. Meneley Constr. Co., 86 Ill. App. 3d 1101, 409 N.E.2d 66 (1980).

[75] *See* Graham v. Clyde, 61 So. 2d 656 (Fla. 1952) (contractor claimed that mistake was caused by the way he manipulated adding machine).

this may be shown if the awarding authority is able to award the bid to the next lowest bidder and if the authority has not taken action in reliance on the inaccurate bid.[76] Thus, promptness in apprising the awarding authority of the bid error is crucial. When notification is provided before the award, lack of prejudice to the awarding authority usually can be shown. However, the fact that notification is not provided until after the award does not necessarily mean that prejudice will result.[77]

Some courts construe this factor as requiring that the awarding authority be restored to the status quo.[78] However, this does not mean that the awarding authority is entitled to the benefit on an erroneous bid.[79]

Obtaining reformation of a bid is difficult under state decisional law. Generally, state courts do not consider reformation an appropriate form of relief for bid mistakes on public contracts.[80] Reformation is not favored because courts are concerned about collusive schemes involving bidders and public officials.[81] One court has held that reformation is appropriate only in cases of mutual mistake.[82] It stated that a court will never rewrite a contract unless there is a clear, convincing, and satisfying proof of a mutual understanding and bargain that has not been accurately expressed.[83]

Another court has indicated, however, that reformation may be available when a plaintiff can show by clear and convincing evidence that the awarding authority was inequitable in not pointing out a possible error.[84]

---

[76] *See, e.g.,* Regional School Dist. v. United Pac. Ins. Co., 4 Conn. App. 175, 493 A.2d 895 (1985); Syracuse v. Sarkisian Bros., Inc., 87 A.D.2d 984, 451 N.Y.S.2d 945 (1982); Mississippi State Bldg. Comm'n v. Becknell Constr., 329 So. 2d 57 (Miss. 1976); Kenneth E. Curran, Inc. v. State, 106 N.H. 558, 215 A.2d 702 (1965); Levine v. Parsons, 258 A.D. 1003, 16 N.Y.S.2d 722 (1940).

[77] *See, e.g.,* Santucci Constr. Co. v. County of Cook, 21 Ill. App. 3d 527, 315 N.E.2d 565 (1974) (project was relet for about $100,000 less than the second lowest of the original bids); Cataldo Constr. Co. v. County of Essex, 110 N.J. Super. 414, 265 A.2d 842 (1970) (awarding authority promptly readvertised and obtained a satisfactory low bid); *see generally* Annotation, *Right of Bidder for State or Municipal Contract to Rescind Bid on Ground that bid was based upon his own mistake or that of his Employee,* 2 A.L.R. 4th 991, 1029–38 (1980).

[78] *See, e.g.,* Kenneth E. Curran, Inc. v. State, 106 N.H. 558, 215 A.2d 702 (1965).

[79] M.F. Kemper Constr. Co. v. City of Los Angeles, 37 Cal. 2d 696, 235 P.2d 7, (1951).

[80] D. Reimer & H. Shipman, *Mistakes or Errors in Bids,* in Construction Bidding Law 98 (R.F. Cushman ed. John Wiley & Sons 1990) (citing Department of Transp. v. Ronlee, Inc., 518 So. 2d 1326, 1328 (Fla. 1987)).

[81] *Id.*

[82] Baltimore v. De Luca Davis Constr. Co., 210 Md. 518, 124 A.2d 557 (1956).

[83] *Id.*

[84] D. Reimer & H. Shipman, *Mistakes or Errors in Bids,* in Construction Bidding Law 98 (R.F. Cushman ed. John Wiley & Sons 1990) (citing Dept. of Transp. v. Ronlee, Inc., 518 So. 2d 1326, 1328 (Fla. 1987)).

However, state contracting agencies usually are not under any obligation to examine bids for errors.[85]

For federal contracts, the rules for obtaining relief from bid mistakes are more distinct. They are codified in 48 C.F.R. § 1414.406, which spells out in detail the showing required for a bidder to rescind or reform its bid. Under the Federal Acquisition Regulation (FAR), that showing varies significantly depending on when the bidder gives notice of the mistake.[86]

§ 20.8 Challenges to Bids and Awards

As mentioned, there may be a number of reasons why a disappointed bidder might wish to challenge a bid or an award. A bidder might claim that its bid was wrongfully rejected, that the low bid should be rejected, or that it is entitled to relief from a bid mistake. Depending on the jurisdiction and the awarding authority, the disappointed bidder may pursue its challenge administratively, through the courts, or both.

Many states provide formal bid protest procedures for enforcing the public bidding laws.[87] These are commonly administered by a regulatory agency that investigates, holds hearings, and decides the dispute. The advantages of such procedures are threefold: informality, speed, and expertise. Adherence to formal rules of procedure and rules of evidence is usually not required. It is not uncommon for the investigation and hearing to be accomplished within a matter of weeks, and the hearing officer is often experienced and knowledgeable in the statutory requirements of the public bidding laws.

Bid protests are usually initiated by filing a written protest with the regulatory agency stating the nature of the dispute and sending a copy to the awarding authority. Timing may be critical. Some jurisdictions may impose time limits for filing, after which the bidder loses its right to protest. Additionally, award and execution of the contract may limit the scope of available relief. Accordingly, the protestor should request the regulatory agency to stay the award and execution as early as possible. If the regulatory agency does not have authority to impose a stay and cannot obtain one voluntarily, the protestor should seek injunctive relief in the courts.

---

[85] *Id.*

[86] The showing varies depending on whether notice of the mistake is given before bid opening, after bid opening but before the award, or after the award. *See generally* 48 C.F.R. § 14.406.

[87] *See, e.g.,* Mass. Gen. L. ch. 149, § 44H (1990).

If the protestor disagrees with the regulatory agency's decision in the bid protest, the protestor usually has a right to appeal. In some jurisdictions, the appeal is administrative; in others, the appeal is to the courts.

In some jurisdictions, it is not required that bid protests be initially brought before an administrative agency. The protestor may seek relief by filing an action in court. The action should include requests for a preliminary injunction and a declaratory judgment.

Bid protests for federal contracts can be made either to the contracting agency,[88] the General Accounting Office (GAO),[89] or the federal courts. Review by the GAO of a challenge to an award is permissive and is not a prerequisite to judicial review of that award.[90]

Before a protestor can bring an action in court, it must be able to show that it has "standing" to assert the action. In some jurisdictions, the protestor need only show that it possesses the potential to obtain the award.[91] In others, the protestor may sue only if it is a taxpayer or joins with a taxpayer to bring suit.[92]

If the awarding authority wrongfully but in good faith executes the contract, the courts will be reluctant to interfere and reverse the status quo. The protestor probably would be entitled to damages, but damages may be limited to the reasonable cost of preparing the bid.[93] However, when the awarding authority in bad faith wrongfully executes the contract, the scope of relief will not be so limited.[94]

---

[88] Smith & Wesson, Div. of Bangor Punta Corp. v. United States, 782 F.2d 1074, 1078 (1st Cir. 1986); Choctaw Mfg. Co. v. United States, 761 F.2d 609, 616 (11th Cir. 1985); Delta Data Sys. Corp. v. Webster, 744 F.2d 197, 204 (D.C. Cir. 1984).

[89] Keco Indus., Inc. v. United States, 492 F.2d 1200, 1203 (Ct. Cl. 1974).

[90] The procedure for prosecuting a bid protest with the contracting agency is usually stated in the part of the Code of Federal Regulations pertaining to that agency.

[91] *See, e.g.,* Quincy Ornamental Iron Works v. Findlen, 353 Mass. 87, 228 N.E.2d 453 (1967); Modern Continental Constr. Co. v. City of Lowell, 391 Mass. 829, 465 N.E.2d 1173 (1984).

[92] Conduit & Foundation Corp. v. City of Philadelphia, 41 Pa. Commw. 641, 401 A.2d 376 (1979).

[93] *See, e.g.,* Paul Sardella Constr. Co. v. Braintree Hous. Auth., 3 Mass. App. Ct. 326, 329 N.E.2d 762 (1975); Swinerton & Walberg Co. v. City of Inglewood—Los Angeles County Civic Center Auth., 40 Cal. App. 3d 98, 103–5, 114 Cal. Rptr. 834 (1974).

[94] *See, e.g.,* Paul Sardella Constr. Co. v. Braintree Hous. Auth., 3 Mass. App. Ct. 326, 332, 329 N.E.2d 762 (1975).

CHAPTER 21

LIABILITY OF ARCHITECTS AND ENGINEERS TO OWNER

Kenneth I. Levin

Kenneth I. Levin is a partner in the law firm of Pepper, Hamilton & Scheetz, Philadelphia, Pennsylvania, specializing in construction litigation. He is vice chair of the American Bar Association's Section of Public Contract Law's State and Local Contract Claims and Remedies Committee, and vice chair of Region II of its Regional Division. He is also a member of the ABA's Section of Litigation, Section of Torts and Insurance Practice, Fidelity and Surety Committee, and Forum Committee on the Construction Industry. He is a contributing author of several chapters in construction law books, including *Construction Litigation: Representing the Contractor* (John Wiley & Sons, Inc., 1985), *Architect and Engineer Liability: Claims Against Design Professionals* (John Wiley & Sons, Inc., 1987) and *Construction Failures* (John Wiley & Sons, Inc., 1989). Mr. Levin has spoken before bar associations and construction industry groups, and also has taught at Villanova Law School on construction contracts. He received his undergraduate degree from Cornell University and graduated *magna cum laude* from Villanova Law School.

BASIS OF LIABILITY AND STANDARDS OF PROOF

§ 21.1 Standard of Care: Negligence, Implied Warranty, or Strict Liability

In the absence of express contractual warranties or stipulations imposing a different standard of care, proof of negligence traditionally has been required as a basis for the imposition of liability in damages upon design professionals.[1]

Although the doctrines of implied warranty and strict liability (liability without fault) are widely applied as a basis for imposing liability upon manufacturers of defective products, the courts, for the most part, have rejected these doctrines in assessing the liability of design professionals.[2]

It is, however, possible for a design professional to contract to a different standard of care, as is illustrated by *Arkansas Rice Growers Cooperative*

---

[1] Pastorelli v. Associated Eng'rs, Inc., 176 F. Supp. 159, 166 (D.R.I. 1959) (quoting Cowles v. City of Minneapolis, 128 Minn. 452, 151 N.W. 184, 185 (1915)).

[2] Del Mar Beach Club Owners Ass'n v. Imperial Contracting Co., 123 Cal. App. 3d 898, 176 Cal. Rptr. 886 (1981); Castaldo v. Pittsburgh-Des Moines Steel Co., 376 A.2d 88 (Del. 1977); Borman's, Inc. v. Lake State Dev. Co., 60 Mich. App. 175, 230 N.W.2d 363 (1975); City of Mounds View v. Walijarvi, 263 N.W.2d 420 (Minn. 1978); Board of Trustees v. Kennerly, Slomanson & Smith, 167 N.J. Super. 311, 400 A.2d 850 (Law Div. 1979); Sears, Roebuck & Co. v. Enco Assocs., Inc., 43 N.Y.2d 389, 372 N.E.2d 555, 401 N.Y.S.2d 767 (1977). Contra Federal Mogul Corp. v. Universal Constr. Co., 376 So. 2d 716 (Ala. Civ. App. 1979) (dicta); Broyles v. Brown Eng'g Co., 275 Ala. 35, 151 So. 2d 767 (1963) (limited to provision of routine services); Bloomsburg Mills, Inc. v. Sordoni Constr. Co., 401 Pa. 358, 164 A.2d 201 (1960) (warranty of fitness). *See also* Doundoulakis v. Town of Hempstead, 42 N.Y.2d 440, 368 N.E.2d 24, 398 N.Y.S.2d 401 (1977) (holding that strict liability could apply when design was for a project which in itself constituted an abnormally dangerous activity as defined in Restatement (Second) of Torts § 520 (1976)).

Association v. Alchemy Industries, Inc.,[3] which arose out of a project to construct an experimental plant for the combustion of rice hulls. When the plant did not perform as anticipated, the owner sued the designer.

The designer had agreed to provide "the necessary engineering plant layout and equipment design and the on-site engineering supervision and start-up engineering services necessary for the construction of a hull by-product facility capable of reducing a minimum of seven and one-half tons of rice hulls per hour to ash and producing a minimum of 48 million BTUs per hour of steam at 200 lbs. pressure."[4] Both the trial and appellate courts concluded that this provision amounted to an express warranty of the design. Accordingly, proof that the plant failed to perform as anticipated was sufficient to establish the owner's case. Additional proof of professional negligence was not required.[5]

Although, as *Arkansas Rice* demonstrates, a professional may by contract agree to a more rigorous standard of care, it has been held that the benefit of such higher standard will run solely to those in privity and not to third-party tort claimants.[6]

§ 21.2 Proof of Professional Negligence

To establish an architect or engineer's liability for professional negligence, a claimant must present evidence (1) establishing the applicable standard of care, (2) demonstrating a violation of the standard, and (3) demonstrating the causal relationship between the violation and the alleged harm.[7]

Ordinarily, proof of professional negligence must be established by expert testimony. The standard of care must be determined from the testimony of experts unless the conduct involved is within the common knowledge of laypersons.[8] Depending upon the jurisdiction in which the claim

---

[3] 797 F.2d 565 (8th Cir. 1986).

[4] *Id.* at 566.

[5] Although it might be tempting for an owner to hold a professional to a warranty of results as in *Arkansas Rice,* such a provision might impair or exceed the scope of coverage afforded by the professional's errors and omissions insurance policy. Such policies usually afford coverage only as to professional negligence.

[6] *See* Peter Kiewit Sons' Co. v. Iowa S. Utils. Co., 355 F. Supp. 376, 394 (S.D. Iowa 1973).

[7] Bell v. Jones, 523 A.2d 982, 987 (D.C. 1986).

[8] *See* Allied Properties v. John A. Blume & Assocs., 25 Cal. App. 3d 848, 102 Cal. Rptr. 259 (1972); Paxton v. County of Alameda, 119 Cal. App. 2d 393, 259 P.2d 934 (1953); Overland Constructors, Inc. v. Millard School Dist., 220 Neb. 220, 369 N.W.2d 69, 76 (1985); R.G. Wood & Assocs. Ltd., 85-1 B.C.A. (CCH) ¶ 17,898 (PSBCA 1985). *See generally* Annotation, 3 A.L.R. 4th 1023 (1981).

Milton J. Womack, Inc. v. House of Representatives, 509 So. 2d 62, 67 (La. Ct. App. 1987), the court held that the failure of architect who drew plans for the renovation of

arises, the design professional's conduct may be measured by a national, rather than a local or regional, standard of care.[9] Although the standard of care is determined with reference to ordinary practices, nevertheless, it has been urged that a failure to adopt new and available technology might constitute professional negligence even though its utilization was not yet customary in the profession.[10]

It has been held that proof of a violation of a municipal building code will constitute evidence of negligence,[11] as may violation of private safety standards.[12] It also has been held that the *Architect's Handbook of Professional Practice* could be considered as evidence of a standard of care, although a violation of its standards would not constitute negligence per se.[13]

§ 21.3 Liability for Errors and Omissions of Consultants

The risks are substantial that a design professional will be held responsible for the errors or omissions of a hired consultant. However, the courts are

---

state capital building to discover a metal x-brace within an interior basement wall scheduled for demolition was an omission from which laypersons could infer negligence without the necessity of expert testimony. The existence of the x-brace was shown in the original blueprints for the capital, which were available on microfilm. The court stated: "It is 'common sense' to conclude that it is the duty of an architect to use reasonable skill and care to determine the location of important structural elements before he completes his plans and authorizes work to begin in accordance with those plans." *Id.* at 67.

[9] *See* Bell v. Jones, 523 A.2d 982, 988 (D.C. 1987).

[10] *See* Peck & Hoch, *Engineer's Liability: State of the Art Consideration in Defining Standard of Care,* 30 Vill. L. Rev. _____, _____ (1985) (citing, inter alia, The T.J. Hooper, 60 F.2d 737, 739–40 (2d Cir.), *cert. denied,* 287 U.S. 662 (1932)), in which Judge Learned Hand stated:

> There are, no doubt, cases where courts seem to make the general practice of the calling the standard of proper diligence. . . . Indeed in most cases reasonable prudence is in fact common prudence; but strictly it is never its measure; a whole calling may have unduly lagged in the adoption of new and available devices. . . . There are precautions so imperative that even their universal disregard will not excuse their omission.

[11] Johnson v. Salem Title Co., 246 Or. 409, 425 P.2d 519 (1967) (Uniform Building Code). Burran v. Dambold, 422 F.2d 133, 135 (10th Cir. 1970) (held that a failure to design in accordance with a state building code constituted negligence per se).

[12] Evans v. Howard R. Green Co., 231 N.W.2d 907 (Iowa 1975) ("Ten-State Standards" promulgated by Great Lakes-Upper Mississippi River Board of State Sanitary Engineers). *But see* Hackley v. Waldorf-Hoerner Paper Prods. Co., 149 Mont. 286, 425 P.2d 712 (1967) (advisory codes or standards of safety without force of law not admissible in evidence).

[13] Taylor, Thon, Thompson & Peterson v. Cannaday, 230 Mont. 151, 749 P.2d 63 (1987).

not uniform in the theories applied. For example, design professionals have been held liable for such errors on the theory that their consultants are their agents.[14] In *Johnson v. Salem Title Co.*,[15] on the other hand, the court characterized an engineering consultant whom an architect had engaged to design a masonry wall as an independent contractor. However, the architect was nevertheless held vicariously liable for the engineer's failure to design the wall in conformity with a city building code, because the code was construed to impose upon the architect a nondelegable duty intended to protect the public. Therefore, notwithstanding the consulting engineer's independent contractor status, the architect was held vicariously liable for his error.

Moreover, even if a consultant should be regarded as an independent contractor, an architect-engineer still could be held liable for negligence in the selection of the consultant or for negligent failure to ascertain deficiencies in the consultant's work.

In a case in which a design professional has been subjected to liability as a result of an error by a consultant, it would appear that the architect/engineer would have a right against the consultant for indemnity.[16]

§ 21.4 Proximate Cause

It is fundamental that for liability to be imposed upon a design professional, negligence must be a causal factor in bringing about the injury for which a recovery is sought. *Bayne v. Everham*[17] is illustrative. A wrongful death action was brought against the designer of a system of reinforced concrete construction for a parking garage after the structure collapsed. There was evidence of negligence in design: the system did not conform to the applicable building code. However, uncontradicted evidence showed that the contractor had deviated from the plans in several respects pertinent to the cause of the failure. Under the circumstances, the court held, the designer could not be held liable.[18] However, a professional will not be relieved of

[14] *See* Scott v. Potomac Ins. Co., 217 Or. 323, 341 P.2d 1083 (1959); Bayuk v. Edson, 236 Cal. App. 2d 309, 46 Cal. Rptr. 49 (1965).

[15] 246 Or. 409, 425 P.2d 519 (1967).

[16] *See, e.g.*, Grossman v. Sea Air Towers, Ltd., 513 So. 2d 686, 689 (Fla. Dist. Ct. App. 1987).

[17] 197 Mich. 181, 163 N.W. 1002 (1917).

[18] 163 N.W. at 1007 (quoting Lake v. McElfatrick, 139 N.Y. 349, 34 N.E. 922, 925 (1893)). *See also* Goette v. Press Bar & Cafe, Inc., 413 N.W.2d 854, 855–56 (Minn. Ct. App. 1987) (architect not liable for injuries resulting from collapse of wall which resulted from contractor's deviation from plans where owner-architect agreement imposed no obligation of supervision on architect).

liability merely because the negligence of the contractor is a concurrent cause with the professional's own negligence in bringing about the harm.[19]

DIRECT ACTIONS BY OWNER

§ 21.5 Owner's Cause of Action: Contract versus Tort Liability

A design professional is potentially liable in both contract and tort to the owner. The malpractice of a design professional may entitle the owner to sue either under a tort theory for negligence or a contract theory for breach of contract.

When an owner proceeds under both tort and contract causes of action, each theory of liability has its own distinct damages and its own distinct statute of limitations. First, damages recovered under a contract theory are measured differently than damages recovered under a tort theory. In certain jurisdictions, this difference may make the tort remedy more advantageous to the plaintiff. Contract damages are governed by the rule in *Hadley v. Baxendale,*[20] which limits generally the recovery for a breach of contract to direct damages deemed to flow naturally from the breach, such as the direct costs of rebuilding a wall that has collapsed due to a design error. *Hadley v. Baxendale* limits additional "special" or "consequential" damages, such as loss of profits resulting from an interruption in the use of a facility, to situations in which the damages were within the reasonable contemplation of the parties at the time they made the contract.[21] By comparison, in an action in tort, "the only limitations are those of 'proximate cause' and the policy which denies recovery to certain types of interests themselves."[22]

Second, contract and tort claims will have different statutes of limitations. For example, in Pennsylvania, there is a two-year statute of limitations[23] for actions in tort and a four-year statute of limitations governs in contract.[24]

The ability of an owner to maintain an action in tort against a design professional, particularly when the damages sought are purely economic in character, however, had been placed in doubt by certain recent decisions

[19] Palmer v. Brown, 127 Cal. App. 2d 44, 273 P.2d 306 (1954).

[20] 156 Eng. Rep. 145 (1854).

[21] *See also* J. Calamari & J. Perillo, Contracts § 14-5 (2d ed. 1977).

[22] W. Prosser & P. Keeton, Prosser and Keeton on Torts § 92, at 665 (5th ed. 1984).

[23] 42 Pa. Cons. Stat. Ann. § 5524 (Purdon Supp. 1988).

[24] *Id.* § 5525.

under New York law. In *Clark-Fitzpatrick, Inc. v. Long Island Railroad Co.,*[25] a contractor sued an owner for breach of contract, in quasi-contract and negligence for delay damages caused by the owner's failure to acquire the rights to a bordering property, to locate and move certain utility lines, and to exercise due care in designing the overall project. The court affirmed the dismissal of both the quasi-contract and negligence causes of action. The court stated that "[i]t is a well-established principle that a simple breach of contract is not to be considered a tort unless a legal duty independent of the contract itself has been violated."[26] A defendant who has entered an express contract is not liable in tort unless the defendant has breached a duty that "springs" from circumstances extraneous to the terms of the contract. In other words, the plaintiff cannot simply reiterate the defendant's breach of the terms of the contract as a basis for negligence liability in a tort action.[27]

However, when professional design services are involved, conduct constituting a breach of contract also may constitute a tort. Then the design professional's conduct constitutes the particular type of negligence known as *malpractice.* A design professional has a legal duty to perform the duties of the contract according to the standards of the profession. Duties imposed by law are tort obligations; therefore, malpractice, which is a breach of a duty imposed by law, is remedied by an action in tort.[28] In *Hotel Utica, Inc. v. Ronald G. Armstrong Engineering Co.,*[29] a case decided before *Clark-Fitzpatrick,* a New York court held that the owner of a hotel could sue an architect who breached his contract to design and supervise construction both in contract and in negligence when the negligent performance of the contract was "malpractice."

This view was recently confirmed in *Carmania Corp., N.V. v. Hambrecht Terrell International,*[30] in which a federal district court, applying New York law, rejected the contention that the rule of *Clark-Fitzpatrick* would bar an

---

[25] 70 N.Y.2d 382, 516 N.E.2d 190, 521 N.Y.S.2d 653 (1987).

[26] *Id.* at 388, 516 N.E.2d at 193, 521 N.Y.S.2d at 656.

[27] *See id.* at 388–90, 516 N.E.2d at 193–94, 521 N.Y.S.2d at 656–57. *See also* Video Corp. v. Frederick Flatto Assoc., 58 N.Y.2d 1026, 448 N.E.2d 1350, 462 N.Y.S.2d 439 (1983); Sears, Roebuck & Co. v. Enco Assoc., Inc., 43 N.Y.2d 389, 372 N.E.2d 555, 401 N.Y.S.2d 767 (1977) for the proposition stated.

[28] *See* W. Prosser & P. Keeton, Prosser and Keeton on Torts § 92 (5th ed. 1984).

[29] 62 A.D.2d 1147, 404 N.Y.S.2d 455, 456 (1978). The court cites the following cases implying an action in both contract and malpractice while deciding the actual issue of statute of limitation: Sears, Roebuck & Co. v. Enco Assoc., Inc., 43 N.Y.2d 389, 372 N.E.2d 555, 401 N.Y.S.2d 767 (1977); Steiner v. Wenning, 43 N.Y.2d 831, 373 N.E.2d 366, 402 N.Y.S.2d 567 (1977); Naetzker v. Brocton Cent. School Dist., 41 N.Y.2d 929, 363 N.E.2d 351, 394 N.Y.S.2d 627 (1977); Paver & Wildfoerster v. Catholic High School Ass'n, 38 N.Y.2d 669, 345 N.E.2d 565, 382 N.Y.S.2d 22 (1976).

[30] 705 F. Supp. 936 (S.D.N.Y. 1989).

owner's action in tort against a design professional with whom it had contracted. The court stated:

> As an architect, HTI must conform to the standard of skill and care that the law demands of professionals who purport to serve the public. Judge Cardozo described that duty's genesis in the leading case of *Glanzer v. Shepard,* 233 N.Y. 236, 239, 135 N.E. 275 (1922): "Growing out of the contract it has nonetheless an origin not exclusively contractual. Given the contract and the relation, the duty is imposed by law." HTI's relationship with Carmania did create a duty independent of the parties' contract. In accusing HTI of violating that duty, Carmania has satisfied *Clark-Fitzpatrick.*[31]

§ 21.6 Economic Loss Defense as Applied to Owner Claims

However, in certain jurisdictions, the mere recognition of the availability of a cause of action in tort may be of little practical significance. This is because, in those jurisdictions, the *economic loss defense* has been held applicable to claims by those in privity with design professionals, as well as those outside the ambit of privity.

Most practitioners are aware of the significance of the economic loss defense as it pertains to tort claims brought by persons not in privity. The defense holds that plaintiffs who have suffered economic loss, but not physical injury to person or property, may not sue in tort to recover for their losses.[32]

The apparent rationale for requiring physical injury to property or person as a predicate to recovery for economic losses is that a "bright line" limitation short of the full range of foreseeability is necessary to protect against a virtually limitless scope of liability for negligence in terms of dollar magnitude and number of potential plaintiffs.[33] Whether the economic loss defense applies to claims by contractors against design professionals is a subject of differing views among the jurisdictions.[34]

---

[31] *Id.* at 938 (footnote omitted).

[32] *See, e.g.,* East River S.S. Corp. v. Transamerica Delaval, Inc., 476 U.S. 858, 106 S. Ct. 2295 (1986).

[33] *See, e.g.,* Louisiana/ex rel./Guste v. M/V Testbank, 752 F.2d 1019 (5th Cir. 1985), *cert. denied,* 477 U.S. 903, 106 S. Ct. 3271 (1986). For example, as a matter of policy, it would be inappropriate for an individual who negligently caused an automobile collision during the morning rush hour to be held liable for lost wages to all commuters who were delayed on their way to work. As a matter of policy, the law has drawn lines short of the broader limits of foreseeability in such circumstances.

[34] *Compare, e.g.,* E.C. Ernst, Inc. v. Manhattan Constr. Co., 551 F.2d 1025 (5th Cir. 1977), *cert. denied,* 434 U.S. 1067 (1978) (applying Alabama law); Donnelly Constr. Co. v. Oberg/Hunt/Gilleland, 139 Ariz. 184, 677 P.2d 1292 (1984); A.R. Moyer, Inc. v.

However, the question of whether the economic loss defense may constitute a defense to tort claims by one in privity with a design professional, that is, the owner, appears only to have been addressed by courts in Illinois and New York. The state courts of Illinois have developed an extensive body of law on the economic loss doctrine. In *Moorman Manufacturing Co. v. National Tank Co.,*[35] the Illinois Supreme Court adopted the economic loss doctrine in a products liability case which held that a plaintiff could not recover damages in a tort action for the cost of repair and the loss of use of a defective grain storage tank. Subsequent decisions in the lower appellate courts of Illinois grappled with the issue of whether *Moorman* precluded an owner or developer from recovering for purely economic losses in a

---

Graham, 285 So. 2d 397 (Fla. 1973); Peter Kiewit Sons' Co. v. Iowa S. Utils. Co., 355 F. Supp. 376 (S.D. Iowa 1973); Gurtler, Hebert & Co. v. Weyland Mach. Shop, Inc., 405 So. 2d 660 (La. Ct. App. 1981); City of Columbus v. Clark-Dietz & Assocs. Eng'rs, Inc., 550 F. Supp. 610 (N.D. Miss. 1982); Owen v. Dodd, 431 F. Supp. 1239 (N.D. Miss. 1977); Lane v. Geiger-Berger Assocs., P.C., 608 F.2d 1148 (8th Cir. 1979) (applying Missouri law); Conforti & Eisele, Inc. v. John C. Morris Assocs., 175 N.J. Super. 341, 418 A.2d 1290 (Law Div. 1980), *aff'd,* 199 N.J. Super. 498, 489 A.2d 1233 (1985); Shoffner Indus., Inc. v. W.B. Lloyd Constr. Co., 42 N.C. App. 259, 257 S.E.2d 50 (1979); Davidson & Jones, Inc. v. County of New Hanover, 41 N.C. App. 661, 255 S.E.2d 580 (1979); Detweiler Bros., Inc. v. John Graham & Co., 412 F. Supp. 416 (E.D. Wash. 1976); Forte Bros., Inc. v. National Amusements, Inc., 525 A.2d 1301 (R.I. 1987); Milton J. Womack, Inc. v. House of Representatives, 509 So. 2d 62 (La. Ct. App. 1987); United States/ex rel. Seminole Sheet Metal Co. v. SCI, Inc., 828 F.2d 671 (11th Cir. 1987); Pritchard Bros. v. Grady Co., 428 N.W.2d 391 (Minn. 1988); Seattle W. Indus., Inc. v. David A. Mowat Co., 110 Wash. 2d 1, 750 P.2d 245 (1988). *See also* COAC, Inc. v. Kennedy Eng'rs, 67 Cal. App. 3d 916, 136 Cal. Rptr. 890 (1977) (holding contractor to be third-party beneficiary of engineer's duty under owner-engineer agreement); John E. Green Plumbing & Heating Co. v. Turner Constr. Co., 742 F.2d 965 (6th Cir. 1984), *cert. denied,* 471 U.S. 1102, 105 S. Ct. 2328 (applying Michigan law) (holding that construction manager owes duty to contractor on third-party beneficiary theory); James McKinney & Son, Inc. v. Lake Placid 1980 Olympic Games, Inc., 92 A.D.2d 991, 461 N.Y.S.2d 483 (1983), *modified on other grounds,* 61 N.Y.2d 836, 462 N.E.2d 137, 473 N.Y.S.2d 960 (1984) (holding that responsibilities of project/construction manager were such as to establish duty in tort to subcontractor) *with, e.g.,* Bernard Johnson, Inc. v. Continental Constructors, Inc., 630 S.W.2d 365 (Tex. Ct. App. 1982); Bryant Elec. Co. v. City of Fredericksburg, 762 F.2d 1192 (4th Cir. 1985); Bates & Rogers Constr. Corp. v. North Shore Sanitary Dist., 128 Ill. App. 3d 962, 471 N.E.2d 915 (1984), *aff'd on other grounds sub nom.* Bates & Rogers Constr. Corp. v. Greeley & Hansen, 109 Ill. 2d 225, 486 N.E.2d 902 (1985); Waldinger Corp. v. Ashbrook-Simon-Hartley, Inc., 564 F. Supp. 970 (C.D. Ill. 1983), *aff'd in part & remanded in part sub nom.* Waldinger Corp. v. CRS Group Eng'rs, Inc., 775 F.2d 781 (7th Cir. 1985).

[35] 91 Ill. 2d 69, 435 N.E.2d 443 (1982). *Economic loss* has been defined as "damages for inadequate value, costs of repair and replacement of the defective product, or consequent loss of profits—without any claim of personal injury or damage to other property" as well as "the diminution in the value of the product because it is inferior in quality and does not work for the general purposes for which it was manufactured and sold." 91 Ill. 2d at 82, 435 N.E.2d at 449.

malpractice claim against a design professional.[36] The issue now seems resolved, however, with the Illinois Supreme Court's decision in *2314 Lincoln Park West Condominium Association v. Mann, Gin, Ebel & Frazier, Ltd.*,[37] holding that there is no architectural malpractice exception to the rule in *Moorman.*

Similarly, in *Carmania Corp., N.V. v. Hambrecht Terrell International,* a district court, predicting New York law, held that an owner could not sue a design professional in tort for purely economic losses.[38] The court expressly rejected the argument that the economic loss limitation was intended to apply only when the parties were not in privity.[39] Shortly after the decision in *Carmania,* however, a state appellate court in New York, in *Robinson Redevelopment Co. v. Anderson,*[40] held that an owner's claim in tort would lie for design malpractice, notwithstanding that the damages sought were purely economic in character.[41] It remains to be seen which view of the scope of the economic loss limitation the New York Court of Appeals will adopt and, further, which view will be adopted in jurisdictions other than New York and Illinois.

§ 21.7 Areas of Liability to Owner

The design professional contracts with the owner for a number of different services over the period of construction.[42] Each of these services is a potential source of liability. The American Institute of Architects (AIA) Standard Form Agreement Between Owner and Architect, Document B141, illustrates the scope of services a design professional may contract to perform for the owner. The agreement divides the architect's service into five phases: the schematic design, design development, construction documents, bidding and negotiation, and construction contract administration. **Sections 21.8** through **21.12** consider the design professional's

[36] *Compare* Palatine Nat'l Bank v. Charles W. Greengard Assocs., Inc., 119 Ill. App. 3d 376, 456 N.E.2d 635 (1983); Bates & Rogers Constr. Corp. v. North Shore Sanitary Dist., 128 Ill. App. 3d 962, 471 N.E.2d 915 (1984); People/ex rel./Skinner v. Graham, 170 Ill. App. 3d 417, 524 N.E.2d 642 (1988); Fence Rail Dev. Corp. v. Nelson & Assoc., Ltd., 174 Ill. App. 3d 94, 528 N.E.2d 344 (1988) *with* Rosos Litho Supply Corp. v. Hansen, 123 Ill. App. 3d 290, 462 N.E.2d 566 (1984); People/ex rel./Skinner v. FGM, Inc., 166 Ill. App. 3d 802, 520 N.E.2d 1024, *appeal denied,* 122 Ill. 2d 593, 530 N.E.2d 263 (1988).

[37] 136 Ill. 2d 302, 555 N.E.2d 346 (1990).

[38] 705 F. Supp. 936, 938 (S.D.N.Y. 1989) (footnotes and citations omitted).

[39] *Id.* at 938 n.3.

[40] 155 A.D.2d 755, 547 N.Y.S.2d 458 (1989).

[41] 547 N.Y.S.2d at 460.

[42] AIA B141-1987.

potential liabilities to the owner in connection with activities performed in these phases.

§ 21.8 —Estimating Errors or Cost Overruns

It has been held that a design professional has an affirmative duty to give a definite idea of the reasonable cost of a project.[43] Liability issues arise when the design professional underestimates the costs of construction. At common law, an architect or engineer does not guarantee the accuracy of cost estimates.[44] However, some jurisdictions have strictly enforced cost limit agreements to hold that the architect is liable for breach when the actual or probable costs of construction exceed the estimates.[45] This rule does not require that the cost limit necessarily be set out in a written contract between the parties.[46] The architect or engineer forfeits his or her fee in a breach of contract action unless the client ordered changes resulting in the increased costs. As one court noted, a cost limitation imposed by an owner can be regarded as a condition precedent to the architect's recovery for her professional services.[47]

In other jurisdictions, the architect or contractor is liable for breach of contract only if the actual cost of that construction does not reasonably approach the amount stated in the cost estimate.[48] In jurisdictions applying this flexible rule, the architect is liable if the actual costs substantially exceed an agreed cost limit.[49] In a jurisdiction requiring substantial departure from the agreed cost figure as a prerequisite to liability for breach, factors that may have a bearing upon the design professional's ability to recover payment when the actual or probable cost of construction exceeds the

---

[43] Williams Eng'g, Inc. v. Goodyear, 496 So. 2d 1012 (La. 1986); Durand Assocs., Inc. v. Guardian Inv. Co., 186 Neb. 349, 183 N.W.2d 246 (1971). (The *Durand* court also held that the architect or engineer has a duty to make full disclosure of all matters important to the client within his knowledge or of which he should have had knowledge.)

[44] *See* Williams Eng'g, Inc. v. Goodyear, 496 So. 2d 1012, 1017–18 (La. 1986). The architect argued that a no-guarantee provision in the contract precluded liability for overrun on costs. However, the architect was liable for breach since he failed to notify the owners of a "cost plus project" that the price had doubled, failed to give the owners other alternatives, and failed to provide revised estimates of cost as the work proceeded. Note that architect's liability under the contract was founded not on the inaccurate estimate figure, but on his failure to adequately perform his contractual duties.

[45] *See* Zannoth v. Booth Radio Stations, Inc., 333 Mich. 233, 52 N.W.2d 678, 682 (1952).

[46] 333 Mich. at 241–42, 52 N.W.2d at 682.

[47] 52 N.W.2d at 684.

[48] Durand Assocs., Inc. v. Guardian Inv. Co., 186 Neb. 349, 183 N.W.2d 246, 247 (1971).

[49] *See* Griswold & Rauma Architects, Inc. v. Aesculapius Corp., 301 Minn. 121, 221 N.W.2d 556 (1974) (architect entitled to compensation when costs exceeded estimate by only 13%).

agreed maximum cost figures include whether (1) the cost figure was expressed as an estimate rather than as a guarantee; (2) the excess was substantial; (3) the excess resulted from orders by the client to change the plans; (4) the client waived objections; and (5) the architect or engineer suggested reasonable revisions after bids in excess of the estimated amount were received.[50]

Cobb v. Thomas[51] is a leading case on the architect's common law liability for construction cost overruns. The owners brought an action for breach of contract and negligence against the architect for failure to keep construction costs below an estimated cost. The court held that the architect could not be held liable for breach of contract when the contract did not stipulate an express construction cost limitation and the only promise made by the architect was to give a "probable" cost of the construction.

> Where the contract, as here, requires the preparation of plans and specifications for the construction of a building according to the express wishes of the owner as to the details of construction without mentioning a cost limitation, the mere non-conformity in the actual cost of construction with the amount so estimated by the architect does not amount to a breach of duty on the part of the architect and therefore forms no basis for a suit to recover the fees paid him.[52]

The court also held that an architect who underestimates the cost of construction cannot be held negligent as a matter of law.[53] The court also stated that, in an action for misrepresentation, a representation as to costs must be knowingly false at the time it was made and affirmed a judgment for the architect in an action for fraud.[54]

The AIA documents limit the circumstances in which an architect will be liable for a cost overrun and, further, the scope of the architect's exposure in the event of liability. Section 5.2.2 of the 1987 AIA Document B141 requires any fixed construction cost limit to be in writing and signed before the fixed limit will be established as a condition of the owner-architect contract. Section 5.2.5 then limits the architect's liability for overruns to redesigning the project without additional charge. This term specifically preserves the architect's right to the agreed fee in the original contract:

> If the Owner chooses to proceed under Clause 5.2.4.4, the Architect, without additional charge, shall modify the Contract Documents as necessary to

---

[50] 301 Minn. at 129–30, 221 N.W.2d at 560–61.

[51] 565 S.W.2d 281 (Tex. Civ. App. 1978).

[52] *Id.* at 286.

[53] *Id.* at 287. *See also* Nelson v. Commonwealth, 235 Va. 228, 368 S.E.2d 239, 246 (1988) (disparity between estimated and actual costs does not of itself establish architect's malpractice).

[54] *Id.* at 290.

comply with the fixed limit, if established as a condition of this Agreement. The modification of Contract Documents shall be the limit of the Architect's responsibility arising out of the establishment of a fixed limit. The Architect shall be entitled to compensation in accordance with this Agreement for all services performed whether or not the Construction Phase is commenced.

§ 21.9 —Errors in Design/Inspection/Shop Drawing Review Functions

Claims by an owner against a design professional often arise from a construction failure due to defective design or inadequate review and inspection of the contractor's work. As noted, an architect does not ordinarily guarantee a perfect plan or satisfactory results. The design professional will not be held accountable for mere errors in judgment and is liable only for a failure to exercise reasonable care and professional skill.[55]

Architects or engineers have been held liable for design defects that resulted in inadequate insulating, waterproofing, or weatherproofing, or in unsuitable piping in a heating system,[56] an inadequate structure,[57] an inaccurate soil report,[58] failure to provide a handrail or otherwise to design a safe staircase,[59] or for selecting defective materials for installation on a construction project.[60]

Reasonable precision is required in the drafting of plans and specifications for the work. In the *Eggers Partnership,*[61] an architect was held

---

[55] See **§ 21.3**.

[56] Bloomsburg Mills, Inc. v. Sordoni Constr. Co., 401 Pa. 358, 360–62, 164 A.2d 201, 202–3 (1960) (unsatisfactory insulating materials in mill roof); Scott v. Potomac Ins. Co., 217 Or. 323, 333–34, 341 P.2d 1083, 1087–88 (1959) (steel tubing used in lieu of copper in heating system).

[57] State v. Wilco Constr. Co., 393 So. 2d 885, 892 (La. Ct. App.), *modified,* 398 So. 2d 1150 (La. Ct. App.), *cert. denied,* 400 So. 2d 905 (La. 1981) (defectively designed weight-bearing walls); Johnson v. Salem Title Co., 246 Or. 409, 411–12, 425 P.2d 519, 521 (1967) (masonry wall blown over by wind); *see* Laukkanen v. Jewel Tea Co., 78 Ill. App. 2d 153, 163, 222 N.E.2d 584, 589 (1966) (pylon toppled by wind).

[58] *See* Mayor of Columbus v. Clark-Dietz & Assocs. Eng'rs, Inc., 550 F. Supp. 610 (N.D. Miss. 1982). *Cf.* Davidson & Jones, Inc. v. County of New Hanover, 41 N.C. App. 661, 255 S.E.2d 580, 584–85, *cert. denied,* 298 N.C. 295, 259 S.E.2d 911 (1979) (finding issue of fact as to whether architects were liable for inaccurate soil reports).

[59] Watt v. United States, 444 F. Supp. 1191, 1195 (D.D.C. 1978) (design of steps made it difficult to perceive change in levels); Montijo v. Swift, 219 Cal. App. 2d 351, 33 Cal. Rptr. 133, 134–35 (1963) (finding issue of fact as to whether design of handrail on stairs was a defect chargeable to architect).

[60] United States/ex rel./Los Angeles Testing Laboratory v. Rogers & Rogers, 161 F. Supp. 132, 136 (D. Cal. 1958); Shoffner Indus., Inc. v. W.B. Lloyd Constr. Co., 42 N.C. App. 259, 257 S.E.2d 50, 57–58, *cert. denied,* 298 N.C. 296, 259 S.E.2d 301 (1979).

[61] 82-1 B.C.A. ¶ 15,630 (IBCA 1982).

negligent for specifying that installation of a particular roofing material should be in accordance with the manufacturer's installation manual, when project conditions, in fact, required a special application technique. It was improper for the architect to rely on the contractor to ascertain that special application techniques were required.

A design professional is not entitled simply to rely upon the assurances of manufacturers or the advice of its consultants. In *Scott v. Potomac Insurance Co.*,[62] an architect was held to be negligent in substituting tin-plated steel tubing for copper tubing in a radiant heating system without changing the method or manner of installation to allow for the different expansion characteristics of the steel tubing. Reliance upon the manufacturer's statement that the steel tubing would be a suitable substitute and a heating consultant's approval of the substitution was not sufficient to satisfy the architect's duty of care. The court held that the architect had an obligation independently to ascertain the true suitability of the substitute material and to determine if it could safely be installed in the manner originally prescribed for the copper tubing. The court stated: "It ill-behooves a man professing professional skill to say I know nothing of an article which I am called upon to use in the practice of my profession."[63] The professional's duty of care and design also extends to the development of solutions to problems arising during the course of construction. In *Clemens v. Benzinger*,[64] the original plans for the erection of steel columns called for the columns to be attached to anchor bolts embedded in concrete floors. However, the concrete contractor neglected to embed the anchor bolts in several locations when the floor was originally poured. The engineer directed the contractor, therefore, to drill holes for the installation of the omitted anchors and then to grout around the bolts with cement. Although the strength of those bolts as supports for the columns was then entirely dependent on the resistance of the cement around the bolts, the engineer thereafter failed to warn the steel erector that the grout was not fully cured. An employee of the erection contractor was killed when anchor bolts to which columns were then attached pulled up out of the floors because the cement grout had not fully hardened. The court stated:

> When the [concrete contractor] deviated from the original plans, a new situation arose which required a new plan, or at least a new direction to the contractors in place of the original plan. The duty to take care of the situation which had then arisen rested on the defendant [engineer], and it recognized such duty and took steps in accordance with it. The superintendent of that company gave direction as to how the problem was to be met. Negligence

---

[62] 217 Or. 323, 341 P.2d 1083 (1959).

[63] 341 P.2d at 1088.

[64] 211 A.D. 586, 207 N.Y.S. 539 (1925).

> in this act is the same as negligence in respect to the original plans, and gives rise similarly to a cause of action in favor of one who receives injury therefrom.[65]

The professional standard of care applies to the duties of contract administration, which can include inspection, supervision, approvals, and shop drawing reviews, as well as to project design. An architect who fails to supervise or adequately inspect the work in violation of the contract may be liable for inadequate, defective, or nonconforming materials or labor.[66] An architect's duty to administer the construction contract can be broadly defined.

In *Nelson v. Commonwealth,* the court held that the architect's duty during the construction administration phase included not only an obligation to assure that the contractor complied with the design specifications and plans, but also the obligation to report to the owner any defects in the design which the architect reasonably should have known of, and to recommend to the owner necessary changes and corrections as the construction progressed.[67] The court held, however, that the failure of the plaintiff to present expert testimony as to the standard of care required of design professionals in the administration of a contract precluded any recovery.[68]

AIA Document B141 does not impose a continuous inspection duty upon the architect. Section 2.6.5 requires the architect only to visit the site at intervals appropriate to the stage of construction (1) to become generally familiar with the progress and quality of the work, and (2) to determine in general if the work is proceeding in a manner indicating that the work, when completed, will be in accordance with the contract documents. The architect is not required to make exhaustive or continuous on-site inspections to check the quality or quantity of the work. He does have a duty to keep the owner informed of the progress and quality of the work and to "endeavor to guard the Owner against defects and deficiencies in the Work." Section 2.6.6 states that the architect is not responsible for the

---

[65] 207 N.Y.S. at 543.

[66] *See* Aetna Ins. Co. v. Hellmuth, Obata & Kassabaum, Inc., 392 F.2d 472, 475–77 (8th Cir. 1968) (surety's claim against architect for defects occurring because of failure to supervise); United States/ex rel./Los Angeles Testing Laboratory v. Rogers & Rogers, 161 F. Supp. 132 (S.D. Cal. 1958) (liability to prime contractor for substandard concrete incorporated into building); Miller v. De Witt, 37 Ill. 2d 273, 285–86, 226 N.E.2d 630, 638–39 (1967) (workmen injured because of inadequate roof shoring); Bayuk v. Edson, 236 Cal. App. 2d 309, 317–18, 46 Cal. Rptr. 49, 54–55 (1965) (defects in private home); Cuttino v. Mimms, 98 Ga. App. 198, 207–12, 105 S.E.2d 343, 350–52 (1958) (defects in private house attributed to failure to supervise).

[67] 235 Va. 228, 368 S.E.2d 239 (1988).

[68] 368 S.E.2d at 245.

contractor's failure to perform the work in accordance with the contract documents.

Under provisions such as these, in general, the courts have rejected efforts to impose "clerk of the works" type supervisory or inspection responsibilities upon design professionals, which would, in effect, make them guarantors of the quality of construction. For example, in *Weill Construction Co. v. Thibodeaux,*[69] an architectural firm was sued by the owner of an ice skating facility. After completion of the facility, water seeped through the concrete slab and damaged the hardwood floor of the rink. The trial court found that the general contractor for the project had poured the slab improperly so as to create a horizontal cold joint through which the seepage had occurred.

The owner's claim for negligent supervision of the construction by the architectural firm was rejected by both the trial and appellate courts, which held that the architect had no duty to supervise the construction of the slab floors. The appeals court relied on the testimony that the architect's fee for the project was 5 percent of the construction costs, when a fee of 6 percent or 7 percent would have been required if it had contracted to supervise the work of the general contractor. Similarly, the court concluded that the language of the general conditions of the contract for construction tended to negate, rather than create, a duty of supervision. The contract provided:

> The Architect will make periodic visits to the site to familiarize himself generally with the progress and quality of the work to determine if the work is proceeding in accordance with the Contract Documents. On the basis of his on-site observations as an Architect, he will keep the Owner informed of the progress of the work, and will endeavor to guard the Owner against defects and deficiencies in the work of the Contractor. The Architect will not be required to make exhaustive or continuous on-site inspections to check the quality or quantity of the work. The Architect will not be responsible for the construction site, means, methods, techniques, sequences or procedures, or for safety precautions and programs in connection with the work, and he will not be responsible for the Contractor's failure to carry out the work in accordance with the Contract Documents. The undertakings of periodic visits and observations by the Architect or his associates shall not be construed as superintendence of actual construction. Neither the provisions of this paragraph nor their failure specifically to exclude other liability shall extend in any way the liability of the Architect to any person whomsoever.

However, even though, as in *Thibodeaux,* an architect has not contracted to provide continuous on-site inspection, the cases demonstrate that the

[69] 491 So. 2d 166 (La. Ct. App. 1986).

architect still owes a duty of care in making periodic observations or inspections.[70] In making periodic inspections or observations, it has been held that an architect has a duty to specifically inspect those aspects of the construction likely to create safety hazards if installation is improper. In *Pastorelli v. Associated Engineers, Inc.*,[71] after completion of construction, an employee of the owner was injured by a falling heating duct. The duct, which was 20 feet long and weighed 500 pounds, was suspended from hangers attached by nails to a ceiling of seven-eighth-inch sheathing. In view of the weight of the duct, good installation practice would have required securing the hangers to the roof joists or the roof itself with lag screws. The evidence showed that the architect was not aware of the defective manner of hanger installation. He had not been present while the duct was being installed and had made no effort afterwards to determine how the duct was installed. The court held that, because it was apparent that the safety of persons in the structure required the ducts to be securely fastened, the architect's failure to take steps to ascertain how they were attached constituted negligence.

In *Dan Cowling & Associates v. Board of Education*,[72] the court allowed the owner to recover damages for the architect's approval of a defective wall because the contract required the architect to periodically visit the site and "endeavor to guard the Owner against defects and deficiencies in the work of the Contractor."

In *First National Bank v. Cann*,[73] the owners entered into the then-current standard agreement with the architect in connection with the renovation of a bank building. The court considered the architect's liability for failing to detect unauthorized welding and cutting of structural steel in the construction of a curtain wall. The court observed that while continuous on-site inspections were not required under the terms of the agreement, "the architect [could not] close his eyes on the construction site, refrain from engaging in any inspection procedure whatsoever, and then disclaim liability for construction defects that even the most perfunctory monitoring would have prevented."[74] The court also noted that its assessment of the appropriate standard for measuring the architect's responsibilities was

---

[70] *See* Dickerson Constr. Co. v. Progress Eng'g Co., 341 So. 2d 646 (Miss. 1977). *But cf.* Mounds View Indep. School Dist. No. 621 v. Buetow & Assocs., Inc., 253 N.W.2d 836 (Minn. 1977) (when architect did not observe deficiencies in installation of roof during periodic visits, summary judgment in favor of architect was appropriate; court will not give owner benefit of "clerk of the works" type inspection when owner paid for less).

[71] 176 F. Supp. 159 (D.R.I. 1959).

[72] 273 Ark. 214, 618 S.W.2d 158 (1981).

[73] 503 F. Supp. 419 (N.D. Ohio 1980), *aff'd*, 669 F.2d 415 (6th Cir. 1982).

[74] 503 F. Supp. at 436.

influenced by circumstances that included the potential for conflict of interest due to the architect's relationship with the contractor, the large amount of the architect's fees and construction costs, the nature of the project (renovation), which made deviations from plans likely in the field, and the cost-incentive character of the job, which might incline a contractor to cut corners. Concluding that even the most general level of observation would have placed the architect on notice of the unauthorized and extensive deviations of the contractor, the court held the architect liable for a failure to satisfy contractual obligations of observation and inspection.

The court, however, affirmed the dismissal of the owner's tort claims against the architect because the owner failed to present any evidence on the scope of supervision demanded by professional standards apart from the language of the contract.[75]

When a design professional is liable for deficiencies in construction by reason of design errors or oversights in inspection responsibilities, there are two traditional rules for measuring damages, depending on whether it is economically feasible to correct the defects. One rule states that the measure of damages is the cost of remedying the defect; the other rule states that the measure of damages is the difference between the value of the building as designed and built and the value it would have had if it had been properly designed and constructed.[76] The former rule is commonly known as the *cost of correction rule* of damages, while the latter is known as the *difference in value* or *diminution in value* rule of damages.

Most jurisdictions state that the owner can recover the actual costs of correcting the defects in the design if it is economically feasible to do so.[77] For example, in *First National Bank v. Cann,*[78] the court held that the owner was entitled to recover the repair costs necessary to conform defective work to the contract specifications because the cost of repairs was only 11 percent of the total project contract price.[79]

However, if the cost to correct the defects is disproportionate in relation to the contract price or economically unfeasible, the correct measure of damages is equal to the difference between the market value of the

---

[75] *Id.* at 439.

[76] *See* 5 Am. Jur. 2d *Architects* § 25 (collecting cases).

[77] *See, e.g.,* Jim Arnott, Inc. v. L&E, Inc., 539 P.2d 1333 (Colo. Ct. App. 1975) (the negligent failure of the architect to provide for water softeners in his design of a motel complex did not make him liable for the total costs of water softeners when error was insubstantial compared to the total cost of the project; architect was liable only for anticipated cost to install the large water softeners).

[78] First Nat'l Bank v. Cann, 503 F. Supp. 419, 441 (N.D. Ohio 1980), *aff'd,* 669 F.2d 415 (6th Cir. 1982).

[79] 503 F. Supp. at 441.

building as designed and constructed and its value if properly designed and constructed.[80]

In some jurisdictions, the owner's recovery for the breach of a construction contract is the lesser of the cost of repair or the diminution of value.[81] However, some jurisdictions permit an owner to recover both cost of repairs and diminution of value damages in the proper circumstances.[82] In *Northern Petrochemical Co. v. Thorsen & Thorshov, Inc.*,[83] the owner of an industrial plant recovered both loss of value and cost of repair damages against the architect and the contractor when the defective design and construction required a partial reconstruction of the structure. The court noted that the building was still worth less after the partial reconstruction than its value would have been if it had been properly constructed. The owner was entitled to recover both the actual costs of repair and the loss of value so long as the total damages did not exceed either the costs of full reconstruction or the diminution of value without any reconstruction.[84]

A complete survey of this area is beyond the scope of this chapter. Several recent cases illustrate some of the issues that arise in the application of these standards. In *Grossman Holdings Ltd. v. Hourihan*,[85] the owner sued a contractor who constructed a "mirror image" of the house the owners' had

---

[80] Bayuk v. Edson, 236 Cal. App. 2d 309, 316, 46 Cal. Rptr. 49, 54 (1965) (applying this measure of damages when the cost to correct defect would have exceeded the cost of rebuilding the house).

See also Restatement (Second) of Contracts § 3482(a) (1981), stating that the owner is entitled to its loss in value if the actual loss can be established with substantial certainty. If the actual loss of value cannot be established with substantial certainty, the damages are the diminution in the market price caused by the breach.

[81] *See* State Property & Bldg. Comm. v. H.W. Miller Constr. Co., 385 S.W.2d 211 (Ky. 1964) (the measure of damages recoverable against contractor is amount that is reasonably necessary to make the building conform to the contract, but it is, in no event, to exceed the difference, if any, between the market value as it should have been constructed and its market value as it was actually constructed.) *But see* Ecksel v. Orleans Constr. Co., 360 Pa. Super. 119, 519 A.2d 1021 (1987) (when cost of repair slightly exceeded difference in market value, homeowner was entitled to recover cost of repairs from contractor when owner had established roots in the community and did not want to relocate.)

[82] *See* Gerodetti v. Broadacres, Inc., 363 So. 2d 265 (Miss. 1978). When some of defects in buildings had been remedied by owner at reasonable cost, some defects were remedied by construction company, and some could not be remedied without great economic waste, "cost rule" could be applied to some defects and "diminished value rule" to others to determine damages on retrial of action by owner against construction company for defective and incomplete performance of construction contract. (Court did not specify what damage rule applied to specific defects.)

[83] 297 Minn. 118, 211 N.W.2d 159 (1973).

[84] 297 Minn. at 125, 211 N.W.2d at 165.

[85] 414 So. 2d 1037 (Fla. 1982).

purchased. The trial court barred the owners from recovering any damages because the repair would have been economically wasteful and because the value of the house had, in fact, increased since the date of the contract. An intermediate appellate court held that the economic waste doctrine did not apply to residential construction and that the proper amount of damages would be the amount necessary to make the house conform to the original plans and specifications. However, the Florida Supreme Court reversed this ruling and held that the proper measure of damages for both residential or commercial construction is either the diminution in value or the cost of repair so long as it does not entail unreasonable economic waste. The court held that reconstruction of this particular structure would involve economic waste; therefore, the proper measure of damage was the difference in value between the house contracted for and the house received.[86] The fact that the house had subsequently increased in value did not bar recovery; the relevant time for measuring diminution in value was the date of completion.[87]

Contract damages are intended to put the party in the same position that she would have been in had the contract been performed. The defense of "betterment" holds that the owner is not entitled to recover damages that would put her in a better position than if the contract had been performed. In *St. Joseph Hospital v. Corbetta Construction Co.,*[88] the architect was liable for negligently specifying paneling that did not meet the "flame spread" requirements of the city building code. The court held that although the hospital was entitled to recover the costs paid for the incorrectly specified defective paneling and its removal, it was not entitled to recover the extra costs and labor expense for installing the more expensive paneling required by the code.[89] The hospital had, in fact, under the construction contract, paid only for the less expensive paneling and it would have been unjustly enriched if it received the more expensive wall paneling free of charge.[90]

§ 21.10 —Errors in Certification of Payments

The design professional's contract usually requires certification of the progress of the construction for payment. In *Browning v. Maurice B. Levien & Co.,*[91] an architect contracted with the lender bank to supervise

---

[86] *Id.* at 1040.

[87] *Id. See also* Pearce & Pearce, Inc. v. Kroh Bros. Dev. Co., 474 So. 2d 369, 371 (Fla. Dist. Ct. App. 1985) ($198,000 not unreasonable economic waste in $4.9 million building).

[88] 21 Ill. App. 3d 925, 943, 316 N.E.2d 51, 64 (1974).

[89] 21 Ill. App. 3d at 935, 316 N.E.2d at 59.

[90] *See also* Grossman v. Sea Air Towers, Ltd., 513 So. 2d 686 (Fla. Dist. Ct. App. 1987).

[91] 44 N.C. App. 701, 262 S.E.2d 355 (1980).

a construction project. The architect's duties included the inspection of the construction at the time of each progress payment request and certification of both the accuracy of the requisition and compliance with the plans and specifications. When the owner sued the architect for the negligent overcertification of payments, the architect asserted a lack of privity as a defense because his contract was with the bank. The court rejected this defense and held that the architect was liable for damages proximately caused by his negligence to anyone who might reasonably be foreseen to rely on his services.[92]

Section 2.6.10 of the 1987 AIA Standard Form Owner-Architect Agreement limits an architect's liability for certifying progress payments. The contract provides that the issuance of the certificate for payment is a representation by the architect that the contractor is entitled to payment in the amount certified. However, the issuance of a certificate for payment shall not be a representation that the architect has (1) made exhaustive or continuous on-site inspections to check the quality or quantity of the work; (2) reviewed construction means, methods, techniques, sequences, or procedures; (3) reviewed copies of requisitions received from subcontractors and material suppliers and other data requested by the owner to substantiate the contractor's right to payment; or (4) ascertained how or for what purpose the contractor has used money previously paid on account of the contract sum.

§ 21.11 —Delay Damages

The design professional has a duty not to delay the construction project.[93] Failure to perform duties in a timely manner can subject the architect to liability.[94] Further, progress on a construction project may be delayed when designs are discovered to be insufficient or incorrect.

---

[92] 262 S.E.2d at 358.

[93] "As a general rule, there is implied in every contract for work or services a duty to perform it skillfully, carefully, diligently, and in a workmanlike manner." Keel v. Titan Constr. Corp., 639 P.2d 1228, 1231 (Okla. 1981) (emphasis added and footnote omitted) (holding architect liable to owner for defective design); 17 Am. Jur. 2d *Contracts* § 371, at 814 (1964).

[94] The following cases illustrate a design professional's liability to contractors for delay damages: E.C. Ernst, Inc. v. Manhattan Constr. Co., 551 F.2d 1026, 1032 (5th Cir. 1977), *cert. denied,* 434 U.S. 1067 (1978) (architect's failure to timely approve equipment to be incorporated into the project); Detweiler Bros., Inc. v. John Graham & Co., 412 F. Supp. 416, 420–21 (E.D. Wash. 1976) (delays associated with approval of piping materials); Normoyle-Berg & Assoc. v. Village of Deer Creek, 39 Ill. App. 3d 744, 746, 350 N.E.2d 559, 560–61 (1976) (failure to timely complete plans, to timely stake project, etc.).

One form of actual damage to the owner is loss of the use of the structure for the period of time attributable to the delay. These damages are marked by the measure of lost rents or lost profit, depending on how the owner intended to use the construction. The owner was entitled to recover lost rents from an architect in *Grossman v. Sea Air Towers, Ltd.*[95] There the architect and structural engineer "underdesigned" a traffic deck for a high-rise apartment complex. The deck collapsed and the owner claimed that the noise and dust of the subsequent repair work caused tenants to vacate the building. The court affirmed an award for lost rents.[96]

American Buildings Co. v. DBH Attachments, Inc.[97] affirms the proposition that lost profits are recoverable in connection with construction failures only to the extent that they can be proved with reasonable certainty and are not remote or speculative.[98] However, other cases illustrate that such damages need not be proved with *absolute* certainty. In *Northern Petrochemical Co. v. Thorsen & Thorshov, Inc.*,[99] an architect was held liable for loss of profits caused by delay in the construction of a new manufacturing plant, when the owner established an industry-wide inability to produce sufficient extruded plastic film to meet the demands of the marketplace. The court noted that damages for loss of use of a facility are available when the loss is a direct and proximate result of the injury and the damages are within the contemplation of the parties at the time of the making of the contract.[100] It also held that increased operating costs resulting from a delay in occupancy were an element of lost profits rather than a distinct type of damages. As one court noted, "the fact that such damages are difficult to measure and by their nature uncertain does not render such damages unrecoverable."[101]

In a recent Virginia case, the court awarded the owner additional interest incurred on a construction loan when the contractor failed to complete the project on time. The rationale of this case, it appears, also could apply when a design professional is responsible for the delay. In *Roanoke Hospital Association v. Doyle & Russell, Inc.*, the owner-contractor agreement stipulated a completion date.[102] Although the owner told the contractor at the bidding

---

[95] 513 So. 2d 686 (Fla. Dist. Ct. App. 1987), *review denied*, 520 So. 2d 584 (Fla. 1988).

[96] 513 So. 2d at 688.

[97] 676 S.W.2d 558 (Tenn. Ct. App. 1984).

[98] *Id.* at 562.

[99] 297 Minn. 118, 211 N.W.2d 159, 166 (1973).

[100] 211 N.W.2d at 166. *See also* Daniel, Mann, Johnson & Mendenhall v. Hilton Hotels Corp., 98 Nev. 113, 642 P.2d 1086 (1982) (jury must consider whether lost profits were foreseeable at time of contract for owner to recover from surveyor).

[101] Natco, Inc. v. Williams Bros. Eng'g Co., 489 F.2d 639, 640 (5th Cir. 1974) (engineer on a pipeline construction project liable for lost profits in an intentional tort claim. The measure of recovery is limited to "the outer limits" of the proof offered).

[102] 215 Va. 796, 214 S.E.2d 155 (1975).

that failure to complete construction by the specified date would result in the owner's paying a higher rate of interest on the construction loan, he did not disclose any of the details of its financial arrangements to the contractor. Construction progress was delayed when the architect had to redesign the foundation and the project was not completed by the date specified. Because the unexcused delay in the completion required an extension of the term of the construction loan, the contractor was liable for interest loss resulting from a longer term of borrowing as direct damages.[103] However, the court held that the damages for interest costs due to higher prevailing interest rates during the construction period and in the permanent loan agreement were consequential damages. The court reversed the award for consequential damages and remanded to the trial level to determine whether the parties had contemplated these damages at the time the contract was executed.[104]

§ 21.12 —Indemnity Against Contractor Claims

The design professional may be liable to indemnify an owner against a contractor's claims against the owner of the construction project. In the *United States v. Skidmore, Owings & Merrill,*[105] the government's contract with the architect for the construction of the Hirshhorn Museum included an express indemnity term, which provided that the architect would be liable to the government "for all costs incurred as a result of [Skidmore's] negligent performance of any of the services furnished under this contract." The contractor sued the government for delay damages when the architect improperly rejected a scale model and refused to approve any shop drawings before a second model was accepted. After settling the contractor's claim, the government sued the architectural firm for indemnity. The tribunal denied the architect's motion for summary judgment, holding the architect could be liable for the delay damages under the indemnity claim even though the statute of limitations had run on direct negligence and breach of contract causes of action.

A common law claim for indemnity also may be implied in a contract between the owner and the design professional when an express provision does not exist. In *Miller v. City of Broken Arrow,*[106] the contractor sued the city for withheld retainage, lost profits, and delay damages when muddy soil conditions made it impossible for him to lay a pipeline. The contractor had consulted the engineer who was under contract to the city in an

---

[103] 215 Va. at 803, 214 S.E.2d at 161.

[104] *Id.*

[105] 505 F. Supp. 1101 (S.D.N.Y. 1981).

[106] 660 F.2d 450 (10th Cir. 1981), *cert. denied,* 455 U.S. 1020 (1982).

attempt to find a solution to the problem. The engineer refused to respond to further requests by the contractor for a design solution after his original suggestion failed. The court held that the engineer was negligent in refusing to respond to the contractor and awarded judgment against the city "over against" the engineer under an implied indemnity theory.[107]

In *Fairbanks North Star Borough v. Roen Design Associates,*[108] a design firm was liable to the borough under a theory of common law indemnification even though a contractor's claim for economic loss against the owner was outside the scope of an express indemnity provision. The court held that the existence of a contractual indemnity clause pertaining to liability for claims for tangible property damage or personal injury as a result of the contractor's acts, whether or not the contractor acted negligently, did not suggest an intent to exonerate the contractor from other losses suffered by the borough as a result of the contractor's negligence.[109]

PROCEDURAL ISSUES AND DEFENSES

§ 21.13 Allocation of Liability among Parties to Construction

Three recent decisions provide interesting insights on the unsettled status of the law concerning the ability to allocate liability for construction failures among parties to a construction project.

In *Hunt v. Ellisor & Tanner, Inc.,*[110] the contract contained a site visit provision much like that found in the 1987 edition of AIA Document B141. The contract stated: "The architect will not be responsible for the contractor's failure to carry out the work in accordance with the contract documents."

Upon completion, the project was impaired by significant construction defects. The owner entered into a settlement with various contractors on the project which covered the cost of repair of many of the defects. The owner then sued the architect for the diminution in value of the project which existed even after the repairs. The theory of the owner's claim was that the architect had breached its obligations to inspect the work. A jury found that the architect did breach the contract, but applying a doctrine of comparative fault, found that the architect was only 5 percent

---

[107] 660 F.2d at 458–59.

[108] 727 P.2d 758 (Alaska 1986).

[109] *Id.* at 761 (citations omitted).

[110] 739 S.W.2d 933 (Tex. Ct. App. 1987).

responsible and the contractors 95 percent responsible for the deficiencies, so that the architect should be assessed only 5 percent of the diminution in value.

On appeal, the architect argued that the contract (in the provision quoted) constituted an absolute bar to liability. However, the contention was rejected. The court observed that although the clause said that the architect was not a guarantor of the quality of construction, it did not exculpate the architect from liability for negligence in carrying out its inspection functions.

The court also held that the architect was not entitled to the benefit of a comparative fault determination, either under statute or common law, because comparative fault does not apply among parties with separate contract obligations: here, on the one hand, the architect's obligation to guard against defects; and, on the other, the contractor's obligation to construct the project in accordance with the plans and specifications. Accordingly, the court held that the architect was liable for the full diminution in value. The court also noted that the damages awarded would not run afoul of the rule against double recovery, because the damages sought by the owner were for the diminution in value that remained even after the repairs were made.[111]

Another decision relevant to the subject of apportionment of liability is *Board of Education of Hudson City School District v. Sargeant, Webster, Crenshaw & Foley.*[112] This case arose out of a roof failure on a school building. The architect's contract had required it, among other things, to supervise construction of the building, to inspect the building, and to advise of measures required to remedy possible defects in the building. Shortly after completion, the roof began to leak because it was not constructed as specified. Several years later, the owner sued both the contractor and the architect for damages for breach of contract. The contractor was successful in obtaining a dismissal because the statute of limitations had expired as to it. The statute of limitations defense, however, was not available to the architect, because of the applicability of the doctrine of tolling to professional malpractice claims, a doctrine that was not applicable to the claim against the contractor.

The architect then sought to assert a third-party claim for contribution or indemnity against the contractor. The court dismissed the third-party claim, holding that the architect could not assert a claim for contribution or indemnity against the contractor, because the liabilities of an architect and contractor arose on separate contractual obligations.

---

[111] Other cases, however, have considered the issue of comparative fault. *See, e.g.,* City of Urbandale v. Frevert-Ramsey-Kobes, Architects-Eng'rs, Inc., 435 N.W.2d 400 (Ia. Ct. App. 1988).

[112] 71 N.Y.2d 21, 517 N.E.2d 1360, 523 N.Y.S.2d 475 (1987).

§ 21.14 Limitation of Liability/ No Consequential Damages

The parties to a professional services agreement may contract to limit the liabilities of the parties. For example, the parties can agree to a clause barring the recovery of any special or consequential damages. However, a limitation on liability may not bind any plaintiff who was not a party to the contract.

One type of limitation of liability clause arises when the parties to the contract with the limitation of liability clause are liable as joint and several tortfeasors and one party asserts the liability limitation clause against a claim for contribution. In *Burns & Roe, Inc. v. Central Maine Power Co.*,[113] the owner-engineer contract provided that the engineer's liability "with respect to services performed hereunder" would be limited to 50 percent of the engineer's fees. In an action for declaratory judgment on the rights of the various parties in a lawsuit instituted by the owner against a subcontractor who participated in the construction of a condenser, the engineering company asserted the liability limitation clause in its contract with the owner against a contribution claim from the subcontractor. The engineer argued that the subcontractor was barred from seeking any contribution from it because the engineer had already settled another claim by the owner for an amount equal to 50 percent of its fee in an unrelated claim. The court, however, held that the subcontractor's right of contribution could not be limited by a contract to which it was not a party.

§ 21.15 Statutes of Limitation and Repose

Statutes of limitation state that no causes of action shall be maintained unless they are brought within a specified time after the right to bring the action accrues. In every jurisdiction, there is a specific statutory time limit within which a claim in contract[114] and in tort[115] must be made. Additionally, some jurisdictions have a specific statute stating the time limit in which a malpractice action against a professional must be brought.[116]

Most litigation pertaining to statutes of limitation addresses the issue of when the limitation period begins to run. A statute may specify that the limitation period begins to run "when the claim for relief arises" or "when

[113] 659 F. Supp. 141, 144 (D. Me. 1987).

[114] *See, e.g.*, 42 Pa. Cons. Stat. Ann. § 5525 (Purdon Supp. 1988) (statute of limitation in contract action is four years).

[115] *See, e.g.*, 42 Pa. Cons. Stat. Ann. § 5524 (Purdon Supp. 1988) (statute of limitation in tort action is two years).

[116] *See, e.g.*, Cal. Civ. Proc. Code § 337(1)(a) (West 1982) (a four-year limitation for patent deficiencies in design or planning of real estate accrues from completion of project).

the cause of action accrues."[117] Traditionally, a cause of action in tort accrues at the time of the injury; a cause of action for breach of contract accrues at the time of the breach. In some jurisdictions, a cause of action in contract against an architect accrues on the date that the architect issues the final certificate of completion.[118] Other jurisdictions apply the "discovery rule" to determine when a cause of action in either contract or tort accrues. Under the discovery rule, the statute does not begin to run on the date that the negligent act or the breach of contract occurred. Rather, the statute runs from the date the injury resulting from the wrongful conduct was either discovered or could have been discovered by an exercise of reasonable diligence.[119] At least one jurisdiction applying the discovery rule states that plaintiff must discover both the injury *and* the causal connection to the defendant's conduct before the statute will begin to run.[120] Furthermore, some jurisdictions recognize the *continuous treatment doctrine,* which tolls the running of the statute of limitations for as long as a confidential relationship exists between the design professional and the client. Therefore, the statute of limitations cannot begin to run until the professional relationship is terminated.[121] However, the continuous treatment doctrine is not universally recognized. Some jurisdictions have held that continuing efforts to repair the problems will not toll the running of the statute against any defendants, including the design professional.[122] Furthermore, a design professional may be estopped from asserting a statute of

---

[117] *See, e.g.,* Ga. Code Ann. § 9-3-30 (1982): "All actions for realty damages shall be brought within four years after the right of action accrues."

[118] Board of Educ. v. Thompson Constr. Corp., 111 A.D.2d 497, 488 N.Y.S.2d 880, 882 (1985) (owner sued architect for breach of contract and warranty to recover for a completely defective roof). *But see* County of Milwaukee v. Schmidt, Garden & Erickson, 43 Wis. 2d 445, 168 N.W.2d 559 (1969) (cause of action in contract accrues from the moment of breach, which more likely than not predates the issuance of the final certificate of completion).

[119] Dillon County School Dist. No. 2 v. Lewis Sheet Metal Works, Inc., 286 S.C. 207, 332 S.E.2d 555, *cert. granted,* 287 S.C. 234, 337 S.E.2d 697 (Ct. App. 1985), *cert. dismissed,* 288 S.C. 468, 343 S.E.2d 613 (1986) (cause of action accrued from time that owners knew that roof leaked and not from time they learned that the roof was irreparable); Pembee Mfg. Corp. v. Cape Fear Constr. Co., 313 N.C. 488, 329 S.E.2d 350, 354 (1985) (cause of action accrued as soon as the leaking roof was apparent or should have reasonably been apparent to plaintiff; plaintiff put on inquiry as to nature and extent of problem).

[120] Lumbermen's Mut. Casualty Co. v. Pattillo Constr. Co., 254 Ga. 461, 330 S.E.2d 344 (1985) (defendant construction company assumed responsibility of an architect by contractual agreement and was liable in tort. Georgia statute requires that plaintiff discover both negligence and damage before statute of limitations begins to run).

[121] *See* Board of Educ. v. Thompson Constr. Corp., 111 A.D.2d 497, 488 N.Y.S.2d 880, 882 (1985).

[122] Dillon County School Dist. No. 2 v. Lewis Sheet Metal Works, 286 S.C. 207, 332 S.E.2d 555, 560, *cert. granted,* 287 S.C. 234, 337 S.E.2d 697 (1985), *cert. dismissed,* 288 S.C. 468, 343 S.E.2d 613 (1986).

limitations defense if promises and efforts to repair a construction defect induce the owner to delay filing suit.[123]

Most jurisdictions also have enacted special construction statutes of limitation called *statutes of repose,* which can be asserted as an affirmative defense by the design professional. A statute of repose differs from a statute of limitations in that a statute of repose begins to run from a date unrelated to the date of injury or discovery, whereas a statute of limitations only begins to run when the plaintiff's cause of action accrues.[124] Therefore, a statute of repose can bar a cause of action before it ever accrues. A statute

[123] 332 S.E.2d at 561; *see also generally* City of Bedford v. James Leffel & Co., 558 F.2d 216, 218 (4th Cir. 1977) (applying Virginia's doctrine of equitable estoppel). A party's assurances that defects can be corrected when coupled with his attempts to correct them may lead the injured party to reasonably believe that it will achieve satisfaction without resorting to litigation.

[124] 42 Pa. Cons. Stat. Ann. § 5536 (Purdon 1981) is an example of a construction statute of repose:

> (a) General rule. Except as provided in subsection (b), a civil action or proceeding brought against any person lawfully performing or furnishing the design, planning, supervision or observation of construction, or construction of any improvement to real property must be commenced within 12 years after completion of construction of such improvement to recover damages for:
>
> (1) Any deficiency in the design, planning, supervision or observation of construction or construction of the improvement.
>
> (2) Injury to property, real or personal, arising out of any such deficiency.
>
> (3) Injury to the person or for wrongful death arising out of any such deficiency.
>
> (4) Contribution or indemnity for damages sustained on account of any injury mentioned in paragraph (2) or (3).
>
> (b) Exceptions.
>
> (1) If an injury or wrongful death shall occur more than 10 and within 12 years after completion of the improvement a civil action or proceeding within the scope of subsection (a) may be commenced within the time otherwise limited by this subchapter, but not later than 14 years after completion of construction of such improvement.
>
> (2) The limitation prescribed by subsection (a) shall not be asserted by way of defense by any person in actual possession or control, as owner, tenant or otherwise, of such an improvement at the time any deficiency in such an improvement constitutes the proximate cause of the injury or wrongful death for which it is proposed to commence an action or proceeding.
>
> (c) No extension of limitations. This section shall not extend the period within which any civil action or proceeding may be commenced under any provision of law.

Another example of a statute of repose is Cal. Civ. Proc. Code § 337.15 (West. 1982) (10-year limitation for latent defects in construction project). The California statute of repose specifically permits a cross-claim for indemnity after the 10-year limit if there was a transactional relationship between the parties to the cross claim. *See* Sandy v. Superior Court, 201 Cal. App. 3d 1277, 247 Cal. Rptr. 677 (1988) (owner's

of repose generally begins to run from the end of the party's involvement with the project or from the date that the project was completed or "substantially completed." In *Witherspoon v. Sides Construction Co.,*[125] the court applied the Nebraska statute creating a 10-year-period of repose in a case in which a homeowner sued both the architect who had contracted to design, supervise, and inspect construction and the engineer who had contracted only to provide design services. The court held that the 10-year statute of repose did not begin to run against the architect until completion of the structure because he was involved in both design and construction. However, because the engineer contracted only to provide design plans, as to him the statute of repose began to run from the date of delivery of the design.

Owners and contractors who are not protected by the statutes of repose have argued these limitations violate the equal protection clause of the Fourteenth Amendment of the United States Constitution[126] when the statutes create special limitations periods for design professionals. Two recent cases are illustrative. The Connecticut Supreme Court recently upheld its seven-year statute of repose for design professionals. The court held that the legislature could rationally create a liability exception for a design professional because the design professional lacks control of the construction after completion of the project, because the likelihood increases that a defect is caused by factors other than design deficiencies as time passes, and because a limit on tort liability is not likely to reduce the care with which a professional exercises duties.[127] However, in that same year, the Alaska Supreme Court held that it could find no substantial relationship between exempting design professionals from liability and the goal of encouraging construction and struck down its six-year statute of repose as unconstitutional.[128]

---

indemnity claim against architect barred by statute of repose because there was no transactional relationship between them).

[125] 219 Neb. 117, 362 N.W.2d 35 (1985).

[126] U.S. Const. amend. XIV.

[127] Zapata v. Burns, 207 Conn. 496, 542 A.2d 700, 709 (1988) (upholding Conn. Gen. Stat. Ann. § 52-584a (West Supp. 1988), which creates a seven-year statute of repose for design professionals' liability in construction).

[128] Turner Constr. Co. v. Scales, 752 P.2d 467 (Alaska 1988) (striking down Alaska Stat. § 09.10.055 (1988) statute of repose for construction design professionals under the equal protection clause of the Alaska Constitution).

CHAPTER 22

LIABILITY OF ARCHITECTS AND ENGINEERS TO THIRD PARTIES

G. William Quatman*

G. William Quatman is of counsel to the Kansas City, Missouri, law firm of Shughart Thomson & Kilroy. He is both a licensed architect as well as an attorney, practicing exclusively in the area of construction law. Mr. Quatman and his firm represent many architectural and engineering firms as well as their insurance carriers. He is an instructor at the University of Kansas School of Architecture on construction law for architects and engineers, and he is legal counsel to the Kansas City Chapter of the American Institute of Architects. Mr. Quatman holds bachelor of environmental design and bachelor of architecture degrees from the University of Kansas and a J.D. from the University of Missouri at Kansas City.

*Mr. Quatman expresses thanks to James D. George, a law student at Indiana University, for his invaluable assistance in preparing this chapter.

§ 22.1 Introduction

The majority of claims against architects and engineers are brought by the owner, the person with whom the design professional has contracted to provide services.[1] When the owner and design professional enter into a contract, they are said to be in *privity* with each other. Outsiders to the contract are said to lack privity. For many years, architect and engineer liability was governed by the rule of *privity of contract.* The privity rule provides that the contracting parties owe a duty to each other, but not to third parties who are strangers to the contract. As applied to architects, the privity rule states that the architect's obligations arising out of a contract are owed only to those who are parties to the contract, that is, typically, the owner. Under this rule, only the other party to the contract can sue for breach of the architect's contract obligations.[2] Outsiders, or third parties, cannot maintain such an action. Whenever damage or an injury arises out of the architect's breach of its contract obligations, the privity rule provides that an

[1] *See* Victor O. Schinnerer & Co., Liability Update 3 (Dec. 1990), indicating 57% of claims are made by the project owner. The term *design professionals* refers to professional architects, engineers, and others who perform design-related functions.

[2] *See* 17 Am. Jur. 2d *Contracts* § 297, at 714 (1964). *See also* Bernard Johnson v. Continental Constructors, 630 S.W.2d 365 (Tex. Ct. App. 1982) (stating the general rule that a suit for breach of contract may be maintained only by the parties to the contract).

action against the architect can be brought only by the other party to the contract.[3] Although the privity rule was rigidly enforced in the past, modern courts are permitting more and more third parties to sue design professionals under a variety of legal theories.

PRIVITY OF CONTRACT AND THIRD-PARTY LIABILITY

§ 22.2 Third-Party Beneficiary

Sometimes a contract is made between two parties specifically to benefit an "outsider" or third party. Under these conditions, the law recognizes that the parties to the contract may owe a duty to that other person who is not in the "chain of privity." When a contract between two parties is intended to benefit such a third party, the third party may maintain an action for breach of contract even though that party is not in privity. For example, a son may contract with a painter to paint his parents' house. Although the contract is between the son and the painter, the parents are intended "third-party beneficiaries" of the contract. The law is well settled that a promise in a contract which creates a duty to an intended third-party beneficiary may be enforced by the third party.[4] As to the third party's rights, courts generally have held that the terms of the contract are controlling.

Not every contract will be found to have third-party beneficiaries. It is not enough that the parties to the contract know, expect, or even intend that some third party may benefit from the contract. Rather, the contract must be undertaken for the third party's *direct benefit* and the contract must contain language which affirmatively makes that intention clear.[5]

Although not common, courts in a few construction cases have held that a general contractor may be a third-party beneficiary to an owner/architect agreement, with the right to enforce that agreement against a breaching party. For example, in a 1987 Minnesota case, *Prichard Bros., Inc. v. Grady Co.,*[6] the court held that although the contractor could not sue the project

---

[3] *See, e.g.,* Delta Constr. Co. v. City of Jackson, 198 So. 2d 592, 597 (Miss. 1967).

[4] Restatement (Second) of Contracts § 304 (1981).

[5] *See, e.g.,* A.R. Moyer, Inc. v. Graham, 285 So. 2d 397 (Fla. 1973); Waterford Condominium Ass'n v. Dunbar Corp., 104 Ill. App. 3d 371, 432 N.E.2d 1009 (1982); Howell v. Fisher, 49 N.C. App. 488, 272 S.E.2d 19 (1980). *See also* C.H. Leavell & Co. v. Glantz Contracting Corp., 322 F. Supp. 779, 783 (E.D. La. 1971) (the objective of establishing an advantage for third persons need not be express, but may be implied).

[6] 407 N.W.2d 423 (Minn. Ct. App. 1987).

architect in tort for delay damages, the contractor could nonetheless maintain an action for breach of contract as a third-party beneficiary to the owner/architect agreement. The court ruled that contract, not tort, law governed the case and that the contractor had a right to enforce the architect's contractual duties. Similarly, in *COAC, Inc. v. Kennedy Engineers,*[7] a general contractor was found to be a third-party beneficiary of the contract between an owner and its engineer.

As a result of these types of cases, the American Institute of Architects (AIA) Standard Form Owner-Architect Agreement contains an express statement that the contract is *not* intended to benefit any third parties.[8] Other than such third-party beneficiary cases, the privity rule barred claims of outsiders for many years.

§ 22.3 History of Privity Doctrine

The rule of privity emerged in an English case decided in 1842, *Winterbottom v. Wright.*[9] For decades thereafter, the rule greatly restricted claims by injured third parties against the wrongdoer. As a result, some have described the case as a "fishbone in the throat of the law."[10] The *Winterbottom* court held that the breach of a contract to keep a mail coach in repair after it was sold could not be the basis for a suit by a passenger who was injured when the coach collapsed. The passenger was not a party to the contract to keep the coach in repair and, therefore, could not maintain an action.

The privity rule prevailed well into the twentieth century. The rule survived primarily upon two grounds. First, the courts believed that the rule would prevent excessive and unlimited liability.[11] Second, courts were concerned that a contrary holding would restrict the right to make contracts by burdening contracting parties with obligations and liabilities to others which the parties would not voluntarily have assumed.[12] Even though these principles underlying the rule were widely accepted, the rule was not followed blindly and without exception. Exceptions became necessary and eventually were carved into the privity rule.

---

[7] 67 Cal. App. 3d 916, 136 Cal. Rptr. 890 (1977).

[8] *See, e.g.,* AIA B141-1987, Owner-Architect Agreement, Art. 9.7.

[9] 10 M&W 109, 152 Eng. Rep. 402 (1842).

[10] W. Prosser & W. Keeton, On The Law of Torts § 93, at 667–68 (5th ed. 1984).

[11] *See* Westerhold v. Carroll, 419 S.W.2d 73, 76 (Mo. 1967).

[12] *Id.* at 77.

§ 22.4 Decline of Privity in Actions for Personal Injury or Property Damage

Over the years, the privity rule has been whittled away by so many exceptions that it has been said that the exceptions have "swallowed the rule."[13] The attack on the privity rule progressed most rapidly in the area of product liability when third parties, injured by a defective product, found their claims against the manufacturer barred for lack of privity. As a legal defense, the rule was dealt a crushing blow in 1916 by the landmark case of *MacPherson v. Buick Motor Co.*[14] In *MacPherson,* the plaintiff purchased a Buick automobile from a car dealer. When a wheel on the Buick collapsed, the plaintiff suffered injury. The plaintiff brought a negligence action against Buick and obtained a favorable judgment. The court rejected Buick's argument that the claim was barred because no privity existed between Buick and the injured plaintiff. The court held that, when a product is "reasonably certain to put life and limb in peril," and the product likely will be used by persons other than the purchaser, the manufacturer owes a duty, by law, to use reasonable care to prevent potential harm.[15] However, the court qualified its holding by stating that a manufacturer or supplier did not have a duty to protect against *every* risk but only against "foreseeable, unreasonable" risks. *MacPherson* spawned the now universally recognized rule that, "a supplier of a product is liable for his negligence which may reasonably be expected to cause injury to another's interests if the product is defective."[16]

The *MacPherson* decision had an immediate impact throughout the United States and, eventually, in cases dealing with liability of architects and engineers. Although slow to abandon the privity rule, construction cases now reflect the development of product liability law. With regard to the construction industry, it has been said that, "this is a field in which the ghost of *Winterbottom v. Wright* died very hard."[17]

§ 22.5 Construction Law and Privity

Early cases held that building contractors were liable only for injuries resulting from their negligence before their work was completed, but once the

[13] Westerhold v. Carroll, 419 S.W.2d 73, 77 (Mo. 1967) (outlines many of the exceptions to the privity rule that have been recognized over the years).

[14] 111 N.E. 1050 (N.Y. 1916).

[15] *Id.* at 1053.

[16] *See* Navajo Circle, Inc. v. Development Concepts Corp., 373 So. 2d 689, 691 (Fla. Dist. Ct. App. 1979).

[17] W. Prosser & W. Keeton, On the Law of Torts § 104 (A), at 722 (5th ed. 1984).

work was finished and accepted by the owner, contractors were not liable to any third person.[18] To some extent, this result still survives except when there are hidden or concealed defects, and when the defect is known to the contractor but not to the owner.[19] But, just as with sellers of goods, exceptions were made to the general rule until *MacPherson* was finally applied with full force to building contractors.[20]

The *MacPherson* rule has been applied not only to building contractors, but also to supervising architects and engineers.[21] *MacPherson* was first specifically applied to architects in the New York case of *Inman v. Binghamton Housing Authority.*[22] In that case, a child suffered injuries when it fell from the porch of an apartment building. Suit was filed against the architect who designed the apartment building. The court rejected the architect's privity defense and, instead, adopted the *MacPherson* holding. Many architect and engineer cases since *Inman* have recognized the principles established in the case.[23]

---

[18] *See, e.g.,* Ford v. Sturgis, 14 F.2d 235 (D.C. Cir. 1926); Galbraith v. Illinois Steel Co., 133 F. 485 (7th Cir. 1904), *cert. denied,* 201 U.S. 643, 26 S. Ct. 759 (1906); Daugherty v. Herzog, 44 N.E. 457 (Ind. 1896); Curtin v. Somerset, 21 A. 244 (Pa. 1891). This completion and acceptance defense relied upon the theory that once the work was completed and accepted by the owner of the project, the contractor is deprived of the opportunity to correct the wrong and, therefore, the owner is substituted as the party responsible for any existing defects that the owner fails to repair.

[19] *See, e.g.,* Forte Towers S., Inc. v. Hill York Sales Corp., 312 So. 2d 512 (Fla. Dist. Ct. App. 1975); Honey v. Barnes Hosp., 708 S.W.2d 686, 701 (Mo. Ct. App. 1986).

[20] *See, e.g.,* Moran v. Pittsburg-Des Moines Steel Co., 166 F.2d 908 (3d Cir.), *cert. denied,* 334 U.S. 846, 68 S. Ct. 1516 (1948); Dow v. Holly Mfg. Co., 49 Cal. 2d 720, 321 P.2d 736 (1958); Hale v. Depaoli, 33 Cal. 2d 228, 201 P.2d 1 (1948); Totten v. Gruzen, 52 N.J. 202, 245 A.2d 1 (1968); Fisher v. Simon, 15 Wis. 2d 207, 112 N.W.2d 705 (1961).

[21] *See, e.g.,* Council of Co-Owners Atlantis Condominium, Inc. v. Whiting-Turner Contracting Co., 308 Md. 18, 517 A.2d 336, 341 (1986); A.E. Inv. Corp. v. Link Builders, Inc., 62 Wis. 2d 479, 214 N.W.2d 764 (1974).

[22] 3 N.Y.2d 137, 143 N.E.2d 895, 164 N.Y.S.2d 699 (1957).

[23] *See* Montijo v. Swift, 219 Cal. App. 2d 351, 33 Cal. Rptr. 133 (1963); Drexel Properties, Inc. v. Bay Colony Club Condo, Inc., 406 So. 2d 515 (Fla. Dist. Ct. App. 1981), *reh'g denied,* 417 So. 2d 328 (Fla. 1982); Council of Co-Owners Atlantis Condominium, Inc. v. Whiting-Turner Contracting Co., 308 Md. 18, 517 A.2d 336, 341 (1986); Totten v. Gruzen, 52 N.J. 202, 245 A.2d 1 (1968); A.E. Inv. Corp. v. Link Builders, Inc., 62 Wis. 2d 479, 214 N.W.2d 764 (1974). *Inman* is famous not only for its expansion of the principles of *MacPherson,* but also for its "patent/latent" defect analysis. The very opinion that overthrew the doctrine of lack of privity of contract as a defense for architects established an equally controversial proposition that the architect is not liable to remote users for a *patent* defect in the structure. In *Inman,* the plaintiff alleged that the porch was unsafe because of the absence of a protective railing, guard, or any device. In denying relief to plaintiff, the court held that the architect owes a duty merely to make the product free from *latent* defects and concealed dangers. The court further held that, because the complaint did not allege the existence of a latent fault or hidden danger in design or construction, it was without legal basis and that the suit was

In negligence actions, most courts hold design professionals to the same standard of care as lawyers, doctors, and other professionals engaged in furnishing skilled services for compensation. The standard of care for design professionals was defined by one court as:

> that of ordinary reasonable care required of a professional skilled architect under the same or similar circumstances in carrying out his technical duties in relation to the services undertaken by his agreement. This includes the knowledge and experience ordinarily required of a member of that profession and includes the performing of skills necessary in adequately coping with engineering and construction problems, which skills are ordinarily not possessed by laymen.[24]

Under current law, a design professional can be found liable to third parties who lack privity if the professional breaches the standard of care, resulting in foreseeable injury to persons or property. The standard of care comes into play when the plaintiff can show that the design professional owed a duty of care to the plaintiff to prevent foreseeable injury or damage. When a design professional's negligent act causes personal injuries or damage to property, the privity rule is no longer a defense, and liability will be determined by applying the *MacPherson* principles.[25]

§ 22.6 Economic Loss Doctrine

Today, it is virtually a universal rule that a design professional may be held liable for personal injuries or for tangible property damage caused by the negligence of the design professional, notwithstanding the lack of privity of contract. However, courts in some states have been less willing to discard the privity requirement when there has been solely an economic loss, rather than a personal injury or property damage. *Economic loss* has been defined as "damages for inadequate value, cost of repair and replacement of the defective product, or consequent loss of profits without any

---

properly dismissed against the architect. The patent/latent distinction has been criticized and eventually rejected by many courts.

[24] Aetna Ins. Co. v. Hellmuth, Obata & Kassabaum, Inc., 392 F.2d 472, 477 (8th Cir. 1968); *see also* Clark v. City of Seward, 659 P.2d 1227 (Alaska 1983); R.H. Macy & Co. v. Williams Tile & Terrazzo Co., 585 F. Supp. 175 (N.D. Ga. 1984); U.R.S. Co. v. Gulfport-Biloxi Regional Airport Auth., 544 So. 2d 824 (Miss. 1989); Forte Bros., Inc. v. National Amusement, Inc., 525 A.2d 1301 (R.I. 1987); *see also* American Fidelity Fire Ins. Co. v. Pavia-Byrne Eng'g, 393 So. 2d 830 (La. Ct. App. 1981) ("[t]he duty owed by those practicing learned professions to their clients, patients or retainers, is that of exercising the degree of professional care and skill customarily employed by others in the same profession in the same general area").

[25] *See generally* White, *Architects' and Engineers' Third Party Negligence Liability—The Fall of the House of Privity,* 10 W. Res. L. Rev. 563 (1959).

claim of personal injury or damage to property."[26] For example, if a warehouse roof leaks due to a design error, and water from the leak damages stored goods or causes a slip-and-fall accident, the personal injury and damaged goods would form the basis of a negligence claim. However, the roof repair or company downtime would be economic losses. Economic loss also can include "the diminution in the value of the product because it is inferior in quality and does not work for the general purposes for which it was manufactured and sold."[27] The refusal of some courts to allow recovery in tort for an economic loss has often been referred to as the *economic loss doctrine.* In those states that recognize the economic loss doctrine, remnants of the privity rule still survive.

At least five jurisdictions recognize the economic loss doctrine as a defense to third-party claims against design professionals. They are Georgia,[28] Illinois,[29] New York,[30] Ohio,[31] and Virginia.[32] In applying the economic loss doctrine, the courts have reasoned that when only economic losses are incurred, the duty breached is contractual in nature. In such actions, the plaintiff is usually suing because of disappointed economic expectations, or for "the benefit of the bargain." Courts have reasoned that "the controlling policy consideration underlying tort [or negligence] law is the safety of persons and property—the protection of persons and property from losses resulting from injury. The controlling policy consideration underlying the law of contracts is the protection of expectations bargained for."[33] When a purely economic loss has been suffered, the law of contracts and warranty, rather than the law of torts, provides the sole remedy.[34]

---

[26] Moorman Mfg. Co. v. National Tank Co., 91 Ill. 2d 69, 435 N.E.2d 443, 449 (1982).

[27] *Id.* at 449.

[28] Malta Constr. Co. v. Henningson, Durham & Richardson, Inc., 716 F. Supp. 1466 (N.D. Ga. 1989).

[29] *See, e.g.,* 2314 Lincoln Park W. Condominium Ass'n v. Mann, Gin, Ebel & Frazier, Ltd., 136 Ill. 2d 302, 555 N.E.2d 346 (1990).

[30] *See, e.g.,* Briar Contracting Corp. v. City of New York, 156 A.D.2d 628, 550 N.Y.S.2d 717 (1989).

[31] *See, e.g.,* Floor Craft Floor Covering, Inc. v. Parma Community Gen. Hosp. Assoc., 54 Ohio St. 3d 1, 560 N.E.2d 206 (1990).

[32] Sensenbrenner v. Rust, Orling & Neale Architects, Inc., 236 Va. 419, 374 S.E.2d 55 (1988); Blake Constr. Co. v. Alley, 233 Va. 31, 353 S.E.2d 724 (1987).

[33] Sensenbrenner v. Rust, 374 S.E.2d at 58.

[34] *Id.* It should be noted that most jurisdictions hold that economic losses are recoverable in tort when one intentionally makes false representations. *See* Moorman Mfg. Co. v. National Tank Co., 91 Ill. 2d 69, 435 N.E.2d 443 (1982); Robert & Co. Assocs. v. Rhodes-Haverty Partnership, 250 Ga. 680, 300 S.E.2d 503 (1983). Economic losses also may be recovered in tort when one who is in the business of supplying information for guidance of others in their business transactions makes negligent misrepresentations. *See* Rozny v. Marnul, 43 Ill. 2d 54, 250 N.E.2d 656 (1969); Oldenburg v. Hagemann,

An example of the economic loss doctrine applied to design professionals is *Blake Construction Co. v. Alley.*[35] In that case, the Virginia Supreme Court held that although a duty may be imposed by contract, there is no common law duty that requires an architect to protect the contractor from purely economic loss. The court held that parties involved in a construction project resort to contracts and contract law to protect their economic expectations. In absence of privity, the court held that there could be no recovery by the contractor against the architect for pure economic loss.

Similarly, the economic loss doctrine worked to the benefit of an engineer in a 1989 Georgia case, in which the court ruled that a contractor could not sue the project engineer for damages based on negligent review of shop drawings due to lack of privity.[36] Under Georgia law, claims to recover economic damages cannot be maintained in tort in absence of privity, except for actions for negligent misrepresentation.[37] The contractor attempted to fit within that narrow exception, stating that an action for negligent review of shop drawings is actually an action for negligent misrepresentation. The court disagreed, finding that the allegations in the suit did not add up to negligent misrepresentation.

In a 1989 New York case, a general contractor was barred from suing the engineering firm that had provided the owner with resident engineering inspection services.[38] The contractor alleged that the engineer had negligently approved work that deviated from the plans and specifications, causing the contractor to incur substantial additional costs. The New York appellate court ruled, however, that "[a]bsent actual privity of contract between the parties or a relationship so close as to approach that of privity, recovery may not be had for pecuniary loss arising from negligent representations of a professional."[39]

The contractor was denied any indemnity or contribution from the engineer for the economic loss suffered as a result of the contractor's breach of its own contractual obligations to the owner.

The Ohio Supreme Court affirmed the dismissal of a flooring contractor's suit against an architect in the 1990 case, *Floor Craft Floor Covering, Inc. v. Parma Community General Hospital Associates.*[40] The contractor

---

159 Ill. App. 3d 631, 512 N.E.2d 718 (1987); Waldor Pump & Equip. Co. v. Orr-Schelen-Mayeron & Assoc., Inc., 386 N.W.2d 375 (Minn. Ct. App. 1986). *See also* Restatement (Second) of Torts § 552 (1977).

[35] 233 Va. 31, 353 S.E.2d 724 (1987).

[36] Malta Constr. v. Henningson, Durham & Richardson, Inc., 716 F. Supp. 1466 (N.D. Ga. 1989).

[37] Robert & Co. Assocs. v. Rhodes-Haverty Partnership, 250 Ga. 680, 300 S.E.2d 503 (1983); Gulf Contracting v. Bibb County, 795 F.2d 980 (11th Cir. 1986).

[38] Briar Contracting Corp. v. City of New York, 156 A.D.2d 628, 550 N.Y.S.2d 717 (1989).

[39] *Id.* at 718.

[40] 54 Ohio St. 3d 1, 560 N.E.2d 206 (1990).

claimed that the architect's defective specifications caused problems with the adhesion of vinyl flooring to a concrete slab, resulting in extra costs. The court concluded that "in the absence of privity of contract no cause of action exists in tort to recover economic damages against design professionals involved in drafting plans and specifications."[41]

Numerous Illinois court decisions have addressed the issue of economic loss, and the opinions have been exceptionally rich in their analysis of this area of the law. The so-called *Moorman doctrine* was announced by the Illinois Supreme Court in a 1982 case, *Moorman Manufacturing Co. v. National Tank Co.*[42] The doctrine has generated a great deal of debate, as well as litigation, because "[l]ike many legal theories, it is understandable in the abstract, but difficult to apply in specific case situations."[43] Essentially, the *Moorman* doctrine is the equivalent of the economic loss rule with some modification. Simply stated, the doctrine bars a plaintiff from suing in tort when there is an alternative action in contract or warranty.

In *Moorman,* the plaintiff had purchased a grain storage tank from the defendant manufacturer. The plaintiff sued the manufacturer after a crack developed in the tank. Plaintiff sought damages for the cost of repairing the tank and for the loss of its use. Plaintiff based its action on the tort theories of strict liability, negligence, and misrepresentation and on the contract theory of breach of express warranty. The Illinois Supreme Court stated that qualitative defects are best handled by the law of contracts rather than the law of torts and that this conclusion applies whether the tort theory is strict liability or negligence. "Tort theory is appropriately suited for personal injury or property damage resulting from a sudden or dangerous occurrence . . . [but] the remedy for economic loss, loss relating to a purchaser's disappointed expectations due to deterioration, internal breakdown or non-accidental cause, on the other hand, lies in contract."[44]

§ 22.7 Application of Economic Loss Doctrine to Design Professionals

One of the first cases to discuss the application of the *Moorman* doctrine to negligence claims against design professionals was *Ferentchak v. Village of Frankfort.*[45] In that case, the plaintiff homeowners were permitted to

---

[41] 560 N.E.2d at 212.

[42] 91 Ill. 2d 69, 435 N.E.2d 443 (1982).

[43] Kishwaukee Community Health Servs. Center v. Hospital Bldg. & Equip. Co., 638 F. Supp. 1492, 1495 (N.D. Ill. 1986). *See generally* Bertschy, *The Economic Loss Doctrine in Illinois After Moorman,* 71 Ill. B.J. 346, 355 (1983).

[44] Moorman Mfg. Co. v. National Tank Co., 91 Ill. 2d 69, 435 N.E.2d 443, 450 (1982).

[45] 121 Ill. App. 3d 599, 459 N.E.2d 1085 (1984), *rev'd on other grounds,* 475 N.E.2d 822 (1985).

recover in tort for the damage to their home against the engineer who, under contract with the project developer, designed and oversaw the construction of a water drainage system. The damages resulted from the foundation grade of the house being set too low and from an inadequate and improper drainage system. The court stated that *Moorman* barred an action in tort only when the plaintiff claims economic loss *and* has an adequate remedy in contract or warranty law. However, *Moorman* should not be applied if to do so would deprive a plaintiff of its *only* cause of action against a defendant.[46]

The Illinois Supreme Court later rejected this limited interpretation of the *Moorman* doctrine. In *Anderson Electric v. Ledbetter Erection Corp.*,[47] the Illinois Supreme Court held that a plaintiff seeking to recover purely economic losses cannot recover from third parties in tort, regardless of whether or not the plaintiff can recover under an action in contract.[48] In 1990, the Illinois Supreme Court clarified the law, holding specifically that the *Moorman* doctrine bars tort claims for economic loss against architects and engineers except for intentional and negligent misrepresentation and intentional interference with contract.[49]

Although some jurisdictions have adopted the economic loss doctrine, the doctrine is not without its critics, and many courts have declined to distinguish between a risk of personal injury or property damage and the risk of economic loss.[50] Courts in most jurisdictions hold that a third party, who is not in privity of contract with the design professional, may recover for negligence that proximately causes a foreseeable injury, economic or otherwise. Generally, courts have discarded the privity rule and now apply a straight negligence analysis to determine liability in actions in which the plaintiff alleges damage to an economic interest.[51] These jurisdictions

---

[46] *See also* Bates & Rogers Constr. Corp. v. North Shore Sanitary Dist., 128 Ill. App. 3d 962, 471 N.E.2d 915 (1984), *aff'd,* 503 N.E.2d (Ill. 1986).

[47] 115 Ill. 2d 146, 503 N.E.2d 246 (1986).

[48] *Id.* at 249. The Illinois Supreme Court relied heavily upon the United States Supreme Court's decision in East River Steamship Corp. v. Transamerica Delaval, Inc., 106 S. Ct. 2295 (1986). In that case, the Supreme Court held that a shipbuilder was not liable to the plaintiff in tort for repair costs and lost income that resulted from alleged design defects in certain oil tankers. The Supreme Court further held that these damages were economic losses for which there is no recovery in tort.

[49] 2314 Lincoln Park W. Condominium Ass'n v. Mann, Gin, Ebel & Frazier, Ltd., 136 Ill. 2d 302, 555 N.E.2d 346 (1990).

[50] Council of Co-Owners Atlantis Condominium, Inc. v. Whiting-Turner Contracting Co., 308 Md. 18, 517 A.2d 336, 344 (1986); *see also* Smith, *The Continuing Decline of the "Economic Loss Rule" in Construction Litigation,* 10 Constr. Law. 1 (1990).

[51] *See, e.g.,* United States v. Rogers & Rogers, 161 F. Supp. 132 (S.D. Cal. 1958); Owen v. Dodd, 431 F. Supp. 1239 (N.D. Miss. 1977); Cooper v. Jevne, 56 Cal. App. 3d 860, 128 Cal. Rptr. 724 (1976); A.R. Moyer, Inc. v. Graham, 285 So. 2d 397 (Fla. 1973); Milton J. Womack, Inc. v. House of Representatives, 509 So. 2d 62 (La. Ct. App. 1987); A.E. Inv. Corp. v. Link Builders, Inc., 62 Wis. 2d 479, 214 N.W.2d 764 (1974).

reason that a distinction between economic loss and personal injury is without merit.

The economic loss defense raises some interesting questions, such as those posed by the Indiana Supreme Court when it asked:

> If there is a defect in a stairway and the purchaser repairs the defect and suffers economic loss, should he fail to recover because he did not wait until he or some member of his family fell down the stairs and broke his neck? Does the law penalize those who are alert and prevent injury? Should it not put those who prevent personal injury on the same level as those who fail to anticipate it?[52]

Aside from Georgia, Illinois, New York, Ohio, and Virginia, most jurisdictions do not distinguish between the risk of personal injury or property damage and the risk of economic loss. The majority holds that when the traditional elements of a negligence or negligent misrepresentation action are satisfied, the design professional may be held liable for economic losses.[53]

LIABILITY TO CONTRACTORS AND SUBCONTRACTORS

§ 22.8 Overview

Whether a design professional will be held liable to a general contractor[54] or to any other individual for a purely economic loss will, of course, depend upon the jurisdiction. As a general rule, most jurisdictions recognize that a contractor or subcontractor has a cause of action in negligence against a design professional if the design professional's negligent conduct is the proximate cause of damages to the contractor, notwithstanding the lack of privity of contract.

---

[52] Barnes v. MacBrown & Co., 264 Ind. 227, 342 N.E.2d 619, 621 (1976).

[53] *See generally* Annotation, *Tort Liability of Project Architect for Economic Damages Suffered by Contractor,* 65 A.L.R.3d 249 (1975).

[54] The courts' treatment of subcontractors mirrors that of contractors. Subcontractors have been permitted to bring a negligence action against design professionals for damages, notwithstanding the lack of privity of contracts. See **§ 22.10**. *But see* Oldenburg v. Hagemann, 159 Ill. App. 3d 631, 512 N.E.2d 718 (1987) (subcontractor did not have a cause of action in negligence against a design professional when the alleged injury was purely economic loss). *See also* Comment, *Architect Tort Liability in Preparation of Plans and Specifications,* 55 Calif. L. Rev. 1361, 1372 (1967).

§ 22.9 General Contractors

In *Forte Bros., Inc. v. National Amusement, Inc.,*[55] a general contractor brought suit against the project owner and architect/engineer alleging that the architect/engineer failed in its duties when measuring the contractor's removal of rock from the construction site. The contractor had agreed with the project owner to perform excavation and grading work. The owner agreed to pay $15 per cubic yard for removal of rock and boulders. The architect/engineer was hired by the owner to oversee the excavation and to report on and measure the removal of rock. No contract existed between the architect/engineer and the contractor. The contractor claimed that as a result of the architect/engineer's negligence, the owner refused to pay for certain excavation. The trial court granted summary judgment in favor of the architect/engineer. However, the Rhode Island Supreme Court reversed the decision, holding that "to deny this plaintiff its day in court would, in effect, be to condone a supervising architect's/engineer's right to do his job negligently and with impunity as far as innocent parties who suffer economic loss are concerned."[56]

In a 1958 case, the architect was found liable to the general contractor even though the contractor had breached its own agreement with the owner by incorporating defective concrete into the building.[57] The court held that the architect was obligated to review test reports on the concrete. Failure to properly review and interpret the test reports caused delay in the project when the architect eventually stopped the job while corrective action was taken. The court held that the architect's authority over the contractor gave rise to a duty to the contractor to use due care.

In *E.C. Ernst, Inc. v. Manhattan Construction Co.,*[58] the general contractor was entitled to recover delay damages from an architect when the project was delayed as a result of design errors and the architect's failure to make timely decisions.

Similarly, in *Donnelly Construction Co. v. Oberg/Hunt/Gilleland,*[59] the court held that the contractor on a school district project properly stated a cause of action for negligence and breach of common law warranty against the project architect despite lack of privity between contractor and architect. The court held that architects have a duty to use due care and skill in providing plans and specifications that are sufficient and adequate for the particular job. The court held that such duty extends "to those with whom

---

[55] 525 A.2d 1301 (R.I. 1987).

[56] *Id.* at 1303.

[57] United States v. Rogers & Rogers, 161 F. Supp. 132 (S.D. Cal. 1958).

[58] 551 F.2d 1026 (5th Cir. 1977), *cert. denied,* 434 U.S. 1067 (1978).

[59] 139 Ariz. 184, 677 P.2d 1292 (1984).

the design professional is in privity and to those with whom he or she is not."[60]

In a 1987 Louisiana case,[61] the court held that a contractor could recover from the architectural firm that drew plans for renovation of the state capitol building when the architect's negligence caused the contractor to suffer delays that prevented the contractor from finishing the job in time to earn its bonus.

In a 1980 New Jersey case,[62] the court noted that the "privity doctrine" is looked on with disfavor and that a design professional can be held liable to third-party contractors. The court stated that as a matter of public policy, design professionals should not be immune from claims for economic damages suffered by third parties.[63]

In a 1973 Florida case, *A.R. Moyer, Inc. v. Graham,*[64] the state supreme court held that a third-party general contractor who is foreseeably injured or sustains economic loss due to the negligence of an architect or engineer has a cause of action against the alleged negligent party, notwithstanding the lack of privity of contract. In *Moyer,* the court held that the design professionals were negligent in the preparation of plans, designs, and specifications and that this negligence was the proximate cause of the economic losses suffered by the contractor.

§ 22.10 Subcontractors

Subcontractors also have had success in suing design professionals despite the lack of privity. For example, a subcontractor sued the project architect for negligent misrepresentation in a 1976 Washington case.[65] The court held that there was no privity of contract between the parties, nor was the subcontractor an intended third-party beneficiary of the owner/architect agreement. However, the court found that absence of privity did not affect the subcontractor's claim and that the architect could be held liable if it breached a duty of due care to the subcontractor.

In *Lane v. Geiger-Berger Associates, P.C.,*[66] a subcontractor was permitted to recover from the structural engineer when the subcontractor's obligation to pay the general contractor for increased costs on the job was proximately caused by the engineering firm's negligence.

---

[60] *Id.* at 1295.

[61] Milton J. Womack, Inc. v. House of Representatives, 509 So. 2d 62 (La. Ct. App. 1987).

[62] Conforti & Eisele, Inc. v. John C. Morris Assoc., 175 N.J. Super. 341, 418 A.2d 1290 (1980), *aff'd,* 199 N.J. Super. 498, 489 A.2d 1233 (1985).

[63] *Id.* at 1292.

[64] 285 So. 2d 397 (Fla. 1973).

[65] Detweiler Bros., Inc. v. John Graham & Co., 412 F. Supp. 416 (E.D. Wash. 1976).

[66] 608 F.2d 1148 (8th Cir. 1979).

The Alabama Supreme Court held in a 1984 case that in a negligence action, a plaintiff-subcontractor, not in privity with the owner and architect, nor a third-party beneficiary of their agreement, may still be owed a duty by the architect. Whether to impose such a duty in construction settings involves an analysis of six factors:

1. Extent to which transaction was intended to affect other person
2. Foreseeability of harm to that person
3. Degree of certainty that the person suffered injury
4. Closeness of connection between defendant's conduct and injury
5. Moral blame attached to such conduct
6. Policy of preventing future harm.[67]

However, when the architect acts as the owner's agent, contractors and subcontractors alike may be unable to sue the architect directly. In *Hogan v. Postin,*[68] the Wyoming Supreme Court held that the project architect was not liable to a subcontractor for economic damages when the architect was acting as agent for the owner, its disclosed principal. This "agency" defense may apply to claims relating to architect actions during the construction phase because the standard AIA Owner-Architect Agreement provides that the architect is the owner's "representative" during construction and "shall have the authority to act on behalf of the Owner."[69] Thus, as agent, the architect generally would not be liable to third parties such as subcontractors for pure economic loss.

§ 22.11 Soils Reports

Several cases have found that design professionals can be held liable to contractors or subcontractors for negligent misrepresentation, despite the lack of privity, when soils reports or soil tests have been negligently prepared or conducted, causing the contractor to incur delays or extra costs.[70] These cases relay primarily on the theory of negligent misrepresentation as set

[67] Berkel & Co. Contractors, Inc. v. Providence Hosp., 454 So. 2d 496, 503 (Ala. 1984); *see also* United States v. Rogers & Rogers, 161 F. Supp. 132 (S.D. Cal. 1958).

[68] 695 P.2d 1042 (Wyo. 1985); *see also* Restatement (Second) of Agency § 357 (1958); State *ex rel.* William Ranni Assoc., Inc. v. Hartenbach, 742 S.W.2d 134 (Mo. 1987) (en banc) (agent not liable to third party for economic loss when principal disclosed).

[69] *See* AIA B141-1987, Owner-Architect Agreement, Art. 2.6.4.

[70] *See, e.g.,* Miller Co. v. Central Contra Costa Sanitary Dist., 198 Cal. App. 2d 305, 18 Cal. Rptr. 13 (1961); Gulf Contracting v. Bibb County, 795 F.2d 980 (11th Cir. 1986) (applying Georgia law); Davidson & Jones, Inc. v. County of New Hanover, 41 N.C. App. 661, 255 S.E.2d 580 (1979); AAA Excavating v. Francis Constr., 678 S.W.2d 889 (Mo. Ct. App. 1984); *see also* Howell v. Fisher, 49 N.C. App. 488, 272 S.E.2d 19 (1980).

forth in the *Restatement (Second) of Torts* § 552, which does not require privity as an element.

LIABILITY TO SURETIES AND OTHER THIRD PARTIES

§ 22.12 Sureties

In an increasing number of negligence cases, architects and engineers are sued for economic losses sustained by sureties who have bonded the general contractor. Frequently, when a contractor defaults in performance, a surety is required to step in and complete the project for the remaining contract balance. If the architect has overcertified payment to the contractor before default, there may not be sufficient funds left in the contract to finish the job. This causes the surety to reach into its own pocket to finance completion. In many cases, the surety then looks to the architect as a source of recovery for the surety's losses. The most common situations giving rise to claims by sureties against design professionals involve negligent certification of pay applications, improper certification of work completed, premature release of retainage, or errors in project administration or supervision.[71] Numerous cases around the country have held that the surety may bring a cause of action against the design professional for negligence in the performance of duties assumed by the design professional's contract with the owner.[72] If the design professional knew that the job was to be bonded, courts have little trouble in ruling that the resulting loss to the surety was foreseeable.

One of the leading cases in this area is the 1954 Mississippi case, *State ex rel. National Surety Corp. v. Malvaney.*[73] In that case, the construction contract stipulated that a certain percentage of the contract price was to be withheld as retainage until the work was satisfactorily completed. The architect had contracted to supervise the construction of the building, to make labor and material estimates, and to issue a certificate of completion authorizing the owner to release the retainage after final inspection and

---

[71] *See* Chapman, *The Liability of Design Professionals to the Surety,* 20 Forum 591, 592-93 (1985); Annotation, *Liability of Architect or Engineer for Improper Issuance of Certificate,* 43 A.L.R.2d 1227 (1955).

[72] *See, e.g.,* Peerless Ins. Co. v. Cerny & Assoc., Inc., 199 F. Supp. 951 (D. Minn. 1961); American Fidelity Fire Ins. Co. v. Pavia-Byrne Eng'g, 393 So. 2d 830 (La. Ct. App. 1981); Calandro Dev., Inc. v. R.M. Butler Contractors, Inc., 249 So. 2d 254 (La. Ct. App. 1971).

[73] 221 Miss. 190, 72 So. 2d 424 (1954).

acceptance of the work. The architect authorized partial payment of the retainage without adequately ascertaining whether the contractor had paid all labor and material bills due on the project. When the contractor notified the surety that he would not be able to pay the outstanding bills, the surety was required under its bond obligations to pay the bills. Obviously, however, the surety could not use the retainage because that money had already been paid to the contractor.

The Mississippi Supreme Court ruled that the architect knew the purpose of the retainage, and that he knew or should have known when he authorized the release of the retainage that the surety would be required to pay in the event of a contractor default. The court stated that "the architect, therefore, undertook the performance of an act which, it was apparent, if negligently done would result in loss to the surety, and the law imposed upon him the duty to exercise due care to avoid such loss."

Similarly, in a 1989 Mississippi case, *U.R.S. Co. v. Gulfport-Biloxi Regional Airport Authority,*[74] the state supreme court found another architect liable to the contractor's surety for negligently certifying release of retainage. The architect in this case had employed a full-time inspector who had been warned twice about deficiencies in the roofing work. After release of the retainage, the roof leaked and had to be replaced. The architect was found to have been negligent in releasing the retainage.

In another 1989 case,[75] the owner sued the architect, contractor, and surety for construction defects. After the architect settled with the owner, the owner was awarded damages against the surety. The surety then sued the architect, alleging negligent inspection of the contractor's work. The architect was held liable to the surety despite its settlement with the owner in the earlier action.

Taking the architect's liability to third parties to the extreme is the Missouri case of *Westerhold v. Carroll.*[76] In that case, the surety was called on to complete the contractor's (Westerhold Construction, Inc.) work after the contractor defaulted. The surety incurred expenses in so doing and, in turn, made demand on its indemnitor (Fred Westerhold, Jr.) under the terms of an indemnity agreement. Mr. Westerhold then sued the architect who had contracted with the owner to supervise the project and to inspect and certify, for the purpose of payment by the owner to the contractor, the amount of work successfully performed and the amount of materials furnished for the project.[77] The plaintiff-indemnitor alleged that the architect negligently

---

[74] 544 So. 2d 824 (Miss. 1989).

[75] Seaboard Sur. Co. v. Walker, 212 Cal. App. 3d 1064, 260 Cal. Rptr. 924 (1989).

[76] 419 S.W.2d 73 (Mo. 1967).

[77] The Missouri Supreme Court held that the indemnitor stood in the position of the surety and could maintain such action against the architect for negligence as the surety could have maintained. *Id.* at 76.

and incorrectly certified the amount of work performed and materials delivered. As a result, when the contractor later defaulted and the surety was required to complete the project, there was less money available to the surety than should have been available. The Missouri Supreme Court held that the rule requiring privity of contract was inapplicable and that the case should be determined by the application of ordinary rules of negligence.[78]

In applying these "ordinary" rules of negligence, the court held that the retainage provisions of the contract were for the benefit of both the owner and the surety and, therefore, the indemnitor, Mr. Westerhold. The court further held that, in issuing its bond, the surety relied upon the inspection and certification of work progress. Finding that all the elements of a cause of action in negligence were present, the court reversed the trial court's dismissal of the suit against the architect.

Another example of the court's willingness to hold design professionals liable to sureties for negligent performance of contractual duties is *Aetna Insurance Co. v. Hellmuth, Obata & Kassabaum, Inc.*[79] In that case, the architect contracted with the owner to prepare the drawings and specifications, and to supervise construction of a terminal plaza at the Lambert-St. Louis Airport. The project was constantly plagued with difficulties. Apparently, the contractor was using funds for the current project to pay debts resulting from the operation of other projects. Upon the certification of the architect, the contractor was paid for work completed on the St. Louis project even though bills on that project were being left unpaid.

The surety alleged that the architect was negligent in failing to ascertain to what use the funds were being put, even after receiving reports that subcontractors and others were not being paid. The surety also sought to recover increased costs and damages for duplicated work. The Eighth Circuit Court of Appeals stated that when the architect knew, or should have known, that the contractor was not paying bills on the work already performed, for which he had been paid, "[t]hen the architect probably would have a duty to make inquiry and take steps to correct the situation before making any further certification on work performed."[80]

Finally, in a 1989 Louisiana case, *City of Houma v. Municipal & Industrial Pipe Service, Inc.*,[81] an engineering firm was held liable to the contractor's surety despite the fact that the contractor had been convicted of *criminally defrauding* the owner. The contractor was awarded a contract to test

[78] *Id.* at 80.

[79] 392 F.2d 472 (8th Cir. 1968).

[80] *Id.* at 472 n.3. *See also* Fabe v. WVP Corp., 760 S.W.2d 490 (Mo. Ct. App. 1988) (holding that an architect was not liable to the surety for having certified payment based, in part, on fraudulent lien waivers provided by the contractor. The architect was not obligated to verify the accuracy of lien waivers presented by the contractor).

[81] 884 F.2d 886 (5th Cir. 1989).

leaky joints in the city's sewer system. The engineer was hired to regularly inspect the work as it progressed so as to assure conformance with contract documents, and to certify work logs reflecting the location of testing and quantity of joint sealing. Upon substantial completion, the contractor requested a change order, which the engineer approved, increasing the contract by 40 percent. Subsequently, the contractor was convicted of fraudulently falsifying work logs on this and other jobs. The city sued the surety for $418,923 for failure of the contractor to perform the work paid for. The surety then sued the engineer for indemnity, and a judgment was entered on the surety's claim against the engineer for the entire $418,923 plus interest.

In affirming the judgment, the court of appeals ruled that the engineer's field representatives were "for the most part untrained, unskilled personnel who employed no reasonable, analytical method calculated to spot performance deficiencies."[82] The court concluded that the engineer was negligent in the performance of its contractual inspection duties, and that it was foreseeable that the surety would rely on the engineer's obligations as stated in its contract with the owner.

These cases reflect the status of the law that design professionals may owe a duty of ordinary and reasonable care to sureties, and that a surety may have a cause of action against a design professional for the negligent performance of duties assumed by the contract.[83] The privity defense has not been successful in barring suits brought by sureties when the design professional has breached its duty of care owed to the surety.

§ 22.13 Condominium Associations

An emerging group that courts now recognize as having a cause of action in negligence against design professionals, notwithstanding the lack of privity of contract, is condominium associations and condominium owners. For example, in *Cooper v. Jevne,*[84] the California Court of Appeals held that the condominium purchaser's complaint stated a cause of action against the architect for professional negligence, even in the absence of privity. In *Cooper,* the architectural firm prepared plans and specifications for the project for the seller of the condominiums, and then supervised the construction of the project. The purchasers alleged that the architect was under a duty to exercise ordinary care to avoid reasonably foreseeable injury to them, and that the architect should have foreseen that the purchasers would

---

[82] *Id.* at 890.

[83] *But see* Murphy, *Impact of the 1976 Edition of AIA Document A201 on the Liability of Architects and Engineers to the Construction Surety,* 45 Ins. Couns. J. 200 (1978).

[84] 56 Cal. App. 3d 860, 128 Cal. Rptr. 724 (1976).

suffer monetary damages if the architect breached its professional duty.[85] The purchasers further alleged that the architect negligently performed its duty and this breach was the proximate cause of their injuries.

The California Court of Appeals held that the architect owed a duty of reasonable care in the performance of its professional services to those who purchased the alleged defectively designed and built condominiums. The court reasoned that:

> The architects must have known that the condominiums they designed and whose construction they supervised were built . . . for sale to the public and that purchasers of these condominiums would be the ones who would suffer economically, if not bodily, from any negligence by the architects in the performance of their professional services.[86]

In *Council of Co-Owners Atlantis Condominium, Inc. v. Whiting-Turner Contracting Co.,*[87] the Maryland Court of Appeals held that the members of a condominium owners' association had a cause of action in negligence against an architect despite the lack of privity of contract. In that case, the condominium owners' association, which was the governing body of a 21-story building housing 198 separate condominium units, sued the general contractor, developer, and architects involved in the construction of the building. The association owners alleged that, as a result of the defendants' negligence, the utility shafts and electrical work did not comply with the requirements of the applicable building code. Furthermore, the owners alleged that these latent conditions created a fire hazard that presented a threat to the safety of the owners and occupants of the condominium building.

The owners specifically alleged that the architects were negligent in their inspection, supervision, and acceptance of the work performed and that the architects, who were to inspect the building for the city, negligently certified to the city inspection department that the building was constructed pursuant to the approved building permit. The plaintiffs sought both compensatory and punitive damages which they alleged were the result of the defendants' negligent conduct.

---

[85] In particular, the purchasers alleged that by reason of the architect's negligent conduct they sustained damages including repair of the condominiums, past and future property damage, past and future loss of use and income of their respective condominiums, and incidental expenses relating to discovery of the alleged structural deficiencies. *See id.* at 728.

[86] *Id.* at 729. *See also* Parliament Towers Condominium v. Parliament House Realty, Inc., 377 So. 2d 976 (Fla. Dist. Ct. App. 1979). *But see* 2314 Lincoln Park W. Condominium Ass'n v. Mann, Gin, Ebel & Frazier, Ltd., 136 Ill. 2d 302, 555 N.E.2d 346 (1990) (architect found to have no duty to condominium association).

[87] 308 Md. 18, 517 A.2d 336, 341 (1986).

Because no personal injury had occurred at the time the action was brought, the court addressed only the issue of whether a tort cause of action exists when the injury is purely economic and no privity of contract exists between the parties. After an exhaustive analysis of the evolution of the privity doctrine, the court of appeals reversed the trial court and held that:

> In following the modern trend, we hold that privity is not an absolute prerequisite to the existence of a tort duty. The duty of the architects . . . to use due care in the design, inspection, and construction of this condominium, extended to those persons foreseeably subjected to the risk of personal injury created.[88]

The court further held that the determination of whether an architect owes a duty should depend upon the risks generated by the negligent conduct, "[r]ather than upon the fortuitous circumstances of the nature of the resultant damage."[89] Thus, the court reasoned that when the risk is of death or personal injury, an action will lie for the recovery of the reasonable cost of correcting the dangerous condition.[90]

As is evident from these cases, courts have recognized that condominium associations and condominium owners, like contractors, subcontractors, and sureties, can have a cause of action in negligence against design professionals, notwithstanding the lack of privity of contract. Like contractors, subcontractors, and sureties, whether condominium owners and condominium associations will have a cause of action against design professionals for purely economic losses caused by the design professional's negligence will depend upon the particular jurisdiction involved.

§ 22.14 Lenders

Similar to the surety cases, some courts have found design professionals liable to construction lenders for negligent certifications. In one such case, *Alley v. Courtney,*[91] the guarantor of a construction loan was found liable to the lending bank on his personal guarantee. The plaintiff-guarantor then sued the project inspector, a professional appraiser, who prepared reports for the bank during construction, upon which the bank advanced payment

---

[88] *Id.* at 344.

[89] *Id.* at 345.

[90] *Id.* The court qualified its holding by stating that, because of the serious nature of the risks involved in the present action, they were willing to recognize a cause of action in the absence of actual injury. The court further noted that when the conditions only present a risk to general health, welfare, or comfort but do not present a risk of death or personal injury, no cause of action would arise.

[91] 448 So. 2d 858 (La. Ct. App. 1984).

to the builder. The inspector had reported to the bank that all foundations were 95 percent complete when, in fact, they were only 15 percent to 60 percent complete. Finding the inspector liable to the guarantor, the court stated:

> As a professional appraiser and inspector, defendant knew or should have known that each of his reports would be relied on to the detriment of a lender if the report was erroneous. Under such circumstances, defendant's duty was not owed solely to the builder, but extended to plaintiff and others that might suffer reasonably foreseeable and direct injury because of a breach of the duty owed by defendant. Privity of contract is not necessary in an action for damages under these circumstances.[92]

Although the defendant in this case was not an architect or engineer, the law could apply equally to design professionals who undertake to inspect and report on the progress of construction for use by lenders or others.

§ 22.15 Construction Laborers

About 8 percent of all claims against design professionals are those brought by construction workers.[93] Fortunately for architect/engineers (A/Es), the overwhelming majority of cases in recent years have found that the design professional has no duty with regard to jobsite safety procedures, nor to provide the worker a safe work place. In large part, this trend is due to usage of standard form contracts that have been drafted to place responsibility for jobsite safety on the general contractor.

Defenses Available

Despite the various theories attempted by plaintiffs' lawyers, most courts have recognized valid defenses available to the design professional. These defenses include:

No duty to insure site safety. In a great many cases, design professionals have been able to successfully defend jobsite injury claims and obtain a dismissal or summary judgment in their favor. These dismissals have been premised on the most basic of all defenses: no duty owed, no duty breached.[94] When standard American Institute of Architects (AIA) or Engineers Joint Contract Documents Committee (EJCDC) contracts are

---

[92] *Id.* at 860.

[93] Victor O. Schinnerer & Co., Liability Update 3 (Dec. 1990).

[94] *See, e.g.,* Kerr v. Rochester Gas & Elec. Corp., 113 A.D.2d 412, 496 N.Y.S.2d 990 (1985); Kemp v. Bechtel Constr. Co., 221 Mont. 519, 720 P.2d 270 (1986); Swartz v. Ford, 469 So. 2d 232 (Fla. Dist. Ct. App. 1985); Young v. Eastern Eng'g & Elevator Co., 544 A.2d 77 (Pa. Super. Ct. 1989).

used, courts have found that the design professional undertook no safety obligations in its contract with the owner. Therefore, no duty ran to foreseeable third parties, such as construction workers, to protect them from harm.

Statutory immunity. As a result of strong lobbying efforts by design professionals, several states have added architects and engineers to the class of persons who are immune from claims under workers' compensation laws. At least 11 states have adopted legislation granting statutory immunity to the design professional for injury claims arising from the contractor's negligence.[95] The design professional is immune unless (1) the design professional contracted for safety duties, or (2) the injury or death was the result of a design defect. In these states, when the accident is the result of the contractor's unsafe construction methods or practices, the design professional will be immune from the worker's suit.

Theories of Recovery

Nearly all damage claims brought against design professionals relating to jobsite accidents are for negligence. The worker typically claims that the architect had a duty to supervise construction and to maintain a safe work place and, that by failing to use due care and skill, that duty was breached, resulting in foreseeable damage to the plaintiff. That duty has been found to arise from a variety of sources, such as contract, statute, ordinance, actions or representations by the design professional, or, in some cases, the duty may even arise out of the architect's or engineer's status as a "professional."[96] The negligence claims fall into the following five classifications:

Negligent supervision. The most common allegation made by workers is that the design professional's contract included certain supervisory duties and, as a result, there was a duty to catch safety errors of the contractor. It is widely recognized, however, that although customary, architects have no common law duty to supervise the contractor's work. That obligation must arise from a contractual undertaking of the architect.[97] Even when the design professional contracts to supervise construction, courts have held that there is no common law duty requiring the architect or engineer to insure

---

[95] Conn. Gen. Stat. § 31-293(b); Fla. Stat. Ann. § 440.09(5) (West); Kan. Stat. Ann. § 44-501(f); Me. Rev. Stat. Ann. tit. 39, § 4; Mo. Rev. Stat. § 287.150; Neb. Rev. Stat. § 25-21, 187; N.D. Cent. Code § 43-03-23; Okla. Stat. Ann. tit. 85, § 12 (West); Or. Rev. Stat. § 30.785; S.D. Codified Laws Ann. § 36-18-28.1; Wash. Rev. Code Ann. § 51.24.035.

[96] *See, e.g.,* Balagna v. Shawnee County, 233 Kan. 1068, 668 P.2d 157 (1983).

[97] 5 Am. Jur. 2d *Architects* § 5 (1962); Geer v. Bennett, 237 So. 2d 311 (Fla. Dist. Ct. App. 1970); Kelly v. Northwest Community Hosp., 66 Ill. App. 3d 679, 384 N.E.2d 102 (1978); Brown v. Gamble Constr. Co., 537 S.W.2d 685 (Mo. Ct. App. 1976).

construction site safety. Before an architect will be held to have agreed to exercise direct control over day-to-day safety precautions, the duty generally must appear in a contract or applicable statute. Absent such a duty, the responsibility for safety falls upon the employer, the contractor, not the design professional.

As part of the negligent supervision theory, plaintiffs have sued architects for failure to "stop the work" when the architect had such authority by contract.[98] In response, contracts published by the AIA and by professional engineering societies no longer give the design professional the contract right to stop the work. Instead, only the owner and the contractor have the right to stop the work due to defective construction or unsafe conditions.[99]

Design errors/omissions. Clearly, if the injury or death is the result of a design error, as opposed to a material failure or defect, construction defect, or failure of the worker to use reasonable care, the design professional will be held liable. As one court stated:

> The engineer or architect owes a duty to the employees of an independent contractor to avoid endangering them by its own negligence. This includes using due care in the preparation of plans and specifications for the direction of the work.
>
> * * *
>
> [I]t is the duty of an engineer or architect to exercise reasonable care, or the ordinary skill of the profession, for the protection of anyone lawfully upon the premises whose injury is reasonably foreseeable as the result of negligent design, plans, orders, or directions.[100]

Examples of design errors alleged to create design professional liability to workers include:

1. Excavation plans requiring a dangerously steep slope[101]
2. Specification of improper sheathing for span between roof rafters[102]
3. Failure to indicate presence of underground high-voltage power lines[103]

---

[98] *See, e.g.*, Erhardt v. Hummonds, 232 Ark. 133, 334 S.W.2d 869 (1960); Miller v. DeWitt, 37 Ill. 2d 273, 226 N.E.2d 630 (1967); Caldwell v. Bechtel, Inc., 631 F.2d 989 (D.C. Cir. 1980); Swarthout v. Beard, 33 Mich. App. 395, 190 N.W.2d 373 (1971).

[99] *See* AIA A201-1987, General Conditions of the Contract for Construction, Arts. 2.3 and 10.3; *see also* EJCDC 1910-8 (1983), Standard General Conditions of the Construction Contract, Arts. 6.22 and 13.10.

[100] Moloso v. State, 644 P.2d 205, 216–17 (Alaska 1982).

[101] *Id.*

[102] Paxton v. Alameda County, 119 Cal. App. 2d 393, 259 P.2d 934 (1953).

[103] Mallow v. Tucker, Sadler & Bennett, 245 Cal. App. 2d 700, 54 Cal. Rptr. 174 (1966).

4. Improper design of wet and dry wells in sewage treatment plant, allowing poisonous gas to seep from one well to the other[104]
5. Design of nonstandard ladder in turbine pit[105]
6. Improper design of steel truss[106]
7. Negligent design of staircase.[107]

Often, it is necessary to distinguish between the architect's design and the contractor's method of construction to determine fault in these types of cases.

Negligent approval of shop drawings. In a 1983 Eighth Circuit case, an architectural firm was sued by two injured workers who fell while welding on a metal stair. Although the specifications called for 10-gauge steel, the architect approved shop drawings that indicated a thinner 14-gauge steel. The stair's metal landing pan collapsed under the workers' weight, causing them to fall. The architect was held liable to the workers for negligent "supervision" of the shop drawings.[108]

By contrast, the Louisiana Supreme Court held in 1961 that an architect who approved a shop drawing for a boiler, which omitted a critical safety device, was not liable for the subsequent death of a worker when the boiler exploded.[109]

In an Oklahoma case, an architect was found not liable for the deaths of two workers and the injury of another allegedly caused by negligent approval of shop drawings for steel erection.[110] The court held that under the AIA General Conditions of the Contract for Construction, Document A201, the contractor, not the architect, was responsible for temporary field connections.

Third-party beneficiary. When an architect or engineer undertakes supervisory duties or responsibility for safety by contract with the owner, the contractor's employees may claim that the architect's contract obligations

---

[104] Evans v. Howard R. Green Co., 231 N.W.2d 907 (Iowa 1975); for a similar case, *see* Van Ornum v. Otter Tail Power Co., 210 N.W.2d 188 (N.D. 1973).

[105] Hackley v. Waldorf-Hoerner, 149 Mont. 286, 425 P.2d 712 (1967).

[106] Swaney v. Peden Steel Co., 259 N.C. 531, 131 S.E.2d 601 (1963).

[107] Gross v. Kenton Structural & Ornamental Ironworks, 581 F. Supp. 390 (S.D. Ohio 1984).

[108] Jaeger v. Henningson, Durham & Richardson, Inc., 714 F.2d 773 (8th Cir. 1983); *see also* Henningson, Durham & Richardson, Inc. v. Swift Bros. Constr. Co., 739 F.2d 1341 (8th Cir. 1984), in which the architect was denied indemnity from the contractor due to a state anti-indemnity statute, S.D. Codified Laws Ann. § 56-3-16 and -17 (1980).

[109] Day v. National U.S. Radiator Corp., 241 La. 288, 128 So. 2d 660 (1961).

[110] Waggoner v. W&W Steel Co., 657 P.2d 147 (Okla. 1982).

are actually intended for their benefit. As "intended" third-party beneficiaries, they will claim damages if injured due to a breach of the architect's supervisory or safety obligations. Such an argument was rejected by the Arkansas Supreme Court in *Walker v. Wittenberg, Deloney & Davidson, Inc.*[111] The court stated:

> The presumption is that parties contract only for themselves, and a contract will not be construed as having been made for the benefit of a third party unless it clearly appears that such was the intention of the parties. Before an architect can be said to have agreed with an owner to exercise direct control over a contractor with respect to day-to-day supervision of a building contract, such agreement must clearly appear from the terms of the agreement, the conduct of the parties, or the nature of the work being performed.[112]

Similarly, in *Williams v. Fenix & Scission, Inc.*,[113] the Ninth Circuit Court of Appeals held that the supervisory duties of the engineer were for the benefit of the owner only, not for the contractor or its injured employee. The court found that, at best, the worker was an "incidental beneficiary" of the owner-engineer contract, and as such, had no rights under the contract against the engineer for injuries suffered in a jobsite accident.

Res ipsa loquitur. In *Day v. National U.S. Radiator Corp.*,[114] the widow of a worker killed in a boiler explosion sued the architect under the theory of res ipsa loquitur. Under this legal theory, negligence need not be proved, only that the accident would not have occurred but for a negligent act. The plaintiff claimed that the boiler would not have exploded if not for the architect's negligence. The architect approved shop drawings for the boiler before its installation. The Louisiana Court of Appeals ruled against the architect under the res ipsa loquitur theory, but the state supreme court reversed on further appeal.

§ 22.16 Pedestrians, Building Users, and Tenants

Insurance statistics indicate that about 16 percent of all claims made against design professionals are asserted by members of the general public

---

[111] 241 Ark. 525, 412 S.W.2d 621 (1966), *on reh'g,* 412 S.W.2d 626, 630 (Ark. 1967).

[112] *Id.* at 630; *see also* Young v. Eastern Eng'g & Elevator Co., 554 A.2d 77, 81 (Pa. Super. Ct. 1989).

[113] 608 F.2d 1205 (9th Cir. 1979).

[114] 117 So. 2d 104 (La. Ct. App. 1959), *rev'd,* 241 La. 288, 128 So. 2d 660 (1961).

injured during or after construction.[115] In addition to bodily injury, members of the general public may suffer foreseeable economic loss due to a design professional's negligence.

For example, a pedestrian who was injured when a masonry wall fell on him in a windstorm successfully sued the project architect for damages in *Johnson v. Salem Title Co.*[116] The architect was found liable for negligence because the wall, designed by the architect's consulting engineer, did not comply with the building code requirements.

When the Kemper Arena roof collapsed in Kansas City in 1979, the circus, the ice follies, the concession vendors, and others brought suit against the arena's designers for economic losses incurred due to lost sales and profits when scheduled events in the arena had to be canceled while repairs were made.[117] The court held that architects can be liable to such third parties even in absence of privity when injury to them is foreseeable.

In a 1983 Kansas Supreme Court case, an engineering firm was held liable for the death of a truck driver whose truck struck a 4-foot by 5-foot-6-inch hole in the Kansas turnpike.[118] The driver was killed when his truck burst into flames after hitting the guardrail and plunging 30 feet to the ground. The engineering firm that had contracted with the state to perform annual inspection of all bridges on the turnpike was found liable for negligent performance of its inspection duties. The court held that, despite the absence of privity, the engineers "had a legal duty to exercise reasonable care in conducting an annual safety inspection which it owed to the [truck driver] and to other members of the traveling public."[119]

The Wisconsin Supreme Court ruled in a 1974 case that an architect, who knew the purpose for which the building was being constructed, could be held liable to a future tenant who suffered loss due to the architect's negligence.[120] The court stated that the architect's failure to properly take into account the condition of the subsoil when designing and supervising construction of a building is an act or omission that could foreseeably cause harm to the tenant. Relying on the *MacPherson* and *Inman* decisions, the court held that privity was no bar to such a third-party claim.

---

[115] Victor O. Schinnerer & Co., Liability Update 3 (Dec. 1990).

[116] 246 Or. 409, 425 P.2d 519 (1967) (en banc).

[117] *See* Chubb Group of Ins. Cos. v. C.F. Murphy Assocs., Inc., 656 S.W.2d 766 (Mo. Ct. App. 1983); Volume Servs., Inc. v. C.F. Murphy & Assocs., Inc., 656 S.W.2d 785 (Mo. Ct. App. 1983).

[118] Ingram v. Howard-Needles-Tammen & Bergendoff, 234 Kan. 289, 672 P.2d 1083 (1983).

[119] *Id.* at 1086.

[120] A.E. Inv. Corp. v. Link Builders, Inc., 62 Wis. 2d 479, 214 N.W.2d 764, 767 (1974).

INTENTIONAL TORTS

§ 22.17 Overview

In addition to negligence and third-party beneficiary cases, design professionals may also be held liable for intentional torts to parties with whom they have no contract. Primarily, these cases deal with fraudulent or malicious conduct that is intended to, and causes, damage to a third party.

§ 22.18 Intentional Interference with Contract

Architects have a "conditional privilege" to interfere with the owner/contractor relationship to the extent that the architect is called on to pass judgment on performance, reject work, rule on claims, and declare the contractor in default. However, when an architect or engineer takes some action maliciously, without just cause, which disrupts a known contractual relationship between two other parties, the courts will impose liability, including punitive damages for "intentional interference with contract." For instance, in *Waldinger Corp. v. CRS Group Engineers, Inc.,*[121] a mechanical subcontractor sued the project engineer for intentional interference with contract when the engineer prepared an exclusionary specification and insisted, without justification, that the subcontractor comply literally with that specification. The court ruled that if the engineer's insistence on strict compliance with the exclusionary specification was malicious, with intent to injure the subcontractor or to merely further the engineer's personal goals, liability would attach.

In a 1981 case, *Juengel Construction Co. v. Mt. Etna, Inc.,*[122] an architect was found liable for only one dollar in actual damages but $10,000 in punitive damages, which were awarded to the contractor for a shopping center when the architect insisted upon rebidding a project after an agreement had been signed with the plaintiff-contractor to build the project. The court held that the architect wrongfully interfered with the owner/contractor relationship, causing the owner to break off its agreement with the contractor.

Courts in New York and Arizona also have found architects and engineers liable to contractors for intentional or "tortious" interference with the owner/contractor relationship.[123]

---

[121] 775 F.2d 781 (7th Cir. 1985).

[122] 622 S.W.2d 510 (Mo. Ct. App. 1981).

[123] Northrup Contracting, Inc. v. Village of Bergen, 139 Misc. 2d 435, 527 N.Y.S.2d 670 (1986); Craviolini v. Scholer & Fuller Assoc. Architects, 89 Ariz. 24, 357 P.2d 611 (1960); Nelson v. Cail, 120 Ariz. 64, 583 P.2d 1384 (1978).

§ 22.19 Libel/Slander

Although the cases are sparse, architects and engineers have been sued for slander or libel by third parties when statements or opinions expressed by the design professional have reflected negatively on the contractor's qualifications as "lowest responsible bidder"[124] or the contractor's ability to complete the job.[125]

In one 1986 New York case, an engineer was sued for libel by another engineer when the defendant had been retained to, and did, prepare a report and critical evaluation of work performed by the plaintiff-engineer on a sewage plant.[126] The court held that opinions, false or not, are not libelous and are constitutionally protected, provided that the facts supporting the opinions are set forth. Finding the statements at issue to be "engineering opinion, adequately supported by a statement of underlying facts," the court concluded that the statements were not defamatory under New York law.

§ 22.20 Fraud

In a 1987 case, the bond purchasers who had invested in a nuclear power project sued the project engineer, claiming that the engineer had fraudulently misrepresented the structural feasibility of the project. The Washington Supreme Court held that the bond purchasers had properly stated a cause of action for fraud because the engineer knew that information it provided to the power company would be passed on to the investors and relied on by them.[127]

In a 1971 soil data case, a contractor alleged that the project engineer hired by the owner performed several subsurface tests but disclosed to bidders only the favorable data, fraudulently concealing the unfavorable results.[128] The court held that such allegations sufficiently stated a claim for fraud against the engineer.

---

[124] Riblet Tramway Co. v. Ericksen Assoc., Inc., 665 F. Supp. 81 (D.N.H. 1987).

[125] Vojak v. Jensen, 161 N.W.2d 100 (Iowa 1968); Alfred A. Altimont, Inc. v. Chatelain Samperton & Nolan, 374 A.2d 284 (D.C. 1977).

[126] Lapar v. Morris, 119 A.D.2d 635, 501 N.Y.S.2d 82 (1986).

[127] Haberman v. Washington Pub. Power Supply Sys., 109 Wash. 2d 107, 744 P.2d 1032 (1987).

[128] Salem Sand & Gravel Co. v. City of Salem, 260 Or. 630, 492 P.2d 271 (1971).

CHAPTER 23

LEGAL DEFENSES OF ARCHITECTS AND ENGINEERS

Larry Selander
Todd Zimmerman

Larry Selander is the partner in charge of construction litigation at the Chicago firm of Keck, Mahin & Cate. He received his B.S. in chemical engineering from the University of Notre Dame and his J.D. from the University of Illinois. Mr. Selander has authored articles in various fields of litigation practice, and he has lectured for the Illinois Institute of Continuing Legal Education. He has taught for the National Institute of Trial Advocacy, and he is an adjunct professor of trial advocacy at the Northwestern University School of Law.

Todd Zimmerman is an associate at the law firm of Keck, Mahin & Cate in Chicago, Illinois. Mr. Zimmerman received an honors B.S. in business administration (economics) from St. Louis University and a J.D. from the University of Virginia.

§ 23.1 Introduction

In considering the defenses available to design professionals against claims arising from the performance of their work, the nature of the relationship between the design professional and the claimant must be kept clearly in mind. The claimant may be someone who has a contract with the design professional for services and, therefore, stands in privity of contract. The claimant may be a noncontracting party who has suffered some kind of loss or damage and believes that the injury was caused, at least in part, by the design professional. The claimant may or may not also have a contractual relationship with another party involved in the construction process, such as the owner or contractor, who may in turn have a contract directly with the design professional. The defenses available to the design professional vary greatly depending upon the identity of the claimant and whether the design professional has a contractual relationship with the claimant or another party to the construction process.

A design professional's specific duties and responsibilities to a client typically are defined by a written contract. The specificity of the contract may vary widely, anywhere from a general agreement to perform vaguely defined services to lengthy, detailed contracts with exacting specificity regarding the nature, extent, timing, and accounting for all work performed.

The American Institute of Architects (AIA) has issued standardized contracts that are in general use within the profession. These contracts attempt to identify precise duties to be performed by the contracting parties. Other bodies, such as the Engineers Joint Contract Documents Committee and many government agencies, also have standard forms for contracts.

However, no matter how precisely a contract is drawn, the final resolution of most disputes between a design professional and a client is usually based on the issue of whether the professional services were provided in accordance with a professional standard of care. A design professional is supposed to act with the degree of skill and learning ordinarily possessed by other similarly situated professionals in the community and apply that knowledge with the diligence ordinarily exercised by reputable designers under similar circumstances.

Nearly all cases involving a claim against design professionals turn on compliance with this standard. Accordingly, in order for a claimant to prevail, expert testimony must be adduced to show that the services performed were inadequate in terms of the local standard. The claimant generally must prove two elements to recover against a design professional:

1. That a duty owed to the claimant was breached; and
2. That the breach of the duty caused the claimant's damages.

Claims against design professionals are sometimes confused and vague in their distinctions between tort and contract principles. Failure to comply with the professional standard gives rise to an action for breach of contract. Often, however, the same failure also can be the basis for a negligence action. Thus, claims for professional misconduct frequently fall under both tort and contract theories.

The primary defense available to the design professional is, of course, that the design professional met whatever standard of care is appropriate. To that end, the defense lawyer must discuss and evaluate a client's performance in light of the testimony of various experts to evaluate that performance against the standard of care that applies in the community.

Other defenses that may be available can be grouped into two categories:

1. Defenses that are independent of the design professional's performance and that might serve to bar the claim. These defenses include standing to bring a lawsuit, the statute of limitations, immunity, protection under laws such as the workers' compensation laws, waiver, and estoppel.
2. Defenses that might shift or reduce the design professional's liability because of the performance and/or responsibility of others. These defenses include contributory negligence, assumption of the risk, contribution, and indemnification and/or hold-harmless agreements.

These defenses will be considered in this chapter, although it is not possible here to provide an extensive treatment of each of these defenses. The rules vary greatly from state to state. The law is very active in this field at present, and both statutory regulation and case law precedent is changing on a regular basis.

Rather, the intent is to review the defenses in general and outline the considerations that might be relevant to each of them. It will be important for the design professional to evaluate these defenses in light of the law of the state in which he or she practices to determine what defenses are available and how they might be applied.

One comment must be made as a matter of general importance. As noted more completely elsewhere in this book,[1] there have been attempts to change the standard of care for design professionals to a standard of strict liability. If this change in the law comes to pass, design professionals essentially would be liable for damages caused by a failure even if the professional were

[1] See **Chs. 6** and **7**.

not guilty of negligence or breach of contract. The care taken by the design professional would become irrelevant for many purposes.

Strict liability has been imposed on many manufacturers of products by courts and legislatures in most parts of the country. In the jurisdictions that have embraced strict liability, manufacturers and sellers of various products have been held liable for damages caused by the use of the product independent of fault.

Thus far, strict liability has not been imposed as a general matter against design professionals. However, the design professional should remain aware of developments in this area of the law that could greatly affect the defenses available from various claims, particularly by claimants who are not in privity of contract with the professional.

STANDING TO SUE

§ 23.2 Liability to Third Parties

For many years, design professionals were primarily concerned with liability for claims made by their clients and not third parties. The trend for a number of years has been to allow third-party claims (those by claimants who are not in privity of contract with the design professional) based on a variety of legal theories, including third-party beneficiary, negligence, indemnity, and contribution.

§ 23.3 —Third-Party Beneficiary Theory

In third-party beneficiary claims, the claimant must show that it was an intended beneficiary of the contract between the design professional and the client.[2] Most courts have stretched rulings to find that third parties are not intended beneficiaries of the design professional's contract with a client.[3] Many parties with close ties to the construction process, including contractors and their workers, have been held to be incidental beneficiaries of the design professional's contract and therefore not entitled to make claims. This is the strongest area for defense against these claims.

---

[2] *See* Restatement (Second) of Contracts § 302 (1982); People *ex rel.* Resnik v. Curtis & Davis, Architects & Planners, Inc., 78 Ill. 2d 381, 400 N.E.2d 918 (1980).

[3] C.H. Leavell & Co. v. Glantz Contracting Corp., 322 F. Supp. 779 (E.D. La. 1971); A.R. Moyer, Inc. v. Graham, 285 So. 2d 397 (Fla. 1973); Waterford Condominium Ass'n v. Dunbar Corp., 104 Ill. App. 3d 371, 432 N.E.2d 1009 (1982).

However, if an intended third-party beneficiary is identified by name in the contract documents, liability may attach.[4]

§ 23.4 —Negligence

A design professional's duty to exercise care in the performance of its work extends to third parties who may foreseeably be harmed by the design professional's failure to exercise that care. The design professional must exercise the ability, skill, and care customarily used by design professionals on the type of project in question. If the design professional breaches the duty of care and this breach directly and proximately causes compensable harm, the injured party may have a claim for negligence.

§ 23.5 —Economic Loss Doctrine

A party not in privity of contract with the design professional may recover damages for personal injury and property damage caused by the professional's negligence. However, a considerable body of law has developed with regard to the type of damages for which recovery may be maintained on a negligence theory. The primary issue revolves around whether damages for *economic loss* can be recovered from the design professional.

> "Economic loss" has been defined as "damages for inadequate value, costs of repair and replacement of the defective product or consequent loss of profits—without any claim of personal injury or damage to other property . . ." as well as ". . . the diminution in the value of the product because it is inferior in quality and does not work for the general purposes for which it was manufactured and sold." These definitions are consistent with the policy of warranty law to protect expectations of suitability and quality.[5]

The meaning and application of the economic loss doctrine has been the subject of extensive litigation over the last few years. In *Moorman Manufacturing Co. v. National Tank Co.,*[6] a seminal case involving the economic loss doctrine decided in 1982 by the Illinois Supreme Court, the plaintiff purchased a grain storage tank that developed cracks, thereby precluding the purchaser from using it as he had intended. The plaintiff's complaint included tort theories and requested damages for purely economic losses calculated by repair costs plus the loss of use of the storage tank. The court

---

[4] *See, e.g.,* People *ex rel.* Resnik v. Curtis & Davis, Architects & Planners, Inc., 78 Ill. 2d 381, 400 N.E.2d 918 (1980).

[5] Moorman Mfg. Co. v. National Tank Co., 91 Ill. 2d 69, 435 N.E.2d 443, 449 (1982).

[6] *Id.*

held that recovery of damages arising solely from economic loss was not permitted under tort law. The court distinguished between remedies that should be allowed by contract law versus remedies that should be allowed under tort law. The court said that:

> The true significance of physical harm is that it usually represents an invasion of a right existing apart from any contract—a tort interest . . . on the other hand, if a product simply fails to live up to its promise, if it does not accomplish what it was supposed to, the way it was supposed to, that is only an invasion of a contract-like interest: the user has lost the benefit of his bargain. If a refrigerator fails, the food inside may spoil, but there is no tort. The product may be inadequate or useless, but it is not dangerous. The only risk is to commercial expectations.
>
> The central test is the relation of the malfunction and the consequent loss to what the product was supposed to accomplish. The product's function is the core of the commercial bargain, and any shortcomings should normally be dealt with by commercial law, unless there is some excellent reason for invoking the less flexible tort system. Hazards peripheral to the product's function, however, were not in the forefront of the minds of the contracting parties, and it is inconvenient to have tort rules about them.[7]

The economic loss doctrine has been litigated widely across the country. Essentially, it divides damages arising from claims into two types:

1. Personal injury and/or casualty losses
2. Damages related to failures of a functional nature.

The first type of claim covers all personal injuries and property damage of a calamitous or catastrophic nature. The second includes damages of a commercial nature that result from the failure of a particular product to perform up to commercial expectations. Examples of these latter types of claims, as they apply to the design professional, might be water leakage from improperly designed structures, cracked concrete or masonry, and heating and cooling system failures.

The impact of the economic loss doctrine is felt when dealing with claims falling within the second category. The economic loss doctrine says that claims based on damages of this nature may not be made in tort. The claimant is instead limited to other types of remedies, such as contract remedies, and, in many cases, may have no remedy at all. The boundaries of the economic loss doctrine are still being explored. Determinations on fact-specific claims can vary from state to state.

The economic loss doctrine is also relevant to claims against a design professional in situations in which the design professional's negligence

---

[7] 435 N.E.2d at 455.

causes a reduction in commercial expectations and also causes incidental property damage. For example, if a design professional negligently designed a basement that leaks, and the leak then causes water damage to other property, the question becomes whether a nonparty to the design professional's contract can bring a tort claim against the design professional for those damages.

Some courts might hold that such a claim is barred because the essence of the defect is qualitative and gradual (a contract law problem) rather than dangerous and sudden (a tort law problem).[8] Other courts may say, however, that the existence of the separate property damage is sufficient to bring the claim within the purview of tort principles.

A recent case of considerable importance addresses the question of whether a tort action for professional malpractice against an architect could be maintained for solely economic loss.[9] The case was brought to a state supreme court specifically for decision on this issue because lower courts had reached widely differing results. The court went through a cogent analysis of case law and various articles by commentators to reach its conclusion that such damage could not be recovered. The case dealt with a suit by a condominium association against an architect for a variety of defects in the design of a high-rise condominium. The court stated:

> We decline to impose on Mann [the architect] a duty in tort to protect the unit owners from the sort of loss asserted. The architect's responsibility originated in its contract with the original owner, and in these circumstances, its duties should be measured accordingly. Recovery of the nature requested here essentially seeks damages for a difference in quality. . . . "[I]f the purchaser buys goods which turn out to be below its expectations, its remedy should be against the person from whom it bought the goods, based upon the contract with that person."[10]

Under this analysis, a count for negligence against an architect was a claim concerning the quality, rather than the safety, of the building, and thus was a matter more appropriately brought under contract law.

The economic loss doctrine is a defense available to design professionals which has substantial importance in defending claims by claimants who are not in privity of contract with the design professional.

---

[8] Wheeling Trust & Sav. Bank v. Tremco, Inc., 153 Ill. App. 3d 136, 505 N.E.2d 1045 (1987).

[9] 2314 Lincoln Park W. Condominium Ass'n v. Mann, Gin, Ebel & Frazier, Ltd., 136 Ill. 2d 302, 555 N.E.2d 346 (1990).

[10] 555 N.E.2d at 353 (citations omitted).

STATUTES OF LIMITATION AND REPOSE

§ 23.6 In General

An important defense to a claim arising from a construction dispute is the applicable statute of limitations. All design professionals should be aware of the statutes of limitation that control claims against them for their actions. A statute of limitations defense is, if successful, a complete bar to the claim and precludes a court from getting to the merits of a case.

The basis for statutes of limitation is public policy. They protect design professionals and others against false or fraudulent claims that can be difficult to disprove because evidence and/or witnesses have become lost or unavailable with the passage of time. They also allow a determination to be made as to when potential liability ceases.

Because the public policy supporting statutes of limitation must be balanced against the countervailing rights of claimants who have suffered damages to seek legal redress, the legislatures of the various states have different statutory schemes, and the design professional accordingly must take care to review the applicable state statute of limitation.

§ 23.7 Statutes of Limitation and Repose Applicable to Design Professionals

In the past, the statute of limitations applying to the design professional has generally been the same as the statute of limitations applying in general to the basic claim being made. Limitation periods are usually different depending upon the type of claim being made. For instance, the limitation period for a contract action is often longer than the limitation period for a negligence action. However, the limitation period might begin to run for a contract action as of the date of the contract, whereas the limitation period for negligence might not begin to run until the claimant actually knew or had reason to know that a negligent act had been committed. This might not happen until a long time after completion of a project. These rules vary widely from state to state.

As a matter of public policy, legislatures also may pass statutes of repose to affix some kind of certainty to things. Statutes of repose say that even if the statute of limitations has not yet run (such as because the claimant does not have actual knowledge of a particular negligent act), the cause of action will expire at the end of a specific time period after the conduct in question was performed. Statutes of repose usually have long time periods before they expire. The theory is that after a certain amount of time a cause of action should die regardless of other circumstances.

The current trend is toward the passage of separate statutes of limitation and statutes of repose that apply solely to construction. These statutes often cover the work of the design professional. Such statutes have been passed in most states.[11]

Construction statutes of limitation vary from state to state. To illustrate some of these differences, reference will be made to the Illinois statute, which provides that:

> Actions based upon tort, contract or otherwise against any person for an act or omission of such person in the design, planning, supervision, observation or management of construction, or construction of an improvement to real property shall be commenced within 4 years from the time the person bringing an action, or his or her privity, knew or should reasonably have known of such act or omission.[12]

The statute also contains a period of repose:

> No action based upon tort, contract or otherwise may be brought against any person for an act or omission of such person in the design, planning, supervision, observation or management of construction, or construction of an improvement to real property after 10 years have elapsed from the time of such act or omission. However, any person who discovers such act or omission prior to expiration of 10 years from the time of such act or omission shall in no event have less than 4 years to bring an action as provided in Subsection (a) of this section.[13]

The Illinois statute of limitations has been held to be constitutional[14] in face of the argument that the statute sets up a particular favored class of persons to give better protection than all other persons for the same type of conduct. The court held that a reasonable basis exists for the special classification in the statute because it differentiates between people based on their activities, not their status.

However, other states have decided that such statutes are not constitutional,[15] and, therefore, reference must be made to the previously existing statutory scheme to determine the limitations period applicable to the particular cause of action.

---

[11] *See, e.g.,* Cal. Civ. Proc. Code §§ 337.1, .15 (West 1990); N.J. Stat. Ann. § 2A:14-1.1 (West 1990); Md. Cts. & Jud. Proc. Code Ann. § 5-108(b) (1990).

[12] Ill. Rev. Stat. ch. 110, para. 13-214(a) (1990).

[13] *Id.* para. 13-214(b).

[14] People *ex rel.* Skinner v. Hellmuth, Obata & Kassabaum, Inc., 114 Ill. 2d 252, 500 N.E.2d 234 (1986).

[15] *See, e.g.,* McClanahan v. American Gilsonite Co., 494 F. Supp. 1334 (D. Colo. 1980).

§ 23.8 When Statute Begins to Run

The Illinois statute of limitations begins to run when the claimant "knew or should reasonably have known" of the conduct in question. The same rule applies in many other states. However, some construction statutes of limitation begin to run upon completion of the project, and others will begin to run when the design professional's services are completed, regardless of whether the project is completed.[16]

There are cases dealing with the timing of when a party knew or should have known of the defect and, therefore, the statute of limitations began to run.[17] The courts in these cases have held that the statute does not commence running simply because there is some knowledge of the defect. If there are routine maintenance problems, for example, the claimant may have at least sufficient time to learn that the routine maintenance problems are not, in fact, routine. Knowledge that a roof leaked does not necessarily constitute knowledge of a wrongful act by someone involved in the construction of the roof which will commence the running of the statute.

In those statutes that refer to completion as the start date for commencement of running of the statute of limitations, some statutes refer to "substantial completion"; others refer simply to "completion." Some statutes define these terms, some do not. The statute should be checked for such definitions and, if none exist, reference should be made to case law to supply the definition.

§ 23.9 Persons Covered by Statute

The Illinois statute of limitations specifically covers persons while acting in the "design" or "planning" of a project, and therefore the design professional's conduct is within the category of persons who are covered by the statute. Broad language covering design professionals is contained in many other such statutes. However, some state statutes of limitation have more restrictive language. Again, reference must be made to the specific statutory scheme in place in the applicable state to determine if the design professional is within the protection of the statute of limitations.

---

[16] *See* N.J. Stat. Ann. § 2A:14-1.1 (West 1990).

[17] *See, e.g.,* Society of Mount Carmel v. Fox, 90 Ill. App. 3d 537, 413 N.E.2d 480 (1980); Knox College v. Cellotex Corp., 88 Ill. 2d 407, 430 N.E.2d 976 (1981).

§ 23.10 Type of Conduct Covered by Statute

The Illinois statute of limitations applies to actions based upon "tort, contract or otherwise," which is very broad language encompassing essentially any type of claim that could be brought. Most construction statutes of limitation contain similarly broad language, but not all.

Some of the more restrictive statutes are, for instance, limited to tort actions only. Some specifically exclude contract claims from those actions that are barred. Reference would then have to be made back to the specific contract statute of limitations present in the state's regulatory scheme to find the contract limitation period.

Construction litigation often involves claims by and against a number of different parties. Cross-claims and third-party claims for indemnification or contribution are typically made among the various parties. Some state statutes of limitation specifically cover actions for construction-related contribution or indemnification. For instance, the Maryland statute provides: "A cause of action for damages does not accrue and a person may not seek contribution or indemnity from any architect, professional engineer, or contractor for damages . . . resulting from a defective and unsafe condition of an improvement to real property."[18] However, most construction statutes of limitation are silent on contribution and indemnity.

Arbitration clauses are contained in many construction contracts. Some of these clauses contain rules relating to the time period within which arbitration must be commenced, others do not. If the construction contract does not contain limitation rules, reference likely will be made to the appropriate statute of limitations.[19] Some construction statutes of limitation specifically apply to arbitration.[20]

§ 23.11 The Future

It is difficult to predict what the future may hold for construction statutes of limitation. It seems safe to say that they will continue to be the subject of attack as special legislation favoring the construction industry, and it is possible that retroactivity rules as applied to court decisions will mean that limitations for particular conduct will change because of court decisions modifying or rejecting particular statutes.

---

[18] Md. Cts. & Jud. Proc. Code Ann. § 5-108(b) (1990).

[19] *See* Young v. Ross-Loos Medical Group, Inc., 135 Cal. App. 3d 669, 185 Cal. Rptr. 536 (1982).

[20] *See, e.g.*, R.I. Gen. Laws § 9-1-29 (1990).

The only course available to the design professional is to watch both legislative changes and the case law in the appropriate state or states and be aware of significant developments in those states.

IMMUNITY

§ 23.12 In General

Immunity grants a complete bar from liability regardless of the otherwise negligent conduct of the design professional. Immunity is a creature of public policy and is available to the design professional in very limited cases. The trend of the law is away from immunity.

There are several types of immunity that might apply to design professionals, including sovereign immunity, statutory immunity, and quasi-judicial immunity.

§ 23.13 Sovereign Immunity

Sovereign immunity may be available to both state and federal governments. For instance, immunity may be available under the Federal Tort Claims Act and similar state statutes for work done in connection with the performance of a "discretionary function or duty" of the government.[21]

This immunity has only limited application to the design professional. The design professional would have to be a government employee whose activities were related to "discretionary" activities. The discretionary part of a project is often limited to the initial decision to do something or not.[22] Immunity would apply to that decision alone. If the project were then implemented negligently, the immunity defense would not be available.

---

[21] 28 U.S.C.A. §§ 1346, 2671–78, 2680 (West 1982); *see also* Ill. Rev. Stat. ch. 85, para. 1-101 (1990); Fla. Stat. Ann. § 768.28 (West 1990).

[22] Neilson v. City of Tampa, 400 So. 2d 799 (Fla. Dist. Ct. App. 1981), *rev'd on other grounds*, 419 So. 2d 1071 (Fla. 1982).

§ 23.14 Statutory Immunity

Some states have statutes that grant immunity in specific situations. The statutes vary greatly from state to state, but are essentially limited to public projects.[23]

Much of the case law involves suits against governmental bodies rather than specific individuals. However, governmental employees who are public officials, such as city engineers or building inspectors, have been sued individually.[24] Immunity has been applied to protect the individuals as well as the governmental body, using an extension of the same public policy.

§ 23.15 Quasi-Judicial Immunity

A limited immunity may be available for design professionals performing services of a quasi-judicial nature during the course of their employment on private jobs.

The basis for this quasi-judicial immunity is once again public policy. It is based on the premise that a design professional is performing a quasi-judicial function when performing the role of an arbitrator of a dispute between other parties to a private contract. The public policy argument is that to allow the arbitrator to fulfill the role of resolving the types of disputes that result in arbitration, the arbitrator must be protected from liability for negligent actions.[25] However, if the charges against the design professional are above the level of negligence, such as willful conduct, immunity will not attach.[26]

This type of immunity has been carefully and cautiously applied by the courts, and only to the design professional's conduct as an arbitrator. The design professional's immunity for the decisions made as an arbitrator does not extend to such acts as delaying or not reaching a decision on the matter being arbitrated.[27]

---

[23] *See, e.g.,* Cal. Gov. Code § 830.6 (West 1990).

[24] *See, e.g.,* Thomas v. Mayor, 391 A.2d 203 (Del. 1978); DiMaggio v. O'Brien, 497 F. Supp. 870 (E.D. Pa. 1980).

[25] Craviolini v. Scholer & Fuller, 89 Ariz. 24, 357 P.2d 611 (1960).

[26] Lundgren v. Freeman, 307 F.2d 104 (9th Cir. 1962).

[27] E.C. Ernst, Inc. v. Manhattan Constr. Co., 551 F.2d 1026 (5th Cir. 1977), *cert. denied,* 434 U.S. 1067 (1978).

WORKERS' COMPENSATION LAWS

§ 23.16 In General

The principal role of workers' compensation laws is to give employees and their families a prompt, definite compensation, in a quick and efficient manner, for injuries or death suffered in the course of their employment and to ensure that the costs of these injuries are borne by the industry itself. The statutes provide financial protection for injured workers and their families. The workers typically may obtain an award without a showing of negligence by the employer or freedom from contributory negligence by the worker.

In return for this prompt, known, efficient handling of claims by workers against employers without complicated trials and determinations of fault, the workers' compensation laws generally give corresponding relief to employers, including design professionals, by granting them immunity from further suits by the employee. Workers' compensation laws set up a statutory scheme for payments to the injured employee. At the same time, workers' compensation laws extinguish the right of an employee to sue an employer for other remedies that might have been available under the common law, most notably a negligence action against the employer.

§ 23.17 Limitations

The injured employee must give notice to her employer that she has sustained an accidental injury arising from her employment within a relatively short period of time.[28]

Giving notice is typically jurisdictional by statute, but lack of notice is not always a strong defense. The governing authorities often have strained themselves to rule that notice was given. If the employer has knowledge from almost any source, notice may be ruled sufficient.[29]

§ 23.18 Third-Party Actions

The principle behind the workers' compensation laws' protection of the employer from common law rights of action is straightforward. In return

---

[28] *E.g.*, 45 days in Illinois, Ill. Rev. Stat. ch. 48, para. 138.6(c) (1990).

[29] *See, e.g.*, Cal. Lab. Code § 5402 (West 1990) ("Knowledge obtained from any source . . . is equivalent" to notice given by an employee).

for the employer's absolute liability for injuries that arise out of and in the course of the employment, the employee gives up her otherwise available statutory and common law rights of action against the employer for unintentional injuries arising out of and in the course of the employment.

However, the workers' compensation laws generally do not bar an employee from suing persons other than an employer for injuries arising out of work-related accidents even if the employee has been paid workers' compensation benefits or has rights to them.

Most states allow a third party sued by an employee for injuries arising from employment to bring a third-party action against the employer. This is generally in the form of an action for contribution by the employer. The doctrine of contribution among joint tortfeasors allows a nonemployer to obtain comparative contribution from the employer in tort actions when the employer was partially responsible for the plaintiff's injuries.[30]

To allow contribution among joint tortfeasors, the requirement that a third-party contributing defendant be liable in tort arising from the same injury does not prevent holding the employer liable for contribution, even though the workers' compensation laws provide an exclusive remedy for the employee against the employer.[31]

§ 23.19 Employer's Right to Subrogation and Compensation Lien

As an additional protection for the employer, workers' compensation laws typically give the employer a right in, and a lien against, the proceeds of an action that an employee might bring against a third party. Thus, the employee is not entitled to a windfall recovery from two sources: both the employer and the third party. If the employee is paid pursuant to the workers' compensation laws by the employer, and then the employee sues a third party, the employer is entitled to the first monies recovered by the employee up to the amount of the employer's lien. This fact creates a certain amount of protection for third parties. Employees are faced with tactical decisions as to whether they will bring an action against third parties or whether they will be satisfied with their workers' compensation claim. If it does not appear that a third-party action will bring sufficient proceeds to the employee to cover both the lien and the costs of proceeding, it is often in the best interests of the employee to walk away from the situation and be satisfied with the workers' compensation award. On the other hand, it is generally allowable for an employer to compromise its lien and thereby

[30] Skinner v. Reed-Prentice Div., Package Mach. Co., 70 Ill. 2d 1, 374 N.E.2d 437 (1977); Doyle v. Rhodes, 101 Ill. 2d 1, 461 N.E.2d 382 (1984).

[31] Gregory v. Garrett Corp., 578 F. Supp. 871 (S.D.N.Y. 1983).

encourage an employee to proceed against third parties because the employer will at least be entitled to the compromised amount of its payment. Additionally, the employer is usually entitled to institute an action on behalf of the employee within a certain time period if the employee elects not to do so.

WAIVER AND ESTOPPEL

§ 23.20 In General

Claims based upon contractual provisions against the design professional may be barred by waiver or estoppel.

A *waiver* occurs when one knowingly and voluntarily relinquishes one's contractual rights.[32] Thus, even if the design professional fails to satisfy certain contractual obligations, acceptance of performance by the other party may constitute waiver, and later attempts to claim inadequate performance by the design professional will be barred.

However, actions need not reach the level of acceptance, for a party who merely indicates that deviant performance would be acceptable may be deemed *estopped* from asserting a claim against the design professional.[33] For example, a contractor or owner who indicates to the design professional that work different from or inferior to that agreed to in the contract will be accepted is estopped from later claiming deviant performance if the design professional relied upon the earlier representations.[34]

Case law in these two areas usually involves disputes between owners and contractors,[35] but waiver and estoppel also should be useful defenses in disputes involving design professionals.[36]

However, waiver and estoppel are two-edged swords. The design professional must be careful not to waive contractual conditions by performance. For instance, if a design professional acts on verbal rather than written orders when written orders are required under the contract, the professional may be deemed to have waived the right to rely on the contract term.

---

[32] J. Calamari & J. Perillo, Contracts § 11-37 (2d ed. 1970).

[33] *Id.* § 11-34.

[34] *Id.*

[35] *See, e.g.,* Anderson Dev. Corp. v. Coastal States Crude Gathering Co., 543 S.W.2d 402 (Tex. 1976) (owner's actions in paying invoices constituted waiver of certain contractual provisions).

[36] *See* Newton Inv. Co. v. Barnard & Burk, Inc., 220 So. 2d 822 (Miss. 1969) (owner waived claim against engineering firm for negligent issuance of erroneous certificates).

§ 23.21 Architect's Certificate

An owner may waive a contract provision requiring that payment for a contractor's work be conditioned upon the issuance of a certificate by a design professional.[37] Such a waiver may occur if an owner accepts and takes possession of a building before the architect issues a certificate, and the owner knew or had reason to know the construction was defective or incomplete.[38] The owner also may waive the certificate requirement by continual failure to assert it. Thus, an owner who makes progress payments throughout the construction period without requiring an architect's certificate may be barred from asserting the requirement at a later time.[39]

Although these examples of the waiver doctrine concern the contractual rights of owners, the design professional should be aware of the implications of a failure to assert the certificate requirement. Moreover, a design professional with a greater interest in the project may be susceptible to the doctrine of waiver. In *Hartford Electric Applicators, Inc. v. Alden,* an architect who was also a partial owner-contractor and codefendant waived the certificate requirement on behalf of all of the owner-contractors by his failure to inspect the work of the subcontractors.[40]

INDEMNITY AND HOLD-HARMLESS AGREEMENTS

§ 23.22 In General

A claim for indemnity is a demand that another party bear the responsibility for damages based upon either a contractual right to be indemnified or an implied right arising from the common law.

There are two types of indemnity that have been traditionally recognized by courts throughout the country: *express indemnity* (arising from some kind of contractual undertaking) and *implied indemnity* (implied by the court because of the circumstances of the case).

[37] Restatement (Second) of Contracts § 303 (1932).

[38] Creith Lumber v. Cummins, 163 Ohio St. 220, 126 N.E.2d 323 (1955).

[39] Palmer v. Watson Constr. Co., 121 N.W.2d 62 (Minn. 1963).

[40] 169 Conn. 177, 363 A.2d 135 (1975).

§ 23.23 Express Indemnity

Contractual indemnification provisions and agreements to hold other parties harmless have been used for many years in many situations, including construction contracts. Such indemnification provisions are matters for negotiation between the parties, including design professionals, and will be interpreted according to the normal rules of construction under the law of the appropriate state.

The indemnification may be limited to amounts of damages that may, in the future, be awarded based upon certain conduct, or it may extend to include obligations to assume the defense of an action, including attorneys' fees. Obviously, the high cost of construction litigation can make this type of provision very important.

The party seeking indemnification should make a request for indemnification pursuant to the contract to the indemnifying party, including a request to take over defense of the case if that is appropriate. If the request is denied, the design professional seeking indemnity must comply with the provisions of the indemnification agreement and the rules of the state in which indemnity is sought to see how much time there is to act and what type of action must be taken. Typically, the design professional will have to file a cross-claim or third-party claim against the indemnifying party if a lawsuit is already under way or, if no lawsuit has been filed, the design professional may have the option of filing a declaratory judgment action seeking a court's declaration that indemnification is owed.

§ 23.24 Indemnification for One's Own Negligence

It is important before negotiating an express indemnification agreement to investigate the law of the jurisdiction that will apply to the agreement to see if there is anything which might render such an agreement void as against public policy. For instance, Illinois, Maryland, and Pennsylvania, among other states, have statutory prohibitions against indemnification clauses whereby one person agrees to indemnify another person for that person's own acts of negligence.[41]

The Illinois Indemnity Act provides that: "With respect to contracts . . . for the construction, alteration, repair or maintenance of a building, structure, . . . or other work dealing with construction, . . . every covenant, promise or agreement to indemnify or hold harmless another person from that person's own negligence is void as against public policy and

[41] Ill. Rev. Stat. ch. 29, para. 61 (1990); Md. Cts. & Jud. Proc. Code Ann. § 5-305 (1990); Pa. Stat. Ann. tit. 68, § 491 (Purdon 1990).

wholly unenforceable." This statute was upheld in *Davis v. Commonwealth Edison Co.*[42] against a constitutional challenge. The supreme court noted that the statute:

> serves to protect workers in the [construction] industry and the public as well from dangers associated with construction work. This statute would thwart attempts to avoid the consequences of liability and thereby ensure a continuing motivation for persons responsible for construction activities to take accident prevention measures and provide safe working conditions.[43]

Thus, even express indemnification provisions, no matter how clearly written, can fail for public policy reasons in some jurisdictions.

If an indemnification clause requires the indemnitor to indemnify for the indemnitee's own acts of negligence, the entire clause may be void. A contractual indemnity claim would be dismissible if based, even in part, on the design professional's own negligence.

The design professional would like to be indemnified for damages from any accident occurring on the job involving bodily injuries or property damage, because safety is usually the responsibility of the contractor, not the design professional. However, if a statutory prohibition against indemnity exists, it may be difficult for the design professional to obtain such protection. If a claim is filed against the design professional based on the professional's action, the complaint would have to allege some kind of negligence or statutory violation. A statute prohibiting indemnification for one's own negligence would thus render the contractual clause void.[44]

It may be possible to avoid the statutory prohibition by requiring the contractor to provide insurance for the design professional. Courts have held that this type of contract does not violate public policy even though the court would be forcing the contractor to essentially assume the role of indemnifying the design professional for its own negligence if the contractor breaches the contract.[45]

§ 23.25 Implied Indemnity

The law often has implied a contract of indemnity in favor of a person who, without her own fault, was placed in a position of possible liability to another by the act or omission of some other person. Such implied indemnity must be clearly justified by the facts present in the case.

---

[42] 61 Ill. 2d 494, 336 N.E.2d 881 (1975).

[43] 336 N.E.2d at 884.

[44] Lloyd C. Ryan v. EAI Constr. Corp., 158 Ill. App. 3d 449, 511 N.E.2d 1244 (1987); Bethlehem Steel v. G.C. Zarnas & Co., 304 Md. 183, 498 A.2d 605 (1985).

[45] Zettel v. Paschea Contractors, Inc., 100 Ill. App. 3d 614, 427 N.E.2d 189 (1981).

Indemnity has been applied primarily to negligence actions when the right to indemnity is not based on a theory of comparative negligence and does not require liability to be apportioned according to comparative fault. Indemnity between tortfeasors has been available when there is a qualitative difference between the negligence of the parties.

When implied indemnity is awarded, it is usually in favor of a person who has been "passively" or "secondarily" negligent in comparison to a second party who has been found to be "actively" or "primarily" negligent towards the third-party claimant. Indemnity is not allowed if the "passively" negligent party is held to have committed any "actively" negligent acts.

In those states where the doctrine of contribution or comparative negligence is applied, the active/passive indemnification theories are restricted, or wholly disallowed, by the courts.

CONTRIBUTORY NEGLIGENCE AND ASSUMPTION OF RISK

§ 23.26 Contributory Negligence

For years, contributory negligence was a defense to claims based on negligence. *Contributory negligence* is conduct essentially amounting to a breach of the duty to exercise reasonable care for one's own safety.[46] Contributory negligence constituted a complete bar to recovery against a claim based on negligence even if the contributory negligence was only slight.[47] However, most jurisdictions have replaced the doctrine of contributory negligence with some form of *comparative negligence* or *comparative fault.* Thus, the harsh rule abolishing claims in their entirety even if a claimant was guilty of a very small percentage of contributory fault has been removed.

To prove the defense of contributory negligence, a defendant must prove that:

1. The claimant failed to exercise the degree of care that a reasonably prudent person would have exercised when acting under similar circumstances
2. The claimant's conduct was a proximate cause of the claimant's injury.

---

[46] *See* Board of Water Works Trustees v. Alvord, Burdick & Howson, 706 F.2d 820 (8th Cir. 1983).

[47] Restatement (Second) of Torts § 467 (1965).

Contributory negligence is generally an affirmative defense that must be raised in an answer or by motion.

§ 23.27 Assumption of Risk

Assumption of the risk is a defense to negligence actions and, in some jurisdictions, strict product liability actions. Assumption of the risk is found in the conduct of a claimant who voluntarily and unreasonably exposes herself to a known danger.[48]

To prove assumption of the risk, it must be shown that the claimant actually knew of the danger and the risk of injury. This may be difficult, because a claimant seldom will admit that she actually knew of a particular danger and risk of injury. The best case for application of the doctrine of assumption of the risk is when a particular danger is open and obvious or commonly known, or when the proof is very strong that the claimant was a knowledgeable user.

Assumption of the risk is established by proving that the claimant knew and appreciated the danger; that she voluntarily encountered it; and that her decision to do so was unreasonable.[49]

Assumption of the risk is an affirmative defense that must be pleaded in an answer or by motion.

CONTRIBUTION AND COMPARATIVE NEGLIGENCE

§ 23.28 In General

Rights of contribution among joint tortfeasors may be created by statute or by case law. In either situation, the law establishes a right of contribution in favor of one person against another person whose tortious action contributed to the injury to the claimant.

Contribution does not affect the common law right of a claimant to recover the full amount of a judgment from any one of multiple tortfeasors. Rather, contribution creates rights among the various joint tortfeasors to recover payments in excess of their pro rata share of the joint liability.

Contribution is not available in all situations involving defendants who are jointly responsible for a claimant's injury. Contribution is generally

---

[48] Restatement (Second) of Torts § 496A (1965).

[49] *Id.* §§ 496D, 496E.

available only among joint tortfeasors. Thus, the economic loss doctrine (see § **23.5**), which may bar certain types of negligence actions, also may preclude contribution rights.

§ 23.29 Effect of Contribution and Comparative Negligence on Liability

Contribution and comparative negligence modify the harsher doctrines of contributory negligence and implied indemnity. In both instances, those rules would completely bar recovery by a party based on its actions contributing to the damage, even if the contribution was only slight. In the case of contributory negligence, plaintiff's claim would be completely barred; in the case of implied indemnity, the otherwise passively negligent defendant would have its implied indemnification rights barred.

Contribution is now used in many states, including New York, California, and Illinois,[50] to apportion relative fault among all the parties to an action.

The way this works in a typical lawsuit is to allow the judge or jury to allocate responsibility for particular injuries among all the parties. Thus, if a claimant sues both the design professional and a general contractor for injuries sustained as a result of problems encountered at the project which were caused in part by both the design professional and the contractor, a determination will be made of the percentage of responsibility attributable to each of those parties. The percentage, if any, of responsibility attributable to the claimant also will be decided. In situations in which the claimant was even slightly responsible, contribution changes the results of the lawsuit enormously because contributory negligence is no longer a bar. Therefore, the claimant is not barred from recovery simply because she was partly responsible for her own injury.

The design professional and the general contractor would be entitled to contribution from each other. The net effect is that each will pay a pro rata share of the total amount of damages reduced by the percentage of fault attributable to the claimant. This shows how contribution changes the previously existing "active/passive" implied indemnification rules because the mere fact of active negligence contributing to the injury on the part of the design professional no longer bars the ability to recover proportionally from the general contractor. In essence, the contribution laws are an effort to establish a fair way to allocate the costs for a particular injury among the parties responsible for the injury.

As noted, until recently, many states used the theory of contributory negligence. Under this body of law, a claimant whose contributory negligence

---

[50] New York: N.Y. Civ. Prac. L. & R. 1401 (McKinney 1990); California: Cal. Civ. Proc. Code § 875 (West 1990); Illinois: Ill. Rev. Stat. ch. 70, para. 301 (1990).

was a partial cause for its injuries, no matter how slight, was barred from recovery against any other negligent parties. This harsh rule has been abrogated in those states that have adopted the doctrine of *comparative negligence,* which provides that claimants who are partially at fault will no longer be barred from all recovery. Rather, the degree to which the claimant's negligence contributed to the injury proportionally reduces the amount of compensation.

CONTRACTUAL DEFENSES

§ 23.30 In General

The design professional may attempt by contract to eliminate or to limit liability for certain types of damages or for damages flowing from certain types of activity. Generally, these limitation provisions will be upheld if they are the subject of fair bargaining and do not violate other laws, such as the laws against indemnification for one's own negligence.

The purpose of these clauses is to provide a reasonable basis for a design professional to evaluate the risks of agreeing to perform certain services for a fee. Often, the fee is low in relation to the potential liability flowing from the services to be performed. Accordingly, the professional may try to limit exposure and, at the same time, try to obtain indemnification for other parts of that exposure.

§ 23.31 Specific Areas of Application

Areas in which contractual limitations are typically negotiated include damages for delay, damages flowing from environmental aspects of the project, contractual provisions specifically defining the design professional's services to limit liability for claims not within those services, and provisions reducing or eliminating claims for consequential damages.

In addition, clauses embodying liquidated damages concepts or limiting liability for certain claims to a specific amount or a specific portion of the design professional's fee are frequently the subject of negotiation and may be enforceable.

It is important to remember that these contractual limitations generally will only work to limit the design professional's liability to the contracting party. They generally will not limit liability to third parties, particularly for personal injuries.

CHAPTER 24

DESIGN PROFESSIONAL'S RIGHTS AND REMEDIES WHEN OWNER BREACHES CONTRACT

Mark C. Friedlander

Mark C. Friedlander is a partner in the law firm of Schiff Hardin & Waite in Chicago. He received his B.A. from the University of Michigan in 1978 and his J.D. from Harvard Law School in 1981. He has been an adjunct professor at the University of Illinois at Chicago School of Architecture and a lecturer at the Illinois Institute of Technology School of Civil Engineering and the Engineering School of the University of Wisconsin. Mr. Friedlander is the author of numerous publications on various topics of architecture, engineering, and construction law. He concentrates his law practice in construction and litigation consulting and representation of design professionals.

§ 24.1 Owner's Obligations under Typical Contract

In a typical contract for architectural or engineering services, the client has very few obligations. (For purposes of this chapter, it is assumed that the design professional is working directly for the owner, but most of the discussion remains valid regardless of the identity of the client.) Obviously, the client's primary obligation is to pay the design professional for his services. Most of this chapter examines what the architect or engineer can do when a client refuses to pay fully for design professional services.

An owner is generally responsible for providing information regarding the property and the project. During the programming phase of the project, information regarding the owner's criteria and intended uses ordinarily comes from the owner, and the architect or engineer cannot proceed with the design without this information. Similarly, owners are frequently responsible for providing reports of investigations performed by other consultants, including surveys, geotechnical reports, environmental reports, and construction cost analyses, as well as legal, accounting, and insurance information.

An owner frequently has additional obligations in the contract with the design professional. The owner may be obligated to purchase and maintain various insurance policies and to name the design professional as an additional insured on those policies; is usually responsible for the coordination of multiple prime contractors; and may be obligated to provide the design professional with access to the finished project for promotional purposes and/or to give the architect or engineer appropriate credit on publicly released materials or the construction sign. The owner/architect agreement also may be worded in such a way as to require the owner to include certain language and provisions in the construction contract. For example, the owner may have agreed to put clauses in the construction contract concerning indemnification or insurance requirements.

Sections 24.2 through **24.5** describe the rules of law governing performance and breach of contracts in the context of an owner's failure to make payment. However, the same principles apply to the owner's breach of any contract provision.

§ 24.2 Basic Contract Law

The law of contracts is part of the common law that America inherited from England in colonial times. Although the law of contracts can be traced back to medieval England (and beyond) and is recognized in virtually every American jurisdiction, it is not a federal law. Except when the federal government is a party, contract law is a part of and depends on the law of each state. The laws and rules that the courts of each state follow are generally uniform, but certain states may have developed specific doctrines or interpretations that differ in subtle ways from those of other states. Accordingly, the contract law principles discussed in this chapter are the common, uniform principles that virtually every jurisdiction follows. However, if specific contract-related issues arise, it is advisable to consult with counsel to determine precisely how a particular jurisdiction interprets and implements the rules and laws described.

§ 24.3 —Types of Contracts

The common concept of a contract is a detailed, written agreement with signature lines at the end. This is one type of contract, but there are three other types which, although not in writing, are equally enforceable if their existence and validity can be established.

One is an *oral contract,* in which the design professional verbally agrees to perform services and the owner verbally agrees to pay for them. Another kind of contract is an *implied contract,* which may be inferred from the circumstances and relationship of the parties, even without any express communications regarding payment or the professional services to be performed. For example, a patient treated in a doctor's office is required to pay the doctor for his services, despite the fact that a contract was never discussed.

The final way of expressing a contract does not really involve a contract at all. Called *quantum meruit,* this legal theory allows a design professional to recover the reasonable value of services performed on another's behalf even without any kind of agreement or understanding with that person.

It is commonly thought that a written contract is ineffective unless both parties have signed it. However, there are other ways to accept and be bound by a written contract without signing it. For example, a written contract can be accepted and agreed to orally, if the party who is sent a contract with one signature says to the other party, "I accept the contract," or words to that effect.

More commonly, a written contract may be accepted by action or performance in accordance with its terms. For example, if the owner, after receiving the contract, authorizes the design professional to proceed and begins making payments under the terms of the contract, the owner ordinarily will be held to have accepted the contract and all of its terms. In one case, a court upheld an arbitration award against a developer pursuant to the arbitration clause in the contract despite the fact that the developer had not signed the contract, because he had authorized the architect to proceed to render services and provided information and made payments to the architect according to the terms of the contract.[1]

In general, oral contracts and implied contracts are just as enforceable as written contracts. The difficulty is ascertaining the precise terms of the contract. The terms that would be set forth in black and white in a written contract may be the subject of disputed or contradictory testimony at trial when the contract is not in writing. This leads to greater uncertainty as to what the judge, jury, or arbitrator will rule.

There are certain specific instances in which a contract will not be enforceable unless it is in writing. These circumstances are set forth in the legal rule called the *statute of frauds.* The statute of frauds requires a contract to be in (or evidenced in) writing if it is for the purchase of goods (not services) valued at more than $500, if it cannot by its terms be performed in less than a year's time, or if the contract calls for one person to guarantee the debt of another. Very few contracts for professional architectural or engineering services fall within these categories.

Even if there is no valid contract between a client and a design professional, the latter is still entitled to be paid the reasonable value of any professional services rendered. The law discourages unjust enrichment, and a client would be unjustly enriched if the benefit and value of services were received without having to pay for them merely because no valid contract existed. Under the doctrine of quantum meruit, the owner is obligated to pay the "reasonable value" of one's services, which may be measured by a regular hourly rate or the economic value of the services to the owner.

Of course, there is bound to be a disagreement about the "reasonable value" of professional services. The client is likely to claim that the services were of little or no value to him for one reason or another, while the design professional values them at usual hourly rates. Therefore, it is preferable to have a clear and detailed written contract for professional services.

What is the reasonable value of professional services if, for example, the owner never goes ahead with the project? The owner will claim that

---

[1] Landmark Properties, Inc. v. Architects Int'l, 172 Ill. App. 3d 379, 526 N.E.2d 603 (1988).

the services were worthless because they did not improve the value of the property, whereas the design professional put time and effort into preparing the plans and specifications. In this situation, the law ordinarily allows a design professional to recover a reasonable hourly rate for the services provided. The usual reasoning is that the property has been made more valuable; it can be improved without having to prepare a new set of plans and specifications. An architect or engineer, as a professional, is paid for the time and effort invested in a project regardless of the ultimate outcome, just as a doctor is paid even though the patient is not cured.

§ 24.4 —Damages When Contract Is Breached

The law does not automatically award a remedy to the innocent party when the other party breaches the contract, even if the breach is deliberate. The law of contracts is not punitive; no one is fined or otherwise punished for breaking a contract. The nonbreaching party is only entitled to compensation if he was harmed or injured in some way by the breach of contract.

This is why the law will recognize a *liquidated damages* clause in a construction contract but will refuse to enforce a virtually identical *penalty clause.* A proper liquidated damages clause recites that breach of the contract (frequently by delay) would almost certainly result in economic loss but that the amount of the loss would be difficult to quantify, and therefore the liquidated damages clause contains a reasonable estimate of the damages to which the parties agree to be bound. In contrast, a penalty clause seeks to create a financial incentive to avoid a breach of the contract (usually late completion) by assessing a fine for the breach, which may or may not have any relationship to actual damages suffered. Most courts will enforce a liquidated damages clause as being a reasonable approximation of actual damages while refusing to enforce a penalty clause on the grounds that penalties unrelated to actual damages are inappropriate in the context of contract law.

The legal theory that virtually every court will try to apply when a contract has been breached is to place the innocent party in the same position that he would have been in had the contract not been breached. Usually this involves an award of money damages. However, in certain circumstances, such as when unique commodities are involved, the court will enter a formal order requiring the breaching party to perform the conditions of the contract. This kind of remedy is called *specific performance.*

Generally, when the owner breaches a contract with an architect or engineer, the breach is a failure to make payment. Thus, an award of money damages ordinarily should compensate a design professional adequately for the owner's breach. A design professional will virtually never be able to obtain a court order forcing the owner to continue to perform the contract, such as by rehiring an architectural or engineering firm that the owner wrongfully terminated.

However, some of the client's duties are unique, possibly justifying a court order of compliance. For example, if an owner refuses to allow the design professional to photograph the completed project for promotional purposes, despite agreeing to allow such photographs in the contract, a court might consider such photographs sufficiently unique to justify an award of specific performance. It is difficult to predict what the financial impact of the promotional photographs would be, so the only adequate remedy may be a court order permitting the photographs to be taken.

The obvious question is: How large an award of monetary damages would the design professional be entitled to? For example, if an owner wrongly terminated an architectural/engineering (A/E) firm exactly in the middle of a $50,000 contract after paying the firm $25,000, to what damages, if any, would the firm be entitled? This is a more difficult question than it might at first seem.

When a court awards money damages for a breach of contract, there are three theories it can use for calculating the damages. By far the most common and preferred theory is *expectation damages.* The goal of this theory is to place the innocent party in the same position it would have been in but for the breach of contract. However, sometimes it is difficult to determine what would have happened in the absence of the breach of contract. In such cases, a court may award the innocent party a sum equal to its costs or losses incurred because of the contract (known as the *reliance theory* of damages) or the benefits that accrued to the breaching party as a result of the contract (known as the *restitution theory* of damages).

Damage awards for breach of contract sometimes contain components intended to compensate the innocent party for the time and cost involved in prosecuting a lawsuit to recover the damages. One frequent component of damage awards is interest on unpaid sums. If the contract stipulates a rate and method of calculating interest, the courts ordinarily will enforce the provision and add interest to any award of damages. Usually, however, the rate of interest must be somewhat reasonably related to the actual time value of the money and not be so high as to be considered penal or usurious. Even if the contract is silent about interest, many jurisdictions have statutes for calculating interest in the absence of a contractual provision both before and after the court renders judgment, at least when there has been a wrongful refusal to pay. Nevertheless, it is wise to make sure the contract contains an interest provision in the case of nonpayment which specifies a rate equal to or higher than that at which money is actually borrowed, because the statutory rates in most jurisdictions are unrealistically low.

Most jurisdictions will award the successful litigant the costs incurred in prosecuting the lawsuit, including filing fees and costs of transcripts. However, the largest component of the cost of prosecuting a lawsuit, the attorneys' fees, are rarely awarded. There are only three instances in which a court can award the prevailing party reimbursement for attorneys' fees: (1) when an applicable statute provides for recovery of attorneys' fees; (2) when the contract provides for reimbursement of attorneys' fees; or (3) when the court finds that the unsuccessful party or its attorney has conducted the lawsuit in such bad faith that the court awards attorneys' fees as a sanction. Therefore, it is prudent to provide in the contract that in a suit to collect unpaid fees, the design professional is entitled to be reimbursed for attorneys' fees.

In the example of the owner who terminated an A/E firm exactly in the middle of a $50,000 contract after paying the firm $25,000, assume that the owner did not have the contractual right to terminate the firm and therefore breached the contract. The court will try to place the A/E firm in the same position it would have been in if it had not been terminated. This does *not* mean that the firm would be entitled to the remaining $25,000; otherwise, it would be unjustly enriched by earning the remainder of the fee without performing the work. The proper award of damages is the remaining $25,000 fee, less the cost to the firm of completing the work. Translated, this would be equivalent to any lost profit, plus unabsorbed overhead, less any savings that accrued to the firm as a result of not having to perform the work. If appropriate, the court would add interest at the contractual or statutory rate on any unpaid sums, plus court costs.

If a client breaches a contract by failing to make timely payments, the second party is entitled to cease or suspend performing its obligations under the contract as well unless or until the breach is cured. The design professional who suspends performance would refuse to continue the design process, send plans or specifications to the client, make additional site visits, sign the lender's certificate, or approve the contractor's applications for payments.

If a client stops making payments, the choice of whether or not to cease performance is the design professional's. One may choose for business or other reasons to continue performing services under the contract, and the right to past or future payments is not lost by doing so. In fact, before deciding to cease performance, one should make certain that the client's nonpayment is wrongful and unjustified under the terms of the contract. If the nonpayment was permissible under the contract and the design professional ceases performance, then it is the A/E who has breached the contract and will be liable to the client for any adverse consequences resulting from delayed performance.

In most jurisdictions, architects and engineers have a special remedy available to make sure they get paid. This remedy is the mechanic's lien. Although many design professionals regularly review contractors' waivers of lien, they are frequently unaware that the same remedy is available to them.

A *mechanic's lien* is a right against a certain piece of property to use that property to secure payment. It is like a mortgage lien. If the client does not make payment, the architect ultimately can have the land sold and use the proceeds to satisfy his fees. The rules governing mechanic's liens vary from state to state, and they are discussed in detail in **Chapter 25**.

It is important not to confuse contract termination with a breach of the contract. Most contracts have *termination clauses* that describe how and under what circumstances either or both of the parties can terminate the contract before its completion. If a client uses the termination clause to terminate a contract before completion, he is merely exercising a bargained-for right and has not breached the contract. The details of compensation in the event of termination should be spelled out in the termination clause.

§ 24.5 —Defenses to Claims for Breach of Contract

When a design professional makes a claim against a client for failure to pay, the client may have certain legal defenses available in addition to simply denying the design professional's version of the facts. These defenses ordinarily go to the enforceability of the underlying contract, and if a defense is successful, then the contract, or the relevant part of the contract, would not be enforceable.

One such defense is the *statute of limitations,* that the claim is barred by the passage of time. Statutes of limitation often consist of two different statutes: a statute of repose (the number of years after a breach of contract in which the claim must be brought) and the statute of limitations (the number of years after discovering the claim during which it must be brought). Statutes of limitation vary from state to state, but many states have adopted a special statute of limitations applicable to construction projects. Some states have held the special statutes to be unconstitutional, but most have not. The design professional should become familiar with the law in the appropriate states to be aware of the extent of the client's and the A/E's legal rights.

Another defense to a claim for breach of contract is that the contract itself is illegal. Specific terms in the contract may violate statutory requirements. For instance, a 25 percent annual rate of interest would be considered usurious and illegal in many jurisdictions. Many well-drafted contracts contain a *severability clause,* which states that if certain provisions are declared illegal, the other provisions would remain unaffected.

Another way in which a contract for architectural or engineering services could be illegal is if the architect or engineer is not properly licensed. Every state licenses architects and engineers and deems it illegal for someone not properly licensed to contract to perform professional services. In some states, corporations are not permitted to practice architecture or engineering or else must meet certain additional requirements before they can be licensed. In theory, a client may be able to avoid payment by claiming that the contract is illegal because the firm has breached some technical requirement of the applicable licensing act. Other states, however, do not recognize this to be a defense to payment, holding that only the state government has the authority to enforce the licensing laws.

Another legal defense to a claim for breach of contract is that the contract was founded upon a mutual mistake of fact. The courts will not recognize the validity of a contract if both parties entered into it on the same mistaken assumption of fact. For example, if an A/E firm and an owner innocently sign an architectural contract on the mistaken assumption that the soil of the property is suitable for building, either party can seek to have the contract declared void on the grounds of mutual mistake of fact. Courts ordinarily will not use this doctrine to sanctify unjust results; if the A/E firm had partially performed the contract, the court would ordinarily award it proportional fees but declare the contract void for any future work.

Another defense to a design professional's claim for payment is a counterclaim for professional malpractice. This is an affirmative claim against the A/E alleging negligent performance of professional services, entitling the owner to offset the payment owed to the A/E by the amount of damages allegedly suffered from the malpractice. The rules governing claims of malpractice against a design professional are covered in **Chapter 7**. However, sophisticated judges and arbitrators know that a sizable counterclaim for malpractice is usually less credible when the owner does not bother to assert the claim until after the design professional has filed a claim for his fees.

§ 24.6 Filing a Claim

When a design professional has a claim for unpaid fees or anything else, the most difficult decision is usually whether or not to pursue it. There are a large number of factors that go into such a decision, some of which are quantifiable and tangible, others of which are intangible personal or emotional factors.

One should consider a claim to be nothing more or less than an asset, and one should determine whether to pursue the claim in the same manner one would determine whether to invest in any asset. If the likely gain outweighs the likely loss, then the investment in the claim is economically worthwhile.

An attorney should be consulted to calculate the likely gains and losses. On the positive side of the equation is the amount the A/E is likely to win multiplied by the likelihood of winning and collecting. On the negative side is the cost of prosecuting the lawsuit, consisting primarily of attorneys' fees and interruption of one's business. If the positive side of the equation is greater than the negative side, then the claim should be pursued.

For example, suppose a client owes $20,000 for services performed. After discussions with an attorney, the design professional concludes that he is two-thirds likely to prevail but that the average cost to prosecute this type of claim would be $10,000 to $15,000. Two-thirds of $20,000 is $13,333, which is approximately the cost of litigating the case. That means pursuing this claim is close to an even proposition economically.

This formula is a guideline only. It can be made considerably more sophisticated by multiplying other possible results by their coefficients of likeliness, by including the effect of any counterclaims the client may have, and by various fee arrangements that can be made with an attorney.

Once the design professional decides to file a claim, the next decision is where to file it. It is ordinarily an advantage to file a claim in the location where one works. Not only is it more economical to litigate on "home turf," but fact finders are sometimes biased in favor of local firms and people.

The decision of whether to file a lawsuit in state or federal court is governed in part by rules of jurisdiction. With rare exceptions, a party can litigate in federal court only if the party being sued is a federal entity or is from a different state and more than $50,000 is at stake. The advantages and disadvantages of federal and state court depend on certain factors unique to the courts. Following are some general considerations:

Federal courts usually have a smaller ratio of cases per judge than state courts in the same district.

Some state court judges are elected or serve fixed terms, making them vulnerable to political pressure.

Federal court is often more formal and scholarly than state court.

It is easier for a case filed in federal court to be transferred to another state than for a case filed in state court.

One may be able to choose the state in which to file the lawsuit. Typically, a lawsuit is filed in the state where the project is located. However, it may be possible and advantageous to file the lawsuit somewhere else, such as in one's home state.

After deciding in which state to file the lawsuit, one may have to choose a particular court system within the state. Especially in states with distinct urban and rural areas, the court systems and the procedures they follow may be quite different. For example, in Illinois, the Chicago (Cook

County) court system is very different from the "downstate" courts or those in surrounding counties. The Cook County Circuit Court is extremely large and unusually structured so that different judges hear different aspects of a single case. The demographic characteristics of the population and, therefore, of potential jurors are different from courts in more rural areas. The caseload per judge is heavier than in the other court systems of the state.

Even if a claim must be decided in arbitration, one still may be able to choose where to file the claim. The American Arbitration Association (AAA), whose procedures are incorporated in the standard American Institute of Architects (AIA) forms, has offices in most major cities. The arbitration clause in a contract can specify the place of the hearing. Typically, in the absence of an agreement specifying a particular location, the arbitration proceeding takes place in the major city nearest to the project. However, the first party to file a demand for arbitration plays the major role in determining the venue of the claim.

The locale for resolving any claims can be specified in the contract. Both courts and arbitrators ordinarily defer to any choice of location specified in the parties' contract.

The location in which the claim is litigated does not necessarily determine which state's law will govern the dispute. A court in one state can legally apply the law of another state to the resolution of a dispute before it. This state law normally will be that of the state in which the project is located, but the parties to the contract may specify that a different state's law will apply provided that the state has some reasonable interest in the performance of the contract.

§ 24.7 Litigation Process

A lawsuit is initiated with a summons and complaint. The complaint is the document stating one's legal claim and requesting the courts to enter judgment in one's favor. The summons is the document that notifies the other party of the lawsuit being filed and is usually served by a sheriff, a process server, or certified mail.

Most jurisdictions give the defendant 20 to 30 days to respond to the complaint. Extensions of time are routinely allowed. The defendant may respond in several ways. He may move to dismiss the complaint, claiming that even if the allegations are accurate, the law does not recognize such a claim; he may file an answer to the complaint, admitting some factual allegations and denying others; or he may file a counterclaim, which is the equivalent of his own lawsuit against the plaintiff. He also has the option of filing third-party claims, which are lawsuits against other parties arising out of the same circumstances as the plaintiff's lawsuit.

The most expensive part of a lawsuit is usually *pretrial discovery.* Discovery involves the production and review of documents, the posing and answering of written questions called *interrogatories,* and the giving and taking of *depositions,* or oral testimony under oath outside the presence of the judge or jury. Most jurisdictions allow relatively free reign in the discovery process, which can therefore be extensive, time consuming, and an invasion of privacy. Before trial, the court ordinarily will hold status hearings, pretrial conferences, and hearings on various motions that the parties may bring to resolve procedural disputes and issues. Some judges view these pretrial conferences as purely administrative, while other courts use them as bargaining sessions to try to reach settlement. The procedures frequently vary from judge to judge, and the only way to know what to expect is to consult with an experienced local attorney.

One especially important kind of pretrial motion is the *motion for summary judgment,* which seeks to have a judge decide the case without a trial on the grounds that there are no disputed issues of fact to resolve. Summary judgment is a powerful tool for resolving disputes quickly and relatively inexpensively. However, it is not available if each side's position is that the other is factually wrong.

Current statistics indicate that less than 1 in every 100 lawsuits is decided by a trial. Most cases are settled before trial, and most of the rest are either dismissed or have judgment entered before trial. Trials are a complicated and sometimes unsatisfactory method of resolving disputes, relying on formal procedures and rules of evidence that often complicate the fact-finding procedure.

One important decision that must be made is whether or not to ask for a jury. When a judge sits without a jury, he finds both the facts and the law. When a jury is present, the jury decides what the facts are and the judge instructs the jury in the applicable law.

In most lawsuits to collect fees, the plaintiff does not request a jury. These are called *bench trials.* Bench trials are faster and therefore usually less expensive than jury trials. A judge is a professional fact finder, whereas a juror hears one case only. Judges are typically better educated than jurors and have more experience in distilling the actual facts from the testimony.

There are, however, some advantages to jury trials. At least in theory, a jury of 12 people is less likely to be biased or arbitrary than a single judge. A jury is more likely than a judge to decide based on "what is fair" rather than based strictly on what the law requires. A jury may treat the case as more important and give it more consideration than a judge who hears hundreds of trials. If there is damaging but inadmissible evidence against a party, a jury will not be allowed to hear it, whereas a judge must hear it first to determine whether it is admissible.

The author prefers a bench trial for a winning case and a jury trial otherwise. Jury trials seem to produce less easily predictable results than trials in front of judges, and it is easier for a lawyer to confuse or obfuscate an issue in front of a jury than in front of a judge.

After a judgment is rendered, either after trial or upon a motion, the lawsuit is not automatically terminated. The losing party always has a right of appeal. Depending on the jurisdiction, the parties must file their notice of appeal within 20 to 30 days of the entry of judgment, after which briefs are filed and an oral argument is made to the appellate court.

The appellate court then issues a written opinion. However, it will only review issues of law and will not reweigh the evidence or substitute its judgment for that of the finder of fact. An appeal is just an opportunity to correct a legal mistake the trial court may have made; it is not an opportunity to retry the case.

An alternative court for small claims is available in many jurisdictions. The rules vary from state to state. A plaintiff ordinarily represents himself without a lawyer and the courts only have jurisdiction to hear claims for relatively small amounts, usually $5,000 or less. The procedural rules are simplified and shortened. Small claims court may be the only means of cost-effectively litigating small claims.

An alternative to the court system is binding arbitration.[2] A dispute is arbitrable only if the parties agree to arbitrate it. This agreement is usually written into the contract for professional services. However, the parties could agree to arbitrate a dispute after it arises even though there is no arbitration clause in the contract.

Furthermore, the dispute must be within the scope of the arbitration agreement. Standard form contracts contain a broad arbitration clause which essentially states that any dispute between the parties pertaining to the contract or project must be resolved in arbitration. However, the arbitration clause may be drafted more narrowly to provide that only certain kinds of claims are arbitrable.

Arbitration is a simplified and streamlined version of courtroom litigation. It is initiated by a demand for arbitration, which is similar to a complaint. There are preliminary and evidentiary hearings, after which the fact finder(s) renders a binding award. However, the parties select the fact finder(s) according to the arbitration rules they have agreed upon.

Opinions are mixed on whether arbitration is a superior alternative to litigation. Although arbitration is gaining support, many lawyers are not familiar with its rules and procedures and therefore tend to avoid it. Following are the major differences between arbitration and litigation:

---

[2] For an excellent discussion of various types of alternative dispute resolution, *see* I. P. Lurie, Alternative Dispute Resolution for Design Professionals (1988). *See also* Arbitration of Construction Disputes (M. Callahan, B. Bramble, & P. Lurie, eds., John Wiley & Sons, Inc. 1990).

Arbitrations are generally resolved more quickly and cheaply than litigation, particularly litigation in congested urban court systems.

Unlike a jury of laypersons, the arbitrators are generally professionals and business people in the construction industry or lawyers with construction law experience.

The courts allow extensive discovery procedures that are ordinarily unavailable in arbitration.

It is more difficult to gather multiple parties in a single arbitration hearing than in court.

Courts follow formal rules of procedure and rules of evidence, whereas arbitration dispenses with most of these formalities.

An error of law made by the trial court can be appealed, but an arbitrator's error generally cannot be appealed.

Many of these advantages and disadvantages cut both ways. The absence of an appeal and of extensive discovery works to the advantage of a party who desires a quick and inexpensive result, but it works to the disadvantage of a party whose case is factually or legally complex. Arbitration is generally the superior method of resolving design professionals' fee disputes because of arbitration's quickness, lesser costs, and fact finders experienced in the construction industry.

There are alternatives to both litigation and arbitration. Frequently called *alternative dispute resolution,* these are nonbinding processes usually facilitated by a third-party neutral.

The weakness of alternative dispute resolution is that it is nonbiding. The party holding the money may choose to view it as just another stalling tactic. Alternative dispute resolution is likely to be more useful when both parties in good faith believe their positions are correct or when the parties have or desire a long-term relationship with each other.

The litigation process is not over after a judgment is obtained. Collecting the money may involve foreclosing on a mechanic's lien or going through another courtroom process to learn what and where a client's assets are. A number of things may happen to make the judgment difficult or impossible to collect. A client may go bankrupt or be a judgment-proof individual or a "shell" corporation with few assets, or there may be a default with the lender taking over the project, which may restrict remedies.

§ 24.8 Hiring a Lawyer to Collect Fees

It is important for a design professional to hire an experienced lawyer in a fee dispute. Collecting an A/E's fee is a specialized kind of legal practice, requiring special skills and experience a business or real estate lawyer may lack.

The biggest decision is usually the fee arrangement. There are two possibilities. The lawyer may bill according to his (and his staff's) hourly rates, with payment due regardless of the result of the lawsuit. Alternatively, the lawyer may charge a contingent fee, usually one-third of whatever is collected (plus expenses off the top), paid only if the case is successful. Some lawyers refuse to work on one basis or the other. If there is a choice, one should consider the likelihood of prevailing with a comparison of likely hourly and contingent fees.

If a lawyer is working on an hourly fee, the A/E should ask about:

1. The lawyer's rates
2. The rates of other lawyers in the office who may work on the case
3. Other office personnel (paralegals, secretaries, word processors, docket clerks): their hourly fees, whether the client is charged for them or if they are overhead, and whether the client can save money by performing some or all of their work with the A/E's own employees
4. Whether the lawyer charges higher "in court" rates
5. Frequency of billing, payment terms, and extension of credit.

When a lawyer works for a contingent fee, it is important to determine the percentage fee and whether the percentage changes depending on the length of the case. For example, if the lawyer succeeds in collecting the fee by writing a letter without ever filing the lawsuit, does he charge the same percentage for his fee? Is there a difference in percentage when the fee is collected after the complaint is filed but before trial, or when the fee is not collected until after an appeal has been resolved?

The rules governing the practice of law ordinarily require the client to pay the expenses (such as filing fees and costs of transcripts) incurred by a lawyer even on an unsuccessful lawsuit taken on a contingent fee. The A/E may want to ask the lawyer what his normal practice is and obtain the names of other clients as references.

In addition to fee structure, the lawyer's background and experience are important. Lawyers familiar with design and construction are more easily able to spot and understand the important issues. It saves time and money when the lawyer does not have to educate himself about procedural matters or construction issues. This is particularly important when the lawyer is charging an hourly fee, but it is also important on contingent fee cases. Most lawyers who charge contingent fees for collection work do not concentrate their practices in architectural or engineering claims and typically litigate a very large number of cases, many of which are uncontested. They frequently do not have the time or background to respond to complex assertions made or positions taken by the defendant against a claim.

Occasionally a dispute may arise between a lawyer and a client regarding legal fees or some other aspect of the litigation. In such cases, the state or local bar association may be able to recommend a special committee that can investigate and resolve the matter.

§ 24.9 Collection Tactics

The best time to avoid a dispute that may result in the withholding of the A/E's fee is before the dispute has arisen. **Sections 24.10** through **24.14** recommend measures the design professional can take in day-to-day practice to minimize the possibility that a fee dispute will develop.

§ 24.10 —Recommended Contractual Clauses

One of the most important contractual clauses to help ensure collection of fees is one that provides for reimbursement of attorneys' fees. The presence of such a clause in the contract will discourage the client from attempting to withhold fees, and if a claim is filed, an attorneys' fees clause is very important in rendering the litigation cost effective.

An attorneys' fees clause favorable to the design professional would be:

> Client shall reimburse Design Professional for any costs and expenses, including attorneys' fees, incurred by Design Professional in any effort to enforce payment.

A more even-handed clause that would have the same effect if the A/E were to successfully sue for fees would be:

> In any lawsuit, claim or other action between the parties arising out of or relating to the contract, the other party shall reimburse prevailing party for all costs and expenses, including attorneys' fees, incurred by the prevailing party in the lawsuit, claim or other action.

An interest clause, with high but realistic rates, helps to ensure that the A/E will truly be "made whole" if a fee dispute is won and will ensure superior bargaining leverage after the dispute arises. One example of such a clause would be:

> Interest shall accrue on all sums due and unpaid at the rate of 1-1/2% per month simple interest from the date on which payment was due.

As discussed in § **24.6**, it may be helpful to specify in the contract the venue for any dispute resolution process that may arise. In conjunction with an arbitration clause, the words "in City, State" can be inserted after the words "shall be . . . decided by arbitration." If there is no arbitration agreement in the contract, the following venue provision can be inserted:

The parties stipulate that any litigation or other dispute resolution process arising out of or relating to this contract shall be venued in City, State, and the parties hereby waive any objections to jurisdiction or venue which they may otherwise have.

A broad arbitration clause such as found in the standard AIA and Engineers Joint Contract Documents Committee (EJCDC) documents, can help collect unpaid fees. Under these clauses, any and all disputes arising out of or relating to the contract must be resolved in arbitration.

It is also possible to draft a much more limited arbitration clause. For example, the following clause is designed to have fee disputes heard in arbitration while major malpractice claims would be litigated through the court system:

All claims, disputes or other matters for which the sum sought to be recovered is less than $50,000 shall be decided by arbitration in accordance with . . . . All claims, disputes or other matters for which the amount sought equals or exceeds $50,000 shall not be subject to arbitration and shall be litigated, if at all, in a court of competent jurisdiction.

Arbitration clauses are very flexible. They can be joined with agreements for other alternative dispute resolution mechanisms. For example, the following clause requires the parties to mediate any dispute and, if unsuccessful, to subsequently arbitrate it:

Any and all claims, disputes or other matters in question between the parties ("controversies") arising out of or relating to this Agreement shall initially be submitted to mediation in accordance with the Construction Mediation Rules of the American Arbitration Association or Endispute, Inc. If the mediation process has not resulted in an agreed settlement within 30 days of submission of the matter to mediation, then the controversy shall be decided by arbitration in accordance with . . . .

It is not necessary to adopt wholesale any published set of arbitration rules. The rules may be modified to provide for the arbitrator to make findings of fact in a written opinion or to allow discovery and prehearing procedures. One frequent modification to standard arbitration clauses is the following:

Any arbitration conducted under this contract shall permit discovery in accordance with the Federal Rules of Civil Procedure. In the event of a discovery dispute, the parties shall submit the dispute to the arbitrator(s), whose decision shall be final and binding.

As discussed in **§ 24.4**, it is important for the design professional to be able to suspend services under a contract when a client ceases making payments. Although the law permits the design professional to suspend services when payment is wrongfully withheld, the A/E runs the risk that the payment would be found to be properly withheld, in which case the A/E would be liable for any resulting delays. The following clause can minimize that risk:

> In the event that the Owner fails to make a payment when it is due, or if the Owner and Design Professional disagree as to whether the Owner has improperly failed to make a payment, the Design Professional shall be entitled to suspend performing services under the contract until either the dispute has been resolved or else the owner places a sum equal to [150% of] the amount in dispute in an escrow account, reasonably satisfactory to both parties, which specifies that the escrow agent shall distribute the escrow sum between the parties in accordance with any arbitration award or court judgment entered resolving the dispute.

Clients are far less likely to withhold payments if they know in advance that they cannot use the money elsewhere and will instead be required to deposit the money in an escrow account.

A problem frequently encountered by design professionals is a client who, near the end of the project, questions billings from long ago to try to negotiate down the overall fee. The following clause can prevent this from happening:

> Within twenty-one days of receipt of Design Professional's invoice, Owner shall examine the invoice in detail to satisfy himself as to its accuracy and completeness and shall raise any questions or objections which he may have regarding the invoice within this twenty-one-day period. After twenty-one days from receipt of Design Professional's invoice, Owner waives any question or objection to the invoice not previously raised.

§ 24.11 —Managing Communications

The major source of claims by owners against design professionals is poor communication resulting in unrealistic owner expectations. One or both parties may be at fault.

One of the most common misunderstandings occurs when the design professional fails to inform the owner of the financial consequences of the owner's decisions. Some unsophisticated owners do not understand normal architectural and engineering practice and expect unreasonable things to be included in basic services. At a minimum, the design professional should carefully explain to the owner at the outset of the project where the line is drawn between basic and additional services. Particularly with an unsophisticated owner, the design professional should obtain the owner's signature on an additional services authorization before performing any such work.

This problem often surfaces when the architect or engineer is designing with a fixed limit of construction costs. It is imperative for the A/E to make the owner aware of the impact of certain design choices on the construction budget. Examples are rampant of design professionals who have been required to value engineer a project at their own expense because they were too accommodating in incorporating the owner's expensive preferences into the design.

Another common mistake design professionals make is to postpone a confrontation on an unpleasant issue. It is always easier to discuss the positive aspects of a project or working relationship than the negative ones. However, it is these negative aspects that are likely to lead a client to withhold payment.

It is natural for an A/E to want to maintain a good working relationship with a client. This is especially true for project managers. Project managers tend to be younger executives, responsible for the project but not the source of the original relationship with the client. Their performance tends to be judged by the outcome of the project, not by success in collecting fees. Rather than confront and resolve an issue when it first arises, project managers often postpone discussing the issue with the client so as not to anger the client or invite closer scrutiny into other decisions previously made. One solution that is gaining popularity among design firms is to link the project manager's compensation in some way with successful collection of fees for the project. In theory, this would give project managers an incentive to pay attention to the business relationship as well as the aesthetic and technical aspects of the project.

A good rule of thumb is never to postpone resolution of a complaint or problem. The earlier in the project that a problem is confronted, the greater number of options for resolving it generally exist. Furthermore, the design professional has greater leverage earlier in the project to negotiate a satisfactory solution.

One common complaint that owners have about design professionals is that they fail to understand the owner's needs and desires. The problem is rarely that architects and engineers do not carefully listen to their clients. Rather, the clients themselves frequently either do not know what they want or have inconsistent desires about the project. The actual source of the misunderstanding is not as important as the fact that the owner perceives that the A/E did not properly perform his duties and withholds part of the fee.

Often the design professional fails to understand the conflicts and limits of authority within an institutional owner. For example, governmental entities, with their high rate of turnover and complex hierarchy, are a major source of conflicting and inconsistent instructions. Large corporations, to a lesser extent, may be subject to similar problems. Condominium associations are famous for inconsistency and deviating from the positions originally taken by the developer or the prior year's condominium association members.

The two-step solution to prevent the development of unrealistic expectations is to communicate and document. It is sometimes difficult for architects and engineers to understand that their clients frequently do not have any real understanding of what design professionals do. A layperson typically and erroneously sees an architect's function as "making sure that the building gets built right." In particular, clients frequently do not understand the differences between a design professional's and a contractor's roles. Following are some suggestions design professionals can follow to improve communications with their clients:

1. Teach the client about the construction process, particularly about the limits and extent of the A/E's duties.
2. Carefully explain which services are considered basic services and which are additional services, illustrating the difference with examples likely to be relevant to the project in question.
3. When a client must make a decision, fully advise him of the various consequences of his options, even if he does not want to hear all of them.
4. If the client is dissatisfied, discuss the reasons for his dissatisfaction as soon as possible, and try to resolve the problem quickly.
5. Take the time to learn an institutional client's command structure, especially who does and does not have the authority to issue instructions or make decisions.

An important rule in performing design services is to document all important communications. If the communications have taken place before the signing of the contract, consider incorporating them into the contract, as described in § **24.12**. If the communications take place after the contract has been signed, there are a number of different ways to document them, described in § **24.13**.

§ 24.12 —Contractual Communications

The best and most reliable source of the rules governing an A/E's relationship with a client is the contract. Most jurisdictions legally define an A/E's duties as those stated or implied in the contract. A letter documenting a conversation is evidence, but not conclusive proof, of what was said; if the same communication or instruction is recited in the contract, it is generally legally conclusive and binding.

Contracts are generally composed of two sections. The second section contains the promises, covenants, warranties, and other provisions that constitute the agreement. The first section often contains recitals of fact that are important in understanding the nature of the relationship between the parties. Any communication, whether it is a simple statement of fact or a complicated set of promises and conditions, can appropriately be included in one of the two sections of the contract.

Even if it is in writing, a client's promise may not be enforceable unless it is included in the contract. For example, suppose a client writes an A/E a letter promising a bonus calculated as a percentage of the amount by which the construction budget exceeds the lowest bid. In reliance on this promise, the A/E agrees to design the project, and the A/E and the owner enter into a standard form contract for architectural services. The owner's promise to pay the bonus probably would *not* be enforceable. Under the legal doctrine of parol evidence, a court would not consider any promises made, even in writing, before entering into the contract on the grounds that the contract supersedes all prior negotiations.

A simple solution is to incorporate such a bonus letter into the contract as an exhibit. Alternatively, a provision could be added to the contract that mirrors the terms of the letter. The point is to make sure the contract accurately reflects all of the important communications and promises made.

The contract also can be used as an educational tool. With the client, the A/E can go through the list of basic services and additional services to make sure the client clearly understands what will be provided and what will be extra. The identity of the client's representative and the extent of his authority should be discussed and included in the contract. If there are any special timing requirements or design features, these should be clearly spelled out as well.

A word of caution: drafting contracts can be a tricky business, and even plain English does not always suffice. For example, a deadline in the contract will have very little effect unless it is accompanied by the legal phrase, "Time is of the essence." When preparing a contract, it is a good idea to consult an attorney, especially when the contract deviates in any important respect from standard form contracts.

§ 24.13 —Post-Contractual Communications

Often it is important to document communications that occur after the contract has been signed. The best way is to put the communication in writing and have it signed or otherwise acknowledged in writing by the other party. An example of this kind of documentation is an additional services authorization form. If the client asks the A/E to perform an additional service, the A/E should send the client a written description of his request, reciting that the work will be billed as an additional service and asking him to initial and return it. This procedure will effectively prevent the client from being able to claim that the A/E is not entitled to additional compensation for the work.

The second best method of documenting a communication is to send a written summary of the communication to the other party, accompanied by a request for that party to notify the first party if he believes the summary is incorrect or incomplete. Probably the best example of this kind of documentation is a confirming letter. Another example would be the minutes of meetings. The advantage of this documentation method is that it creates a clear record of the communication in a less formal and confrontational manner than requiring signature or initialing as acknowledgement. The disadvantage is that there still may be an adversarial element to the documentation. The other party is alerted to the fact that a written record of the communication is being made for some reason, and the other party may be able to claim that he never received or paid attention to the document circulated.

The least effective form of documentation is to take notes or make a record of the communication but to keep the record without circulating it to the other party. Its major disadvantage is that because the written record was never shared with the other party, that party may deny its accuracy when confronted. This method of documentation is most effective if there is a regularly established procedure (such as a telephone log) for taking notes and filing them. A further advantage of this method is that one can keep a written record of communications without the other party's knowledge.

Making an audio or tape recording of oral communications is not always effective and has several drawbacks. In some states, it is illegal to surreptitiously record a conversation without the other party's consent. If it is known that a tape is being made, people sometimes speak "for the record," distorting what would otherwise be said. Tape-recording a meeting or conversation is frequently interpreted as adversarial and confrontational. Finally, unless the tape is routinely transcribed, which is time consuming, it is difficult to organize or index tape-recorded conversations. A tape recording is most effective when one knows in advance that the communication in question will be very important and likely the source of future disputes.

§ 24.14 —Financial Considerations

Another way the design professional can help ensure payment is to check the client's financial situation. Because of the realities of the marketplace, virtually no design professionals are paid in advance or work against a retainer. The industry standard is to bill at the end of the month for services performed earlier that month. Accordingly, design professionals routinely advance credit to their clients.

Very few architects or engineers adequately investigate their client's creditworthiness, feeling they are fortunate to have been awarded the project and fearing they would insult the owner by seeking financial assurances.

There are numerous means of verifying a client's creditworthiness. There are companies that issue credit reports on businesses and individuals. The design professional also can solicit information from the client's bank, review the client's financial statements, or ask the client for references to other design professionals, contractors, or other business people. A credit check is probably unnecessary if the client is a major corporation such as General Motors or IBM.

However, government agencies can pose a trap for the unwary. Just because the client is a municipal or public agency does not mean that it has the money to pay the A/E's fees. Many agencies have statutory limits on their expenditures, and money may not have been properly appropriated for design fees. With private clients, a mechanic's lien can usually secure one's right to payment; however, most jurisdictions do not permit mechanic's liens to be filed against real property owned by governmental agencies.

It is also important to pay attention to the precise legal entity with which one is contracting. Considerable development is performed by corporations or land trusts established specifically for the project and which may not possess any uncommitted assets with which to pay design fees. Just because the owners or others affiliated with the corporation or trust have substantial money does not mean that the corporation or trust will have access to that money. In the eyes of the law, with very few exceptions, a corporation or trust is considered a distinct legal entity, just like an individual person, and the owners of the corporation and beneficial owners of trusts are not personally liable for the corporation's or trust's debts.

This does not mean that one should never enter into a contract with a *shell* entity (one with few or no assets of its own). However, before advancing credit to the shell entity by performing services against future billings, one should make sure that the right to payment is secure from some source. For example, if the services the A/E is performing give him mechanic's lien rights, the lien against the real estate may be sufficient security. Otherwise, the client may be able to give the design professional a security interest in the real estate (that is, mortgage) or in some other real or personal property to secure payment. The structuring of secured transactions of this kind can be quite complicated and should not be attempted without a lawyer's advice.

Perhaps the simplest way of securing fee payments owed by a shell entity is to have another responsible person or entity guarantee the payments. The client would require a similar guarantee of any tenant that is a shell entity in a building he is developing; he would ordinarily require the entity's owner(s) to guarantee the entity's obligations under the lease. The same thing can be done in the contract for professional services by a signature at the end and the following language immediately preceding it: "The undersigned hereby guarantees all of the obligations of Shell Entity under this Agreement."

A related concern involves contracts with partnerships. The law of partnerships is more favorable to the design professional than the law of corporations because it renders each partner personally responsible for the partnership debts. However, there are two different kinds of partnerships. The typical one is a *general partnership* in which all general partners are individually liable for the partnership's debts. Some partnerships are called *limited partnerships* and consist of both general and limited partners. Limited partners are essentially investors, and they are *not* liable for partnership debts beyond the amount of their financial contribution to the partnership. Every limited partnership must have at least one general partner who is individually responsible for partnership obligations. With the responsibility comes authority: ordinarily, only a general partner, not a limited partner, has the authority to bind the partnership to a contract or to hire a design professional to perform services. However, caution is advisable when the only general partners of a partnership are shell entities.

When entering into a contract with a government agency or public body, it is necessary to make sure that the agency or public body is acting within its authority. The statutes and regulations governing these entities are published, and the law holds the design professional responsible for being familiar with them. The A/E should verify that the agency is acting within the scope of its authority, that the individual who will be signing the contract has the authority to do so, that the necessary funds have been appropriated, and that the agency has followed the proper rules and procedures in entering into the contract. When in doubt, consult with an attorney.

Especially in private development, the source of the money to pay design fees frequently will be a construction loan from a bank or other financial institution. When possible, one should verify the terms of the loan agreement to make sure the client has met or can meet all conditions required to draw on the loan. The size, duration, and other aspects of the loan should be realistic and sufficient and provision should be made for payment of design fees. The A/E frequently will be asked to sign a document consenting to a collateral assignment of the contract to the lender if the developer defaults. It is reasonable to sign such a document, but one should make sure that its provisions require the lender to make payment on a current basis plus all past due invoices if the lender takes over the project after the developer's default and requires the A/E's services.

One more word of caution: beware of the private developer with the bad reputation. Ask for references and check them out. Smaller, private developers who frequently operate "on a shoestring" are the kind of client most likely to wrongfully withhold professional fees. Especially as profit margins shrink, some private developers are unscrupulous and unethical and try to make additional money at the design professional's expense. They believe it is acceptable to slow down or withhold the last payment(s) in order to negotiate the fee down after the work has been done. They fabricate claims against the design professional to offset sums owed, and they make disingenuous and unreasonable demands for supporting documentation solely for the purpose of delaying payment.

Even honest and ethical private developers frequently believe they have a right to withhold fees for reasons not the A/E's fault. They frequently refuse to make overdue payments they acknowledge are owed merely because they have not yet themselves received the money (such as a draw on a construction loan) to pay the A/E. Unless a specific provision in the contract allows the developer to delay payment for this reason, it is not proper to do so. However, developers usually get away with the delay because the design professional does not want to alienate the client and because the collection process, even at its fastest, is usually too slow to expedite the payment. It is wise to make sure the contract contains a strong "interest on late payments" clause, and the design professional should do what contractors do: formally calculate and make a claim for the interest owed on account of the late payments.

Some developers feel entitled to withhold sufficient money to cover any dispute, even if the design professional did nothing wrong. The client may blame the A/E for failing to catch construction mistakes, or the entire draw on a construction loan may be held up because of disputes involving parties having nothing to do with the design professional. If there is a question or dispute concerning a small portion of the A/E's invoice, developers frequently refuse to pay even the undisputed sums until the question or dispute has been resolved.

One partial solution to this problem is to require that sums withheld because of a dispute be placed in escrow. If there is a legitimate, good faith dispute, the client is probably justified in withholding the disputed amount, at least until the dispute is resolved. However, the A/E wants to eliminate any incentive for the client to artificially exaggerate the amounts in dispute and to use the withheld sums to finance the project. See § **24.10** for a sample contract clause that effectuates this solution.

Working for developers who practice these "sharp" tactics is shortsighted. The job is unlikely to be profitable because the developer's decision on how much to wrongfully withhold without spurring the A/E to legal action will take that profit into account. The administrative time and expense the A/E will expend trying to collect fees may be a major drain on the firm and is virtually certain to offset any profit. Even if business is slow, the A/E's time usually would be better spent marketing to clients who will pay fully.

§ 24.15 —Quality Control

A further way to maximize the likelihood of being fully paid is to emphasize quality control and claims avoidance. Quality control is not only a professional obligation, but a good financial investment as well. It pays off in greater and faster collections and improves internal efficiency. Although there is no way to guarantee perfect work, the best way to minimize client dissatisfaction is to anticipate problems and avoid mistakes.

Following are some time-tested methods for improving quality control:

Make sure the firm's principals stay highly involved in the work.

Perform honest self-evaluations.

Encourage frank and full discussion among employees.

When problems occur, keep records of them and look for patterns in the types of problems and the people involved.

Participate actively in professional societies' peer review processes.[3]

Originally developed by the American Consulting Engineers Council, many professional societies now conduct formal peer review programs in which similarly situated design professionals conduct in-house analyses of other firms and their procedures.

§ 24.16 —Statement of Completion

One final recommendation is to create and obtain the client's signature on a statement of completion. The statement of completion is a certificate signed by the client reciting that services have been satisfactorily completed. It is analogous to a contractor's certificate of substantial or final completion. The statement of completion might use the following language:

> Design Professional has performed all of its contractional services in accordance with its contract with the undersigned in a manner acceptable to the undersigned [except as may be noted below].

Ideally, a sample form should be attached to and incorporated in the design professional's contract, along with a provision stating that the client shall sign and deliver it to the design professional with final payment.

---

[3] American Consulting Engineers Council, Professional Liability Risk Management (1990).

§ 24.17 Resolving a Dispute

Despite the design professional's best efforts to avoid a dispute, a problem may develop that causes the owner to withhold payment. The A/E's approach will depend to a great extent on how confrontational he is willing to be.

The first stage of resolving such a dispute is the talking stage. The A/E asks the client why he is withholding payment, and he gives his reasons. Presumably, the A/E disagrees with those reasons and tries to persuade the client they are improper. If neither party changes his position, the dispute escalates to the next stage.

The design professional usually threatens the client with some form of protective or retaliatory action including:

Stopping work or otherwise withholding services

Informing the lender or other interested parties of the nonpayment

Informing the code authority of the cessation of the design professional's participation

Informing the code authority of existing code violations

Filing a law suit or going to arbitration.

In most jurisdictions, the law does not permit one to threaten to report a violation of the law to achieve an objective like enforcing payment. In many states, making such a threat is a crime called *intimidation* or *blackmail.* One may have an independent legal or moral obligation to report a violation of the law, but one cannot offer to forego making the report in exchange for payment.

The design professional may threaten to take civil action to enforce payment, such as filing suit or a demand for arbitration. Similarly, there is nothing improper about threatening to inform other interested parties, such as the lender or surety, if payment is not received. It is likely to be in the A/E's interest to inform the client's lender of nonpayment because the lender may insist that the A/E be paid or else declare the loan agreement in default. In fact, if the A/E has signed a lender's consent to collateral assignment form, he may be contractually obligated to report nonpayment to the lender. Also, depending on the law in that jurisdiction, the A/E may be obligated to report the cessation of his firm's involvement in the project to the applicable authorities.

The law also allows the design professional to threaten to stop work or withhold other services. Wrongful nonpayment is a material breach of the contract, and when one party materially breaches a contract, the other party is no longer obligated to continue performing. It is not usually necessary to formally terminate the contract in accordance with the termination clause; however, the contract itself can limit or modify one's right to suspend performance for nonpayment.

Common examples of withholding services include:

Stopping work during the design phase
Refusing to transmit the plans and specifications to the client
Refusing to sign a lender's certificate
Refusing to sign or evaluate a change order
Refusing to visit the construction site

The design professional should consult with an attorney to make sure his position is correct before deciding to withhold services. If the client can ultimately prove that withholding payment is justified, the A/E is the one who breached the contract and will be liable for the delays and extra cost caused by withheld services. The decision to withhold services is similar to "raising the stakes" in a poker game. Although the A/E increases the pressure on the client to pay him, the A/E also increases his own liability if the client's decision to withhold payment is ultimately proved to be justified.

§ 24.18 —Negotiation

The major alternative to a confrontational course of action is negotiation. Negotiation has a good chance of succeeding if both parties are proceeding in good faith. Beware of the client who professes to be willing to negotiate but takes unreasonable positions. The client may be using negotiation as a stalling tactic.

Three important considerations are common to all negotiations. First, be aware of what the alternative to negotiation is and what its consequences would be. Frequently, the only alternatives to negotiation are capitulating or filing a lawsuit (or demand for arbitration). In any negotiation, when deciding whether or not to accept an offered settlement, keep in mind the transaction costs and other consequences of the alternatives to negotiation. Both parties are likely to incur substantial attorneys' fees and related costs if the negotiation is ultimately unsuccessful and a lawsuit ensues. The ultimate goal of the negotiation should be to duplicate the result that would be reached if the claims were submitted to the appropriate dispute resolution process, with the resulting savings in attorneys' fees and other transaction costs.

The second consideration is for the design professional to put himself in the client's shoes to understand his interests from his perspective. The client may be operating from a totally different set of facts or assumptions, focusing on different goals. Talking with the client may help correct misunderstandings.

For example, a developer may try to withhold a portion of the architect's fee equal to the change order he was forced to grant the contractor because of a design omission. From the developer's point of view, he may only be aware that the design omission resulted in him paying the contractor for an extra, so it may seem logical to withhold that sum from the architect. The architect should educate the developer that this was a "betterment" situation in which the developer would have had to pay the same amount as part of a higher original contract price if the omission had not occurred in the first place. The developer would be "getting something for nothing" if allowed to withhold the cost of the extra. The developer who is acting in good faith may then pay the architect or agree to a much more satisfactory compromise.

The third consideration is the importance of devising a solution other than *zero-sum.* A zero-sum solution is one in which an improvement in the result for one party is directly counterbalanced by an equivalent worsening of the other party's result. A good example is the distribution of a fixed sum of money; the more one party receives, the less the other gets.

Creative solutions may be necessary. For example, if an owner is withholding design fees because of a consultant's error, the A/E might offer the owner something that does not cost any money. The A/E might offer to assign his claim against the consultant to the owner and to assist in prosecuting the claim in exchange for payment of all but the fees owed to the consultant. Or, if an owner is withholding money because he claims the A/E specified a poor quality or inappropriate product, the A/E may try to secure a manufacturer's warranty or the A/E or his insurer might warrant the product to avoid having to defend against a claim.

The secret to devising creative non-zero-sum solutions is in understanding the client's real interest. The A/E should learn what the client's true concerns are and search for ways to satisfy them without having to pay as much (or any) money as the client has been withholding. The successful negotiator is the one who gives in on the non-zero-sum issues to obtain concessions on the zero-sum issues like payment of fees.

There are two major types of negotiations. The first is *unstructured bargaining,* in which both parties exaggerate their positions in order to meet somewhere in the middle. The other kind of negotiation is *principled negotiation,* which involves agreeing on the legal/equitable principles governing the dispute and applying the facts to those principles to suggest a solution.

The most common example of "random number bargaining" is "splitting the difference." For no particular reason, the two parties agree to "meet in the middle" so they are each compromising to an equal extent. The major advantages of this kind of negotiation are that it is quick and simple, requiring a minimum of time or effort, and thus useful for small disputes. It tends to favor the party with the superior leverage, regardless of the relative merits of the parties' positions.

This style of negotiating has several disadvantages. The result does not reflect the merits of each party's position, it provides an unfair advantage to the party with the greater leverage, it encourages the parties initially to take unrealistic positions in order to have more room to compromise, and it provides no guidelines for determining what offers to make or accept.

Principled negotiation is a very different process. It requires more thought and creativity, but it ultimately leads to a more logical and satisfactory result. The procedure varies depending on the circumstances, but four steps ordinarily are involved:

1. Determining what the applicable rules of law or custom in the industry are
2. Applying the facts to the rules and determining whether and the extent to which the parties' positions and/or conduct comply with or violate those rules
3. Assigning responsibility/liability in accordance with deviations from the rules
4. Calculating the consequences of responsibility/liability and settling the dispute accordingly.

For example, an owner may withhold money equivalent to the cost of repairing a construction defect, claiming that the architect should have detected the defect. The first step is to determine the applicable legal rules and principles. In this case, the rule is that an architect is not responsible for contractors' mistakes unless he knew or reasonably should have known of the mistake. However, in this example, the architect was only hired to be on the jobsite two days per month and could only have prevented the mistake had it occurred when he was at the site. There are two conclusions to be drawn in assigning responsibility: the architect had only a 2/30 chance of spotting the defect, and even if the architect were on site on the day in question, the owner's and architect's positions that the architect should/would not have been able to spot the defect have equal merit at this stage in the negotiation. The negotiation results in the compromise that the architect is held responsible for 1/30 (half of 2/30) of the cost of repairs.

Another example of principled negotiation occurs when an owner withholds part of a civil engineer's fee because he omitted a water line required by code. The applicable principle might be that the owner should be restored to the same financial position that he would have been in had there not been any omission. The contractor's labor and materials cost $10,000, including $1,000 for having to remobilize the excavator who had otherwise completed his work. The liability conclusions are fairly clear: the owner would have had to pay for the actual cost of the pipe and installation, even without the omission, because the cost would have been included in the contractor's original price, but the owner would not have had to pay for remobilization of the excavator. The calculation follows logically: the owner should absorb $9,000 of the cost, and the engineer is responsible for $1,000.

Principled negotiation has several advantages. Its resolutions are based on the merits of the parties' positions, and it is the fairest approximation of what the results of the dispute resolution process would have been. It provides strong guidance as to appropriate settlements and leaves the parties feeling as satisfied as possible with the results.[4]

Alternative dispute resolution, as discussed earlier, is a very useful supplement to negotiation. Most of the various types of alternative dispute resolution are designed to facilitate one or more aspects of negotiation. For example, mediation is little more than negotiation assisted by a neutral third party. Minitrials are a tactic for compelling the other party to understand the strength and details of one's position (and vice versa). A professional alternative dispute resolution organization can make the initial contacts and organize the alternative dispute resolution process without revealing which party asked the organization to get involved.[5]

§ 24.19 —Negotiated Forbearance

It is quite common for a client to ask for some additional time to pay the design professional's fees. The reason may be that the developer's cash flow does not permit immediate payment or that the source of the payment will be the opening of or the next draw on a construction loan. Architects and engineers routinely assent to the delayed payment, particularly when the developer has been forthcoming about the reasons. However, very few design professionals protect themselves properly in this kind of situation by taking steps to increase the likelihood that the payment will be made.

When a client asks for additional time to pay design fees, it is prudent to condition approval on the client's providing satisfactory (or at least additional) security for the payment. In effect, the design professional is financing the client's operations. If the client were to go to a bank or other financial institution and ask for a similar extension of time to make payment, some kind of collateral or additional security likely would be required.

If the client is requesting the extension of time in good faith, then he is unlikely to object to a request for additional security, particularly as long as it does not cost him anything. Following are examples of additional security the A/E may want to request:

1. A personal guarantee by the principal(s) of the client
2. A collateral pledge of specific property, such as a certificate of deposit

[4] For an excellent and more detailed description of principled negotiations, *see* R. Fisher & W. Ury, Getting to Yes (1981).

[5] *See* I. P. Lurie, Alternative Dispute Resolution for Design Professionals (1988).

3. A letter of credit from a financial institution or surety company
4. Signature on a formal note or confession of judgment form, which includes recovery of attorneys' fees and collections costs
5. A stipulation as to the adequacy of design services.

The purpose of a certificate stipulating that the design professional performed services adequately is to make it difficult for the client to fabricate a claim to offset the payments owed. It is probably not fair to ask for a complete release, because a legitimate claim may yet be undiscovered, but the client can be asked to stipulate that he is not aware of any inadequacies in the performance of design services. A simple version of such a certificate might read as follows:

In exchange for Design Professional's forbearance in collection of his fees, the undersigned hereby bindingly stipulates that as of the date shown below, he is not aware of any facts, incidents or other problems which might tend to indicate that Design Professional's services were not performed in accordance with the highest standards of professional care.

§ 24.20 Consultants' Pass-Through Claims

A common problem caused by an owner's withholding of fees is a design professional's liability to consultants. Typically, this problem occurs when a developer refuses to pay the architect's invoice, which includes the invoices rendered to the architect by the engineering consultants. It is particularly vexing for a consultant whose work has nothing whatsoever to do with the dispute between the owner and architect to have his fee withheld until unrelated design issues are resolved.

Philosophically, in the absence of contractual language to the contrary, the architect should pay the consultant regardless of whether the owner has paid the architect, unless the reason for the owner withholding the money pertains to the consultant's work. The reason is that the architect, rather than his consultants, is responsible for checking and ensuring the owner's creditworthiness, because there is no direct contractual relationship between the consultants and the owner. However, as a practical matter, most architects' cash flow does not enable them to pay consultants before being paid themselves.

The best way to resolve this problem is to include a provision in the architect-consultant agreement that states how this problem will be handled if it arises. The following are by no means exhaustive, but they represent the three most popular contractual resolutions of this problem:

1. *Pay-when-paid clause:* "Architect shall promptly submit consultant's invoices to Owner and shall make payment to Consultant within

______ business days after receiving payment from owner for Consultant's services; provided, however, that Architect shall not be liable for making payments to Consultant unless and until Architect has received payment from Owner on account of Consultant's services."

2. *Absolute obligation clause:* "Architect shall pay Consultant within ______ business days of Consultant's invoice, regardless of whether or not Architect has received payment from Owner for Consultant's services."

3. *Hybrid clause:* "Architect shall pay Consultant's invoices within ______ business days of receipt of the invoice, except that if Owner withholds any sums from Architect allegedly on account of Consultant's work, Architect shall not be obligated to pay that sum to Consultant unless or until Owner pays said sum to Architect."

CHAPTER 25

LIEN AND BOND RIGHTS AND OTHER SPECIAL COLLECTION REMEDIES

Arthur A. Park, Jr.

Arthur A. Park, Jr., is a graduate of the Georgetown University Law Center and holds a B.S. from the University of California. He spent several years in Washington, D.C. as a trial attorney with the Foreign Claims Settlement Commission and the Federal Maritime Commission. Now in private practice, Mr. Park is a partner in the San Francisco law firm of Ottenweller, Solan, Park and King, where he specializes in construction, surety and fidelity, and maritime matters. He is a member of the California bar, the International Association of Defense Counsel, and the Defense Research Institute.

§ 25.1 Introduction

One who bestows labor, material, or services for the benefit of another's property is entitled to compensation therefor. An individual may institute an action in personam for breach of express or implied contract and may recover under theories of quantum meruit or unjust enrichment. Assuming a favorable judgment, the creditor may be distressed to find that the debtor is insolvent. At the very least, enforcement and collection proceedings may drag out over a considerable period of time, with nonrecoverable costs diluting the eventual reward. However, architects and engineers may, in appropriate circumstances, have or gain the benefit of security for their labors either by way of a secured interest in real property or direct rights against funds held by a third party or against the promise of a third party to answer for the debt of those with whom the architect or engineer contracted. This chapter examines the architect's and engineer's lien and bond rights and other special collection remedies.

§ 25.2 Mechanic's Liens

A *mechanic's lien* is a statutory lien attaching to buildings and other improvements on realty, and to the realty itself, ensuring material suppliers and other laborers of payment for their work or material.[1] The Internal Revenue Code (IRC) defines a *mechanic's lienor* as "any person who under local law has a lien on real property (or the proceeds of a contract relating to real property) for services, labor, or materials furnished in connection with the construction or improvement of such property."[2]

Mechanic's liens were unknown in the common law or in English equity practice.[3] On considerations of equity and prevention of unjust enrichment,[4] statutes providing for mechanic's liens were first enacted in the

---

[1] Tommasi v. Bolger, 114 A.D. 838, 100 N.Y.S. 367 (1906).

[2] I.R.C. § 6323(h)(2) (1988).

[3] Durling v. Gould, 83 Me. 134, 21 A. 813 (1890); J.J. Henry Co. v. United States, 411 F.2d 1246, 1253 (Ct. Cl. 1969), Note, *Mechanics Liens in Virginia,* 29 Va. L. Rev. 121, 122 (1942).

[4] Dagit v. Radnor Convalescent & Nursing Home, Inc., 38 Pa. D. & C.2d 389, 53 Del. 225, 227 (1965).

United States as early as 1791.[5] They have subsequently been codified in every state of the union.[6] Generally, provisions providing for mechanic's liens appear in each state's general civil legislation. However, certain states mandate the right to a mechanic's lien in their constitution.[7]

In most jurisdictions, land and improvements thereon are the subject of a mechanic's lien. Liens may attach against any interest that is transferable, assignable, or conveyable in the realty of the person at whose instance the work of improvement was done. The interest must be such that it may be sold under execution as a separate and distinct entity.[8] Real estate held in joint tenancy or as community property may be the subject of a mechanic's lien.[9] A lien may attach to an equitable estate or interest, including a beneficial interest under a trust agreement.[10] Most states provide that a leasehold interest is subject to a mechanic's lien for an improvement erected by or under a contract with the lessee.[11]

In the majority of jurisdictions, a mechanic's lien has priority against a bona fide purchaser of the property when it has attached before the conveyance was made. When the conveyance is made after the contract for improvements has been entered into, but before the lien has been recorded or otherwise perfected, there are at least four different theories as to priority:

1. When, by the terms of the statute, the lien relates back to the beginning of the actual work of improvement, the lien takes priority over a subsequent conveyance.
2. In other jurisdictions, the lien is in a priority position to conveyances made subsequent to the delivery of material to or the rendering of labor on the job.
3. The lien does not attach until it is recorded and perfected, and conveyances are free and clear of any encumbrance even though the work has been done.
4. The lien, when properly perfected or recorded, relates back to the date when the contract for the work was entered into between the owner and the contractor.[12]

---

[5] Freeform Pools, Inc. v. Strawbridge Home for Boys, Inc., 228 Md. 297, 179 A.2d 683 (1962); Chesbro-Whitman Co. v. Edenboro Apartments, Inc., 86 N.J. Super. 422, 207 A.2d 186 (1965).

[6] Note, *Mechanics Liens in Virginia,* 29 Va. L. Rev. 121, 122 (1942).

[7] *See, e.g.,* Tex. Rev. Civ. Stat. Ann. art. 16, § 37 (Vernon 1976).

[8] McClintic-Marshall Co. v. Ford Motor Co., 254 Mich. 305, 236 N.W. 792 (1931).

[9] Littell & S. Mfg. Co. v. Miller, 3 Wash. 480, 28 P. 1035 (1892).

[10] Amatrudi v. Blake, 117 So. 2d 416 (Fla. Dist. Ct. App. 1960).

[11] Annotation, *Right to Mechanics Lien upon Leasehold,* 42 A.L.R.2d 685, 687 (1955).

[12] Note, *Mechanics Liens in Virginia,* 29 Va. L. Rev. 121, 127 (1942).

Under the terms of the IRC,[13] a mechanic's lien on property perfected before the imposition of the government's tax lien is in a priority position to the tax lien.

On the proposition that it is against public policy to permit public property to be sold in satisfaction of a private debt and that general statutes are not to be construed to apply to the sovereign unless expressly made to do so, the general rule is that a mechanic's lien does not attach to and cannot be enforced against property of the United States,[14] a state,[15] a county,[16] or, generally, a municipality.[17] New Jersey's Municipal Mechanic's Lien Law provides for a lien for labor and materials on a public work of improvement that attaches to the funds appropriated but not to the public land or buildings.[18]

Although the proscription is not as broad as it is with respect to public property, the prevailing rule is that in the absence of a statute granting the right, a mechanic's lien cannot be imposed on property owned by a religious or charitable organization.[19]

Although there was at one time a Uniform Mechanic's Lien Law,[20] great diversities exist in the state statutes as to the scope of the lien, the conditions of its creation, and the manner of its preservation and enforcement.[21] Obviously, a detailed review of all or even a majority of the 50-odd mechanic's lien statutes is beyond the scope of this chapter. Suffice it to say that all mechanic's lien statutes provide a method for impressing a lien on real property, procedures for instituting suit to enforce the lien, and, following a judgment for foreclosure, directing the sale of the property to which the lien attached, with payment of the proceeds made available to the lienor/judgment creditor. Perhaps typical of the general statutes is California's:

> Mechanics, materialmen, contractors, subcontractors, lessors of equipment, artisans, architects, registered engineers, licensed land surveyors,

[13] I.R.C. § 6323 (1988).

[14] United States v. Munsey Trust Co., 332 U.S. 234, 67 S. Ct. 1599 (1947).

[15] Artukovich & Son, Inc. v. American Fidelity Fire Ins. Co., 72 Cal. App. 3d 940, 946, 140 Cal. Rptr. 434 (1977).

[16] J.E. Moss Ironworks v. County Court, 89 W. Va. 367, 109 S.E. 343 (1921).

[17] Union Reddi-Mix Co. v. Speciality Concrete Contractor, 476 S.W.2d 160 (Mo. Ct. App. 1972).

[18] N.J. Stat. Ann. § 2A:44-128 (West 1933).

[19] Cain v. Rea, 159 Va. 446, 166 S.E. 478 (1932) (allowed); Eureka Stone v. First Christian Church, 16 Ark. 212, 110 S.W. 1042 (1908) (not allowed).

[20] The statute was adopted by only one state and was later withdrawn as a uniform law. Geiser v. Permacrete, Inc., 90 So. 2d 610, 612 (Fla. 1956).

[21] Le Grand v. Hubbard, 216 Ala. 164, 112 So. 826 (1927); Note, *Mechanics Liens in Virginia,* 29 Va. L. Rev. 121 (1942).

> machinists, builders, teamsters, and draymen, and all persons and laborers of every class performing labor upon or bestowing skill or other necessary services on, or furnishing materials or leasing equipment to be used or consumed in or furnishing appliances, teams, or power contributing to a work of improvement shall have a lien upon the property upon which they have bestowed labor or furnished materials or appliances or leased equipment for the value of such labor done or materials furnished and for the value of the use of such appliances, equipment, teams, or power whether done or furnished at the instance of the owner or of any person acting by his authority as a contractor or otherwise. For the purposes of this chapter, every contractor, subcontractor, sub-subcontractor, architect, builder, or other person having charge of a work of improvement or portion thereof shall be held to be the agent of the owner.[22]

The lien attaches to the work of improvement and the land on which it is situated.[23] The amount of the lien is limited to the claimant's contract price or the reasonable value of the labor, services, equipment, or materials furnished, whichever is less.[24] To be entitled to enforce the lien, all claimants except those under direct contract with the owner or those performing actual labor for wages, must file with the owner a preliminary 20-day notice describing the labor or materials furnished, the name of the claimant, the name of the person who contracted for the labor or materials, and a description of the jobsite and must specifically note that if the bill is not paid, the improved property may be subject to a mechanic's lien.[25] Recognizing that an architect's or engineer's services may occur a considerable time before work on the project actually commences, the statute provides that architects or engineers who have furnished services for the design of the work are allowed to give their 20-day preliminary notice 20 days after the work of improvement actually commences.[26] Thereafter, the claimant must record the mechanic's lien with the county recorder within a certain time period. The lien stands in priority to any other lien, mortgage, deed of trust, or other encumbrance on the work of improvement on the site that attaches subsequent to the commencement of the work of improvement.[27] An action to enforce the mechanic's lien must be commenced within 90 days of its recording.[28]

---

[22] Cal. Civ. Code § 3110 (West 1986).

[23] *Id.* § 3128.

[24] *Id.* § 3123.

[25] *Id.* § 3097.

[26] *Id.*

[27] *Id.* § 3134.

[28] Cal. Civ. Code § 3144 (West 1986).

§ 25.3 Benefits of Mechanic's Lien Statutes for Architects and Engineers

It has long been considered that an architect's or engineer's plans and specifications or other drawings are not "material."[29] Thus, the applicability of and benefit to the architect and engineer of a mechanic's lien statute is for "labor." That the architect and engineer supply labor has been well said:

> If they did not labor, what word will characterize the service they furnished? When the architect idealized the structure and put it upon paper, what was his effort if not labor? . . . . [A] critical examination of the words of the statute reveals that it gives the lien to any person to whom a debt is due for labor performed or furnished. The word "furnished" is not synonymous with performed. One person may perform labor with his trowel; another may furnish labor with his mind.[30]

Another court stated:

> That our statute was not intended to apply alone to those who do toilsome or manual labor is apparent from its terms. . . . So, too, it seems to us the architect who furnishes the painstaking care and skill necessary in the preparation of plans for a building or other improvement of the kind mentioned in the statute, and which actually are employed in constructing the same, has "performed labor" within the meaning of our statute and is therefore entitled to a lien.[31]

As noted, the mechanic's lien statutes of the several states vary greatly. However, for purposes of this chapter, the statutes may be categorized as (1) those expressly delineating architects and engineers as beneficiaries; (2) those granting lien rights to "a person," "any person," or "every person" who provides labor or material on a work of improvement; and (3) hybrid statutes expressly delineating certain beneficiaries (but not specifically architects and engineers) and "others;" or delineating "mechanics," "laborers," and "materialmen" but not "others."

§ 25.4 —Statutes Expressly Granting Lien Rights to Architects and Engineers

Typical of statutes granting lien rights to architects and engineers is that of Florida:

---

[29] Stephens v. Hicks, 156 N.C. 239, 72 S.E. 313, 315 (1911).

[30] Williamson v. Hotel Melrose, 110 S.C. 1, 96 S.E. 407 (1918).

[31] Gaastra, Gladding & Johnson v. Bishop's Lodge Co., 35 N.M. 396, 402, 299 P. 347 (1931).

713.03. Liens for Professional Services.

(1) Any person who performs services as an architect, landscape architect, interior designer, engineer or land surveyor, subject to compliance with and the limitations imposed by this part, shall have a lien on the real property improved for any money that shall be owing to him for his services in preparing plans, specifications, or drawings used in connection with improving the real property or for his services in supervising any portion of the work of improving the real property, rendered in accordance with his contract and with the direct contract.

(2) Any architect, landscape architect, interior designer, engineer, or land surveyor who has a direct contract and who in the practice of his profession shall perform services, by himself or others, in connection with a specific parcel of real property and subject to said compliances and limitations, shall have a lien upon such real property for the money owing to him for his professional services, regardless of whether such real property is actually improved.[32]

In cases from those jurisdictions specifically allowing a mechanic's lien to architects and engineers, courts have merely stated the obvious.[33] However, the real issue that the courts have struggled with is whether or not the architect/engineer (A/E), in order to be entitled to a lien, need only have prepared plans and specifications or whether the A/E also must have supervised the work. Obviously, in those jurisdictions granting lien rights to architects and engineers, where those professionals have rendered supervisory and inspection services in addition to drafting plans and specifications, lien rights are granted.

Decisions granting mechanic's lien benefits to an architect or engineer who supervised work do not go into detail as to the nature of the supervision. Either the scope of the supervision was spelled out in the underlying contract or its nature was that normally recognized in the profession. Supervising test borings has been held not to be supervision subject to mechanic's lien security.[34] Nor may an architect or engineer be deemed to have supervised a work of improvement when such duties were not mandated by the underlying contract and the professional's acts were undertaken only for the purpose of coming within the terms of a statute requiring supervision.[35] It has been held that an architect's attendance at zoning

---

[32] Fla. Stat. Ann. § 713.03 (West 1972).

[33] Design Assocs., Inc. v. Welch, 224 Cal. App. 2d 165, 36 Cal. Rptr. 341 (1964); Dagit v. Radnor Convalescent & Nursing Home, Inc., 38 Pa. D. & C.2d 389, 53 Del. 225, 227 (1965); Bankers Trust Co. v. El Paso Pre-Cast Co., 560 P.2d 457 (Colo. 1977).

[34] Dagit v. Radnor Convalescent & Nursing Home, Inc., 53 Del. Co. 225, 227 38 Pa. D. & C.2d 389 (1965).

[35] United States *ex rel.* Charles H. Thayer v. Metro Constr. Corp., 330 F. Supp. 386 (E.D. Va. 1971).

board meetings does not constitute supervision of the sort to acquire mechanic's lien rights.[36]

A California case, *Nolte v. Smith,*[37] discusses a fact pattern falling somewhat between drawing plans and supervising work and drawing plans only. In that case, the California Court of Appeal was faced with an issue of first impression as to whether or not an engineer who had rendered services consisting of surveying, planning, and mapping property for a subdivision and preparing a subdivision map for and erecting permanent markers and monuments upon the property was entitled to a mechanic's lien. The landowner argued that these services did not constitute any improvement to the land as required by the mechanic's lien statute. The court upheld the engineer's lien rights, finding that the setting of permanent monuments in the ground following extensive engineering services "is similarly the commencement of a work of improvement, or improvement, and an integral and essential part of the scheme of improvement as those terms are used [in the statute]."[38]

In those jurisdictions allowing the imposition of a lien for the drawing of plans only, issues remain as to whether or not the plans must be actually used on a work of improvement.

Those cases allowing the imposition of a mechanic's lien when the A/E drew plans later used in the work of improvement rely on and point out the equitable nature of the remedy: to prevent unjust enrichment.[39] In one case,[40] it was argued that the architectural services were performed off the premises and as such were not the proper subject of a lien, or, more specifically, they were not "work and labor upon" any building. The court found it inconceivable that when the legislature used the term "architect" it qualified the application by meaning that the actual labor must be done upon the premises. The correct interpretation would be that the legislature contemplated the services as they were usually performed, including the architect who works at a home office in another city.

Those cases allowing the imposition of a mechanic's lien when the A/E drew plans that were *not* used on the work of improvement not only point out the equitable nature of the remedy to prevent unjust enrichment, but also rely on a liberal interpretation of the mechanic's lien law. Thus, in *O'Hara v. Architects Hartung & Association,*[41] foreclosure on a mechanic's

[36] Stratford v. Boland, 306 Pa. Super. 475, 452 A.2d 824 (1983).

[37] 189 Cal. App. 2d 140, 11 Cal. Rptr. 261 (1961).

[38] 189 Cal. App. 2d at 150.

[39] McDonald v. Filice, 252 Cal. App. 2d 613, 60 Cal. Rptr. 832 (1967); Construction Eng'g Co. v. Village Shopping Center, Inc., 168 So. 2d 826 (La. Ct. App. 1964); Parklane Properties v. Fisher, 89 Colo. 591, 5 P.2d 577 (1931).

[40] Carid Eng'g Works v. 7-Up Gold Mining Co., 111 Mont. 471, 111 P.2d 267 (1940).

[41] 163 Ind. App. 661, 326 N.E.2d 283 (1975).

lien was sanctioned when the architect's plans and specifications were ordered to facilitate accurate cost estimates and helped in the decision of whether to construct the proposed building. Similarly, when architects and engineers performed site inspections and topographical work and made presentations before administrative bodies, and when the plans were used in the actual conversion of the building, it was held that an architectural and engineering firm was entitled to a lien against the building.[42] In *Zions First National Bank v. Carlson,*[43] it was held that an architect may file a lien upon the property concerning which the architect has rendered professional service, although the plans may not be brought into fruition by erection of a building. The Utah statute provided that architects and engineers "who have furnished designs, plats, plans, maps, specifications, drawings, estimates of cost, surveys or superintendence, or who have rendered other like professional service, or bestowed labor shall have a lien upon the property upon which or concerning which they have rendered service."[44] The court held that the words "bestowed labor" were purposely broad in order to give a lien for the drawing of plats, plans, maps, or specifications which are not done directly upon the property. The liens are created for services "usually performed before the visible to the eye commencement of construction."[45] In so determining, the court noted that the prior statutes providing a lien for plans illustrating a structure of work done "or to be done" had been consolidated into the present statute.[46] In *McDonald v. Filice,*[47] the court denied the enforcement of a mechanic's lien when the architect had drawn plans that were never used on the work of improvement when it was found that the parties had rescinded the original written contract of employment and had substituted an agreement that the architect would be compensated according to the reasonable value of his services. Implicit in this act was a determination that the project contemplated by the written employment agreement was abandoned by mutual consent. Under these circumstances, no lien attached to the land.[48]

McDonald v. Filice was closely followed by *Tracy Price Associates v. Hebard,*[49] in which the California court held that when no actual

---

[42] GRW Eng'rs, Inc. v. Elam, 504 So. 2d 117 (La. Ct. App.), *cert. denied,* 506 So. 2d 1230 (1987).

[43] 23 Utah 2d 395, 464 P.2d 387 (1970).

[44] Utah Code Ann. § 38-1-3 (1953).

[45] Zions First Nat'l Bank v. Carlson, 23 Utah 2d 395, 398, 464 P.2d 387 (1970).

[46] 23 Utah 2d at 398.

[47] 252 Cal. App. 2d 613, 60 Cal. Rptr. 832 (1967).

[48] 252 Cal. App. 2d at 620. *See also* James H. Stewart & Assoc., Inc. v. Naredel of Colo., Inc., 39 Colo. App. 552, 571 P.2d 738 (1977); Chambliss/Jenkins Assoc. v. Forster, 650 P.2d 1315 (Colo. Ct. App. 1982).

[49] 266 Cal. App. 2d 778, 72 Cal. Rptr. 600 (1968).

improvement on the land had commenced, a lien for architectural services did not attach as against a trust deed or other attachment lien.

In 1984, the United States District Court for the Northern District of California in *In re Morrell*[50] distinguished *McDonald v. Filice* and *Tracy Price* and held in a Chapter 11 case that an architectural firm that had completed drawings could properly assert a mechanic's lien under the California statute even though no visible improvement had ever commenced. The facts as stated in the decision indicate that an architectural firm contracted with the bankrupt party to prepare drawings and specifications. These were completed, but the bankrupt party never commenced construction and failed to pay the architect the contract price. Thereafter, the architect recorded its mechanic's lien. Some months later, an involuntary petition under Chapter 7 was commenced against the debtor, which was later converted to Chapter 11. The trustee filed an adversary proceeding to determine the validity of various claims, including the mechanic's lien. The trustee contended that the mechanic's lien was invalid because there was no improvement on the land against which a lien could attach. The bankruptcy court granted the architect's motion for summary judgment and upheld the lien.

On review, the district court initially noted that California courts had never squarely decided whether an architect's claim for services rendered in the preparation of plans was lienable against the interest of one who contracted for the services when, through the fault of the owner of such interest, no actual work on the ground commenced.[51] The court acknowledged the general rule in California that a mechanic's lien attaches only upon commencement of a work of improvement and, as no work ever commenced, it would appear that the architects could not successfully assert the mechanic's lien. However, the court was receptive to the architect's citation to *Lamoreaux v. Andersch,*[52] in which the Minnesota Supreme Court upheld an architect's lien even though no actual work of improvement had been done. The court acknowledged that *Lamoreaux* was not controlling in California but accepted that it was in actuality "an extension of the doctrine recognized in California that where an improvement is not completed or is destroyed through the fault of the person whose interest is sought to be impressed with a lien, he [the landowner] is estopped to deny benefit."[53] The court went on to note that several California courts had considered *Lamoreaux* but, owing to differing factual scenarios, none had explicitly

---

[50] 42 Bankr. 973 (1984).

[51] *Id.* at 975.

[52] 128 Minn. 261, 150 N.W. 908 (1915), discussed in § **25.5**.

[53] *In re* Morrell, 42 Bankr. 973, 977 (1984) (citing Tracy Price Assocs. v. Hebard, 266 Cal. App. 2d 778, 787, 72 Cal. Rptr. 600 (1968)).

adopted or refuted the decision.[54] The *Morrell* court concluded that the case was distinguishable in that it did not involve a dispute over the priority position of the lien claimant and other parties. In such a situation, the lien should attach. The court stated:

> Thus, California precedents do not maintain that for a lien to be enforceable against the interest of an owner, actual work on the ground must begin. Rather, they only hold that commencement of construction is a condition precedent to giving a mechanic's lien priority over subsequent liens and encumbrances. In the present case, there is no question of priorities; Appellee seeks a lien only against the interest of appellant, successor-in-interest to debtor. Application of *Lamoreaux* is therefore appropriate in this case.[55]
>
> * * *
>
> Architects have little or no control over the construction of their designs; they can do nothing themselves to begin work on the ground to make their liens valid. Consequently, this Court adopts the holding of *Lamoreaux,* and rules that as against an owner who prevents commencement of a work of improvement, no actual or visible work on the ground is necessary for an architect to attach a mechanic's lien if the lienable work is completed.[56]

In 1986, legislation was introduced in the California Assembly that would have provided separate and distinct lien remedies for architects and engineers when there had been no actual commencement of the work of improvement. The governor vetoed the legislation.[57] At the behest of the California Council of the American Institute of Architects, the California Council of Civil Engineers and Land Surveyors, and the California Land Surveyor's Association, another bill[58] was introduced, considered, and signed by the governor in 1990. This legislation amends the California Civil Code as of January 1, 1991, and specifically grants certain lien rights to architects and engineers when the work of improvement for which they have drawn plans does not actually commence.[59]

---

[54] *Id.* (citing Nolte v. Smith, 189 Cal. App. 2d 140, 11 Cal. Rptr. 261 (1961) and McDonald v. Filice, 252 Cal. App. 2d 613, 60 Cal. Rptr. 832 (1967)).

[55] *Id.* at 978.

[56] *Id.* at 979.

[57] Comments of the staff of the California Senate Insurance, Claims and Corporations Committee to Assembly Bill No. 1789, introduced in 1990 [hereinafter Staff Comments].

[58] Assembly Bill No. 1789.

[59] Cal. Civ. Code §§ 3081.1 to .10 (West 1986). The governor, in vetoing the earlier proposed legislation, had said that he had not received any compelling evidence to support the expansion of the existing mechanic's lien laws proposed by the measure. Design professionals could, under existing law, require a property owner to secure their right to receive payment, and they could also sue a property owner for breach of contract should the owner fail to pay for services rendered. However, the architect, engineer, and land surveyor sponsors to Assembly Bill No. 1789 contended that surveys of their members presented abundant evidence showing that plans were often sold with

The legislation pertains to "design professionals" defined as certified architects, registered professional engineers, or licensed land surveyors.[60] If the landowner has taken out a building permit, the design professional shall, from the date of recordation, have a lien upon the real property for which the work of improvement was planned to be constructed, notwithstanding the absence of commencement of actual construction, if the landowner contracted for the design professional's services and is also the owner of the real property at the time of recordation of the lien. The lien shall be for the amount of the design professional's fee for services rendered before commencement of the work of improvement or the reasonable value of those services, whichever is less.[61] In order for the design professional to be entitled to a lien, it is necessary that (1) the landowner default in payment and (2) not less than 10 days before recordation of the lien, the design professional must mail to the landowner written demand for payment and (3) record with the appropriate county recorder a notice of lien.[62] The lien shall expire either on the commencement of the work of improvement or 90 days after recording the notice of lien unless the design professional files suit to enforce the lien within that time period.[63] The lien is cumulative to other remedies and shall not affect the ability of a design professional to obtain a mechanic's lien under existing law.[64] The design professional's lien provided in this legislation does not apply to a work of improvement relating to a single-family owner-occupied residence for which the construction costs are less than $100,000 in value.[65] Finally, the legislation notes that it is the intent of the legislature to establish an exclusive lien remedy for design professionals in cases in which no actual construction of a planned work of improvement is commenced before recordation of the notice of lien, and to thereby disapprove and supplant any lien remedy provided by the court decision in *In re Morrell.*[66]

A number of jurisdictions would deny the imposition of a lien when the plans and specifications were not actually used in the work of improvement.[67]

---

a property and the design professional submitting the plans was not compensated. Staff Comments.

[60] Cal. Civ. Code § 3081.1 (West 1986).

[61] *Id.* §§ 3081.2, .7.

[62] *Id.* § 3081.3.

[63] *Id.* § 3081.4.

[64] *Id.* §§ 3081.6, .8.

[65] *Id.* § 3081.10.

[66] Cal. Civ. Code § 2, ch. 8, tit. 14, pt. 4, div. 3 (West 1986).

[67] McDonald v. Filice, 252 Cal. App. 2d 613, 60 Cal. Rptr. 832 (1967); Ohrenstein v. Howell, 227 Ill. App. 215 (1922); Construction Eng'g Co. v. Village Shopping Center, Inc., 168 So. 2d 826 (La. Ct. App. 1964); Clark v. Smith, 234 Wis. 138, 290 N.W. 592 (1940).

Florida courts have construed that state's mechanic's lien statute to require that the plans be actually used on the work of improvement,[68] unless the services were rendered under a direct contract with the owner, as distinguished from a subcontract.[69]

§ 25.5 —Statutes Granting Lien Rights to "Any Person"

Typical of statutes granting lien rights to "a Person," "Any Person," or "Every Person" is that of Hawaii: "Any person or association of persons furnishing labor or material in the improvement of real property shall have a lien upon the improvement as well as upon the interest of the owner of the improvement in the real property upon which the same is situated."[70] A variation is found in Minnesota: "Whoever contributes to the improvement of real estate by performing labor, or furnishing skill, material or machinery for any of the purposes hereinafter stated . . . shall have a lien upon the improvement, and upon the land on which it is situated or to which it may be removed."[71]

The modern line of cases emanating from those states that have enacted this type of statute uniformly hold that architects and engineers fall within the term "persons." Minnesota statute using the word "whoever" has been specifically construed to apply to architects.[72]

The following is typical of the thinking in some of the older cases in which such a connection was not made:

> [W]e do not suppose that architects would classify themselves as "mechanics or laborers." One class is of as high dignity as the other in every way, but they are disassociated in our mental conception of the two; and when we think and speak of them they are naturally differentiated as belonging to separate and distinct callings, or avocations, though held in the same estimation, so far as the worthiness of the pursuit is concerned.[73]

This holding has been specifically criticized and rejected.[74]

Accepting that architects and engineers constitute "persons," a split of authority still remains as to whether or not the design professional can enforce a mechanic's lien for the mere preparation of plans and specifications or whether the A/E is also required to perform certain supervisorial work.

---

68 Miami Highland Park, Inc. v. Leslie, 142 So. 2d 754 (Fla. 1962).

69 Warshaw v. Pyms, 266 So. 2d 355 (Fla. 1972).

70 Haw. Rev. Stat. § 507-42 (1955).

71 Minn. Stat. Ann. § 514.01 (West 1986).

72 Dunham Assoc., Inc. v. Group Invs., Inc., 223 N.W.2d 376 (Minn. 1974).

73 Stephens v. Hicks, 156 N.C. 239, 72 S.E. 313, 315 (1911).

74 Gaastra, Gladding & Johnson v. Bishop's Lodge Co., 35 N.M. 396, 299 P. 347 (1931).

When the design professional seeks to impose and enforce a mechanic's lien for services incorporating both the drawing of plans and specifications and supervising the work, the jurisdictions are virtually unanimous in granting the lien.[75]

However, a number of jurisdictions limit enforcement of the lien to design professionals who have supervised the work and exclude the protection from those who have drawn plans only.[76] These decisions appear to be based on the perception that the work and labor of preparing plans and specifications, being "usually performed in the office of the architect, far removed from the site of the building," is not the type of work and labor contemplated in the statute, which work and labor "must be performed upon the structure, or at least upon the premises where the structure is being erected."[77]

Cases involving a "plans only" scenario are divided between those in which the plans were used on the work of improvement and those in which they were not.

The majority of jurisdictions recognizing lien rights when the A/E drew plans but did not supervise the work narrow their holding to situations in which the plans were actually used on the work of improvement.[78]

Within the jurisdictions granting liens to "persons," there are arguably only two decisions granting lien rights to design professionals for drawing plans that were not used on the work of improvement. Both were issued by Minnesota courts. In *Lamoreaux v. Andersch,*[79] the court very liberally construed its statute, and under a concept of "constructive improvement" held that an architect was entitled to a lien for services in preparing plans and specifications even though no work of improvement had commenced and even though the land itself was not benefitted thereby. A close reading of the case points out that the court was clearly swayed by the fact that the owner had repudiated his contract with the architect and had abandoned the project before work could commence. In a later case,[80] the Minnesota

---

[75] 35 N.M. at 396; Wilkinson v. Rowe, 266 Ala. 675, 98 So. 2d 435 (1957); General Air Conditioning Corp. v. Stewe, 156 Kan. 182, 131 P.2d 638 (1942); Freedman v. Stein, 4 N.J. 34, 71 A.2d 346 (1950); Lancaster v. McKenzie, 439 S.W.2d 728 (Tex. Ct. App. 1965); Nakashima Assoc. v. Pacific Beach Corp., 3 Haw. App. 58, 641 P.2d 337 (1982).

[76] Furlong v. Housing Auth., 132 N.J. Eq. 341, 28 A.2d 424 (1942); Robert V. Clapp Co. v. Fox, 124 Ohio St. 331, 178 N.E. 586 (1931); Stark v. McConnell, 22 Ohio Op. 123 (1940); Chesnow v. Gorelick, 246 Mich. 571, 225 N.W. 4 (1929).

[77] Stark v. McConnell, 22 Ohio Op. 123, 125 (1940).

[78] Gaastra, Gladding & Johnson v. Bishop's Lodge Co., 35 N.M. 396, 299 P. 347 (1931); Buckingham v. Flummerfelt, 15 N.D. 112, 106 N.W. 403 (1906); Gollehon, Schemmer & Assoc., Inc. v. Fairway-Bettendorf Assoc., 268 N.W.2d 200 (Iowa 1978); Sullivan v. Thomas Org., P.C., 88 Mich. App. 77, 276 N.W.2d 522 (1979).

[79] 128 Minn. 261, 150 N.W. 908 (1915).

[80] Dunham Assoc., Inc. v. Group Invs., Inc., 223 N.W.2d 376 (Minn. 1974).

Supreme Court found that if the plans were not used, they were lienable against the owner, but a bona fide purchaser or mortgagee without notice had priority over the lien claimant.

§ 25.6 —Hybrid Statutes

Some state mechanic's lien statutes provide protection to certain designated beneficiaries (but not specifically including architects and engineers) and "others" or specifically delineate "mechanics, laborers, and materialmen" but do not add "others."

The cases indicate that a majority of the jurisdictions using these statutes grant mechanic's lien rights to architects and engineers who have rendered supervisorial duties in addition to drawing plans.[81] Some of the jurisdictions grant the right only when the plans drawn were used on the work of improvement.[82] A very few would extend mechanic's lien rights when the plans were not used to prevent the inequitable result that would otherwise ensue.[83]

It must be remembered that whatever the wording of the statute, if the jurisdiction requires architects and engineers to be licensed to lawfully render their services, as virtually all states do, then a necessary condition precedent to any action to enforce a mechanic's lien is that the architect or engineer was properly licensed when the services were rendered.[84] The relationship of the architect or engineer to the original contractor also may have a negative impact on the A/E's rights. An architect or engineer cannot recover on a mechanic's lien if the A/E is in a joint venture with the original contractor.[85]

§ 25.7 Stop Notices

A state may provide that a design professional who would qualify as a proper mechanic's lien claimant under the particular statute may file a stop notice or a "notice to withhold" with the owner (public or private) or construction lender. The stop notice directs the owner or lender to withhold payments to the claimant's debtor until the claimant is paid for its labor,

---

[81] Beeson v. Overpeck, 112 Ind. App. 195, 44 N.E.2d 195 (1942).

[82] Rivers v. Pastro, 11 P.2d 491 (Alaska 1948).

[83] Korsunsky Krank Erickson Architects, Inc. v. Walsh, 370 N.W.2d 29 (Minn. 1985); Design Assoc., Inc. v. Powers, 86 N.C. App. 216, 356 S.E.2d 819 (1987).

[84] O'Kon & Co. v. Reidel, 540 So. 2d 836 (Fla. Dist. Ct. App. 1989); McDonald v. Filice, 252 Cal. App. 2d 613, 60 Cal. Rptr. 832 (1967).

[85] National State Bank of Newark v. Terminal Constr. Corp., 217 F. Supp. 341, 361 (D.N.J.), *aff'd per curiam,* 328 F.2d 315 (3d Cir. 1964).

material, or services. Most such statutes provide for a direct right of action by the claimant on the funds that were the subject of the stop notice or notice to withhold.[86]

§ 25.8 —Private Works

The California statute on stop notices on private works was drafted in response to mortgage lender protests against state court decisions holding that even after completion of construction, a lien claimant might have an equity interest in the building loan account superior to both the lender and the builder. The present stop notice statute specifically provides that claims upon construction loan funds by persons furnishing labor, material, or services are confined and limited to the statutory mechanic's lien and stop notice procedures and that no person may assert any other legal or equitable right with respect to the contract funds.[87]

The right to proceed with the stop notice does not depend on the establishment of a mechanic's lien.[88] It is an additional or cumulative remedy.[89] Its value as a cumulative remedy is particularly noteworthy in that the stop notice is directed to and attaches to the unexpended balance of the loan, not to the land, and as such survives foreclosure of a trust deed that could wipe out mechanic's liens.[90]

On receipt of a timely and properly prepared stop notice, the owner is required to withhold from the original contractor sufficient funds due to or to become due the original contractor to cover the claim. Failure to do so may render the owner personally liable to the claimant.[91]

A stop notice may be served on the construction lender. On receipt of the stop notice, the lender has the right but not the duty to withhold disbursements to the owner or original contractor. However, if the stop notice is accompanied by a bond indemnifying the lender for subsequent liability to the owner or original contractor, the lender must withhold the funds.

If there are two or more stop notices filed and the amount withheld is insufficient to pay all claims in full, a pro rata distribution is to be made without preference to the order in time in which the stop notices were filed.

---

[86] Ind. Code § 5-16-5-1 (19); Miss. Code Ann. § 85-7-181 Cal. Civ. Code § 372 (private work), § 3210 (public work) (West 1986).

[87] Cal. Civ. Code § 3264; Pankow Constr. Co. v. Advance Mortgage Corp., 618 F.2d 611, 614 (9th Cir. 1980).

[88] Diamond Match Co. v. Silberstein, 165 Cal. 282, 131 P. 874 (1913).

[89] Korherr v. Bumb, 262 F.2d 157 (9th Cir. 1958).

[90] Connolly Dev., Inc. v. Superior Court, 17 Cal. 3d 803, 533 P.2d 637, 132 Cal. Rptr. 177, *appeal dismissed,* 429 U.S. 1056, 97 S. Ct. 778 (1977).

[91] *Id.*

In the case of a stop notice directed to a lender, the stop notice will have priority over any assignment the owner or original contractor may have given the lender, whether before or after the date of the stop notice.[92]

§ 25.9 —Public Works

Public property may not be the subject of a mechanic's lien. To protect those whose labor, material, or services have resulted in a public benefit, some states have enacted stop notice remedies covering public works.[93] As is the case with private works stop notices, the state's mechanic's lien statute defines who is entitled to serve a public works stop notice and for what labor, material, or services.[94] The statutes provide that on the receipt of a timely and properly prepared stop notice, the public entity is obligated to withhold from the original contractor sufficient funds to cover the claim. Should the public entity disregard the stop notice, it may subject itself to a suit in equity filed by the claimant.[95] Provisions allow for pro rata distribution of conflicting claims in excess of the contract balance and for enforcement by litigation against the original contractor and the public entity.

§ 25.10 Construction Trust Funds

Some states provide by statute that amounts paid by a public body to a general contractor on public works are trust funds intended to protect persons who have furnished labor, material, or services on the job and that such persons are to be preferred to creditors whose claims bear no relationship to the public improvement. Typical of such a statute is that of New Jersey:

> All money paid by the state of New Jersey or by any agency, commission or department thereof, or by any county, municipality or school district in the state, to any person pursuant to the provisions of any contract for any public improvement made between any such person and the state or any agency, commission or department thereof, or any county, municipality or school district in the state, shall constitute a trust fund in the hands of such person as such contractor, until all claims for labor, materials and other charges

---

[92] A-1 Door & Material Co. v. Fresno Guar. Sav. & Loan Ass'n, 61 Cal. 2d 728, 394 P.2d 829, 40 Cal. Rptr. 85 (1964).

[93] Cal. Civ. Code § 3179 (West 1986).

[94] *Id.* § 3181.

[95] United States Fidelity & Guar. Co. v. Oak Grove Union School Dist., 205 Cal. App. 2d 226, 231, 22 Cal. Rptr. 907 (1962).

> incurred in connection with the performance of such contract shall have been fully paid.[96]

The trust attaches on payment by the public body of funds to the contractor.[97]

Statutory trust provisions are similar to stop notice remedies in that, unlike mechanic's liens that attach to the land, stop notices and statutory trusts that are impressed upon funds either held by the owner or paid over by a public owner to the contractor, which funds are for the benefit of those providing subcontracted labor, material, and services to the work of improvement.

Beneficiaries of trust fund statutes include those entitled to file mechanic's liens or who could properly recover against a public contractor's payment bond.[98] However, it has been held that claims under these statutes are more comprehensive than mechanic's liens and as such may include nonlienable items so long as those items relate to performance of a contract on public work.[99] Under this line of thinking, in those jurisdictions where the mechanic's lien would not attach for an architect's or engineer's services in drawing plans only, the architect could arguably recover for those services under a construction trust statute if such was in force in the particular jurisdiction.

In those jurisdictions providing for the imposition of a trust on funds paid to a contractor, should the contractor transfer the funds to a third party to the detriment of an unpaid architect or engineer, the architect or engineer could institute suit against the transferee to recover the funds. Depending on the procedural requirements of the jurisdiction, the architect or engineer might be able to argue that the transferee, in turn, holds the funds as a constructive trust for the benefit of the unpaid architect or engineer and as such take advantage of prejudgment attachment remedies to secure the claim. However, some jurisdictions have held that no trust arises from the mere fact that the contractor received money for a public improvement. Thus, in that situation, for a claimant to recover from a transferee, the claimant must show that at the time the claim was liquidated, there was a diversion of funds paid to the contractor and that the transferee was not a bona fide purchaser for value.[100]

---

[96] N.J. Stat. Ann. § 2A:44-148 (West 1932).

[97] Wilson v. Stretch, Inc., 44 N.J. Super. 52, 129 A.2d 599 (1957). *See also* Wis. Stat. § 779.16.

[98] Key Agency v. Continental Cas. Co., 31 N.J. 98, 155 A.2d 547 (1959).

[99] Morris F. Fox & Co. v. State, 229 Wis. 44, 281 N.W. 666 (1938).

[100] Gramatan-Sullivan, Inc. v. Koslow, 240 F.2d 523 (2d Cir. 1952) (applying New York statute).

Finally, when the contractor has transferred or wrongfully dissipated payments deemed to be a trust fund and then filed for bankruptcy in an action for breach of contract, debt, or otherwise against the contractor seeking to recoup compensation, the architect or engineer could allege that the contractor's debt was not dischargeable in bankruptcy.

§ 25.11 Surety Bonds

A surety or guarantor is one who promises to answer for the debt, default, or miscarriage of another.[101] The relationship is stipulated in a written instrument referred to as a *bond,* usually a performance or payment bond, in which the principal obligor and the surety bind themselves to a specific obligee or class for a certain sum of money. If the principal obligor fails to perform or pay, the surety will so perform or pay.

Surety bonds include private payment bonds, state public works bonds, and Miller Act payment bonds.

§ 25.12 —Private Payment Bonds

Private owners or a contractor subcontracting out certain work on a private job may or may not require a payment bond for the benefit of those supplying labor, material, or services. Pertinent provisions of the American Institute of Architects (AIA) standard form payment bond[102] provide that proper claimants on the bond include architects and engineers providing "services required for performance of the work of the contractor and the contractor's subcontractors, and all other items for which a mechanic's lien may be asserted in the jurisdiction where the labor, materials or equipment were furnished."[103] Clearly, should the AIA form payment bond be used, an architect or engineer will be deemed a beneficiary. The scope of the recovery, that is, for drawing plans and providing supervisory services only, or merely for drawing plans, will depend on the particular jurisdiction's consideration of the architect's or engineer's right to recover for those services under the particular mechanic's lien statute.

Procedurally, the AIA form payment bond treats certain claimants differently. Claimants who are employed by or have a direct contract with the contractor, to enforce their claim on the bond need only give notice to the surety and the owner stating that a claim is being made under the bond and in what amount. However, claimants who do not have a direct

---

[101] Cal. Civ. Code § 2787 (West).

[102] AIA A312-1984.

[103] *Id.* § 15.1.

contract with the contractor must furnish written notice to the contractor and owner within 90 days of having last performed labor; must have either received a rejection in whole or in part from the contractor, or not received within 30 days of furnishing notice any communication from the contractor indicating that the claim will be paid; and not having been paid within 30 days, must have sent a written notice to the surety and the owner stating that a claim is being made on the bond.[104]

A surety and, on occasion, a contractor may have its own form payment bond. The bond may or may not specifically refer to architects and engineers as beneficiaries. In this situation, assuming a contest as to whether or not architects or engineers are covered by the bond, the courts will usually review the general mechanic's lien statute in the particular jurisdiction to determine if the design professional has rights under the bond. If the provisions of the bond as to beneficiaries are ambiguous, the architect or engineer may have the benefit of the generally accepted principle that ambiguities are to be construed against the drafter of the document.

§ 25.13 —State Public Works Bonds

As lien rights do not extend to public works, statutory obligation to file a payment bond on public works contracts was established to protect laborers, materialmen, and others.

Some public works bond statutes merely provide that the agent contracting on behalf of the public entity shall require a bond securing the payment of all labor performed or materials supplied to or consumed on the particular work of improvement without specifically delineating the beneficiaries.[105] Others, such as the Kansas statute,[106] provide that the bond is for the benefit of "all persons" in whose favor liens might accrue. Therefore, architects and engineers probably would be the beneficiaries of public works payment bonds. California's public works bond statute[107] is for the benefit of those individuals and entities who could file stop notices. As noted in **§§ 25.2** and **25.9**, in California architects and engineers may file stop notices on public works.

Rights on public works payment bonds are cumulative and in addition to other rights. Thus, it is not necessary that a claimant on a public job file a stop notice before seeking recovery on the public works payment bond.[108]

Each jurisdiction will have its own particular conditions precedent to enforcement of rights against a state public works payment bond. Preliminary

[104] *Id.* § 4.

[105] N.J. Stat. Ann. § 2A:44-143 (1980).

[106] Kan. Stat. Ann. § 60-1110 (1964).

[107] Cal. Civ. Code § 3248(c) (West 1986).

[108] *Id.* § 3250.

notice to the contractor may be required,[109] and the statute may provide a period limiting the time to institute suit on the bond, usually a period less than that which would be allowed for an ordinary suit for breach of a written contract.[110]

Some state public works bond statutes specifically provide for the recovery by the prevailing party of attorneys' fees.[111] Even in those jurisdictions where the statute is silent on this issue,[112] when the underlying contract between the contractor and the persons supplying labor or services provided for the recovery of attorneys' fees, such fees have been ordered to be recovered from the bond.[113]

§ 25.14 —Miller Act Payment Bonds

Because the property of the United States is not subject to mechanic's liens, Congress has recognized that protection should be afforded to those whose labor, material, and services render a benefit to the public, and security should be given to secure the compensation owing those individuals and entities. At the federal level, this security is reflected in the Miller Act,[114] mandating that on all contracts exceeding $25,000 for the construction, alteration, or repair of any federal building or work the original contractor shall furnish to the United States payment and performance surety bonds. By the terms of 40 U.S.C. § 270b(a):

> Every person who has furnished labor or material in the prosecution of the work provided for in such contract, in respect to which a payment bond is furnished under this Act . . . and who has not been paid in full therefor . . . shall have the right to sue on such payment bond for the amount, or the balance thereof, unpaid at the time of institution of such suit and to prosecute said action to final execution and judgment for the sum or sums justly due him.

Although the statute speaks of "every person," it has been construed to in fact cover two classes of persons that are given benefits under the Act:

> The right to bring suit on a payment bond is limited to (1) those materialmen, laborers and sub-subcontractors who deal directly with the prime contractor and (2) those materialmen, laborers and subcontractors who, lacking express or implied contractual relationship with the prime contractor, have

[109] *Id.* § 3091.

[110] *Id.* § 3250 (six months after the period in which stop notices may be filed).

[111] *Id.*

[112] *See, e.g.*, Idaho Code § 54-192 (1986).

[113] Consolidated Supply Co. v. Babbitt, 96 Idaho 636, 534 P.2d 466 (1975).

[114] 40 U.S.C. § 270(a) (1978).

> direct contractual relationship with a subcontractor and who give the statutory notice of their claims to the prime contractor.[115]

The second class of persons, those who have no direct contract with the general contractor, are often referred to as *second-tier subcontractors*. These must give proper notice to the general contractor as a condition precedent to instituting suit on the bond. Notice must be forwarded to the general contractor within 90 days from the date the claimant performed the last of the labor or services or furnished the last of the material for which the claim is made.[116]

A plaintiff suing under the Miller Act is entitled to recover according to the terms of the contract, and the Miller Act surety is bound by the contract price rather than the reasonable value.[117] The statute specifically requires[118] that suit must be commenced on the bond within one year after the day on which the last of the labor was performed or material was supplied by the claimant.

Another federal statute, the Capehart Act,[119] covering the construction of military housing, also calls for the posting of a payment bond. Generally speaking, rules developed in Miller Act litigation will be applied when the Capehart Act is at issue.[120] However, the Capehart Act bond may have different notice requirements and mandate duties on the claimant not found in the Miller Act.[121]

A number of cases have addressed the issue of whether architects and engineers are beneficiaries of the Miller Act. Cases interpreting the Heard Act, the predecessor statute to the Miller Act, had held that an architect or other skilled individual who actually superintended the work was "furnishing labor."[122]

The case of *J.J. Henry Co. v. United States*[123] involved the Miller Act claim of a naval architect who had prepared plans for a ship contractor. The

---

[115] Clifford F. MacEvoy Co. v. United States *ex rel.* Calvin Tomkins, 332 U.S. 102, 107, 64 S. Ct. 890 (1944).

[116] Bowden v. United States *ex rel.* Malloy, 239 F.2d 572 (9th Cir. 1956), *cert. denied,* 353 U.S. 957 (1957); McWaters & Bartlett v. United States *ex rel.* Wilson, 272 F.2d 291 (9th Cir. 1959).

[117] Royal Indem. v. Woodbury Granite Co., 101 F.2d 689 (D.C. Cir. 1938) (construing predecessor statute).

[118] 40 U.S.C. § 270b (1978).

[119] 42 U.S.C. § 1594 (1967).

[120] D&L Constr. Co. v. Triangle Elec. Supply Co., 332 F.2d 1009 (8th Cir. 1964).

[121] Continental Casualty Co. v. Allsop Lumber Co., 336 F.2d 445 (8th Cir. 1964), *cert. denied,* 379 U.S. 968, 85 S. Ct. 662 (1965).

[122] American Sur. Co. v. United States *ex rel.* Barrow-Agee Labs, 76 F.2d 67, 68 (5th Cir. 1935).

[123] 411 F.2d 1246, 188 Ct. Cl. 39 (1969).

work was to be performed in Florida. The court, in discussing whether or not the architect's services fell within the purview of the statute, initially held that the plans and drawings were not material incorporated into the construction of a building or, in this case, a vessel.[124] As to whether the services classified the architect as a "laborer," the court looked to Florida law. Under Florida law, an architect's lien can only attach to land. The claimant in *J.J. Henry* could not have impressed a lien on land for his services and, thus not being a person who could impress a lien, could not in that case be deemed a beneficiary of the Miller Act. The *Henry* court, at least impliedly, recognized that an architect or engineer could be a beneficiary of the Miller Act, and the ultimate decision is probably correct. However, the methodology used (review of state law) in reaching the decision is suspect. The Miller Act provides a federal cause of action, and the scope of the remedy as well as the substance of the rights created thereby are matters of federal rather than state law; therefore, state law is not an appropriate reference when the Miller Act is being construed.[125]

Subsequent to *J.J. Henry,* a federal court examined the claim of an engineer under the Miller Act in which the engineer's sole function was to prepare the design, drawings, and specifications for a water tower. Save and except an occasional telephone call, the engineer had nothing further to do other than collect his bill for services rendered. The court determined that these were not sufficient services to render the engineer the beneficiary of the Miller Act. The court was not swayed by the engineer's argument that he performed his services under a duty to see to it that the owner obtained a structure in accordance with the plans and specifications. To follow this reasoning through to a conclusion, such a holding would require architects charged only with the duty of drawing plans and specifications to serve as supervising architects.[126]

Any doubt as to the applicability of the Miller Act to architects and engineers was resolved with a decision in *United States ex rel. Naberhaus-Burke, Inc. v. Butt & Head.*[127] The facts recited in *Naberhaus* are skimpy, but it appears that the engineer claimant drew plans and specifications but did not render any job supervision. Specifically rejecting any reliance on state law, the court held, without citation:

> While case law interpreting the word "labor" in section 270b(a) is relatively sparse, the word has been construed to include physical toil, but not

---

[124] 411 F.2d at 1252.

[125] F.D. Rich Co. v. United States *ex rel.* Industrial Lumber Co., 417 U.S. 116, 127, 94 S. Ct. 2157, 2164 (1974).

[126] United States *ex rel.* Charles H. Thayer v. Metro Constr. Corp., 330 F. Supp. 386 (E.D. Va. 1971).

[127] 535 F. Supp. 1155 (S.D. Ohio 1982).

> work by a professional, such as an architect or engineer. However, the term does include an architect or another professional who actually superintends the work as it is done on the jobsite.[128]

Definitively, an architect or engineer is a proper beneficiary under the Miller Act when a claim is made for services rendered in supervising all or a portion of the work of improvement. The design professional may not recover when services consisted only of the drawing of plans and specifications.

This certitude as to the architect's and engineer's position under the Miller Act is in direct contrast with the more uncertain status as a mechanic's lien, trust fund, or stop notice claimant or as a beneficiary under a private or state public works bond. However, even in those categories, the architect or engineer rendering supervisorial services in addition to or in lieu of drawing plans and specifications will, in the majority of jurisdictions, be the beneficiary of secured rights. Indeed, the architect and engineer, as a mechanic's lien, trust fund, or stop notice claimant, may be the beneficiary of rights for services rendered in drawing plans only, which is not the case under the Miller Act.

Security has been defined as something "so strong, stable or firm as to ensure safety."[129] Although the rights extended to an architect or engineer under mechanic's lien, trust fund, and stop notice statutes or private or public works payment bonds may not exhibit the degree of security set forth in this definition, they do, when applicable and properly perfected, give a reasonable degree of assurance that an architect or engineer will be compensated for labors performed.

---

[128] *Id.* at 1158.

[129] Wenzel & Henoch Constr. Co. v. Industrial Comm., 202 Wis. 595, 233 N.W. 777, 799 (1930).

PART VI

SPECIAL ISSUES OF THE 1990s

CHAPTER 26

DEALING WITH HAZARDOUS WASTE AND ENVIRONMENTAL ISSUES

Donald G. Gavin
J. Kent Holland, Jr.*

Donald G. Gavin is a partner in the law firm of Wickwire Gavin in Washington, D.C.; Vienna, Virginia; and Madison, Wisconsin. His practice in Virginia emphasizes public contract law, environmental issues, construction and surety matters. He lectures frequently throughout the country on subjects dealing with hazardous waste and treatment facilities, construction, and government contracts. He has authored and coauthored numerous books, articles, and other publications on construction, environmental, procurement, and surety subjects and has served on advisory panels to several federal grantor agencies concerned with construction under federal assistance. Mr. Gavin is a Fellow of the American Bar Association. He earned a degree in economics from the University of Pennsylvania's Wharton School, a J.D. degree from the University of Pennsylvania Law School, and a masters of law degree in government procurement law from George Washington University.

J. Kent Holland, Jr., is a partner in the law firm of Wickwire Gavin in Vienna, Virginia. His practice emphasizes federal assistance, government contracts, construction law, EPA grants, and hazardous waste law. He received a B.S. degree in earth sciences from West Chester University in Pennsylvania and earned his J.D. from the Villanova University School of Law. Mr. Holland is chairman of the Superfund Procurement Committee of the American Bar Association Public Contract Law Section. He is the author and coauthor of numerous articles and books on the subjects of procurement, contract management, construction claims, environmental construction projects, and liability and indemnification under hazardous waste cleanup actions.

*The authors gratefully acknowledge the research and writing assistance of Scott A. Fenske, an associate with Wickwire Gavin, P.C., and the assistance of David J. Dybdahl of Corroon & Black with this chapter's insurance discussion.

§ 26.1 Introduction

According to the United States General Accounting Office (GAO), more than 425,000 hazardous waste sites potentially need cleanup. By some estimates, it is projected that the cost of cleaning up America will be between $400 and $700 billion over the next 50 years.

This chapter identifies important opportunities available for engineers to participate in the cleanup effort. It also addresses some of the major risks involved for those performing consulting services or contracting on hazardous waste cleanup projects.

The largest sector for potential cleanup work appears to be the projects to be managed by the potentially responsible parties (PRPs) that are liable for cleanup costs pursuant to the Comprehensive Environmental Response Compensation and Liability Act (CERCLA or Superfund).[1] Whereas the Environmental Protection Agency (EPA) was initially the principal agency responsible for cleanup actions and spending monies for engineers to perform remedial investigation/feasibility studies (RI/FS) and design services, there are now increasing contracting opportunities directly with PRP groups and other federal agencies, including the Department of Defense, the Department of Energy, and the United States Army Corps of Engineers.

CERCLA defines *removal actions* to include initial monitoring and assessment activities, the cleanup disposal and removal of hazardous substances, provision of alternative water supplies, site security, and temporary evacuation and housing of threatened individuals not otherwise provided for.[2] *Remedial actions,* on the other hand, are actions necessary to

---

[1] 42 U.S.C. §§ 9601–9675 (1990).

[2] *Id.* § 9601(23).

accomplish a permanent remedy and are taken instead of or in addition to the removal action. They may include perimeter protection using dikes, trenches, or ditches, the cleanup of released hazardous substances, destruction and disposal of wastes, and on-site incineration.[3] Removal actions are considered to be those designed for short-term abatement, whereas remedial actions are intended to restore long-term environmental quality.[4]

Concern about risk management is a significant barrier to entering the remedial action contracting industry. Before entering this field, the contractor, whether an engineer or general construction contractor, must carefully consider the risk versus the opportunity. Because the hazardous waste cleanup business is in its infancy and many unique liability issues surround this type of work, there is no clear body of legal precedent providing direction on how legal issues will be resolved, nor is there a body of case precedent for insurance carriers to look to in determining the likelihood of loss.

In choosing to perform this work, the response action contractors (RACs) must depend on a multifaceted approach to handle the unique risks. Insurance will not be the exclusive solution. This chapter explains some of the risks facing RACs and provides suggestions for dealing with those risks.

§ 26.2 Environmental Statutes

An exhaustive discussion of the environmental statutes creating opportunities and risks for engineers could fill a book. **Sections 26.3** through **26.5** briefly discuss a few of the key statutes pertaining to hazardous wastes and toxic pollutants.

§ 26.3 —Resource Conservation and Recovery Act

The Resource Conservation and Recovery Act (RCRA) was originally passed by Congress in 1976 and was significantly amended in 1980 and 1984.[5] This statute creates a regulatory scheme to address hazardous wastes from generation to final disposal. This is sometimes known as the *cradle-to-grave* system to regulate the movement of hazardous wastes.

RCRA deals with both solid waste and hazardous waste, which are broadly defined to include not only solids, but also liquids and contained gaseous substances. The terms have been defined by EPA to include any

---

[3] *Id.* § 9601(24).

[4] T&E Indus., Inc. v. Safety Light Corp., 680 F. Supp. 696, 706 (D.N.J. 1988).

[5] Pub. L. No. 94-550, 90 Stat. 2796 (1976), *amended by* Pub. L. No. 96-482, 94 Stat. 2334 (1980); Hazardous and Solid Waste Amendments of 1984, Pub. L. No. 98-616, 98 Stat. 3221 (codified at 42 U.S.C. §§ 6901–6992 (1990)).

discarded material, whether the material is disposed of, treated in lieu of disposal, burned, or recycled.[6] Pursuant to RCRA, EPA has listed, in the Code of Federal Regulations, specific waste that it deems to be hazardous.[7] Waste has been identified as being hazardous by EPA if it exhibits any of four specified characteristics, including reactivity, ignitability, corrosivity, or toxicity.[8]

RCRA is prospective in scope, applying to ongoing waste production and disposal and not to inactive hazardous waste sites. Penalties for violation of RCRA range from civil liability to criminal penalties.

§ 26.4 —Comprehensive Environmental Response Compensation and Liability Act (CERCLA)

EPA deals with inactive waste sites through its programs under the Comprehensive Environmental Response Compensation and Liability Act (CERCLA or Superfund).[9] The principal purpose of Superfund is to deal with uncontrolled releases of hazardous substances to the environment, including those occurring before 1980 and, therefore, outside the regulatory program established under the Resource Conservation and Recovery Act (RCRA). Under Superfund, the federal government has been authorized to clean up hazardous wastes and toxic pollutants in water, air, and on land and to recover the costs of these cleanup actions from the parties responsible for the pollution (potentially responsible parties or PRPs). The classes of persons potentially liable under Superfund include owners and operators of facilities contaminated by or containing hazardous substances; persons who arranged for disposal or treatment of hazardous substances; and persons who accepted hazardous substances for transportation or selected the disposal facility.

Hazardous substance is defined broadly to include any substance that has been designated as hazardous or toxic under the Clean Water Act, any hazardous waste designated under RCRA, any hazardous air pollutant listed under the Clean Air Act, any eminently hazardous chemical substance under the Toxic Substances Control Act (TSCA), and any other substance listed by EPA.[10] Oil, natural gas, or synthetic gas of pipeline quality is not included in the definition of hazardous substance and is, therefore, not addressed by the Superfund law.

---

[6] 40 C.F.R. § 261.2 (1990).

[7] *Id.* § 261.

[8] 42 U.S.C. § 6921 (1990); 40 C.F.R. §§ 260–261 (1990).

[9] 42 U.S.C. §§ 9601–9675 (1990).

[10] *Id.* § 9601(14).

Liability under Superfund is based on the strict liability standard, meaning liability without regard to negligence or fault.[11] Liability under Superfund also may be joint and several, meaning that each responsible party is individually liable for all costs and damages related to the site contamination and cleanup.[12]

§ 26.5 —Toxic Substances Control Act

The Toxic Substances Control Act (TSCA) addresses chemical substances and mixtures.[13] In addition to applying to manufacturers and processors, it poses restrictions on use or handling of chemicals and mixtures and contains specific provisions applying to the manufacture, use, and disposal of polychlorinated biphenyls (PCBs), which are commonly used in electrical transformers and equipment.[14]

TSCA requires manufacturers to notify the EPA before producing a new chemical substance that is on EPA's list of chemicals. A second regulatory feature of TSCA is the regulation of the production, use, distribution, and disposal of hazardous chemical substances.

§ 26.6 Contracts Available from EPA

The EPA has awarded six basic categories of Superfund contracts. These are:

1. **Removal action.** The removal action contractor provides EPA with technical and management assistance for EPA's removal action program under Superfund. Contracts are also available to provide such assistance for the corrective action program financed by the Leaking Underground Storage Tank (LUST) Trust Fund.

   EPA has awarded emergency response technical assistance team (TAT) contracts, whereby contractors monitor response activities, provide special services (such as aerial survey and mapping support), collect samples, and provide temporary administrative support. Under emergency response cleanup services (ERCS) contracts, the

---

[11] *Id.* § 6901(32); Bulk Distrib. Centers, Inc. v. Monsanto Co., 589 F. Supp. 1437 (S.D. Fla. 1984).

[12] *See, e.g.*, United States v. Chem-Dyne Corp., 572 F. Supp. 802 (S.D. Ohio 1983); United States v. A&F Materials Co., 578 F. Supp. 1249 (S.D. Ill. 1984); O'Neil v. Picillo, 883 F.2d 176 (1st Cir. 1989).

[13] 15 U.S.C. §§ 2601–2629 (1990).

[14] *Id.* § 2605(e).

contractor provides cleanup personnel, equipment, and materials for purposes such as containing, recovering, and disposing of hazardous substances, analyzing samples, and restoring areas after cleanup is completed.

2. **Remedial response.** The response action contractors (RACs) provide EPA with technical assistance and resources for cleanup activities and may perform the actual cleanup work. Field investigation team (FIT) contracts are awarded to groups of multidisciplinary professional and technical personnel. The preremedial activities conducted under these contracts are for the purpose of conducting preliminary assessments and site inspections needed to determine the nature of the problem at a site and to gather information to support EPA's hazard ranking system. Remedial engineering management (REM) contracts are awarded by EPA to engineering firms to perform tasks such as remedial investigation/feasibility studies (RI/FS) to determine the type and extent of contamination at a hazardous waste site. They also include engineering design and construction of small remedial actions, community relations activities, and support of enforcement actions. EPA no longer awards these contracts, but instead awards alternative remedial contract strategy (ARCS) contracts.

3. **Support services.** Support services contractors provide special technical support to EPA regional offices and headquarters. These contracts cover safety and technical training, demonstration of new or novel technology, laboratory analysis and sample control, quality assurance, aerial survey and mapping, and remote sensing.

   EPA awards environmental emergency response unit (EERU) contracts in two distinct groups. The first is concerned with operating and maintenance of field ready equipment and with providing support services to EPA's environmental response teams. The second group is for research and development aimed primarily at shakedown and demonstration of prototype equipment and transfer of information on research and development projects to user communities.

   Other support contracts awarded by EPA are for the contract laboratory program providing analytical services for Superfund and aerial survey and mapping support used to assess areas of danger, characterize the extent of the problems, and assist in determining a need for cleanup.

4. **Technical enforcement support.** Contractors provide technical enforcement support (TES) to EPA regions and headquarters to assist in enforcing the Comprehensive Environmental Response Compensation and Liability Act (CERCLA) and the Resource Conservation and Recovery Act (RCRA). These contracts include tasks such as providing expert witnesses, searching for those responsible for problems at a

hazardous waste site, evaluating comprehensive ground water monitoring data, and inspecting RCRA facilities and reviewing their closure plans.

5. **Policy, program management, and administrative services.** Contracts are awarded by EPA headquarters to support the formulation of Superfund policy and program implementation. Contracts are also awarded for development and maintenance of automated data processing (ADP) systems and data handling services for EPA headquarters and regional offices. EPA has awarded contracts entitled Technical Support for Superfund Policy Formulation, Support for Superfund Implementation and Evaluation, Policy/Analytical Support for Superfund Implementation, and ADP Services. Each of these contracts, despite their names, is essentially intended to provide technical services by engineering consultants. It is on these contracts, however, that EPA has been accused of permitting outside contractors to run the Superfund program. These allegations have been based largely on a misunderstanding of the nature of the work performed under the contracts. Even on so-called policy contracts, the contractors are only providing information, review, comments, support, and technical data and information and services to assist EPA in rendering EPA policy decisions. Only EPA can make policy. Consequently, contracting out for these services seems appropriate and necessary.

6. **ARCS contracts.** The principle contract type used by EPA for remedial action today is the ARCS contract. This contract requires the engineering consultant/contractor to have a full-service capability from the RI/FS through the remedial implementation. In what is essentially a design-build contract, EPA believes it will achieve the benefit of continuity of performance, increased contractor accountability, accelerated cleanup, and improved performance incentives. EPA awards multiple contracts in each EPA region or zone. Under these indefinite-quantity contracts the base award is relatively small, but EPA holds out the carrot of options for additional work based on EPA's capacity requirements and the contractor's performance. When this type of contract was initiated, numerous engineering firms competed for the contracts, believing this would be the primary vehicle for EPA to clean up remedial action sites. Although this has been the case, the contracts have been underfunded and far fewer than expected work assignments have been awarded to the chosen contractors. Much of the responsibility for cleaning up projects has been transferred to the Army Corps of Engineers by EPA, and EPA is opting to emphasize enforcement actions under Superfund to cause potentially responsible parties (PRPs) to design and implement their own cleanups. EPA also has steered more funds into cooperative agreements with the states, whereby the states in turn award contracts to consulting firms.

The specific functions to be performed by the ARCS contractor include:

a. **Site-specific project management.** This includes planning project activities; monitoring and controlling project activities; providing project coordination with other EPA offices, states, and other agencies; and providing community relations and coordination.
b. **Remedial planning.** This includes conducting RI/FS; characterizing site conditions; developing and evaluating remedial alternatives; and recommending a remedy or a range of remedies for EPA's consideration.
c. **Remedial design.** This includes developing plans, drawings, and specifications for the selected remedy and preparing invitations for bids for construction contractors.
d. **Remedial implementation/construction management.** This involves selecting subcontractors or support contractors for general construction, earth moving, well drilling, fence building, and other activities necessary for the project. It also includes providing construction management and technical engineering services during construction.

Under the ARCS contracts, the general construction contracts may be directly between EPA and the general contractor, between the ARCS contractor and the general contractor, or between the Corps of Engineers or state government and the general contractor. When the construction contract is held by the ARCS contractor, the ARCS contractor is responsible for selecting the subcontractors based on competitive sealed bidding, managing the construction, and providing technical engineering services. When the construction contract is held by EPA, the ARCS contractor is expected to assist, but not be a party to the procurement; manage the construction; and provide technical engineering services. When the construction contract is held by the Corps of Engineers or the state, the ARCS contractor could be asked only to provide technical engineering services.

The ARCS contracts are based on cost-plus award fee and are level-of-efforts contracts. They vary in size and are for a 10-year period of performance plus an option period.

§ 26.7 Contracts with Potentially Responsible Parties and Federal Agencies

Due to EPA's current "enforcement first" policy, the emphasis at EPA is on having the potentially responsible parties (PRPs) take the lead in procuring services to perform remedial actions. Providing services for PRPs could be the largest source of business in the 1990s. There appears to be growing sentiment in the PRP community against retaining the same engineers who work for EPA. This may, in part, be due to the fact that the PRP may seek an engineer who, in performing work on the site, will be aggressive in challenging the record of decision (ROD) issued by EPA which the PRP may believe creates an excessively expensive remedy.

Before accepting contracts with EPA, an engineer must, therefore, decide what aspect of the market the firm desires to serve. This is particularly important due to EPA's proposed conflict of interest (COI) rules, which it has been enforcing through contract provisions and guidance documents.[15] Under the COI rules, an engineer's future contracting opportunities are limited. Before accepting work for a PRP or state or other federal agency, the engineer may be required by EPA to apply to the agency for permission to do so. Engineers are being required by EPA to disclose the names of their clients and provide other information to demonstrate that they have no COI. The burdens and limitations on future contracting opportunities, when combined with the significant reduction in contracting funds being spent by EPA on cleanups it is managing, is contributing to the decision of many engineers to choose not to work for EPA and instead provide services exclusively to PRPs and other federal agencies.

§ 26.8 Traditional versus Hazardous Waste Engineering

In traditional engineering work, if a project involves design and construction of a wastewater treatment plant or a complex building, the procedure probably will include investigation, study, design, and finally construction. A study is typically conducted by the engineer within the parameters of the objectives, cost constraints, and operating conditions dictated by the client. The engineer assesses the possible alternatives and recommends the option deemed to be most suitable in consideration of the client's objectives. The preliminary and final designs are then produced and bids for construction are accepted. The contract is awarded to the contractor who will proceed in accordance with the specified design details. The experienced engineer can determine when enough information has been obtained in the study phase and can proceed with relative confidence into design and implementation. This confidence comes from knowing that uncertainties are manageable and can be accommodated through minor (low cost/schedule/quality impact) changes.

It appears that the majority of relevant parties, including engineers, have assumed that hazardous waste engineering can be conducted in the same manner as traditional engineering practice. Specifically, they have assumed that by the exercise of due care, the uncertainties inherent in the work may be reduced to manageable levels, thereby permitting design and construction to proceed routinely as they would on any other type of project.

---

[15] 48 C.F.R. §§ 1509, 1510, 1512, 1527, 1552 (1990).

Although the steps the engineer follows during hazardous waste site remediation are similar to those described, the risks are far greater. During the remedial investigation/feasibility studies (RI/FS), the engineer conducts investigations to determine the level and extent of site contamination. The information derived from the investigations is used to estimate the risk the contamination poses to public health and the environment. EPA uses a risk assessment mechanism to estimate the risk posed by contamination at the hazardous waste site to justify the need for remediation and determine the appropriate remedy—that which reduces risk from contamination to *acceptable* levels. The importance of this step cannot be overstated. In the absence of a firm body of knowledge and experience or a slate of standards to apply to specific sites, EPA employs a site-specific risk assessment to show that the selected remedy will protect public health and the environment while being cost effective.

Understandably, risk assessment plays a key role in the remedial process. Its purpose is to discriminate among remedial approaches (types of remedies employed, the extent of cleanup needed) in a very high stakes game. Overscoping the remedy may waste millions of dollars; underscoping may leave unacceptable levels of contamination and consequential residual risk. Thus, the risk assessment process must be well refined and capable of producing convincing evidence of the adequacy of the remedy. Unfortunately, it cannot.

The risk assessment process derives an estimate of overall risk by estimating the location, composition, and quantities of contaminants that reside underground, and by estimating the movement, fate, and effects of exposure of those contaminants on the public or the environment. Although the process can derive a value for risk with relative ease, there are huge uncertainties present in each of the risk parameters: location, composition, toxicity, movement, fate, exposure effects. These uncertainties are caused by the inability of current technology to provide accurate estimates. The net result is a risk assessment that does not offer convincing evidence of remedy adequacy.

Major engineering firms with the most significant experience performing hazardous waste site remediation work believe that uncertainties are not eliminated, nor are they even sufficiently reduced.[16] The nature of the hazardous waste contamination problem is not yet fully understood.

Major residual uncertainties at hazardous waste sites that cannot be reduced to manageable levels using current RI/FS technologies include (1) an incomplete understanding of the location of significant contamination, (2) insufficient characterization of the subsurface stratigraphy, and (3) insufficient understanding of the transport and fate of contaminants.

---

[16] W. Wallace & D. Lincoln, *How Scientists Make Decisions about Ground Water and Soil Remediation,* Colloquium 5: Ground Water and Soil Contamination Remediation: Toward Compatible Science, Policy, and Public Perception (1990).

Remedial projects entering the design and implementation phases consequently carry a considerable degree of risk and exposure from claims arising out of the discovery of additional contamination, misdirection of the cleanup implementation, or unexplained health effects.

Except for very small and simple sites, it is not always possible for the engineer to accurately locate the contamination and estimate its transport and fate using the normal exploratory methods available. The technologies generally available include taking soil borings and analyzing ground water. These methods can, at best, sample a small area of the site. To sample the soil on an entire site would destroy the site at a great expense. Moreover, engineers experienced in this field maintain that due to the highly variable nature of the subsurface, it is necessary to take samples over many intervals to provide the necessary resolution to address the problem. Data gathering using these methods is extraordinarily expensive, and owners typically are not willing to pay for and do not expect an engineer to perform tests extensive enough to fully and accurately analyze a site.

Thus, the risk exposure to the response action contractor (RAC) and the design engineer working on a hazardous waste project is significant. The design professional must take appropriate action through management and field activities and contract drafting to reduce the risk as much as possible. For example, some branches of engineering explicitly recognize the problems of uncertainty early in the design process. Geotechnical engineers who deal with substantial physical uncertainty in soil and foundation engineering and dam design have used an "experimental" or "observational" method for conducting their work. In this work, the uncertainties are explicitly identified during the study phase and accounted for in the design and implementation phases. Site models are developed with the recognition that deviations to the model may exist. The observational method formally recognizes such deviations and incorporates contingency plans into the design and implementation phases. This method is now being applied to hazardous waste remediation with good results.[17]

§ 26.9 Loss Prevention Programs

To reduce exposure to financial loss, architect/engineers (A/Es) active in the hazardous waste site remediation field have found it essential to establish loss prevention programs including business practices evaluation, training, supervision, control, and monitoring.

[17] D. Mark, L. Holm, & N. Ziemba, Application of the Observational Method to an Operable Unit Feasibility Study, presented at Hazardous Materials Control Research Institute Tenth National Conference (1989).

At the inception of the work, the engineer must evaluate the project to determine and identify potential sources or causes of liability that may include performance failures and property damage, damage to the environment and natural resources, subcontractor disputes, employee claims and third-party claims alleging injuries, and damage from environmental impact or impairment. The engineer must exercise care in all communications with the client to avoid creating great expectations that cannot be satisfied along with any express or implied guarantees or warranties concerning the ability of the design or work to alleviate hazardous waste problems at the site.

Site owners and those potentially responsible for the cleanup of a site often do not understand that the engineer has greater concern about risks than on a normal construction project. In contract negotiations on behalf of engineers and contractors, the negotiating positions of certain owners, as well as their attorneys, have failed to reflect the unusual exposure involved in this work. Consequently, such owners have sought express guarantees and warranties not only as to performance, but also that the contract actions will correct the environmental problems. Such owners have demanded that at the conclusion of the work, the response action contractor (RAC) sign a certification attesting that all contaminated soils and pollutants have been removed from the site and that the site is in complete conformance with all federal and state laws. Some owners also have demanded that the contractor indemnify the owner for any and all damages and liabilities arising out of work on the site. Finally, such owners typically demand that the contractor be responsible for exercising a standard of care that is the "best" or "state-of-the-art" practiced nationally.

The more knowledgeable the client and the client's attorney with hazardous waste site remediation, the more likely it is that the owner will negotiate contract terms more favorable to the engineer by shifting certain risks to the owner and by accepting the uncertainties that are inherent in the work. Important arguments for why an engineer should not accept responsibility for indemnifying the owner are: (1) the owner of the site is otherwise responsible for the environmental damage pursuant to relevant federal and state laws and (2) the owner is not paying the RAC to be an insurance company. Certainly the fees paid to the RAC are approximately equal to or not significantly greater than fees paid on other types of engineering and contracting work, and thus provide no basis for a major contingency.

§ 26.10 Cleanup Standards

The engineer or contractor performing cleanup work must give proper priority to compliance with all statutory requirements and accurate documentation of the scope and cost of the cleanup. This responsibility is significant because response costs are often so substantial that few potentially responsible parties (PRPs) can easily negotiate a satisfactory resolution of Superfund cases.

As a guideline, the engineer or contractor will want to ensure that its work is in compliance with applicable technical standards. For example, § 104(c)(4) of the Comprehensive Environmental Response Compensation and Liability Act (CERCLA) states that remedial measures selected in government cleanups financed by Superfund must be practicable, in accordance with the National Contingency Plan (NCP), and cost effective. Section 105(7) of CERCLA requires that the NCP include "means of assuring that remedial action measures are cost-effective over the period of potential exposure to the hazardous substances or contaminated materials." Section 107(a)(4)(A) also states that response costs the United States government or state may recover must be "not inconsistent" with the NCP.

Because these statutory requirements essentially do not set an environmental standard, however, the prudent engineer or contractor will want to ensure that any action on a cleanup site is confirmed with an individual from the governmental entity (such as the Corps of Engineers or the EPA) who has actual contractual authority. As part of this effort, engineers and construction contractors will want to confirm any deviations, directives, guidance, criteria, or other information that may relate to compliance with the statutory requirements. Of course, remedial actions that involve destruction, treatment, off-site storage, or secured disposition of hazardous substances also must comply with the hazardous waste management regulations of Subchapter III of the Resource Conservation and Recovery Act (RCRA).

Additionally, remedial action under CERCLA, as amended by the Superfund Amendments and Reauthorization Act of 1986 (SARA), must conform with applicable or relevant and appropriate requirements (ARARs).[18] The remedial actions also must comply with the ARARs promulgated under more stringent state laws, provided the state has consistently applied them in similar circumstances at their sites. EPA has explained and interpreted the meaning of the ARARs in the NCP preamble.[19] EPA also has issued interim guidance interpreting the ARARs.[20] An EPA manual entitled "CERCLA Compliance with Other Laws Manual" (August 8, 1988) and an EPA guidance entitled "RI/FS Guidance" (October 1989) provide additional information on cleanup standards. Guidance on the overall remedy selection process is provided in "Interim Guidance on Superfund Selection of Remedy" (December 24, 1986) and "Additional Interim Guidance for FY 87 Records of Decision" (July 23, 1987). All of these are available from EPA. ARARs may be ambient or chemical-specific requirements

[18] 42 U.S.C. § 9621(d) (1990).

[19] 40 C.F.R. § 300 (1990).

[20] 52 Fed. Reg. 32,496 (1987).

(such as maximum contaminant levels under the Safe Drinking Water Act); performance, design, or other action-specific requirements (such as RCRA closure regulations); or location requirements (such as laws for hazardous waste facilities).

There is a statutory preference for remedies involving treatment that permanently and significantly reduce volume, toxicity, or mobility of hazardous substances and use permanent treatment technologies or resource recovery technologies to the maximum extent practicable.[21]

On Superfund-sponsored cleanups, EPA is required to review cleanups at least once every five years when hazardous waste substances have been left on-site. This is to assure that human health and the environment are being adequately protected.[22] EPA has perpetual oversight authority enabling it to require further remedial work. As a result of this continued EPA oversight, an engineer's work may be inspected and found inadequate years after performance was completed. Consequently, a sight remediation may be called into question a decade later and an engineer may be subject to liability for hazardous waste that may be leaking onto the land, into the water, or into the environment.

§ 26.11 Areas of Potential Liability for Response Action Contractor

The response action contractor (RAC) has exposure to third-party liability from individuals claiming injuries as a result of the RAC's work at a site. Injured third parties could include employees of the RAC, other contractors or subcontractors, or even the owner. Because most employees are restricted in their recovery for work-related injuries by state workers' compensation laws, there is incentive to look to the engineer on the site as having failed in its duty to locate or identify contaminants or provide job-site safety. Claims also may arise from third parties off-site, claiming that a hazardous waste or contaminated material has been released or migrated off-site into ground water or wells, causing environmental impact damage or damage to natural resources.

Another area of claims against the RAC stems from owner dissatisfaction with the RAC's performance. This can occur because of the owner's false expectations concerning what the RAC was to accomplish. In particular, the RAC is sometimes asked or expected to devise an investigation and a design that will guarantee that the site is completely clean and in compliance with all applicable federal and state laws. As discussed, such complete guarantees are not technically feasible and are unwise.

---

[21] 42 U.S.C. § 9621(b) (1990).

[22] *Id.* § 9621(c).

§ 26.12 —Consultant Liability for Negligent Misrepresentation Concerning Hazardous Waste

As discussed in § **26.8**, using the current state of the art and standard of due care, it is generally impossible within time and budget confines to ascertain the exact locations of hazardous wastes under or in the soil or ground water of a site. To the extent that a consultant breaches its standard of care and negligently investigates and reports the types and quantities of wastes at a site, however, liabilities may arise to the other contracting party under the theory of negligent misrepresentation. An early and important case applying this theory was *Gagne v. Bertran.*[23] In *Gagne,* the California Supreme Court held that a soil tester was liable for misrepresentation for stating that there was "nothing to worry about, o.k., 12 to 16 inches is about all," when, in fact, it was determined that the land in question contained 3 to 6 feet of fill. The court found that this was a statement of fact made by the soil scientist, with knowledge that it would be relied upon by the owner to his detriment. However, the scope of the damages suffered by the owner was limited by the court.

On the other hand, there are cases holding that mere nondisclosure of soil conditions does not constitute misrepresentation. In *Nei v. Boston Survey Consultants, Inc.,*[24] the court held that the surveyor had no duty to warn property purchasers about potential problems caused by a high water table when the surveyor had no contractual relationship to the purchasers. It is clear that the professional who makes a negligent misrepresentation also may be held liable to other contractors. In *Craig v. Everett M. Brooks Co.,*[25] an engineer incorrectly placed offset stakes that were relied upon by the general contractor. It was held that despite the lack of privity of contract between engineer and contractor, the contractor nevertheless could recover against the engineer on theories of negligence, reckless misrepresentation, or intentional misrepresentation.

§ 26.13 —Responsibility of Parties and Recognition of Risk

Due to the uncertainties inherent in the environmental and geologic site conditions and the potential for damage to the environment, in spite of the engineer's exercise of due care during site investigations or remedial work, some engineers have negotiated into the contract a clause whereby the client expressly states that it recognizes the risk inherent in the work. A

[23] 43 Cal. 2d 481, 275 P.2d 15 (1954).

[24] 388 Mass. 320, 446 N.E.2d 681 (1983).

[25] 351 Mass. 497, 222 N.E.2d 752 (1967).

typical clause provides that the client recognizes that environmental, geologic, and geotechnical conditions can vary from those encountered at the times when and locations where data are obtained by consultants, and that the limitation on available data results in some level of uncertainty in interpreting these conditions, despite the use of due professional care. The client also states its recognition of the fact that within the times and budgets provided for the work and without excavating or destroying the entire site, there is a potential for failure to detect hazardous substances or underground tanks despite the use of reasonable care in the performance of the service.

Recognition-of-risk clauses also may state that the client recognizes that the commonly used exploration methods themselves involve an inherent risk. For example, while drilling the contractor may penetrate through an aquifer of contaminated fluid and thereby contaminate otherwise noncontaminated ground water. Finally, clients have been asked to recognize that projects such as contaminated waste sites and sanitary and landfill sites may not perform as anticipated by the client even if consultants' services are performed with due care.

§ 26.14 —Warranties and Guarantees

Some site owners attempt to obtain a guarantee from the engineer that would require the engineer to make any design changes and corrections to the design or work at its own expense regardless of whether the design or other work was performed in accordance with the appropriate standard of care. Such a warranty provision is similar to that contained in a standard construction contract. It is not appropriate, however, for particular engineering work on hazardous waste projects. Nevertheless, in the administration of its alternative remedial contract strategy (ARCS) contracts, EPA has attempted to unilaterally insist on the use of strict warranty provisions after contract award and without additional compensation, causing contract disputes with contractors.

The nature of hazardous waste work dictates that there will be an evolving design and changes throughout the project as conditions are encountered differing from those initially anticipated and as proposed technologies do not appear to resolve the waste problem as favorably as anticipated.

§ 26.15 Law Applicable to Standard of Practice

The A/E is expected to perform in accordance with the usual and accepted standards of the profession at the time and place in question. The standard is becoming more commonly a "national" as opposed to a "local" standard of care. This does not mean there is a guarantee that, in performing work in accordance with that standard, a satisfactory result will ensue. The responsibility of an architect or engineer has been described as being essentially the same as that of a lawyer to a client or a physician to a patient. The architect's duty was well described in *Koombs v. Beede,* which stated:

> The undertaking of an architect implies that he possesses skill and ability, including taste, sufficient to enable him to perform the required services at least ordinarily and reasonably well; and that he will exercise and apply in the given case his skill and ability, his judgment and taste, reasonably and without neglect. But the undertaking does not imply or warrant a satisfactory result. It will be enough that any failure shall not be by the fault of the architect. There is no implied promise that miscalculations may not occur. An error of judgment is not necessarily evidence of a want of skill or care, for mistakes and miscalculations are incident to all the business of life.[26]

In the absence of an express contractual provision to the contrary, an architect has been held to be not liable for faulty or defective plans unless the problems are caused by neglect in exercising skill or care.[27] Again, in *Friendship Heights Associates v. Vlastimil Koubek, AIA,*[28] it was held: "an architect does not, by agreeing simply to perform work for a client, guaranty the ultimate results, only that he or she will perform with the requisite degree of care and skill."

In *Clark v. City of Seward,* the standard of practice was defined as follows:

> In performing professional services for a client, an engineer has a duty to have that degree of learning and skill ordinarily possessed by reputable engineers, practicing in the same or a similar locality and under similar circumstances. It is his further duty to use the care and skill ordinarily used in like cases by reputable members of his profession practicing in the same or a similar locality under similar circumstances, and to use reasonable diligence and his best judgment in the exercise of his professional skill and in the application of his learning, in an effort to accomplish the purpose for which he was employed.[29]

There is a random element that is inherent when dealing with hazardous waste. Due to the presence of a similar random element, the case of *City of Mounds View v. Walijarvi*[30] held that the A/E is not responsible as a guarantor of the results of its services. The court stated that assuming that the

---

[26] 89 Me. 187, 36 A. 104 (1896).

[27] Weill Constr. Co. v. Thibodeaux, 491 So. 2d 166 (La. Ct. App. 1986).

[28] 573 F. Supp. 100 (D. Md. 1983).

[29] 659 P.2d 1227 (Alaska 1983).

[30] 263 N.W.2d 420 (Minn. 1978).

architect possesses the skill and ability requisite to performing the required services at least ordinarily and reasonably well and that the architect practices those services without neglect, "the undertaking does not imply or warrant a satisfactory result." The court specifically rejected the plaintiff's theory of implied warranty, stating that adoption of such a theory "would in effect impose strict liability on architects for latent defects in the structures they design." The court stated that:

> even in the present state of relative technological enlightenment, the keenest engineering minds can error in their most searching assessment of the natural factors which determine whether structural components will adequately serve their intended purpose. Until the random element is eliminated in the application of architectural services, we think it fair that the purchaser of the architect's services bear the risk of such unforeseeable difficulties.[31]

In the hazardous waste arena, it has appeared that some owners seek through the services of the A/E to rid themselves of all liability for their hazardous waste problems. It is, therefore, not uncommon that an owner will seek, through its contract language, to obtain a higher standard of practice than the general standard of due care in effect when and where the work is performed. Because the standard of technical knowledge and understanding is evolving on a daily basis in the hazardous waste industry, it is possible and perhaps likely that a lawsuit will be filed at some point in the future concerning a latent defect at the project. There will, therefore, be a temptation when the lawsuit is filed to apply the then existing standard, rather than the standard that existed when the work was performed.

To protect against that situation, some engineers include a clause in their contract specifically stating that the standard is that which applies to the time when and the place where the work is performed and that they will not be judged by some higher future standard. An example of such a clause is as follows:

> Standard of Care/Professional Responsibility
>
> The services provided by consultant shall be performed in accordance with generally accepted professional consulting practice at the time when, and the place where, the services are rendered. No other representations to client, express or implied, and no warranty or guaranty is included or intended in this agreement, or in any report, opinion, document or service performed. In reporting the results of its services, consultant assumes no responsibility for conditions undetected and not discovered after reasonable investigation.

---

[31] *Id.* at 423–24. *See also* Paxton v. Alameda County, 119 Cal. App. 2d 393, 259 P.2d 934 (1953). *See generally* Annotation, *Responsibility of One Acting as an Architect for Defects or Insufficiency of Work Attributable to Plans,* 25 A.L.R.2d 1085 (1952).

> Client recognizes that the state of practice, particularly with respect to contaminated sight and waste conditions, is changing and evolving. For example, the long-term effect of chemicals on soils or manufactured or constructed liner systems is not well established or known at this time. While consultant is required to perform in reasonable accordance with the generally accepted standards at the time and place when its services are performed, it is recognized that those standards may subsequently change because of improvements in the state of practice and that the consultant is not responsible for anticipating such subsequent improvements and shall not be judged by such subsequent standards of practice.

§ 26.16 Causes of Action Against Engineer by Contractors

As mentioned, owners who have a contractual agreement with an engineer may use the contract language to modify and, in fact, increase the duty of care owed by the engineer to the owner. Normally, a third-party contractor may not rely on the contract language between the engineer and the owner to create a third-party beneficiary right in the contract.

Cases such as *Davidson & Jones, Inc. v. County of New Hanover*[32] limit the engineer's duty to a contractor not a party to the contract between the engineer and the owner. Other cases, even in the same state, such as *Shoffner Industries, Inc. v. W.B. Lloyd Construction Co.,*[33] have allowed suit directly against engineers by a contractor on the theory that every person who enters upon an active course of conduct has a positive duty to use ordinary care to protect others from harm.

§ 26.17 Suits by Contractor's Employees Directly Against Engineers

Because a contractor's employees may be barred from recovery by workers' compensation limitations, they may seek to impose greater liability on any available additional party.

In *Miller v. DeWitt,*[34] the court found that the A/E was negligent for not being present to inspect the work during the critical shoring and bracing of a structure. However, in *Evans v. Howard R. Green Co.,*[35] the court held that the A/E is not responsible for the safety of the finished product of

---

[32] 41 N.C. App. 661, 255 S.E.2d 580, 584, *cert. denied,* 298 N.C. 295, 259 S.E.2d 911 (1979).

[33] 42 N.C. App. 259, 257 S.E.2d 50, *cert. denied,* 298 N.C. 296, 259 S.E.2d 301 (1979).

[34] 37 Ill. 2d 273, 226 N.E.2d 630 (1967).

[35] 231 N.W.2d 907 (Iowa 1975).

the construction, but is responsible for the safety of the project during construction.

In *Henshaw v. Edward E. Clark Engineers-Scientists,*[36] an engineer was responsible for making recommendations for the cleanup and control of toxic waste. The engineer had issued a report representing that all remedial action had taken place and that only traces of toxic substances remained on the employer's property. During a regulatory agency site inspection several years later, it was discovered that the site, in fact, contained heavy contamination. In that case, the court declined to grant summary judgment in favor of the engineer, and found that there was a material question of fact as to whether employees who later worked at the jobsite were within the class of persons foreseeably harmed by the negligence of the engineering firm.

Liability for site safety and the health of workers at a site is another issue that may be of increasing concern for design professionals and construction managers. It has been held that construction workers who are injured as a result of the collapse of construction design by an engineer were not third-party beneficiaries of the contract between the engineers and the state and, therefore, had no cause of action.[37] There are other decisions, however, holding that a construction manager cannot delegate away responsibility for site safety and thereby avoid liability to injured workers. It appears that to the extent that the design professional is deemed to have assumed responsibility for the supervision of site safety or workers, the firm may be liable for injuries sustained to workers.

It has been held in numerous cases, however, that when there is a clear division of duties among the parties and the architect was not specifically retained to supervise performance of the job, the architect may not be liable to the owner for damages sustained to project materials and work that were within the contractor's responsibility.[38] Likewise, when a worker fell from a 15-foot-high concrete platform after crawling through an unfinished window, it was held that the engineers who did not directly control the work activities of the contractor were not liable to injured workers.[39]

When a steel beam collapsed causing death to a laborer, it was held that the engineer was entitled to summary judgment because it had no power to supervise or control the work site or to establish construction methods or safety procedures.[40] On the other hand, when a supervisor for the architect was on the job daily and had the power to stop the work, it was held that the

---

[36] 490 So. 2d 161 (Fla. Dist. Ct. App. 1986).

[37] Zukowski v. Howard Needles Tammen, & Bergendoff, Inc., 657 F. Supp. 926 (D. Colo. 1987).

[38] Jewish Bd. of Guardians v. Grumman Allied Instruments, Inc., 96 A.D.2d 465, 464 N.Y.S.2d 778 (1983), *aff'd,* 62 N.Y.2d 684, 465 N.E.2d 42, 476 N.Y.S.2d 535 (1984).

[39] Sherwood v. Omega Constr. Co., 657 F. Supp. 345 (S.D.N.Y. 1987).

[40] Hamby v. High Steel Structures, Inc., 134 A.D.2d 884, 521 N.Y.S.2d 926 (1987).

architect was in charge of the construction and liable to a workman under the State Structural Work Act for an injury sustained when a sewer trench collapsed.[41]

Many engineers now insert specific safety provisions in their contracts with contractors. An example of such a contract clause provides:

> In performance of Work under this subcontract the subcontractor shall, as a minimum, satisfy all federal, state, and local statutes, regulations, ordinances, etc. regarding health and safety. Beyond this minimum requirement, the subcontractor shall develop and submit to the contractor for review a site-specific safety and health plan in accordance with 29 CFR 1910.120 [the Occupational Safety and Health Administration (OSHA) regulations for the protection of hazardous waste workers] peculiar to the particular site.

Another common contract clause also provides that "the subcontractor shall be solely and completely responsible for conditions of the job site, including safety of all persons (including employees) and property during performance of the work." Contractors should be aware of the effectiveness of such provisions. In the recent case of *Stute v. P.B.M.C., Inc.,*[42] the general contractor P.B.M.C. subcontracted the installation of gutters to S&S Gutters. The subcontractor's employee (Stute) was working on the jobsite when he slipped off the roof. There was no scaffolding or other safety equipment and Stute was badly injured. The general contractor knew that safety devices were not being used.

Stute sued P.B.M.C. alleging that a duty was owed to a subcontractor's employee by the general contractor to provide safety devices. The lower court found that the general contractor did not owe a duty to provide safety equipment because it had not assumed the responsibility in its contracts with the owner or the subcontractor.

On appeal, the general contractor argued that it would be erroneous to impose upon it a duty to protect all employees unless it controlled the subcontractor's work. P.B.M.C. further alleged that the subcontractor was an independent contractor, and was responsible for the safety of its own employees. The Washington Supreme Court stressed the existence of the exception in cases in which an employer retains control. The court, in reversing the decision of the lower court, placed the primary responsibility for complying with safety regulations on the general contractor "because the general contractor's innate supervisory authority constitutes sufficient control over the workplace."[43] This was based upon the finding that because of

---

[41] Bisset v. Joseph A. Schudt & Assocs., 133 Ill. App. 3d 356, 478 N.E.2d 911 (1985).

[42] 114 Wash. 2d 454, 788 P.2d 545 (1990).

[43] 788 P.2d at 550.

the general contractor's supervisory authority, the general contractor was in "the best position to ensure compliance with safety regulations."[44]

§ 26.18 Suits by General Public Against Engineers and Contractors

Contractors and A/Es are increasingly looked to by the general public as a source of potential recovery in the event of injury. Exposure to claims from third parties is the single greatest threat of liability exposure to engineers and contractors. In *United States Fidelity & Guaranty Co. v. United States,*[45] EPA hired OH Materials Company as the contractor for cleanup operations at an abandoned chemical facility. A tank car containing oleum posed a threat of fire, explosion, and release of oleum into the air. The EPA on-scene coordinator determined it was necessary to drain the tank, but proceeded with the activity when conditions contradicted the recommendation of the state hydrogeologist that certain wind conditions be present to minimize the danger to a nearby town. Two accidents ensued, and the nearby town and its inhabitants made various claims against the contractor, which its insurance company paid. Obviously, the contractor was seen as a target for such claims and a source of recovery. The insurance company brought suit under the Federal Tort Claims Act for the EPA on-scene coordinator's negligence. The Third Circuit found that the on-scene coordinator's actions fell within the discretionary function exception for liability and therefore, the United States was not liable to the insurance company. The Supreme Court has recently declined to review this case.[46]

In the case of *Inman v. Binghamton Housing Authority,*[47] it was determined that the A/E who designed a housing project in the City of Binghamton could be liable in negligence for designing stoops at the project that allegedly directly contributed to the injury of a plaintiff.[48]

Various states have imposed statutes of limitation and statutes of repose in an attempt to limit causes of action by remote third parties against A/Es after specific periods of time. However, a number of states have held such statutes unconstitutional, while other states have refused to apply the statutes to late-manifesting injuries until the illness was reasonably

---

[44] *Id.*

[45] 837 F.2d 116 (3d Cir. 1988).

[46] 487 U.S. 1235 (1988).

[47] 3 N.Y.2d 137, 143 N.E.2d 895, 164 N.Y.S.2d 699 (1957).

[48] *See also* Fox v. Stanley J. Howe & Assocs., Inc., 309 N.W.2d 520 (Iowa 1981), and Klein v. Catalano, 386 Mass. 701, 437 N.E.2d 514 (1982).

discoverable. For example, *Turner Construction Co. v. Scales*[49] found Alaska's statute of repose unconstitutional. Most states apply these statutes to "building construction," and thus a significant question is whether or not such statutes would apply to cleanup contractors.

§ 26.19 Ultrahazardous Theories of Liability

Claimants have been largely unsuccessful at this time in arguing that an A/E or contractor is to be held *strictly liable* in tort for injuries caused by allegedly defectively designed and inherently dangerous structures. The rejection of such a theory often occurs because the courts define the engineer's role differently from that of a manufacturer of goods who might have impliedly warranted that the goods are free from defects. An engineer makes no absolute warranty to the general public, usually precluding strict liability.[50]

In some cases, the issue has been permitted to go to a jury. In *Hyman v. Gordon,*[51] a gas-fired water heater located at floor level in the garage of a home exploded when gasoline from a can was tipped over, injuring a child. The proximity of a gas-fired heater to the possible location of flammable liquids influenced the court in an action against the designer/builder.

It is not clear how much greater the liability will be when the prime contractor has contracted for the performance of ultrahazardous activities. There is little case law yet in which the courts have been asked to decide whether the investigation and cleanup of a hazardous waste site is "ultrahazardous." Manufacturers of asbestos have been held strictly liable for many of the injuries and illnesses resulting from exposure to their products even without a showing of negligence. In many cases, the insurance industry has been found liable for such damages, causing in part a general reappraisal of their willingness to write coverage in the future in all areas of potential strict liability.

In the event of a finding of ultrahazardous activity, a prime contractor may not be able to hide behind the "independent contractor" defense that it is not responsible for the activities of its subcontractors. In the same sense, the duty of care of an engineer to third-party members of the public likewise may be considered significantly greater and strict liability may be imposed even without a showing of negligence. At this point, there is no way to fully predict the course of this legal development.

---

[49] 752 P.2d 467 (Alaska 1988).

[50] City of Mounds View v. Walijarvi, 263 N.W.2d 420, 424 (Minn. 1978).

[51] 35 Cal. App. 3d 769, 111 Cal. Rptr. 262 (1973).

§ 26.20 Liability after Contract Has Been Performed

There is a great deal of uncertainty as to the potential liability of the engineer and contractor even after completion and acceptance of their work. The present contractual forms do not specifically release in full the engineer or contractor from potential liability upon completion of the work. However, the "Inspection of Construction" clause (Federal Acquisition Regulation (FAR) 52.246-12) and other similar language generally provides for correction or replacement of nonconforming work, rather than for consequential damages or damages providing for loss of use and loss of business profits. In particular, the FAR clause provides "Acceptance shall be final and conclusive except for latent defects, fraud, gross mistakes amounting to fraud, or the Government's right under any warranty or guaranty."

Obviously, an engineer or contractor will seek to obtain releases at some appropriate point. However, the fixing of a time and scope for such a release before entering into the contract would greatly facilitate an assessment of the contractor's risk.

Even more significant is the long-term risk for materials remaining on the site or sent off the site to be disposed of or transported, unless some form of indemnification is provided. See §§ **26.27** through **26.30**.

§ 26.21 Confidentiality of Business or Site Information and Duty to Warn Public

When performing a hazardous waste investigation or remedial design work, an engineer is typically required by its client to maintain information discovered during performance of the services as strictly confidential.

Both parties to the contract may have valid reasons for desiring confidentiality. There are occasions, however, when the engineer needs to disclose facts learned while performing services to protect innocent third parties from potential hazardous waste injury or to comply with reporting requirements of various federal, state, or local laws and regulations. For example, while investigating a site near a state highway, the consultant may discover that numerous toxic substances have been deposited along the roadside. The contract with the owner of the land along the highway strictly prohibits the consultant from divulging such information to anyone. Disclosure of the information could adversely affect the proposed sale of the land, reduce the value of the property, and subject the owner to various cleanup responsibilities.

When the consultant learns that the state is planning to perform work in the near future, the consultant may reasonably conclude that its duty to protect the health of the state's laborers must prevail over its contract barring the disclosure. The California attorney general has issued an opinion addressing a similar issue.[52] That opinion states that a design professional who is retained to investigate the integrity of a building and who determines that there is an eminent risk of serious injury to the occupants has a duty to warn the occupants of the danger and must discharge that duty even if the owner requests that the engineer treat the results of the investigation as confidential.

A clause that has been proposed by one consulting engineer for use on hazardous waste contracts is as follows:

> Notwithstanding anything to the contrary set forth herein, it is understood by Client that the Engineer is or may be subject to certain legal and ethical requirements and obligations depending upon the nature and scope of services rendered hereunder which may impose upon the Engineer an obligation to disclose facts observed by the Engineer to third parties. The Engineer shall advise Client or Client's representatives in the event the Engineer believes it has such an obligation, but shall, subject to any legal obligation on the Engineer to immediately disclose such facts, refrain from making any such disclosure until the Engineer and Client have conferred with respect to such obligation and the facts giving rise to same. If the Engineer believes on the advice of counsel that it must disclose such facts to third parties, then and in such event, any such disclosure shall not be deemed a violation of this Agreement and Client agrees that the Engineer shall be and hereby is released from any liability, claim or cause of action whatsoever with respect to such disclosure.

§ 26.22 Liability to Contractors

An engineer may be liable for damages caused to a contractor arising out of the negligent manner in which the engineer performed supervision of the contract and for tortious interference with the contractor's contract. In *Northrup Contracting, Inc. v. Village of Bergen,*[53] it was held that when an engineer had been retained by a municipality to design a wastewater collection project and the contractor used plans and specifications and test borings prepared by the engineer to determine subsurface conditions in preparing its bid, the engineer was liable for denying the contractor's claim and advising the contractor to move to another part of the job when the contractor encountered excessive subsurface water entitling him to additional compensation. On the other hand, there are cases in numerous jurisdictions holding that a general contractor for construction cannot recover

---

[52] Cal. Op. Att'y Gen. No. 85-208 (1985).

[53] 139 Misc. 2d 435, 527 N.Y.S.2d 670 (Sup. Ct. 1986).

for economic loss arising from the A/E's breach of contract or negligent performance of the contract with the owner.[54]

In another case that may shed light on liabilities arising on hazardous waste cleanup projects, a contractor suffered damages because of subsurface debris and alleged that the project architect and engineer were contractually obligated to the owner to supervise the work of a wrecking company that had been employed to prepare the site for construction. The contractor alleged that the A/E had received notice through soil test reports of the existence of subsurface debris, but had failed to disclose that information to the contractor by way of final plans and specifications. In that case, the court held that the case could go forward on the theories that the A/E was liable for negligent misrepresentation, despite lack of privity of contract, because the A/E supplied the false information, and it was foreseeable that the general contractor for the project would be injured by reasonable reliance on the false information. The court also held that A/Es may be liable to a general contractor for failure to accurately describe construction requirements, even in the absence of privity of contract, when such accuracy is vital to the bidding process.[55]

§ 26.23 Liability to Lenders

Much of the investigative work being performed on sites for the purpose of determining pollution and contamination is done to facilitate property transfers. Although the consultant may be retained by one party to the transaction, there are potential liabilities that may flow to other parties to the transaction or other nonrelated parties that may reasonably rely upon reports and conclusions generated by the consultant. Lending institutions and subsequent purchasers of mortgages, for example, could make their financial decisions on the basis of reports generated by the consultant.

In the case of *Mears Park Holding Corp. v. Morse-Diesel, Inc.*,[56] a developer employed an architect to prepare drawings for a project. When the developer defaulted on certain loans, it transferred title to the project to its lender in lieu of foreclosure. The court held that the lender was not an intended third-party beneficiary under the contract and could not have reasonably relied upon the consultant's professional services because the possibility of liability to the lender following the developer's default and foreclosure was too remote to be foreseeable. In the context of hazardous waste, and in particular regarding liability under the Comprehensive

[54] Blake Constr. Co. v. Alley, 233 Va. 31, 353 S.E.2d 724 (1987).

[55] Gulf Contracting v. Bibb County, 795 F.2d 980 (11th Cir. 1986). *See also* Bacco Constr. Co. v. American Colloid Co., 148 Mich. App. 397, 384 N.W.2d 427 (1986).

[56] 427 N.W.2d 281 (Minn. Ct. App. 1988).

Environmental Response Compensation and Liability Act (CERCLA), the cases appear to be developing in such a way that a secured creditor or lender may stand in the shoes of its borrower despite little involvement on the project and that lender reliance upon the consultant's reports would be foreseeable.

A dramatic change has recently been made in the risk of liability for lenders. According to *United States v. Fleet Factors Corp.,*[57] the secured creditor may be liable even though it is not an operator of a hazardous waste facility if it participated in the management of a facility "to a degree indicating a capacity to influence the corporation's treatment of hazardous waste."[58] The court further concluded that "a secured creditor will be liable if its involvement with the management of the facility is sufficiently broad to support the inference that it could affect hazardous waste disposal decisions if it so chose."[59] *Fleet Factors'* petition for writ of certiorari to the United States Supreme Court has been denied and at least one other circuit has held that mere oversight or ability to influence management is not enough to find a secured creditor liable, but that in order to be liable, the secured creditor "must exercise actual management authority."[60]

As a result of these recent decisions, there is much uncertainty as to the liability of secured creditors whose real property collateral is found to contain hazardous waste. As a consequence, it is likely that lenders and secured creditors will require more extensive phase one and phase two audits before completing financial transactions and that their reliance upon the professional services of consulting firms providing such environmental audits will increase.

When the seller or purchaser is securing the services of a design professional, it is reasonably foreseeable that lending institutions and other creditors will rely to their detriment on the work product produced by the consultants. To the extent that a consultant seeks to limit who can rely on the written product and thereby limit its risk exposure to its own client, various contract language and disclaimers may be included in both the contract and final written report. A clause clearly stating that nothing contained in the agreement shall create a contractual relationship with or cause of action in favor of a third party against the owner or consultant has become almost standard. Moreover, some consultants have included a disclaimer at the beginning of their written environmental audit report stating that the report was prepared for the exclusive use and benefit of the consultant's client and is not intended to be nor shall be relied upon by any other individual or party, and that to the extent that other party does act in reliance, such party

[57] 901 F.2d 1550 (11th Cir.), *reh'g denied,* 911 F.2d 742 (11th Cir. 1990).

[58] *Id.* at 1557.

[59] *Id.* at 1558.

[60] *In re* Bergsoe Metal Corp. v. East Asiatic Co., 910 F.2d 668 (9th Cir. 1990).

shall indemnify and hold the consultant harmless for any damages, losses, or expenses arising out of the work or report.

A caveat or disclaimer that is sometimes included in these reports provides as follows:

> The potential contamination which is the subject of a report such as this report would typically be hidden in the subsurface materials making up the site, and the hazardous materials, if any, would likely have been introduced by man at random locations. Given these conditions, there are no scientific methods, short of sampling and testing the entire site to some undefined depth limit, that can provide substantial certainty in evaluating the total absence of all types of hazardous site contamination. The act of sampling the entire site, would, of course, destroy the site. It is consequently impossible to state conclusively, "no contamination exists at the site."

Generally, in order to recover as an intended third-party beneficiary, the plaintiff must show that there was a duty owed by the engineer and that there was an intent that the third party benefit. When a contract between an engineer and municipality expressly stated that there would be no third-party rights arising under the contract, it was held that no third-party beneficiary rights arose in favor of the project contractor, because the contractor was not, in fact, an "intended beneficiary."[61] Likewise, when the contract did not demonstrate an intent to confer rights on ultimate owners of buildings that the engineer was designing for a developer, it was held that the owners had no right to assert a cause of action against the architect.[62]

§ 26.24 Economic Loss

Although there are numerous jurisdictions and cases holding that economic loss cannot be claimed against an engineer by a third party based on the engineer's alleged breach of contract with the owner,[63] the majority view in negligence cases against design professionals is that an economic loss is recoverable.[64]

Due to the likelihood of diminution in value of a property either resulting from services performed on the property during hazardous waste investigation or remedial action or from the discovery of pollutants that were not found by the design professional during its services, economic loss recovery

[61] Edward B. Fitzpatrick, Jr. Constr. Corp. v. County of Suffolk, 138 A.D.2d 446, 525 N.Y.S.2d 863 (1988).

[62] Lake Placid Club Attached Lodges v. Elizabeth Town Builders, Inc., 131 A.D.2d 159, 521 N.Y.S.2d 165 (1987).

[63] Blake Constr. Co. v. Alley, 233 Va. 31, 353 S.E.2d 724 (1987).

[64] Rosos Litho Supply Corp. v. Hansen, 123 Ill. App. 3d 290, 462 N.E.2d 566 (1984); Donnelly Constr. Co. v. Oberg/Hunt/Gilleland, 139 Ariz. 184, 677 P.2d 1292 (1984); and Huang v. Garner, 157 Cal. App. 3d 404, 203 Cal. Rptr. 800 (1984).

should be a major concern to the engineer. For this reason, many engineers include a clause in their contract expressly stating that the engineer is not liable to the owner for consequential damages or that neither party shall be liable to the other for consequential damages, including economic loss due to diminution of value of the property.

§ 26.25 Contractual Liability of Engineer for Redesign Costs

Government agencies may base claims against their engineers on the theory of breach of contract or failure to perform. Usually such claims assert a failure to carry out a particular duty specified in the contract. With EPA, the Corps of Engineers, and the potential responsibility party's frequent reliance on a single contractor to do both engineering and removal, an engineering/construction firm often faces the combined liability of both an engineer and contractor.

The clause found in Federal Acquisition Regulation (FAR) 52.236-23 applicable to the engineer provides:

> Responsibility of the Architect-Engineer Contractor (APR 1984)
>
> (a) The Contractor shall be responsible for the professional quality, technical accuracy, and the coordination of all designs, drawings, specifications, and other services furnished by the Contractor under this contract. The Contractor shall, without additional compensation, correct or revise any errors or deficiencies in its designs, drawings, specifications, and other services.
>
> (b) Neither the Government's review, approval or acceptance of, nor payment for, the services required under this contract shall be construed to operate as a waiver of any rights under this contract or of any cause of action arising out of the performance of this contract, and the Contractor shall be and remain liable to the Government in accordance with applicable law for all damages to the Government caused by the Contractor's negligent performance of any of the services furnished under this contract.
>
> (c) The rights and remedies of the Government provided for under this contract are in addition to any other rights and remedies provided by law.
>
> (d) If the Contractor is comprised of more than one legal entity, each such entity shall be jointly and severally liable hereunder.

The clause's duty to correct designs, drawings, and specifications *without compensation* can be costly and must be considered and budgeted for out of profit. According to FAR 36.609-2(b), the clause at 52.236-23 is to be used in *fixed price* contracts. Federal Acquisition Circular 84-8[65] states that

---

[65] 50 Fed. Reg. 26,902 (1985).

the clause is to be inserted *only* in fixed price A/E contracts. EPA, however, has been requiring the alternative remedial contract strategy (ARCS) contractors to agree to the application of the clause even on cost-reimbursable contracts without recognition of a change or payment of additional compensation. As of January 30, 1991, EPA has indicated that it will continue to give work orders to contractors who do not accept the clause and will be willing to consider negotiating contract adjustments when the clause is added.

The language is significant because it denies the engineer many of the defenses that would ordinarily apply. The fact that EPA or some other government body approves the design does not limit the engineer's responsibility. This is critical when decisions by the applicable lead regulatory agency are aimed, in part, at obtaining a "cost effective" remedy within the language of the National Contingency Plan (NCP) § 104 (40 C.F.R. § 300.68(j) (1990)). This does not necessarily mean that the remedy most likely to work or the safest solution will be approved.

The engineer could fail to supervise the work of a contractor and thus permit the contractor to not perform some critical aspect of the work. If a government agency requires the use of FAR 52.236-24, "Work Oversight in Architect-Engineer Contracts," this risk becomes acute. A question arises whether it is the engineer's responsibility for not having observed and required correction during performance. Cases such as *Moundsview Independent School District No. 621 v. Buetow & Associates, Inc.*[66] draw a distinction between the engineer's duty to perform inspection services with reasonable care and competence and acting as "clerk-of-the-works." In *Moundsview,* the engineer offered a greater degree of inspection services to the owner than required, and the owner declined to accept and pay for them. Therefore, the court was reluctant to impose the higher standard of care on the engineer, illustrating the importance of the contractual definition of the engineer's duties. There are many clauses that can create liability concerns beyond those dealing with insurance and indemnification, such as "Health and Safety," EPA Acquisition Regulations 52.223-3; "Hazardous Material Identification and Material Safety Data" and "Design Within Funding Limits," FAR 52.236-22; and there are clauses that may limit liability, such as "Limitation of Liability," FAR 52.246-25.

§ 26.26 Relationship of Contractor's Liability with Duty Owed by Engineer

If the contractor is going to be relieved of the responsibility for successful performance when it complies with the design of the engineer, then the

[66] 253 N.W.2d 836 (Minn. 1977).

engineer assumes some responsibility for the adequacy of the design. In *Board of Education v. Del Biano & Associates, Inc.*,[67] the contractor's failure to achieve successful performance effectively brought to the owner's attention the responsibility of the engineer. Here an engineer was held responsible for a breach of an implied obligation to the owner when the mortar specified was unsuitable for Chicago weather conditions.

§ 26.27 Forming Corporate Subsidiaries

Creating a separate subsidiary corporation to perform hazardous waste work may provide some protection to the parent corporation. In forming a subsidiary, however, it is important that the contractor carefully follow the proper guidance and rigidly adhere to the practices indicated by the law of the applicable jurisdictions. Otherwise, there is a possibility that the subsidiary will be deemed what is known as a *mere instrumentality* of the parent corporation. This could result in the assets of the parent corporation being exposed to the substantial risks that the contractor sought to avoid by forming the subsidiary.

The list of factors that are considered by the courts in evaluating whether or not to permit "piercing of the corporation veil" in the subsidiary-parent situation include:[68]

1. The parent corporation owns all or most of the capital stock of the subsidiary
2. The parent and subsidiary corporations have common directors or officers
3. The parent corporation finances the subsidiary
4. The parent corporation subscribes to all the capital stock of the subsidiary or otherwise causes its incorporation
5. The subsidiary has grossly inadequate capital
6. The parent corporation pays the salaries and other expenses or losses of the subsidiary
7. The subsidiary has substantially no business except with the parent corporation or no assets except those conveyed to it by the parent corporation
8. In the papers of the parent corporation or in the statements of its officers, the subsidiary is described as a department or division of the

---

[67] 57 Ill. App. 3d 302, 372 N.E.2d 953 (1978).

[68] Jackson v. General Elec. Co., 514 P.2d 1170, 1173 (Alaska 1973); *see also* Dewitt Truck Brokers, Inc. v. W. Ray Flemming Fruit Co., 540 F.2d 681 (4th Cir. 1976); 18 Am. Jur. 2d *Corporations* § 14 (1990).

parent corporation, or its business or financial responsibility is referred to as the parent corporation's own

9. The parent corporation uses the property of the subsidiary as its own
10. The directors or executives of the subsidiary do not act independently in the interest of the subsidiary, but take their orders from the parent corporation in the latter's interest
11. The formal legal requirements of the subsidiary are not observed.

One of the most important considerations is the adequacy of capitalization of the subsidiary. The capitalization is measured against the nature and magnitude of the corporation's undertaking.[69] The greatest number of cases piercing the corporate veil have done so because the courts found fraud. In such cases, the legal function of the corporation is not maintained because it would protect someone who has defrauded customers or creditors.[70]

Perhaps the factor most asked about by contractors who are forming subsidiaries is how much of the subsidiary's stock the parent can own. A parent's stock ownership alone may not necessarily render the parent liable for the subsidiary's actions or omissions, regardless of whether the subsidiary is wholly owned by the parent corporation.[71] One court stated that control through ownership of a majority or even all the subsidiary's stock, and the use of power incident to that ownership to elect officers and directors, does not necessarily, in and of itself, result in liability of the parent, but that liability depends on whether dominion and control is so complete that the subsidiary corporation has no will, mind, or existence of its own, and operates as a mere department of the business of the stockholder.[72]

Exercise of dominion and control is an important factor considered by the courts. Courts have applied the rule that when a parent corporation exercises its right to control its subsidiary, the corporate entity of the subsidiary will be pierced and the parent may be held liable for its actions.[73]

Stated simply, an injured party seeking to sue a parent corporation for a subsidiary's actions will attempt to demonstrate as many conditions as possible that indicate control or dominion by the parent. To avoid parental liability, the contractor should take appropriate steps to demonstrate that the subsidiary stands on its own feet and that the parent lacks control or dominion. The less control the parent has over the subsidiary, the less the

---

[69] National Marine Servs., Inc. v. C.J. Thibodeaux, 501 F.2d 940 (5th Cir. 1974).

[70] Parker Peanut Co. v. Felder, 200 S.C. 203, 20 S.E.2d 716 (1942).

[71] Califf v. Coca-Cola Co., 326 F. Supp. 540 (N.D. Ill. 1971).

[72] Lowendahl v. Baltimore & O.R. Co., 247 A.D. 144, 287 N.Y.S. 62, *aff'd,* 272 N.Y. 360, 6 N.E.2d 56 (1936), *reh'g denied,* 273 N.Y. 584, 7 N.E.2d 704 (1937).

[73] Henderson v. Rounds & Porter Lumber Co., 99 F. Supp. 376 (D. Ark. 1951).

likelihood of the parent being tagged with the liability for the contracts or torts of the subsidiary.[74]

§ 26.28 Indemnification

The need for indemnification arises from the unavailability of commercial liability insurance in sufficient amounts and coverage to respond to the real risks of cleanup contracting. The almost universal presence of the "absolute pollution exclusion" in available third-party liability policies may mean that very little risk shifting can be achieved through insurance.

§ 26.29 —Indemnification under Section 119 of Superfund Amendments and Reauthorization Act

An indemnification agreement may be provided by the EPA only if the agency determines that each of the following requirements of § 119(c)(4) of the Superfund Amendments and Reauthorization Act (SARA) are met:

> The liability covered by the agreement exceeds or is not covered by insurance available, at a fair and reasonable price, to the RAC [response action contractor] at the time of contract execution, and "adequate insurance to cover such liability is not generally available at the time the response action contract is entered into."
>
> The RAC has made diligent efforts to obtain insurance coverage from nonfederal sources to cover such liability.
>
> In the case of a response action contract covering more than one facility, the RAC agrees to continue to make such diligent efforts each time the contractor begins work under the contract at a new facility.

The EPA requires that RACs seeking federal indemnification meet the following requirements:

> Within a specified time after signing an indemnification agreement with the EPA, RACs must submit to the agency (or to the appropriate state contracting officer) written documentation concerning the efforts they have made to secure pollution liability coverage.
>
> A RAC that has obtained pollution liability coverage must submit a copy of the policy and declaration page to the EPA (or to the state contracting officer).

---

[74] Holland, *Indemnification and Risk Reduction Strategies,* 2 Envtl. Claims J. 59 (1989).

The RAC must periodically submit written documentation reporting additional efforts it has made to secure pollution liability insurance coverage since execution of the indemnification agreement. The EPA expects RACs to continue monitoring the insurance market for pollution liability insurance, and to continue to seek insurance coverage from commercial insurance carriers or through alternative risk transfer mechanisms, such as self-insurance pools.

EPA published a proposed rule for indemnification in 1989.[75] This rule is still being debated and revised at this writing. The proposed regulations would limit indemnification of contractors by establishing a dollar limit of available indemnification (sliding scale up to $50 million); limiting the time period of indemnification coverage (10 years); establishing high deductible amounts; eliminating indemnification if a plaintiff recovers on a complaint that charged liability under both strict liability and negligence; and establishing procedural requirements that are difficult to satisfy.

Indemnification by EPA will not be a viable risk reduction solution for most contractors. Other strategies consequently will be essential.

§ 26.30 —Indemnification under Public Law 85-804

Another possible source of indemnification for the contractor working directly for the federal government on the cleanup of certain military installations or facilities of the Department of Energy concerned with nuclear weapons development is the indemnification clause found in Federal Acquisition Regulation (FAR) 50.403-1, entitled "Indemnification Under Public Law 85-804." To avail itself of such indemnification, the contractor must make a request under FAR 50.403 and then complete all the information required by FAR 50.403-1. The request should be submitted and acted upon in the negotiation of the contract. The contract language in FAR 52.250-1 provides for indemnity of the contractor against:

> (1) Claims (including reasonable expenses of litigation or settlement) by third persons (including employees of the Contractor) for death; personal injury; or loss of, damage to, or loss of use of property;
>
> (2) Loss of, damage to, or loss of use of contractor property, excluding loss of profit; and
>
> (3) Loss of, damage to, or loss of Government property, excluding loss of profit.

[75] 54 Fed. Reg. 46,012 (Proposed Oct. 31, 1989).

It appears that such indemnification might include claims for strict liability. Excluded from coverage are claims, loss, or damage caused by willful conduct or lack of good faith on the part of any of the contractor's principal officials. The contractor shall not be indemnified for the government's claims against the contractor.

FAR 50.203(b) provides the following language concerning the funding of indemnification under Public Law 85-804:

> No contract, amendment, or modification shall be made under the Act's authority— . . . (3) except within the limits of the amounts appropriated and the statutory contract authorization (however, indemnification agreements authorized by an Agency head, (50.403) are not limited to amounts appropriated or to the contract authorization).

It should be cautioned that obtaining contractual indemnification not subject to the limitation of amounts appropriated or to contract authorization requires, under FAR 50.201, the express approval of the agency head, which approval for indemnification is difficult to obtain and has at this time not readily been available to response action contractors (RACs).

§ 26.31 —Indemnification in Private Party Contracts

A key method used for reducing or shifting the risk of the parties is the indemnification clause and limitation-of-liability clause that may be included in the contract. In some contracts, owners require contractors to indemnify them. Others provide that the owner indemnifies the engineer, and yet others provide that the general contractor indemnifies the owner and the engineer. The substance and style of indemnification clauses are as varied as the imaginations of the attorneys and principals drafting them.

From an engineer's perspective, the owner should be providing indemnification for all claims and damages arising out of the work because of the uncertainties involved with performing the work and the inability of the engineer to obtain meaningful insurance. Again, from the engineer's perspective, the indemnification should be as broad and as inclusive as legally permissible. It should protect from and against all claims, damages, losses, and expenses, whether direct, indirect, or consequential. It should include attorneys' fees and court and arbitration costs. It should extend the claims that arise out of, are related to, or are based upon actual or threatened dispersal, discharge, or escape of any contaminant or pollutant. Finally, the indemnification to be written should apply to the full extent permitted by law regardless of the fault, negligence, breach of warranty or contract, or strict liability of the engineer. In drafting indemnification clauses, careful attention must be paid to the numerous state anti-indemnification laws.

Some states, such as Texas, permit an engineer to be indemnified by owners, even when the damages arose as a result of the engineer's sole negligence. Note, however, that Texas law prohibits indemnification or "hold-harmless" agreements between engineers and contractors.[76] Other states, such as New Jersey, prohibit a contractor from being indemnified for its sole negligence.[77]

To comply with anti-indemnity statutes while obtaining the benefit of an owner defending an engineer against claims, even when those claims are allegedly based on the engineer's negligence, some engineers use an indemnification clause requiring the owner to defend, hold harmless, and indemnify the engineer against all claims and damages except those "finally determined" to have resulted from the engineer's sole negligence or willful misconduct. This has the benefit of providing protection right up until the time of a final judgment by a court or other trier of fact. Because many of the claims will be resolved through settlement, there will not be a "final determination" and the engineer may, therefore, obtain a complete indemnification for its attorneys' fees and damages paid to a claimant through settlement.

§ 26.32 Consultant's Liability under Superfund Law

A consultant that becomes involved at a hazardous substance or hazardous waste generating facility to the extent of managing day-to-day operations, directing cleanup personnel, signing manifests, selecting transporters, selecting disposal facilities or disposal methods, and taking other management responsibilities for the operation and cleanup of a facility, may inadvertently become liable under the strict joint and several liability aspects of the Superfund law. With the recent decision in the case of *United States v. Fleet Factors,*[78] holding that a secured creditor could be liable as a facility operator merely because it had the capacity to influence the owner's treatment of hazardous waste without regard to the fact that it did not actively involve itself in day-to-day operations, consultants should be concerned about the extent to which they likewise will be deemed by the courts to be operators of facilities. Under the Superfund liability scheme, if the consultant is found to fall within the definition of "operator," it would be liable for the full cost of the site remedial action, subsequent monitoring, and any natural resources damages. It is, therefore, imperative that a consultant take extraordinary care to limit the scope of its work to avoid or reduce risks of exposure to the draconian measures of the Superfund law.

---

[76] Texas Civ. Prac. & Rem. Code Ann. § 130.002 (Vernon Supp. 1991).

[77] N.J. Stat. Ann. § 2A:40A-2 (West 1987).

[78] 901 F.2d 1550 (11th Cir.), *reh'g denied,* 911 F.2d 742 (11th Cir. 1990).

§ 26.33 Liability under CERCLA

Section 107(d) of the Comprehensive Environmental Response Compensation and Liability Act (CERCLA) contains language exempting from liability persons rendering care, assistance, or advice in accordance with the National Contingency Plan (NCP) or at the direction of an on-scene coordinator, with respect to an incident creating damages to public health and welfare or the environment as a result of any release of a hazardous substance or the threat thereof. Gross negligence is not exempted. Nevertheless, this exemption is not either sufficiently clear or broad to satisfactorily be relied upon for limiting the liability of most response action contractors (RACs), although it probably is of assistance at least to those contractors performing emergency response contracts.

The passage of the Superfund Amendments and Reauthorization Act of 1986 (SARA) strengthened the RAC exemption from liability under the Act with the inclusion of the following language in the newly enacted § 119(a)(1):

> RESPONSE ACTION CONTRACTOR - A person who is a response action contractor with respect to any release or threatened release of a hazardous substance or pollutant or contaminant from a vessel or facility shall not be liable under this title or under any other Federal law to any person for injuries, costs, damages, expenses, or other liability (including but not limited to claims for indemnification or contribution or claims by third parties for death, personal injury, illness or loss of or damage to property or economic loss) which results from such release or threatened release.

However, paragraph (2) goes on to provide:

> NEGLIGENCE, ETC. - Paragraph (1) shall not apply in the case of a release that is caused by conduct of the response action contractor which is negligent, grossly negligent, or which constitutes intentional misconduct.

Additionally, subparagraph (3) provides;

> EFFECT ON WARRANTIES; EMPLOYER LIABILITY - Nothing in this subsection shall effect [sic] the liability of any person under any warranty under Federal, State, or common law. Nothing in this subsection shall effect the liability of an employer who is a response action contractor to any employee or such employer under any provision of law, including any provision of any law relating to worker's compensation.

It is obvious that the RAC, whether it is an engineer or construction contractor, is exempted from § 107 strict liability provided that such contractor is not negligent or grossly negligent or does not perform in such a way that constitutes intentional misconduct. Likewise, warranties are unaffected by this language.

§ 26.34 Avoid Selecting Disposal Site

Anyone who decides where hazardous waste will be disposed of or treated is subject to liability under Superfund.[79] "The relevant inquiry is who decided to place the waste into the hands of a particular facility that contains hazardous waste."[80] When working on a site containing hazardous substances or wastes that must be treated or disposed of, the consultant should insure that the owner makes the final decisions concerning disposal and treatment and that the owner sign all manifests for the transport and disposal.[81]

Even when the consultant does not sign the manifest for hazardous waste, the consultant still may be liable as an arranger for the treatment, transportation, or disposal of hazardous waste if he was negligent. A contractor or consultant will not be liable under the Superfund law unless his work has been performed negligently or intentionally wrong.[82] This effectively protects the consultant from the strict liability aspect of the Superfund law, but does not eliminate liability when negligence is proved.

The consultant may be vulnerable for mistakes in site assessments, particularly for missing wastes or underestimating wastes. Missing waste in a site assessment may result in an unexpected major legal liability for remedial action on contaminated land. The cleanup costs can be tremendous. The average cost of a site cleanup has been estimated to be approximately $14 million, and EPA estimates that the average cost may be closer to $30 million in the near future.

§ 26.35 Tips to Reduce Liability Exposure

As the country moves forward with a major financial commitment to hazardous waste cleanup, there are tremendous opportunities for architects and engineers. To enjoy these opportunities, it is wise to minimize the perils inherent in providing necessary services.

---

[79] Jersey City Redev. Auth. v. PPG Indus., 655 F. Supp. 1257 (D.N.J. 1987).

[80] United States v. A&F Materials Co., 582 F. Supp. 842, 845 (S.D. Ill. 1984).

[81] United States v. Hardage, 1990 U.S. Dist. Lexis 16401, 32 Env't Rep. Cas. (BNA) 1073 (W.D. Okla. 1990) (trucking company that hauled waste and selected disposal site in Oklahoma was liable under Superfund).

[82] SARA § 119(a)(2) (1986).

Following are some of the things an A/E may do to reduce risks:

1. Carefully define the scope of work and the standard of care to be applied under the contract
2. Price the job to reflect the liability risk
3. Negotiate indemnification and limitation-of-liability clauses in the contract
4. Obtain insurance that fills the gap created by the pollution exclusion typically contained in errors and omissions insurance policies and obtain a comprehensive insurance program to cover all liabilities in the various aspects of one's services
5. Require the client to sign all hazardous waste manifests and to take responsibility for selecting the disposal site
6. Avoid signing certifications stating that all wastes have been removed from a site or that all wastes and quantities of waste have been discovered at a site, or that as a result of the A/E's services, the site has been put into a condition that meets all requirements of federal, state, and local laws and regulations
7. Maintain a risk assessment program, health and safety program, and training program for employees.

§ 26.36 Insurance for Environmental Impairment

The hazardous materials contractors' insurance program for a firm providing design/build or single-source environmental contracting, including asbestos abatement services, includes numerous basic insurance coverage parts. These policies interface with each other to complete the insurance protection. Some of the policies are, in effect, duplications of policy forms except that exclusions within one or the other make the purchase of the second policy necessary. Particular attention must be paid to the rating basis on all policies to avoid duplicating premiums without gaining duplicate coverage. The rates for some of these coverages may exceed the normal operating margins of a contracting firm; therefore, mistakes on the coordination of rates and revenue streams could potentially bankrupt a firm through audit premiums at the end of the policy period.[83]

The insurance coverages used on hazardous waste and asbestos work are summarized briefly in §§ **26.37** through **26.45**.

---

[83] D. Dybdahl, Advanced Environmental Risk Management (1990).

§ 26.37 —Commercial General Liability

The general liability (GL) insurance policy is designed to provide insurance coverage for bodily injury, property damage, and defense costs arising out of the insured's premises, operations, products and completed operations. It is the equivalent of all-risk protection, subject to exclusions. The resulting gaps in coverage created by the exclusions make it necessary to purchase other forms of liability insurance if the response action contractor (RAC) intends to be insured for hazardous waste contracting work. The exclusions typically eliminate coverage for claims arising out of (1) pollution, (2) operations at a hazardous waste site, (3) maintenance, operation, and use of automobiles, (4) injuries to the insured's employees, and (5) professional errors, acts, or omissions.

§ 26.38 —Contractors' Pollution Liability

Due to the exclusion in the general liability (GL) policy for pollution, contractors' pollution liability (CPL) coverage was developed. The traditional CPL policy contains an endorsement that amends environmental impact liability (EIL) policy coverage to more closely reflect the exposure to the contracting firm. In this regard, it should be noted that the standard EIL policy provides little or no insurance protection for a "contracting" exposure. A manuscript CPL policy also may be purchased without an endorsement onto an EIL policy.

The protection provided by the CPL policy is stop-gap coverage for the GL exposure. It is not an all-risk policy. It provides pollution liability coverage for bodily injury, property damage, defense costs, and cleanup costs for the contractor's described operations. Coverage can be purchased on a blanket, reported sites, or project-specific basis.

§ 26.39 —Architects' and Engineers' Professional Errors and Omissions

For design professionals, the purchase of errors and omissions (E&O) coverage has historically been necessitated by a special exclusion endorsed onto the general liability (GL) policy excluding claims for design errors. To fill this gap in coverage, the purchase of a professional E&O policy is necessary. The typical insuring agreement of these policies states that it will indemnify the insured for negligent acts, errors, or omissions arising out of the rendering of a described professional service. Most E&O policies currently on the market contain an exclusion for claims arising out of a pollution incident. There are some standard policies, however, that provide coverage for pollution by deleting the pollution exclusion as it relates to the design of potable water systems or sewage wastewater treatment plants. It is also possible to purchase "package" policies that provide coverage for pollution claims as part of the traditional E&O coverage.

§ 26.40 —Specialty Environmental Engineers' Errors and Omissions Policy Forms

There are a number of custom-tailored errors and omissions (E&O) policy forms for use by firms that provide environmental remediation services. These policies usually start off with a traditional E&O policy and, by amending or deleting the pollution exclusion, extend the professional liability (PL) coverage to claims arising out of a pollution incident.

§ 26.41 —Asbestos Abatement Liability

The asbestos abatement liability (AAL) insurance policy provides coverage for asbestos abatement operations generally by amending the pollution exclusion on a general liability (GL) policy. Both the GL policy and AAL policy use payroll and receipts as the rating basis to determine premiums. The coverages are redundant for premium computation purposes and the insured should make sure that it obtains an endorsement enabling it to avoid paying double the necessary premium.

§ 26.42 —Asbestos Consultants' Errors and Omissions

Professional errors and omissions (E&O) liability insurance policy coverage is provided by the asbestos consultants' E&O policy. It deletes the pollution exclusion to the extent necessary to provide coverage for professional errors, acts, or omissions arising out of the design of asbestos projects. Asbestos consultants' E&O coverage has the potential to be redundant to the engineers' pollution liability (EPL) coverage. This coverage may be unnecessary if the EPL policy or the standard E&O policy has sufficiently broad wording so as not to exclude the asbestos hazard.

§ 26.43 —Commercial Automobile Liability

As mentioned, the general liability (GL) insurance policies exclude claims arising out of the maintenance, use, or operation of motor vehicles. The business automobile liability (BAL) policy form excludes claims arising out of pollution. If the insured transports materials that could lead to an environmental claim, it is therefore imperative to procure appropriate insurance coverage to fill this gap. Pollution coverage for upsets and overturns is available, but must be specifically requested by the insured and added by a specific endorsement.

§ 26.44 —Workers' Compensation

The workers' compensation (WC) policy pays for claims arising out of injury, death, or disability of employees while performing within the scope of their employment. Although WC policies do not contain a pollution exclusion, it appears that most insurance carriers will not knowingly write WC coverage on the higher-risk classes of hazardous materials contractors.

§ 26.45 —Structuring the Insurance Program

A response action contractor (RAC) must decide whether to use blanket or project-specific insurance coverage for the hazardous waste work. Under the blanket approach to insuring a firm, the firm obtains coverage for all of its described operations. The blanket coverage provides insurance to the firm on a number of sites and generally for a number of different operations. Site-specific insurance, on the other hand, provides insurance only for the specified site and for the specified operations at that site.

The insurance available under the various pollution policies is on a claims-made basis. Unlike the occurrence basis policies, the insurance only provides protection against those claims made during the period that the policy is in place. Consequently, due to the long period of time in which a claimant such as a third party might allege an injury, it is necessary to continuously renew the policies to cover the loss exposure following the completion of the work.[84]

---

[84] EPA's proposed indemnification policy, for example, establishes indemnification by EPA for a period of 10 years after completion of the work.

TABLE OF CASES

Case	*Book §*
American Ins. Group v. McCowin, 7 Ohio App. 2d 62, 218 N.E.2d 746 (1966)	§ 14.15
American Mach. & Foundry Co., ASBCA No. 15037, 74-1 B.C.A. (CCH) ¶ 10,409 (1973)	§ 11.20
American Sur. Co. v. United States *ex rel.* Barrow-Agee Labs, 76 F.2d 67 (5th Cir. 1935)	§ 25.14
Anderson Dev. Corp. v. Coastal States Crude Gathering Co., 543 S.W.2d 402 (Tex. 1976)	§ 23.20
Anderson Elec., Inc. v. Ledbetter Erection Corp., 115 Ill. 2d 146, 503 N.E.2d 246 (1986)	§ 22.7
Anderson-Ross Floors, Inc. v. Scherrer Constr. Co., 62 Ill. App. 3d 713, 379 N.E.2d 786 (1978)	§ 18.9
A-1 Door & Material Co. v. Fresno Guar. Sav. & Loan Ass'n, 61 Cal. 2d 728, 394 P.2d 829, 40 Cal. Rptr. 85 (1964)	§ 25.8
APAC-Va. v. Department of Highways & Transp., 9 Va. 450, 388 S.E.2d 841 (1990)	§ 15.5
Apple Computer, Inc. v. Formula Int'l, Inc., 562 F. Supp. 775 (C.D. Cal. 1983)	§ 19.14
Apple Computer, Inc. v. Microsoft Corp., 709 F. Supp. 925 (N.D. Cal.) *summary judgment granted in part* 717 F. Supp. 1428 (N.D. Cal. 1989)	§ 19.14
Arkansas Kraft Corp. v. Boyed Sanders Constr. Co., 298 Ark. 36, 764 S.W.2d 452 (1989)	§ 8.3
Arkansas Rice Growers Coop. Ass'n v. Alchemy Indus., Inc., 797 F.2d 565 (8th Cir. 1986)	§ 21.1
Arkansas State Bd. of Architects v. Bank Bldg. & Equip. Corp. of Am., 225 Ark. 889, 286 S.W.2d 323 (1956)	§ 14.5
Armco Steel Corp. v. Cox (Roy H.) Co., 103 Cal. App. 3d 929, 163 Cal. Rptr. 330 (1980)	§ 8.6
A.R. Moyer, Inc. v. Graham, 285 So. 2d 397 (Fla. 1973)	§§ 18.10, 19.5, 21.6, 22.2, 22.7, 22.9, 23.3
Arthur Rettenberg Corp. v. Dawney, 647 F. Supp. 1214 (M.D. Fla. 1986)	§ 17.5
Artukovich & Son, Inc., v. American Fidelity Fire Ins. Co., 72 Cal. App. 3d 940, 140 Cal. Rptr. 434 (1977)	§ 25.2
Asher v. Broadway-Valentine Center, Inc., 691 S.W.2d 478 (Mo. Ct. App. 1985)	§ 8.8
Associated Eng'rs, Inc. v. Job, 370 F.2d 633 (8th Cir. 1966), *cert. denied,* 389 U.S. 823 (1967)	§§ 8.5, 15.5
Atlantic Coast Dev. Corp. v. Napoleon Steel Contractors, Inc., 385 So. 2d 676 (Fla. Dist. Ct. App. 1980)	§ 8.4
Atlantic Richfield Co. v. Petroleum Personnel, Inc., 768 S.W.2d 724 (Tex. 1989)	§ 8.3
Audlane Lumber & Builders Supply, Inc. v. D.E. Britt Assocs., Inc., 168 So. 2d 333 (Fla. Dist. Ct. App. 1964)	§ 14.9
Bacco Constr. Co. v. American Colloid Co., 148 Mich. App. 397, 384 N.W.2d 427 (1986)	§ 26.22

Case	*Book §*
Baird v. Chesapeake & Potomac Tel. Co., 208 Md. 245, 117 A.2d 873 (1955)	§ 14.16
Baker v. Selden, 101 U.S. 99 (1879)	§ 19.14
Balagna v. Shawnee County, 668 P.2d 157 (Kan. 1983)	§ 22.15
Balaban-Gordon Co. v. Brighton Sewer Dist., 41 A.D.2d 246, 342 N.Y.S.2d 435 (1973)	§ 20.7
Baldwin Elec., Inc., ASBCA No. 19683, 76-2 B.C.A. (CCH) ¶ 12,199 (1976)	§ 11.20
Baltimore v. De Luca Davis Constr. Co., 210 Md. 518, 124 A.2d 557 (1955)	§ 20.7
Baltimore County v. John K. Ruff, Inc., 281 Md. 62, 375 A.2d 237 (1977)	§ 20.7
Bank of Cal. v. Connolly, 36 Cal. App. 3d 350, 111 Cal. Rptr. 468 (1973)	§ 16.1
Bankers Trust Co. v. El Paso Pre-Cast Co., 560 P.2d 457 (Colo. 1977)	§ 25.4
Barker v. Colorado Regents Sports Car Club, 35 Colo. App. 73, 532 P.2d 372 (1974)	§ 8.8
Barker S.S. Lines, Inc. v. Quinn Bros., Inc., 104 F. Supp. 78 (D. Mass. 1952)	§ 8.4
Barnes v. MacBrown & Co., 264 Ind. 227, 342 N.E.2d 619 (1976)	§ 22.7
Barondon Corp. v. Kunika Nakawatase, 196 Cal. App. 2d, 16 Cal. Rptr. 472 (1961)	§ 14.5
Bartlett v. Davis Corp., 219 Kan. 148, 547 P.2d 800 (1976)	§ 8.8
Bates & Rogers Constr. Corp. v. North Shore Sanitary Dist., 92 Ill. App. 3d 90, 414 N.E.2d 1274 (1980)	§ 14.20
Bates & Rogers Constr. Corp. v. North Shore Sanitary Dist., 128 Ill. App. 3d 962, 471 N.E.2d 915 (1984), *aff'd on other grounds sub nom.* Bates & Rogers Constr. Corp. v. Greeley & Hansen, 109 Ill. 2d 225, 486 N.E.2d 902 (1985)	§§ 21.6, 22.7
Bayne v. Everham, 197 Mich. 181, 163 N.W. 1002 (1917)	§ 21.4
Bayuk v. Edson, 236 Cal. App. 2d 309, 46 Cal. Rptr. 49 (1965)	§§ 21.3, 21.9
Beacon Constr. Co. v. United States, 161 Ct. Cl. 1, 314 F.2d 501 (1963)	§ 18.9
Bedford, City of v. James Leffel & Co., 558 F.2d 216 (4th Cir. 1977)	§ 21.15
Beeson v. Overpack, 112 Ind. App. 195, 44 N.E.2d 195 (1942)	§ 25.5
Bell v. Jones, 523 A.2d 982 (D.C. 1986)	§ 21.2
Bergsoe Metal Corp., *In re* v. East Asiatic Co., 910 F.2d 668 (9th Cir. 1990)	§ 26.23
Berkel & Co. Contractors v. Providence Hosp., 454 So. 2d 496 (Ala. 1984)	§ 22.10
Bernard Johnson, Inc. v. Continental Constructors, Inc., 630 S.W. 2d 365 (Tex. Ct. App. 1982)	§§ 21.6, 22.1

Case	*Book §*
Bernard McMenamy Contractors, Inc. v. Missouri State Highway Comm'n, 582 S.W.2d 305 (Mo. Ct. App. 1979)	§ 20.3
Bethel Plumbing & Heating Co. v. General State Auth., 81 Dauph Co. 173 (Pa. 1963)	§ 20.7
Bethlehem Steel v. G.C. Zarnas & Co., 304 Md. 183, 498 A.2d 605 (1985)	§ 23.24
Bisset v. Joseph A. Schudt & Assocs., 133 Ill. App. 3d 356, 478 N.E.2d 911 (1985)	§ 26.17
Bissett-Berman Corp., NASA No. 1270-19, 73-2 B.C.A. (CCH) ¶ 10,346 (1973)	§ 11.21
Black Mountain Ranch v. Black Mountain Dev. Co., 29 Wash. App. 212, 627 P.2d 1006 (1981)	§ 8.6
Blake Constr. Co., GSBCA No. 2477, 71-1 B.C.A. (CCH) ¶ 8,870 (1971)	§ 11.13
Blake Constr. Co. v. Alley, 233 Va. 31, 353 S.E.2d 724 (1987)	§§ 22.6, 26.22, 26.24
Bloomsburg Mills, Inc. v. Sordoni Constr. Co., 401 Pa. 358, 164 A.2d 201 (1960)	§§ 21.1, 21.9
Board of Educ. v. Del Biano & Assocs., Inc., 57 Ill. App. 3d 302, 372 N.E.2d 953 (1978)	§ 26.26
Board of Educ. v. Joseph J. Duffy Co., 97 Ill. App. 2d 158, 240 N.E.2d 5 (1968)	§ 8.6
Board of Educ. v. Sargeant, Webster, Crenshaw & Foley, 71 N.Y.2d 21, 517 N.E.2d 1360, 523 N.Y.S.2d 475 (1987)	§ 21.13
Board of Educ. v. Thompson Constr. Corp., 111 A.D.2d 497, 488 N.Y.S.2d 880 (1985)	§ 21.15
Board of Educ. v. Valden Assocs., Inc., 46 N.Y.2d 653, 389 N.E.2d 798 (1979)	§ 17.2
Board of Trustees v. Kennerly, Slomanson & Smith, 167 N.J. Super. 311, 400 A.2d 850 (Law Div. 1979)	§ 21.1
Board of Water & Sewer Comm'rs v. Spriggs, 274 Ala. 155, 146 So. 2d 872 (1962)	§ 20.7
Board of Water Works Trustees v. Alvord, Burdick & Howson, 706 F.2d 820 (8th Cir. 1983)	§ 23.26
Bob Neiner Farms, Inc. v. Hendrix, 141 Ill. App. 3d 499, 490 N.E.2d 257 (1986)	§ 14.12
Boenning v. Brick Township Mun. Utils. Auth., 150 N.J. Super. 32, 374 A.2d 1214 (1977)	§ 18.3
Bonebrake v. Cox, 499 F.2d 951 (8th Cir. 1974)	§ 14.12
Borman's, Inc. v. Lake State Dev. Co., 60 Mich. App. 175, 230 N.W.2d 363 (1975)	§ 21.1
Bowden v. United States *ex rel.* Malloy, 239 F. 2d 572 (9th Cir. 1956), *cert. denied,* 353 U.S. 957 (1957)	§ 25.14
Branecky v. Seaman, 688 S.W.2d 117 (Tex. Ct. App. 1984)	§ 17.6
Briar Contracting Corp. v. City of New York, 156 A.D.2d 628, 550 N.Y.S.2d 717 (1989)	§ 22.6
Bridston v. Dover Corp., 352 N.W.2d 194 (N.D. 1984)	§ 8.8

Case	*Book §*
Broadway Maintenance Corp. V. Rutgers, 90 N.J. 253, 447 A.2d 906 (1982)	§ 18.5
Brown v. Gamble Constr. Co., 537 S.W.2d 685 (Mo. Ct. App. 1976)	§§ 7.5, 22.15
Brown v. Maryland Casualty Co., 246 Ark. 1074, 442 S.W.2d 187 (1969)	§ 18.12
Browning v. Maurice B. Levien & Co., 44 N.C. App. 701, 262 S.E.2d 355 (1980)	§§ 18.14, 21.10
Broyles v. Brown Eng'g Co., 275 Ala. 35, 151 So. 2d 767 (1963)	§§ 14.9, 19.8, 21.1
Bryant Elec. Co. v. City of Fredericksburg, 762 F.2d 1192 (4th Cir. 1985)	§ 21.6
Buckingham v. Flummerfelt, 15 N.D. 112, 106 N.W. 403 (1906)	§ 25.5
Bulk Distrib. Centers, Inc. v. Monsanto Co., 589 F. Supp. 1437 (S.D. Fla. 1984)	§ 26.4
Burns & Roe, Inc. v. Central Me. Power Co., 659 F. Supp. 141 (D. Me. 1987)	§§ 17.2, 21.14
Burran v. Dambold, 422 F.2d 133 (10th Cir. 1970)	§ 21.2
Cain v. Rea, 159 Va. 446, 166 S.E. 478 (1932)	§ 25.2
Calandro Dev., Inc. v. R.M. Butler Contractors, Inc., 249 So. 2d 254 (La. Ct. App. 1971)	§ 22.12
Caldwell v. Bechtel, Inc., 631 F.2d 989 (D.C. Cir. 1980)	§§ 18.10, 22.15
Califf v. Coca-Cola Co., 326 F. Supp. 540 (N.D. Ill. 1971)	§ 26.27
California Steel Co., *In re,* 21 B.R. 383 (N.D. Ill. 1983)	§ 17.6
Cantrell v. Woodhill Enter., Inc., 273 N.C. 490, 160 S.E.2d 476 (1968)	§ 18.15
Carid Eng'g Works v. Seven-Up Gold Mining Co., 111 Mont. 471, 111 P.2d 267 (1940)	§ 25.4
Carmania Corp., N.V. v. Hambrecht Terrell Int'l, 705 F. Supp. 936 (S.D.N.Y. 1989)	§§ 21.5, 21.6
Carrier Corp. v. United States, 6 Cl. Ct. 169 (1984)	§ 20.7
Castaldo v. Pittsburgh-Des Moines Steel Co., 376 A.2d 88 (Del. 1977)	§ 21.1
Cataldo Constr. Co. v. County of Essex, 110 N.J. Super. 414, 265 A.2d 842 (1970)	§ 20.7
CCTW&M v. United States Envtl. Protection Agency, 452 F. Supp. 69 (D.N.J. 1978)	§ 15.4
Central Nat'l Bank v. McDaniel, 734 P.2d 1314 (Okla. Ct. App. 1986)	§ 8.2
Central Navigation & Trading Co., S.A., ASBCA No. 23946, 82-2 B.C.A. (CCH) ¶ 16,074 (1982)	§ 11.20
Chambliss/Jenkins Assocs. v. Forster, 650 P.2d 1315 (Colo. Ct. App. 1982)	§ 25.4
Charlebois v. J.M. Weller Assocs., Inc., 72 N.Y.2d 587, 535 N.Y.S.2d 356, 531 N.E.2d 1288 (1988)	§§ 14.4, 14.5
Charles N. White Constr. Co. v. Department of Labor, 476 F. Supp. 862 (S.D. Miss. 1979)	§ 20.5

Case	*Book §*
Chatlos Sys., Inc. v. National Cash Register Corp., 479 F. Supp. 738 (D.N.J. 1979), *aff'd,* 635 F.2d 1081 (3d Cir. 1980)	§§ 19.9, 19.11
Chesbro-Whitman Co. v. Edenboro Apartments, Inc., 86 N.J. Super. 422, 207 A.2d 186 (1965)	§ 25.2
Chesnow v. Gorelick, 246 Mich. 571, 225 N.W. 4 (1929)	§ 25.5
Chevron Oil Co. v. E.D. Walton Constr. Co., 517 F.2d 1119 (5th Cir. 1975)	§ 8.6
C.H. Leavell & Co. v. Glantz Contracting Corp., 322 F. Supp. 779 (E.D. La. 1971)	§§ 19.5, 19.8, 22.2, 23.3
Choctaw Mfg. Co. v. United States, 761 F.2d 609 (11th Cir. 1985)	§ 20.8
Christy v. Menasha Corp., 297 Minn. 334, 211 N.W.2d 773 (1973)	§ 8.3
Chubb Group of Ins. Cos. v. C.F. Murphy Assocs., Inc., 656 S.W.2d 766 (Mo. Ct. App. 1983)	§ 22.16
Churchill Chem. Corp. v. United States, 602 F.2d 358 (Ct. Cl. 1979)	§ 20.5
Clark v. City of Seward, 659 P.2d 1227 (Alaska 1983)	§§ 22.5, 26.15
Clark v. Smith, 234 Wis. 138, 290 N.W. 592 (1940)	§ 25.4
Clark-Fitzpatrick, Inc. v. Long Island R.R. Co., 70 N.Y.2d 382, 516 N.E.2d 190, 521 N.Y.S.2d 653 (1987)	§ 21.5
Clemens v. Benzinger, 211 A.D. 586, 207 N.Y.S. 539 (1925)	§ 21.9
Clifford F. MacEvoy Co. v. United States *ex rel.* Calvin Tompkins, 322 U.S. 102, 64 S. Ct. 890 (1944)	§ 25.14
Clinton v. Boehm, 139 App. Div. 73, 124 N.Y.S. 789 (1910)	§ 15.6
COAC, Inc. v. Kennedy Eng'rs, 67 Cal. App. 3d 916, 136 Cal. Rptr. 890 (1977)	§§ 21.6, 22.2
Cobb v. Thomas, 565 S.W.2d 281 (Tex. Civ. App. 1978)	§ 21.8
Cofell's Plumbing & Heating, Inc. v. Stumpf, 290 N.W.2d 230 (N.D. 1980)	§ 18.9
Coller v. St. Paul, 223 Minn. 376, 26 N.W.2d 835 (1947)	§ 20.5
Columbus, City of v. Clark-Dietz & Assocs. Eng'rs, Inc., 550 F. Supp. 1239 (N.D. Miss. 1982)	§ 21.6
Commonwealth Dept. of Transp. v. Cumberland Constr. Co., 90 Pa. Commw. 273, 494 A.2d 520 (1985)	§ 20.3
Community Consol. School Dist. v. Meneley Constr. Co., 86 Ill. App. 3d 1101, 409 N.E.2d 66 (1980)	§ 20.7
Comptroller *ex rel.* VMI v. King, 217 Va. 751, 232 S.E.2d 895 (1977)	§ 18.6
Computer Network Corp., 55 Comp. Gen. 445, 75-2 CPD 297 (1975)	§ 17.4
Computer Servicenters, Inc. v. Beacon Mfg. Co., 328 F. Supp. 753 (D.S.C. 1970), *aff'd,* 443 F.2d 906 (4th Cir. 1971)	§ 19.9
Conduit & Foundation Corp. v. City of Philadelphia, 41 Pa. Commw. 641, 401 A.2d 376 (1979)	§ 20.8

Case	*Book §*
Cone Bros. Contracting Co. v. Ashland-Warren, Inc., 458 So. 2d 851 (Fla. Dist. Ct. App. 1984)	§ 8.6
Conforti & Eisele, Inc. v. John C. Morris Assocs., 175 N.J. 341, 418 A.2d 1290 (1980), *aff'd,* 199 N.J. Super. 498, 489 A.2d 1233 (1985)	§§ 21.6, 22.9
Connolly Dev., Inc. v. Superior Court, 17 Cal. 3d 803, 533 P.2d 637, 132 Cal. Rptr. 177, *appeal dismissed,* 429 U.S. 1056, 97 S. Ct. 778 (1977)	§ 25.8
Consolidated Supply Co. v. Babbitt, 96 Idaho 636, 534 P.2d 466 (1975)	§ 25.13
Construction Eng'g Co. v. Village Shopping Center, Inc., 168 So. 2d 826 (La. Ct. App. 1964)	§ 25.4
Consulting Eng'rs Council v. State Architects Licensure Bd., 560 A.2d 1375 (Pa. 1989)	§ 2.4
Consulting Serv. Corp., ASBCA No. 20288, 76-2 B.C.A. (CCH) ¶ 12,124 (1976)	§ 11.21
Continental Casualty Co. v. Allsop Lumber Co., 336 F.2d 445 (8th Cir. 1964), *cert. denied,* 379 U.S. 968, 85 S. Ct. 662 (1965)	§ 25.14
Contract for Route 280 Section 7U Exit Project, *In re,* 179 N.J. Super. 280, 431 A.2d 848 (1981)	§ 20.5
Contract Steel Sales, Inc. v. Freedom Constr. Co., 321 N.C. 215, 362 S.E.2d 547 (1987)	§ 17.6
Cool-Rite Corp., 48 Comp. Gen. 369 (1968)	§ 20.5
Cooper v. Jevne, 56 Cal. App. 3d 860, 128 Cal. Rptr. 724 (1976)	§§ 22.7, 22.13
Corpus Christi v. Acme Mechanical Constr., Inc., 736 S.W.2d 894 (Tex. 1987)	§ 15.5
Council of Co-Owners Atlantis Condominium, Inc. v. Whiting-Turner Contracting Co., 308 Md. 18, 517 A.2d 336 (1986)	§§ 22.5, 22.7, 22.13
County Asphalt, Inc. v. State, 40 A.D.2d 26, 337 N.Y.S.2d 415 (1972)	§ 20.3
Cowles v. City of Minneapolis, 128 Minn. 452, 151 N.W. 184 (1915)	§ 21.1
Craig v. Everett M. Brooks Co., 351 Mass. 497, 222 N.E.2d 752 (1967)	§§ 19.4, 26.12
Craviolini v. Scholer & Fuller Assocs. Architects, 89 Ariz. 24, 357 P.2d 611 (1960)	§§ 22.18, 23.15
Creswell Iron Works v. Camden Hous. Auth., 449 F.2d 557 (3d Cir. 1971)	§§ 18.11, 18.12
Crigler v. Salac, 438 So. 2d 1375 (Ala. 1983)	§§ 8.5, 8.8
Crouch v. Tourtelot, 350 S.W.2d 799 (Mo. 1961)	§ 8.5
Crown Cent. Petroleum Corp. v. Jennings, 727 S.W.2d 739 (Tex. Ct. App. 1987)	§ 8.3
Cunningham v. Government of Nashville, 476 S.W.2d 641 (Tenn. 1972)	§ 8.2
Curtin v. Somerset, 21 A. 244 (Pa. 1891)	§ 22.5
Cutlip v. Lucky Stores, 325 A.2d 432 (Md. 1974)	§ 7.5
Cuttino v. Mimms, 98 Ga. App. 198, 105 S.E.2d 343 (1958)	§ 21.9

Case	*Book §*
C.W. Regan, Inc. v. Parsons, Brinkerhoff, Quade & Douglas, 411 F.2d 1379 (4th Cir. 1969)	§ 15.6
Dagit v. Radnor Convalescent & Nursing Home, Inc., 53 Del. Co. 225, 38 Pa. D. & C.2d 389 (1965)	§§ 25.2, 25.4
Dale Constr. Co. v. United States, 168 Ct. Cl. 692 (1964)	§ 14.11
Dalton, Dalton, Little v. Mirandi, 412 F. Supp. 1001 (D.N.J. 1976)	§ 2.8
Dan Cowling & Assocs. v. Board of Educ., 273 Ark. 214, 618 S.W.2d 158 (1981)	§§ 18.10, 21.9
Daniel, Mann, Johnson & Mendenhall v. Hilton Hotels Corp., 98 Nev. 113, 642 P.2d 1086 (1982)	§ 21.11
Daugherty v. Herzog, 44 N.E. 457 (Ind. 1896)	§ 22.5
Davidson & Jones, Inc. v. County of New Hanover, 41 N.C. App. 661, 255 S.E.2d 580, *cert. denied,* 298 N.C. 293, 259 S.E.2d 911 (1979)	§§ 19.2, 19.8, 21.6, 21.9, 22.11, 26.16
Davis v. Commonwealth Edison Co., 61 Ill. 2d 494, 336 N.E.2d 881 (1975)	§ 23.24
Day v. National U.S. Radiator Corp., 117 So. 2d 104 (La. Ct. App. 1959), *rev'd,* 241 La. 288, 128 So. 2d 660 (1961)	§§ 15.6, 18.11, 22.15
Deel v. United States Steel Corp., 105 Ill. App. 2d 170, 245 N.E.2d 109 (1969)	§ 8.3
Del Mar Beach Club Owners Ass'n v. Imperial Contracting Co., 123 Cal. App. 3d 898, 176 Cal. Rptr. 886 (1981)	§ 21.1
Delta Constr. Co. v. City of Jackson, 198 So. 2d 592 (Miss. 1967)	§ 22.1
Delta Data Sys. Corp. v. Webster, 744 F.2d 197 (D.C. Cir. 1984)	§ 20.8
Demetriades v. Kaufman, No. 88 Civ. 0848 (S.D.N.Y. Mar. 8, 1988)	§ 17.5
Department of Transp. v. Ronlee, Inc., 518 So. 2d 1326 (Fla. 1987)	§ 20.7
Design Assocs., Inc. v. Powers, 86 N.C. App. 216, 356 S.E.2d 819 (1987)	§ 25.6
Design Assocs., Inc. v. Welch, 224 Cal. App. 2d 165, 36 Cal. Rptr. 341 (1964)	§ 25.4
Detweiler Bros., Inc. v. John Graham & Co., 412 F. Supp. 416 (E.D. Wash. 1976)	§§ 19.4, 21.6, 21.11, 22.10
Dewitt Truck Brokers, Inc. v. W. Ray Flemming Fruit Co., 540 F.2d 681 (4th Cir. 1976)	§ 26.27
Diamond v. Diehr, 450 U.S. 175, 101 S. Ct. 1048 (1981)	§ 19.13
Diamond Match Co. v. Silberstein, 165 Cal. 282, 131 P. 874 (1913)	§ 25.8
Dickerson Constr. Co. v. Process Eng'g Co., 341 So. 2d 646 (Miss. 1977)	§ 21.9
Dickinson Co. v. Des Moines, 347 N.W.2d 436 (Iowa 1984)	§ 20.4

Case	*Book §*
E.C. Ernst, Inc. v. Manhattan Constr. Co., 551 F.2d 1026 (5th Cir. 1977), *cert. denied,* 434 U.S. 1067 (1978)	§§ 18.9, 18.11, 18.13, 20.2, 20.3, 21.6, 21.11, 22.9, 23.15
Ecksel v. Orleans Constr. Co., 360 Pa. Super. 119, 519 A.2d 1021 (1987)	§ 21.9
Edward B. Fitzpatrick, Jr. Constr. Corp. v. County of Suffolk, 138 A.D.2d 446, 525 N.Y.S.2d 863 (1988)	§ 26.23
Eggers Partnership, 82-1 B.C.A. ¶ 15,630 (IBCA 1982)	§ 21.9
E.H. Morrill Co. v. State, 65 Cal. 2d 787, 423 P.2d 551, 56 Cal. Rptr. 479 (1967)	§§ 15.7, 20.3
80-82 Greene St. Corp. v. AFA Protective Sys., Inc., 100 Misc. 2d 334, 418 N.Y.S.2d 971 (Sup. Ct. 1979)	§ 17.2
Electronic & Missile Facilities, Inc., ASBCA No. 9031, 1964 B.C.A. (CCH) ¶ 4,338 (1964)	§ 11.13
Electro Optics, Inc., ASBCA Nos. 24235, 24390, 81-2 B.C.A. (CCH) ¶ 15,181 (1981)	§ 11.18
Eley v. Brunner-Lay S. Corp., 289 Ala. 120, 266 So. 2d 276 (1972)	§ 8.3
Elsbach v. Mulligan, 58 Cal. App. 2d 354, 136 P.2d 651 (1943)	§ 16.1
Emberton v. State Farm Mut. Auto Ins. Co., 71 Ill. 2d 111, 373 N.E.2d 1348 (1978)	§ 18.10
Emerald Forest Util. Dist. v. Simonsen Constr. Co., 679 S.W.2d 51 (Tex. Ct. App. 1984)	§ 20.2
Emery Waterhouse Co. v. Lea, 467 A.2d 986 (Me. 1983)	§§ 8.8, 17.2
Employers Liab. Assurance Corp. v. Tebbs, 137 F. Supp. 869 (D. Wyo. 1956)	§ 14.14
Erhardt v. Hummonds, 232 Ark. 133, 334 S.W.2d 869 (1960)	§§ 7.5, 22.15
Estes Co. v. Aztec Constr., Inc., 139 Ariz. 166, 677 P.2d 939 (Ct. App. 1983)	§ 8.8
Ethyl Corp. v. Daniel Constr. Co., 725 S.W.2d 705 (Tex. 1987)	§ 8.6
Etowah Mfg., ASBCA No. 23521, 80-1 B.C.A. (CCH) ¶ 14,438 (1980)	§ 11.13
Eureka Stone v. First Christian Church, 16 Ark. 212, 110 S.W. 1042 (1908)	§ 25.2
Evans v. Howard R. Green Co., 231 N.W.2d 907 (Iowa 1975)	§§ 8.8, 21.2, 22.15, 26.17
Eveleth, City of v. Ruble, 302 Minn. 249, 225 N.W.2d 521 (1974)	§§ 18.10, 19.2
Fabe v. WVP Corp., 760 S.W.2d 490 (Mo. Ct. App. 1988)	§ 22.12
Fairbanks N. Star Borough v. Roen Design Assocs., 727 P.2d 758 (Alaska 1986)	§ 21.12
Falcon Research & Dev. Co., ASBCA No. 26853, 87-1 B.C.A. (CCH) ¶ 19,458 (1986)	§ 11.21

Case	*Book §*
Farris Eng'g Corp. v. Service Bureau Corp., 406 F.2d 519 (3d Cir. 1969)	§ 14.16
F.D. Rich Co. v. United States *ex rel.* Industrial Lumber Co., 417 U.S. 116, 94 S. Ct. 2157 (1974)	§ 25.14
Federal Ins. Co. v. Community State Bank, 905 F.2d 112 (5th Cir. 1990)	§ 17.6
Federal Mogul Corp. v. Universal Constr. Co., 376 So. 2d 716 (Ala. Civ. App. 1979)	§§ 14.9, 21.1
Federal Screw Works v. Interface Sys., Inc., 569 F. Supp. 1562 (E.D. Mich. 1983)	§ 17.3
Fence Rail Dev. Corp. v. Nelson & Assocs., Ltd., 174 Ill. App. 3d 94, 528 N.E.2d 344 (1988)	§ 21.6
Ferentchak v. Village of Frankfort, 121 Ill. App. 3d 599, 459 N.E.2d 1085 (1984), *rev'd on other grounds,* 475 N.E.2d 822 (1985)	§ 22.7
Fidelity & Casualty Co. v. J.A. Jones Constr. Co., 325 F.2d 605 (8th Cir. 1963)	§ 19.6
Fifteenth Ave. Christian Church v. Moline Heating & Constr. Co., 131 Ill. App. 2d 766, 265 N.E.2d 405 (1970)	§ 18.9
First Nat'l Bank v. Cann, 503 F. Supp. 419 (N.D. Ohio 1980), *aff'd,* 669 F.2d 415 (6th Cir. 1982)	§§ 18.3, 18.10, 18.14, 21.9
Fisher v. Simon, 15 Wis. 2d 207, 112 N.W.2d 705 (1961)	§ 22.5
Floor Craft, Inc. v. Parma Community Gen. Hosp. Assoc., 560 N.E.2d 206 (Ohio 1990)	§ 22.6
Florida Power Corp. v. Taylor, 332 So. 2d 687 (Fla. Dist. Ct. App. 1976)	§ 8.5
Florida Power & Light Co. v. Mid-Valley, Inc., 763 F.2d 1316 (11th Cir. 1985)	§§ 8.7, 14.16, 17.2
Ford v. Sturgis, 14 F.2d 235 (D.C. Cir. 1926)	§ 22.5
Formigli Corp. v. Fox, 348 F. Supp. 629 (E.D. Pa. 1972)	§ 17.6
Forte Bros., Inc. v. National Amusements, Inc., 525 A.2d 1301 (R.I. 1987)	§§ 21.6, 22.5, 22.9
Forte Towers S., Inc. v. Hill York Sales Corp., 312 So. 2d 512 (Fla. Dist. Ct. App. 1975)	§ 22.5
Foshay, *ex parte,* 7 U.S.P.Q. (BNA) 121 (1930)	§ 17.5
Foster v. Keating, 120 Cal. App. 2d 435, 261 P.2d 529 (1953)	§ 16.1
Foster Constr. C.A. v. United States, 435 F.2d 873, 193 Ct. Cl. 587 (1970)	§ 20.3
Fox v. Stanley J. Howe & Assocs., Inc., 309 N.W.2d 520 (Iowa 1981)	§ 26.18
Freedman v. Stein, 4 N.J. 34, 71 A.2d 346 (1950)	§ 25.5
Freeform Pools, Inc. v. Strawbridge Home for Boys, Inc., 228 Md. 297, 179 A.2d 683 (1962)	§ 25.2
Friendship Heights Assocs. v. Vlastimil Koubek, AIA, 573 F. Supp. 100 (D. Md. 1983)	§ 26.15
Frischertz Elec. Co. v. Hous. Auth., 534 So. 2d 1310 (La. Ct. App. 1988)	§ 18.6

Case	*Book §*
Fuchs v. Parsons Constr. Co., 172 Neb. 719, 111 N.W.2d 727 (1961)	§ 18.14
Funderburg Builders, Inc. v. Abbeville County Memorial Hosp., 467 F. Supp. 821 (D.S.C. 1979)	§ 20.4
Furlong v. Hous. Auth., 132 N.J. Eq. 341, 28 A.2d 424 (1942)	§ 25.5
Gaastra, Gladding & Johnson v. Bishop's Lodge Co., 35 N.M. 396, 299 P. 347 (1931)	§§ 25.3, 25.5
Gagne v. Bertran, 43 Cal. 2d 481, 275 P.2d 15 (1954)	§§ 12.8, 14.8, 26.12
Galbraith v. Illinois Steel Co., 133 F. 485 (7th Cir. 1904), *cert. denied,* 201 U.S. 643, 26 S. Ct. 759 (1906)	§ 22.5
Garden City Floral Co. v. Hunt, 126 Mont. 577, 255 P.2d 352 (1953)	§ 15.6
Geer v. Bennett, 237 So. 2d 311 (Fla. Dist. Ct. App. 1970)	§ 22.15
Geiser v. Permacrete, Inc., 90 So. 2d 610 (Fla. 1956)	§ 25.2
General Air Conditioning Corp. v. Stewe, 156 Kan. 182, 131 P.2d 638 (1942)	§ 25.5
General Elec. Corp. v. United States, 194 Ct. Cl. 678, 440 F.2d 420 (1971)	§ 11.21
General Time Corp., ASBCA No. 18962, 75-2 B.C.A. (CCH) ¶ 11,462 (1975)	§ 11.21
General Utils. & Operating Co. v. Helvering, 296 U.S. 200 (1935)	§§ 3.12, 3.13
George A. Fuller Co. v. Chicago College of Osteopathic Medicine, 719 F.2d 1326 (7th Cir. 1983)	§ 19.7
Georgia, Fla., Ala. Transp. Co. v. Deaton, Inc., 293 Ala. 359, 304 So. 2d 168 (1974)	§§ 8.3, 8.8
Gerodetti v. Broadacres, Inc., 363 So. 2d 265 (Miss. 1978)	§ 21.9
Gilson v. Republic of Ireland, 606 F. Supp. 38 (D.D.C. 1984)	§ 17.3
Glassman Constr. Co. v. Maryland City Plaza, Inc., 371 F. Supp. 1154 (D. Md. 1974)	§ 14.3
Glamorgan Pipe & Foundry Co. v. Washington Suburban Sanitary Comm'n, 183 F. Supp. 840 (D. Md. 1960)	§ 20.7
Glanzer v. Shepard, 233 N.Y. 236, 135 N.E. 275 (1922)	§ 21.5
Goette v. Press Bar & Cafe, Inc., 413 N.W.2d 854 (Minn. Ct. App. 1987)	§ 21.4
Gollehon, Schemmer & Assocs., Inc. v. Fairway-Bettendorf Assocs., 268 N.W.2d 200 (Iowa 1978)	§ 25.5
Gottschalk v. Benson, 409 U.S. 63 (1972)	§ 19.13
Grade-way Constr. v. United States, 7 Cl. Ct. 263 (1985)	§ 20.5
Graham v. Clyde, 61 So. 2d 656 (Fla. 1952)	§ 20.7
Gramatan-Sullivan, Inc. v. Koslow, 240 F.2d 523 (2d Cir. 1952)	§ 25.10
Grass Range High School Dist. v. Wallace Diteman, Inc., 155 Mont. 10, 465 P.2d 814 (1970)	§ 18.15
Gravely v. Providence Partnership, 549 F.2d 958 (4th Cir. 1977)	§ 19.4

Case	*Book §*
Green v. Brookins, 23 Mich. 48 (1871)	§ 8.2
Greenfield Erectors & Builders, Inc. v. Feleure, 443 N.E.2d 87 (Ind. Ct. App. 1983)	§ 17.6
Gregory v. Garrett Corp., 578 F. Supp. 871 (S.D.N.Y. 1983)	§ 23.18
Grenier v. Compratt Constr. Co., 189 Conn. 144, 454 A.2d 1289 (1983)	§§ 18.9, 18.13
Griswold & Rauma Architects, Inc. v. Aesculapius Corp., 301 Minn. 121, 221 N.W.2d 556 (1974)	§ 21.8
Gross v. Kenton Structural & Ornamental Ironworks, 581 F. Supp. 390 (S.D. Ohio 1984)	§ 22.15
Grossman v. Sea Air Towers, Ltd., 513 So. 2d 686 (Fla. Dist. Ct. App. 1987), *review denied,* 520 So. 2d 584 (Fla. 1988)	§§ 8.4, 21.3, 21.9, 21.11
Grossman Holdings Ltd. v. Hourihan, 414 So. 2d. 1037 (Fla. 1982)	§ 21.9
GRW Eng'rs, Inc. v. Elam, 504 So. 2d 117 (La. Ct. App.), *cert. denied,* 506 So. 2d 1230 (1987)	§ 25.4
Guardian Constr. Co. v. Tetra Tech Richardson, Inc., 583 A.2d 1378 (Del. 1990)	§ 20.2
Gulf Contracting v. Bibb County, 795 F.2d 980 (11th Cir. 1986)	§ 22.6, 22.11, 26.22
Gurtler, Hebert & Co. v. Weyland Mach. Shop, Inc., 405 So. 2d 660 (La. Ct. App. 1981)	§ 21.6
Haberman v. Washington Pub. Power Supply Sys., 109 Wash. 2d 107, 744 P.2d 1032 (1987)	§ 22.20
Hackley v. Waldorf-Hoerner Paper Prods. Co., 149 Mont. 286, 425 P.2d 712 (1967)	§§ 21.2, 22.15
Hadley v. Baxendale, 156 Eng. Rep. 145 (1854)	§ 21.5
Haith & Co. v. Ellers, Oakley, Chester & Rike, Inc., 778 S.W.2d 417 (Mo. Ct. App. 1989)	§ 2.8
Hale v. Depaoli, 33 Cal. 2d 228, 201 P.2d 1 (1948)	§ 22.5
Hall v. Union Indem. Co., 61 F.2d 85 (8th Cir. 1975)	§ 18.14
Hamby v. High Steel Structures, Inc., 134 A.D.2d 884, 521 N.Y.S.2d 926 (1987)	§ 26.17
Hardy v. Monstano Enviro-Chem Sys., Inc., 414 Mich. 29, 323 N.W.2d 270 (1982)	§ 8.4
Hartford Elec. Applicators of Thermalux, Inc. v. Alden, 169 Conn. 177, 363 A.2d 185 (1980)	§§ 18.10, 18.13
Heimsath & Assocs., NASA BCA No. 180-1, 83-1 B.C.A. (CCH) ¶ 16,133 (1982)	§ 11.12
Henderson v. Rounds & Porter Lumber Co., 99 F. Supp. 376 (D. Ark. 1951)	§ 26.27
Henningson, Durham & Richardson, Inc. v. Swift Bros. Constr. Co., 739 F.2d 1341 (8th Cir. 1984)	§ 22.15
Henry & John Assocs. v. Demmilo Constr. Corp., 137 Misc. 2d 354, 520 N.Y.S.2d 340 (1987)	§ 17.6
Henry Hope X-Ray Prod., Inc. v. Marron Carrel, 674 F.2d 1336 (9th Cir. 1982)	§ 17.3

Case	*Book §*
Henshaw v. Edward E. Clark Eng'rs-Scientists, 490 So. 2d 161 (Fla. Dist. Ct. App. 1986)	§ 26.17
Herman Frankel Org. v. Wolfe, 184 U.S.P.Q. (BNA) 819 (E.D. Mich. 1974)	§ 17.5
Hickey v. Polachack, 63 Or. App. 784, 666 P.2d 294 (1983)	§ 17.6
Hill v. Polar Pantries, 219 S.C. 263, 64 S.E.2d 885 (1951)	§§ 12.8, 14.9, 19.8
Hill Behan Lumber Co. v. American Nat'l Bank & Trust Co., 101 Ill. App. 3d 268, 427 N.E.2d 1325 (1981)	§ 17.6
Hoagland v. Celebrity Homes, Inc., 40 Colo. App. 215, 572 P.2d (1972)	§ 14.11
Hogan v. Postin, 695 P.2d 1042 (Wyo. 1985)	§ 22.10
Hollerbach v. United States, 233 U.S. 165, 34 S. Ct. 553 (1914)	§ 20.3
Holtz v. United Plumbing & Heating Co., 49 Cal. 2d 501, 319 P.2d 617 (1957)	§ 16.1
Honey v. Barnes Hosp., 708 S.W.2d 686 (Mo. Ct. App. 1986)	§ 22.5
Hood v. Welch, 249 Ark. 1159, 463 S.W.2d 362 (1971)	§ 8.8
Hotel Utica, Inc. v. Ronald G. Armstrong Eng'g Co., 62 A.D.2d 1147, 404 N.Y.S.2d 455 (1978)	§ 21.5
Houma, City of v. Municipal & Indus. Pipe Servs., Inc., 884 F.2d 886 (5th Cir. 1989)	§ 22.12
Housing Auth. v. Pittman Constr. Co., 264 F.2d 695 (5th Cir. 1959)	§§ 20.4, 20.6
Howell v. Fisher, 49 N.C. App. 488, 272 S.E.2d 19 (1980)	§§ 22.2, 22.6, 22.11
Huang v. Garner, 157 Cal. App. 3d 404, 203 Cal. Rptr. 800 (1984)	§§ 14.9, 26.24
Huber, Hunt & Nichols v. Moore, 67 Cal. App. 3d 278, 136 Cal. Rptr. 603 (1977)	§§ 14.8, 18.12
Huggin v. Atlanta Tile & Marble Co., 98 Ga. App. 597, 106 S.E.2d 191 (1958)	§ 18.9
Hughes Aircraft Corp., ASBCA No. 24601, 83-1 B.C.A. (CCH) ¶ 16,396 (1983)	§ 11.21
Hunt v. Ellisor & Tanner, Inc., 739 S.W.2d 933 (Tex. Ct. App. 1987)	§§ 8.7, 21.13
Hyman v. Gordon, 35 Cal. App. 3d 769, 111 Cal. Rptr. 262 (1973)	§ 26.19
IDG Architects, B-235487 (Sept. 18, 1989), 89-2 CPD ¶ 236 (1989)	§ 11.8
IFR, Inc., Comp. Gen. B-203391.4, April 1, 1982, 81-1 CPD 292	§ 17.4
Independent Consol. School Dist. No. 24 v. Carlstrom, 277 Minn. 117, 151 N.W.2d 784 (1967)	§ 14.11
Ingram v. Howard-Needles-Tammen & Bergendoff, 234 Kan. 289, 672 P.2d 1083 (1983)	§ 22.16
Inman v. Binghamton Hous. Auth., 3 N.Y.2d 137, 143 N.E.2d 895, 164 N.Y.S.2d 699 (1957)	§§ 19.2, 22.5, 26.18
Insurance Co. of N. Am. v. Universal Mortgage Corp., 82 Wis. 2d 170, 262 N.W.2d 92 (1978)	§ 17.2

Case	*Book §*
Inter-National Research Inst., ASBCA No. 24212, 80-1 B.C.A. (CCH) ¶ 14,345 (1980)	§ 11.21
Irondequoit Bay Pure Water Dist. v. Nalews, Inc., 123 Misc. 2d 462, 472 N.Y.S.2d 842 (1984)	§ 8.4
ITT Defense Communications Div., ASBCA No. 14270, 70-2 B.C.A. (CCH) ¶ 8,370 (1970)	§ 11.20
ITT Gilfillon v. United States, 200 Ct. Cl. 367, 471 F.2d 1382 (1973)	§ 11.19
Jackson v. General Elec. Co., 514 P.2d 1170 (Alaska 1973)	§ 26.27
Jackson v. Hooper, 76 N.J. Eq. 592, 75 A. 569 (1910)	§§ 16.1, 16.14
Jacksonville Port Auth. v. Parkhill-Goodloe Co., 362 So. 2d 1009 (Fla. Dist. Ct. App. 1978)	§ 20.3
Jaeger v. Henningson, Durham & Richardson, Inc., 714 F.2d 773 (8th Cir. 1983)	§ 22.15
James H. Stewart & Assocs., Inc. v. Naredel of Colo., Inc., 571 P.2d 738 (Colo. Ct. App. 1977)	§ 25.4
James McKinney & Son, Inc. v. Lake Placid 1980 Olympic Games, Inc., 92 A.D.2d 991, 461 N.Y.S.2d 483 (1983), *modified on other grounds,* 61 N.Y.2d 836, 462 N.E.2d 137, 473 N.Y.S.2d 960 (9184)	§ 21.6
Jasper Constr., Inc. v. Foothill Jr. College Dist., 91 Cal. App. 3d 1, 153 Cal. Rptr. 767 (1979)	§§ 18.4, 20.2
J.A. Thompson & Son, Inc. v. State, 51 Haw. 529, 465 P.2d 148 (1970)	§ 20.3
J.D. Hedin Constr. Co. v. United States, 347 F.2d 235, 171 Ct. Cl. 70 (1965)	§ 20.2
J.E. Moss Ironworks v. County Court, 89 W. Va. 367, 109 S.E. 343 (1921)	§ 25.2
Jersey City Redevelopment Auth. v. PPG Indus., 655 F. Supp. 1257 (D.N.J. 1987)	§ 26.34
Jewish Bd. of Guardians v. Grumman Allied Instruments, Inc., 96 A.D.2d 465, 464 N.Y.S.2d 778 (1983), *aff'd,* 62 N.Y.2d 684, 465 N.E.2d 42, 476 N.Y.S.2d 535 (1984)	§ 26.17
Jim Arnott, Inc. v. L&E, Inc., 539 P.2d 1333 (Colo. Ct. App. 1975)	§ 21.9
J.J. Henry Co. v. United States, 411 F.2d 1246, 188 Ct. Cl. 39 (1969)	§§ 15.3, 25.2, 25.14
J.L. Manta, Inc. v. Braun, 393 N.W.2d 490 (Minn. 1986)	§ 20.4
J.L. Simmons Co. v. United States, 412 F.2d 1360, 188 Ct. Cl. 684 (1969)	§ 20.2
J.M. Thomson, Jr., 39 Comp. Gen. 259 (1959)	§ 20.5
John Carlo, Inc. v. Corps of Eng'rs, 539 F. Supp. 1075 (N.D. Tex. 1982)	§ 20.6
John E. Green Plumbing & Heating Co. v. Turner Constr. Co., 742 F.2d 965 (6th Cir. 1984), *cert. denied,* 471 U.S. 1102, 105 S. Ct. 2328 (1985)	§ 21.6
John F. Miller Co. v. George Fichera Constr. Corp., 7 Mass. App. Ct. 494, 388 N.E.2d 1201 (1979)	§ 20.3

Case	*Book §*
John Grace & Co. v. State Univ. Constr. Fund, 99 A.D.2d 860, 472 N.Y.S.2d 757 (1984)	§ 8.4
John J. Brennan Constr. Corp. v. Shelton, 187 Conn. 695, 448 A.2d 180 (1982)	§ 20.4
Johnson v. Salem Title Co., 246 Or. 409, 425 P.2d 519 (1967)	§§ 15.2, 21.2, 21.3, 21.9, 22.16
Johnson, Drake & Piper, Inc., 39 Comp. Gen. 468 (1959)	§ 20.6
Jones v. J.H. Hiser Constr. Co., 60 Md. App. 671, 484 A.2d 302 (1984)	§ 18.3
Jones v. Strom Constr. Co., 84 Wash. 2d 518, 527 P.2d 1115 (1974)	§ 8.3
Jordan v. City of Beaumont, 337 S.W.2d 115 (Tex. 1960)	§ 20.7
Joseph Pickard's Sons Co., ASBCA Nos. 13585, 15537, 73-1 B.C.A. (CCH) ¶ 10,026 (1973)	§ 11.15
Juengel Constr. Co. v. Mt. Etna, Inc., 622 S.W.2d 510 (Mo. Ct. App. 1981)	§ 22.18
Keco Indus., Inc. v. United States, 492 F.2d 1200 (Ct. Cl. 1974)	§ 20.8
Keel v. Titan Constr. Corp., 639 P.2d 1228 (Okla. 1981)	§ 21.11
Kellogg Bridge Co. v. Hamilton, 110 U.S. 108, 3 S. Ct. 537 (1884)	§ 14.9
Kelly v. Northwest Community Hosp., 66 Ill. App. 3d 679, 384 N.E.2d 102 (1978)	§ 22.15
Kemp v. Bechtel Constr. Co., 221 Mont. 519, 720 P.2d 270 (1986)	§ 22.15
Kennedy v. Bowling, 319 Mo. 401, 4 S.W.2d 438 (1928)	§ 14.9
Kennedy v. Columbia Lumber & Mfg. Co., 299 S.C. 335, 384 S.E.2d 730 (1988)	§ 12.8
Kenneth E. Curran, Inc. v. State, 106 N.H. 558, 215 A.2d 702 (1965)	§ 20.7
Kerr v. Rochester Gas & Elec. Corp., 113 A.D.2d 412, 496 N.Y.S.2d 990 (1985)	§ 22.15
Ke-Wash v. Stauffer Chem. Co., 177 N.W.2d 5 (Iowa 1970)	§ 8.4
Key Agency v. Continental Cas. Co., 31 N.J. 98, 155 A.2d 547 (1959)	§ 25.10
Kilbride v. Moss, 113 Cal. 432, 45 P. 812 (1896)	§ 8.2
Kinetic Structures Corp. v. United States, 6 Cl. Ct. 387 (1984)	§ 20.4
King v. Alaska Hous. Auth., 512 P.2d 887 (Alaska 1973)	§ 20.5
Kingston v. Preston, Lofft 194, 2 Doug. 684 (K.B. 1773)	§ 18.9
Kirschner Assocs., Inc., ASBCA No. 24958, 81-1 B.C.A. (CCH) ¶ 14,834 (1980)	§ 11.21
Kishwaukee Community Health Servs. Center v. Hospital Bldg. & Equip. Co., 638 F.2d 1492 (N.D. Ill. 1986)	§ 22.6

Case	*Book §*
Leo A. Daly Co., Eng. BCA No. 4463, 85-1 B.C.A. (CCH) ¶ 17,740 (1984)	§ 11.12
Levine v. Parsons, 258 A.D. 1003, 16 N.Y.S.2d 722 (1940)	§ 20.7
Liberty Mut. Ins. Co. v. Altfillisch Constr. Co., 70 Cal. App. 3d 789, 139 Cal. Rptr. 91 (1977)	§ 17.2
Lipman v. Well-Mix Concrete, Inc., 138 N.Y.S.2d 316 (1954)	§ 8.4
Littell & S. Mfg. Co. v. Miller, 3 Wash. 480, 28 P. 1035 (1892)	§ 25.2
Lloyd C. Ryan v. EAI Constr. Corp., 158 Ill. App. 3d 449, 511 N.E.2d 1244 (1987)	§ 23.24
Long Island Lighting Co. v. IMO Delaval, Inc., 668 F. Supp. 237 (S.D.N.Y. 1987)	§§ 14.16, 17.2
Lotus Dev. Corp. v. Mosaic Software, Inc., No. 87-0074K	§ 19.14
Lotus Dev. Corp. v. Paperback Software Int'l, 740 F. Supp. 37 (D. Mass. 1990)	§ 19.14
Louisiana *ex rel.* Guste v. M/V Testbank, 752 F.2d 1019 (5th Cir. 1985), *cert. denied,* 477 U.S. 903, 106 S. Ct. 3271 (1986)	§ 21.6
Lowendahl v. Baltimore & O.R. Co., 247 A.D. 144, 287 N.Y.S. 62, *aff'd,* 272 N.Y. 360, 6 N.E.2d 56 (1936), *reh'g denied,* 273 N.Y. 584, 7 N.E.2d 704 (1937)	§ 26.27
Lumberman's Mut. Casualty Co. v. Pattillo Constr. Co., 254 Ga. 461, 330 S.E.2d 344 (1985)	§ 21.15
Lundgren v. Freeman, 307 F.2d 104 (9th Cir. 1962)	§§ 18.8, 23.15
MacPherson v. Buick Motor Co., 111 N.E. 1050 (N.Y. 1916)	§ 22.4
Madison v. Superior Court (Sulejmanagic), 203 Cal. App. 3d 589, 250 Cal. Rptr. 299 (1988)	§ 17.2
Magnolia Constr. Co. v. Mississippi Gulf S. Eng'rs, Inc., 518 So. 2d 1194 (Miss. 1988)	§ 18.14
Malan Constr. Corp. v. Board of County Comm'rs, 187 F. Supp. 937 (E.D. Mich. 1960)	§ 20.6
Mallow v. Tucker, Sadler & Bennett, 245 Cal. App. 2d 700, 54 Cal. Rptr. 174 (1966)	§ 22.15
Malta Constr. Co. v. Henningson, Durham & Richardson, Inc., 716 F. Supp. 1466 (N.D. Ga. 1989)	§ 22.6
Manson-Osberg Co. v. State, 552 P.2d 654 (Alaska 1976)	§ 8.6
Markborough Cal., Inc. v. Superior Court, 91 C.D.O.S. 1165 (1991)	§ 12.3
Markel v. Florida State Bd. of Architecture, 268 So. 2d 374 (Fla. 1972)	§ 14.4
Marshall Constr. Co. v. Bigelow, 29 Haw. 641 (1927)	§ 20.4
Martin Co., Comp. Gen. B-178540 (May 8, 1974)	§ 20.5
Maryland Nat'l Capital Park & Planning Comm'n v. Lynn, 514 F.2d 829 (D.C. Cir. 1975)	§ 15.2
Mason v. Rose, 176 F.2d 486 (2d Cir. 1949)	§ 16.1
Massman Constr. Co. v. United States, 60 F. Supp. 635 (Ct. Cl.), *cert. denied,* 325 U.S. 866 (1945)	§ 20.4

Case	*Book §*
Mayor & City Council v. Clark-Dietz & Assocs. Eng'rs, 550 F. Supp. 610 (N.D. Miss. 1982)	§§ 20.2, 21.9
McClanahan v. American Gilsonite Co., 494 F. Supp. 1334 (D. Colo. 1980)	§ 23.7
McClintic-Marshall Co. v. Ford Motor Co., 254 Mich. 305, 236 N.W. 792 (1931)	§ 25.2
McCloskey & Co. v. Wright, 363 F. Supp. 223 (E.D. Va. 1973)	§ 19.6
McDonald v. Filice, 252 Cal. App. 2d 613, 60 Cal. Rptr. 832 (1967)	§§ 25.4, 25.6
McGovern v. Standish, 65 Ill. 2d 54, 357 N.E.2d 1134 (1976)	§ 7.5
McWaters & Bartlett v. United States *ex rel.* Wilson, 272 F.2d 291 (9th Cir. 1959)	§ 25.14
Mears Park Holding Corp. v. Morse-Diesel, Inc., 427 N.W.2d 281 (Minn. Ct. App. 1988)	§ 26.23
Metropolitan Supply Dist. v. Anthony Pontarelli & Sons, Inc., 7 Ill. App. 3d 829, 288 N.E.2d 905 (1972)	§ 18.9
M.F. Kemper Constr. Co. v. City of Los Angeles, 37 Cal. 2d 696, 235 P.2d 7 (1951)	§ 20.7
Miami Elevator Co. v. La Concha Motor Inn, 462 So. 2d 511 (Fla. Dist. Ct. App. 1985)	§ 8.4
Miami Highland Park, Inc. v. Leslie, 142 So. 2d 754 (Fla. 1962)	§ 25.4
Midland, City of v. Waller, 430 S.W.2d 473 (Tex. 1968)	§ 18.15
Miller v. City of Broken Arrow, 660 F.2d 450 (10th Cir. 1981), *cert. denied,* 455 U.S. 1020 (1982)	§ 21.12
Miller v. DeWitt, 37 Ill. 2d 273, 226 N.E.2d 630 (1967)	§§ 15.5, 21.9, 22.15, 26.17
Miller Co. v. Central Contra Costa Sanitary Dist., 198 Cal. App. 2d 305, 18 Cal. Rptr. 13 (1961)	§ 22.11
Milton J. Womack, Inc. v. House of Representatives, 509 So. 2d 62 (La. Ct. App. 1987)	§§ 21.2, 21.6, 22.7, 22.9
Milwaukee, County of v. Schmidt, Garden & Erikson, 43 Wis. 2d 445, 168 N.W.2d 559 (1969)	§ 21.15
Mississippi Meadows, Inc. v. Hodson, 13 Ill. App. 3d 24, 299 N.E.2d 359 (1973)	§ 19.4
Mississippi State Bldg. Comm'n v. Becknell Constr., 329 So. 2d 57 (Miss. 1976)	§ 20.7
Modern Continental Constr. Co. v. City of Lowell, 391 Mass. 829, 465 N.E.2d 1173 (1984)	§ 20.8
Modern Controls, Inc. v. Andreadakis, 578 F.2d 1264 (8th Cir. 1978)	§ 17.3
Mohawk Drilling Co. v. McCullough Tool Co., 271 F.2d 627 (10th Cir. 1959)	§§ 8.7, 14.16
Moloso v. State, 644 P.2d 205 (Alaska 1982)	§ 22.15
Montijo v. Swift, 219 Cal. App. 2d 351, 33 Cal. Rptr. 133 (1963)	§§ 21.9, 22.5
Moorman Mfg. Co. v. National Tank Co., 91 Ill. 2d 69, 435 N.E.2d 443 (1982)	§§ 21.6, 22.6, 23.5

Case	*Book §*
Moran v. Pittsburg-Des Moines Steel Co., 166 F.2d 908 (3d Cir.), *cert. denied,* 334 U.S. 846, 68 S. Ct. 1516 (1948)	§ 22.5
Morehouse v. Crangle, 36 Ohio St. 130 (1880)	§ 8.2
Morgan v. Good Humor Corp., 54 A.D.2d 560, 386 N.Y.S.2d 888 (1976)	§ 8.6
Morrell, *In re,* 42 Bankr. 973 (1984)	§ 25.4
Morris F. Fox & Co. v. State, 229 Wis. 44, 281 N.W. 666 (1938)	§ 25.10
Motorists Mut. Ins. Co. v. Jones, 9 Ohio Misc. 113, 223 N.E.2d 381 (1966)	§ 8.7
Mounds View, City of v. Walijarvi, 263 N.W.2d 420 (Minn. 1978)	§§ 14.9, 14.20, 18.10, 19.2, 19.8, 21.1, 26.15, 26.19
Mounds View Indep. School Dist. No. 621 v. Buetow & Assocs., Inc., 253 N.W.2d 836 (Minn. 1977)	§§ 19.2, 21.9, 26.25
Mountain Fuel Supply v. Emerson, 578 P.2d 1351 (Wyo. 1978)	§ 8.8
Mountain Home Contractors v. United States, 192 Ct. Cl. 16, 425 F.2d 1263 (1970)	§ 18.9
M-R-S Mfg. Co. v. United States, 203 Ct. Cl. 551, 492 F.2d 835 (1974) *aff'g* 71-1 B.C.A. (CCH) ¶ 8,821 (ASBCA 1971)	§ 11.20
Naetzker v. Brocton Cent. School Dist., 41 N.Y.2d 929, 363 N.E.2d 351, 394 N.Y.S.2d 627 (1977)	§ 21.5
Nakashima Assocs. v. Pacific Beach Corp., 3 Haw. App. 58, 641 P.2d 337 (1982)	§ 25.5
Natco, Inc. v. Williams Bros. Eng'g Co., 489 F.2d 639 (5th Cir. 1974)	§ 21.11
National Comics Publications v. Fawcett Publications, 191 F.2d 594 (2d Cir. 1951)	§ 16.1
National Marine Servs., Inc. v. C.J. Thibodeaux, 501 F.2d 940 (5th Cir. 1974)	§ 26.27
National Parks & Conservation Ass'n v. Klepp, 547 F.2d 673 (D.C. Cir. 1976)	§ 17.4
National Parks & Conservation Ass'n v. Morton, 498 F.2d 765 (D.C. Cir. 1974)	§ 17.4
National State Bank v. Terminal Constr. Corp., 217 F. Supp. 341 (D.N.J.), *aff'd per curiam,* 328 F.2d 315 (3d Cir. 1964)	§ 25.6
Navajo Circle, Inc. v. Development Concepts Corp., 373 So. 2d 689 (Fla. Dist. Ct. App. 1979)	§§ 18.10, 22.4
NCH Corp. v. Broyles, 563 F. Supp. 142 (E.D. La. 1983)	§ 17.3
Nei v. Boston Survey Consultants, Ins., 388 Mass. 320, 446 N.E.2d 681 (1983)	§ 26.12
Neilson v. City of Tampa, 400 So. 2d 799 (Fla. Dist. Ct. App. 1981), *rev'd on other grounds,* 419 So. 2d 1071 (Fla. 1982)	§ 23.13

Case	*Book §*
Nelson v. Cail, 120 Ariz. 64, 583 P.2d 1384 (1978)	§ 22.18
Nelson v. Commonwealth, 235 Va. 228, 368 S.E.2d 239 (1988)	§§ 21.8, 21.9
Nelson, Inc. v. Sewerage Comm'n, 72 Wis. 2d 400, 241 N.W.2d 390 (1976)	§ 20.7
N.E. Redlon Co. v. Franklin Square Corp., 89 N.H. 137, 195 A. 348 (1937)	§ 18.9
Newport News Shipbuilding & Drydock Co. v. United States, 226 F.2d 137 (4th Cir. 1955)	§ 8.5
New Terminal Warehouse Corp. v. Wilson, 589 S.W.2d 465 (Tex. Civ. App. 1979)	§ 8.5
Newton Inv. Co. v. Bernard & Burk, Inc., 220 So. 2d 822 (Miss. 1969)	§§ 18.3, 23.20
New York Cent. R.R. v. General Motors Corp., 182 F. Supp. 273 (N.D. Ohio 1960)	§ 8.2
Niver v. Nash, 7 Wash. 558, 35 P. 380 (1893)	§ 14.9
Nolte v. Smith, 189 Cal. App. 2d 140, 11 Cal. Rptr. 261 (1961)	§ 25.4
Normoyle-Berg & Assocs. v. Village of Deer Creek, 39 Ill. App. 3d 744, 350 N.E.2d 559 (1976)	§§ 7.6, 21.11
Northeast Constr. Co. v. Romney, 485 F.2d 752 (D.C. Cir. 1973)	§ 20.5
Northern Petrochemical Co. v. Thorsen & Thorshov, Inc., 297 Minn. 118, 211 N.W.2d 159 (1973)	§ 21.9, 21.11
Northrup Contracting, Inc. v. Village of Bergen, 139 Misc. 2d 435, 527 N.Y.S.2d 670 (Sup. Ct. 1986)	§§ 22.18, 26.22
Northwestern Marble & Tile Co. v. Megrath, 72 Wash. 441, 130 P. 484 (1913)	§ 18.9
Nucor Corp. v. Tennessee Forging Steel Servs., Inc., 476 F.2d 386 (8th Cir. 1973)	§ 17.5
Obray v. Mitchell, 98 Idaho 533, 567 P.2d 1284 (1977)	§ 18.12
O'Brien v. Carney, 6 F. Supp. 761 (D. Mass. 1925)	§ 20.6
O'Hara v. Architects Hartung & Ass'n, 163 Ind. App. 661, 326 N.E.2d 283 (1975)	§ 25.4
Ohio River Pipline Co. v. Landrum, 580 S.W.2d 713 (Ky. Ct. App. 1979)	§ 8.8
Ohrenstein v. Howell, 227 Ill. App. 215 (1922)	§ 25.4
O'Kon & Co. v. Reidel, 540 So. 2d 836 (Fla. Dist. Ct. App. 1988)	§ 25.6
Old Dominion Dairy Prods., Inc. v. Secretary of Defense, 631 F.2d 953 (D.C. Cir. 1980)	§ 20.6
Oldenburg v. Hagemann, 159 Ill. App. 3d 631, 512 N.E.2d 718 (1987)	§§ 22.6, 22.8
Olsen v. Molzen, 558 S.W.2d 429 (Tenn. 1977)	§ 17.2
O'Neil v. Picillo, 883 F.2d 176 (1st Cir. 1989)	§ 26.4
Optimum Sys., Inc., B-183039, 75-1 CPD ¶ 166	§ 15.4
Optonetics, Inc., ASBCA No. 17015, 73-2 B.C.A. (CCH) ¶ 10,173 (1973)	§ 11.21
Ordinary v. Connolly, 75 N.J. Eq. 521, 72 A. 363 (1909)	§ 8.2

Case	*Book §*
Orlopp v. Willardson Co., 232 Cal. App. 2d 750, 43 Cal. Rptr. 125 (1965)	§ 16.1
Oster v. Medtronic, Inc., 428 N.W.2d 116 (Minn. Ct. App. 1988)	§ 8.5
Overland Constructors, Inc. v. Millard School Dist., 220 Neb. 220, 369 N.W.2d 69 (1985)	§ 21.2
Overstreet v. Norden Laboratories, Inc., 669 F.2d 1286 (6th Cir. 1982)	§ 19.10
Owen v. Dodd, 431 F. Supp. 1239 (N.D. Miss. 1977)	§§ 21.6, 22.7
Owings v. Rose, 262 Or. 247, 497 P.2d 1183 (1972)	§ 8.6
Pacific Architects & Eng'rs, Inc. v. United States, 491 F.2d 734 (Ct. Cl. 1974)	§ 15.2
PAE Int'l, ASBCA No. 20595, 76-2 B.C.A. (CCH) ¶ 12,044 (1976)	§ 11.20
Palatine Nat'l Bank v. Charles W. Greengard Assocs., Inc., 119 Ill. App. 3d 376, 456 N.E.2d 635 (1983)	§ 21.6
Palmer v. Brown, 127 Cal. App. 2d 44, 273 P.2d 306 (1954)	§ 21.4
Palmer v. Watson Constr. Co., 121 N.W.2d 62 (Minn. 1963)	§ 23.21
Pankow Constr. Co. v. Advance Mortgage Corp., 618 F.2d 611 (9th Cir. 1980)	§ 25.8
Parker v. Tharp, 409 N.W.2d 915 (Minn. Ct. App. 1987)	§ 8.2
Parker Peanut Co. v. Felder, 200 S.C. 203, 20 S.E.2d 716 (1942)	§ 26.27
Parklane Properties v. Fisher, 89 Colo. 591, 5 P.2d 577 (1931)	§ 25.4
Parks v. Atkinson, 19 Ariz. 111, 505 P.2d 279 (1973)	§ 18.10
Parliament Towers Condominium v. Parliment House Realty, Inc., 377 So. 2d 976 (Fla. Dist. Ct. App. 1979)	§ 22.13
Pastorelli v. Associated Eng'rs, Inc., 176 F. Supp. 159 (D.R.I. 1959)	§§ 21.1, 21.9
Paul Krebs & Assocs. Matthews & Fritts Constr. Co., 356 So. 2d 638 (Ala. 1978)	§§ 8.4, 8.6
Paul Sardella Constr. Co. v. Braintree Hous. Auth., 3 Mass. App. Ct. 326, 329 N.E.2d 762 (1975)	§ 20.8
Paver & Wildfoerster v. Catholic High School Ass'n, 38 N.Y.2d 669, 345 N.E.2d 565, 382 N.Y.S.2d 22 (1976)	§ 21.5
Paxton v. County of Alameda, 119 Cal. App. 2d 393, 259 P.2d 934 (1953)	§§ 21.2, 22.15, 26.15
Pearce & Pearce, Inc. v. Kroh Bros. Dev. Co., 474 So. 2d 369 (Fla. Dist. Ct. App. 1985)	§ 21.9
Pearlman v. Pittsburg, 304 Pa. 25, 155 A. 118 (1931)	§ 20.6
Peerless Ins. Co. v. Cerny & Assocs., Inc., 199 F. Supp. 951 (D. Minn. 1961)	§ 22.12
Pembee Mfg. Corp. v. Cape Fear Constr. Co., 313 N.C. 488, 329 S.E.2d 350 (1985)	§ 21.15
People *ex rel.* Department of Pub. Works & Bldgs. v. Southeast Nat'l Bank, 226 N.E.2d 778 (Ill. 1971)	§ 20.7

Case	*Book §*
People *ex rel.* Department of Transp. v. Superior Court, 26 Cal. 3d 814, 608 P.2d 673, 163 Cal. Rptr. 585 (1980)	§ 8.4
People *ex rel.* Resnik v. Curtis & Davis, Inc. 78 Ill. 2d 381, 400 N.E.2d 918 (1980)	§ 23.3
People *ex rel.* Skinner v. FGM, Inc., 166 Ill. App. 3d 802, 520 N.E.2d 1024, *appeal denied,* 122 Ill. 2d 593, 530 N.E.2d 263 (1988)	§ 21.6
People *ex rel.* Skinner v. Graham, 170 Ill. App. 3d 417, 524 N.E.2d 642 (1988)	§ 21.6
People *ex rel.* Skinner v. Hellmuth, Obata & Kassabaum, Inc., 114 Ill. 2d 252, 500 N.E.2d 234 (1986)	§ 23.7
Peoples Gas Sys., Inc. v. RSH Constructors, Inc., 563 So. 2d 107 (Fla. Dist. Ct. App. 1990)	§ 8.6
Pero Bldg. Co. v. Smith, 6 Conn. App. 180, 504 A.2d 524 (1986)	§ 17.6
Perry, Dean, Hepburn & Stewart, DOTCAB Nos. 67-24C, 67-24D, 70-1 B.C.A. (CCH) ¶ 8293 (1970)	§ 15.6
Peter Kiewit Sons' Co. v. Iowa S. Utils. Co., 355 F. Supp. 376, (S.D. Iowa 1973)	§§ 19.5, 21.1, 21.6
Peter Kiewit Sons' Co. v. O'Keefe Elevator Co., 191 Neb. 50, 213 N.W.2d 731 (1974)	§ 8.8
Peter Kiewit Sons' Co. v. United States, 109 Ct. Cl. 517, 74 F. Supp. 165 (1947)	§ 18.3
Peter Kiewit Sons' Co. v. Washington State Dept. of Transp., 30 Wash. App. 424, 635 P.2d 740 (1981)	§ 20.7
Petkas v. Staats, 501 F.2d 887 (D.C. Cir. 1974)	§ 17.4
Pezzillo v. General Tel. & Elec. Information Sys., Inc., 414 F. Supp. 1257 (M.D. Tenn. 1976), *aff'd per curiam,* 572 F.2d 1189 (6th Cir. 1978)	§ 19.11
Philippines Airlines v. McDonnell Douglas, 189 Cal. App. 3d 234, 234 Cal. Rptr. 423 (1987)	§ 17.2
Phil Rich Fan Mfg. Co., ASBCA No. 12770, 71 B.C.A. (CCH) ¶ 8,694 (1971)	§ 11.18
Pickens-Bond Constr. Co. v. North Little Rock Elec. Co., 249 Ark. 389, 459 S.W.2d 549 (1970)	§ 8.8
Pierce v. Pacific Gas & Elec. Co., 166 Cal. App. 3d 75, 212 Cal. Rptr. 283 (1985)	§ 12.8
Pine Bluff Hotel Co. v. Monk & Ritchie, 122 Ark. 308, 183 S.W. 761 (1916)	§ 20.2
P.J. Maffei Bldg. Wrecking Corp. v. United States, 732 F.2d 913 (Fed. Cir. 1984)	§ 15.7
Planning Research Corp. v. Federal Power Comm'n, 555 F.2d 970 (D.C. Cir. 1977)	§ 17.4
PNM Constr., Inc. v. United States, 13 Cl. Ct. 745 (1987)	§ 20.6
Pollard v. Sacks & Yolles Dev. Co., 12 Cal. 3d 374, 525 P.2d 88, 115 Cal. Rptr. 648 (1974)	§ 12.8
Porter v. Stevens, 24 Wash. App. 624, 602 P.2d 1192 (1979)	§ 7.5
Potomac Eng'rs, Inc. v. Walser, 127 F. Supp. 41 (D.D.C. 1954), *aff'd,* 223 F.2d 95 (D.C. Cir. 1955)	§ 2.6

Case	*Book §*
Precision Prod., Inc., ASBCA No. 14284, 70-2 B.C.A. (CCH) ¶ 8,447 (1970)	§ 11.18
Prichard Bros., Inc. v. Grady Co., 407 N.W.2d 423 (Minn. Ct. App. 1987) 428 N.W.2d 391 (Minn. 1988)	§§ 21.6, 22.2
Primrose v. Western Union Tel. Co., 154 U.S. 1, 14 S. Ct. 1098 (1894)	§ 14.16
Quincy Ornamental Iron Works v. Findlen, 353 Mass. 87, 228 N.E.2d 453 (1967)	§ 20.8
Randolph Eng'g, Inc., B-192375, 79-1 CPD ¶ 465 (GAO)	§ 15.4
Ranger Constr. Co. v. Dixie Floor Co., 433 F. Supp. 442 (D.S.C. 1977)	§ 14.12
Rayco Constr. Co. v. Vorsanger, 397 F. Supp. 1105 (E.D. Ark. 1975)	§ 20.6
Raymond Int'l, Inc. v. Baltimore County, 45 Md. App. 247, 412 A.2d 1296 (1980)	§ 20.3
Raza Eng'g Corp. v. Daubon, 86 P.R.R. 182 (1962)	§ 2.6
R.C. Hedreen Co., ASBCA No. 20599, 77-1 B.C.A. (CCH) ¶ 12,328 (1977)	§ 11.15
Reber v. Chandler High School Dist. No. 202, 13 Ariz. App. 133, 474 P.2d 852 (1970)	§ 7.5
Regional School Dist. v. United Pac. Ins. Co., 4 Conn. App. 175, 493 A.2d 895 (1985)	§ 20.7
Renel Constr. Inc. v. Brooklyn Coop. Meat Distrib. Center, 59 A.D.2d 391, 399 N.Y.S.2d 429 (1977)	§ 20.2
Residential & Indus. Loan Co. v. Weinberg, 279 Md. 43, 369 A.2d 563, *cert. denied,* 434 U.S. 876 (1977)	§ 17.6
Reynolds Metal Co. v. I.W. Schickli & Bros., 548 S.W.2d 841 (Ky. 1977)	§ 8.8
R.G. Wood & Assoc. Ltd., 85-1 B.C.A. (CCH) ¶ 17,898 (PSBCA 1985)	§ 21.2
R.H. Macy & Co. v. Williams Tile & Terrazzo Co., 585 F. Supp. 175 (N.D. Ga. 1984)	§ 22.5
Riblet Tramway Co. v. Ericksen Assoc., Inc., 665 F. Supp. 81 (D.N.H. 1987)	§ 22.19
Ricciuti Assoc., AGBCA No. 289, 73-2 B.C.A. (CCH) ¶ 10,133 (197)	§ 15.6
Riter-Conely Mfg. Co. v. Aiken, 203 F. Supp. 669 (3d Cir. 1913)	§ 17.5
Rivers v. Pastro, 11 Alaska 491 (1948)	§ 25.5
Roanoke Hosp. Ass'n v. Doyle & Russell, Inc., 215 Va. 796, 214 S.E.2d 155 (1975)	§ 21.11
Robert & Co. Assocs. v. Rhodes-Haverty Partnership, 250 Ga. 680, 300 S.E.2d 503 (1983)	§ 22.6
Robert R. Jones Assocs. v. Hino Homes, Corp. L. Rep. (CCH) 26,165 (E.D. Mich. 1987)	§ 17.5
Robertson Lumber Co. v. Stephen Farmers Coop. Elevator Co., 274 Minn. 17, 143 N.W.2d 622 (1966)	§ 14.9

Case	*Book §*
Scherr & McDermott, Inc. v. United States, 175 Ct. Cl. 440, 360 F.2d 966 (1966)	§ 11.21
Schipper v. Levitt & Sons, Inc., 44 N.J. 70, 207 A.2d 314 (1965)	§§ 14.10, 19.8
Schrier v. Beltway Alarm Co., 73 Md. App. 281, 533 A.2d 1316 (1987)	§ 17.2
Schuchart & Assocs., Professional Eng's, Inc. v. Solo Serv. Corp., 220 U.S.P.Q. (BNA) 170 (W.D. Tex. 1983)	§ 17.5
Scott v. Potomac Ins. Co., 217 Or. 323, 341 P.2d 1083 (1959)	§§ 21.3, 21.9
SDK Medical Computers Servs. Corp. v. Professional Operating Management Group, Inc., 371 Mass. 117, 354 N.E.2d 852 (1978)	§ 19.9
Seaboard Sur. Co. v. Walker, 212 Cal. App. 3d 1064, 260 Cal. Rptr. 924 (1989)	§ 22.12
Seal & Co. v. A.S. McGaughan Co., 907 F.2d 450 (4th Cir. 1990)	§ 15.5
Sears, Roebuck & Co. v. Enco Assocs., Inc., 43 N.Y.2d 389, 372 N.E.2d 555, 401 N.Y.S.2d 767 (1977)	§§ 21.1, 21.5
Seattle W. Indus., Inc. v. David A. Mowat Co., 110 Wash. 2d 1, 750 P.2d 245 (1988)	§ 21.6
Seaview Hosp., Inc. v. Medicenters of Am., Inc., 570 S.W.2d 35 (Tex. Civ. Ap. 1978)	§ 14.4
Secretary of Commerce, 37 Comp. Gen. 186 (1957)	§ 20.5
Secretary of the Army, 37 Comp. Gen. 780 (1958)	§ 20.5
Secretary of the Navy, 42 Comp. Gen. 96 (1962)	§ 20.5
Sefton v. Pasadena Waldorf School, 219 Cal. App. 3d 359, 268 Cal. Rptr. 335 (1990)	§ 12.8
Sensenbrenner v. Rust, Orling & Neale Architects, Inc., 236 Va. 419, 374 S.E.2d 55 (1988)	§ 22.6
Shannon Holloway Constr. Co. v. Louisville & Jefferson County Metro. Sewer Dist., 674 S.W.2d 523 (Ky. Ct. App. 1983)	§ 20.5
Shaw v. Williamsville Manor, Inc., 38 A.D.2d 442, 174 U.S.P.Q. (BNA) 277 (1972)	§ 17.5
Shay v. McCormack, 167 A.D. 854, 153 N.Y.S. 808 (1915)	§ 20.4
Shea v. Bay State Gas Co., 383 Mass. 218, 418 N.E.2d 597 (1981)	§ 19.6
Shelby Mut. Ins. Co. v. City of Grand Rapids, 6 Mich. App. 95, 148 N.W.2d 260 (1967)	§ 17.2
Shell Oil Co. v. Birnkerhoff-Signal Drilling Co., 658 P.2d 1187 (Utah 1983)	§ 8.8
Sherwood v. Omega Constr. Co., 657 F. Supp. 345 (S.D.N.Y. 1987)	§ 26.17
Shoffner Indus., Inc. v. W.B. Lloyd Constr. Co., 42 N.C. App. 259, 257 S.E.2d 50, *cert. denied,* 298 N.C. 296, 259 S.E.2d 301 (1979)	§§ 7.6, 19.2, 19.4, 21.6, 21.9, 26.16

Case	*Book §*
Siders v. Schloo, 188 Cal. App. 3d 1217, 233 Cal. Rptr. 906 (1987)	§ 12.8
Sierra v. Garcia, 106 N.M. 573, 746 P.2d 1105 (1987)	§ 8.6
Sierra Diesel Injection Serv., Inc. v. Burroughs Corp., 874 F.2d 653 (9th Cir. 1989)	§ 19.10
Skinner v. Reed-Prentice Div., Package Mach. Co., 70 Ill. 2d 1, 374 N.E.2d 437 (1977)	§ 23.18
S&M Constr., Inc. v. City of Columbus, 70 Ohio St. 2d 69, 434 N.E.2d 1349 (1982)	§ 20.3
Smith v. Chevron Oil Co., 517 F.2d 1154 (5th Cir. 1975)	§ 8.6
Smith v. Little Brown & Co., 273 F. Supp. 870 (S.D.N.Y. 1967), *aff'd,* 396 F.2d 150 (2d Cir. 1968)	§ 17.5
Smith & Wesson v. United States, 782 F.2d 1074 (1st Cir. 1986)	§ 20.8
Society of Mount Carmel v. Fox, 90 Ill. App. 3d 537, 413 N.E.2d 480 (1980)	§ 23.8
Soucie v. David, 448 F.2d 1067 (D.C. Cir. 1971)	§ 17.4
South Dakota Bldg. Auth. v. Geiger-Berger Assocs., 414 N.W.2d 15 (S.D. 1987)	§§ 8.4, 15.2
South Tippecanoe School Bldg. Corp. v. Shambaugh & Son, Inc., 182 Ind. App. 350, 395 N.E.2d 320 (1979)	§ 17.2
Stanwick Corp., ASBCA No. 14905, 71-1 B.C.A. (CCH) ¶ 8,777 (1971)	§ 11.21
Stark v. McConnell, 22 Ohio Op. 123 (1940)	§ 25.5
State v. Beck, 156 Me. 403, 165 A.2d 433 (1960)	§ 2.4
State v. Wilco Constr. Co., 393 So. 2d 885 (La. Ct. App.), *modified,* 398 So. 2d 1150 (La. Ct. App.), *cert. denied,* 400 So. 2d 905 (La. 1981)	§ 21.9
State Bd. of Architects v. North, 197 N.J. Super. 385, 484 A.2d 1297 (1984)	§ 2.4
State Bd. of Control v. Clutter Constr. Corp., 139 So. 2d 153 (Fla. App. 1962)	§ 20.7
State Bldg. Comm'n v. Becknell Constr., Inc., 329 So. 2d 57 (Miss. 1976)	§ 20.7
State *ex rel.* Missouri State Highway Comm'n v. Hensel Phelps Constr. Co., 634 S.W.2d 168 (Mo. 1982)	§ 20.7
State *ex rel.* National Sur. Corp. v. Malvaney, 221 Miss. 190, 72 So. 2d 424 (1954)	§ 22.12
State Highway Comm'n v. Canion, 250 S.W.2d 439 (Tex. Civ. App. 1952)	§ 20.7
State Highway Comm'n v. DeLong Corp., 9 Or. App. 550, 495 P.2d 1215 (1972)	§ 20.3
State Property & Bldg. Comm'n v. H.W. Miller Constr. Co., 385 S.W.2d 211 (Ky. 1964)	§ 21.9
Steffek v. Wichers, 211 Kan. 342, 507 P.2d 274 (1973)	§§ 18.9, 18.13
Steiner v. Wenning, 43 N.Y.2d 831, 373 N.E.2d 366, 402 N.Y.S.2d 567 (1977)	§ 21.5
Stephens v. Hicks, 156 N.C. 239, 72 S.E. 313 (1911)	§ 25.3, 25.5
Stewart Petroleum Co. v. United States, 438 F. Supp. 527 (D.D.C. 1977)	§ 20.6

Case	*Book §*
Stratford v. Boland, 306 Pa. Super. 475, 452 A.2d 824 (1983)	§ 25.4
Straw v. Williamsport, 286 Pa. 41, 132 A. 804 (1926)	§ 20.4
Stuart v. Crestview Mut. Water Co., 34 Cal. App. 3d 802, 110 Cal. Rptr. 543 (1973)	§ 14.10
Stuart v. Hertz Corp., 351 So. 2d 703 (Fla. 1977)	§ 8.5
Stute v. P.B.M.C., Inc., 114 Wash. 2d 454, 788 P. 2d 545 (1990)	§ 26.17
Sullivan v. Thomas Org., P.C., 88 Mich. App. 77, 276 N.W.2d 522 (1979)	§ 25.5
Sundstrand Turbo v. United States, 182 Ct. Cl. 31 (1968)	§ 11.19
Surf Realty Corp. v. Standing, 195 Va. 431, 78 S.E.2d 901 (1953)	§ 20.2
Svenson v. Miller Builders, Inc., 74 Ill. App. 3d 75, 392 N.E.2d 628 (1979)	§§ 8.4, 8.5
Swaney v. Peden Steel Co., 259 N.C. 531, 131 S.E.2d 601 (1963)	§ 22.15
Swan Wooster Eng'g, AGBCA Nos. 83-104-1, 83-124-1, 87-2 B.C.A. (CCH) ¶ 19,894 (1987)	§ 11.12
Swarthout v. Beard, 33 Mich. App. 395, 190 N.W.2d 373 (1971)	§ 22.15
Swartz v. Ford, 469 So. 2d 232 (Fla. Dist. Ct. App. 1985)	§ 22.15
Sweet v. Colborn School Supply, 39 Mont. 168, 639 P.2d 521 (1982)	§ 8.8
Swett v. Gribaldo, Jones & Assocs., 40 Cal. App. 3d 573, 115 Cal. Rptr. 99 (1974)	§ 14.11
Swinerton & Walberg Co. v. City of Inglewood-Los Angeles County Civic Center Auth., 40 Cal. App. 3d 98, 114 Cal. Rptr. 834 (1974)	§ 20.8
Sylvania Elec. Prod., Inc., ASBCA No. 13622, 70-2 B.C.A. (CCH) ¶ 8,387 (1970), *aff'd,* Sylvania Elec. Prod., Inc. v. United States, 202 Ct. Cl. 16, 479 F.2d 1342 (1973)	§ 11.20
Syracuse v. Sarkisian Bros., Inc., 87 A.D.2d 984, 451 N.Y.S.2d 945 (1982)	§ 20.7
Tamarac Dev. Co. v. Delamater Freund & Assocs., P.A., 234 Kan. 618, 675 P.2d 361 (1984)	§§ 12.7, 12.8
Tandem Computers, B-221333 (Apr. 14, 1986), 86-1 CPD ¶ 362 (1986), *modified on other grounds,* 86-2 CPD ¶ 315 (1986)	§ 11.9
Taylorcraft Aviation Corp., *In re,* 168 F.2d 808 (6th Cir. 1948)	§ 17.6
Taylor, Thon, Thompson & Peterson v. Cannaday, 230 Mont. 151, 749 P.2d 63 (1987)	§ 21.2
T&E Indus., Inc. v. Safety Light Corp., 680 F. Supp. 696 (D.N.J. 1988)	§ 26.1
The T.J. Hooper, 60 F.2d 737 (2d Cir.), *cert. denied,* 287 U.S. 662 (1932)	§ 21.2
Third Swansea Properties, Inc. v. Ockalund Constr. Co., 41 Ill. App. 3d 894, 354 N.E.2d 148 (1976)	§ 17.2

Case	*Book §*
United States v. Penn-Olin Chem. Co., 378 U.S. 158 (1964), *later review,* 389 U.S. 308 (1967)	§§ 4.3, 16.10
United States v. Rogers & Rogers, 161 F. Supp. 132 (S.D. Cal. 1958)	§§ 22.7, 22.9, 22.10
United States v. Skidmore, Owings & Merrill, 505 F. Supp. 1101 (S.D.N.Y. 1981)	§ 21.12
United States v. Spearin, 248 U.S. 132, 39 S. Ct. 59 (1918)	§§ 18.4, 20.2
United States *ex rel.* Charles H. Thayer v. Metro Constr. Corp., 330 F. Supp. 386 (E.D. Va. 1971)	§§ 23.4, 25.4, 25.14
United States *ex rel.* Los Angeles Testing Laboratory v. Rogers & Rogers, 161 F. Supp. 132 (D. Cal. 1958)	§§ 18.10, 21.9
United States *ex rel.* Naberhaus-Burke, Inc. v. Butt & Head, 535 F. Supp. 1155 (S.D. Ohio 1982)	§ 25.14
United States *ex rel.* Seminole Sheet Metal Co. v. SCI, Inc., 828 F.2d 671 (11th Cir. 1987)	§ 21.6
United States Fidelity & Guar. Co. v. Continental Casualty Co., 153 Ill. App. 3d 185, 505 N.E.2d 1072 (1987)	§ 7.28
United States Fidelity & Guar. Co. v. Long, 214 F. Supp. 307 (D. Or. 1963)	§ 15.2
United States Fidelity & Guar. Co. v. Oak Grove Union School Dist., 205 Cal. App. 2d 226, 22 Cal. Rptr. 907 (1962)	§ 25.9
United States Fidelity & Guar. Co. v. United States, 837 F.2d 116 (3d Cir.), *review denied,* 487 U.S. 1235 (1988)	§ 26.18
University Plaza Shopping Center, Inc. v. Stewart, 272 So. 2d 507 (Fla. 1973)	§ 8.3
Urania, Town of v. M.P. Dumesnil Constr. Co., 492 So. 2d 888 (La. 1986)	§ 20.2
Urbandale, City of v. Frevert-Ramsey-Kobes, Architects-Eng'rs, Inc., 435 N.W.2d 400 (Iowa Ct. App. 1988)	§ 21.13
U.R.S. Co. v. Gulfport-Biloxi Regional Airport Auth., 544 So. 2d 824 (Miss. 1989)	§§ 22.5, 22.12
Valley Contractors, ASBCA No. 9397, 1964 B.C.A. (CCH) ¶ 4,071 (1964)	§ 11.18
Van Ornum v. Otter Tail Power Co., 210 N.W.2d 188 (N.D. 1973)	§ 22.15
Varigas Research, Inc., ASBCA No. 28610, 84-1 B.C.A. (CCH) ¶ 17,154 (1984)	§ 11.21
Venturi, Inc. v. Austin Co., 681 F. Supp. 584 (S.D. Ill. 1988)	§ 8.3
Video Corp. v. Frederick Flatto Assocs., 58 N.Y.2d 1026, 448 N.E.2d 1350, 462 N.Y.S.2d 439 (1983)	§ 21.5
Virginia Petroleum Jobbers Ass'n v. Federal Power Comm'n, 259 F.2d 921 (D.C. Cir. 1958)	§ 11.9
Vojak v. Jensen, 161 N.W.2d 100 (Iowa 1968)	§ 22.19

Case	*Book §*
Wheeler v. Bucksteel Co., 698 P.2d 995 (Or. Ct. App), *review denied,* 404 P.2d 513 (Or. 1985)	§ 2.8
Wheeler & Lewis v. Slifer, 195 Colo. 291, 577 P.2d 1092 (1978)	§ 7.5
Wheeling Trust & Sav. Bank v. Tremco, Inc., 153 Ill. App. 3d 136, 505 N.E.2d 1045 (1987)	§ 23.5
Whelan Assocs., Inc. v. Jaslow Dental Laboratory, 797 F.2d 1222 (3d Cir. 1986), *cert. denied,* 479 U.S. 1031 (1987)	§ 19.14
White Constr. Co. v. Commonwealth, 11 Mass. App. Ct. 640, 418 N.E.2d 357 (1981), *aff'd,* 385 Mass. 1005, 432 N.E.2d 104 (1982)	§§ 14.16, 15.6, 17.2
Whitfield Constr. Co. v. Commercial Dev. Corp., 392 F. Supp. 982 (V.I. 1975)	§ 18.12
Whittle v. Pagani Bros. Constr. Co., 383 Mass. 796, 422 N.E.2d 779 (1981)	§ 8.6
W.H. Lyman Constr. Co. v. Village of Gurnee, 84 Ill. App. 3d 28, 403 N.E.2d 1325 (1980)	§§ 17.2, 19.2
Wichita Falls, City of, HUD BCA No. 76-13, 77-2 B.C.A. (CCH) ¶ 12,764 (1977)	§ 11.21
Willey v. Minnesota Mining & Mfg. Co., 755 F.2d 315 (3d Cir. 1985)	§ 8.4
Wilkinson v. Rowe, 266 Ala. 675, 98 So. 2d 435 (1957)	§ 25.5
Williams v. Fenix & Scission, Inc., 608 F.2d 1205 (9th Cir. 1979)	§ 22.15
Williams Eng'g, Inc. v. Goodyear, 496 So. 2d 1012 (La. 1986)	§§ 18.3, 18.4, 21.8
Williamson v. Hotel Melrose, 110 S.C. 1, 96 S.E. 407 (1918)	§ 25.3
Wilson v. Stretch, Inc., 44 N.J. Super. 52, 129 A.2d 599 (1957)	§ 25.10
Winterbottom v. Wright, 10 M&W 109, 152 Eng. Rep. 402 (1842)	§ 22.3
Witherspoon v. Sides Constr. Co., 219 Neb. 117, 362 N.W.2d 35 (1985)	§ 21.15
W.L. Dev. Corp. v. Triford Realty, Inc., 484 N.Y.2d 29, 370 N.E.2d 969, 406 N.Y.S.2d 437 (1978)	§ 17.6
Wolfe v. Ford Motor Co., 386 Mass. 95, 434 N.E.2d 1008 (1982)	§ 19.8
W. William Graham, Inc. v. City of Cave City, 289 Ark. 105, 709 S.W.2d 94 (1986)	§§ 14.16, 17.2
W. Wright, Inc. v. Korshoj Corp., 197 Neb. 692, 250 N.W.2d 894 (1977)	§ 15.5
Wyman v. Hooker, 2 Cal. App. 36, 83 P. 79 (1905)	§ 18.12
Young v. Eastern Eng'g & Elevator Co., 381 Pa. Super. 428, 554 A.2d 77 (1989)	§ 22.15
Young v. Ross-Loos Medical Group, Inc., 135 Cal. App. 3d 669, 185 Cal. Rptr. 536 (1982)	§ 23.10

Case	***Book §***
Zannoth v. Booth Radio Stations, Inc., 333 Mich. 233, 52 N.W.2d 678 (1952)	§ 21.8
Zapata v. Burns, 207 Conn. 496, 542 A.2d 700 (1988)	§ 21.15
Zettel v. Paschea Contractors, Inc., 100 Ill. App. 3d 614, 427 N.E.2d 189 (1981)	§ 23.24
Zions First Nat'l Bank v. Carlson, 23 Utah 2d 395, 464 P.2d 387 (1970)	§ 25.4
Zukowski v. Howard Needles Tammen & Bergendoff, Inc., 657 F. Supp. 926 (D. Colo. 1987)	§ 26.17
Zurn Eng'rs v. State Dep't of Water Resources, 69 Cal. App. 3d 798, 138 Cal. Rptr. 478 (1977)	§ 18.13

INDEX